# THE SOCIAL WORLD:

*An Introduction to Sociology*

# THE SOCIAL WORLD:
## An Introduction to Sociology

*Edited by:*

**Lorne Tepperman**
*University of Toronto*

**R. Jack Richardson**
*McMaster University*

## CONTRIBUTORS

Anton L. Allahar, *The University of Western Ontario*
Maureen Baker, *formerly of Scarborough College, University of Toronto*
Robert Brym, *University of Toronto*
Gordon Darroch, *York University*
Edward Harvey, *Ontario Institute for Studies in Education*
Peter Li, *University of Saskatchewan*
Nancy Mandell, *Atkinson College, York University*
William Michelson, *University of Toronto*
Raymond Murphy, *University of Ottawa*
Peter Sinclair, *Memorial University*
Austin T. Turk, *University of Toronto*
Susannah Wilson, *Wilfrid Laurier University*
Willem H. Vanderburg, *University of Toronto*

McGRAW-HILL RYERSON LIMITED
*Toronto Montreal New York Auckland Bogotá Cairo Guatemala Hamburg Johannesburg Lisbon London Madrid Mexico New Delhi Panama Paris San Juan São Paulo Singapore Sydney Tokyo*

Cover Design and Sculpture: Susan Hedley

Cover Photograph: Dave Hader

ISBN 0-07-548971-6

1 2 3 4 5 6 7 8 9 0 THB 5 4 3 2 1 0 9 8 7 6

Printed and bound in Canada

Care has been taken to trace ownership of copyright material contained in this text. The publishers will gladly take any information that will enable them to rectify any reference or credit in subsequent editions.

CANADIAN CATALOGUING IN PUBLICATION DATA
Main entry under title:
The Social world
Bibliography: p.
Includes index.
ISBN 0-07-548971-6

1. Sociology. I. Tepperman, Lorne, date
II. Richardson, R. J.

HM51.S63 1986          301          C85-099831-X

# ACKNOWLEDGEMENTS

Putting a book like this together can be difficult. However, we had a great time putting this one together because of the excellent people we worked with.

Our first thanks go to the contributing authors. They are all fine scholars and, more than that, professionals. They took our criticism and requests for revision with good humour and grace. Needless to say, the book could not have existed without their scholarship, creativity, hard work and co-operation.

We are also grateful to the editors of this book. Joan Blishen, sponsoring editor at McGraw-Hill Ryerson, enthusiastically supported the project from its beginnings and saw it through the mass of paperwork, correspondence, and demands for encouragement that accompany any project of this scope. Alan Wain, our style editor, honed our first and second drafts into clearer and more engaging prose, showing a large amount of "sociological imagination" all along the way. Carol Soloman, the production editor, took yet another bash at our prose and made it both more readable and consistent from one chapter to another. Finally, dozens of reviewers advised us on ways to improve our sociological content at each stage.

The resulting book is, of course, imperfect, but we accept responsibility for the flaws that remain. We hope the book will achieve the purpose for which it was written: namely, to better inform our students, a new generation of sociologists, about the history, goals and methods of this most interesting enterprise in which we share, the discipline of sociology.

# TABLE of CONTENTS

# SOCIOLOGY
## and
# SOCIETY

Sociology is the science that constructs theories about the social relations making up a society. Let's consider what this means.

This apparently simple definition hides some important difficulties. For sociologists, the word *science* means much the same as for physicists or biologists: namely, the construction and validation of theories about the real world. A science of social relations is more complex than one concerned with atoms or amoebae. But, in principle, the goals of all sciences are the same.

*Theories* are, for sociologists as for physicists, tentative explanations of observable reality and the basis for predicting future events. Every theory is judged against competing theories in terms of thoroughness and economy of explanation. A science tests and retests its theories to improve and even discard them in favour of better ones.

*Social relations* are any relationships between people that are somehow binding. In this sense, the subject matter of sociology is the *social bond*, which connects individuals in groups and societies.

*Societies*, then, are collections of social relationships. A society is made up of all the families, clubs, groups, corporations, understandings, arrangements and rules that its members share. Seeing the boundaries of a given society is sometimes difficult, for many social relationships may span an international border, like the one between Canada and the United States. Indeed, some writers have wondered whether Canada and the United States, which are certainly distinct nation-states, are really distinct societies. (Others, for similar reasons, have wondered whether the two are distinct economies, since they are so closely tied by trade and the flow of migrants.) Yet, in principle, the idea of a "Canadian society" still has value to sociologists, as to others.

## The Character of Sociological Theories

The theories sociologists construct have certain characteristics. As noted earlier, they are tentative, thorough and economical. But they should also be *true*, as far as we can tell. Sociologists, being human, may become blinded to what is true and false. Our intellectual shortcomings, personal interests and values may mislead us. To reduce the risk of this, sociologists use agreed-upon methods of discovering, confirming, and communicating their findings and theories.

Sociological theories should not be circular or tautological, i.e. true by definition. A theory that "satisfied workers are happy with their jobs" is tautological if what we mean by "satisfied" is "happy with their jobs." Foolish as it may sound, many students and even professional sociologists make theories which prove tautological on inspection. A tautological theory, though true, has no value to science because it cannot be disproved.

A theory that is not tautological is open to *verification* or validation. Scientists, including sociologists, never prove a theory absolutely right; they only prove contending theories wrong. The theory that best survives multiple attempts at disproof and shows itself thorough and economical is considered the most valid.

Some of Einstein's theories in physics waited for decades until equipment was developed to test their mathematically derived predictions. Likewise, some sociological theories are not immediately verifiable because they predict future events: for example, Marx's theories about the coming of communism to industrial societies. Others cannot be validated because they assume the existence of invisible (i.e. unmeasurable) forces: for example, Freud's theory of the unconscious. How remarkable that these very theories have taken a central position in social science, despite their problems of verification. On the other hand, Marx's theoretical importance was established largely through analyses of past and present societies, and Freud's through the treatment of neuroses, not through prediction.

Whatever the difficulties, verification must always be sought. Every theorist must appeal to objective evidence and reason over intuition, emotion and good intention in promoting his/her ideas.

Two other aspects of sociological theories are worth mentioning. First, theories should be *important* or socially relevant. Sociologists aim ultimately to understand the whole social world and not simply its smallest, most readily accessible parts. To sociologists, all social relations are of interest. But, as sociologists/citizens, we should keep our eyes on the public problems of our times. Sociology's history shows the best work has been done by "middle range" researchers moving back and forth between pure theory and an active concern with on-going events. Still, sociologists should avoid promising results prematurely. Nothing undermines popular faith in any science more than false claims, even if motivated by good intentions.

Sociology that influences the way some portion of society is working is called *applied sociology*. Applied sociology is being taught in more and more North American universities, largely because sociological application is becoming a bigger part of sociologists' on-going work. Each year, more graduate sociologists take jobs outside universities, applying their sociological knowledge to government and corporate decision-making. The chapter on applied sociology in this section describes how sociological theory and methods can be made socially relevant.

Finally, sociological theories should be *nonobvious* or counter-intuitive. Many accuse sociology of dressing up common sense in impenetrable jargon. This unfortunate idea, though apparently justified by many published works, is inherently wrong. Good theories do *not* just give us back what we already know. On the contrary, a good theory, by connecting previously unconnected facts, yields insights no one anticipated. The degree to which sociology succeeds in making such non-obvious theories is a measure of its maturity as a science. If sociology falls short, the failure is not for want of trying.

Like other scientists, sociologists create a conceptual language to work in: a set of terms, precisely defined, whose value may not be immediately obvious to the layperson. Like theory itself, theoretical language need not justify itself at every turn. It may not be obvious or easily penetrated, yet it will still withstand the charge of being jargon if, finally, it yields insights harder to reach in some other language. In this respect, mathematics is the prime example of a theoretical language that is not jargon; but it is not the only example. Sociology, too, has its own language.

## Sociology Contrasted With Other Disciplines

Sociologist Kenneth Westhues has helped us better understand sociology by comparing it with other, similar activities. For example, sociology is different from journalism and history. Both journalism and history describe real events and to some degree base their descriptions on an interpretation or implicit theory. Sociology is different. It makes its theories explicit in order to test them. Telling a story is, for sociologists, less important than testing the interpretation on which the story is based. Sociology may be a good preparation for doing history or journalism, but it differs from these disciplines.

Sociology also differs from philosophy. Both are analytical — that is, concerned with making and testing theory. However, theorizing is quite different in these two fields. Sociology is resolutely *empirical*, or concerned with evidence grasped by the senses, and philosophy is not. This does not mean philosophy has a greater concern with the internal logic of its arguments. Sociological theories must stand up logically, but they must *also* stand up to observable evidence in a way philosophical theories need not. A sociological theory whose predictions are not supported by evidence gathered in an agreed-upon way will not be accepted by sociologists, no matter how logical the theory may be.

Finally, sociology differs from psychology, which is also analytical, reflective and empirical. The difference here lies in the units of analysis. Psychologists study the behaviour of individual humans (or, occasionally, animals) under varied experimental conditions. Sociology's subject is the social relationship or group of relationships observed in nature: the family, group, or total society. Sociology and psychology come together in a field called social psychology; but even it is defined differently by sociologists and psychologists.

To summarize, sociology is concerned with making scientifically valid theories about social relations. These theories should be "scientific" in the usual meanings of the word. But certain methodological problems make the scientific study of social relations more difficult than the scientific study of atoms, amoebae, or even individual monkeys and humans.

## Some Methodological Difficulties

First, we can rarely, if ever, experiment on groups or families, let alone societies. By "experiment" we mean the random assignment of cases to experimental and control groups, the careful manipulation of the experimental group, and the comparison of the two groups before and after manipulation. (This procedure is described further in Chapter 2.) Yet experimentation is the basic method of testing theories in physical and to a lesser degree in biological sciences.

The impossibility of experimentation in sociology leads us to develop alternative methods, none completely satisfactory. The sociologist must know and use a large variety of research methods. Any sociological theory must withstand a battery of weak tests, using many approaches, since strong (experimental) tests are not possible.

The second main difficulty lies in the existence of competing paradigms in sociology. *Paradigms* are ways of thinking. Different paradigms not only define which problems are key to understanding social relations; they also define which research procedures are most appropriate and which evidence most relevant. Paradigms have multiplied in sociology for many reasons, including: a strong philosophical (deductive) tradition in European sociology and an empirical (inductive) one in America and Britain; the rising and falling popularity of particular research techniques; and fluctuating political radicalism in the public mind and in the universities. The ambiguity of sociological method also contributes. If a sociological proof *must* consist of many weak approximations, room exists for many approaches, many paradigms.

A third main difficulty lies in the reactive nature of the sociologist's object of study. Sociologists and the people being studied all hold views likely to affect research outcomes. Usually these preconceptions bias the outcomes in favour of what the investigator expects. Some researchers think this reactivity is desirable. They believe the sociologist's role is to combine study with social action: to discover, study and eliminate problems at the same time. Most, however, prefer to separate these activities in the interest of scientific precision. People, unlike atoms or guinea pigs, can and do monitor what scientists say about them. Indeed, most people have their own theories about how society works. Their actual or expected reaction to scholarly analysis contributes to the climate of disagreement within sociology.

A fourth problem is the nonrepetitiveness of history. If our subject is society itself, we must study many societies under different conditions, in hopes of finding "natural experiments." But sociologists will never find two societies identical in every respect except the one of theoretical interest. Always, new kinds of societies are found in new historical contexts. Consider the Industrial Revolution. It will never be repeated. For this reason, no theory about the Industrial Revolution can be tested as a physicist or chemist might test a theory. Of course, there are many different theories about industrialization, growth and development, even theories about why the Industrial Revolution first occurred where and when it did. Yet, theories about societies industrializing today are dealing with a different phenomenon: industrial development in the midst of an already industrialized, colonized world. Sociologists can apply their understanding of eighteenth-century England to studying industrialization in twentieth-century India, but only by making a great deal of allowance for the different contexts. In this respect, sociology faces a problem similar to the one facing biologists and ecologists, among others.

## The Notion of a Social System

These methodological problems which prevent sociology from using true scientific method may never be fully overcome. On the other hand, several other factors make the scientific study of social relations somewhat easier. Social relations are *systemic*: they contain arrangements of parts that sustain one another in a given pattern over time. Some theorists have argued that all sociologists study social systems, and all social systems, large and small, have common features. If this is true, an understanding of social systems in general can be used to understand a particular case that is hard to study directly. Information about smaller, more accessible social systems can be used to develop and test theories about larger, less accessible ones.

Not all sociologists would accept this view. Many reject the explicit focus on social systems; they find the concept too limiting. Yet, a compelling result of system thinking is the discovery of the "unanticipated consequence," of which Robert Merton (1910- ) has written a great deal. Research demonstrates that people are often constrained by the social relationships in which they participate, despite their own plans and wishes to the contrary. People (alone or in groups) are part of a larger, complex reality beyond their easy control. They are part of a *social structure*, as discussed in the next chapter and elsewhere in this book.

This observation has led sociologists to a unique understanding of public planning. More and more, applied sociology helps planners guard against the unanticipated consequences of their actions: against plans that will inevitably fail, produce undesirable social side-effects, or even prove "fatal remedies," killing the patient in the process of curing. Only by understanding societies as social systems can planners intervene in ways that will actually work.

Unanticipated consequences prove a society is more than the simple sum of people and things, each with distinct properties that mix together. The combination of people produces complex interactions, as in chemistry and ecology. Eventually sociologists will fully understand these interesting, complex interactions.

The three chapters that follow develop some of the ideas put forward in this Introduction. "Sociology: The Science of Society" clarifies the discipline's competing paradigms and discusses their historical background. It discusses two issues central to our discipline: namely, "free will versus determinism" and the concept of "social structure." The second chapter extends our understanding of experimental and nonexperimental methods of research. Chapter 3, on applied sociology, shows how theory and method can be brought to bear on pressing current problems. These chapters come first in the book because they are the most basic. A good understanding of sociology's subject matter and purpose means, first, understanding the discipline's theory and method.

# 1

# Sociology: The Science of Society

## *Anton L. Allahar*

# INTRODUCTION

It is exceedingly difficult, if not pointless, to attempt an exhaustive and all-encompassing definition of sociology. This is not to imply that what sociology is or what sociologists do is totally incomprehensible. Rather, it is meant to sensitize the reader to the fact that the scope of the discipline is wide-ranging, rich, complex and continually growing. For these reasons, a single definition will never suffice. It would be so broad and general that it would say very little. For example, defining sociology as "the study of social order, social disorder and social change," though essentially accurate, is so general that it has little practical utility.

As a point of departure, therefore, it seems more appropriate to talk of such things as the aims, methods and uses of sociological inquiry — in other words, what sociologists do. Generally, sociologists try to make sense of that noisy blur of human activity called "society." They try to define, describe, explain and interpret human behaviour within the contexts of social groups and institutions. Unlike the psychologist, who focuses on individual motivations and purposes underlying human behaviour, the sociologist is interested primarily in general and recurrent behaviour patterns, whether in small groups, specific social institutions, regions of a country or entire societies.

One thing that becomes immediately apparent to the student of sociology is the infinite complexity of the term "society." It is so vast and dynamic that sociologists often compartmentalize various aspects of societal relations in smaller, more manageable units. One of the traditional divisions is between *macrosociological* and *microsociological* areas. The former refers to large-scale social interactions, such as the impact of unemployment on marriages or the relationship between religion and economic development. Microsociological issues, on the other hand, are small-scale behaviour patterns within groups and institutions. For example, how is power distributed within the family, or how are decisions made and implemented in specific office settings? Both the macro- and microsociological areas of concern share fundamental characteristics that serve to define the sociological outlook or approach.

# SOCIOLOGY AND HISTORY

## WHY HISTORY IS IMPORTANT

Many of the essential insights of sociology are drawn from history. Most sociologists agree that individuals are not born with ideas, nor do ideas drop from the sky. Our basic modes of interaction, our social institutions, patterns of organization, communication, and conventions, in a word, our cultures, are history-laden. What occurs in any given society, therefore, usually takes history as its point of departure and builds on historical knowledge. As will be seen in the chapter on culture, the concept of society also implies language and communication.

Sociologists, then, may choose to ignore history at their own peril. For history is indispensable as a means of understanding future ways of behaving. History, understood as a social process that has generated a stock of knowledge relating to past failures and triumphs, is thus a lucrative repository of information. This does not mean, however, that understanding history alone is sufficient to understand society.

The sociologist must also realize that humans are rational, thinking beings possessed of a will. Hence, whether individually or in groups, they may choose to act contrary to the established historical pattern. In fact, they may not even know that a given pattern exists. It is the task of the sociologist to identify the pattern of social convention and then *explain* why it persists or dies out.

## THE INDUSTRIAL AND THE FRENCH REVOLUTIONS AS HISTORICAL WATERSHEDS

Of the major modern historical processes, the Industrial Revolution and the French Revolution have received the most sociological attention. Indeed, several social theorists have argued that sociology as a formal discipline was born as a reaction to the events surrounding these two major social developments (Zeitlin, 1981b; Collins and Markowsky, 1984:28; Nisbet, 1966; Seidman, 1983). The Industrial Revolution, which first took hold in England in the early eighteenth century, is generally described in terms of the social and economic changes which it wrought.

Among these were: the displacement of the peasantry from the land and their replacement by agricultural wage workers; the growth of industrial towns that drew people away from the self-sufficient villages of the countryside; the widespread production of marketable commodities, which changed informal barter and simple exchange relations in the absence of a formally constituted market; and finally, the creation of huge numbers of urban dwellers (both employed and unemployed) who were totally dependent on wage labour for their survival.

If the Industrial Revolution was characterized by sweeping social and economic changes, the French Revolution of 1789 is most remembered for its social and political consequences. The watchwords of the revolution — liberty, individuality, fraternity and equality — heralded a new way of life for French men and women in virtually all aspects of society and made possible the cry for political democracy. The bourgeoisie, a relatively new class of manufacturing, commercial, and industrial entrepreneurs, rivalled the monarchy, aristocracy and nobility for power. They challenged established authority and tradition and called for new rules of conduct that would free them to pursue their economic and political goals. The destruction of French feudalism thus became the *precondition* for the rise of this class, as well as other new classes.

# HISTORY OF SOCIOLOGICAL THOUGHT

## ENLIGHTENMENT VERSUS ROMANTICISM

Out of the ferment created by the French Revolution, some of the major forerunners of sociological thinking were born. The eighteenth-century Enlightenment produced an unprecedented interest in science and rationality. Instead of resorting to intuition, introspection, tradition, authority and revelation as sources of truth, many philosophers and thinkers embraced a faith in science, which promised to liberate the human being from superstition and fear of the unknown.

Driven by a deep-seated humanitarianism, Enlightenment thinkers attempted to show that the universe was intelligible, that the laws governing its operation could be discovered and manipulated to the benefit of man. They criticized the divine right of kings to rule, traditional authority and privilege and religion as sources of human bondage. Taking account of the social situation in France during the eighteenth century, the forerunners of sociological thought analysed French social institutions, practices and beliefs with a view to explaining the nature and logic of the human condition. They were convinced that only by constructive social criticism and appeals to rationality could men and women create a more just and equal social order. Their concerns were eminently sociological, and these thinkers helped shape sociological thought down to the present.

But while Enlightenment thinkers such as Montesquieu and Rousseau set the tone for much present-day sociological scholarship, they also provoked a countercurrent that, too, made a significant contribution to the development of the discipline. That countercurrent has been called the romantic and conservative reaction to the French Revolution and the Enlightenment philosophy which followed in its wake. In essence, the romantic-conservatives, also deeply concerned with human behaviour and interaction, disagreed with the heavy emphasis Enlightenment thinking placed upon science and rationality. They argued that significant components of social behaviour were nonrational but nevertheless crucial for analysing social interaction.

Specifically, the romantic-conservatives reacted to the lack of respect for religion, morality and the wisdom of established tradition and custom, and the subjection of imagination, feeling and sentiment to rational ridicule. They cherished the old order and saw progress or change as something that should come about, not via revolution, but through slow and gradual reform. And herein lay their conservatism.

Out of the clash between these two major philosophical orientations, the two founding fathers of sociology forged their seminal ideas. Henri de Saint-Simon (1760-1825) and Auguste Comte (1798-1857) blended some tenets of Enlightenment philosophy with certain aspects of romantic-conservative thought to produce a *positive science of society* — a means for uniting what may otherwise appear to be two opposing currents: order and progress. Their writings deal with some of the concerns that have remained central even in contemporary sociological literature: social class, power, religion, ideology, the family, property, inequality and politics.

These themes were later seized upon by three men who are today regarded as the main pillars of the discipline of sociology: Karl Marx (1818-1883), Émile Durkheim (1858-1917) and Max Weber (1864-1920).

## SOCIOLOGY'S THREE PILLARS — MARX, DURKHEIM AND WEBER

Harbouring a deep-seated humanitarian concern, Marx analysed the operations of the capitalist economic system, which he saw as inherently unjust, dehumanizing and destined to be overthrown. Employing a class analysis, he argued that the capitalist class, whose sole economic motive is the pursuit of profit, exploits the working class to a point where the latter is eventually moved to react violently. From the point of view of the working class, exploitation creates both the *objective* conditions of misery and the *subjective* conditions for the developing class consciousness which combine to make the workers revolutionary. The inevitable clash between

*Marx was born and educated in Germany. He studied law and philosophy at the universities of Bonn and Berlin, but, owing to his radical views, was blacklisted and never managed to practise either. In 1842 he met Friedrich Engels, with whom he collaborated on many of his writings. Marx spent many years at the British Museum while writing **Das Kapital** (1867), an analysis of the exploitive aspects of capitalism.* By permission of the Bettman Archive, New York, N.Y.

*Karl Marx (1818-1883)*

the two principal classes of capitalist society ultimately results in victory for the workers and the establishment of a socialist society, where private property and exploitation are eliminated, social inequalities are greatly reduced, and human dignity is restored to the worker.

In Durkheim one can see some broad similarities to Marx. Both were interested in the rise of capitalism, the impact of economic changes on individuals and their communities, the origins and consequences of social inequality, and the problem of social order. But whereas Marx was more directly concerned with class and power struggles, Durkheim posed the prior question: "How are the social structures within which power and class struggle operate even possible in the first place?" (Grabb, 1984:74). Or, stated differently, "How is society possible"?

From this question, Durkheim was led to develop some of his central sociological ideas. Beginning with the concept of *solidarity*, he wanted to explain how, in spite of all the tensions and conflicts in society, human beings nevertheless are bound together in stable and enduring relationships. Depending on the society in question, solidarity or social cohesiveness for Durkheim was of two types: mechanical and organic.

He associated *mechanical solidarity* with primitive societies. It is a solidarity based on "likeness" or "sameness," for in such societies, where people are organized into

*Durkheim was born in France, where he studied philosophy and history at the École Normale Supérieure and the University of Paris. In his doctoral dissertation, **The Division of Labour in Society** (1893), he developed his core ideas concerning mechanical and organic solidarity, and in some circles this earned him the title "the father of sociology." He also wrote extensively on law, morality and religion, and his study of suicide is still regarded as a classic in sociological methodology.* By permission of the Bettman Archive, New York, N.Y.

*Émile Durkheim (1855-1917)*

clans, tribes, extended families and other such units, they all share basic similarities, e.g., they are self-sufficient, employ simple tools, are deeply religious. But what binds these separate groups together, what gives them solidarity, is what Durkheim refers to as a *collective conscience* — a totality of beliefs and sentiments common to average citizens of the same society (Durkheim, 1933:79). Further, Durkheim tells us, the collective conscience, which embodies the moral rules that make solidarity possible in primitive society, is rooted in religion. For primitive religion "contains in a confused mass, besides beliefs properly religious, morality, law, the principles of political organization, and even science. . . . " (Durkheim, 1933:135). He thus argues that law is essentially religious in its origin and that legal or judicial rules gradually develop out of the collective conscience through the influence of religious beliefs. When there is a close correspondence between the laws and the collective conscience of a society, that society is a moral one (Grabb, 1984:75).

*Organic solidarity*, on the other hand, is linked with modern societies. For Durkheim, the principal cause of the transition from primitive to modern society was the increasing specialization of tasks and activities associated with the division of labour. As opposed to primitive society, where most people worked at similar jobs, held similar beliefs, possessed similar amounts and types of knowledge, modern society is characterized by *social dissimilarity*, the rise of individualism, and a corresponding variety of values and norms to suit the new circumstances.

*Weber was born in Germany, where he studied law but later switched to an academic career. He went on to study and teach economics and political science at the universities of Freiburg and Heidelberg before becoming actively involved in politics. Later in life he became interested in the questions of sociological theory and methods, and in 1919 he accepted a teaching position at the University of Munich. Among his many sociological writings **The Protestant Ethic and the Spirit of Capitalism** (1905) is the best known.* The Granger Collection, New York.

*Max Weber (1864-1920)*

Hence, in modern society mechanical solidarity is gradually undermined, and the collective conscience is eroded by the growth of a "personal conscience." For this change to occur, Durkheim tells us, the individual must be freed from the pervasive hold which the collective conscience has on him in primitive society:

> . . . the individual personality must have become a much more important element in the life of society, and in order for it to have acquired this importance, it is not enough for the personal conscience of each to have grown in absolute value, but also to have grown more than the common conscience (Durkheim, 1933:167).

The decline of mechanical solidarity, then, is accompanied by "a growing multitude of individual differences" (Durkheim, 1933:172); and in order that society not fall apart, "another solidarity must slowly come in to take the place of that which has gone" (Durkheim, 1933:173).

The new form of solidarity Durkheim terms "organic." Stemming from the division of labour, organic solidarity refers to the fact that society, like a living organism, is made up of distinct parts that must be *integrated* if the whole is to survive. And this task of integration falls to the division of labour, which replaces the collective conscience as the glue of society because it requires that members of a society be dependent on each other (Durkheim, 1933:181). In conclusion, therefore, we can see that Durkheim, like Marx, looks to the economic structure of modern society as the source of both order and change.

Weber, finally, appears unfamiliar with Durkheim's works, but he certainly read Marx. And although he accepted some of the main tenets of Marxism regarding class inequality and conflict, he disagreed with Marx's basic two-class schema. Weber's work was largely concerned with the structures of domination in capitalist society, particularly the bureaucratic structures. Using *bureaucracy* as his principal unit of analysis, Weber reasoned that bureaucrats and managers, who are not necessarily members of the capitalist class as it is defined by Marx, nonetheless wield a great deal of *power*. They are able to issue commands and have them obeyed, owing to the type of *authority* conferred upon them by the structure of bureaucratic organization in capitalist society. Unlike the traditional and charismatic forms of authority prevalent in earlier societies, modern society is characterized by increasing bureaucratization and the rational-legal type of authority. Such authority is based on the general acceptance by people of impersonal bureaucratic laws and rules. Interestingly, also, Weber argued that even in a socialist society, bureaucratic domination is inescapable.

In the final section of this chapter, we will take another look at the contributions of Marx, Durkheim and Weber.

# THE SOCIOLOGICAL IMAGINATION

## THE INFLUENCE OF THE PAST

Awareness of the relationship between history and sociology and the ability to appreciate the historical context of the origins of sociological thought are indispensable to an understanding of what sociology is. Indeed it is in this precise sense that C. Wright Mills (1959:146) observed that "all sociology worthy of the name is 'historical sociology'." As one of the most celebrated sociologists of the twentieth century, Charles Wright Mills (1917-1962) left an indelible stamp on the discipline. In his now classic monograph, *The Sociological Imagination*, Mills speaks of that quality of mind which characterizes the true sociologist.

It is only by carefully cultivating "the sociological imagination," Mills argues, that one can grasp the infinite complexity of social life. Such an imagination can simultaneously comprehend history and personal biography and understand how they intersect in society. By the intersection of history and biography he means realizing how individuals live their personal lives within the context of historical sequences (Mills, 1959:6). For Mills, therefore, the sociological imagination is developed through the rigorous application of social scientific methodology to an understanding of historical and contemporary social processes.

## MAN IS BOTH A CREATURE AND A CREATOR

As individuals, we are born into a world that is not of our own making. The society, norms and culture we inherit have definite histories to them, and those histories impinge on our lives, whether or not we like it, whether or not we are conscious of it. But this is a two-way street. Although we have no direct input into our societies before birth, the moment we are born we start acting as historically specific beings who influence our worlds. We are transformed from mere *creatures* of history into *creators* of history. To become aware of our personal biographies, our destinies, ourselves, then, we must understand the larger historical forces operating around us, even those forces and the particular conditions which called us into existence.

> The sociological imagination enables us to grasp history and biography and the relations between the two within society. That is its task and its promise. To recognize this task and this promise is the mark of the classic social analyst (Mills, 1959:6).

Neither individual biographies nor social histories can be understood in and of themselves. The two fields of investigation must be combined with the one informing the other. And the key to undertaking the entire project lies in the cultivation of that quality of mind referred to by Mills as the sociological imagination.

All too often in Western, liberal societies, where such emphasis is placed on the individual being self-motivated, self-supporting, self-fulfilled, self-confident and so on, the individual forgets that there is a wider social context within which he or she operates. Surely all of our behaviours and aspirations contain an element of individual or personal initiative. But the point is to recognize that such initiative is socially and culturally conditioned.

# THE IDEA OF SOCIAL STRUCTURE

Saying social behaviour is somehow "conditioned" immediately suggests a "conditioner." How does the wider social context affect human behaviour? The answer lies in the concept of *social structure*, which Coulson and Riddell (1980:33) described as "a key leadoff point, and the anchorage idea of sociology."

## STATUSES, ROLES AND NORMS

The concept of social structure recognizes that much of our everyday behaviour is regular and patterned. Such behaviour occurs within various social groups and generally follows set conventions. As members of society we each occupy several *statuses* and fulfill a variety of *roles*. For example, the status of student, daughter or policeman is accompanied by a series of behaviours expected of a student, daughter or policeman. These behaviours include a variety of rights and responsibilities that others associate with persons occupying such statuses and fulfilling their specific roles. According to the established *norms* of our society and culture, we have a fairly clear idea of how students, daughters and police officers should behave. In sociological terminology, we refer to these as *normative expectations*, i.e., those aspects of social interaction that can be taken for granted in a "normal" situation.

It is clear, too, that any given individual will occupy a number of different statuses. For example, one can be a daughter, a mother, an engineer and a teacher all at the same time. One's different statuses and roles often complement each other, but there is always the possibility of a conflict, as in the case of the police officer who sells illegal drugs. The statuses of police officer and drug dealer are incompatible, and hence we do not normatively expect them to be associated. But this does not mean to say they never are. Statuses also are either ascribed or achieved. An *ascribed* status is one into which we are born, for example, our gender status. It is relatively fixed and unchanging. *Achieved* status, on the other hand, is one we enter through purposive action, for example, our occupational status. It is subject to change because it can be gained or lost. Statuses and roles are important aspects of social structure.

## SOCIETY AS A COLLECTION OF INTERACTING PARTS

To more clearly illustrate what is meant by this concept, Coulson and Riddell (1980: 34-46) use the analogy of a watch. A watch can only tell us the time if its parts are *arranged in a particular way*. If we take a watch apart and hold its pieces in our hand, we cannot tell the time from all the screws, springs, wheels and hands that are thrown together in a haphazard fashion. The parts of the watch only reveal the time when placed in a set relationship to specific other parts, when structured in a definite manner. And while we may be unable to physically *see* that structure or the relationship among the parts, it nevertheless is real.

The same applies to human social behaviour. Human interaction is never the mere sum of the number of people or behaviours involved, but rather the patterns, the ways in which individual behaviours are displayed in relation to the whole. Our behaviour is never quite as haphazard as it may sometimes seem. It is, as was said above, patterned, fairly regular and highly structured; and it is the task of the sociologist to uncover that structure and make sense of it. For if our behaviour were totally unstructured and left up to individuals' whims and fancies, not only would it be impossible to study it, but *social* living itself would be impossible.

# FREE WILL VERSUS DETERMINISM

Since our behaviours are so conditioned by social structure, one may well wonder if individuals have any choice in the courses of action they pursue. Indeed, it may appear that we are so subject to this pervasive invisible force called social structure that we are wholly passive creatures devoid of will or initiative. Nothing is further from the truth.

Free will and determinism are not all-or-nothing phenomena. They are not either-or propositions, for human behaviour is clearly guided by elements of both. Surely we conform *generally* to group pressure, laws, norms, expectations and so on, but, as curious, thinking beings possessed of a will, we also at times, (consciously or unconsciously) resist group pressure, break laws, violate norms and defy expectations. Social life is not so tightly programmed that every facet of our behaviour can be prescribed. In fact, we are the ones who consciously make laws, collectively produce culture and determine what is appropriate and inappropriate behaviour for a given situation. The margin for social maneuverability is usually quite wide, and the various norms or social conventions are often loosely defined.

As social beings we have a need for belonging, we desire acceptance by friends and family, seek social approval and generally conform to the expectations of the group(s) to which we belong or want to belong. In this sense, social structure clearly influences us. But, as active social beings, we also drop out of groups, join others that we seek to change from the inside, or even establish our own groups with accompanying laws and norms.

Recognizing the importance of social structure for moulding behaviour does not imply a denial of free will. These are matters of degree. Human beings are, and have always been, limited to achieving those things which our physical and intellectual capacities permit. Not only are we limited by climate and geography, but also by physical strength, height, age *and* existing levels of skill, knowledge and scientific development. So a certain degree of "unfreedom" has always been with us. Freedom is relative.

To produce our basic needs — food, clothing and shelter — we have had to adapt to physical and biological limitations and overcome them with our intellects to survive. Thus, survival is a more or less constant struggle against nature, against traditionally established patterns of social organization, even against other human beings.

If we did not *actively* produce our own means of subsistence, no one would have done so for us. We would have died out, and the human species would have disappeared from the earth. In other words, we have never been free *not* to produce, *not* to become actively involved with each other, *not* to create.

In this sense, we can agree with Coulson and Riddell (1980:18), who argue that, far from being a depressing science that only shows us how we are prisoners of social structure, sociology is a liberating science. By helping us to understand the hidden constraints on our behaviour, by identifying the invisible mechanisms governing much of our social interaction, sociology lets us make meaningful choices regarding specific courses of action. And this is where free will, or *voluntarism*, enters the picture and serves to counterbalance determinism. Whether dealing with individuals in small-scale interpersonal relationships, or with groups operating at the larger societal level, sociological insight helps us avoid pitfalls hidden to the casual observer who relies primarily on common sense to guide his or her behaviour.

This does not mean there is anything inherently wrong with common sense as a mode of reasoning. But sociological insight is more systematic and rigorous. It penetrates surface appearances and gets to the underlying causes of social behaviour in a way that common sense, intuition, revelation, tradition and references to sacred and secular authorities can not. As Nisbet and Perrin (1977:10-12) point out, sociological explanation relies on the logic of verification, whereas the above-mentioned ways of arriving at knowledge do not. For example, some people believe that Canadian Indians have less respect for law than other Canadians; men are smarter than women; blacks make better athletes than whites; doctors are smarter than nurses. For such people, the so-called facts speak for themselves; the statistics do not lie. The task of sociology, however, is to question such "facts" and, as in the case of these examples, expose their falsity.

# APPROACHING SOCIETY

Apart from using historical data, sociologists have also employed a number of other techniques for gathering information on relevant issues. These techniques will be discussed more fully in Chapter 2, but, for the present, a brief introduction is in order.

The types of research questions addressed by sociologists will determine, to a large degree, the types of data that they will collect. Sociological questions, as we saw, can be of a macro or micro nature. But it must not be assumed that one is divorced from the other. For example, Marx's (macro) concern with the impact of economic exploitation on the development of revolutionary consciousness among workers is directly related to Weber's (micro) interest in how individuals socially construct *meanings* of their world. Revolutionary consciousness is intimately connected to people's religious orientations and values, which are linked with their family and class backgrounds, which in turn are filtered through their personal and individual life experiences and finally balanced by their subjective assessments of the likelihood that revolution is in their best interests.

It is clear, therefore, that to determine which individuals, groups and classes are most likely to develop revolutionary ideas is no simple matter. Or similarly, if we wish to know what kinds of people move to suburbia, which segments of the elderly population will protest specific types of governmental legislation, which economic groups will be more prone to a particular type of deviant behaviour or which religious groupings will favour abortion, a wide variety of data on individuals, groups, classes, organizations, beliefs, occupations, residential location and so on will have to be collected, interpreted and analysed.

In this context, we can think of how the research on a specific group can have implications for the larger society. A case in point is a recent Toronto study of occupational discrimination against blacks in that city. The research findings pointed clearly to the existence of extensive discriminatory practices in both the private and public spheres. Apart from the psychological and economic consequences at the level of individuals, such discrimination also has serious familial, political, social, and even constitutional (human rights) implications. Clearly, no single sociological study, no one theoretical or methodological approach will suffice to capture the complexity and magnitude of the problems involved in that situation. As a result, sociologists, whether working independently or hired for example, by government, will gather relevant information using a variety of methods.

Since all members of the society, black and non-black, are affected, the sociologist in this study will be interested in *interviewing* samples of the population, administering *questionnaires* or conducting *surveys* and *participating* with people on an overt or covert basis in order to experience directly the situation, all with a view to collecting data on the extent of discrimination. After such data are scientifically analysed, recommendations are made to the proper authorities, and specific policies aimed at correcting the situation can then be implemented. These, in turn, can affect individuals, groups, organizations, communities or society as a whole.

Thus, in addition to historical methods, sociologists also collect a great deal of contemporary data on various aspects of social life through a multiplicity of methods. And it is a direct consideration of those methods and research techniques that we address in the next chapter.

# SOCIOLOGY AS A SCIENCE

## EMPIRICAL KNOWLEDGE

The reason sociological knowledge claims superiority to knowledge derived from common sense observations, intuition, biblical revelation and so on is that sociological knowledge is scientifically generated. But, before proceeding further, some clarification of the term "science" is necessary. Originating from the Latin verb *scire*, to know, the term "science" refers to the acquisition of systematized knowledge based on observation, study and experimentation. Scientific knowledge is thus *empirically* derived, for it comes to us via sensory perception: seeing, feeling, hearing, smelling and tasting.

Generally speaking, when we hear the word science, we think of natural or physical sciences such as botany, geology, physics or chemistry. We also think of the scientist as someone making precise and accurate predictions about his or her subject matter. In a sense, the subject matter of the natural or physical scientist — plants, rocks, metals or gases — lends itself neatly to observation, experimentation, testing, weighing, measurement and manipulation. It is relatively uncomplicated to study such things within controlled laboratory settings, where the scientist can observe the behaviour of matter in response to the careful manipulation of specific conditions or variables.

## NATURAL VERSUS SOCIAL SCIENCE

The physicist studying the strength of a given physical structure, say, a bridge, may build a model to scale in her laboratory and simulate normal conditions, applying weights, calculating for wind pressure, erosion and so on. In this way she obtains a reasonably accurate idea of how much weight the bridge can support, the potentially weak points and the types of safety measures that should be implemented. This is all possible because her subject matter is always *compelled to react* in the same manner when subjected to the same conditions. For sociology, a social science, however, the situation is different. The subject matter of the social scientist is *qualitatively* different. It does not lend itself readily to controlled laboratory testing, for the subject matter of the social scientist is the human being, the human group, the human society. For the sociologist in particular, his laboratory is the society at large. And that society is so highly complex and variable that it is often difficult to predict precisely how every individual or group will behave at any given time. Such precise prediction, however, is *not* the concern of the sociologist.

What distinguishes the subject matter of the natural scientist from that of the social scientist is precisely what distinguishes natural science from social science. Whereas the subject matter of the former is devoid of consciousness and a will, the subject matter of the latter is possessed of consciousness and will. As was stated above, the structure of the bridge will *always* react in the same way to set or fixed conditions. It cannot choose *not* to buckle under too much pressure. The human being, on the other hand, if punched in the nose today, may choose to run away; but tomorrow, the same punch may elicit the opposite response — he or she may *choose* to punch back.

Because the sociologist's subject matter is comprised of rational, thinking beings with emotions, feelings, sentiments, values, morals, consciousness and will, studying it calls for different methods than those employed by the natural scientist. Further, since humans are primarily subjective beings, they interact and communicate through symbols to *interpret* and *assign meanings* to the multiplicity of phenomena that make up the natural and social universe. And this sets them apart not only from rocks and trees, but also from lower forms of animal life that do not possess the capacity for abstract thought. Nisbet and Perrin state the matter succinctly. What really serves to differentiate the social from the natural sciences, they say, is that

> only individuals assign meanings to the world around them and act in terms of such meanings. The difference between mere water and holy water, or between mere oil and anointing oil, lies in the meaning conferred (1977:4).

Sociology, then, as the science of society, seeks to make sense of those meanings, to uncover what is regular or patterned about them, to identify when and where they can be expected to influence behaviour.

As a social scientist, the sociologist specializes in generalities, whereas the natural scientist specializes in the particular. The former aims not to make precise predictions of how a given individual will react in a given situation, but rather to identify general behaviour patterns within and among groups, explain how and why those patterns emerge, how they persist, why they may break down, and under what conditions new ones may be established. This social forecasting is never aimed at one hundred percent accuracy, for the complex and variable nature of social behaviour does not permit it.

As a social science, sociology recognizes that all individuals are unique, but this does not mean that such uniqueness rules out making accurate general statements about group attributes. In fact, as Sorokin (1969:7-8) correctly points out, sociology even distinguishes itself from the other social sciences in this respect. Whereas economics, politics, religion and psychology deal narrowly with *homo economicus*, *homo politicus*, *homo religiosus* and *homo psychologicus*,

> *homo socius* of sociology is viewed as a generic and manifold *homo*, simultaneously and inseparably economic, political, religious, ethical and artistic, partly rational and utilitarian, partly non-rational and even irrational, with all these aspects incessantly influencing one another.

Therefore individual uniqueness is not a barrier to sociological explanation. Surely each individual possesses unique qualities and personality traits, but social behaviour never takes place solely on the basis of those qualities and traits that distinguish individuals one from the other. As Coulson and Riddell state:

> There is no incompatibility between a thing being unique and sharing characteristics with others . . . an individual does not respond to a situation in terms of one characteristic alone, but as a whole person. (1982:18)

Hence, while an individual's *total* combination of characteristics may make him or her unique, that individual shares many characteristics with others. And those common characteristics make it possible to identify general patterns and permit sociological explanation and prediction.

The above speaks to sociology's dual task. Firstly, we can see that, while sociology differs from the other social sciences in its scope and content, it is also related in various degrees and combinations to the other social sciences. The first challenge to sociology, then, is to explain the common elements and relationships in a given social phenomenon. The second challenge is to account for the differences. Since almost every sphere of social interaction will encompass economic, political, religious and other elements, it is evident the sociologist's ability to make informed generalizations places him or her in an advantageous situation. In sum, while the economist is narrowly concerned with considerations of prices and wages, while the political scientist studies patterns of vote distribution, and while the specialist in religious behaviour investigates how people's present-day behaviour is influenced by their views of the hereafter, only the sociologist brings them all together to render a genuinely *social* explanation of human behaviour. This is what distinguishes sociology as a separate discipline within the social sciences.

## CONTENDING PERSPECTIVES WITHIN SOCIOLOGY

So far, we have been discussing the sociological outlook or perspective as being common to all practitioners of sociology. Though helpful, this may prove misleading if the reader assumes all sociologists agree on all things. As Wilson (1983:10) has argued, there is "no single all-embracing theory that has proven adequate to deal with the wide range of problems sociologists identify as theirs." Sociologists aim to understand society, critique it and suggest how it may be reformed. However, one must not assume, as was stated in the introduction to this chapter, that the variety and complexity of social living somehow indicate that sociological insight is a mere hodgepodge of inconclusive and unconnected information. Rather, instead of viewing the abundance and variety of sociological theory as a sign of sociology's weakness and ineptitude, it must be regarded as a sign of its vitality and strength (Wilson, 1983:10). For it is through the free interplay of opposing ideas that we can gain a fuller understanding of our complex social world.

Hence, sociologists, though they may agree on what constitutes a social problem or issue, do not always agree on the ways to deal with it. In essence, this is a philosophical matter concerning differences in ontology and epistemology. *Ontology* refers to a theory of essence or being — it talks about what *is* or what is real. Epistemology, on the other hand, refers to method: how do we come to *know* what is or what is real?

At first sight these differences may seem trivial. But not so, for our ontological and epistemological premises often determine which problems we deem relevant and their appropriate solutions. More crucially, if two sociologists, coming from distinct ontological and epistemological positions, study a common problem, it is highly unlikely they will ever agree on a common solution.

Consider, for example, the question of human aggression. The researcher who makes the ontological assumption that aggression is natural and *instinctual*, will clearly never agree with the researcher who thinks aggression is *learned* behaviour. This is the old nature versus nurture argument, and, depending on one's position in this argument, the epistemological questions can vary greatly.

The sociologist who assumes human aggression is natural will design a totally different plan of investigation from the sociologist who sees aggressive behaviour as the result of social learning processes. And as each delves more deeply into his or her respective study, the questions asked will become increasingly dissimilar. In the end, since the kinds of questions we ask tend to determine the kinds of answers we receive, our two sociologists will present us with two diametrically opposed sets of research findings on the same problem. The two researchers, and others within the scholarly community, must then determine which findings are more adequate. Then the process snowballs and generates all types of debates, subsidiary studies, conferences, refutations, confirmations and so on, and these collectively make up and define the stuff of sociology.

To get a clearer idea of the main contending perspectives in sociology today, however, it would be helpful to identify a specific theme and examine how it has been addressed by various sociological schools of thought. One issue of interest to all such schools is that of social order and social change. We will, therefore, examine how functionalists, Marxists and symbolic interactionists conceive of the problem of order in society.

## STRUCTURAL FUNCTIONALISM

As one of the leading schools of thought in sociology, structural functionalism has had a long history. The term "function" itself, is one

> which came into the foreground of philosophic discourse in the last quarter of the nineteenth century and has maintained an increasingly strong position there ever since (Kallen, 1937: 523).

Though difficult to trace directly, its overall origins may be found in the disciplines of biology, art, law and architecture. But as far as its use in the social sciences goes, we must look to anthropology and the works of such men as Bronislaw Malinowski and A.R. Radcliffe-Brown. Among sociologists specifically, Durkheim is viewed as the first to have applied systematically functionalist principles to the analysis of society.

The structural functionalist approach has been characterized by much confusion and disagreement, both among its practitioners and its critics; and much of this confusion stems from the definitions of the terms "structure" and "function." Before discussing these terms, however, two points must be made: a) The questions addressed by structural functionalists are eminently sociological, and, like the questions of Marxists and symbolic interactionists (to be discussed next), concern the general relationship between social order and social change; and b) it is misleading to identify the structural functionalist approach exclusively with any *one* theorist, for many structural functionalists make different assumptions about society, ask different questions and employ different research procedures to answer them.

Why, then, are they grouped together in a single school of thought? The answer lies in their *teleological* approach to understanding society: They all seek to analyse social structures and practices by reference to the ends or purposes they serve. Structural functional analysis, for example, argues that specific social institutions (e.g., marriage, religion) exist because they contribute to the overall survival of the social system. Those institutions that do not function toward this end will ultimately disappear.

Structural functionalism is based on the notion that society is more than just the sum of its individual parts. For society, like an organism, has a structure of its own, over and above its constituent elements. And in the same way that a living organism

*Parsons was born in the United States and studied at Amherst College and the London School of Economics. Though initially interested in biology, he later switched to social science and came to distinguish himself internationally in sociology. For several years he held the chair of sociology at Harvard, during which time his name became synonymous with the school of structural functionalism. His book, **The Structure of Social Action** (1937), was the first of 150 books and articles that spanned a career of over 50 years.* Photo courtesy of Harvard University New Office.

*Talcott Parsons (1902-1980)*

has *needs* that must be met if it is to survive, so too with society. Continuing this *organismic analogy*, society's needs are seen to include such things as reproducing the species, regulating the behaviour of individuals and providing for the physical subsistence of the population.

The strategy of social inquiry adopted by this school treats society as a *system* whose various parts are organized into *structures* or institutions, each of which fulfills some *function* for the system as a whole (Grabb, 1984:71). Let us, then, examine what is meant by these terms and see how they inform this particular sociological approach.

Talcott Parsons (1902-1980) is the structural functionalist best known for his use of the concept of "social system." For him society or the social system is viewed as

> a set of related and interdependent phenomena which have boundaries that are maintained; it exists in a state of equilibrium or balance with its environment and has certain mechanisms for maintaining this state (Cashmore and Mullan, 1983:180).

The "mechanisms" referred to are social institutions which are related to a number of subsystems that in turn are connected to the larger social system. Every social system or subsystem must fulfill four basic *needs* that are key to its survival: a) adaptation; b) goal attainment; c) integration; and d) pattern maintenance.

At the level of society, these *vital system needs* correspond to four subsystems of the larger social system: the economy, the polity, the community and the fiduciary. As subsystems, however, each of these contributes to the maintenance and survival of the larger whole, which is society. But subsystems are still systems, and as such must also ensure that their respective needs of adaptation, goal attainment, integration and pattern maintenance are met. For the social system, then, the economic subsystem that encompasses the economic institutions contributes to adaptation by ensuring the effective production and allocation of disposable resources. The political subsystem and its related institutions set overall goals for the society and provide for their realization. The community functions as an integrative subsystem by promoting a sense of social cohesiveness or solidarity. And finally, the fiduciary is that subsystem concerned with pattern maintenance at the cultural level. It deals with such things as promoting value commitment and shared social goals.

Hence, the idea of the social system is one of a social whole in which the various structures or institutions function in harmony to maintain it in a state of equilibrium. This is how the concept of "structure" becomes relevant to structural functionalism. For structures refer to organized patterns of relationships or practices between parts of a system. Structure also implies that there is some continuity to the pattern, that it is enduring.

Thus, if we look at the economic *structure* of society, we are concerned with the economic institutions and the specialized tasks or functions they perform in the economic division of labour: in the area of energy, for example, we can think of the oil companies that extract the oil from the ground; the processing of oil into gas; the use of gas to power cars; the use of cars in getting people to work. All of these specialized economic tasks and the adaptations and interconnections they imply constitute the *economic structure* of a society. And the same can be done for the political, juridical, educational and religious institutions.

To discuss social institutions as structures automatically implies a consideration of the people who populate them. The activities of these people are themselves structured in a hierarchy of *statuses* that cover a multiplicity of *roles*. The statuses or positions that individuals occupy in an institution correspond to the goals of the institution, and each individual has a role with its accompanying rights, duties and responsibilities. Thus, from the micro level of the individual to the macro level of the social system as a whole, one can trace the many links that integrate the society.

This then brings us to the last key concept in structural functional analysis: the idea of *function*. Here the term refers to the contributions that an institution or structure makes in relation to the whole. In other words, we are told that the function of a social institution has to be understood in terms of its contribution to the survival of the social system: The institution of marriage functions to ensure orderly procreation and the nurturing of children, which enable the society to maintain itself from generation to generation.

But as Robert K. Merton (1957), himself a structural functionalist, has pointed out, this view is conservatively biased in favour of a strict, orderly view of society. It leaves little room for considerations of change and conflict. For if all institutions function positively to promote system survival, how does change come about? Thus, while Merton acknowledged the fact that a given social structure may be functional for some, he also recognized that it will not necessarily by functional for all. And in his analysis of the political machine, he came to appreciate the existence of conflicts between competing interest groups in society, though he never dealt with how they might be eliminated. In addressing the conservative bias, however, Merton introduced the notions of *functions* and *dysfunctions* of social structures: Those structures that help the system adapt to its environment are said to be functional; those that impede such adaptation are labelled dysfunctional.

However, although Merton recognized that the same structure could have both functional and dysfunctional effects, he and other structural functionalists usually assume that a given pattern or institution would not survive unless its functions outweighed its dysfunctions (Wilson, 1983:76). And to this he added one further refinement: The functions and dysfunctions of an institution can be *manifest* or *latent*. If they are intended and recognized by members of society, they are manifest; if they are unintended and unrecognized, they are latent. For example, the institution of religion has the manifest function of giving the individual spiritual support and comfort, while it functions latently to maintain group solidarity (Cashmore and Mullan, 1983:152).

In sum, therefore, structural functionalism contributes many insights into the operations of society that are not necessarily provided by other sociological approaches. And given its conservatism, its inability to deal with questions of radical change in society, it makes for an interesting backdrop against which to examine the more radical perspective of Marxism. [For a more elaborate and systematic exposition of structural functionalism and the important criticisms of it, see Coulson and Riddell (1980) and Wilson (1983)].

## MARXISM

The school of sociology that draws its main lines of reasoning from the work of Karl Marx (1818-1883) is radically opposed to functionalism. Whereas functionalists are preoccupied with the questions of order and stability in society, Marxists stress disorder and conflict as equally integral aspects of social living. Some key concepts employed by Marxists are social class, exploitation, struggle and revolution.

Like the functionalists, Marxists study social order, but they disagree with the functionalists on how social order is achieved. Instead of assuming order is automatically generated on the basis of commonly shared values, Marxists think that order is largely *coerced* — it comes about, directly or indirectly, through force. And the ability to use force or to threaten to use force belongs to certain groups and classes owing to their positions in the social structure.

In essence, Marxists argue that order is secured by one of, or a combination of, three elements (Zeitlin, 1981a:112-114). The first element is fear, pure and simple. We behave properly, obey the laws and do what is expected of us because we fear the consequences of arrest, imprisonment and punishment. Of course, some people willingly break the law and flout social conventions, but such people are few, and their collective deviance does not disrupt the general social order. The second element is more narrowly economic. In our society, the vast majority of people depend on wages and salaries to survive. Without a job many of us would be unable to feed and clothe ourselves. Hence, as Weber (1961:208-209) says, we go to work and do what is expected, for "under the compulsion of the whip of hunger" we cannot afford to risk being fired. Finally, the third element that promotes an ordered society according to Marxists is ideology. Those in power maintain control, not by force alone, but by encouraging us to view the world as they see it. Their definitions of justice, morality and propriety become our definitions. This point will be developed further in the chapter on ideology, which discusses the Marxian notion of false consciousness and the Weberian idea of the legitimation of authority.

Society, for the Marxists, is not made up simply of a variety of individuals and groups that co-operate and work together in pursuing common social ends. Quite the contrary: Society is composed of hostile and antagonistic classes pursuing incompatible ends. For example, among the many social classes, Marx focused on the two principal ones: the bourgeoisie, or the property-owning capatalist class, and the proletariat, or propertyless working class. The primary goal of the capitalists is accumulating capital in the form of money, land, livestock, factories, machinery or raw materials. And in pursuing this goal, the capitalists' interests conflict with those of the workers.

The conflict of class interests is seen to reside in the fact that the capitalists own and control the bulk of the property in society, and if the mass of the people are to survive, they must seek employment in the factories, farms, corporations and other enterprises of the capitalists. But, in pursuing profit and accumulating capital, the capitalists cannot afford to pay their workers the *full value* of everything that the latter produce. Hence, the wages paid to the workers represent what is left after the capitalist has deducted his profit and reinvested part of it, paid his rent, bought new raw materials, replaced and repaired his machinery, and put aside some for his personal consumption.

Realizing they live quite differently from the capitalists and that their lot in life does not improve over time in the same way as the capitalists', the workers become understandably upset. Some form unions to secure better wages, better working conditions, better benefits; they may even go on strike to achieve these ends. Reasoning that the factories, farms, corporations and businesses cannot work without them and that the wealth and general well-being of the capitalist are derived from their labour and the products of it, the workers start seeing their own interests as opposed to those of the capitalists. They argue that they are *exploited*, i.e., that they are giving more in labour than they receive in wages, and demand a more equal share of the profits.

Out of this situation, the Marxists say, revolutions are born. To maximize profits, capitalists aspire to pay low wages and to crush unions, since higher wages and benefits imply lower profits. When such a situation is widespread, when wages are so depressed that workers can barely afford decent food, clothes, housing, education for their children and adequate health care, society runs the risk of a working-class uprising. The Marxists insist, further, that such a risk increases when the *objective* conditions of poverty and misery combine with the worker's *subjective* awareness that they could take matters into their own hands and make things better for themselves. This is called *developing class consciousness*.

This is generally how Marxists view a breakdown of social order. There comes a time when fear of the police, fear of losing one's job and the appeal of the prevailing ideology can no longer function to preserve the social order.

To Marxists, then, capitalist industrial society represents a curious mix of order and conflict. The institutional framework responsible for preserving order and regulating conflict is called the *state*. For Marx, the state is a committee of men making decisions, developing laws and taking action *in support of the interests of the capitalist class*. The state is not an impartial body governing society in the interests of all individuals, groups and classes. Hence, Marx argues that the advent of socialism will mean the disappearance of the class-based capitalist state. In a socialist society, the workers are supposed to hold both economic and political power after over-throwing capitalism. Socialism is a transition stage between the unequal capitalist society and the final stage, communism, in which all men and women will be equal.

We will have more to say about capitalism, socialism and equality in the chapter on historical patterns of development. For the moment, an insight into Marxist views of the capitalist state and society can be found in Miliband (1969) and the response to Miliband by Poulantzas (1973). Good summaries of both positions are contained in Giddens (1982).

## SYMBOLIC INTERACTIONISM

While the concerns of functionalists and Marxists are macrosociological, owing to their focus on whole societies or large subsections of them, the perspective known as symbolic interactionism deals with more microsociological issues. Symbolic interactionists pay less attention to the impact of social structure on human behaviour, while emphasizing the moment of social interaction at the individual level.

As a separate perspective within the discipline, symbolic interaction draws its main teachings from the works of Max Weber, George Herbert Mead and Herbert Blumer. Although it would be inaccurate to characterize Weber as a symbolic interactionist and nothing more, it is clear that Weber's writings on "social action" provide the basis upon which this tradition was built. For Weber, the sociological enterprise deals with an *interpretive* understanding of human social behaviour. To correctly interpret behaviour, Weber argues, sociologists must realize that human beings are *subjective* actors who attach *meaning* to their acts. In fact, interaction is only possible if subjective meanings are shared by the participants in an interactive situation — and this is what makes it specifically *social* interaction.

According to Weber, social structure alone cannot explain the totality of behaviour. As mentioned earlier, the subject matter of sociology is the living, thinking, acting, conscious human being. And human behaviour, though constrained by social structure, is also infused with purpose, motive and subjective intent. Hence, no accurate assessment of behaviour can ignore human choice and will, for these invariably intermingle with social structure to produce set patterns of social action.

For Mead (1934) and Blumer (1962), however, social structure is of less importance in understanding behaviour. For them, social living is "symbolic" in that we communicate, co-operate and socialize using common symbols, e.g., language. As Haralambos and Heald observe:

> Symbols provide the means whereby man can interact meaningfully with his natural and social environment. They are man-made and refer not to the intrinsic nature of objects and events but to the ways in which men perceive them (1980:544).

Because human beings do not have instincts to guide their behaviour, they rely almost entirely on *learning* what is appropriate or inappropriate behaviour. Such learning, however, can only take place on the basis of shared symbols whose meanings

*Mead was born in the United States to a comfortable middle-class family. He studied philosophy and psychology at Oberlin College and Harvard University. As he came to see the influence of societal forces on the development of mind, self, and language, his work increasingly assumed a sociological orientation. In 1893 he joined the faculty of philosophy at Chicago, where he deepened his interest in sociology. Though not a prolific writer, Mead's **Mind, Self and Society** (1932) is an authoritative statement on the symbolic interactionist dimension of human life.* The Granger Collection, New York.

*George Herbert Mead (1863-1931)*

are communicated to the actors involved in a continuous process of interaction. Thus, to survive, make plans and develop society, men and women consciously construct and live within a world of meaning. And most importantly, at the level of interacting individuals these meanings are *negotiated* — they are defined and refined by social actors in specific situations.

For the sake of social order, therefore, actors must interpret the meanings and intentions of others and respond in an *inter-subjective* manner. To explain this, Mead developed the concept of "role-taking," whereby an individual imaginatively places herself in the position of the person with whom she is interacting. For example, if you observed someone walking briskly toward you with a stern look on his face and shouting verbal abuse, you consciously (or unconsciously) put yourself in that person's place by using your imagination in order to interpret his intention and meaning. And based on the interpretation you assign to such symbolic action, you choose to (re)act: You may run away, prepare for a fight, attempt to pacify that person, and so on. In the meantime, the person is also observing and interpreting your behaviour, for he is also role-taking; and depending on his interpretation of your behaviour, he may choose to strike you, to talk out the problem, or to threaten you verbally. Hence, we see how the symbolic interactionist, who analyses human interaction at the level of individuals, views interaction as a more or less continuous process of interpretation and reinterpretation of meanings.

In sum, then, social order is maintained when the various parties to any given interactive situation have similar interpretations and definitions of that situation. In the words of Haralambos and Heald:

It is a 'negotiated order' in that it derives from meanings which are negotiated in the process of interaction and involves the mutual adjustment of the actors concerned. The net result is the establishment of social order, of an orderly, regular and patterned process of interaction (1980:553).

For a more detailed exposition and critique of symbolic interactionism, refer to Meltzer, Petras and Reynolds (1975).

## A BRIEF ASSESSMENT

While each of the sociological perspectives discussed above has its own great strengths, none is perfect. Structural functionalism, for example, has been criticized at several levels; such criticism will be discussed in greater detail in the coming chapters. For the moment, however, some of the general features can be mentioned. The most telling criticism levelled at this school concerns its inability to account for radical social change. The conservative bias inherent in this approach leads to a one-sided emphasis on questions of social order, system integration, equilibrium and consensus. Structural functionalism has also been faulted for its use of the organismic analogy. All too often, structural functionalists tend to forget that they are dealing with an analogy and treat society as if it were, in fact, a living organism with all the characteristics that living organisms share. Two other criticisms that may be noted here concern the imprecise definition of key terms and the tendency toward circular reasoning. Terms such as structure, function and system, for example, are neither clearly nor consistently operationalized, and this leads to much confusion. On the question of circularity or tautological reasoning, the structural functionalists argue that only those social institutions that function positively to maintain the social system will continue to survive. The problem here is that one cannot tell the difference between the cause and the effect: How do we know that a given institution has functioned positively? Because it has survived! Why did it survive? Because it functioned positively! We are left neatly enclosed in a circle.

Shifting our focus to the orthodox Marxist approach, three common criticisms are encountered. The first concerns the blurring of class boundaries in an advanced capitalist society. Surely we can distinguish the owners of productive property from the nonowners, but there have been very significant increases in the white collar, managerial and technical sectors that serve to confound greatly the Marxian schema. Though not owners of productive property in the direct sense, these sectors wield a great deal of power in the day-to-day operations of capitalist enterprises. And although their interests may often complement those of the direct owners, the orthodox Marxist approach has great difficulty explaining just how those interests intersect in their class model. Related to the above is the charge that the orthodox Marxist view of the capitalist state is far too mechanical. It is simplistic and inaccurate to assert that the state is nothing more than a tool in the hands of the capitalist class that can be manipulated at will. Finally, there is the oft-repeated criticism that Marx did not foresee the extent to which capitalism could deflect or even accommodate many of the contradictions which he felt would lead to its demise. Contrary to the expectation of Marx, the socialist revolution simply has not occurred in advanced capitalistic societies.

Regarding the microsociological approach of symbolic interactionism, the two major criticisms of this school concern its tendency to neglect the importance of social structure and its overemphasis on the conscious and subjective actions of individuals. Symbolic interactionists generally assume that individual behaviour is guided by inner states and personal motives that override the constraints of social structure. By doing so, they open themselves up to the charge that their work is more psychological. Also, by making the conscious, individual actor their unit of analysis, they are unable to claim objectivity, and this calls into question the scientific status of their work.

## CANADIAN SOCIOLOGY

If sociology has often been described as a young science, one that is still in its infancy, then Canadian sociology will have to be described as a mere fetus. As recently as the 1960s, the only autonomous department of sociology in Canada was at McGill University. This meant, as Clark (1979:399) has pointed out, that up until around 1965 the ranks of sociology teachers in this country were very thin, and what might be called a body of Canadian sociological literature was even thinner. Apart from McGill and the University of Toronto, where sociology was but an appendage to the department of political economy, Canadians wishing to study sociology usually did so at American universities.

When one talks of the pioneers of Canadian sociology, the names of Carl Dawson, Harold Innis (an economist), S.D. Clark and John Porter immediately spring to mind. These men left an indelible stamp on the development of the discipline in Canada and served to give it a focus distinct from American sociology as it was conceived and practised at the University of Chicago. Dawson's work on Canadian ethnic communities, Innis' writings on the fur trade and metropolis/hinterland relations, Clark's research on diverse aspects of Canadian society and economy and Porter's analyses of culture and stratification in the Canadian mosaic served to define the beginnings of an indigenous sociology of Canada. Building on these pioneering efforts, contemporary Canadian sociologists have begun to develop a truly Canadian sociological literature.

Canadian sociology, however, did not develop along a single path. As a result of the French-English cleavage in Canadian society, there also emerged distinct Francophone and Anglophone sociological orientations. In French Canada, the strong links between educational and religious institutions obstructed the initial acceptance of sociology, which often challenged religious beliefs and teachings and counselled a more secular approach to life (Rocher, 1977:495). In English Canada, on the other hand, as in Britain, sociology was viewed as an upstart social science and in the early years reluctantly was attached to more traditional departments such as history, anthropology and political economy. Having to contend with the influence and opposition of the Catholic Church, Francophone sociology came to develop a more critical and activist side in comparison to its Anglophone counterpart, which was characterized by the conservative, functionalist and Chicago-based teachings of such men as Hughes and Park.

In discussing sociology in English Canada particularly, one cannot fail to take note of the "Canadianization debate" of the early 1970s. That debate, Hiller tells

*Carl Dawson (left), Everett Hughes (right) and sociology graduate students at McGill, 1931. The work of Dawson and his students was the earliest in Canadian sociology and focused primarily on the development of ethnic communities in greater Montreal and the Prairies. Everett Hughes, an eminent American sociologist, taught at McGill for many years. His study of the ethnic division of labour in an Eastern Townships community influenced Quebec sociology for decades.* Courtesy of Dennis William Magill.

*The work of S.D. Clark has left an indelible mark on Canadian sociology. His early work incorporated historical and economic analysis into sociological explanations of the development of Canadian social institutions. He later added elements of American structural functionalism to his repertoire. One of Clark's unique strengths has been his ability to discover and explain nonobvious and often surprising relationships between economy and society.*

us, can be divided into two stages: The first concerned matters of *personnel*, while the second related specifically to *content* or *perspective* (1979:126; 132). The personnel dispute accompanied a rising tide of economic and political nationalism and was especially aimed at the large numbers of foreigners, mainly Americans, who occupied key academic positions in Canadian universities. The issue over content and perspective, however, was more fundamental. It called for a genuine Canadian orientation to understanding this society and sought to reject foreign models, foreign theoretical formulations and foreign case studies. Canadian sociology, it was maintained, must be rooted in an appreciation of Canada's unique history and must address Canadian problems. According to Hiller, the Canadian sociology movement sought

> to develop different or at least additional theoretical perspectives than currently typical of sociology in Canada, and which should change sociology from an imported to a more indigenous discipline (1979:133).

As we will see in the following chapters, then, both the development of sociology in Canada and the development of Canadian sociology, though still nascent, have already generated a rich tradition upon which to build.

## SUMMARY

In this chapter we have examined sociology from a wide-angle perspective, sacrificing detail for a more panoramic view of the discipline. We have seen that the laboratory of the sociologist is society at large, with all of its infinite variety and complexity. Further, sociologists are not only concerned with present-day forms of social organization, but also study history in a search for possible future trends and patterns.

Generally speaking, sociologists of all persuasions agree that society is the product of human beings interacting in social situations. Culture, norms, values, laws, religion and politics are just some of the major social conventions studied by sociologists. These make up the "stuff" of society, for more than anything else they distinguish human beings from other animals. Sociologists, therefore, concern themselves with human beings and the wide variety of behaviour people display as individuals, in groups, as members of social classes, as citizens and so on.

Sociologists want to know whether such behaviour is regular and predictable. To what extent do our groups, classes and associations influence our behaviour? This question acknowledges the pervasiveness of social structure, which largely patterns our behaviour. On the other hand, sociologists also study behaviours that occur in spite of the fact that our interactions are highly structured. This raises the question of free will versus determinism. For our society to be an ordered one, some patterned response or predictability is necessary; but the human being, as a conscious and thinking animal, is never totally passive. Hence, sociologists, as social scientists, seek to understand both social order and the factors sustaining it and social disorder and change and the factors promoting them. The active, curious, restless human being is both a creature and a creator of society, pursues both stability and change, is conditioned by social structure and possessed of free will; and out of this point-counterpoint interplay sociologists derive the subject matter of their discipline.

# DISCUSSION QUESTIONS

1. In what sense are human beings simultaneously creatures and creators of society?

2. How does sociological insight differ from insight yielded by common sense, intuition and revelation?

3. How does the concept of "social structure" relate to the debate concerning free will and determinism?

4. What is the basis upon which sociology claims to be a science?

5. Though instructive as an analogy, what are some of the potential problems and/or limitations that can result from viewing society as a living organism?

# 2

# Sociological Methods of Research

*Peter Li*

# INTRODUCTION

Sociologists use several methods to approach social facts, the choice of which depends on the nature of the research problem, the preference of the researcher and the scope of the study. The basic objective of these methods, however, is the same. All methods accomplish two tasks: they collect accurate empirical evidence and discard incorrect explanations.

Science questions the obvious. This means questioning what has been taken for granted, re-examining facts and advancing novel explanations based on new observations and insights. To challenge what others have accepted require weeding out unreliable and irrelevant facts from voluminous evidence and building new concepts and theories from the empirical findings.

In this chapter, we shall examine the following methods of investigation: experimental design, historical/comparative research, survey method, participant observation and the use of secondary materials. The experimental design provides the framework for scientific proofs and disproofs, although its direct application to sociological problems is often not feasible. Thus, sociologists must often use comparisons to approximate the logic of experimentation. Comparing similar cases yields a general type, while contrasting different cases permits specifying typological differentiations. In a case study where explicit comparisions are absent, sociologists use detailed information gathered to refute or refine existing theories. We shall also study measurement and sampling problems which affect all types of research. But before we proceed, we must understand the logic of sociological inquiry and how to formulate a sociological question.

## THE LOGIC OF SOCIOLOGICAL INQUIRY

All sciences have certain standards and rules of research practice. These standards represent coherent traditions of scientific research and are referred to as *paradigms* (Kuhn, 1970). Put simply, paradigms are examples or models representing points of view expressed in scientific schools of thought. They represent basic assumptions, philosophies and cumulative findings upon which scientists conduct their research.

Underlying scientific development is what Kuhn (1970) calls the *structure of scientific revolution*, that is, the transformation of one paradigm into another. The catalyst for a scientific revolution is the appearance of anomalies, or gaps, between facts and the theories that supposedly explain them. When the anomalies recur systematically, scientists are forced to search for new solutions which the old paradigm fails to provide. New ideas, previously rejected, may be re-examined. Questions never raised before may now be asked. Out of this confusion come new theories to explain the anomalies. Some theories survive testing, others are discarded. Through repeated experiments and trials, new ideas are advanced and gradually forged into a new paradigm which will serve as a new guideline for research and for problem-solving until anomalies surface again.

Sociology today is a multi-paradigm discipline (Ritzer, 1975) with several competing schools coexisting. Examples include structural functionalism, symbolic interactionism and dialectical materialism. One way of evaluating the validity of paradigms is to rely on empirical evidence. To understand how theories are tested, we must examine the research cycle.

## The Research Cycle

The research cycle basically works on two levels: theory and facts. One goal of science is to develop more general theories that may be applied more universally. Sociologists are constantly theorizing about human interactions and relationships. In such an exercise, a sociologist checks for logical inconsistencies until he comes up with a rational explanation of the phenomena he is investigating. This exercise, however, is largely a mental construct. The way to find out whether the explanation or theory has an empirical basis is to check it against concrete facts. If the facts are inconsistent with the theory, the sociologist must re-evaluate his mental construct and modify it. After the modification, testing begins again.

As an example, let us consider a study of suicide by Émile Durkheim, a prominent French sociologist. Durkheim (1951) noted that suicide rates varied from one country to another, and he wanted to explain this variation. He suspected suicide might be related to psychological states of mind, cosmic factors (climatic and seasonal variations) and social factors. He developed measurements for his concepts and gathered data bearing on each set of factors. His analysis led him to discard cosmic factors and focus on certain social forces. He found suicide rates higher among Protestants than Catholics and higher among nonmarried people than married ones. These findings were the empirical generalizations of his study. His next step was to explain these general observations. He concluded that suicide is related to how much an individual is integrated into meaningful and cohesive groups. On the one hand are those who are overly integrated into a social group. They may commit suicide because they perceive themselves as insignificant compared to the group. On the other hand, there are those who are isolated from social groups, and the absence of goals in stressful times is also conducive to suicide. Furthermore, clearly stated goals and well-defined norms provide guidelines for people's behaviour. The absence of norms during rapid social change confuses individuals about how to behave. This, according to Durkheim, also increases the likelihood of suicide. Following this theory, suicide rates are lower among Catholics and married people because they are more integrated normatively and socially than their counterparts.

As the foregoing example shows, the research cycle usually begins with an analytical question. Hypotheses, or tentative answers, are then developed, and key concepts are *operationalized*, a process that translates abstract concepts into a set of procedures allowing empirical measurement. For example, suicide was operationalized by Durkheim (1951: 44) to mean "all cases of death resulting directly or indirectly from a positive or negative act of the victim himself, which he knows will produce this result." Data are then collected, coded and analysed. The outcome of data analyses is to arrive at summary statements about the empirical observations. Through repeated observations, these summary statements become *laws*. Although a law describes a relationship, it does not explain it. To do that we have to move to the higher level of theorization. Explanations or theories are subject to further research and verification. Figure 2-1 summarizes the steps in the research cycle. The cycle is a never-ending process, with each research project answering some questions and leaving others open for further inquiry.

Figure 2-1   The Research Cycle

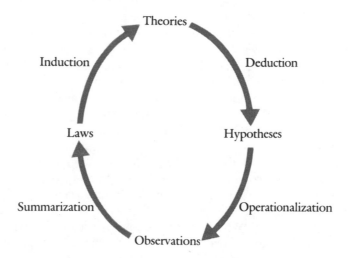

# FORMULATING A RESEARCH PROBLEM

In attempting to understand society, sociologists often study a class or category of people, in the hope of discovering some regularities about the group (Li, 1981). Thus, sociologists are not so much concerned with the behaviours and attitudes of an individual person, but with how similar people would behave. There are certain implications of this approach. When a sociologist finds that people belonging to a social category have a distinct view towards a social issue, he is implying that people not belonging to the same social group do not have the same view towards the issue. For example, if one shows that those with a university education are more likely to support legalizing marijuana because education tends to liberalize people's orientation, then one should expect to find that others without a university education are less likely to support legalizing marijuana.

The above example also shows that there has to be some variation across groups before meaningful questions can be raised. Sociologists speak of age, sex, income, education, ethnic origin and occupation as *variables* because these characteristics vary from one individual to another. The variable a researcher wishes to explain in a study is called the *dependent variable*. Variables which are used as explanations are called *independent variables*. "Explanations" here simply means relationships, in that when an independent variable varies, so does the dependent variable. For example, a sociologist may wish to explain why some wage earners are more committed to their jobs than others. The dependent variable is job commitment, and it varies from high to low from person to person. Job commitment may be related to job incentives, one of which is income. The variation in job commitment may be explained by income levels (independent variable) if the higher the income a person receives, the greater is his commitment to the job.

To think of social phenomena as variables is similar to thinking of individuals or groups as having certain characteristics. You may describe an acquaintance as tall, about twenty-five years old, Caucasian and male. If you can describe the same types of characteristics, that is, height, age, race and sex of five other people, you would have data on four variables for six individuals. The *unit of analysis*, or the unit to which the characteristics refer, may be individual or group, although the unit remains the same throughout a research project. The unemployment rate of regions and the size of the family are two examples in which the unit of analysis is a group.

Sociology is a discipline of comparison, in that sociologists are always interested in learning why some groups have certain characteristics and not others. For example, why are suicide rates higher among Protestants than among Catholics? Why are younger people more likely to move than older people? The way these questions are raised necessitates a comparison. Protestants have to be compared to Catholics to find out how these religions make a difference in suicide rates. Older people must be compared to younger people, and so on. The way a question is raised influences the answer. The question "Why do people smoke marijuana?" implies that there is a motive for smoking marijuana. The typical layperson's response is that people smoke marijuana because they are lonely. For beginners in sociology, it is frequently tempting to attribute motives to behaviour. Examples are: People go to university because they are motivated to study; people smoke because they are nervous; people are unemployed because they lack the motivation to work. However, people do many things without necessarily having a motive. Motives are hard to define and empirically test, and arguments based on loosely defined motives often produce circular explanations.

To consider marijuana smoking in a sociological way would involve comparing people who smoke regularly with those who don't smoke marijuana. The basic approach is to see how the ones who smoke marijuana differ from those who don't. One may find, for example, that the ones who smoke marijuana regularly do so as a group. They are therefore more likely to be sociable than socially isolated. In contrast, the ones who don't smoke regularly may have no group support. Social isolation from a support group explains why they do not smoke regularly. The sociological question "Why do some people smoke marijuana regularly, while others do not?" permits a much wider basis of comparison between the two groups and leads to answers not necessarily confined to commonly assumed motives.

There is often a difference between issues of public concern and sociological problems. For example, the question of the legalization of abortion is a controversial one. Sociology does not answer moral questions or pass value judgements on be-haviours. Sociologists may study the beliefs of a pro-life group and how their beliefs affect their behaviour. It is quite possible to study an anti-abortion group without being an advocate of its position. This does not mean, however, that sociological findings cannot be applied to promote social causes or change social policies. Applied sociology is dealt with in Chapter 3.

Now that we have seen how sociologists raise questions, we will be able to understand how they conduct research. But first, we must understand the logic of scientific tests through experimentation.

# EXPERIMENTAL DESIGNS

## Classic Experimental Design

In conducting an experiment, observations are usually taken in laboratory settings, where the conditions are artificially contrived. The researcher manipulates one variable at a time to observe its effect on another variable. The basic idea is to see whether the presence or absence of a *test variable* changes the variable being studied.

The logic of experiments is best illustrated in the classical experimental design in which two groups are exposed to identical conditions before the experiment. During the experiment, the test, or independent, variable, is introduced to one group but not the other. Subsequent comparisons are made to see how this manipulation affects the dependent variable under investigation.

For example, a researcher may be interested in studying the effectiveness of television instruction on the arithmetic performance of school children. Arithmetic performance is the dependent variable, and it may be measured by testing each child. The independent variable is exposure to television instruction. The experiment tests whether exposure to a television instruction program makes the students perform better or worse than those not viewing such a program.

There are seven steps in the classical experimental design. They are: 1. selecting a sample; 2. randomly assigning subjects to the experimental and control groups; 3. ensuring all conditions are equal; 4. pretesting; 5. introducing the treatment to the experimental group; 6. posttesting; and 7. making comparisons.

The procedure of the classical experimental design is given in Figure 2-2. Points $O_1$ and $O_2$ represent observations of the dependent variable in the experimental group during pretest and posttest respectively. Points $O_3$ and $O_4$ represent observations of the dependent variable in the control groups during pretest and posttest respectively. T represents the treatment or the independent variable.

Figure 2–2  The Classical Experimental Design

| | Pretest | Treatment | Posttest | Comparison |
|---|---|---|---|---|
| Experimental Group | $O_1$ | T | $O_2$ | $O_2 - O_1$ |
| Control Group | $O_3$ | | $O_4$ | $O_4 - O_3$ |

The classical experimental design requires that both the experimental and control groups be exposed to identical conditions, except that the independent variable is introduced only into the experimental group and not into the control group. By comparing the dependent variable before and after the test, any change observed in the experimental group and not in the control group can be attributed to the independent variable.

## Quasi-experimental Designs

Although the classical experimental design is a convincing method of establishing relationships, it is often not feasible to use it. It is for example, impossible to induce a revolution in one country and not another to study its effects. Thus, a researcher may have to modify the experimental design to accommodate a specific problem. As he relaxes the restrictions of the design, he is introducing a greater likelihood of errors in his research. We shall discuss three variations of the classical experimental design, called quasi-experiments, which produce less conclusive results.

The *one-shot case study* is a design in which a single group is measured on a dependent variable at one point in time, after an event that supposedly has changed the dependent variable — as, for example, the effect of a race riot on racial attitudes. The one-shot case study may be summarized as follows:

$$\text{Occurrence of } X \longrightarrow \text{Posttest of } Y$$

The main drawback of this design is that the researcher isn't sure whether Y would be at a certain level with or without the occurrence of X. Suppose a study following a riot finds a high level of racial tension. One cannot conclusively attribute such a level to the riot because tensions may already have been high before the riot.

In a *static-group comparison*, observations of the dependent variable are taken in two groups after an event has occurred in one group but not the other. For example, one may compare the centralization of government administration in a country that has experienced a coup d'etat within the past five years to the administration in another country that has not experienced such an abrupt change of government. The design may be summarized as follows:

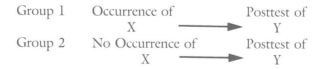

Without a baseline comparison, we are not sure whether it is indeed the independent variable which makes a difference in the two groups or whether the difference existed prior to the occurrence of the independent variable. If, using the above example, we find a high level of centralization in the country with the coup d'etat, we are still not sure whether the coup led to centralization because we have no measurement of centralization before the coup. Indeed, if such a difference existed before the coup, high centralization may well be a cause and not a consequence of radical political change.

The *one-group pretest-posttest design* compares one group before and after an event takes place. If we want to study the effectiveness of a media campaign encouraging birth control, we can take a survey prior to the campaign to find out what attitudes exist among the population, then administer the campaign and conduct the posttest to measure any change in attitudes. The design may be represented as follows:

Pretest on         Occurrence of        Posttest on
X   ⟶   Y   ⟶   X

The problem here is that there is no way of knowing whether the change would have happened with or without the occurrence of the event being studied. In the above example, something else, and not the media campaign, may have caused changes in attitudes.

## Sources of Invalidity

Many factors can invalidate experimental results. Quasi-experimental designs are more vulnerable to these factors. The issue of *internal validity* refers to whether it is the experimental treatment, and not something else, that makes a difference in the dependent variable. *External validity* refers to the extent to which the experimental results may be generalized to a larger population or a different setting. The sources of internal validity include the effects of 1. history; 2. maturation; 3. testing; 4. instrumentation; 5. statistical regression; 6. selection biases; 7. experimental mortality; and 8. selection-maturation interaction (Campbell and Stanley, 1970). The sources of external validity are 1. representativeness of sample; and 2. reactive effects of experimental arrangements.

The problem of *history* refers to events, other than treatments, that occur between the pretest and the posttest of an experiment and that are competing explanations for changes in the dependent variable. The government may announce incentives for small families in the middle of a media campaign for family planning, thus confounding the effect of the campaign on respondents. *Maturation* refers to natural changes among the subjects of an experiment over time, such as becoming tired. The effect of *pretesting* refers to sensitizing the subjects to a test, making it unclear whether an improvement is caused by the experimental treatments or the subjects' increased awareness. The problem of *instrumentation* concerns the instability of the measuring instruments, so that changes in the dependent variable may be attributed to faulty instruments and not necessarily to the experimental treatment. The problem of instrumentation also includes inconsistencies of the observer, who may use different standards for recording the subjects. *Statistical regression* refers to the tendency towards the average performance when subjects are selected on the basis of their extreme scores on the dependent variable. For example, if a group of under-achievers is selected and is placed in a learning program, the students will most likely improve over time, since they have reached the lower limit in performance. *Selection biases* result from differentially assigning subjects to experimental and control groups so that the subjects are not comparable. If, for example, the subjects in the experimental group are more intelligent than the ones in the control group, then the improvement in the experimental group may be attributed to the biased characteristics of the subjects and not to the treatment. *Experimental mortality* refers to subjects dropping out of an experiment before it is completed. The remaining subjects taking the posttest may be radically different from those in the group for the pretest. *Selection-maturation interaction* refers to a complicated change produced by the joint problem of selection and maturation, as, for example, when under-achievers are bored easily during the experiment.

Even if there is internal validity in an experiment, the findings cannot be applied to a larger group if the sample is not representative of a population. This is a problem of external validity influenced by the *representativeness* of the sample. Another problem is the *reactive effects* of experimental arrangements, which must be considered when applying experimental results to real life. Although a researcher may establish the internal validity of an experiment and its external validity to people under similar experimental conditions, it is doubtful whether people react the same way in a real life situation.

## The Limitations of Experimentation

Experimental designs offer a formal procedure to isolate the effects of variables, but they require a researcher to artificially manipulate the conditions of an experiment. Such manipulations are often impractical for sociological problems. For example, if a sociologist wants to study the effect of the Great Depression on the union movement, it is impossible to reproduce past events. The effect of a revolution can only be studied after the revolution has taken place. In short, historical events cannot be randomized, and their effects on behaviour are difficult to assess in laboratory settings. Cross-national studies also create insurmountable problems in applying experimental designs, as historical, cultural and social variations make laboratory control impossible. Even on the individual level, there is a potential difference between subjects' responses under contrived conditions and those in real life situations. In the following sections, we shall see how sociologists use alternative methods to pursue their scientific inquiry.

## HISTORICAL/COMPARATIVE RESEARCH

Sociologists study phenomena which they themselves have not artificially induced. This requires examining situations *ex post facto*. As Durkheim (1964: 125) put it:

> When . . . the production of facts is not within our control and we can only bring them together in the way that they have been spontaneously produced, the method employed is that of indirect experiment, or the comparative method.

This sociological method involves comparing similar and different cases to show the presence or absence of a relationship. For example, why did capitalism develop in Europe and not elsewhere? This is one of the fundamental questions Weber addressed in his comparison of world religions. Weber concluded that the Protestant ethic teaches that economic accumulation in this world is consistent with salvation in the next, thus giving support to capitalist development (Weber, 1958). In contrast, none of the other major world religions promotes accumulation of capital for investment (Bendix, 1962).

The historical/comparative method is evident in Marx's analysis of various types of society. Each type, to Marx, has its own characteristics and logic of development.

To understand a particular class structure at a specific historical juncture requires studying the material conditions of society. Each productive system is characterized by a definite set of social relationships. A preclass system exists in hunting and gathering societies because there is little division of labour and a low capacity to produce more than basic needs (Marx, 1965). Ancient society, as in Rome and Greece, created a ruling class based on landed property (Giddens, 1971). Capitalism is characterized by ownership of capital and the need of workers to sell labour power as a commodity, so that capitalists and wage labourers are the two predominant classes (Marx, 1967). Accordingly, as the mode of production changes in a society, so do social relationships.

The method of comparing similarities and differences can be misleading in historical cases, as each situation is unique in terms of its occurrence in a given time and location. The comparative method sometimes requires a researcher to abstract the common grounds of seemingly different situations and to specify subtle differences in similar cases. This is how explanations are refined. For example, in Brinton's (1964) study of four revolutions — England's in 1640, America's in 1776, France's in 1789 and Russia's in 1917 — he shows certain common characteristics in all four situations, despite their historical differences. His case studies demonstrate the typical conditions before a revolution, and the assumption is that the absence of those conditions would make a revolution unlikely. Durkheim's (1951) study of suicide shows that there is more than one cause, leading him to conclude that there is more than one type of suicide. In other words, although all suicides are related to social integration, specific comparisons show the conditions under which different types of suicide are likely to occur.

The historical/comparative method basically ascertains the presence of a relationship in similar cases and the absence of a relationship in very different cases. Further comparisons may indicate how cases are similar in some ways and different in others, thus producing changes in the relationship under study. The logic is best illustrated in survey research.

## SURVEY RESEARCH

Survey research is widely used in sociology. Its basic feature is the systematic collection of data from sample populations by means of questionnaires or structured interviews. A researcher approaches a group of people who are exposed to a set of events or experiences and asks them questions about these experiences. Variations in the independent variable are not controlled but statistically manipulated after the fact. For example, a researcher may study how urbanites and rural dwellers vote in federal elections. The independent variable, in this case, is statistically manipulated. Changes in the dependent variable are not observed directly over time. Instead, its variations from one individual to another are analysed in connection with variations in the independent variable.

### Logic of Survey Research

Like other designs, survey research aims at discovering relationships between variables. A researcher uses survey answers to group the respondents into categories. To the extent the dependent variable changes from one category of the independent variable to another, there is a relationship. Assume, for example, that the respondents are divided by sex and that 70 percent of the males and 20 percent of the females have incomes over $35 000. As we move from one category of the independent variable (male) to another category (female), we find a corresponding change in the dependent variable (incomes over $35 000) from 70 percent to 20 percent respectively. In other words, there is a relationship between gender and income.

The problem with this type of analysis is that we do not know whether the variation in gender leads to the variation in income, or whether some other factors are operating. These competing variables are called *rival causal factors*. We have rival causal factors because, when we first group our subjects into categories of the independent variable, we have no way of controlling for other variations. The males may have different levels of education, aspiration and experience than the females.

One way of *controlling* for rival factors is to identify them and divide the categories of our independent variable into subgroups for comparison. If, for example, we suspect the education of the respondents, and not gender, may make a difference in income, then we can divide the male and female respondents further into two educational groups. By comparing the high-education-female group to the high-education-male group, we make education a constant, and gender becomes the characteristic which is varying. These subgroup comparisons then tell us what changes, if any, occur in the dependent variable. If, by varying education and controlling for gender, we do not observe a change in the dependent variable, then we know education is not a relevant independent variable. Conversely, if, by varying gender and controlling for education, we find a change in the dependent variable, then we know gender is the relevant variable, and we have eliminated education as a rival causal factor.

This process of comparing subgroups and eliminating variables can be tedious. But it reveals the relevant variables in explaining the dependent variable.

The rival causal factors have to be tested individually. After testing and eliminating several rival factors, we will still be uncertain as to whether there are other factors we may have ignored. Researchers often make assumptions about these unknown factors. One assumption is to consider the effects of these factors, if any, to be randomly distributed among the categories of our independent variable so that they do not disturb or interfere with our dependent variable.

## Bivariate Analysis

One widely used method of studying survey data is *contingency table analysis* (Davis, 1971). It may be employed to study *bivariate* and *multivariate* relationships. In the simplest form, a contingency table has two variables, with two or more categories in each variable. The table has several boxes or cells. The number in each cell indicates the number of cases which have a shared attribute as determined jointly by the two variables. Each case can only appear in one cell. Table 2-1 is an example of a contingency table. It cross-tabulates two variables, attitude toward uranium development by age.

To facilitate comparisons, it is always more convenient to convert raw figures to percentages. There are two ways the percentages can run, either by row or by column. The rule to follow is to compute the percentages in the same direction as the categories of the independent variable. Thus, comparisons of percentages can be

## TABLE 2-1 Attitude Toward Uranium Development by Age

"DO YOU APPROVE OR DISAPPROVE OF BUILDING A URANIUM REFINERY 100 MILES FROM YOUR COMMUNITY?"

|  | UNDER 30 | 30 AND OVER |
|---|---|---|
| Approve | 56% | 68% |
| Disapprove | 44 | 32 |
| Total | 100 | 100 |
|  | (200) | (250) |

made between categories of the independent variable. For example, Table 2-1 shows 56 percent of the respondents under 30 years of age approve of the statement, while 68 percent of the respondents 30 years of age and over approve of it. The percentages indicate that older people are more likely to approve of building a uranium refinery. In other words, there is a relationship between age and attitude towards uranium development.

A bivariate table tells us whether a relationship exists or not, but it does not explain the relationship. In the above example, it is not clear why younger people are more likely to disapprove of the building of a uranium refinery. Are younger people more concerned about environmental pollution? Do older people have something to gain by supporting a refinery? These are questions which require us either to refine or to explain the original relationship. We may suspect, for example, that property owners have more to gain from uranium development because such development would inflate property values. If we can demonstrate that older people are more likely to own property, then perhaps we can explain why they are more likely to support uranium development.

Table 2-2 cross-tabulates home ownership by the age of the respondent. It shows 30 percent of the respondents under age 30 own their home, compared to 72 percent of the respondents 30 years of age and over who own their home. In other words, the older people are more likely to own their home than the younger people. This table provides evidence to support our explanation of the uranium refinery survey.

## TABLE 2-2 Home Ownership by Age

DO YOU OWN YOUR PRESENT DWELLING?

|  | UNDER 30 | 30 AND OVER |
|---|---|---|
| Own | 30% | 72% |
| Not Own | 70 | 28 |
| Total | 100 | 100 |
|  | (200) | (250) |

## Multivariate Analysis

Multivariate analysis controls for those variables which we suspect may affect the relationship under study. In our example, we want to control for the variation in home ownership to see whether it affects the original relationship between attitude towards uranium development and age. Table 2-3 shows such a control table.

TABLE 2-3    Attitude Towards Uranium Development by Age and Home Ownership

|  | OWN | | NOT OWN | |
|---|---|---|---|---|
|  | UNDER 30 | 30 AND OVER | UNDER 30 | 30 AND OVER |
| Approve | 75% | 75% | 48% | 48% |
| Disapprove | 25 | 25 | 52 | 52 |
| Total | 100 | 100 | 100 | 100 |
|  | (80) | (190) | (120) | (60) |

The original sample is divided into two groups: those who own their home and those who do not own their home. Within each group, we cross-tabulate attitude towards uranium development and age. If, for example, we find no relationship between attitude towards uranium and age among the respondents who own their home, then we know that age is really not the variable which explains the attitude.

Table 2-3 shows 75 percent of the younger age group who own their homes *and* the same percentage of the older age group approve of the statement. Simply put, younger and older respondents who own homes are just as likely to approve of the statement. We notice also that younger and older respondents who do not own homes are just as likely to approve the statement as well. However, when we compare the first column to the third column, we find a change in percentages. The respondents in these two columns belong to the same age group but differ in home ownership. In other words, as we vary home ownership, holding age constant, we find home owners are more likely to support uranium development. Specifically, among home owners, 75 percent of those under age 30 favour development. In contrast, among those who do not own homes, 48 percent of those younger than 30 approve of the development. In short, home ownership, and not age, makes a difference in the response to the statement.

When we are analysing three or more variables, it is often convenient to put them into a system which allows causal relationships to be specified. Such a system is referred to as a model (Blalock, 1972). In the previous example, we find two relationships on the basis of Tables 2-1 and 2-2. The relationships may be summarized as follows:

Table 2-1        Age ⟶ Attitude
Table 2-2        Age ⟶ Home Ownership

In a subsequent analysis of Table 2-3, however, we find home ownership, and not age, affects the attitude towards uranium development. Taken together, these relationships suggest the following model:

Age ——————▶Home Ownership——————▶Attitude

This model indicates that the original relationship between age and attitude is spurious. The way to test for a spurious relationship is to control for the intervening variable, home ownership. If, by controlling the intervening variable, the original relationship disappears, as in Table 2-3, then the relationship is spurious.

We have seen how, when statistical controls are used, survey research approximates the logic of experimentation. The inability to use laboratory controls calls for multivariate analyses to eliminate spurious relationships. Although survey results are not as conclusive, such findings are strengthened if they are replicated in other studies and supported by theories. Furthermore, survey research gives more flexibility to the study of sociological problems in real life situations. In the next section, we shall learn another sociological method that provides the greatest flexibility for the study of people in their daily life.

## PARTICIPANT OBSERVATION

A *participant observer* "gathers data by participating in the daily life of the group or organization he studies" (Becker, 1958: 652). He observes the interactions of people in situations, how they behave, what they do and what they say. In addition, a participant observer also talks to the participants and finds out their interpretations of various events. He inquires about past events and about other situations he may not have a chance to observe. He also interprets events and makes decisions about what to follow up on, and whom to speak to. In short, a participant observer is an active researcher in the field.

In general, participant observation is effective in studying small groups. Historically, sociologists have successfully applied participant observation to the study of ethnic organizations, street crimes and urban ghettos. Some classic studies include *Street Corner Society* by Whyte (1955); *Tally's Corner* by Liebow (1967); *Boys in White* by Becker *et al.* (1961); *Urban Villagers* by Gans (1962).

### Gaining Entry Into the Field

It is often difficult for a researcher to be accepted initially by the people he wants to study, especially if he is a total stranger. One way of gaining entry is to establish contacts with some members of the group. These contacts may be made indirectly through a friend or an acquaintance who may in turn know the members of the group. It is important to recognize at what level the contact is made. In a voluntary organization, for example, it is more useful to have the leader of the group, rather than other members, introduce the researcher to the group. The leader usually is identified more closely with the group and its accomplishments, and he may be more willing to speak to a researcher. Being introduced by the leader also suggests to the members that the researcher has been endorsed by the leader.

Depending on the nature of the group one is studying, sometimes there is a good reason to participate in disguise. For example, Griffin (1977), a white researcher, wanted to study the experience of being black. The only way he could experience being black was to hide his white identity by dyeing his skin. The researcher, however, has to resolve the ethical questions involved. Is it ethical for a researcher to lie to the people he is studying in order to obtain data? Can scientific research justify misleading the people being studied?

## What the Observer is Looking For

A participant observer is looking for facts, facts that tell him about the lives of people, how they behave in various situations, how they interpret events and individuals in their daily experiences. Out of all these facts, an observer hopes to develop more general concepts that help him understand the group. As his study progresses, the researcher hopes to make summary statements about the group and to find evidence supporting these statements. Since what the observer is looking for depends so much on the concrete situation, it is helpful to study an example.

Elliot Liebow spent one and a half years studying a group of black men who congregated around a corner carry-out store in Washington, D.C. (Liebow, 1967). Before entering the field, he had only a vague idea about investigating low-income families. Shortly after he moved into the field, he found himself completely submerged in the research. We describe his experiences as follows:

> My initial excursions into the street . . . seldom carried me more than a block or two from the corner where I started. From the very first weeks or even days, I found myself in the middle of things; the principle lines of field work were laid out, almost without my being aware of it (Liebow, 1967:237).

His field observations were centred around twenty or so men. He found out what they did for a living, what they had done in the past, who their friends and relatives were, and how they felt about things. He summarized his field approach:

> Throughout this period, my field observations were focused on individuals: what they said, what they did, and the contexts in which they said them or did them. I sought them out and was sought out by them (Liebow, 1967: 248).

The final report of his field work is a brilliant analysis of the inner world of street-corner black men and its relation to the outer world. He described the marginal employment of the men, their transient relationships with wives and lovers and their phantom ties with friends and pseudo-kin. Liebow concluded that these relationships had a lot to do with the economic instability of the men, and that the inner world of these people was closely tied to the world outside, a world they had little hope of entering.

## Recording and Analysing Field Notes

It is important for a field worker to take detailed notes of his experiences. These notes represent the researcher's records of what happened in the field, whom he spoke to and what they said on each occasion. In short, the field notes are the data base for subsequent analyses. They can effectively illustrate one's analysis and provide a context to the readers.

Field materials and notes are analysed throughout the field research and not just at the end of the project. In analysing the notes, a researcher is looking for concepts and statements which best summarize the empirical situation. One way of developing such concepts and statements is to search for similarities among the cases. Sometimes it is impossible to develop a concept or statement that fits all cases. A researcher may quantify his field materials by stating how many cases fit a particular pattern, while other cases fall into other patterns. These other patterns, or exceptions, are *deviations* from the dominant pattern. It is just as important to account for the deviant cases as for the major social type.

In studying a group or an organization, a researcher is frequently looking for underlying norms, relationships and structures. Often, by seeking an answer that is the opposite of what we are looking for, we find meaningful information. For example, what holds a social group together may not be readily seen. The question, however, may be answered by inquiring into the conditions under which the group breaks down (Whyte, 1955).

## THE USE OF EXISTING DATA IN SOCIAL RESEARCH

Aside from collecting data first-hand, a researcher can use existing data sources such as official statistics, public documents and private records. These methods of data collection are sometimes called *unobtrusive measures* because the researcher is removed from the events being studied.

### Official Statistics

All modern governments collect official statistics for planning, administration and other purposes. These statistics include unemployment figures, divorce rates, population changes, labour-force characteristics, health service records and a host of others.

Since most official statistics are not collected for research purposes, researchers must use ingenuity in applying these statistics to a particular research problem. Marriage records, for example, may contain information on the family backgrounds of the couples, which may be used to study intergenerational mobility. Birth certificates and death records may contain brief descriptions of family histories, which can be used to reconstruct genealogies. Tax returns have information on income, which can be used to study inequality. Rogoff's study of occupational mobility in Indiana (1953) was based on occupations given in marriage records, and Johnson's analysis of income inequality in Canada (1977) shows how official statistics may be applied to social research.

There are several problems in using official statistics. First, official statistics are compiled by government agencies for classifying people into the statistical categories. By changing the definitions of classification, official statistics can be manipulated. Unemployment figures are good examples. If the definition of an unemployed person is one who has been unemployed for four weeks and actively looking for a job, then the unemployment figures would not include those unemployed for less than four weeks or those not actively looking for work. Changing the definitions of statistical categories also means figures compiled at different times may not be totally comparable. Stirling and Kouri (1979) produced unemployment rates in various provinces of Canada that are almost twice as high as the official figures by using a different definition of unemployment. Similarly, crime rates as compiled by law-enforcement agencies are subject to changes in legislative bills which redefine violations of the law. An increase or decrease in drug-related convictions may reflect a tightening or loosening of laws pertaining to drug addiction and possession.

Criminologists know that official crime statistics often reflect the law-enforcement agencies' capacity to handle criminals more than changes in criminality in society. This observation suggests another aspect of official statistics. Since they are compiled by officials, government statistics sometimes reveal as much about the people compiling the figures as about the people the statistics supposedly describe. Cicourel and Kitsuse (1963), for example, discovered in their investigation of a school that the teachers' evaluations of students revealed more about the subjective standards used by teachers than about the students themselves.

## Public Documents

Aside from official statistics, all government departments and agencies have correspondence, memoranda and other written documents. Many of these materials are classified for reasons of security and confidentiality. But, after a certain time, some government materials are declassified and placed in public archives. These materials provide valuable sources for studying government policies, political parties, public administration and other related topics.

Archival materials provide a context for many social events. The letters and memoranda of politicians, for example, often reveal much about their lives over and above what is evident from their public appearances and records, as the diaries of Prime Minister Mackenzie King show (Pickersgill and Forster, 1970). Internal government records often reveal why certain policies were made.

Judicial and political records provide another source of materials for social research. Both the Congress in the United States and the Parliament in Canada maintain extensive records of the bills and statutes passed, the debates that took place, the voting patterns of legislators and minutes of various committee meetings. Another type of public record are the reports compiled by congressional hearings or royal commissions. These hearings and commissions generally deal with a specific social or political issue. The reports contain interesting accounts or testimonies and briefs presented by the public, as well as recommendations and analyses by officials. They record the views of different interest groups on public issues.

## Private Documents and Other Sources

Other sources of unobtrusive measures are private documents produced by private citizens or voluntary associations. Many people keep letters, diaries, biographies and essays. These materials provide insights into the private lives of people and their interpretations of events and experiences. For example, private collections can provide valuable data for studies of immigrants' experiences — their interpretations of the new world, their ties to the old one, their aspirations and disappointments. A classic study in this area is the work of Thomas and Znaniecki (1958) on Polish peasants in North America and Europe, which is based on many private documents of Polish immigrants.

Newspapers, novels, cartoons, television and radio programs are additional sources of unobtrusive measures. For example, relying largely on old newspapers, Ward

(1978) analysed anti-Orientalism in British Columbia from the 1860s to the 1940s. Haskell (1974) studied female stereotypes in movies.

In the sections that follow, we shall examine sampling and measurement problems which affect the external and internal validity of all research methods.

# SAMPLING PROBLEMS

Research is always limited by the resources available. Given that we only have the resources to study a segment of the entire population, how should we select the sample so that we can speak with some confidence about the rest of the population? This is the question sampling theories try to answer.

Whenever we must rely on a sample to generalize to a population, the question of external validity becomes an issue. External validity refers to the extent to which a generalization is valid or biased because of our particular sample. Putting it another way, the external validity of research is determined by the population to which we can generalize our findings, based on a sample. Probability sampling theories provide the methods for drawing samples which have greater likelihood of accurately reflecting the characteristics of the population.

## PROBABILITY SAMPLING DESIGNS

**1. Simple Random Sampling.** In a simple random sample, every element of the population has an equal and independent chance of being selected. To draw a simple random sample, one must have a complete list of all the elements in the population. Each element can only appear once on the list. For each element, a unique number is assigned. The students of a university campus may be seen as the population, from which a sample may be randomly selected. A complete list of student numbers is a good source from which to draw a random sample. Random numbers can be generated from a table of random numbers. A student is selected into the sample if his or her number matches with a number from the table.

**2. Systematic Sampling.** A systematic sample is one in which every $n$th case is selected from a list of all cases in the population after the first case has been randomly selected. For example, randomly pick a first case from a telephone directory and thereafter pick every $n$th case. A systematic sample may be treated, in practice, as a simple random sample. In general, systematic sampling is simple to use and highly practical. It is a procedure often used in selecting a sample from a telephone directory, a voters' list or other compilations of names.

**3. Stratified Sampling.** Instead of drawing cases from the general population, a stratified sample divides the population into various homogeneous subgroups and then randomly or systematically selects cases within each subgroup. This design increases the efficiency at a given cost level and can be more accurate than a simple random sample in estimating population characteristics. Assume we wish to study university students on a campus of 10 000 students, with 4 000 in the first year, 3 000 in the second year, 2 000 in the third year, and 1 000 in the fourth year. Also assume we have the resources to study 1 000 students. Using a simple random sample, we may not obtain an accurate representation of each of the four years because of sampling error, that is, fluctuation from one random sample to another.

If it is important to have such representation, a better way to select our cases is to divide the students into four subgroups, according to their year of registration. Within each subgroup, we can then select 250 students, using either random sampling or systematic sampling.

Stratified sampling requires prior knowledge of the population in order to stratify the subgroups. Generally, one should use a major independent variable as a criterion of stratification. In our example, the independent variable was the student's year of registration.

**4. Cluster Sampling.** Cluster sampling divides the population into geographic areas and then draws probability samples within these areas. A cluster sample is like a stratified sample, but instead of using the characteristics of the population to subdivide the population, a cluster sample uses *geographic locations*. Census tracts and census districts are good examples of geographic subdivisions. Cluster sampling reduces the transportation cost of interviewing. Within each geographic cluster, cases may be selected randomly by simple random sampling or systematic sampling.

## NONPROBABILITY SAMPLING DESIGNS

**5. Quota Sampling.** Quota sampling ensures that a given proportion of the elements in the sample has certain characteristics, irrespective of how the elements are selected. For example, if we want to have 60 percent males and 35 percent Catholics in our sample, we can set these figures as quotas for sampling. In selecting the cases, we would make sure our sample had these characteristics.

**6. Availability Sampling.** In an availability sample, the elements in the sample are easily available to the researcher. The criterion of selection is not based on known probability, but upon how accessible the elements are. If we want to study illegal immigrants, it is not likely that a comprehensive list of names is available for sampling, and we have to select subjects as they become available. Although restrictive in terms of generalizing the results, this procedure can be very informative about the group under study.

**7. Snowball Sampling.** Snowball sampling relies on the subjects referring other subjects to the researcher. Its name evokes a snowball accumulating more snow as it rolls down a hill. In the same way, a researcher gathers more cases through referrals while studying available subjects. This procedure cuts down the refusal rate, especially when the subjects are somewhat apprehensive about participating. For example, criminals and social deviants may be reluctant to speak to researchers for fear of revealing their identity.

## MEASUREMENT PROBLEMS

Measurement may be defined as the assigning of numerals to objects, events or persons according to rules (Stevens, 1951). In sociology, measurement involves quantifying the social properties of individuals and groups as variables. All variables have two definitions: theoretical and operational. The *theoretical* definition delineates the variable's conceptual boundaries, while the *operational* definition allows the variable to be classified into empirical categories. For example, education may be conceptualized as the formal schooling a person receives, and, operationally, it may be measured in three categories: (1) elementary; (2) secondary; and (3) post-secondary. To the extent that the categories bear quantifiable relationships to each other, a scale can be developed. In the above case, people in the post-secondary category have more education than those in the secondary, or elementary categories. Otherwise, the measurement remains at the level of classification, as, for example, the classification of respondents into 1. male and 2. female.

In developing the categories of a variable, there are two principles to follow. The first principle is that the categories must be mutually exclusive, that the boundaries of categories cannot overlap. Secondly, the categories should be totally exhaustive. All the categories taken together should account for all the empirical cases.

## LEVELS OF MEASUREMENT

Although measurement involves the assignment of numbers to attributes, or categories, of variables, the meanings of these numbers may vary, depending on the variables. In some cases, as when sex is a variable, the numerals representing male and female are symbolic and are merely used to classify the subjects into two groups. In other cases, as when education varies, the numbers may represent the actual years of schooling, and so they have numeric properties. Variables may represent different levels of measurement. There are four levels of measurement to consider: nominal, ordinal, interval and ratio.

A *nominal* level of measurement can classify objects or people into categories. When numbers are used for such a classification, they are merely symbols representing the qualitative categories and do not carry any numeric properties. For example, one can use the number (1) to represent Catholics, (2) for Protestants, and (3) for other religious affiliation.

An *ordinal* level of measurement can rank-order the categories as well as classify them. The variable "education," as defined earlier, has these categories. Those in group (3) have an education that is higher than those in group (2) and group (1). There is, therefore, a rank-order among the three groups. Although we can differentiate the ones with a higher education from those with a lower education, we have no measurement of how much more or less education one group has compared to others.

An *interval* level of measurement has all the properties of a nominal and an ordinal measure. In addition, the distances separating the categories or units are equal intervals. The Fahrenheit temperature scale is an example of interval measurement. The difference between 50° and 51° is 1°, and so is the difference between 49° and 50°. An interval level of measurement, however, does not have an absolute zero, so that one cannot speak of 90° being twice as hot as 45°. An example of an interval level of measurement in social science is the intelligence quotient.

The only difference between a *ratio* measure and an interval measure is that the former has an absolute zero, as, for example, in age and years of formal schooling.

## QUESTIONNAIRE CONSTRUCTION

Students constructing a questionnaire for the first time often find it difficult to decide on which questions to include or exclude and how to phrase the questions to accurately measure the sociological concepts they have in mind. Some of the difficulties are not just technical but relate to theoretical confusions. Confusion may arise from the specification of the research problem, the develoment of hypotheses and the operationalizations of variables. After all, a questionnaire is no more than a tool to be employed for a clearly stated purpose.

A questionnaire may contain both open-ended and close-ended questions. *Open-ended* questions are those which do not provide a choice of answers; the respondents are free to answer any way they wish. *Close-ended* questions, on the other hand, have a set of answers from which the respondents must choose. An example of an open-ended question is: "What is the most serious problem facing the country today?" A close-ended question is: "Last week, how many hours did you work for pay? 1. None; 2. Less than 10 hours; 3. 10 to 19 hours; 4. 20 to 29 hours; 5. 30 hours and over."

Although open-ended questions are flexible, in that they allow the respondents to answer any way they desire, they are difficult to code or to summarize. To analyse the answers of open-ended questions, a researcher must first do a content analysis and develop a set of categories for sorting the answers. Open-ended questions, however, are sometimes useful to elicit quotations from respondents, which may be used to substantiate statistical discussions. Close-ended questions produce results which are easy to code. Sequential numbers are often assigned to the categories so that they can be directly entered into a computer.

Questions should not be worded in a way that appears to support a particular choice. For example, "Do you think Canada has been harmed by immigrants coming into this country?" is a biased question because it implies that our country has been harmed by immigrants. A proper way to phrase the question is to include both sides of the issue: "Do you think this country has benefited or been harmed by immigrants coming into the country?"

*Double-barrelled* questions are ambiguous because there are two things contained in a single question, and answers to such questions are hard to interpret. Here is an example: "Would you or would you not support legalizing abortion and marijuana?" If a respondent answers yes, it is not clear whether he or she supports legalizing abortion or marijuana or both.

All questionnaires should be pretested before they are applied to the actual sample. To the greatest degree possible, respondents in the pretest sample should be similar to those in the actual sample. It is often necessary to pretest the questionnaire more than once. During the pretest, the researcher should see how the respondents react to the questions and determine which ones are too difficult, unclear, too lengthy and so on. The aim is to improve both the reliability and validity of the survey. A poorly constructed questionnaire not only has large measurement errors, but is also less likely to be completed by respondents.

# SUMMARY

All research methods are concerned with collecting accurate empirical evidence and with discarding incorrect explanations. Sociologists, like other scientists, follow the *research cycle* in using empirical evidence to verify theories.

The *classical experimental design* provides a basis for testing the effect of an independent variable on a dependent variable in a laboratory setting. The basic approach is to expose the experimental group, but not the control group, to a treatment to see if a subsequent change is produced, while holding other experimental conditions constant. *Quasi-experimental designs* are deviations from the classical experiments and consequently subject to various threats to their *internal and external validity*.

Sociologists must often use alternative methods to approximate the logic of experimentation. The *historical/comparative* method compares similar and different cases to show the presence or absence of a relationship. This method is evident in the works of classical sociologists like Durkheim, Weber and Marx.

Survey methods also employ comparisons. Instead of artificially controlling for the independent variables, as in experimentation, survey methods statistically manipulate them after the fact. Changes in the dependent variable at different levels of the independent variable are compared, and controls are introduced statistically.

*Participant observation* allows a researcher to participate in the daily life of the people that he studies. This method is suitable to the study of small groups. It allows the blending of theoretical conceptualization with field research.

Besides collecting data first-hand, sociologists use *unobtrusive measures* such as official statistics, public records, private documents and other sources.

Problems of sampling and measurement affect the validity of all methods. In *probability samples*, the probability of selection is known. The four types are: *simple random sample*, *systematic sample*, *stratified sample* and *cluster sample*. *Non-probability sampling designs* include *quota samples*, *availability samples* and *snowball samples*.

Measurement involves quantifying observations. The four levels of measurement are *nominal*, *ordinal*, *interval* and *ratio* measurement.

In developing a questionnaire, a researcher should pretest the questions.

## DISCUSSION QUESTIONS

1. What is the relationship between sociological theory and research method?

2. What are the sources of invalidity in an experimental design in which there is no control group?

3. How does one control for the variations of independent variables in comparative and survey research?

4. What are the major problems in using secondary data and official statistics?

5. What are the advantages and limitations of: a stratified sample; a cluster sample; and a snowball sample?

# 3

# The Practice of Applied Sociology

## Edward Harvey

INTRODUCTION

USES OF APPLIED SOCIOLOGY
*Social Impact Assessment*
*Surveys*
*Evaluation Studies*

STAGES IN A RESEARCH PROJECT
*Problem Definition*
*The Fundamentals of Applied Sociological Research*
*Analytical Strategies*
*After the Research is Done*

THE APPLIED SOCIOLOGIST'S ROLE

SUMMARY

# INTRODUCTION

Increasingly, we live in an information rich, data-oriented world. As societies become more economically developed, there is a corresponding growth in the desire to predict and control many aspects of life. In less developed parts of the world, "fate" is still often used to explain societal catastrophes or personal misfortunes. By contrast, people in the economically developed, highly industrialized world strongly believe that such events can be controlled and eliminated or ameliorated by science and technology (Whitehead, 1948). Medical research into cures or therapies for disease is one example of this. As societies become more industrialized and modernized, people become more aware of how the applications of science and technology can benefit their lives. Social science has not been excluded from this trend.

In post-World War II Canada, for example, the growing interest in applied sociology has taken many forms. For approximately 25 years after the end of the World War II, Canada enjoyed strong economic growth (Drummond, 1972). Of course, there were cyclical ups and downs during this period, but, overall, sustained economic growth was the dominant trend. During this period, the real after-tax income of Canadians doubled. This presented governments with a greatly expanded base of tax revenues without raising taxes. Particularly during the 1960s, a growing proportion of these expanded government revenues were invested in social programs. Between 1960 and 1970, for example, expenditures on education rose from about $1.7 billion to $7.4 billion, the latter figure representing nearly 9 percent of the Gross National Product in 1970 (Statistics Canada, 1973). In post-war Canada, large public expenditures and investments were made in health care, job creation and unemployment insurance.

This great growth in publicly funded social programs caused a corresponding growth in the need for sociological data and research of all kinds. Such sociological information is required for many purposes, including: 1. to determine how large a program may be required to meet the needs of the relevant population; 2. to make sure an existing program is reaching the people for whom it is intended; 3. to see if program costs and benefits are in reasonable balance.

One way governments met their needs for such research, particularly during the 1960s and 1970s, was to hire more people with skills and experience in applied sociology. Although government hiring has slowed considerably in recent years, it appears there is still a reasonable market for well-developed, applied sociological research skills. Another way governments meet their requirements for applied sociological research is to hire consultants to study specific issues.

When governments consider significant new developments or shifts in policy, the issues generated are often complex and politically sensitive. Royal commissions of inquiry, with their emphasis on extensive public hearings, have been used by Canadian governments to gauge the feasibility and acceptability of major new policy directions (Wilson, 1971). Besides holding public hearings, such commissions are usually large consumers of applied social research. Examples of significant royal commissions include: the Royal Commission on Health Services (Govt. of Canada, 1964), which was a prelude to the creation of Medicare; the Commission on Bilingualism and Biculturalism (Govt. of Canada, 1969), the basis for the development of Canada's official languages policy; and the Commission of Inquiry on Equality in Employment (Govt. of Canada, 1984), which appears to have set the stage for introducing mandatory affirmative action in Canada.

The private sector is also an extensive user of applied sociological research. It is well known, for example, that changing social and demographic conditions influence the markets for various products and services. For example, the baby-boom generation, because of its large size, has had a major impact over the past several years on many service and product markets (Russell, 1982). Now that they are entering their 30s and have more disposable income, their consumption interests and capabilities are quite different from when they were teenagers. Today's baby-boomers are probably more interested in investment counselling services than rock music. An aging population, a more highly educated population, and an increasing proportion of women in the labour force all have an effect on product and service markets today (Statistics Canada, 1980).

Figure 3-1 Age Pyramid of the Population of Canada, 1971 and 1981

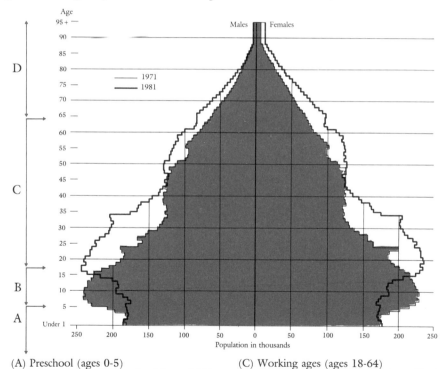

(A) Preschool (ages 0-5)      (C) Working ages (ages 18-64)
(B) Elementary and high school (ages 6-17)    (D) Retirement age population (ages 65+)

1971 Census of Canada, Catalogue 92-716, Table 14. 1981 Census of Canada, Catalogue 92-901, Table 2.

*The changing population has implications for many product and service markets.*

*Highlights: 1981 Census of Canada*, Ottawa, Statistics Canada, April 1984, p. 2. Reproduced by permission of the Minister of Supply and Services Canada.

Many private enterprises monitor these trends to ensure that their product development and marketing strategies are adjusted to current trends. Market research surveys—a form of applied sociology—provide the private sector with this type of information.

Apart from market surveys, the private sector uses other forms of applied social research. In recent years, more employers have been developing programs in such areas as quality of working life (Jenkins, 1981; Mansell and Rankin, 1983) and affirmative action or equal employment opportunity (Govt. of Canada, 1984). Such programs require periodic evaluation to determine if they are accomplishing their objectives. Applied social research, such as organization-specific surveys or evaluation studies, fulfill this function.

The need for and application of sociological research and information will continue to grow. This trend is reflected in the fact that sociology is now taught in many professional schools, including schools of law, medicine and library science. Increasingly, physicians recognize that the state of one's health is affected by one's family and/or employment situation (Duff and Hollingshead, 1968). Many librarians now realize that important sociological variables such as education, occupation and income are powerful determinants of library use and information needs and interests. A 1981 study, for example, discovered that over a selected 12-month period, people with professional or semi-professional jobs were more than four times as likely to visit a library as people in blue-collar occupations; it was concluded that special outreach programs were required if libraries were to become more socially representative in their user base (Harvey, Marsden and Woodsworth, 1981).

Recently there has been a growing interest in developing programs in applied sociology at many North American universities, including the University of Michigan, the University of California at Los Angeles and the University of Toronto. This is a reaction partly to the trends just described and partly to the economically troubled times we have been experiencing of late. College and university students are much more concerned about job prospects, and it seems that, within sociology, applied sociology is perceived as one area of study that leads to better employment prospects. In addition, it seems that the demand for certain types of applied sociological research grows during economically difficult times. Governments, for example, often expand their program evaluation studies during recessions as a means of enhancing efficiency or achieving savings. Similarly, as business competition intensifies, companies do more—not less—market research as they seek better ways to reach their target markets.

# USES OF APPLIED SOCIOLOGY

We have already alluded to some ways in which applied sociology may be useful. We will now examine this issue in greater detail by looking at three specific approaches: 1. social impact assessment; 2. surveys; 3. evaluation studies.

## SOCIAL IMPACT ASSESSMENT

There has been substantial growth recently in the use of applied sociology to assess the social impact of large-scale development projects. Broadly speaking, social impact assessment examines the likely consequences of these developments—for example, natural resource extraction projects—and suggests the appropriate planning or ameliorative strategies.

As is well known, natural resources are the foundation of the Canadian economy. Indeed, our history has been significantly shaped by the way these resources have been developed (Buckley, 1958; Marsden and Harvey, 1979). Often, such development has been uneven and poorly planned. A typical scenario proceeds as follows. First, changes in marketplace conditions (often outside Canada), make it economically viable to exploit one of our natural resources. This development is carried out rapidly, with a great infusion of technology, capital and labour. Dislocation of the population and damage to the environment are often extensive. Finally, when the exploitation of the resource ends (or economic marketplace conditions change), the boomtowns that sprung up become ghosttowns as labour, technology and capital move on to new areas of opportunity (Neill, 1972).

In the early 1970s, the success of OPEC (the Organization of Petroleum Exporting Countries) dramatically raised the world price of oil. In Canada, this meant that the Alberta tar sands—a petroleum source both expensive and technologically complicated to exploit—became more valuable. Simply put, the higher world oil price made this previously unattractive resource much more attractive. Communities close to the tar sands, such as Fort McMurray, Alberta, have borne the social and economic brunt of rapid development of the tar sands. The consequences of the development included cultural and economic dislocation for many native people in the area, rapid population growth with resultant imbalance between social needs and the capacity of the health, recreation and education infrastructures to respond and a broad impact on the ecology (Nichols et al., 1980; Larson, 1977).

The growing concern for and regulation of use of the environment during the 1960s, however, meant the end of such large-scale, completely unregulated natural resource developments.

In Alberta, for example, the government now requires private corporations planning large-scale tar sands development to prepare lengthy and detailed social impact assessment reports. These reports cover a wide range of impact areas—including housing, employment patterns, health, education and recreation—and set out plans for dealing with such impacts. A considerable amount of applied sociological research is involved in preparing these reports. The completed reports are subjected to extensive review by government officials, who usually perform or commission their own social impact assessment studies in order to identify deficiencies in the private sector plans.

The data contained in these studies provide the Alberta government with valuable information for the planning and development of social services. Information on family size and age of children, for example, has been used in determining future requirements for school-rooms and teachers. Similarly, surveys of existing recreational facilities, combined with information on peoples' interests and level of disposable income, provides useful input to the planning of cultural and sports programs in fast-growing communities.

The applied sociological research methods used in connection with social impact assessment studies are exceedingly varied, ranging from surveys and interview and observational studies to analyses of existing statistical data on employment, housing, health services and other relevant topics.

## SURVEYS

Politicians commission opinion surveys to assess how the electorate may react to specific policy positions. Private corporations use market surveys to assess how a given product or service is performing or how a planned new product or service might perform in the future. Departments of government are constantly performing or commissioning surveys to monitor policy and program issues, such as the kinds of jobs obtained by young graduates, the adequacy of pension plans, and the extent to which women would use subsidized training programs to facilitate their entry into nontraditional jobs.

It should be emphasized that market surveys are not just used by the private sector. Philip Kotler, in his recent book, *Marketing for Non-Profit Organizations* (1975), shows that many types of organizations—universities, hospitals, libraries and museums—are becoming increasingly interested in learning more about the marketplace for their services and programs. During the affluent 1950s and 1960s, such organizations could virtually count on automatic increases in their base of public funding. With the onset of slower economic growth in the 1970s and 1980s, many such organizations have had to supplement operating revenues through their own fundraising initiatives. Marketing surveys have become useful in helping such organizations determine the segments of the public to which they can turn for support and how they can best shape their programs to meet changing public needs.

A major metropolitan library system recently surveyed several hundred members of various groups in the community, including frequent users of the library system, nonusers and special interest groups such as students, teachers and businesspeople. The survey results showed that the professional librarians had not always recognized the best ways for making the library system attractive and accessible. There was much more interest than had been imagined in program areas such as computerized information searching, flexible library hours and newsletters publicizing upcoming library-related events. The information is now being used to rethink and redesign many programs.

## EVALUATION STUDIES

As noted earlier, we are living in an era of government programs. Moreover, many government policy and program initiatives create a need for program development in the private sector. Affirmative action or equal employment opportunity programs are cases in point. Such programs require periodic evaluation for several reasons (Weiss, 1972; Leonard, 1978). First, such programs imply substantial commitment of financial and personnel resources. Such commitments require periodic review and assessment to determine if they are still cost-effective. It must also be borne in mind that the groups or populations served by a particular program are not static entities. Their needs change over time, and, accordingly, the related programs must also change.

Employment and retraining programs are another good example of private-sector programs. During the 1970s, job opportunities for youth were a leading concern of government policymakers as the baby-boom generation reached working age. Although youth unemployment remains an important issue, it has been joined by other pressing concerns. An increasing number of women, and not just the young, are returning to the labour force, and this trend is straining the economy's ability to create jobs. In addition, many jobs are being affected—or will be affected—by fast-moving technological changes such as computerization and the development of robotics. Many observers predict a massive need for retraining programs in the future. Evaluation studies will help set directions for these new programs. Like social impact assessment, evaluation research draws upon a wide range of applied sociological methods. Evaluation research often implies a time dimension, that is, it makes an attempt to determine if the desired results have been obtained over time as a consequence of a specific program rather than other extraneous developments. It is, of course, difficult to measure changes over time, given the difficulty (or impossibility) of establishing controlled settings in the social environment.

The evaluation researcher also finds that the effects of social programs are usually gradual and not dramatic. Our institutionalized society channels most change through social organizations that inhibit great fluctuations. Part of the challenge for the applied sociological evaluation researcher is to determine which effects may be of significance despite their apparently limited impact.

Social impact assessment, surveys and evaluation studies are three important areas of research to which applied sociology contributes. Of course, many other situations also call for the application of different sociological techniques and analyses. In many cases, these situations may not be covered in any textbook. One skill required by the effective applied sociologist is the ability to determine how best to "custom tailor" sociological theories and methods to a given problem or situation.

# STAGES IN A RESEARCH PROJECT

## PROBLEM DEFINITION

The essence of applied sociology is the bringing together of sociological techniques and data so that they can be used to solve practical problems. Although this reality permeates all aspects of the applied sociological research project, it is particularly critical in the initial, or *problem-definition*, stage. Here a clear understanding must be worked out between the applied sociologist, who will be providing the information and the techniques, and the client whose central concern will be with translating information or techniques into an operational application.

The breakdown of effective communication between the applied sociologist and the client can occur in various ways. For example, the sociologist may have a clear idea of how best to conceptualize, organize and perform a research project that will meet the client's needs. The client, however, may be under organizational, financial or time pressures that preclude using the ideal approach. The effective applied sociologist develops an understanding of these constraints and presents alternatives to find the best possible compromise between methodological perfection and practical necessities and/or limitations.

A further problem is that, in the applied setting, most problems are inter-disciplinary Consider, for example, implementing an affirmative action plan designed to achieve equal employment opportunity for women, disabled people and visible minorities. Developing and implementing such a plan requires experience and skill in several areas. For example, designing such a program involves employee testing and evaluation practices, which are often dependent on skills in psychology and personnel science.

The internal demographics of the organization's workforce may also be significant. An organization that has a relatively young age structure and plans little future hiring may have difficulty realizing the degree of personnel flexibility necessary to achieve the affirmative action program goals (Morgan, 1981).

Increasingly, particularly in large organizations, personnel records systems are computerized. Therefore, planning and developing an affirmative action program in a large organization may well require expertise in computer systems and analysis.

Effective development and implementation of an affirmative action program also draws extensively on the skills of the applied sociologist in analysing career and training ladders within the organization, determining areas of systematic bias in recruitment and promotion, identifying the attitudes and practices of supervisors and gathering—through surveys and other means—information required for the effective evaluation of the program.

The practice of sociology in applied settings is very like the merging of two cultures. Sociologists, whether or not they are interested in applied work, are trained in particular ways and develop specific modes of communication. The effective applied sociologist will remember that the language of sociology may be unfamiliar to many potential users of applied sociological knowledge. Similarly, the language and conventions of the user may be unfamiliar to the applied sociologist. If the sociologist is to be accepted by such users, she must develop an understanding of their conventions and language.

From the point of view of the applied sociologist, clarity and precision at the problem-definition stage are central to developing an appropriate research strategy. It may well be, however, that many clients will be hard pressed to provide such precise information. In both private and public organizations, program goals are often deliberately stated in very general or vague terms. Managers or bureaucrats may not wish to be held too closely to account. Furthermore, given the career interests of individuals in organizations, official and private objectives may become entangled in complicated and obscure ways. All of these patterns are part of the reality of organizational life. The fundamental challenge for the applied sociologist is to identify and understand these organizational complexities and subtleties and then come up with research procedures that will produce relevant results. In sum, dealing with the dynamic complexities of the applied setting is more likely to trouble the applied sociological researcher than the sociologist occupied with basic research.

The sociologist engaged in basic research defines his or her problem by locating it in an existing body of theory and research. Does this mean that existing theory and research literature is of less concern to the applied sociologist? Not at all. In fact, the effective use of theory and/or previous research can be an enormous time-saver to the applied sociologist in identifying what the really critical issues are and what methodologies or techniques to use in exploring those issues. The effective use of theory helps the applied sociological researcher develop an overall perspective on the problem.

Developing such an overall view permits a more systematic and integrated selection of appropriate research methodologies, which increases the likelihood that the applied research study can be kept on track and on schedule. Basic research sometimes allows the researcher the luxury of abandoning an ineffective approach and starting again. Given the time and financial constraints invariably associated with applied sociological assignments, this option is seldom available to the applied researcher.

The development at the conceptual level of a clear over-view of the direction the project will follow permits the development of secondary specifications, such as the overall critical path, which will influence when and where the key research decisions are made and how research staff (in large projects) are trained and deployed (Kidder, 1981).

## THE FUNDAMENTALS OF APPLIED SOCIOLOGICAL RESEARCH

An applied sociological researcher is attempting to learn something in order to produce information that will be of practical value in resolving a given problem. Generally, when trying to find something out, we ask questions and, indeed, the sociological research methodology has many different ways of asking questions. Two notable examples are surveys and interview studies. It should be observed, however, that we are also asking questions when we consult existing data, such as government statistical records, or when we engage in observation.

Questions, however, can be posed in many ways. There is no guarantee that the questions ultimately posed by the applied researcher will properly relate to the questions asked initially. This is because the research process contains several stages which must be passed through, and at each stage it is possible for issues to be subtly redefined or distorted. A typical applied sociological research project passes through the following stages:

1. Basic definition of the problem.
2. Translation of this definition into more specific hypotheses or research questions.
3. Development of the operational measurements to be used in carrying out the research.
4. Development of the research instruments (such as survey questionnaires, interview schedules, protocols for recording observational data).
5. Definition of the population, sample or other data source from which the required information will be obtained.
6. Gathering the data and preparing it for analysis.
7. Analysis, interpretation and presentation of the results.

When we understand what it is we want to do, including, perhaps, a set of hypotheses or research questions, we have established the conceptual foundations for our project. But one cannot go into the field until these conceptual foundations have been translated into operational procedures. When we operationalize our concepts, we sometimes find that our procedures subtly change or distort the essence of what we were seeking to learn.

As one moves through the stages of a research project, there is always the possibility of redefinitions or distortions entering the process. The applied social researcher must try to avoid such "drift" over the life of the research project, so that the ultimate conclusions and recommendations will correspond to the original concerns or questions to which the research was addressed.

If asking the right questions is one critical building block of the applied sociological research study, then knowing of whom the questions should be asked is the other. In this case, the "whom" includes not only the individuals or groups surveyed or interviewed, but also the sources that may be drawn upon in consulting existing data sources or in conducting observations.

Given the usual constraints of time and money, it is seldom possible to consult all the data sources that might bear on the issue under investigation. Generally, the applied sociologist examines some, rather than all, of the data: for example, interviewing or surveying a sample of individuals rather than an entire population. Of course, once we start to rely on samples rather than entire populations, the possibility of sampling error arises and this can affect the validity of our results. Fortunately, there are sampling techniques which estimate and minimize these risks (Kidder, 1981; see also pages 53 and 54 of this text).

One difficulty the applied sociological researcher often faces is that clients will worry about the constraints of time and money and, at the same time, insist that the research study results provide a strong basis for their future actions. Complicated tradeoffs may have to be discussed. For example, additional interviews may improve the data base, but they will unquestionably add to the cost and length of the study. The effective applied sociologist learns to explain to clients, in common-sense terms, the relationship between different methods and different levels of confidence and the implications of choices in method for cost and time considerations.

In working with clients, the applied sociologist often encounters different understandings of the same problem. For example, it may be clear to the applied sociologist—from a theoretical or methodological point of view—why certain data should be gathered. The concerns of the client may be quite different. The client may not understand the theoretical reasons for obtaining certain data and be worried about the cost of obtaining it, the effects on the organization of gathering such data, or the administrative obstacles to gathering such data.

There are several areas where potential conflict can arise between the client and the applied researcher. For example, the researcher may wish, for theoretical or methodological reasons to extend the research process over a longer time. The clients, on the other hand, often want immediate results that can be translated into immediate action. Because of his professional expertise, the applied sociologist is usually certain about the appropriate course to be taken in a given applied research project. Not infrequently, the client has an equally certain, if substantially different, understanding of the situation. If these differences are not reconciled early, the research may deteriorate into a futile conflict between the client and the sociologist.

## ANALYTICAL STRATEGIES

All of the statistical and data analysis strategies appropriate to basic research in sociology are potentially useful in applied sociology. It should be borne in mind that the users of applied sociological research will likely be laypeople who are unfamiliar with the technical or methodological procedures of sociological research.

Therefore, it is sometimes desirable to present at least some results of research in the form of graphs, which help make the results clear and easily understood (Statistics Canada, 1980). Figure 3-2 shows the changing age profile of the Grand Oil Company between 1984 and 1989. The exhibit is taken from a study performed to help the company's management understand possible implications of an aging corporate workforce. This mode of presenting data, called a histogram, is readily understandable without extensive training in statistics. Variations on this straightforward approach to results presentation are illustrated in Figure 3-3. These include pie diagrams, bar charts and graphs.

Figure 3-2   The Changing Age Structure of the Grand Oil Company

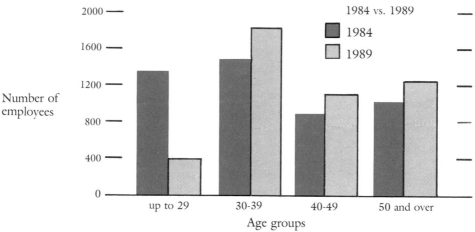

Another effective strategy is to present research results in an ascending order of complexity. A common starting point is the basic distributional information on the characteristics of the data gathered. In the report of a survey, information on the sex, age and income distribution of respondents gives the reader an immediate sense of how broadly representative (or unrepresentative) the data are.

In studies designed to provide policy makers with decision-making information, simple statistics may have important implications. A 1980 study comparing firms that provided training opportunities for their workforce with firms that did not found that 69 percent of managers in firms offering training said they did so because they felt it produced a good return on the investment made. In sharp contrast, 71 percent of managers in firms not offering training said they feared a loss of investment if workers moved on to other jobs shortly after participating in company subsidized training programs. In fact, the study showed that fewer than 10 percent of employees left within two years of receiving training. Clearly, if government was to realize its objective of expanding employer commitment to training programs, informational programs were urgently needed to clear up significant misconceptions.

As useful and interesting as such *basic distributions* may be, the relationships they point to can be made clearer by introducing other factors into the analysis. In the training study referred to above, further important differences were found when

## Figure 3-3

The pie diagram is an effective means for data presentation:

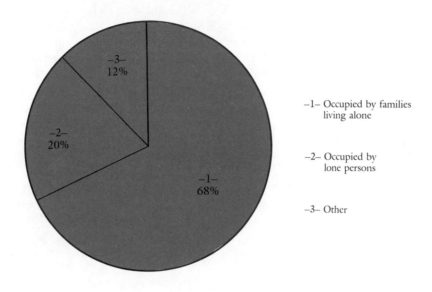

-1- Occupied by families
    living alone

-2- Occupied by
    lone persons

-3- Other

As are graphs:

Average Persons per Household

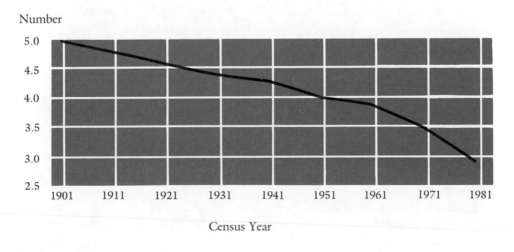

Census Year

*Highlights: 1981 Census of Canada*, Ottawa, Statistics Canada, pp. 5, 30. Reproduced by permission of the Minister of Supply and Services.

other factors, such as size of firm, type of industry, and geographical location of the company, were introduced.

Both simple and complex forms of analysis can serve the applied sociological researcher. By starting with the simple and proceeding to the complex, however, the applied sociologist increases the likelihood that her audience will have some sense of what the more complex analyses mean.

In sociological research, one will periodically hear debated the merits of quantitative versus qualitative research. Table 3-1 sets out the principal differences between the two approaches. In the applied setting, the sociologist will often have to work with, and effectively reconcile, very different types of data. Generally speaking, however, the *qualitative* approach is most appropriate when the applied sociologist is working with exploratory or pilot project situations. The *quantitative* approach works best when large-scale data are needed to evaluate an established program or to determine broad new directions in market planning or service delivery.

TABLE 3-1    The Qualitative and Quantitative Paradigms Compared

| QUALITATIVE PARADIGM | QUANTITATIVE PARADIGM |
| --- | --- |
| Advocates the use of qualitative methods. | Advocates the use of quantitative methods. |
| Naturalistic and uncontrolled observation. | Obtrusive and controlled measurement. |
| Subjective. | Objective. |
| Close to the data: the "insider" perspective. | Removed from the data: the "outsider" perspective. |
| Grounded, discovery-oriented, exploratory, expansionist, descriptive and inductive. | Ungrounded, verification-oriented, confirmatory, reductionist, inferential and hypothetico-deductive. |
| Process-oriented. | Outcome-oriented. |
| Valid: "real," "rich," and "deep" data. | Reliable: "hard" and replicable data. |
| Ungeneralizable: single case studies. | Generalizable: multiple case studies. |
| Holistic. | Particularistic. |
| Assumes a dynamic reality. | Assumes a stable reality. |

Adapted from Charles S. Reichardt and Thomas D. Cook, "Beyond Qualitative Versus Quantitative Methods" in T.D. Cook and C.S. Reichardt (eds.) *Qualitative and Quantitative Methods in Evaluation Research*, Beverly Hills, Sage Publications 1979.

## AFTER THE RESEARCH IS DONE

### Writing a Report

Applied sociological research gathers information that will permit action to be taken. The applied sociologist must, therefore, present his or her results clearly and draw from these results the implications for action.

In most cases, the applied sociologist presents the results to the client in a research report. There are several requirements for a successful report. Although it may seem obvious, an important feature of any such report is a *title* that succinctly conveys the essence of what has been done. The *introductory chapter* should clearly set forth the background situation that led to the research being undertaken. Also, if other research studies were used in conducting the research being reported, these too should be discussed. The introductory section of the report should also provide the reader with an overview of what the entire report contains.

The introductory section is generally followed by the section or sections that outline the *data and research methods used*. If the audience for the report is nontechnical, much of this information may be presented in appendices to the main report. Still, even a nontechnical audience needs enough information to form a general idea of the nature of the data being used and of how they were obtained.

The stage is now set for presenting *results*. At this point, it is often useful to present again—in a concise statement of research objectives—the basic issues to which the research was directed. The form in which the results will be set forth will, of course, be determined by the research questions and the data obtained. Nevertheless, as suggested earlier, it is often effective to start with the basic results and then proceed to the more specific or particular findings.

In reports which may become the basis for action, it is particularly important to discuss the strength of the findings or, put another way, the degree of confidence the client can have in the findings. Statistical procedures, such as tests of significance, can be helpful, but it is also possible—and sometimes desirable—to deal with the issue of confidence by examining your results in the light of other related research or information to define the limits within which your results can be reasonably applied. This may be more understandable to the lay user of your research than a purely statistical approach.

After presenting the results, it is necessary to pull together the major themes of what has been discovered and translate these into practical proposals for action. This process produces the *conclusions and recommendations* section of the report. The conclusions should succinctly summarize what has been discovered and clearly address the original questions posed. Conclusions may vary from "weak" to "strong," and, as has been said, it is important that the issue of confidence be addressed. During a research study, unexpected or unanticipated findings often arise. These should also be discussed in the concluding section of the report, particularly to explain how such findings might affect the original questions addressed by the research. Finally, recommendations should be presented in point form, so that each can be assessed on its own merits. The amount and kind of evidence in support of a recommendation, should also be clearly stated.

The applied sociologist should realize that this report will probably be read by three quite different audiences. The senior management of the organization for whom the work was done will be most interested in the specific recommendations for action and the brief overview of the research. Thus, the research report should also include an *executive summary* which—in six pages or less—sets out the essence of what has been discovered and what should be done. The interest of middle management will no doubt extend to the entire main body of the report. Technical appendices dealing with sample design or survey instrumentation may be referred to specialists within the organization. The effective applied sociologist will structure a report to make these main sections easily identifiable and readily accessible to the reader.

Two other general principles are important in preparing an effective research report. First, jargon should be avoided. The following paragraph shows how to quickly lose your reader's interest and/or understanding:

> Recent research in the forced-compliance paradigm has focused on the effects of predecisional choice and incentive magnitude (Kidder, 1981).

Clear, straightforward language and examples that are meaningful to your audience are the most effective way to communicate your results. The second principle involves ethical issues. In applied work, the sociological researcher often receives confidential, sensitive information. Moreover, in applied work, results are likely to be acted upon. It is therefore essential that the researcher take every precaution to protect sources and to present results in such a way that specific individuals cannot be identified.

## Oral Presentations

In addition to preparing a report, the applied sociologist will often be asked to make a presentation based on the study results. The techniques used for an effective presentation are quite different from those used for an effective report. First, most presentations have time limits. Second, such presentations are often attended by people with very different levels of understanding of sociological research and—more often than not—very different ideas on how such research should or should not be applied.

Handing out copies of the report to the audience and pointing out the salient results is usually not effective. Complex points that may be understood after an undisturbed reading of the report are often exceedingly difficult to explain in a brief seminar. Unfortunately, the applied sociologist can never assume that the people at a presentation have read the report in detail. In addition, it is difficult to control the direction of a presentation by "walking" participants through a report. When you want to deal with something on page 20, someone else has moved on to page 35 and is asking questions about material presented there.

A far more effective strategy is to plan out what you want to say and then say it in short, to-the-point statements. It is often desirable to prepare these statements on overhead transparencies or slides. This way, presentation participants can be taken sequentially and systematically through the results of the study.

In some cases, the applied sociologist's involvement with the client will end with the tabling of a report that sets out the research findings and recommends appropriate action. In other cases, the applied sociologist may become involved in implementing the recommendations of his report.

## Implementing Recommendations

Implementing change in an organization is a complex and challenging task. Change, no matter how it is introduced, usually causes anxiety. People worry about how changes may affect them personally—their job, their workload, their prospects for future promotion. If these anxieties cannot be relieved, the general reaction to the proposed changes is likely to range from apathy to active resistance.

Two further difficulties complicate the implementation of applied sociological research findings in organizations. First, organizations are dynamic and continue to change during the research process. Members leave and are replaced by new people with new ideas. Sometimes, the applied sociologist finds that the original sponsor or sponsors of a study leave the organization or move to new areas of responsibility. A second problem area involves *weak effects* (Rossi and Wright, 1977). People do not create and enter into patterns of social organization by accident. Social organizations ensure continuity and predictability in most aspects of our lives. Consider, for example, the many layers of social organization involved in education, health care, employment, the legal system and so on. The need for continuity and predictability is mirrored in the research results applied sociologists typically obtain. People usually react conservatively toward change. Often, they prefer to live with what they know—despite its limitations—rather than face the anxieties that arise when they pursue a new course of action. Where a willingness to consider change does exist, people generally prefer change to be incremental and gradual.

This does not mean weak effects are unimportant. It means that the applied sociologist must be careful to establish with clients a common context of understanding within which the research results may be interpreted. The applied sociologist who fails to do this will likely find that research results are dismissed as trivial or insignificant, whereas in fact they may be important—albeit subtle—indicators of problem areas demanding further action.

The applied sociologist who wants to become effective at implementing results will develop certain approaches to the work. First, during the research, he or she will establish and maintain contact with the people who represent key sectors or interests within the research setting. This sustained contact helps the applied sociologist create a context of understanding for the research being performed. Second, the effective applied sociologist will recognize the important difference between what is *feasible* and what is *acceptable* within a given organization or research setting. Particular recommendations for action may well be feasible, in a technical sense, but quite unlikely to be adopted given the interests or ideology of influential members of the organization.

For example, applied sociological studies of organizations often recommend ways of improving efficiency by reorganizing or reducing staff and/or budgets. Managers, however, measure their organizational status in terms of such things as staff and budget size and almost invariably emerge as powerful opponents to such recommendations. This is why the applied sociologist, apart from conducting the required research, must also develop a dynamic sociological understanding of the organization or research setting involved. This is even more critical if the researcher is expected to become involved in the implementation process.

# THE APPLIED SOCIOLOGIST'S ROLE

Within applied sociology there are, broadly speaking, three roles a sociologist can play. The first is that of researcher. In this role, the sociologist gathers data or otherwise establishes facts and makes them available to the client. The decision about whether to implement action based on the results is made and carried out by the client.

A second role the applied sociologist can fill is that of change agent. In this case, the sociologist may also conduct research and gather data, but, once the results are in place, he or she becomes actively involved with the client in developing and carrying out the implementation strategies discussed earlier.

A third role the applied sociologist may perform is that of facilitator. Dealing with and adapting to change is a regular feature of organizational life. However, the different interests or points of view of the members of an organization make it difficult to develop coherent and systematic strategies to deal with change. Here, the applied sociologist—as a neutral observer equipped with skills for organization analysis—can help to identify the conflicting points of view and develop mechanisms which promote examination and discussion within the organization of obstacles to change and adaptation.

To perform applied sociology effectively, the sociologist needs several kinds of training or experience. A strong grounding in both sociological theory and research methods is essential. Often, the applied sociologist must work quickly to define the problem to be dealt with and to match that definition with an appropriate research strategy.

The applied sociologist should also have training in organizational theory, given that most problems a researcher will be involved with occur within organizations. Also important, particularly for sociologists working in government, is an under-standing of policy studies, the discipline that focuses on how governments formulate new public policies and translate new policies into practice.

Besides the skills described above, the applied sociologist will find it useful to know how to use statistics and computers. Management skills will also prove useful, since, particularly in large projects, the applied sociologist may be called upon to train and supervise field staff, develop and monitor the critical path for the research program, and deal with many other administrative and budgetary problems that arise.

Over and above these basic skills, the applied sociologist may be highly specialized in a particular area such as crime and deviance, health studies or industrial sociology.

The applied sociologist should be flexible and creative in combining these various skills. A researcher cannot afford to be doctrinaire. This creativity and flexibility should be matched by a well-developed ability to work and communicate effectively with people in a wide range of settings and at all levels within those settings. Although certain skills can be acquired through university study, the training and development of an effective applied sociologist also requires practical, in-the-field experience in the form of an internship or apprenticeship.

More generally, the applied sociologist has a dynamic role that will continue to evolve in response to changes in society and the discipline of sociology. To place this evolution in perspective, it is important to realize that applying sociological knowledge is not a new development. Auguste Comte (1798-1857)—often regarded as the founder of sociology—was preoccupied with identifying general sociological laws or principles that could then be applied to achieve social progress. Our un-derstanding of social problems and needs is different today from what it was in Comte's time and will be different in the future from what it is today. But we are still searching for sociological knowledge that can be applied to changing needs and problems.

In the performance of this work, does the applied sociologist become simply a tool of established interests and/or policy? In fact, many applied sociological research studies point to an important role for the applied sociologist as a social critic. Applied social research has, for example, helped document conditions of inequality for women and racial and linguistic minorities and has helped to identify directions for needed social change (Govt. of Canada, 1969; 1984). As with many other forms of knowledge, applied sociological research can be used to support a wide range of political and/or ideological positions. An open and continuing discussion of ethical issues is the best safeguard against abuse or misuse of sociological knowledge and should be welcomed by all those working in the field.

# SUMMARY

With industrialization and modernization, people increasingly expect science and technology to solve their problems. Social science has been no exception to this trend. In addition, beginning in the 1950s and reaching a zenith in the 1960s, government-funded social programs have expanded enormously. These developments have expanded the demand for applied sociological research.

Population changes in such areas as aging, family size and patterns of education and employment have major implications for many product and service markets. Both governments and private corporations use applied sociological research to monitor these trends and develop appropriate responses.

Applied sociological research can assume many forms. Three major types are: 1. social impact assessment, which determines the probable consequences of large-scale developments; 2. surveys, which are frequently used for assembling broadly based data on attitudes and behaviours; 3. evaluation studies, which determine if programs are meeting their objectives.

The problems the sociologist faces in the applied setting are usually multidisciplinary in nature. This often makes it difficult to arrive at common understandings during the critical problem-definition stage of a project. The effective applied sociologist learns how to communicate well with different disciplines and will develop skills in communicating his or her perspective in terms readily understood by people who are unfamiliar with sociological theories and methods.

It is sometimes thought that applied sociology is atheoretical. In fact, using theory is essential in defining a research problem and in establishing an overall, coherent direction for a project. Establishing of such clear, overall research directions is particularly critical in applied work, where time and cost pressures are invariably present. Applied work can also contribute to theory development. In the mid-1960s, the sociologist James S. Coleman was commissioned by the U.S. government to conduct a wide ranging study of equality of educational opportunity designed to provide information for the development of civil rights programs and policies (Coleman et al, 1966). *The Coleman Report* and reactions to it by other researchers have improved our understanding of social stratification and achievement (Jencks et al., 1972).

The applied sociological research process rests on two fundamental building blocks: 1. the questions to be answered; 2. the sources of data to be sampled or drawn upon in answering the questions. A frequent problem in the applied setting is

effectively reconciling methodological concerns and cost, time and other administrative considerations. The sociologist will develop skills that facilitate the tradeoffs
which must often be made.

The applied sociologist can use all the statistical and data analysis techniques
employed in basic research. However, the applied sociologist's audience will often
lack in-depth training in sociological theory and method. Thus, the applied sociologist will learn to communicate research results in common-sense terms readily
understood by a lay audience. Using graphs for data presentations often serves this
objective. In addition, many applied sociologists find it useful, in dealing with lay
audiences, to gradually develop their analysis from the more basic to the most
complex findings.

A competent researcher should also have strong skills in report writing and oral
presentations. It is essential that the sociologist learn how to simplify without being
simplistic.

In applied work, the sociologist will be expected to formulate recommendations
for action. The people who may ultimately implement these recommendations will
legitimately be concerned about the strength of the evidence on which recommendations rest. Once again, the researcher must find clear and understandable ways of
presenting the evidence that supports his recommendations.

If the applied sociologist becomes involved in implementing research results, she
will find that, in many cases, proposals for change generate anxiety or resistance
among those who will be affected. Here, an understanding of organization dynamics
can be helpful in finding the most effective ways of explaining changes and enlisting
co-operation. A researcher cannot assume that recommendations will be welcomed
simply because they are technically sound or based on strong data.

The future for applied sociology and sociologists seems bright. Work in this area
requires a strong grounding in theory and methods, an understanding of how
organizations are structured and how they work, an ability to work with people,
computer skills and an ability to be flexible and creative while working under pressure.

## DISCUSSION QUESTIONS

1. Describe some of the constraints or problems the applied sociologist must
   deal with and what strategies might be appropriate in response to them.

2. What are the major social trends of the past ten years, and how have they
   affected the requirements for applied sociological research? What future
   trends and requirements do you envision?

3. What are the major uses to which applied sociology can be put? What kinds
   of questions or problem areas can sociological analysis and research help
   to resolve?

4. Compare and contrast the role of sociological theory in basic and applied
   sociological research.

5. What steps should the applied sociologist take to ensure that his or her research will be properly understood and acted upon by a client?

# PROCESSES of SOCIAL ORGANIZATION

What ties people together in groups? What makes them behave in predictable ways? How are people assimilated into on-going social organizations?

These questions will all be addressed in this section of the book. The following chapters examine basic processes of social organization: population, acculturation, socialization, progress through the "life stages," control and deviance.

To a large degree, the answers to the above questions also answer opposite questions: What severs the ties between people or prevents ties from forming? Why do people sometimes behave unpredictably? What keeps them from assimilating into on-going organizations? To understand social conflict, deviance and change is also to understand social consensus and stability. The two differ only in their emphasis, as in the question, "Is the waterglass half empty or half full?" However, theorists who approach society from the opposing standpoints of order and change differ in important ways. For this reason, this book devotes an entire section to change. (See page 547.) The related topic of social conflict is discussed throughout this text. (See, for example, the chapters on social movements, stratification and class and law and society.)

The problem of order is, for sociology, a central one. English political theorist Thomas Hobbes (1588-1679), for example, declared that, in a state of nature, lacking government, people's selfish desires would run wild; they would lead lives that were "solitary, poor, nasty, brutish and short." This was why a sovereign ruler was needed. People could not rely on "society" to protect its members: only the nation-state could do so.

The nineteenth century saw an upsurge of anarchist and utopian philosophies opposing this Hobbesian view. They held that nation-states were unnecessary and repressive and that social order could emerge naturally from people's co-operative instincts. Unlike Hobbes, utopian and anarchistic theorists believed selfishness was learned and artificial and co-operativeness and sociability, natural. In large part, their views led to the study of society as an entity distinct from the state.

The sociologists studying "community," a topic discussed in the next section, supported this distinction. With industrialization and urbanization, social relations changed markedly. No longer were they based on tradition and blood ties but on impersonal, temporary, more limited kinds of bonds. Such changes within an enduring nation-state proved that social order was distinct from political order and that it contributed in a unique way to human well-being. This observation led toward the systematic study of social order, what establishes and what disrupts it.

## Population Processes

The most basic aspect of a society (or a social relationship) is its population. The people in a particular society (or social relationship) are of certain kinds. In some relationships, they are more often male, in others female, in some both male and female. In some relationships, they are young, in others old, in some both young and old. Likewise, societies vary markedly from one to another in their population characteristics.

During the nineteenth and twentieth centuries, Western societies industrialized, urbanized and underwent radical population changes. Their populations grew and redistributed geographically; the ratio of young to old altered; and the presence of males and females, old and young, in particular relationships also changed. These population shifts put great pressure on such social institutions as marriage and the family, education and the workplace. New kinds of people had to be assimilated into on-going social organizations. New organizations were established to accommodate the new population groups. The flood of immigrants that filled North American society and its institutions made keeping the social order a problem.

## Culture and Acculturation

Not only population change affected social order in the nineteenth and twentieth centuries. The *culture* of the entire Western world also *modernized*. By "culture" we mean the entire collection of values and behaviours that characterize life in a society. "Modernization" is complex. It grows out of industrialization, urbanization, the rise of modern science and technology, secular religion, mass literacy and a new public awareness of the world. By a "modernized" culture we mean one that accommodates these new developments. According to researchers like sociologist Alex Inkeles, such a culture produces new kinds of personalities: people who are more inclined to plan, reason, grant equality to others and interest themselves in other parts of the world. By some definitions, modernization expands human horizons beyond past and present to future, beyond narrow interest in self, family and community to an interest in nation, world and cosmos.

Other images of modernization are less favourable. Karl Marx (1818-1883) and Max Weber (1864-1920) depicted modern society as exploitive, alienating, immense and impersonal, over-organized but with insufficient concern for human beings, obsessed with technology and efficiency, faddish and overcrowded with meaningless gadgetry. Modernity, in this view, is a worldwide consumer's market characterized by the fetish for commodities—an obsession to acquire material possessions as a proof of personal value.

Whichever assessment seems more accurate, and both apply in some instances, Western culture has changed significantly in the last two centuries. Culture, like population, is an important part of the context within which a society maintains or changes its way of maintaining order. Accordingly, the social relations that make up society in the West have also changed significantly.

*Acculturation* is the process by which members of a society learn their culture. The process usually occurs in an unstructured, often unconscious way, the way language is learned. Babies learn to speak their society's language without knowing they are learning it. They practice, imitate, use trial and error. The learning of cultural values probably also proceeds this way. For example, research by sociologists Bernd Baldus and Verna Tribe has shown that, by an early age, Canadian schoolchildren have learned to associate good manners and morals with symbols of high social standing (for instance, a nice car, a large home).

Where and how did they learn this? Perhaps unconsciously, from the mass media portrayals of rich and poor people, or from unspoken cues provided by their parents and other adults.

Acculturation is related to two other important processes. One is *assimilation*, the process by which adult members of foreign cultural groups learn the values and behaviours of a culture into which they have immigrated. In a society like Canada's, so heavily composed of immigrants, a smooth assimilation process is crucial. Despite our commitment to multiculturalism, some consensus is necessary among Canadians of varied cultural origins.

## Socialization

The second related process is *socialization*, by which people learn the social rules defining relationships into which they will enter. Socialization goes on throughout life, but in childhood the changes are most dramatic and visible. A child is born without any knowledge of social rules. Yet, by the time he or she begins school, the child has learned to follow the orders given by people in authority (chiefly adults), to co-operate (chiefly with peers), to accept certain responsibilities and to carry out assigned tasks at home.

Typically, the roles and rules learned in socialization are suited to the values learned in acculturation. For example, in our society a child is acculturated to believe that children must obey authority. They are trained to associate authority with adults, and particularly with specific adults: parents, grandparents, teachers and policemen, among others. Peers, by contrast, must establish their authority. Since none of the learned bases for authority seem to apply, obedience among peers must be established by fighting, which is the way animals accomplish this task. Once a rough hierarchy has been established, children "know their place" in the playground just as they do at home.

In some situations, no rules exist. Rules must be hammered out by the interacting group, then learned and obeyed. In other situations, participants must follow the existing rules, even if they conflict with earlier experiences. This conflict is experienced by the workman promoted to foreman, for example. As workman, he may have felt loyal to the workers and opposed management; as foreman, he *must* feel loyal to management and, equivalently, opposed to the workmen. The structure of the worker/foreman relationship creates this conflict. People must solve it through resocialization, and research shows they generally weather the transition, if not always smoothly.

## Aging and the Life Process

Some change in situations comes about through simple aging. Our responsibilities as schoolchildren differ markedly from those of newlyweds, young parents, new grandparents or retired people. Maintenance of the social order depends no less on learning these roles than on learning job roles; yet the requirements of these roles are usually much less clear. People are often reluctant to discuss the problems they have understanding, learning and fulfilling them.

Paradoxically, for these roles, some of the most difficult and important we play as adults, we usually receive the least formal preparation. No one is educated for retirement. Few take courses in being a good spouse or parent. Who needs to pass an examination or get a licence (except a marriage licence) to pass from one such role to another? The consequences of this lack of preparation are dire. High divorce rates illustrate, among other things, many people's inadequacy as spouses, while high rates of child abuse attest to the strains of parenthood entered into without preparation.

The problems of aging and the life process go well beyond marriage and parenthood. Aging brings many life crises: changes in the sense of self worth or life purpose. We must find our way through the problems of young adulthood, full maturity and social obsolescence largely on our own. Many people seek social supports and form groups to help them cope . The deviant and self-destructive behaviours of people who do not cope socially with these strains—who retreat instead into alcohol, drugs or even suicide—attest to the importance of social order for a happy and productive life.

## Control and Deviance

Yet societies also bring restrictions aplenty. Social life and social relationships require rules. Rules imply control, and control in turn implies authority, the right to impose and enforce rules. Differential authority creates social inequality. This suggests that no society, whether capitalist, socialist or communist, will ever be wholly egalitarian, for no society can operate without rules and authority. This theme will be developed more thoroughly in other chapters.

An early, surprising discovery by Émile Durkheim (1858-1917) is that any society needs deviance. This statement seems paradoxical, since any society also needs order, and deviance implies disorder. Yet deviance, like conflict, offers an opportunity to reaffirm order, an occasion to remind society's members of the limits of proper behaviour. Punishment of deviance, like the conduct of a war with outsiders, strengthens social solidarity and group cohesion, and thus is a process of social organization.

The question of why particular people break the rules is the object of continuing attention from criminologists. Many reasons can be given for deviance, ranging from chemical, physiological, psychological, up through social and cultural factors. What is surprising is not that deviance happens so often, given the tremendous number of reasons for its occurrence; but rather that it happens so rarely. Of course, everyone deviates in some way, at some time or another (perhaps daily). In this sense, deviance is amazingly common, the norm and not the exception in human societies. Yet most deviance is minor and hidden. Furthermore, most deviance is prevented, minimized or hidden not because of coercion but because of acculturation, socialization and an unwillingness to risk exposure to ridicule, criticism or ostracism.

The material basis of social life should not be ignored in explaining conformity. We all depend upon the good will and co-operation of others for money, information and other kinds of assistance. Without these, we find it hard to carry out our social roles, hold jobs or participate in social life. Thus, excommunication, communal expulsion, the "silent treatment" and other forms of banishment have been used with great success by religious and secular organizations to control their members. The example of an expelled member helps a great deal to pull the other group members back into line.

Having said that, we must remember the importance of formal social controls. These include laws and law enforcement agencies, which punish serious deviations. Whether informal social controls would be sufficient without formal ones backing them up, we shall never know. No societies of any complexity lack formal social controls, any more than they lack inequalities. The role and character of these formal controls will be discussed in a later section in a chapter on law and society.

## A Summary and Look Ahead

To summarize, people are gathered into social relationships by processes of social organization. These include population processes, acculturation, socialization, progress through the life stages, control and deviance. These processes are similar in social organizations of differing size and complexity. All social systems require smooth functioning of these processes. Yet social organizations of different sizes and complexity differ in other important ways. Thus, the science of society cannot be reduced, as some would wish, to a science of human individuals or groups. To move from individuals to groups to societies, sociologists must understand a great deal more than they do about the effects of size and complexity on social functioning.

The next section will take us from social roles, the basic building blocks of social relationships, to communities and cities, which are very large and complex sets of social relations. The section following this one will deal with the still more complex social relations that make up society's central institutions.

# 4

# Population Processes

*Lorne Tepperman*

# INTRODUCTION: POPULATION PROCESSES AND SOCIAL STRUCTURE

A society's population shapes its social, economic and political life. In turn, social organization shapes a population.

Viewed one way, a population is just a set of people. But sociologists see more than that. They want to know what affects the number and types of people making up a population, the rate at which numbers and types of people are changing and how these and related changes affect social organization.

Three main aspects of a population are: size, composition and distribution. *Size* refers to the number of people living in a given area; *composition*, to their characteristics; and *distribution*, to their location. These three aspects of population result from fertility, mortality and migration. *Fertility* refers to the average number of children women bear; *mortality*, to the deaths in the population; and *migration*, to people's changes of location. The three population processes—fertility, mortality and migration—determine the rate at which people move through social structures, the effects of population on social structures and vice versa.

By *social structure* we mean social relationships which keep the same form as people move through them. Take the relationship between parents and their children. Naturally, families differ due to class, ethnic background or other variables. But if a Martian asked how average Canadian parents and their children interact, sociologists could answer with considerable accuracy. The answer would reveal important similarities among families and differences between Canadian families and, for example, the average Chinese (or Martian) families.

Making this relationship predictable from one family to another are: *laws*, which punish offences against the relationship (e.g., child abuse); *social values* learned and relearned throughout life; *role expectations* parents and children hold about one another; and *social pressures* to conform that outsiders—friends, relatives, neighbours, school teachers and others—constantly bring to bear on the family members.

Relations between parents and their children change as the culture changes. But no pattern is altered suddenly by new people entering into the roles of parent and child. Children are born daily, grandparents die and adults enter and leave the role of parent, yet it is remarkable how little the continuing flow of people in and out of these roles affects the social relationship. The same behaviours and emotions are thus repeated day after day, year after year.

## HOW POPULATION FLOW AFFECTS SOCIAL RELATIONS

But what if the flow of people through these roles changed? In fact, it has. Today people are slower to become parents than they used to be. They are also slower to leave the role of parent, due to an increase in average life expectancy. Fewer people are becoming parents at all, as greater numbers choose to remain childless. And fewer people are fulfilling the role of child, because of reductions in the size of families.

These changes are dramatically altering the number of "conventional" families and thereby weakening the base of predictable family relations. Traditional patterns

In 1851, a "representative village" of one thousand people would experience forty-six births per year, while in 1976 it would count only sixteen births. In 1851 the village would experience a death of a child under one year of age every month and a half, while in 1976 they would have one every five years. By contrast, survival to age eighty or over has become much more common. The changed levels of fertility and mortality have important consequences for families. Couples spend considerably fewer years in the childbearing and childrearing part of their lives. Couples who marry in their early twenties might, on average, be expected to celebrate their fiftieth wedding anniversary, thus changing dramatically the meaning of the phrase "till death do us part." In effect, the instabilities caused by death have been replaced by the instabilities in the marital relationship itself.

Excerpt from pp. 135-6 GROWTH AND DUALISM by R. Beaujot and K. McQuillan. Copyright © 1982 Gage Publishing Limited. Reprinted by permission of GAGE EDUCATIONAL Publishing Company (A Division of Canada Publishing Corporation).

are dying out, and traditional expectations do not apply as well as they once did. But new expectations have not yet formed. People today feel confused about what "proper" family relationships are. We are passing through a period of social change induced by population change.

Population processes not only affect families, they affect all social relationships which make up social structures, large and small. To understand this, it is useful to think of society as a large, fully furnished hotel.

As time passes, people check in and out in an orderly procession. But what if the rate of movement sped up? If twice as many people crowded into the same number of rooms? Or if new kinds of people arrived, lacking knowledge of or respect for the hotel rules? People might move the furniture around, perhaps vandalize or destroy the building. Certainly, the hotel would change. How *much* it might change is partly decided by the size, composition and distribution of the hotel population.

At bottom, population processes are only the addition and subtraction of people: the births and deaths, in-migrations and out migrations and the relocation of people within a society. Any social role or institution can be studied from a population perspective. That is what sociologists do when they study *social mobility*, people moving from one social class into another; or *careers*, people moving through a series of jobs or organizations; or any other institution (e.g., a university) through which people move in a predictable way. As economist Kenneth Boulding has put it (1981:55), a population is merely "the stock of a species with throughput"!

# AN OVERVIEW OF POPULATION CHANGE

Good theories about population processes demand good historical data. Population data include censuses, vital statistics and national and international migration records. All four types of data are found in their most developed form in modern Western societies. Population theories often reflect the experiences of these societies. Even after World War II, good data were drawn almost entirely from European and North American populations. This bias led sociologists to believe that population change in the Third World would follow the pattern observed in Europe for several centuries.

However, by collecting reliable data in developing countries, our theories have changed. *Demographers*, who study population scientifically, have helped governments improve the quality of their data and interpret this information more effectively. They have developed techniques for judging and correcting flawed data (United Nations, 1967; Shyrock and Siegel, 1973).

Recent advances in methodology and data quality have also helped historical analysis. An example is the new method of analysing parish records by computer in order to study the populations of historic communities. In this way, we can make excellent guesses about family structures, household composition and population processes hundreds of years ago. The work by Peter Laslett and his Cambridge (England) Group (Laslett, 1971; Wrigley, ed., 1966; Laslett, ed., 1972) is especially notable in this area. In Canada, Charbonneau (1975) has used a similar technique to study the entire population of seventeenth century New France. This is part of an on-going project that will eventually reveal a lot about the demographic history of French Canada through parish records, early censuses, genealogies and other archival materials.

The creative use of historical censuses is found in a great many studies by demographers and historians. Perhaps the most advanced and systematic work has been done by researchers associated with Princeton University's European Fertility Study, under the guidance of Ansley Coale. Already, volumes have been published on the demographic history of France, Germany, Spain, England, Russia and a number of other countries.

With reliable statistics, we can begin to discover past and present population trends. One feature of a population that interests social planners greatly is its growth rate. The growth rate is the number of people added to (or subtracted from) a population in a given period of time, expressed as a proportion of the total population in that same period. Demographers also measure population increase in terms of *doubling time*, or the number of years a population will take to double its size if it grows at its current rate. For example, growing at the current rate of about 2 percent per year, the world's population will double in less than 35 years. An easy way of estimating doubling time is to divide the growth rate, in this case .02, into .69. (This works only if growth is unaffected by migration, as in the earth's population.) If our estimate is right, the world will contain more than 8 billion people early in the next century.

According to demographer Philip Hauser (1964: 17), if growth continues at the present rate, by the year 3530 the human population will outweigh the earth it stands on! This hypothetical result is clearly absurd. But it illustrates the speed at which our species is approaching its territorial limits on earth. Sooner or later, growth must stop. But when and how? Will the change be sudden or gradual, chosen or forced upon us? Will it be accompanied by a drastic decline in childbearing or a rise in the number of deaths? World population increase results from an excess of births (fertility) over deaths (mortality). This excess is called *natural increase* (as distinct from increase due to migration). There are only two ways for population

> It is possible quickly to summarize the remarkable acceleration of his growth rate which man has experienced. It took most of the millennia of man's habitation of this planet to produce a population as great as one billion persons simultaneously alive. This population was not achieved until approximately 1850. To produce a population of two billion persons simultaneously alive required only an additional seventy-five years, for this number was achieved by 1925. To reach a population of three billion persons required only an additonal thirty-seven years, for this was the total in 1962. Continuation of the trend would produce a fourth billion in about fifteen years and a fifth billion in less than an additional ten years.
>
> If man's precursors prior to the old Stone Age are ignored, it has been estimated that since the beginning of that era there have been perhaps 77 billion births. Of this number only 12 billion, or less than 16 percent of the total, occurred during the approximately 8000 years encompassing the Neolithic period and history up to the middle of the seventeenth century. Some 23 billion births, or 30 percent of the total, occurred during the three centuries of the Modern Era. Of the total number of persons that have ever been born, according to these estimates, about 4 percent, therefore, are now living.
>
> Excerpt from "The Population of the World," by Philip M. Hauser from the book POPULATION: THE VITAL REVOLUTION by Ronald Freedman. Copyright 1964 by Doubleday & Company, Inc. Reprinted by permission of the publisher.

growth to slow (or stop): the fertility rate falls or the mortality rate rises. What changes in human death and birth rates have caused such dramatic changes in natural increase in the recent past?

# THREE THEORIES OF POPULATION GROWTH

## MALTHUSIAN THEORY

One of the earliest and most influential theories about population growth was put forward by Thomas Robert Malthus (1766-1834), an English clergyman and economist. Malthus (1959; originally 1798) sees the human condition as tied to the "principle of population." He argues that the population tends to grow faster than the means of food production. At best, Malthus claims, the means of subsistence can increase only arithmetically, as in the series 1,2,3,4,5. But population will increase geometrically, as in the series 1,2,4,8,16. The gap between these two series gets wider and wider if population growth goes unchecked.

Malthus develops his ideas from several assumptions. First, people want sex. Uncontrolled sexual passion, according to this theory, must result in childbearing. Second, people need food. But the human needs for food and sex conflict, since more sex, resulting in more children, will increase the total need for food. As one constraint is lifted, the other operates more strongly. If fewer children are born,

*Malthus wrote his first Essay on Population in 1798 at the age of 32. He directed it against the optimistic, utopian views of his father and the revolutionary thinkers his father admired: William Godwin and Jean-Jacques Rousseau.*

*His view of utopian theories is captured in the following words: "A writer may tell me that he thinks man will ultimately become an ostrich. I cannot properly contradict him . . . (But) till the probability of so wonderful a conversion can be shown, it is surely lost time and lost eloquence to expatiate on the happiness of man in such a state."*

*Thomas Robert Malthus (1766–1834)*

more food will be available. But as more food becomes available, more people marry and produce children. Populations, Malthus argues, will always increase to the limit of subsistence, catching up to and consuming any food surplus. Thus, material progress—in the production of food and other areas—can have no lasting effects. Population, unless prevented by powerful checks, will always increase when the means of subsistence increases. For Malthus, these checks are either preventive or positive.

*Preventive* checks are actions people take to reduce births. For Malthus, postponing marriage was the preferred preventive check. In a society not practising contraception, the later a woman begins bearing children, the fewer children she will bear in total. Calling for abstinence struck Malthus as useless, because passion between the sexes needs expression. And voluntary birth control by artificial means was widely, though not universally, held to be immoral.

*Positive* checks result from human action or from natural causes: wars, famines, plagues and other disasters. Malthus thought positive checks would eventually come into play since humans, like other living creatures, reproduce beyond their means of subsistence. In his early works, Malthus stressed positive checks and the value (especially for the poor) of religious faith in helping people accept life's inevitable hardships. This aspect of his work has caused people to link Malthus's name with doom and gloom.

But in his later work, Malthus emphasized preventive checks to avoid the positive ones. His name became associated with birth control, even though, as we have noted, Malthus did not favour birth control by artificial means. Later editions of his *Essay* (1970; originally 1830) were more and more optimistic that education would strengthen the preventive check, and for this reason Malthus pushed for

> Malthus wrote his famous *Essay on the Principle of Population* in 1798 at the age of 32. He directed it against the optimistic, utopian views of his father and the revolutionary thinkers his father admired: William Godwin and Jean-Jacques Rousseau.
>
> His view of utopian theories is captured in the following words:
>
> A writer may tell me that he thinks man will ultimately become an ostrich. I cannot properly contradict him. . . . (But) till the probability of so wonderful a conversion can be shown, it is surely lost time and lost eloquence to expatiate on the happiness of man in such a state (Malthus, 1959:4).

general education in an era when even enlightened people thought it might prove dangerous to the social order.

## Criticisms of the Theory

The debate about Malthusian theory rages on. Malthus's most dire predictions did not come to pass in the century after his death. One reason was the opening of new land for food production and improved agricultural methods. Another was the widespread adoption of contraception as a preventive check. A third was the shift from an agricultural to an industrial economic base, which has proven better able to bring prosperity.

However, some observers point pessimistically to swelling population figures to recurring famines in many parts of the world and to growing shortages of nonrenewable resources (even shortages of water) in the developed world (Meadows et al., 1972; Higgins, 1980). Some see these things as signs that the alarm Malthus raised was well founded. After all, he didn't say *when* disaster would strike, only that it was inevitable.

How many people can the earth support? The earth's "carrying capacity" is limited by the resources available on it, our technology and the standard of living people will accept. Some say that all the world's people cannot possibly share the level of affluence enjoyed in North America today, given our present level of technology. Either we must find many more resources (an unlikely event), accept a lower standard of living for ourselves and others (an undesirable choice), or improve our technology. Evidence suggests that technology will continue to improve, but technology also produces harmful social and environmental side effects. In any event, we cannot know in advance what technology will do for us.

Population control is the most cautious type of social planning. Controlling population and lowering our expectations are surer means of protecting our future than relying on technological innovation and new resources. Thus, some people equate all cautious social policy-making with "Malthusianism."

Malthus's theory marks the beginning of scientific thinking about population. Despite its flaws, his *Essay on the Principle of Population* helped establish two ideas. First, it showed that population was growing rapidly in his day and argued that controlling fertility was better than accepting higher mortality rates as inevitable.

He was an early social planner, using data to develop and defend his policy positions. Second, Malthus reminded us that people are biological as well as social beings. Humans cannot create perfect societies without dealing with the sex drive and the need for food.

## THE MARXIST PERSPECTIVE

After Malthus, no one could deny human well-being was determined by the ratio of resources (especially food) to population, and the ratio was changing rapidly (Wrigley, 1969). But did this change demonstrate a law of population that held good at all times and places? Or was it the result of historically specific conditions and, primarily, of a capitalist economy?

In his first essay, Malthus attacked the socialist doctrine that stated that if the world's wealth were shared equally, everyone would have plenty. Marx and Engels, writing two generations later, abandoned that simple view (Meek, 1954). They argued that the capitalist system is the most likely system to produce an excess of population and a shortage of food. It is in the interest of the capitalist employer to have a large, impoverished "reserve army of the unemployed," since an increased supply of labour lowers wages. As a seller of food, it is in his interest to maintain scarcity and thereby ensure the highest possible price for his wares. Therefore, the capitalist produces an apparent population crisis.

The appearance of overpopulation is exaggerated by other trends in capitalist development. As capital grows, it comes to be concentrated in fewer hands. The demand for workers also grows, but much more slowly than the demand for new technology. In effect, the proportion of capital invested in workers, compared with that invested in machines, declines at an ever-increasing rate. Jobs are eliminated; workers are displaced. But there only *seem* to be too many workers for the available jobs. According to this theory, capitalism creates too few, indeed, ever fewer, jobs, *not* too many people.

Marxists today use their arguments to analyse relations between the capitalist powers and the Third World. They show that colonialism has forced poor nations to organize their agricultural production for export, in order to benefit rich nations. In the short run, poor countries deprive their own people of needed food; and in the long run, they fail to develop their economies (Gunder Frank, 1966; Wilber, 1973). An underdeveloped economy based on manual labour and a low level of technology encourages people to have large families to achieve some measure of material security. Thus, overpopulation is not the cause of poverty; instead, poverty and exploitation cause overpopulation.

### Criticisms of the Theory

Much can be said for this argument. However, many communist countries suffer food shortages without ever having suffered colonial exploitation. The People's Republic of China remains so overpopulated that family planning is now strongly promoted there. So the problems Malthus pointed to are not automatically solved by a socialist redistribution of wealth or by ending capitalism.

When Marx and Engels criticized Malthus in the mid- to late nineteenth century, industrial capitalism was in its early stages. Low wages and high subsistence costs seemed likely to continue. Yet, later capitalists realized that creating a large market of consumers would be profitable. Creating such a market meant paying higher wages and charging lower prices.

Under these conditions, children are not needed to contribute to the family income. As England moved into mature capitalism, the "Malthusian problem" seemed to take care of itself. Population growth declined, and the standard of living rose. Workers left the poverty and insecurity of the nineteenth century for the mass consumer society and welfare state of the twentieth. In doing so, they took a new approach to affluence. Rather than increasing the size of their families, they limited them, as Malthus would have recommended. World fertility has been declining for the last 20 years, *despite* general improvements in health and material well-being.

To understand this change, we must turn to the theory of the demographic transition.

## THE THEORY OF DEMOGRAPHIC TRANSITION

The demographic transition theory is based on observed changes in Western European societies. It relates historical changes in population to social and economic modernization.

According to this theory (Davis, 1945; Stolnitz, 1964), changing from a traditional to a modern population pattern involves three stages. During the first stage, called *pretransition*, a population's fertility and mortality rates are high. However, both rates are greatly affected by such Malthusian positive checks as famines and epidemics. Equally high birth and death rates mean little, if any, population growth. The *transitional* is the second growth stage and begins with a decline in the death rate. Initially, the birth rate remains high; the population grows rapidly. Then, the birth rate begins falling while the death rate continues its decline. Because the mortality rate started falling earlier, it remains lower than the birth rate. The population continues to grow rapidly. Stage three, *posttransition* completes the changeover to low birth and death rates. Finally, population growth slows dramatically.

Both the pretransition and the posttransition populations are in balance with their environment. But in one case the population turnover is very rapid, in the other, very slow. In stage one, the death rate fluctuates widely and the birth rate is relatively stable, often near a biological maximum. In stage three, the death rate is relatively stable: public health, improved medical techniques, better housing and nutrition have all but eliminated epidemics, famines and many infectious diseases. Now only fertility varies widely through changes in desired family size, and family size is influenced by changes in prosperity. Shifts in economic opportunities influence career decisions, the timing of marriages and the timing and frequency of childbearing. To see this, compare fertility in the prosperous baby-boom years of the 1950s with fertility in the austere 1970s and 1980s, when couples delay childbearing and often avoid it altogether.

According to this theory, demographic transition is irreversible. Societies may differ in *when* they begin the transition, how fast it proceeds and which factors start the process. But no society returns to high mortality or to high fertility after reaching stage three. The reasons are plain: No society would willingly accept higher death

## Figure 4-1  Graphic Depictions of the Malthusian and Demographic Transition Models

The Malthusian Curves

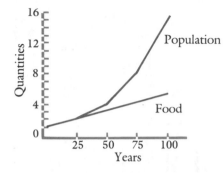

| Period | 1 | 2 | 3 | 4 | 5 | 6 | 7 | 8 |
|---|---|---|---|---|---|---|---|---|
| Year | | 1 | 25 | 50 | 75 | 100 | 125 | 150 | 175 |
| Growth of Population | 1 | 2 | 4 | 8 | 16 | 32 | 64 | 128 |
| Growth of Food | | 1 | 2 | 3 | 4 | 5 | 6 | 7 | 8 |

Model of Demographic Transition

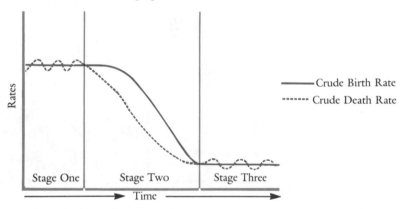

Overbeek, J. *History of Population Theories*. Rotterdam: Rotterdam University Press, 1974, p.42.

Reprinted with permission of Holt, Rinehart and Winston of Canada from *Sociology*, Second Edition by Gee/edited by Hagedorn.

rates; and no society can long afford high birth rates once it has lowered its death rates.

## How Population Change is Related to Socio-Economic Change

What has most interested sociologists is that the demographic transition theory relates population changes to social and economic changes. Each demographic stage has its own social and economic context.

Stage one, with high fertility and mortality, is typical of a preindustrial society. Such societies cannot ensure their member's survival, due to the unpredictability of crops, the lack of a regular food surplus, the absence of a market where food can

Figure 4-2  A Hypothetical Model of Relationships Between Demographic, Social and Economic Change in a Preindustrial Society.

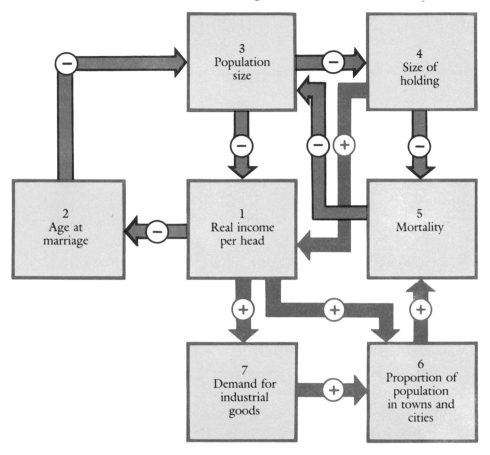

A (+) sign in the model means that two variables are increasing (or decreasing) together. A (−) sign means that, as one is increasing, the other is decreasing. Like any negative-feedback model, this one keeps returning to equilibrium, or balance. Test it by increasing or decreasing any one of the variables, then following the effect of change through the model until it returns to the starting point.

Reprinted with permission of World University Library from E.A. Wrigley's *Population and History*.

be bought if necessary. Conditions are also ripe for spreading contagious diseases, especially in cities. The bubonic plague of 1348-50 killed an estimated one-quarter of Europe's population in the worst of many serious epidemics in European history. Under such circumstances, death rates cannot be controlled. High fertility is essential; any population with a low fertility rate would simply die out.

Improved technology upsets the balance between birth and death rates. England from roughly 1850 to 1950 offers a prime example of this. During this time, medicine and public sanitation caused a rapid decline in mortality, particularly among infants and children, and a long, steady decline in childbearing occurred.

In about 1775, England had begun its industrial revolution. Manufacturing was concentrated in factories, and around these factories new urban centres developed. New technology increased productivity and improved transportation and communication, helping to create mass markets, mass literacy, a mass culture and the modern nation-state. This set the stage for the population explosion of the second (or transitional) stage, which took place between 1850-1950.

Fertility, according to the theory, declines more slowly than mortality because it is affected by social mores and traditional values. Nevertheless, modernization finally leads to a lower birth rate. The economic reasons for having large families disappear; in cities, added children prove more costly and less useful than on farms. Fewer children need to be born to ensure that one or two will survive to care for their parents. More and more, the state steps into family life to require that children be educated (and to prevent child labour) and to ensure old-age security which undercuts one reason for childbearing. Parents shift from childbearing for gain to childbearing for pleasure.

## Criticisms of the Theory

A theory so obviously correct in its overview of English and European historical change is difficult to attack. But closer analysis, using preindustrial parish records, other historical artifacts and observation of demographics in the Third World has raised many questions.

One criticism is that the theory is not universally valid. It does not explain current changes in the Third World. There, availability of Western technology has cut the link between modernization and population change (Kirk, 1971). Since World War II, better medicine and inexpensive birth control have been available worldwide. This has given rise to an international debate over whether birth control must be preceded by modernization or whether Third World nations should control births more effectively before getting economic aid from developed countries (Coale and Hoover, 1958; Coale, 1963).

The transition theory may also prove inadequate as a summary of historical experience in Europe. Evidence from many preindustrial societies has shown a wide variation in *nuptiality*, or marriage patterns by age (Hajnal, 1965), and marital fertility (Coale, 1969). Each preindustrial society seems to have uniquely combined preventive and positive checks to control its population growth.

Some assertions made about stage two also seem doubtful. It is not clear whether the burst of population growth during that stage was primarily due to a decline in deaths. Demographers disagree over whether growth resulted mainly from a fall in the death rate (McKeown and Brown, 1965) or a rise in the birth rate (Habakkuk, 1965). Each argument may be partly correct. Birth and death rates were probably rising and falling in different parts of the same population. Contrary to the theory, a rise in births may have resulted from several factors, including the breakdown of traditional social controls on childbearing and increasing prosperity. To argue that declining mortality always or usually started the population growing would require more reliable statistics than we have.

Finally, regarding stage three, the best research has not found any simple correlation between modernization and fertility decline. Fertility did decline in the West, it is true; but the causes of this and the particular sequence of events seem to vary from one locale to another.

These failings in the theory of demographic transition may indicate that demographers, with few exceptions, have exaggerated the importance of economic factors and underplayed the cultural ones. New ways of thinking about family structure and behaviour may significantly influence childbearing without being related directly to economic change, as Philippe Ariès (1962) has shown in his classic study of changing European conceptions of childhood (see also Van de Walle and Knodel, 1980).

One value of the theory, more ideological than scientific, lies in its presentation of change as proceeding from one condition of stability (high fertility/high mortality) to another (low fertility/low mortality). Such a story is quite different from the one Malthus told, for it is a story with a happy ending. In this story, material progress not only takes root, it solves the Malthusian problem. But, like Malthusian theory, it leaves many questions unanswered.

## POPULATION GROWTH IN CANADA

So far, we have paid attention only to the size of the global population, while ignoring its composition and distribution. But this does not teach us much about the history of Canada's population, whose composition and distribution have changed greatly over time.

> Canada is not the only society which has been created by large numbers of human beings moving into vacant areas, but it is unlikely that any other society has resembled a huge demographic railway station as much as has the non-French part of Canada. As well as a society receiving immigrants it has been one producing emigrants, either naturally or by harbouring the "birds of passage" who have stopped over in Canada while making the move from Europe to the United States. What is likely to be the effect on social institutions, and in particular on class structure, of such a kinetic population?
>
> John Porter, *The Vertical Mosaic*, University of Toronto Press (Toronto 1965) p. 33.

Canada's population has grown a lot in some periods and very little in others. Times of rapid growth include the decade before World War I and the decade after World War II; times of slower growth include the later nineteenth century, the 1930s, and the 1970s and 80s. The reasons for these shifts lie in changing patterns of natural increase and international migration. (For a good overview of these changes, see Beaujot and McQuillan, 1982.)

When Europeans "discovered" North America in the early 1600s, 200 000 to 1 000 000 natives lived in what is now Canada. By 1763, immigrants and their descendants had increased the local population by about 100 000. The growth of Canada's population to more than 25 000 000 has taken two centuries, thanks to a growth rate of about 4 percent in the century before Confederation and 2 percent in much of the century that followed. The population grew because of high rates of childbearing and high rates of immigration. These two factors have created an extremely high ratio of *newcomers* to *tradition carriers*.

Almost all Canadians are descended from immigrants, particularly immigrants who arrived in the last 50 to 100 years. But emigration was sometimes so common in Canada that it largely offset the effects of immigration. In 1982 alone, more than 45 000 people left Canada to live elsewhere. Demographers estimate that between 1851 and 1971, about 9 500 000 immigrants entered Canada while 6 500 000 left, for a net gain through immigration of about 3 000 000 people. Yet in this same period, 28 000 000 children were born and 11 500 000 people died, for a net gain through natural increase of about 16 500 000. Overall, fertility has influenced Canada's population history much more significantly than immigration (especially in French Canada).

## THE WIDE FLUCTUATIONS OF IMMIGRATION

However, the effects of immigration have fluctuated widely over time, while those of natural increase have not. Mirroring Western Europe's demographic transition, Canada's birth and death rates have dropped slowly but smoothly and predictably since about 1851. True, the economic depression of the 1930s pushed childbearing below the expected level, and the postwar baby boom of the 1950s pushed childbearing above it. But overall, the downward trend has been slow and steady.

By contrast, migration in and out of Canada has varied a great deal from one decade to another in response to various influences. Canadian economic development has proceeded rapidly, almost crazily, from one resource-driven economic boom-and-bust to another. (For an overview of this "staples approach" to Canadian history, see Watkins, 1963.) With each resource discovery comes the opening of a new portion of the country. Willing workers extract the resource, whether it is fish, furs, timber, wheat, gold or oil. Developing a resource industry creates new communities and new jobs in manufacturing, services, communications and transportation. Often more jobs are created than can be filled by native Canadians with the right skills. At these times, Canada opens its doors to immigrants, liberalizing legislation, increasing quotas, even searching out immigrants in preferred countries (Kalbach, 1970; Hawkins, 1972).

How long this need for workers lasts depends on the persistence of foreign demand for the resource at Canadian prices. When the demand dies down, as it usually does, the need for immigrant labour collapses. Immigration laws tighten up again and fewer immigrants are admitted. As opportunities evaporate, more people leave, chiefly for the United States.

This migration is most striking when confined to one small region. Remember the rapid population growth of Edmonton and Calgary in the 1970s and the slow-down in the 1980s? Or the recent massive shift of migrants away from increasingly separatist Quebec? More dramatic still are the effects of migration on the resource-based, single-industry company towns (Lucas, 1972). As John Porter (1965) has

Figure 4-3   Level of Immigration and Unemployment Rates, Canada, 1946-1980

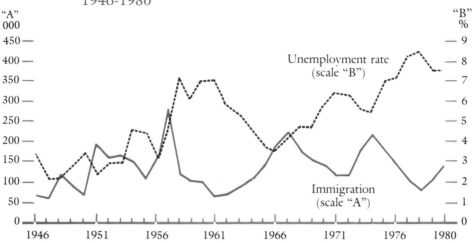

Employment and Immigration Canada, Immigration and Demographic Policy Group, *Immigration Statistics, 1981* (Annual) Statistics Canada, Labour Force Survey Division, *The Labour Force* (Monthly), Catalogue No. 71-001. Reproduced by permission of the Minister of Supply and Services Canada.

said, a psychology of population instability results from (and perhaps causes) the movement of migrants; its effect is out of all proportion to the number of migrants in the population.

Migration has been particularly problematic for French Canada, from two standpoints. Up through the early part of this century, the continuing migration of many French Canadians to the United States (documented by Lavoie, 1972) led some to believe emigration could end the French presence in Canada. More recently, French Canada has suffered an opposite problem: an influx of immigrants from abroad who cannot speak French and are unwilling to learn. This, combined with the clear evidence of French language loss outside Quebec, has led to concern among Francophone demographers (e.g. Henripin, 1974) and policymakers. However, more recent analysis (Lachapelle, 1980) suggests that this anxiety may be premature. The French language within Québec is apparently alive and well.

In recent years the biggest population change in Canada, as elsewhere, was caused by the baby boom of the 1950s. During that decade, parents and governments were chiefly concerned with providing adequate primary schooling. In the 1960s and 1970s, concern focused on jobs and housing for the baby-boomers. In the early twenty-first century, old-age pensions, retirement rules and nursing-home vacancies will probably be of great interest to most Canadians (see, for example, Foot, 1982).

Finding it harder to get jobs than in the past, members of the baby-boom generation are having smaller families. In the 1970s and 80s, Canadian women are postponing marriage and childbearing and having fewer children. Dual-earner families are increasingly common. But difficulties in providing for themselves will not stop at age 65. Baby-boomers will also have had more difficulty earning and saving for old age. Younger age groups supporting them through contributions to pension and social security funds will be too small to do the job. As a result, the tempestuous

> The baby boom is consumer society's R&D division—testing new products, new fads, new drugs, new morality, even new ideas about marriage and children . . .
>
> Now, as it washes up in the 1980s, the baby-boom generation is experiencing a shift in the way it thinks about itself and its future. Optimism is yielding to pessimism. Altruism is yielding to narcissism. The generation that grew up convinced of its special place in society is not finding it. The maternity wards were too crowded; the schools were crowded; they were sent to Vietnam; they couldn't find jobs; they couldn't get promoted. Instead they found themselves causing booms in crime, in suicide, in divorce, in childlessness, in venereal disease, in housing prices, and in property taxes . . .
>
> The faith in the future that powered the boom generation through the sixties is shattered.
>
> From *Great Expectations: America and the Baby Boom Generation*, by Landon Y. Jones, pp. 387-89. Reprinted by permission of publisher Putnam Publishing Group

generation that blasted open traditional institutions by its force of numbers may go out, somewhat subdued perhaps, breaking Canada's health and welfare piggy bank.

# SOCIAL EFFECTS OF POPULATION PROCESSES

In many respects, the social effects of changes in population composition and distribution are the most interesting. Two compositional features demographers always discuss, for several reasons, are sex and age. Sex and age composition are biologically based in birth and death processes. This is why sex and age composition theories can hold good for all societies. Also, sex and age are central bases of social differentiation. Most social roles in any society are age- and sex-specific. They are filled by people of one sex, not the other, and by one age group, not others.

What is men's work in one society may be women's work in another. What is forbidden in one society may be acceptable in another and so on. Such age and sex differentiation has a limited basis in biology and no universality of practice. What is striking, however, is the universal occurrence of some kinds of differentiation. Thus, social planners will always need to know the number of males and females and the number of young and old in a population.

Returning to our example of the imaginary hotel: Studying how different kinds of people fill social roles is like studying how rooms have been filled in the hotel. Some rooms may house too few people, others too many. But what do "too few" and "too many" mean?

## SEX COMPOSITION AND ITS EFFECTS

The sex composition of a population refers to the ratio of males to females or the number of males per hundred females. In every human population, more males are born than females: In Canada, the ratio at birth is about 105 males per 100 females. But this ratio is not found at every age. In Canada, the ratio begins falling almost immediately after birth. In cities, for example, women outnumber men in every age group after age 40.

Women are hardier than men, as Madigan (1957) showed in his comparative study of nuns and monks. As well, their relative longevity is partly due to differences in behaviour. Until recently, men smoked many more cigarettes than women. Smoking has been a major cause of the longevity gap, which today is about seven years of life expectancy at birth. Also, men typically play more hazardous (e.g., military, industrial) or reckless (e.g., highway speeding) roles in society.

For all these reasons, women live longer, and the excess of women at each adult age increases progressively. One result of this is that women are more likely to die as widows than men as widowers. Another result is that male companionship is harder for women to find with each passing year. This difficulty is increased by our culture, since women in our society (as in many others) usually marry older men. In general, age is a greater handicap for women than for men in the marriage market.

These problems are often further complicated by events. For example, during wartime, it is usually men who are killed, increasing the imbalance of the ratio of males and females in the population. As well, men usually leave first for foreign lands, causing shortages of men in the home countries and surpluses in the new ones. Internal migration also causes imbalances. Today, women are more likely to migrate within Canada, typically from rural regions or small towns to large cities. This creates an excess of females in cities and a shortage in the less populated areas.

People respond to such problems creatively. Wherever men suffer a shortage of women, they find ways to deal with it, including importing mail-order brides and patronizing prostitutes. When women suffer shortages of men, they relax the rules about appropriate age, ethnic, racial or other characteristics of potential spouses or find ways to live comfortably while remaining unmarried.

## The Marriage Squeeze

Most recently, imbalances in the sex ratio have stemmed from the baby boom and bust, creating a problem known as the *marriage squeeze*. Between the late 1930s and 1959, more babies were born each year; after 1959, fewer were born. Was it better for a female to be born before or after 1959, in terms of her chances of finding a mate? Remember that in our culture, women usually marry men two to three years older than themselves. A woman born in 1959 would typically select her mate from among men born in 1956. But fewer men were born in 1956 than women in 1959. Women born in 1959 (or any year before 1959) would suffer a marriage squeeze, or shortage of eligible men. On the other hand, a woman born in 1965 would typically select her mate from among men born in 1962. By 1962, births had already begun to decline. More men were born in 1962 than women in 1965. Thus, women born in 1965 (or any year after 1959) could choose from a relative surplus of men. Conversely, men born after 1959 would suffer the marriage squeeze: a shortage of women of the right age.

The results of such shortages are not fully known. People make do with what they can get. Yet the "market value," or the attractiveness, of a scarce social type is bound to be higher than that of a common social type. Some have suggested that the less numerous men born before 1960 were able to impose their point of view

## Figure 4-4 Total Nuptiality Rate, Canada, 1921-1982

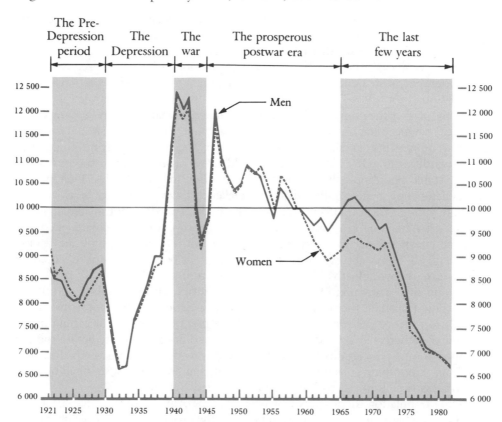

"The decrease in first marriages is not due to a drop in the number of persons of marriageable age but to the fact that fewer young adults are 'taking the plunge' (for the moment at least). . . . Indeed, it is now safe to say that this decline in nuptiality will be seen as one of the most remarkable in Canada's history."

*Current Demographic Analysis: Report on the Demographic Situation in Canada 1983.* Prepared by Jean Dumas, Demography Division, Catalogue 91-209E. Reproduced by permission of the Minister of Supply and Services Canada.

on courtship and marriage contracts: They could be in favour of free sex, though against a more general women's liberation.

Such imbalances in the sex ratio also affect family formation. During periods of severe imbalance, fewer than usual families will be formed, depressing population growth. One solution is *serial monogamy*, or people entering into and leaving several marriages per lifetime. Extramarital sex, romantic affairs, and divorce and remarriage have also increased in the last two decades. They reflect a change in sexual morality. But they may also represent a solution to demographic imbalance, to the marraige squeeze, since they also make scarce males available (however partially) to a larger number of females.

# AGE COMPOSITION AND ITS EFFECTS

The age composition of a population is harder to describe because ages can be grouped in many ways. Still, sociologists know a lot about the age differentiation of roles and the processes that produce age imbalances.

Life expectancy, or how long a person will probably live, can be predicted from a demographer's life table, which is based on large numbers of lives in a particular population. In a "closed" population, one without migration, demographers can perfectly predict the numbers of people at each age, if that population is *stable*. By "stable," we mean the birth rate and the mortality rate at each age are unchanging. These requirements of stable population theory may seem extremely limiting. Since these conditions rarely exist in the real world, why construct such a theory?

The stable population theory meets this objection in several ways, First, all scientific laws apply better to ideal than to actual circumstances. Newton's laws ignore friction, though friction affects every moving body. This does not invalidate Newton's laws. When we formulate a theory, we expect to eventually eliminate, or correct for, the effects of "outside" factors. A theory is not intended to duplicate reality, warts and all, but to abstract from it the relationships between groups of variables: in this case, between births, deaths and age structure.

Beyond this, many preindustrial populations have been fairly stable; and, if demographic transition theory is correct, modern societies will be too. Thus, stable population theory will prove useful in studying past populations (or certain bands of hunter-gatherers living today in premodern conditions) or in predicting the age composition of populations that have achieved zero population growth. It is also useful in "smoothing" or correcting data obtained in flawed censuses or in birth or death registries (Keyfitz and Flieger, 1971; United Nations, 1967).

Stable population theory was first developed by Alfred Lotka in the 1920s. It shows mathematically the relationship between the proportion of people in any age category (for example, the proportion of people who are 22 years old), the birth rate, the probability of surviving to a given age, and the growth rate. By this formula, we can estimate the proportion of people in any age category. Therefore, we can also estimate the ratio between any two categories and the relative size of one age group compared to another. This method helps us to distinguish common from unexpected features of observed populations.

## Measures of Age Composition

Measures of age composition include the median age, the dependancy ratio, and the age-sex pyramid. The *median age* is the age of the middle-ranked person in the population. In Canada, the median age is currently about 30 and should reach 37 by the year 2001. Populations get older mostly through falling fertility, not rising life expectancy. Reflecting the aging of the Canadian population are two startling facts. In the near future, deaths will temporarily overtake births in Canada; and by the year 2031, the percentage of Canadians over age 65 will equal the percentage under age 15 (Foot, 1982: Chapter 4).

The *dependancy ratio* is the ratio of "dependant" people (ages 0-17 and 65 plus) to working-age people (ages 18-65). As a population ages, the youth dependancy ratio (the ratio of people ages 0-17 to those 18-65) drops and the elderly dependancy ratio (the ratio of persons 65 and over to those 18-65) rises. Taken together, these two ratios give an overall dependancy ratio today of about 58 "dependants" per 100 persons of working age, the lowest in Canada's history. In an older population, a larger segment produces the national wealth through work. Today, almost two Canadians in three are adults of working age. A smaller part is dependant on, or supported by, such work and is actively consuming health, educational and welfare services. Of course, other factors influence national wealth, including the participation rate (the proportion of working-age people actually working in paid jobs) and the productivity rate (the dollar-value produced by each worker per unit time). Still, up to a point, an older population is more productive.

Actually, the matter is more complicated. A successful enterprise—whether a family, a sports team or a society—requires just the right mix of old people and young, youth and experience. So, whichever age group is in shortest supply gains greatest value and enjoys the most opportunity for advancement. Examples of this abound. The trouble the baby-boom generation is having today in finding good jobs results largely from the surplus of young, inexperienced people compared to old, experienced workers (Easterlin, 1980). Today, experience is in short supply, and older workers will be paid more. In general, scarcity brings high rewards.

But no accurate statement can be made about which part of the social mix will be scarce, and therefore most rewarded, 50 or 100 years from today.

## The Population Pyramid

A third way to summarize the age-sex structure of a society is with a population pyramid. Demographers have distinguished three common forms of pyramid. The *expansive* pyramid has a particularly broad base, indicating a high proportion of children in the population. Such a pyramid results from high fertility levels; it characterizes a young, rapidly growing population. The *stationary* pyramid has a narrower base and nearly equal proportions of all ages. Such a pyramid results from prolonged low fertility and characterizes an old, nongrowing population. Finally, the *constrictive* pyramid has a base narrower than its middle, indicating a recent, rapid decline in fertility.

A population pyramid has several attractive features. It readily communicates complex information. Our eyes can quickly examine a country's population pyramid and tell what kind of population it is. As well, we can readily see gross deviations: age categories that are too large, probably indicating a period of migration, or too small, probably indicating a population loss due to war or reduced childbearing. We can note imbalances between the ratios of the sexes at particular ages. Fluctuations involving both sexes usually result from changes in prosperity, while those increasing the numbers of one sex more than another usually are the consequence of migration or war. The timing of major social and economic changes is thus reflected in a modern population's age structure. By contrast, a preindustrial or transitional population has more regular demographic features. Gross distortions usually point to incorrect age or gender reporting or to administrative confusion and a need to improve data collection

A demographer can read a population pyramid for signs of change the way a geologist reads layers of rock. Each observer is guided by a theory of how process creates structure, of what normal structures look like and what leads to deviations.

Figure 4-5  Population Pyramids

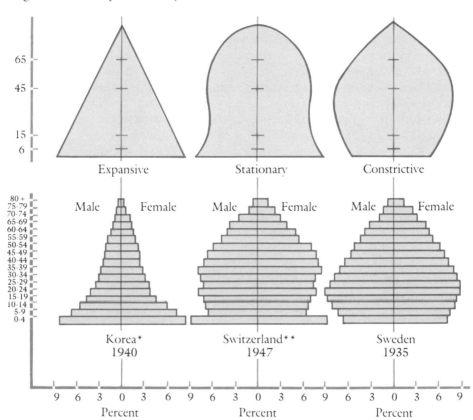

*Most Third World countries today
**An increasing number of developed (European and North American) countries

Reprinted with permission of Macmillan Publishing Company from POPULATION, third edition by William Petersen. Copyright © 1975, by William Petersen.

However, populations and layers of rock differ in at least one important way. Layers of rock offer a permanent record of historic changes over thousands of years. Population structures, conversely, do not preserve their history for long. Two populations with very different age-sex pyramids will eventually become identical if subjected to the same birth and death processes. (This remarkable fact is known to us through stable population theory.) Population processes are steadily eroding and recreating population structures.

## OTHER COMPOSITIONAL EFFECTS

Besides age and sex composition, variables of interest include ethnicity, birthplace, language and educational attainment. These are commonly (and inappropriately) referred to as "demographics" in public opinion surveys. Survey designers assume that these variables will predict a variety of things: voting, consumer behaviour and life styles, among others.

These variables have all demonstrated their value in what are sometimes called *demographic explanations* (Stinchecombe, 1968). A demographic explanation of behaviour has two parts. One part focuses on the size of a causal force; the other, on the number and kind of people to whom that force is applied. It matters whether an observed change in behaviour is due to a change in the composition of a population or a shift in causal forces applied to the population. Consider an imaginary by-election in which a seat formerly held by the NDP is lost to the Progressive Conservatives. Does this electoral loss demonstrate the causal force of a "swing to the right"? Or has there merely been a change in the population composition of the riding, such that people normally inclined to vote NDP are fewer and those inclined to vote PC, more numerous? If the latter, only the composition or mixture of people, not the size of a causal force (i.e., the inclination to vote PC) had changed. There had been no "swing to the right."

Sociologists who study demography become very aware of such compositional issues. They become used to calculating rates and ratios that eliminate the effects of compositional change in order to reveal the causal forces: changes in attitudes and behaviours, among others. But for demographers, changes in composition are interesting in themselves. Demographers explain them by reference to changes in fertility, mortality and migration.

## Tradition-Carriers and Newcomers

One important compositional variable is birthplace. People born in another country are likely to have been socialized into different values, and they will have learned Canadian culture less thoroughly than people born and raised here. Canadian culture, already weak and fragmented, has been under steady attack by people favouring multiculturalism, regionalism and the American way of life. What, then, are the added effects of changes in demographic composition resulting from shifts in the ratio of adult, native-born *tradition-carriers* to *newcomers*, both newborns and immigrants?

Historically, Canada's immigration and fertility rates have risen together during economic booms and fallen together during economic depressions. Booms tend to be localized around some resource extracting activity. Thus, the variations in immigration and fertility have been especially marked in Province A at one time, Province B at another time.

During the last hundred years, the overall Canadian ratio of tradition-carriers to newcomers has varied markedly. It has been highest in periods of economic depression: for example, from 1891-1911 and 1931-1951. Renewed economic prosperity has always lowered the ratio. Today, the current ratio is fairly high: As always, low fertility, low immigration and, ultimately, economic depression are the cause. The ratio has been continuously higher in the United States, which may help explain the weakness of a Canadian identity or the strength of the American one. However, the recent rise in the number of tradition-carriers offers Canada the chance for a renewed attempt at cultural integration. This change in demographic composition will never *create* a Canadian identity; it will only provide a context that is more favourable than usual to the promotion of one (Bell and Tepperman, 1979). Language use among Canada's ethnic, and particularly immigrant, subpopulations is a major factor in cultural assimilation. When the immigrant language is lost, ethnic social cohesion and cultural values are likely to go, too. Therefore, demographers study data on the language use of ethnic subgroups, and, particularly, what language people use at home (Henripin, 1974; and Lachapelle, 1980). Many ethnic groups keep up their traditional language and culture. But "interaction in linguistically plural communities . . . appears to ignore linguistic boundaries, and . . . individuals adapt to these conditions by becoming bilingual" (de Vries and Vallee, 1980: 73). Linguistic assimilation leads to marriage outside one's own group. In particular, Canadian-born people are more likely than foreign-born people to marry outside their own group. If the general decline in immigration to Canada continues, intermarriage is expected to increase, creating an increasingly homogenous population.

## SUMMARY

A good deal more could be written about population processes. Entire books have been devoted to the construction and use of life tables. Government, the health professions and the insurance industry all depend on good demographic data and theories to monitor public demand for their services. Their need has been met by a vast number of specialized reports and studies which we have not begun to examine. And the discussion of long-term population policy has occupied a great deal of expert and public attention (for example, Stone and Marceau, 1977).

A lot has been written elsewhere about the social factors influencing fertility and mortality, topics not dealt with here. Nor have we given much consideration to fertility decline in Canada, a topic which will, however, receive some attention in the chapter on families. A thorough discussion of these topics would go well beyond the space available here. Instead, the reader is directed to excellent discussions of this important topic elsewhere. Material on Quebec can be found in Henripin and Lapierre-Adamcyk (1974). Material on Canada can be found in Beaujot and McQuillan (1982), Bouma and Bouma (1975) and Kalbach and McVey (1979). Finally, Petersen (1975), Wrigley (1969) and the United Nations (1973) examine the issue from a worldwide perspective.

Nor has this chapter thoroughly discussed migration. We have no good theories of migration in Canada that are not political-economic ones. Some related themes will come up in the chapters on urbanization and social deveopment in this book.

We have resisted the opportunity to state a great many population facts about Canada and the world. Instead, we have examined some central theories and methods in the analysis of population processes. The purpose of the sociological and demographic enterprise is to create and examine theories. Sociologically valuable facts are a useful by-product of demography. But the central goal of demography is to understand how a population functions. And for a sociologist, the study of population processes is part of the study of social structures and the effects of population and social processes on one another.

This chapter has shown that demography is guided by central theories. Some, for example, the demographic transition theory, relate population processes to social processes like modernization. Others, like the stable population theory, relate population processes to population structures such as the age pyramid. Together, these theories enhance our understanding of what Malthus pointed out: The human need for food and sex have social, cultural, economic and political consequences.

None of the theories we have explored is complete or above attack. Demography, like other sciences, is always refining its theories. Few social sciences have created as much sustained, international interest and co-operation. Demography is a truly interdisciplinary enterprise, yet it is central to sociology, the study of societies.

## DISCUSSION QUESTIONS

1. The same shortages result if there are too many people or too few resources (food, land, jobs). Marx and Malthus might, therefore, have analysed the same situation in opposite ways. How can we tell who was right?

2. What other countries are likely to have the same psychology of population instability as Canada? Do some research on these countries to find out whether the effects on social and cultural organization are similar.

3. How much has the liberalization of sexual norms (e.g., premarital and extramarital sex, open homosexuality, easier divorce) resulted from demographic imbalances, like the marriage squeeze, and how much from other causes? What might these other causes be?

4. Does Canada need a population policy? If not, why not? If so, what should this policy encompass: numbers, growth rates, composition, distribution? How should it be administered?

5. In a society practising contraception, the number of children a woman has already borne predicts whether she will have another. In a noncontraceptive society, it does not. Explain this difference. How is it useful in studying primitive or historical societies?

# 5

# Culture, Change and Autonomy

## Susannah Wilson

# INTRODUCTION

Canada's history, ethnic composition and proximity to the United States make us particularly aware of debates about Canadian culture and Canadian identity. Our sense of ourselves comes partly from appreciating cultural differences within Canada. While it may be difficult to describe what Canadian culture is, we sense we are unlike our American neighbours in important ways. In this chapter, we will explore how sociologists have approached the nebulous topic of culture and what these findings reveal about ourselves as Canadians.

Bronislaw Malinowski, (1939:588) one of anthropology's founding fathers, described culture as "the most central problem of all social science." Most sociologists would say it is one of the most, if not *the* most, central concept in sociology. The concept of culture was introduced into the English language in the 1880s by two anthropologists, Matthew Arnold and Edward B. Tylor, although its origins can be traced to the fourteenth century (Langness, 1974). Tylor (1924:1) defined culture as "that complex whole which includes knowledge, belief, art, morals, law custom and any other capabilities and habits acquired by man as a member of society." Since Tylor's time, the concept has been developed and altered (and, as Boon [1973] suggests, "obscured and misunderstood") by social scientists in many disciplines.

The major difficulty in defining culture is that it is so all encompassing. As Hall (1976:14) explains, "There is not one aspect of human life that is not touched and altered by culture." Another anthropologist, Schneider (1973) said that culture seems to refer to everything, including the kitchen sink, since the kitchen sink is part of *material culture*. Anthropologists customarily distinguish *material culture*, or cultural artifacts, from *nonmaterial culture*, which refers to values, ideas and beliefs. Edward Hall notes that when anthropologists study another culture, their focus will be influenced by what they define as important in their own culture. Nevertheless, there is general agreement that culture is learned, that aspects of culture are interrelated and that culture is shared to the extent that cultural differences define group boundaries (Hall, 1976).

Generally, discussions of culture focus on four elements: *norms, values, beliefs* or *ideologies* and *expressive symbols*. Over time, the emphasis given to these elements has changed. Now, more attention is paid to expressive symbols. The current focus of many studies is the symbolic representation or meaning of both the material and nonmaterial culture. Culture then, is "the symbolic-expressive aspect of human behavior" (Wuthrow et al., 1984:3).

## MAJOR THEMES IN THE STUDY OF CULTURE

In this section, we will look briefly at the differing emphases given to the study by the major theoretical traditions in sociology. Generally, functionalists emphasize the basis and reinforcement of value consensus. The way Parsons connects the cultural and social systems to individual behaviour is an example of this. For *Marxists*, aspects of culture are part of the superstructure of society and are reflected in ideology. Ideologies serve to frame and legitimize the existing economic order. *Interactionists* focus primarily on symbolic expressive aspects of culture, such as language. Using a common language, saluting a flag or attending a religious ceremony confirms our identity as members of a culture or group. At the same time, these expressive symbols perpetuate the group's existence as new members are introduced to them.

## CULTURAL VALUES AND NORMS

Talcott Parsons described culture as one of four interrelated systems of action. The other three action systems are the *social system*, the *personality system* and the *biological system*. The social system "is a way of organizing human action" (Parsons, 1973:36), the "master example" of which is society. Societies consist of individuals who interact within the framework of a common culture. Collective identity is expressed in our readiness to include ourselves in particular groups. For example, we might identify ourselves as "we" Canadians, "we" Memorial University students, "we" Roman Catholics, "we" sociologists and so on. We are all members of many such groups. Some groups will be small, but some will be large and cut across national boundaries. Over 5000 sociologists attend meetings of the International Sociological Association.

According to Parsons, values, norms and beliefs are the most important distinguishing characteristics of a social system. Institutionalized values, or value systems, "constitute relatively generalized patterns of orientation" which "focus on the normative regulation of social relationships" (Parsons, 1973:37-38). In complex, differentiated systems such as ours, subsystems, or collectivities, will have particular value systems, although Parsons assumed that these are more or less congruent with widely held values. Norms, unlike values, are situation specific. They define desirable patterns of interaction and come to be regarded as standards against which behaviour is evaluated. Beliefs are existential statements about how the world operates and often serve to justify values and norms.

Individuals learn norms, values and beliefs during socialization. For example, North Americans are taught to value equality of opportunity and personal freedom, and we believe these should be protected. Canadians and Americans may differ in the emphasis placed on core values and in the symbolic expression of these. In a classic study, Lipset (1963) found that Canadians are more conservative, more authoritarian and more oriented to tradition, hierarchy and elitism than Americans. Some values, such as the incest taboo, and norms, such as those restricting public nudity, are shared by most cultures. On the interpersonal level, our interactions with others are predictable because we have learned to accept and expect certain standards of behaviour.

Subcultures are identifiable because they share norms, values and beliefs which differ from those of the core culture. Some argue our lives are far more influenced by subcultural norms and values than by those shared by the society as a whole. In pluralistic and fragmented societies like ours, it is difficult to determine the extent of shared meanings. Our emphasis on individualism, fueled by the human potential movement of the 1970s, gives us a great deal of flexibility within the boundaries imposed by formal and informal sanctions.

In one sense, cultural values are implicit in the choice of topics covered in this textbook and the ways issues are analysed. The study of sociology in the West is carried on in a milieu which reflects particular cultural values. In China, sociology is much more directly connected to social policy than it is in Canada or the United

States. The section of this text that describes Canadian political, legal, economic and educational institutions reveals a great deal about how cultural values in Canada have become institutionalized.

## IDEOLOGY

Functionalist sociologists emphasize the integrative role of common cultural elements. For Marxists, the impression of a shared culture is the result of a complex process of social construction and legitimation, with strong ideological support. Ideologies as defined by Marchak (1981:xi) are "beliefs about realities which are by their nature held on faith . . . . The function of ideology is to direct the members of the society to a shared understanding of what their collective lives are all about." Marchak described the two major ideologies in Canada now as *liberalism* and *socialism*.

> The first describes Canada as a liberal democracy governed by representatives elected by a majority of adult citizens. The society is maintained by a stable and self-sufficient free-enterprise economy staffed by reasonably happy and affluent workers. The second describes Canada as a society ruled by an hereditary oligarchy and multi-national imperialist corporations, maintained by a large and increasingly impoverished working class (Marchak, 1981:ix. Permission granted by McGraw-Hill Ryerson Limited.)

Marchak argues that the 1980s saw the emergence of a third ideology: *corporatism*. Corporatism is an ideology of "legitimate authority, the natural hierarchy of persons and skills, and of the subordination of the individual not only to society but as well to the state" (Marchak:170).

Bourdieu and Passeron (1977) argue that the function of education is to reproduce the dominant culture. Educational success is largely determined by how well individuals internalize the dominant culture. It is, in Bourdieu's words, the most important means of accumulating *cultural capital*. Cultural capital consists of symbolic elements valued by the dominant class, including speech, rules of etiquette, knowledge and experience.

## EXPRESSIVE SYMBOLS

In the postwar period, a number of social movements expressed dissatisfaction with the dominant culture and with basic structural inequalities. Youth, students, blacks, women and even middle-class professionals involved in the human potential movement criticized several generally held social values. The civil rights movement and the women's movement focused on unique and previously undervalued aspects of their own cultures. The introduction of native, black and women's studies programs in North American Universities is in part a response to this kind of demand. Many groups expressed their differences symbolically, in their dress and hair styles. Peterson (1979) suggests that the attention now paid by sociologists to expressive symbolization coincided with the increased visibility of countercultures in our society.

Generally, our collective identity is represented in the symbolic expression of our cultural traditions, in language and in the countless rituals which punctuate our lives as citizens, employees, members of families and so on. In confirming our group membership, these symbols reinforce our sense of ourselves. We identify with and feel comfortable with familiar symbols. We feel we belong. When we travel, we find important cultural differences, even in such taken-for-granted aspects of social interaction as how much personal space we can claim when talking to others, eye contact and touching behaviour. And, as many of us have experienced with some frustration, different cultures attach different meanings to the notion of time and of being "on time."

## Time Difference

Hall (1976) describes Westerners' orientation to time as *monochronic*. In other words, we prefer to do one thing at a time. Monochronic time emphasizes schedules and promptness. A *polychronic* orientation to time, typical of Latin America and the Middle East, is characterized by several things happening at once (1976:14). Typically, Westerners tend to compartmentalize their lives and prioritize their activities. Monochronic time is tangible: "They (Westerners) speak of it as being saved, spent, wasted, lost, made up, accelerated, slowed down, crawling and running out" (1976:15). As Hall explains, these differences are learned, but they are learned so well and are so well integrated with other aspects of culture that they are treated as natural.

The fast pace of life in North America makes it tempting to disparage the Spanish idea of "mañana." In fact, Peace Corp volunteers found that, next to language, their greatest difficulties in adjusting to a foreign culture were in dealing with "the general pace of life and the punctuality of others" (Levine and Wolff, 1985:32). Attempts to explore different meanings attached to social time cross-culturally are limited by linguistic comparisons. Cultures which place a high priority on punctuality have more specific words to describe time dimensions than cultures in which time is less important. For example, "esrerar" in Portuguese means "to hope for," "to wait for" and to "expect." (Levine and Wolff, 1985:34) To circumvent these problems, Levine and Wolff used unobtrusive measures to estimate the pace of life in six countries. These researchers found important differences in the accuracy of the country's bank clocks, pedestrian walking speed and the average time it took to buy a stamp.

## Language

Perhaps the most useful expressive symbol is language. In addition to being an efficient means of communicating, language is an expression of group membership. This is obvious when we think about French and English Canadians. But language can also distinguish members of smaller groups: professionals, students, punkers or even members of families. Whether in the form of family "nicknames" or technical jargon, we all develop peculiarities of speech which symbolically differentiate members from nonmembers. At the same time, these unique ways of talking help to establish rapport between members of the group.

Several anthropologists have concluded that language also shapes our perceptions of the world. The *Sapir-Whorf Hypothesis* assumes that language helps define experience because it orients us to certain aspects of our environment. Thus, when people acquire language, they also acquire a way of organizing their experience. Cultural differences rooted in the very structure of language make cross-cultural communication difficult.

Feminists argue that language is based on male experience and therefore describes a masculine view of the world. When we use generic terms such as "he" and "man,"

Table 5-1 The Pace of Life in Six Countries

|  | Accuracy of Bank Clocks | Walking Speed | Post Office Speed |
|---|---|---|---|
| Japan | 1 | 1 | 1 |
| United States | 2 | 3 | 2 |
| England | 4 | 2 | 3 |
| Italy | 5 | 4 | 6 |
| Taiwan | 3 | 5 | 4 |
| Indonesia | 6 | 6 | 5 |

Numbers (1 is the top value) indicate the comparative rankings of each country for each indicator of time sense.

Reprinted by permission from *Psychology Today Magazine* © 1985.

we are, in effect, reinforcing this masculine view. Furthermore, people who hear generic terms envision a male referent. Students asked to select pictures to illustrate an introductory sociology text chose more pictures of males when the chapter titles used generic terms such as "Urban Man" than when the chapters had neutral titles like "Urban Life" (Schneider and Hacker, 1973).

## Mass Mediated Culture[1]
Although the media are the focus of a later chapter, we cannot discuss culture without considering the role of the media in the social construction of reality. The media, particularly television, are pervasive cultural influences. Continuity is preserved by the production and reproduction of cultural symbols, and the media are active in this process.

You have probably heard that by the time you graduate, you will have spent more hours watching television than in school. In fact, in your lifetime, you will spend more time watching television than doing anything else except working or sleeping. More than 98 percent of American homes have television sets, and these are turned on for an average of *seven* hours a day. Television viewing has increased steadily among all age, educational and ethnic groups in the last decade (Neuman, 1982:471)

In Gerbner's view, television is a unique medium because it is so pervasive. He feels (1978) that television has assumed the role once occupied by religion in preindustrial societies in that we are born into its symbolic environment and rarely

[1] This term is borrowed from the title of a book by Real (1977).

NOT JUST GOOD CHRISTIAN MEN REJOICING NOW
By Kelley Teahen

God is not a she, at least not in the language of churches of the Christian tradition. And ever since the first righteous monk translated the Greek word for "humanity"—anthropos—as "man" in the scriptures, it has sounded like the Holy Writ is addressed to only the male half of the Christian community.

During the past decade a sensitivity has developed to so-called exclusive language within the songs, prayers and scripture translations used in churches. Such language excludes womanhood in two ways. The community of worshippers is often described as "sons of God" or "the brethren," not taking into account the women in the congregation. And God is understood to be He Himself—the lord, king, master and father of all.

Some churches do not feel this kind of language poses a problem for the women of their communities.

"Sexist language is not a dominant issue with the evangelicals," said Rev. Brian Stiller, executive director of the Evangelical Fellowship of Canada, which represents such denominations as the Pentecostal Assembly, the Salvation Army and some Mennonite groups. "Women have been very involved in our ministry over the years and there's an implicit acceptance of women when we say 'mankind.'"

In other churches however—notably the United and Roman Catholic—women have felt set apart in worship and, during the past few years, have brought about changes in the words sung and spoken in prayer and praise. . . .

"All language about God is inadequate, but somehow we always think of God as 'He,'" she said.

Although many may fear the richness of traditional language in liturgy and in standard hymns such as Faith Of Our Fathers will be diminished by exclusive adaptations, the churches—notably the Roman Catholic, whose women are not allowed to enter into the higher callings of its ministries—feel the changes in language are needed to reflect the Church's growing awareness of women's roles in the community.

"I may not be happy, grammatically, with a word like humankind," said Father Poirier.

"But it sure is a lot fairer than saying mankind."

*The Globe and Mail*, Toronto, August 3, 1985.

question its cultural assumptions. "Television is the ritual that dramatizes the myths underlying American culture, it explains and justifies the major social institutions of American society and socializes individuals into their life roles" (White, 1983:286).

In a series of continuing studies begun in 1967, Gerbner and his associates have studied the cultural environment of television. They have regularly monitored television content and compared these trends with attitude studies of the television audience. The symbolic environment of television is analysed by what Gerbner calls *cultural indicators*. His focus is on the priorities, values and relationships in television drama. His studies found heavy viewers internalized a world and a value system congruent with the world of television. For example, heavy viewers who witness a great deal of televised violence see the world as more threatening than light viewers. Therefore, they are more inclined to support greater measures of social control (Gerbner and Gross, 1976). The media thus act as an instrument of social control, reinforcing and legitimizing certain kinds of social relationships. (These ideas are taken up in more detail in Chapter 20.)

This has been a brief introduction to the major concepts in the study of culture. Next we will look at some ways sociologists have found these concepts useful for understanding social behaviour.

# SUBCULTURES

As described in the section above, subcultures are groups whose norms, values and expressive symbols differ from ones more generally held. In the section below, we will look at several ways of conceptualizing these groups. Lewis's analysis of the culture of poverty emphasizes value differences, whereas the description of British youth culture focuses on symbolic expressive differences.

## THE CULTURE OF POVERTY

Anthropologist Oscar Lewis coined the phrase *culture of poverty* to describe

> a subculture of Western society with its own structure and rationale, a way of life handed on from generation to generation along family lines. It is a culture in the traditional anthropological sense in that it provides human beings with a design for living, with a readymade set of solutions for human problems, and so serves a significant adaptive function. This style of life transcends national boundaries and regional and rural-urban differences within nations (Lewis, 1966:19).

Lewis identified 70 traits which characterize the culture of poverty. These traits describe: the relationship between the subculture and the larger society; the nature of the slum community; the nature of the family; and the attitudes, values and character structure of the individual. There is a lack of integration between the subculture and the larger community as a result of segregation, discrimination, fear, suspicion and apathy. The community itself is characterized by unemployment, underemployment, low wages and a chronic shortage of cash. Marriage is typically unstable, and families are mother centred. "The individual who grows up in this culture has a strong feeling of fatalism, helplessness, dependence and inferiority" (Lewis, 1966:23).

Lewis's solution—"slowly to raise their level of living and incorporate them in the middle class"—is typical of the 1950s and early 60s approach to social problems. The assumption was that cultural deficiencies could be identified and altered. The same assumption used to explain global underdevelopment. Thus, foreign aid included an exchange of personnel to train Third World people in the ways of Western industrial capitalism. In the 70s these ideas gave way among sociologists to more critical and radical analyses of development and underdevelopment, although the legacy of the 50s and 60s remains in some quarters. In the more radical social climate of the late 1960s and 1970s, many challenged the presumption that our middle-class, Western way of life should be a model of social development.

The term *ethnocentrism* describes this seemingly universal tendency to rate one's own group or culture more positively than any other group or culture. A Canadian study (Kehoe, 1982) found that, among grade five students, subjects who perceived themselves positively were most likely to appreciate cultural diversity, and those who most appreciated cultural diversity were least ethnocentric.

## YOUTH CULTURES

A different way of looking at subcultures focuses on groups that develop around some sort of expressive symbolism. A number of studies of British youth culture have been done along these lines. As Brake (1980) explains, British youth culture arises out of a concern with masculinity, which is reflected in expressions of male superiority and disdain for homosexuality.

According to Brake, an important element of subcultures is the symbolic use of style. Style consists of: image (appearance enhanced by costume, hair-style and jewellery); demeanor (expression, gait and posture); and argot (a special vocabulary). These help to differentiate insiders from outsiders and full-timers from pretenders. In postwar Britain, there has been a discernible turnover of youth cultures, as mods replaced teddy-boys and skinheads replaced mods. Each group has had its own distinctive style. The teddy-boy dress code was a unique adaptation of upper-class style. Teddy-boys wore long, velvet-collared Edwardian jackets, tight drainpipe trousers, bootlaced ties and thick, crepe-soled shoes known as "brothel-creepers." Their heroes were James Dean and Elvis Presley. Hairstyles imitated early Elvis—sideburns and duck-tails, or DAs as they were called. Skinheads of the 60s (a group which re-emerged a few years ago) were self-consciously working-class and ardent football (soccer) fans. They focused their aggression on three groups: Asian immigrants, hippies and homosexuals.

## THE TSIGOLOICOS

Professional groups might also be considered as subcultures. In 1956, Horace Miner wrote a wonderfully facetious article called "Body Ritual Among the Nacirema," which poked fun at this "backward" American tribe. Recently, an "elite clan" of the Nacirema, the Tsigoloicos, were the subject of a similar analysis. (See page 124.)

## CORPORATE CULTURE

In recent years, the business community has begun to understand problems of organizational change in terms of *corporate culture*. An article in *Business Week* (October 27, 1980) describes how understanding an organization's culture can have important consequences for business decisions.

> "Culture implies values, such as aggressiveness, defensiveness, or nimbleness, that set a pattern for a company's activities, opinions, and actions. That pattern is instilled in employees by managers' example and passed down to succeeding generations of workers."

Managers are beginning to understand that company values are well entrenched and therefore difficult to change.

The *Business Week* article explains how the culture of PepsiCo Inc. changed as the company decided to become a more aggressive competitor. In an ad campaign familiar to us all, Pepsi challenged Coke's domination of the market.

> "That direct confrontation is reflected inside the company as well. Managers are pitted against each other to grab more market share, to work harder, and to wring more profits out of their businesses. Because winning is the key value at Pepsi, losing has its penalties. Consistent runners up find their jobs gone."

# CULTURAL CHANGE

Cultures change because of technological innovations, economic or environmental change, the introduction of new members through migration or as a result of internal conflicts. In this section we will look at the impact of technological innovation on Canadian society, the process of cultural diffusion and some important symbolic changes.

Rosengren (1981) has described four positions to categorize theories of cultural change: materialism, idealism, interdependence and autonomy. The *materialist* position assumes that cultural changes follow structural changes; this is the classic Marxist stance. The theories of Innis and McLuhan, which describe cultural changes resulting from changes in communication technology, are also materialist. The *idealist* position is that cultural changes precede structural changes. For example, Weber's thesis, which states that the cultural values of Calvinism created an environment in which capitalism could thrive, could be called idealist. Other positions assume that culture and structure are *autonomous*, although perhaps most discussions of their relationship focus on their *interdependance*. In other words, most analysts claim that culture and structure are not related to one another holistically. Rather, various aspects of both interact at different times in the ongoing process of change.

## TECHNOLOGY AND CHANGE

Innis and McLuhan, two Canadians, are called *technological determinists* because of their focus on technological innovation as a source of change. Both were primarily interested in innovations in communication technology. Innis argued that the modes of communication influence the nature of social organization. Oral cultures, where communication is by speech alone, will have a strong temporal bias and will focus on the past. These societies will emphasize tradition and have a strong moral order. Cultures with a written language will be present and future oriented and will favour the growth of science and technical knowledge.

McLuhan took from Innis the centrality of communication technology but focused on how these changes influence the way we perceive the world around us. According to McLuhan, print cultures depend on sight to acquire knowledge and confirm experience. Print organizes experience in a linear fashion. Because reading is a private

## MYTH AND SYMBOL AMONG THE NACIREMA TSIGOLOICOS: A FRAGMENT

The Tsigoloicos are a large, decentralized clan distributed throughout that geographical area occupied by the Nacirema. Though nomadic in disposition, the group has recently accepted more permanent settlement as a consequence of gradual exhaustion of natural resources. The clan has a relatively short history, and has only recently claimed elite status and conceived elaborate rituals whereby this is conferred upon new members. It is thus difficult to classify the Tsigoloicos in either of the two great Nacirema phratries (i.e., the Secneics and the Seitinamuh), a fact which probably explains the disdain in which they are held by the more firmly established clans of each.

The life of the Tsigoloicos seems to pass alternately through the two distinct phases observed among the central Australian tribes by Spencer and Gillen (1904). In the first phase, economic activity is indeed the preponderating one, and the Tsigoloicos limit themselves to the two primary occupations for which they are rewarded—i.e., the production and exchange of ritual inscriptions, and the preparation of neophytes for initiation into the clan. These occupations are typically pursued with only mediocre intensity and the dispersed condition of the clan results in a life which is uniform, languishing, and dull [*EF*, p. 246]. Periodically, however, the Tsigoloicos come together at a designated location to participate in a ceremony remarkably similar to the Arunta corrobori. Here, on the contrary, the reason and will of the primitive give way to his passional faculties, and he is caught up in the collective effervescence of communal life [*EF*, pp. 246, 258]. And while the ostensive function of such gatherings remains the exchange of ritual inscriptions, it is clear that their latent function is to reaffirm the solidarity of the clan—i.e., to give it a sense of itself and to reassure its members that it does, in fact, exist [*EF*, p. 257].

Our interest here, however, is in the religious institutions of the Tsigoloicos and especially in the bizarre mythologies which underly them. These myths apparently grow out of the daily, profane activities of the Tsigoloicos themselves. As indicated above, each clan member is expected to periodically produce and exchange certain ritual inscriptions. For the most part, these inscriptions have little of the sacred about them; their utility is temporal and generally confined to the individual who produces them; and they are quickly deposited in the large vaults of Tsigoloicos temples, where they are soon forgotten.

A very few Tsigoloicos inscriptions, however, seem to have acquired and retained sacred status—i.e., they inspire collective sentiments of awe and respect, and are set aside from profane inscriptions and treated with special precautions [*EF*, pp. 56, 301]. The Tsigoloicos themselves appear confused over how this sacredness came into existence; for these are typically very old inscriptions, written in oblique, turgid styles and even strange languages (ironically, the inscription seems to gain in dignity as its meaning is more

> obscure). As a result, the Tsigoloicos maintain a small class of priests, called *stsiroeht*, whose functions include the interpretation of sacred inscriptions and concoction of fantastic myths to account for their special powers. The result is a set of representations which express the nature of these sacred things and the relations which they sustain, either with each other, or with profane things [*EF*, p. 56]. At the same time, the Tsigoloicos have established rites which prescribe how a man should comport himself in the presence of these sacred objects [*EF*, p. 56].
>
> Mones, Robert; "Myth and Symbol Among the Nacirema Tsigoloicos;" *American Sociologist*; Vol. 15: 207-212; (1980).

activity, it encourages individual confirmation of experience. The electronic media develop different ways of organizing experience. Television viewing is multisensory and involves the viewer more than print does. Because television is a shared experience, it draws individuals together as members of the global village. McLuhan described the generation gap of the 1960s as a conflict between these two modes of thought. Parents who grew up in a print culture and children who grew up with television inevitably saw the world differently.

Alvin Toffler, in *Future Shock* (1971), described changes in social patterns resulting from technological and environmental change. A film explaining his main points was released soon after his book. Shortly after the film's release, many of the changes Toffler described had become "old hat." Sociology students who had grown up in the electronic age were accustomed to Toffler's formerly radical ideas and saw nothing new in his thesis.

## CULTURAL DIFFUSION

The influence of the media, the ease of international travel and the multinational corporation have all contributed to a blurring of international cultural distinctions. In a way never before possible, we witness international events in politics or sports as they happen. We are surrounded by evidence of cultural diffusion. American popular culture is really a universal popular culture. One can eat Kentucky Fried Chicken in Nairobi, watch *I Love Lucy* in Scandinavia and discuss American films in Bulgaria. And even in the heart of West Africa, one need never go without Coca-Cola.

As business is increasingly conducted in an international environment, the idea of cultural diffusion has taken on a more popular meaning. For example, part of Japan's great economic success in the postwar years is attributed to that country's uncanny ability to adopt those Western business techniques which could be easily integrated into Japanese life and reject others. Indeed, many Japanese managers travelled to the United States in the 1950s and 60s to study the successful American management model. Ironically, by the 1980s the pattern was reversed. Western managers were seeking ways of adapting Japanese techniques to the North American business environment. Recently several books[2] have praised the Japanese model, which places far more emphasis on human resource development than has been typical in North America. About 35 percent of Japan's workforce will spend their entire working life with the same employer. Employees are usually reassigned or retrained rather than laid off when jobs become obsolete or the economy slumps. Management–worker relations are more apt to be collaborative than adversarial. These more egalitarian relationships are symbolized by such practices as uniform dress for all, line workers and managers alike.

According to some analysts, the success of a few exemplary American companies results from their use of management techniques similar to those employed in Japanese companies: for example, quality circles, semiautonomous work groups and job rotation.

## SYMBOLIC CHANGE

Raymond Breton (1984) argues that much of the recent change in Canada is change in the symbolic order. In a society where most people share a symbol system, attempts to reinforce that system will have an integrating effect. Breton's point is that Canada is different because Canada is a binational, multicultural country. Restructuring the symbolic environment involves introducing new symbolic elements and breaking with the past to form a new collective identity.

From Breton's perspective, the symbolic environment of Canadian society until World War II was primarily British. This was reflected in Canada's social institutions, language, customs and the symbols which represented Canadian culture. Various conflicts developed as non-British groups struggled to control their own educational systems or media, but, except for the French, none of these were particularly successful. Once this symbolic environment was well established, cultural pluralism was less threatening. In the postwar years, Quebec's Francophone protest increased. "Their intense feeling was that Canadian society was not their society, its institutions not their institutions, its meanings and symbols, not their meanings and symbols" (Breton, 1984:129).

The institutional elites responded by trying to change the symbolic environment. Some of the changes involved changing the symbols themselves: The flag was changed; *O Canada* was named the national anthem; money and stamps were redesigned and the constitution (the *British* North America Act) was repatriated.

Public response to these changes was mixed. Some saw them as positive developments, but others resisted or opposed them. Those who opposed felt a sense of symbolic loss, a reaction which is understandable since symbolic change inevitably involves conflict.

In the following section, we will focus specifically on several dimensions of Canadian culture: Americanization, regionalism, ethnic pluralism and multiculturalism. Breton's discussion of symbolic change is an apt introduction to these themes.

[2] For example, William Ouchi, *Theory Z: How American Business Can Meet the Japanese Challenge* (Addison-Wesley, 1980); and Richard T. Pascale and Anthony Athos, *The Art of Japanese Management* (Simon and Schuster, 1981).

# CANADIAN CULTURE

It is quite difficult to describe the cultures of complex, highly differentiated modern societies such as ours. The extent of cultural diffusion in technology and in popular culture via the mass media makes the material and nonmaterial cultures of the advanced industrial countries very homogenous. Furthermore, in countries like Canada, the United States and Australia, with large immigrant populations, distinctive elements of culture are difficult to identify. In Canada, the overwhelming presence of the United States makes it even more difficult to define our uniqueness.

It was popular in the past to describe Canadian society as a *mosaic* and the United States as a *melting pot*. This was supposed to convey the importance of ethnic pluralism in Canada, as opposed to the assimilation model in the United States. More recent comparisons found that the differences between these two countries in their policies towards immigrants are not as distinct as they once appeared. Some groups are more readily assimilated, and some groups resist assimilation in both Canada and the United States. Furthermore, the recent phenomenon of "ethnic rediscovery" is more or less universal, related more to an increased awareness of ethnic and racial inequalities than to a celebration of culture (Porter, 1979b). Nevertheless, both our proximity to the United States and our ethnic composition are fundamental aspects of our sense of ourselves as Canadians. In the following sections, we will describe how Americanization, regionalism and multiculturalism have shaped and continue to shape the Canadian identity.

## THE AMERICANIZATION OF CANADIAN CULTURE

In a recent article, Ogmundson (1980:1) argued that "a central aspect of the Canadian experience—Americanization—has received insufficient attention from academic social scientists in Canada, especially those involved in the study of culture and ethnicity." He thinks Canadian sociologists recognize our economic and political dependance on the United States but not that country's cultural domination of Canada. Unlike the analyses of bilingualism, multiculturalism or discrimination, Americanization has been all but ignored. Yet, American domination of our cultural industries, such as publishing, (including textbook publishers), film making, art and television means that Canadian popular culture is largely American. Thus, Ogmundson argues, we can study anglophone Canadians with the models used to study other American minority groups. In his view,

> It may well make very little sense to study Canada as a separate sociological entity. Rather it seems more sensible to study Canadian culture, and its various subcultures, in the same way that we study the disappearing cultures of the Inuit, the Indian, the Franco-Manitoban—as declining group(s) within a larger system (1980:3).

This analysis seems particularly negative to Canadian nationalists. On the other hand, it is clear that the media—the purveyors of our culture—*are* indisputably American dominated.

# THE MEDIA AND CANADIAN IDENTITY

Frederick Elkin (1983) looked specifically at the question of the media and our national identity. He argues that there are powerful internal and external forces that support a strong national identity and other forces which work against it. Elkin considered those forces which stem from mass communications. He began by describing what he means by a Canadian national identity.

> We assume a close link between culture and identity. An identity that stems from any collectivity implies some distinctive cultural elements. To experience the Canadian identity implies at least a concern with some things considered Canadian, and may imply a complete absorption in Canadian institutions and Canadian problems. For most Canadians it probably includes a concern with Canada vis-à-vis other countries on the international scene; an interest in federal government politics, federal-provincial relationships, political parties, and leading political figures; an awareness of problems associated with the Arctic, Quebec, western energy resources, and the native peoples; a familiarity with a unique history and geography; an enjoyment of the popular culture associated with Canadian entertainment stars and distinctive holidays; and an interest in Canadian participation in international and professional sports such as hockey, football (including the Grey Cup), baseball, and soccer—all of which are given considerable attention in the mass media.
>
> We assume too a close link between the collective identity applied to a nation, large group or institution and the individual identity, experienced by those who make up the collectivity. For the individual, the image of the group is internalized and is part of the psychological world that enters into his or her sentiments, thoughts, and behavior. A Canadian success is experienced with pleasure and a Canadian failure with a sense of loss (Elkin, 1983:148). (This material is copyright of Addison-Wesley Publishers Ltd. and is used here by permission of the Publisher. All rights reserved.)

When Canadians are free to choose, most prefer American films, magazines, television programs and books, and the Canadian government has been disinclined to restrict the amount of American media penetration in Canada. The availability of American products "reinforces American influence and presumably weakens Canadian identity as such" (Elkin, 1983:149). The strongest internal force mitigating against a strong national identity is the French-English duality of language and culture. Separate public and private media organizations serve these two communities, and the separateness of communities is emphasized by language differences. Multiculturalism also operates against a strong national identity. For many of the 25 percent of Canadians whose cultural heritage is neither English nor French, maintaining their own language and culture has become an important concern. What we commonly call the ethnic media serve audiences which Elkin estimates number into the millions. Finally, Elkin describes how regional sentiments, particularly those expressed in separatist movements, act, in some contexts, as divisive forces. Opposing these divisive elements are the integrative forces of public institutions and regulating bodies. The Canadian Radio-Television and Telecommunications Commission, the CRTC, regulates all broadcasting in Canada. This agency controls the amount of foreign ownership (limited to 20 percent) and foreign content (30 percent of all music played on Canadian radio stations and 60 percent of all television content must be Canadian). Organizations such as the CBC and the Canadian Press have especially emphasized Canadian content.

## REGIONALISM

Canadian sociologist Bernard Blishen (1978) asked a large sample of Canadians the following question: "Some people say they are (name of province of residence) first, and Canadian second, while others say they are Canadian first and (name of province of residence) second. How would you describe yourself? Canadian first, provincial first, both equally, neither, other (specify), don't know." French-speaking Quebec residents were asked the following question. "Comment vous définessez-vous *en tout premier lieu*: comme un Canadien-français, un Québecois, un Canadien tout simplement, ou autrement?" The results of this study indicate that most Canadians have a stronger national than regional identity. The two groups with strong regional identities were French-speaking residents of Quebec and non-French residents of the Maritimes. Interestingly, at the time of this survey, when separatist sentiment in Quebec was high, only 30 percent of the respondents identified themselves as Quebecois first.

If these attitudes are representative, many Canadians feel a strong regional identity. In the past, regional differences have been described in terms of economic indicators, but, as Matthews (1982:91) argues, regional disparity is also a social and cultural phenomenon. "Regionalism . . . refers to a sense of identification of consciousness-of-kind which inhabitants of a particular territorial area feel for that territorial area, and/or for their fellow inhabitants of that region" (1982:86). While the study of regional cultures has not been a major thrust in Canadian sociology, it seems that most Canadians recognize regional inequality but nevertheless prefer their own region, regardless of its economic opportunities (Schwartz, 1974).

## ETHNIC PLURALISM

One important dynamic of Canada's population structure described in Chapter 4 is its ethnic composition. In the early years of this century, 90 percent of Canada's population were British or French. Now these two groups account for less than 75 percent of the population. Of the remaining 25 percent, the largest immigrant groups are Germans, Italians and Ukrainians. All other immigrant groups, as well as Canada's two indigenous populations, account for 2 percent or less of the current population. In Chapter 14, you will consider Canadian ethnic and racial relations in detail. Here we will look briefly at the issue of *ethnic identity*.

Ethnic identity has been defined as "a socio-psychological process by which individuals or groups subjectively include themselves in a community of their alleged ancestors or predecessors, who shared a distinct culture" (Isajiw, 1983:108). Ethnicity is one among several social categories, including age, sex, social class, nationality and so on, the total of which constitutes an individual's *social identity*. In a sense, these categories help us "locate" ourselves and those with whom we interact. Sometimes these categories are based on *stereotypes*—the positive and negative images we have of ourselves and others. Depending on the nature of our social interaction, some social categories will be more important than others. In other words, some categories have greater salience than others at different times. *Ethnic salience*, as defined by Mackie and Brinkerhoff (1984:117) is "the importance an individual attaches to being ethnic," a definition which draws attention to the fact that "ethnicity is a variable, whose salience is situational" (1984:117). In other words, ethnic identity will be more important in some situations than in others.

Mackie and Brinkerhoff (1984) used a sample of University of Calgary students to investigate ethnic salience. When the students were asked how they usually thought of their own identity, 54.8 percent responded, "Canadian"; 19.2 percent named an ethnic group; and the remaining 19.2 percent gave a hyphenated response (i.e., Italian-Canadian)—if these response categories were provided. But, when asked how they would define their ethnicity, 33 percent of the students gave no response when the question was open-ended. Only 4.4 percent of the group chose ethnicity from a list of five social identities as the "most important aspect" of themselves. The other more important identities were gender (62.3 percent), citizenship (17.1 percent) and religion (12.5 percent). Ethnicity was more salient for women than for men, for working-class than for middle-class students and predictably was higher for those born outside of North America.

As noted earlier, the cross-cultural diffusion of technologies and ideas and the "internationalization" of popular culture has tended to blur differences between cultures. Within Canada, these same processes promote assimilation. In Porter's view (1979a:125), both Canada and the United States face a similar dilemma over ethnic identity. "(O)n the one hand if they value and emphasize ethnicity, mobility and opportunity are endangered, on the other hand if they emphasize mobility and opportunity, it will be at the cost of submerging cultural identity." Perhaps this dilemma is most acute for indigenous groups. Although many Native Americans remain isolated from mainstream Canadian society, Gerber's (1979) research shows that others are making some economic headway, either as individuals or through community development projects. In most cases, Gerber argues, this has not threatened the survival of reserve communities, nor does it necessarily diminish ethnic identity. "The elaborate provincial and national organizations and the proliferation of developing Indian communities indicate that assimilation and integration at one level are accompanied by ethnic differentiation at another" (Gerber, 1979:420). As Isajiw (1983:109) says: "Assimilation and retention of ethnic identity are not necessarily contradictory, zero-sum processes, that is, that the more one assimilates, the less one retains identity, and vice versa." Rather, he argues, ethnic identity will have a different meaning for each generation. Ethnic subcultures are no more resistant to change than are dominant cultures. While we all tend to romanticize the past, or in Marshall McLuhan's terms, see life in "the rear-view mirror," no modern culture remains static. For young people, ethnic identity may be more a matter of not wanting to lose sight of cultural traditions and historical roots without necessarily wanting to retain traditional life styles or life patterns.

## MULTICULTURALISM

In October, 1971, Prime Minister Trudeau announced the initiation of a policy of "multiculturalism within a bilingual framework." This policy was to encourage the expression of non-English, non-French cultures in Canada. The incentive for such a policy arose out of the Royal Commission on Bilingualism and Biculturalism. Representatives of Canada's "other" ethnic groups told the commission that their interests would be overshadowed by a policy of dualism. A policy of multiculturalism, on the other hand, would better reflect Canada's ethnic diversity.

The federal government's multicultural policy supported ethnic publications, conferences, festivals and so on. Critics argue that most of the support has been for specific projects and that long term effects are difficult to determine. Isajiw (1983) has said that there are two other important conceptions of multiculturalism. The first calls for the institutionalization of selected minority-ethnic activities within the mainstream of Canadian society. For example, in academic circles, we have seen the formation of the Canadian Ethnic Studies Association. The other way of thinking of multiculturalism, according to Isajiw, is as a set of values which oppose prejudice and discrimination and which support equal opportunity. While this has not been a major thrust of Canada's attempt at multiculturalism, some initiatives have been taken to reduce interracial or interethnic tensions through public education.

Perhaps it is too soon to judge the Canadian government's policy on multiculturalism. The amount of money allocated has not been great, and the issue has been overshadowed by fundamental economic problems. Certainly, the criticisms have been strongly stated. Those on the left argue that the policy only serves to appease. Others, including John Porter (1979:133), an eminent Canadian sociologist, oppose multiculturalism because they feel that, while bilingualism may survive (given enough support), neither biculturalism nor multiculturalism are compatible with the post-industrial phase we are entering in the 1980s.

## SUMMARY

Two seemingly contradictory points have been made about the study of culture. First, culture is a fundamental concept in sociological analysis. But the current generation of sociologists has neglected the systematic study of culture partly because culture is such an all-encompassing feature of social life. On the other hand, the research cited throughout this chapter shows that culture remains a key reference point in any sociological analysis.

While most sociologists agree about the importance of values, norms, beliefs, ideologies and expressive symbols, these are given more or less emphasis by different researchers. *Functionalists* tend to emphasize core values, norms and beliefs and the ways these are institutionalized. *Marxists* focus on the way dominant ideologies frame and legitimize existing social arrangements. *Interactionists* focus on the symbolic expressive aspects of culture.

In complex societies such as ours, some values and beliefs will be shared (more or less) universally. But unless these are challenged, we are usually unaware of their strength. Our day-to-day interactions are more directly influenced by the norms of the subcultures or groups of which we are members. Four subcultures were discussed in this chapter: the culture of poverty, youth culture, the culture of a professional group and corporate cultures.

The section on cultural change described the effects of the introduction of new technologies and new symbols. However, neither of these factors alone can account for the rhythms of cultural change, for their influence cannot be isolated from the myriad other factors that affect us. Perhaps the complexity of modern social life and the interdependancy of modern cultures eludes traditional analysis. John Porter may have been right when he suggested:

> What of cultures? Cultures are traditionbound. Anthropologists view cultures as established ways of doing things, or of viewing the world, or as designs for living and survival passed from generation to generation, and, while for societies more simply organized than those of today, the role that cultures played and for many continue to play was important, they are less and less relevant for the postindustrial society because they emphasize yesterday rather than tomorrow. Can cultures of the past serve societies facing the coming of post-industrialism? The one recurring theme in many of the analyses of the next twenty-five years is the rapidity of change, of the shock of the future. One can almost speak of the end of culture, as some have written of the end of ideology. Many of the historic cultures are irrelevant to our futures. Opportunity will go to those individuals who are future-oriented in an increasingly universalistic culture. Those oriented to the past are likely to lose out. (From THE MEASURE OF CANADIAN SOCIETY by John Porter, p. 133. Copyright © 1979 by Gage Publishing Limited. Used by permission.)

## DISCUSSION QUESTIONS

1. Describe a subculture you are familiar with. Your family might be an interesting group to focus on. What norms, values, beliefs and expressive symbols characterize this group?

2. What symbols differentiate Canadian, American and British cultures? How are these different from non-Western cultural symbols?

3. Compare stereotypes of Americans and Canadians. Think of the stereotypes you hold of other cultural groups. Where do these ideas originate? How are they perpetuated?

4. Working with a group of students from different faculties (music, arts, business, etc.) develop an inventory of style differences which characterize members of different faculties in your school. Do professors implicitly encourage these differences?

5. Observe people in a public area of your university. How do differences in dress, demeanor and argot serve as symbols of exclusion and inclusion?

6. Consider the feminist claim that language is sexist. In your next written assignment, consciously avoiding using sexist terminology (i.e., the generic "he").

7. Consider your initiation to university life as a process of acculturation. How did initiation week activities help to establish group cohesion? In what ways could this adjustment be made easier?

8. Gerbner feels that the media create a symbolic environment which defines a world view and a value system. While watching your favourite television drama, imagine what someone unfamiliar with Western culture would learn from it. Try to list some of these *cultural indicators*.

9. Discuss the issue of assimilation with a first-generation immigrant. How does he or she feel about the dilemma of maintaining cultural identity described by Porter?

10. Using Mackie and Brinkerhoff's study as a guide, do a mini-study to measure ethnic salience among your colleagues.

# 6

# Socialization

## *Susannah Wilson*

# INTRODUCTION

Peter Berger (1975:55) called socialization the process by which we learn to become members of society. For all of us this process starts at birth an continues throughout our lives. Because much of this learning goes on in the early years of an individual's life, sociologists distinguish primary from secondary socialization. *Primary socialization* occurs from birth to adolescence. And, as Berger points out, because children have less power than adults and because they are unaware of alternatives, early socialization is largely imposed. In satisfying a newborn infant's needs—even such a basic need as food—parents respond within a framework of culturally defined expectations. If an infant is fed according to a schedule, the baby will learn to be hungry at "feeding time." "The same observation pertains to elimination, to sleeping and to other physiological processes that are endemic to the organism" (Berger, 1975:50). Consequently, while we will all develop individual likes and dislikes, even our early experiences of hunger, pain and comfort are mitigated by the social world into which we are born.

*Secondary socialization* is the ongoing process of learning to adjust to new situations. At key transition points, such as entering or leaving the labour force or becoming parents or grandparents, we learn new role expectations and adjust our behaviour to these. While sociologists have been most concerned with primary socialization, socialization continues throughout the life cycle. In effect, we are not talking about one, but a series of processes. Because adults bring to new situations the accumulated learning of their previous experiences, including certain preconceptions about each new role, secondary socialization differs from primary socialization.

During childhood, members of our family have the greatest influence on our socialization. But, beginning sometimes at an early age, child-care workers, teachers, friends and the mass media also help shape our basic beliefs and values.

Socialization establishes boundaries of behaviour. Because of this, there are similarities in the way individuals in certain cultural settings mature. But we are all individuals, so people react differently to similar experiences. Some children thrive on routine; others resent it. Some grow up wanting to be like their parents; others react against these models. As children mature, and their interactions outside the family increase, they recognize differences in the behaviour, speech and values of the people they encounter. Even within our families there are fundamentally different behavioural expectations for men and women, old and young. We gradually learn how our own views are relative. One interesting thing about meeting people from different cultural backgrounds is learning how their definitions of social reality differ from ours. In fact, much of social research, particularly studies using participant observation, is designed to make these differences explicit.

In the previous chapter, we called socialization the process by which we internalize cultural norms. In large part, cross-cultural differences in language, customs and values reflect differences in how we have been socialized. While recognizing that parents are individuals who have specific goals and expectations for their children, we can see that socialization is also influenced by structural variables. How we are socialized will depend on whether we grew up in Vancouver or Moncton; whether we spoke English or Ukrainian at home; and whether we worshipped at a church or a synagogue. In a sense, socialization is a restriction. "The values, beliefs, assumptions, and ways of life that come to be 'second nature' to children make it difficult for them to function effectively in some kinds of social situations involving persons who have been socialized in other subcultures" (Elkin and Handel, 1978:74). This is particularly important when we consider class and sex differences in socialization. For example, if early socialization is based on traditional assumptions about the sexual division of labour, young women will place less importance on acquiring the kind of education most likely to lead to future job security. Some of the implications of gender differences in socialization are addressed in detail in Chapter 10.

Perhaps because of the intensity and importance of early learning, much of the socialization literature has focused on children. However, socialization can also be reciprocal. The idea of mutual learning seems evident when we consider the role of peer groups in socialization. It also seems clear that much of adult socialization involves reciprocity. As Peters (1985) argues, reciprocal socialization need not be restricted to interaction between peers. For example, in many ways children influence their parents or teachers. According to Peters, parental socialization (the socialization of parents by their children) will be optimal in families where affectivity is high, respect is good and where excessive parental power is not exercised. He also believes that parents' self-image will be influenced by their children's reactions to them as parents. Peters used a sample of parents of undergraduate students to test how adolescents socialize their parents. While several parents responded to questions by saying "I learned nothing from my adolescents," others said that their children influenced them. The area of greatest influence was sports, although adolescents also influenced parental involvement in politics, leisure and personal care. They also influenced their parents' attitudes to sexuality, handicapped persons, minorities and drugs.

In summary, we can make four general points about socialization. First, socialization continues throughout the life cycle. Secondly, it is a reciprocal process. Thirdly, how we are socialized will depend largely on our social class, our ethnicity, our sex, our religion. Finally, although we normally refer to parents, the media, education and peer groups as the most important agents of socialization, socialization involves all of our interactions, whether formal or informal, conscious or not.

## THEORIES OF SOCIALIZATION

As you become more familiar with sociology, you will see sociologists often disagree about the best way to analyse any social situation. This, of course, is not unique to sociology, although it has been argued that sociology differs from some other sciences in that no one perspective dominates. In the first chapter of this book, you read about several theoretical points of view within sociology and learned that the question sociologists ask and often the research methods they use depend on their theoretical orientation. Not all sociologists make the same distinctions when categorizing the extensive body of theoretical and empirical work done in their field.

Some sociologists begin with social structure as the unit of analysis, and others begin with individuals. The difference between them largely depends on what assumptions are made about human nature and the nature of social organization.

Dawe (1970:214) called these two approaches (1) the sociology of social system and (2) the sociology of social action. "One views action as the derivative of system whilst the other views system as the derivative of action."

In the past, some sociologists viewed socialization as more or less imposed on individuals. Others (likely most sociologists today) understand individuals are actively engaged in the process of socialization.[1]

In the following section, we will describe more specifically two contrasting views of socialization. The "action as derivative of system" approach is best represented in the work of American sociologist Talcott Parsons. The other way of understanding socialization, which focuses on individual actors creating meaning while involved in myriad social interactions relies most heavily on the perspective described in Chapter 1 as symbolic interactionism. George H. Mead (1863-1931) and Charles H. Cooley (1864-1929), two American sociologists, were key influences in developing the symbolic interactionist perspective. Perhaps more than any other theorists, these two men have influenced the way most sociologists understand socialization.

Socialization is a fundamental concern of sociologists because it provides a link between the individual and society. "From the point of view of the individual, interaction with other people is the means by which human potentialities are actualized. From the point of view of society, socialization explains how commitment to the social order is maintained over time" (Mackie, 1982:83).

## PARSONS' FUNCTIONALIST VIEW

For Parsons and for other functionalist sociologists, socialization is the process whereby individuals *internalize* socially approved norms and value. When individuals are properly socialized, they develop into "normal, conforming, socially acceptable and socially approved adults" (Boughey, 1978:104). Deviants have failed to internalize accepted codes of behaviour. Thirty years ago, deviants were assumed to have been improperly socialized. Now it seems simplistic to assume that, even within certain social groups, there are established and generally agreed upon rules of behaviour. Critics of this "top-down" view of socialization point out that the meanings we attach to social behaviour are not universal but are situated in many social contexts. The emphasis on individual conformity to group norms amounts, as Wrong (1961:183–193) pointed out, to "an oversocialized view of man" and presumably of women as well. To say that we are all socialized does not, however, imply that we have been completely moulded by the norms and values of our culture.

## THE SYMBOLIC INTERACTIONIST PERSPECTIVE

Symbolic interaction focuses on the *processes* of socialization and the ways individuals actively participate in this process. Both Charles H. Cooley and George H. Mead were interested in how individuals develop a sense of self and the importance of family interaction in this process. Cooley believed children were born with an instinctual capacity for *self* development and that this matured in interactions in primary

[1] On the other hand, empirical studies of socialization seem to be dominated by the determinist viewpoint, perhaps because of the strong influence functionalism has played in the professional socialization of most academic sociologists.

groups. For Cooley, primary groups are "characterized by intimate face to face association and cooperation" (1909:23). These interactions Cooley called *nursuries of human nature*. Once infants have gained control over their immediate environment, they begin to develop a sense of self, or what Cooley called an *I-feeling*.

Adults communicate their attitudes and values to their children primarily through language, and children understand themselves based on these interactions. In other words, we begin to see ourselves as we imagine others see us. This feeling, "I feel about me the way I think you think of me," Cooley called the *looking-glass self*, which he said has three elements. This awareness involves: "the imagination of our appearance to the other person; the imagination of his judgement of that appearance; and some sort of self-feeling, such as pride or mortification" (1902:184). Cooley was pointing out the importance of the *perceptions* of others' reactions to us in determining how we feel about ourselves. No doubt we can all think of instances where our intentions were misread or when we have misunderstood the approval or disapproval of others.

One important problem raised by Mead deals with how we become sensitive to the responses of others (Campbell, 1975:10). How do we learn to present ourselves in different social situations? According to Mead, we learn symbolically, through role-taking. At first, a child's behaviour is a combination of instinctual behaviour and imitation. This Mead called the *pre-play stage*. Later, during the *play stage*, children learn to assume the roles of others and to objectify that experience by seeing themselves from the others' point of view. In the next stage, the *game stage*, children learn to handle several roles at once and thus to anticipate the behaviour of others. Finally, children learn to internalize general social expectations by imagining how any number of others will act and react. At this *generalized other stage*, the child has a sense of self and can react in a socially approved way.

As young children experience the approval and disapproval of those around them, they begin to understand what is expected of them. This more conventional, controlled and socially conscious part of self Mead called the *me*. The *I*, on the other hand, is more impulsive and individualistic.

The concepts of the self introduced by Cooley and Mead are difficult to substantiate with empirical investigation and have been criticized for this reason. However, two studies of students' self-concepts tested the idea that the self is developed through social interaction. Miyamoto and Dornbusch (1956) asked students to rate themselves and other members of their group in terms of intelligence, self-confidence, physical attractiveness and likeableness. Each student was also asked to rate how they thought each other group member would rate them. The researchers found more similarity between the students' ratings of themselves and their *perceptions* of how others would rate them than between their perceptions and the actual ratings given by their peers. In a more recent replication of this study, Quarentelli and Cooper (1966) followed a panel of dental students from entrance to graduation. This second study found that the correspondence between self-concept and the perceptions of others' opinions remained the same for the duration of the study, indicating that this relationship is not transitory. Their general conclusion supports Mead's theory. The *perceived* views of others, not their actual opinions, influence our self-concepts.

The views of Erving Goffman will be discussed in a later chapter. However, he added an important twist to the understanding of socialization which bears mentioning here. Goffman agreed with Mead that the self is created in social interaction. As we have seen, for Mead, this involved a relatively straightforward process of role-taking. Goffman, on the other hand, saw social interaction as something individuals learned with difficulty. He called this process *impression management*.

## CLASS AND SOCIALIZATION

In the previous chapter, we described Oscar Lewis's ideas about a culture of poverty. Lewis argued that poor children in Western countries are socialized to respond to their environment in certain ways. "By the time slum children are six or seven they have usually absorbed the basic attitudes and values of their subculture" (Lewis, 1966:21). Lewis's critics say that the behavioural patterns he observed are just adaptations to a particular set of circumstances. Whether or not one agrees with Lewis, there do seem to be class differences in socialization.

A series of sociological studies done in the United States has found consistent differences in parental values which seem related to the occupations of parents. "White-collar occupations are characterized by low supervision, an emphasis on people or ideas rather than objects, and a relatively high degree of self-reliance" (Ellis, Lee and Petersen 1979:387). Consequently, white-collar parents tend to place a high value on self-reliance in their children. In contrast, the occupational experiences of blue-collar parents mean they will place a high value on conformity in their children. Anthropologists studying cross-cultural patterns of socialization have found similar differences. It seems that self-reliance is valued in hunting and gathering societies, whereas conformity is valued in agricultural societies. Thus, research in both disciplines suggests that "where adults are closely supervised in their economic, political or family roles, they tend to value conformity in their children; where they are more autonomous in these roles, self-reliance becomes a primary socialization value" (Ellis, Lee and Petersen, 1979:390). Ellis, Lee and Petersen tested this idea with data from 122 different cultures and found a universal relationship between autonomy for adults and the value of self-reliance in children.

Another study (Alwin, 1984) found that parents now place a higher value on autonomy than they did a generation ago. Public opinion surveys done in Detroit in 1958, 1971 and 1983 revealed some interesting differences. Parents were asked:

> If you had to choose, which thing would you pick as the most important for a child to learn to prepare him for life?
> a) to obey
> b) to be well-liked or popular
> c) to think for himself
> d) to work hard
> e) to help others when they need help

Respondents were asked to rank their top four choices. Alwin found "To think for himself" was the most preferred quality and that the number of parents citing this as most important increased over time. Being well-liked was the least preferred and this became less important over time. Obedience decreased in importance, but hard work increased. The number of parents who valued being helpful remained stable. Since the change was due primarily to shifting attitudes among Roman Catholic respondents, Alwin concluded that the differences were due to the increased assimilation of ethnic group members who were Roman Catholic.

Another way to look at the relationship between class and socialization is to focus on children's perceptions of social class differences and the ways these are legitimized. An American study (Lauer, 1974) discovered that even children in grade two could rank occupations by prestige. Furthermore, the children's ranking closely resembled the rankings established in national studies, and the accuracy of the ranking increased with the ages of the children. "By the time we reach grade six, the rank correlation is nearly .9 and the children are quite capable of legitimating the ranking by reference to occupational functioning, prerequisites, and rewards. . . . Thus, beginning in the home and continuing in the school, these children have been socialized to accept the inequalities implied in the ranking and to perpetuate them through legitimating reasons (Lauer 1974:179, 181).

In a study of Toronto-area children, Baldus and Tribe (1978) used pictures and stories to assess young children's perceptions of social inequality. The pictures were presented in sets. The first set showed two men, one well dressed and one casually dressed. The children were also shown pictures of two houses (one taken in a high-income area of the city, one in a working-class area), two different living rooms, and two cars (one old and one new and expensive). Children in grades one, three and six played a game matching the sets of pictures. Children's ability to match correctly increased with age but was not affected by the children's sex, their school environment or their parents' social class. The children also provided ready evaluations of the two men. The well-dressed man was described as cheerful, nice, intelligent and well liked. They described the casually dressed man as tough, lazy, likely to swear, steal or drink and not caring much about his family.

The researchers felt one of their most important findings was the similarity of response despite social class differences among the children, for these evaluations are keys to the children's self-concepts as well as to their evaluations of others.

There are, however, important social class differences in the socialization of boys and girls. Research evidence (summarized in Weitzman, 1984) concludes that working-class and lower-class families are more concerned about cultivating differences between boys and girls. Middle-class parents seem more concerned with developing a range of behavioural traits in their children, whether boys or girls. In the following section, we will look more specifically at these kinds of differences.

# SEX-ROLE SOCIALIZATION

Three main determinants of status in most cultures are age, sex and social class. The preceding section described how social class differences are related to differences in socialization. While many sociologists do not agree with Lewis, accumulated research findings describe social class differences in socialization *practices*. Later in this chapter, we will describe how socialization changes throughout the life cycle. This analysis assumes that as we learn new roles, we internalize society's expectations about *age specific* behaviours. In this section, we will focus on sex-role socialization, a topic which has received a great deal of research attention.

Traditionally, differences between men and women were assumed to be based on natural or biological differences between the sexes. Much research was devoted to specifying the nature of these differences. In the 1970s this presumption was carefully scrutinized. Analysis of previous research findings by Maccoby and Jacklin (1974)— who reviewed over 1400 studies—and others, revealed that many behavioural and attitudinal differences once thought to be based on biological propensities were, in fact, learned capacities. Recently, biological determinism has received a new lease on life. However, when we encounter determinist views, we should keep in mind that scientific discoveries have a political context. The current swing back to determinism should be seen as a reflection of deep-seated resistance to change (Oakley, 1981). Feminists like Rossi (1984) also argue that some sex differences are influenced by biology, and that at certain points in time (i.e., during puberty or pregnancy), biological processes are more important than at other times. Rossi feels that if we correctly identify these differences, they can be the basis of compensatory socialization for both females and males. Chapter 10 will describe these findings in greater detail.

Research evidence suggests that *gender* (learned) differences are much more significant than *sex* (biological) differences. Gender differences refer to psychological traits such as intuition, dependance or aggression usually associated with masculinity or femininity.

Most societies attach importance to both sex and gender differences. Some expectations will be more or less universal (usually those related to childrearing and economic roles); others will vary from culture to culture. In every society, these expectations are based on stereotypes. Sex stereotyping begins before birth. The size, the activity and the position of the fetus are presumed to be related to its sex. While prenatal sex differences may largely be based on folklore, it is clear that strong reinforcement of gender stereotypes takes place almost from the moment of birth. Rubin, Provenzano and Luria (1974) interviewed parents of newborn children within 24 hours of the birth. Although the babies were similar in size and other physical characteristics, they were described very differently by their parents. Daughters were described as "softer, finer featured, weaker, smaller, prettier, more inattentive, more awkward, and more delicate." Sons, on the other hand, were described as "firmer, larger featured, better co-ordinated, more alert, stronger and hardier." Thus, the stage is set within the first hours of life. Furthermore, the male children are still seen as more desirable than female children. Oakley (1981:95) asked London women expecting their first child what sex they preferred. Fifty-four percent said boys; 22 percent said girls and the rest didn't care. After the children were born, 93 percent of those who had boys were pleased, but 44 percent of those who had girls were disappointed. When my own daughter was born in 1979, I was stunned when one of the nurses remarked, "Oh well, maybe you'll have better luck next time."

Cooley and Mead identified the importance of early interaction with family members, or *significant others*, to use Mead's phrase. They did not, however, explore the process of developing a sexual identity. The following paragraphs describe several psychological theories of personality development as they relate to gender identification. (More detailed descriptions are found in O'Connell, 1979; and Mackie, 1982.)

## PSYCHOANALYTIC THEORY

Freud identified several stages of psychological development: oral, anal, phallic, latent and genital. Sexual differences in development began, for Freud, with the phallic stage, when both boys and girls resolve their early attachment to their mothers. A boy sees his father as a rival for his mother's affection, but fears this rivalry will lead to castration—as he assumes it has for girls. Fear of castration is the mechanism for resolving a boy's Oedipal complex. Resolving the Oedipal complex by identifying with his father develops a strong superego in a boy. A girl's discovery that she is missing a penis leads her to blame her mother and desire her father. For a girl, however, the Oedipal complex is not easily resolved. Consequently, female superegos are weaker. Thus, for Freud, personality differences are rooted in physiological differences, specifically, in the awareness of having or not having a penis. Such biological determinism was strongly criticized by Freud's contemporaries and by others who agree with other tenets of his psychoanalytic theories. The theories of penis envy and fear of castration simply do not have empirical justification.[2]

## IDENTIFICATION THEORY

Many psychologists have pursued the idea that normal development depends on identification with the same-sexed parent. However, it is difficult to demonstrate that young children will identify with a parent before they are aware of themselves as either male or female. Nor is it clear why boys would necessarily identify with fathers when, in most cases, they have more contact with mothers. For most children, parents are but two of many people they encounter, including, of course, the ever-present models on television.

## SOCIAL LEARNING THEORY

Social learning theory says gender roles are learned through *reinforcement*. The process of gender learning presumably begins at birth, when children are labelled according to sex, and is reinforced throughout childhood. This reinforcement encourages children to generalize some behaviours and to avoid others. However, research has not found a strong association between the behaviour of children and the behaviour of their same-sexed parent. Children learn sex-specific behaviour, but it is not clear that they learn it exclusively, or even primarily, from their same-sexed parent, as the theory suggests.

## COGNITIVE DEVELOPMENT THEORY

Cognitive development theory assumes that gender identity begins when children categorize themselves as either a boy or a girl. Usually this occurs late in the child's

[2] I cannot resist countering Freud's anecdotal evidence of penis envy with an observation made by my five-year-old daughter. As she said when she noticed her young brother pulling his penis in the bath: "Maybe he wants to pull it off so he can be like me."

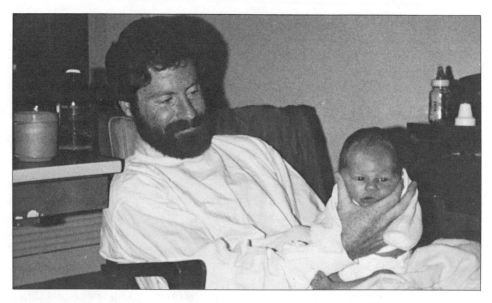

*Changing gender roles have blurred the rigid distinctions of the 1950s.*

second year. After this, children are moved to behave in ways consistent with the gender label, and their attention is focused on same-sexed models. So for Kohlberg, the main proponent of this theory, social reinforcement is far less important in learning gender roles than cognitive development. While the social learning and cognitive development theories seem to correspond to our sense of how gender identity is acquired, both focus on *differences* in male/female behaviour.

Some recent approaches to sex-role socialization move beyond dichotomizing gender roles. For example, a series of studies (Bem, 1974) have focused on individuals who appear to have a balance of masculine and feminine characteristics. Bem calls such individuals *androgenous* and reports that one-third of those she has studied fit this description. Recent recognition of the restrictive nature of traditional male and female roles make alternative conceptualizations such as this attractive. Changes in women's roles, particularly in labour force participation, and the consequent increased involvement of men in domestic tasks have blurred the rigid sex-role distinctions of the 1950s. Even 20 years ago, it would have been impossible to imagine that, by the mid-1980s, thousands of young boys would be caring for their own Cabbage Patch dolls.

The women's movement has been responsible for many changes in what is expected of women and men. Both structural and ideological changes challenge traditional sex-role socialization, although some people will always prefer the "good old days." Kimball (1975) feels that there is some ambivalence in the messages young girls are receiving. They still seem to be presented with two choices: to be feminine *or* to be competent. The conflict this ambivalence produces, particularly in the face of the adolescent desire to be popular, may cause young women to make choices that will not maximize their future economic security. When journalist Ann Pappert (1980) visited a Toronto high school in 1979, she found that the main goal of most young women was marriage. They expected, perhaps like their mothers, to be gainfully employed for a short time before they had children. Lindell (1982) found that *working-class* high-school women were realistic about their probable future in the labour force (although they had no specific career plans) and so accepted the inevitability of day-care for their children. *Middle-class* students expected to leave the labour force when children arrived, an expectation which current labour-force trends suggest may not be realistic.

## THE MASS MEDIA

The media has been strongly criticized for contributing to the stereotyping of gender roles. The results of hundred of studies of media content support this conclusion. Women are underrepresented, stereotyped and trivialized by the media. In an extensive study of sex-role socialization, Fischer and Cheyne (1977) concluded that the media are far more consistent in stereotyping women than either parents or the educational system. And children spend more time watching television than they do at school.

The role of the media in establishing similar stereotypes about social class differences has been less extensively studied. We know that the media exaggerate the number of professionals in the population. Younger "middle-Americans" are the most numerous protagonists in media drama. Nonwhites, like women, are underrepresented and stereotyped.

George Gerbner, whose studies of American television content were described in Chapter 5 feels strongly about the influence of television in socializing young people.

> Television is the central and most pervasive mass medium in American culture and it plays a distinctive and historically unprecedented role. Other media are accessible to the individual (usually at the point of literacy and mobility) only after the socializing functions of home and family life have begun. In the case of television, however, the individual is introduced virtually at birth into a powerful flow of messages and images. The television set has become a key member of the family, the one who tells most of the stories most of the time. Its massive flow of stories showing what things are, how things work, and what to do about them has become the common socializer of our times. These stories form a coherent if mythical "world" in every home. Television dominates the symbolic environment of modern life.(From Gerbner et al. "The Mainstreaming of America," *Journal of Communication* 30(3) p. 14.)

## ADOLESCENT SOCIALIZATION

Some have suggested that adolescence was a creation of advertisers who "discovered" that young people had money to spend. Others have argued that the identification of this age group as distinct from others accompanied the latter stages of industrialization and the introduction of compulsory education. Whatever its origins, adolescence is clearly a social construct and not a natural stage of development.

In North America, we see adolescence as a period of change and ambivalence, growth and experimentation, in which young people gain independance from their families and prepare for adult reponsibilities. Simmons (Mortimer and Simmons, 1978) suggests that childhood socialization is primarily concerned with regulating biological drives, whereas adolescent socialization focuses on values and self-image. Because the period of economic dependence is prolonged in our society by increased education (and high youth unemployment), adolescence stretches well into the 20s.

Lyell (1973) argues that adolescent feelings of ambivalence and low self-esteem occur because, until people enter the labour force, their activities are not generally highly regarded. She used a *semantic differential scale* to test this assumption. She asked young people to score themselves on 25 adjective pairs (i.e., active-passive, strong-weak, good-bad), first, as they would like to be and second, as they really are. A high correspondence between these two ratings was taken to indicate high self-esteem. The four groups in the study were: young adult working males; young female adults who were not working; female adolescents who were not working; and male adolescents who were not working.

She found that working adult males felt more positively about themselves than the other three groups, all of whom showed considerable evidence of low self-esteem. Thus, Lyell argues, when adolescents are aloof, indifferent or apathetic, we should understand that these feelings result from their subordination to and exclusion from the formal occupational system.

The socialization theories described earlier relate specifically to childhood social-ization and to the development of the self. Childhood socialization is presumed to be closely tied to interactions within the family, whereas adolescence, as Campbell (1975) describes it, involves a period of *unlearning*, as young people develop a sense of autonomy and independence. According to Campbell, the most significant ex-perience of adolescence is "the demise in *relative* influence of the family as a reference group and the central emotional pillar" (1975:34). This does not mean that the family becomes unimportant. But the influence of peers, the media and the school is greater than ever before.

Parsons (1942) introduced the term *youth culture* over 40 years ago. Since then, sociologists and psychologists have debated whether adolescence is a transition period or whether this age group has a distinct culture. In Chapter 5, the study of British youth culture was described from the point of view of expressive symbols. North American studies of adolescent culture have usually adopted the framework of more traditional studies of subcultures as groups with distinct norms and values. In his study of Illinois high schools, Coleman (1961) described students as sharing an adolescent culture. Because adolescents spend a lot of time at school, or in school-related activities, many of which are unrelated to their formal education, and because most of their interactions involve others of the same age group, Coleman concluded that these young people have a distinct adolescent subculture. In this environment, popularity and athletics were valued above academic achievement, a finding Campbell sees as convincing evidence of a strong youth culture. "Only a youth culture of considerable strength could sustain antieducational and antiintellectual values in the very setting of an institution established to serve educational purposes!" (Campbell, 1975:40).

Tanner (1978) studied youth culture in five secondary schools in Edmonton, Alberta. Based on the findings of an earlier British study (Murdock and Phelps,

1973), Tanner hypothesized that "commitment to school is inversely associated with the two main variants of 'youth culture,' namely pop-media culture and street culture" (1978:91). The British study found that working-class boys with low commitment to school were likely to be oriented to a street culture, whereas middle-class students with low commitment (mainly girls) chose the pop-media culture as an alternative. Tanner's study tested this relationship in a Canadian setting.

Tanner operationally defined street culture as self-reported delinquency. He found that low commitment to school was related to high involvement in self-reported delinquency, that this was inversely related to socioeconomic status and that the relationship was stronger for boys than girls. In other words, working-class boys were the most likely to be involved in delinquent behaviour—if their commitment to school was low—and middle-class girls were least likely. No such straightforward relationship emerged concerning student commitment to school and their interest in popular music. School-rejecting boys were more involved in music than school-rejecting girls, but this was unrelated to social class. Tanner suggested that music *may* provide a more acceptable form of revolt for girls and middle-class school rejectors—although the two aspects of youth culture are not mutually exclusive.

Other sociologists are skeptical about the notion of a distinct youth culture. As Elkin and Handel (1978:231) argue, "With regard to fundamental values, the continuity of adolescent socialization with adulthood outweighs the discontinuity." Campbell's (1975:41-2) point is that there is considerable correspondence between parental and adolescent values. Because parents want their children to be well liked and because they want good relationships with their children, they are unlikely to strongly oppose too many aspects of the youth culture. In addition, the peer group's influence is tempered because parents control "scarce and valued resources," including their approval. Furthermore, Campbell says that early socialization has created important *cultural boundaries*. "By virtue of membership in a family, one is *assigned* to a social class, to a residential area, to a race, to a moral system, to a religion, to an ethnic tradition, to a social space" (1975:43). As children mature, they increase their contacts and experiences, but these will not be random events or associations. By and large, they will be compatible with previous experiences. It is, therefore, unlikely that the school environment will be very different from the environment the child already knows. Middle-class children will attend a high school with other middle-class children, who will likely value school achievement. Certainly, some students will rebel, but usually their defiance will not pose a significant challenge to parental values. In a later chapter, this point will be reconsidered in the context of social inequality, when the discussion will focus on how the schools reproduce the existing social class structure.

## ADULT SOCIALIZATION

In the introductory paragraphs of this chapter, we noted that socialization is a life-long process. While this assumption meets with little argument, adult socialization has not been a major focus of research. Adult socialization differs from childhood socialization because children are more malleable. The accumulated learning of adults makes them more resistant to change. Nevertheless, as we change our jobs, marry,

*Rituals like graduation or marriage ceremonies help to signal changing status.*

have children, cope with middle-age and so on, we are continually being socialized. Many of these changes are life-cycle changes, although the fact that we can predict childbirth, retirement or widowhood does not mean that the adjustment will be easy. When these changes occur, individuals go through a period of *disengagement* as they change roles. The idea of disengagement has been used to describe the experience of widowhood and divorce, although it can describe any role change (Mortimer and Simmons, 1978). Rituals like graduation or marriage ceremonies help to signal changing status.

Some socialization is formal, as in the training we receive in professional schools or in work-related courses. Increasingly, formal training is available in areas previously left to the family, the schools or to other agents of socialization, or for which socialization was once taken for granted. Thus, new parents may feel inadequate without training in childbirth and later in child-care, and people anticipating retirement sign-up for courses in retirement training. In many ways, adult socialization is informal. Without being told, we quickly learn what standards of behaviour are expected in new social or work situations. Students, for example, are adept at cataloguing these kinds of differences in behaviour and using them in comparing universities.

In some cases, we can learn to adjust to new situations because our previous experiences gave us the capacity to imagine what new experiences will be like. Sociologists call this preparation *anticipatory socialization*. "Anticipatory socialization refers to training in skills and values that is oriented toward a new role that one will enter at some future time" (Campbell, 1975:47). The effectiveness of anticipatory socialization will depend on how ambiguous the new situation is and how similar to our previous experience.

Professional schools are important socializing agents for adults, and medical schools in particular have been studied in this regard. What students learn during these years goes beyond acquiring technical skills. They are learning how to behave like doctors. Some researchers have questioned whether professional schools play an important role in socializing students. They argue that the similarity of attitudes and values results from selective recruitment of middle- and upper-class students rather than socialization. In their panel study of Canadian medical students, Chappell and Colwill (1981) found that medical schools effectively change some attitudes. But they also found that students recruited to medical schools shared certain attitudes at the outset. Interestingly, these seemed unrelated to social class or sex. Although these researchers do not describe their findings in terms of anticipatory socialization, it seems that a medical student's orientation to the profession begins long before she enters medical school. If so, she will enter medical school with an orientation which is reinforced during her prolonged training period.

In most cases, we cannot anticipate what it will mean to our sense of self to experience the sudden death of someone we love, our parents' divorce or being fired. When we encounter these situations, we have to learn new rules. There are, however, occasions when people choose to, or are required to, change their behaviour in rather dramatic ways. This process is called *resocialization*. For example, when families or individuals relocate for school or work, they may find that their previous world view is fundamentally challenged. Wives of men who go to work in Arab countries find it extremely difficult to adjust to the many social restrictions placed on women there. Companies often expand considerable energy preparing employees for this culture shock. Sometimes, resocialization is occasioned by social changes that individuals cannot control, as when the nature of a job is completely altered by technology.

Generally, the term "resocialization" applies to the kind of learning that goes on in what Goffman (1967) called *total institutions*. Total institutions, like prisons, boarding schools or mental hospitals, make considerable effort to alter existing values and self-concepts. Because individuals are removed from familiar surroundings and because their daily routines are altered to conform to the goals of the institution, the changes in behaviour can be dramatic.

Seiber and Gordon (1981) introduced the idea of *socializing organizations* as a way of understanding socialization. Socializing organizations include total institutions, as well as schools, job-training programs, counselling centres and voluntary associations. These organizations are formally chartered to bring about some change in their members, but often the explicitly stated aims are less important than the latent messages they send. "As recruits participate in the organization they learn its social and speech etiquettes, modes of self-presentation, rituals, routines, symbolic codes of deference, and other patterns of social relations" (Seiber and Gordon, 1981:7). Sometimes, there is a formal period of orientation designed to facilitate this kind of learning. An extreme example is the introduction to military training usually referred to as "boot camp." Universities customarily hold orientation weeks, where "recruits" are introduced to the informal side of university life.

Much of adult socialization is self-initiated. When adults join organizations like Weight Watchers, Parents Without Partners or homophile groups, for example, they do so because they seek the social support these groups provide. It is during transition periods that this support is most needed. The consciousness raising groups that characterized the women's movement in the 1960s provided forums for women to discuss the changes they were experiencing. The human potential movement of the 1970s also had a significant impact on changing values and beliefs. One social analyst (Yankelovich, 1981) estimated that as many as 80 percent of Americans were involved in a search for self-fulfillment in the 1970s. He estimated that 17 percent were deeply committed to the search. Whether adults change as a result of these experiences will depend on the extent of the changes sought and the other kinds of demands placed upon them (Mortimer and Simmons, 1978).

## SUMMARY

In this chapter, you have been introduced to several concepts used by sociologists to better understand socialization and also to a number of studies that develop these concepts. Generally, sociologists view socialization as a process that continues throughout life and that is influenced by all of our social interactions. Social class and sex differences in socialization were related to behavioural differences among adults.

In the past, some sociologists described socialization as if it were imposed on individuals. Some argued that different personality types developed in different cultural settings. In contrast, Cooley and Mead helped to shed light on ways in which individuals are actively engaged in their own socialization process. Socialization is not something that simply happens to us. The messages we receive during socialization are inconsistent and sometimes contradictory, and we all draw our own conclusions from these competing influences as we establish our own life course. Individual life chances are strongly affected by structural variables, the most important of which are sex, race and social class.

## DISCUSSION QUESTIONS

1. Talk to your parents about what they considered to be important values for your early development. What differences do you anticipate in the raising of your children?

2. Some people have argued that the entertainment media provide lessons in "who counts" in our society. The next time you are watching television, think about what power relations are implied in the program.

3. Interview a foreign student in one of your classes to find out what resocialization he or she experienced in coming to a North American university.

4. Is Alwin correct in assuming that the socialization values of immigrants are changing? What aspects of traditional socialization remain?

5. Feminists object to the use of the generic "he" or "man" because they argue that people hearing these terms envision a male referent. The study by Alwin (page 141) contains examples of such usage. Would Alwin's results have been different if a nonsexist term had been used? What if "she" was substituted for "he" in the questionnaire? Would more parents have cited being helpful as most important?

6. The underrepresentation of women in educational materials is an important socializing experience. Compare this text to other sociology texts and to introductory texts in other disciplines to see if women are underrepresented in them. Consider such things as the number of pictures and other references to women.

# 7

# Aging and the Life Process

## *Maureen Baker*

# INTRODUCTION: CHANGING AGE STRUCTURES

Aging involves more than wrinkles, grey hair and diminished strength. It also implies psychological changes, different social treatment and retirement. Since the turn of the century, Canada's population has been aging. As in other industrialized countries, birth rates have fallen, infant mortality has declined and life expectancies have increased. The "baby-boomers," born from 1945 to 1965, are grown up and will constitute a huge group of older citizens by the year 2000. These demographic changes have led to increased political concern about, and academic interest in, aging.

In the 1930s, when birth rates plunged, demographers and policy makers became concerned about the aging population. But after World War II, when birth rates bounced back they became preoccupied with the construction of facilities for the large numbers of school-aged children. Since 1965, birth rates have fallen again for several reasons. For one thing, the birth-control pill, licensed in 1960 and marketed in 1961, was soon widely used. Expanding economic opportunities have enticed married women into the labour force, and new methods of contraception allow couples to more reliably plan their family size. Increasing costs of childrearing and an ideology promoting self-development discourage large families. Continuing urbanization and industrialization have decreased the benefits of having large families and have actually made them a liability.

Since the 1960s, the average age of the population has been gradually rising. But compared to some European nations, Canada's population is relatively young. The more developed and industrialized countries tend to have a higher proportion of older citizens than the developing countries. In 1981, when 9.7 percent of Canada's population was 65 and over, 11.4 percent of the United States', 13.5 percent of France's, 14.4 percent of Denmark's and 16.3 percent of Sweden's population were 65 and over (National Council of Welfare, 1984:19). These countries provide proof that an aging population need not cause economic stagnation, insufficient pension funds or intergenerational hostility (Myles, 1982:36).

The major reasons for Canada's aging population have been declining fertility rates and increased life expectancy. The crude birth rate fell from 29.3, in 1921, to 15.0 births per 1000 population in 1983 (Statistics Canada, 1985:2; Kalbach and McVey, 1979:96). Consequently, the proportion of the population aged 0 to 19 has dropped from 43.7 percent in 1921 to 32.0 percent in 1981 and is expected to decline to 26.7 percent in 2001 (Science Council of Canada, 1976:8). We have already experienced some of the consequences of this decline in the form of recent school closures and fewer jobs for teachers.

Increased life expectancy is also enlarging the proportion of elderly in this country. Infant mortality and maternal death rates have declined. From 1941 to 1981, the life expectancy at birth increased from 62.9 to 71.87 years for males and from 66.30 to 78.94 years for females (Statistics Canada, 1983a, 1984). Women's life expectancy is increasing faster than men's, a fact we will return to in our discussion of poverty among the elderly. But until our social policies change, longer lives mean a prolonged retirement and a reduced standard of living for many elderly. Our social institutions

TABLE 7-1  Percentage of the Canadian Population 65 and Over,
1901-2051*

|  | % 65 AND OVER |
| --- | --- |
| 1901 | 5.0% |
| 1911 | 4.7 |
| 1921 | 4.8 |
| 1931 | 5.6 |
| 1941 | 6.7 |
| 1951 | 7.8 |
| 1961 | 7.6 |
| 1971 | 8.1 |
| 1981 | 9.7 |
| 1991 | 11.1 |
| 2001 | 12.0 |
| 2011 | 13.1 |
| 2021 | 16.4 |
| 2031 | 19.6 |
| 2041 | 18.9 |
| 2051 | 18.2 |

* Figures after 1981 are projections.

Derived from National Council of Welfare. *Sixty-Five and Older*, Ottawa, February 1984, Table 1, p. 4.
Reprinted by permission of the National Council of Welfare.

are ill suited to accommodate even today's elderly, much less those of the future (Myles, 1982:36).

In periods of high immigration, such as the 1920s, the late 1940s and the 1960s, Canada received young people who produced fewer children than native-born Canadians. As these immigrants became older and immigration rates declined, these factors helped lower birth rates and raise life expectancies. Since the 1950s, the median age of the Canadian population has risen from 27.7 years in 1951 to 29.1 years in 1981, and it is expected to be about 36 years in 2001 (Science Council of Canada, 1976:14).

The postwar baby boom (1945-1965) recently led to an emphasis on young people and their needs. Yet now that these "boom babies" are approaching middle-age, the emphasis on youth is giving way to concern about the elderly. For one thing, business people can no longer assume that the "young look" will attract buyers. Facilities for children, especially schools, have experienced declining enrollment and funding cutbacks. More of society's resources will be allocated to older people as their numbers increase. Policies toward mandatory retirement are changing and accusations of age discrimination are brought before the courts. The connotations of "young" and

TABLE 7-2  Life Expectancy at Birth in Selected Countries, 1975-80

|  | MALE | FEMALE |
|---|---|---|
| Bangladesh | 46 years | 46 years |
| Brazil | 60 | 64 |
| Canada | 70 | 77 |
| Cuba | 71 | 74 |
| Ethiopia | 38 | 41 |
| France | 70 | 78 |
| Japan | 73 | 78 |
| Mexico | 62 | 67 |
| United Kingdom | 69 | 75 |
| United States | 69 | 77 |
| Sweden | 72 | 79 |

Selected from United Nations, *World Statistics in Brief*, New York, 1983. Copyright, United Nations (1983). Reproduced by permission.

"old" will change with the times, just as our images of childhood and adolescence have varied with demographic and economic trends.

# STAGES IN THE LIFE PROCESS
## CHANGING IMAGES OF CHILDHOOD

The ways in which adults have viewed childhood have varied with the economic importance of children to the family, infant mortality rates, and cultural and religious beliefs. In times of high infant mortality, parents could hardly afford to become emotionally involved with their children. If they relied on child labour to help support the family, they could not coddle their children or treat them much differently than adults. If children were "born evil," as was once believed, then strong discipline and education were necessary to produce Christian adults.

In preindustrial society, children were often treated as the property of their parents and were seen as an investment (Mackie, 1984:39). In the early stages of British industrialization, children's labour was required, but their exploitation led in the 1830s to legislation restricting the age of child workers to six years and over (Synnott, 1983). By 1847, British laws granted women and child workers a ten-hour day.

In Canada, children's labour was essential to the family on farms and in the working-class urban family. Through child emigration schemes, British children were brought to Canada and given room and board in return for their labour on family farms. After the restriction of child labour and the advent of compulsory education in the twentieth century, the economic value of children declined. Lower birth and infant mortality rates led to parents having stronger emotional attachment to children and an increased investment in their education and upbringing. More attention was paid to childrearing techniques, the protection of children from exploitation and their psychological development.

Increasingly today, children are segregated from adults and from children of other ages in day-care centres, nurseries and schools. Their play activities and organized leisure are similarly structured. The state protects them from most forms of paid labour and from adult abuse. Compulsory education until age 16 provides them with necessary training yet keeps them financially dependant on their parents. For middle-class children, childhood is viewed as a period of innocence, indulgence and play, but many working-class children still contribute to the family income, have little opportunity for play and little protection from the realities of adult life.

Since the upbringing of North American children is now assumed to cover much more than food, clothing and education, the cost of having children rises. Child-rearing expenses depend on the family's resources, and some parents feel compelled to provide a private school education, extra lessons and expensive clothes and leisure activities. Recent studies suggest that, in 1981, raising a child to age 18 could cost between \$84 000 and \$200 000, depending on the income of the parents (Eichler, 1983:262). We can no longer send our children away to work as apprentices or servants but must keep them at school until age 16. Compulsory schooling and the need for postsecondary education have raised the costs of childrearing and made people think twice about having large families. More people are having one child or are opting for childless marriage.

The experience of childhood varies considerably in different parts of the world. In developing countries, such as Pakistan or Haiti, many children die at an early age. Those who survive are sometimes forced by family circumstances to leave school before they reach adolescence in order to contribute to the family income. The separation between childhood and adult life is not as great in these countries as in North America. Only financially secure families can afford to allow their children to play and retain the innocence we attribute to this period of life.

## THE EMERGENCE OF ADOLESCENTS AS A UNIQUE GROUP

At the end of the seventeenth century, the development of formal education seg-regated children from the adult world. Yet most young people from about eight years old to their mid-twenties (or the age of marriage) lived in a state of semi-independence from their families as servants, apprentices or students boarding away from home (Gillis, 1974:2). Since children were usually assigned responsible roles at early ages, the onset of puberty was not particularly significant (Mackie, 1984:41). But as infant mortality and birth rates dropped, first among the higher classes and then among the working classes, parents were less likely to send their children to live elsewhere. Continued dependency on parents caused by a lengthened formal education led to the recognition of adolescence as a separate period (Ariès, 1960).

Although formal schooling increases young people's dependence on their parents, until a few decades ago only wealthier young people attended college or university. With the expansion of higher education in North America in the 1960s and 1970s, a larger proportion of the population continued their education beyond high school.

In 1951, 6 percent of 18- to 24-year-olds were in school, but by 1981, this figure increased to 22 percent (Statistics Canada, 1983:65).

Although many North American students work part-time to help finance their education, they often continue to live with their parents. Until the first full-time job or marriage, many young people rely on their families for housing, food and spending money. As jobs become increasingly scarce, adolescent dependence is prolonged.

Even though many young people live with their parents, the world of adolescence is often far apart from the adult world. Particularly for immigrant parents, the "youth culture," with its emphasis on sexuality, drugs and popular music, may be difficult to comprehend. Despite this apparent rift, many young people of the 1980s, like their parents, value marriage, children, steady work and home ownership (Baker, 1985).

As with childhood, however, adolescence is less likely to be recognized as a distinct stage of life in developing countries, where young people enter the work world at an earlier age. For example, in African countries, over 90 percent of 18- to 23-year-olds are not in school (UNESCO, 1984) and are either working at home, in the labour force or unemployed. Lack of government support for education and the need for family income make adolescence and adult life very similar in these countries.

## SYMBOLS OF ADULT STATUS

The coming of age ceremony has many variations, depending on the culture and the historical period. The bar mitzvah has been the Jewish ritual for the boy who reaches adult status, even though age 13 now seems remarkably young. In some social circles, the debutante ball introduces the young lady into society. High school or college graduation ceremonies play a similar role in the less affluent classes. But marriage remains a strong symbol of adult status and is accompanied by many rituals. The groom's stag party indicates his fun is now over as he takes on the adult responsibilities of a husband. Symbols of fertility (confetti or rice) are still thrown at the bride to indicate that her childbearing phase can now officially begin. Also surrounded by ceremony is the birth of the first child, an event often seen as the beginning of maturity and acceptance of adult responsibility.

Although marriage and childbirth are accompanied by social rituals, little formal preparation for either event exists in our society. We can easily buy a marriage licence, and we need no formal training to become a spouse or parent. This lack of preparation may be partially responsible for high rates of divorce and child abuse, as more complex demands are placed on modern families.

For those who do not marry, moving away from home and setting up an independent household usually is perceived as an indication of adult status. However, this is a relatively recent phenomenon. Unmarried people prior to the Second World War generally boarded with another family or lived with relatives. Living alone would have been considered improper, especially for women. The unmarried person, however, has sometimes been treated as less adult or responsible than a married person (Veevers, 1980). Yet the life of an unmarried adult certainly has changed over the past two generations, allowing greater independence from family and more opportunity for nonmarital sex. Celibacy is no longer expected of unmarried people. Fewer adults now fit into the nuclear family, even though the marriage rate remains high. More people marry, but an increasing number also divorce.

Most adults' middle years are occupied with raising a family and earning a living. About 85 percent of Canadians marry, and about 90 percent of these have children. The strains of parenting are apparent in increasing rates of child abuse and delinquency. Yet there are few places for the modern parent to learn childrearing skills, apart from psychology books or personal experience.

Whereas middle-class women used to be expected to care for the home or do volunteer work after their children reached school age, an increasing proportion of middle-aged women return to paid work in clerical or service occupations. The two-earner family has increased the standard of living of Canadian families and raised women's aspirations for more involvement in public life. When their children reach their teens and prepare to leave home, working mothers experience fewer personal anxieties than they used to when they remained at home as housewives. The "empty-nest" syndrome of the 1960s seems less prevalent in the 1980s.

Both sexes apparently experience mid-life and aging crises but for slightly different reasons. Men sometimes experience psychological problems when their work becomes less personally rewarding, when they realize that they have grown apart from their wives and children, or when they retire. Because women have been associated with youth, beauty, sexuality and fertility, their crises may come when their hair colour fades or their figure broadens. Menopause confronts them with loss of fertility, and children leaving home allows them more leisure but makes them less important at home. When the "nest" empties, many women begin second careers. Because so many women have worked at home for no pay and have been financially dependant on their husbands, they often find themselves alone and poor in their later years.

Although social scientists have gathered numerous facts about adult life (such as statistics on marriage, divorce, labour-force participation and unemployment rates), few have investigated adult development. We now realize that socialization occurs throughout life, but only a few authors have focused on crisis points or transition periods in adult life (Sheehy, 1974; Levinson, 1978). The developmental approach has been used mainly to study children.

## VARYING DEFINITIONS OF AGING

Definitions of "old" are sometimes based on changes in physical or mental functioning. Wrinkles form, muscles slacken, hair turns grey or falls out and activity declines. Reflexes slow and memory may lapse. But there is also a social and cultural aspect of aging. Many traditional cultures honour the aged, whereas most "modern" cultures do not. A society's definition of "old" is relative to life expectancy, which has generally increased over this century. Our society provides us with an official definition of old age: the age of 65, when we begin to receive Old Age Security cheques. This may also coincide with retirement, although many people in occupations requiring physical beauty or skill are considered old much before 65. But part of being old is seeing ourselves as old and behaving as if we were old (Roadburg, 1985:4-6).

Different perceptions of aging are apparent for men and women. While older men with greying temples and business suits have been used in advertising as symbols of knowledge and authority, older women have been associated with a loss of sexuality and attractiveness and with loneliness. Products to eradicate wrinkles, colour grey hair and smooth out "middle-age spread" have been sold to women to a much greater extent than to men. Women have been taught to associate youth with beauty and beauty with love. This double standard "perpetuates the view that women have nothing to offer but their bodies, and that no amount of intelligence, learning and wisdom can make up for their lost bloom of youth" (Dulude, 1978:4,5).

## Retirement

For men, retirement is often seen as the beginning of old age. While the nineteenth-century life style involved a more gradual winding down of work, without any official retirement (Synge, 1980), mandatory retirement in the twentieth century has made the transition to old age abrupt. Most retirement research focuses on males. However, for an increasing number of women, retirement from paid work is also important. But some have argued that women are more likely to have retained interests other than paid work. And fewer women officially retire. Only 35 percent of women 55 to 64 years old, compared to 70 percent of men, were in the labour force in 1985 (Statistics Canada, 1985). Most people experience a drop in income when they leave their jobs. Since not all workers receive employer-sponsored pensions, many must retire on Old Age Security, Canada Pension Plan, the Guaranteed Income Supplement or their own savings or investments.

Preretirement courses and planning are becoming more common, especially among government workers. New policies of having older employees work two or three days a week and receive partial pension for the rest of the week have been tried in Sweden and are being discussed in Canada. This gradual retirement may ease the unemployment situation for younger workers and assist retiring employees to psychologically adjust to more leisure time.

Since retired men are more likely than retired women to be married and still living with their spouses, the retired man can often enjoy greater companionship with his wife and take a more active role in the home. But wives of retired men sometimes find that their newly retired husbands disrupt their daily routines, and an adjustment period is necessary for both partners. Retired women are less likely to have living spouses or to be married at all, and so having a network of friends or relatives is even more important for retired women. Women who have reached retirement age are more likely than their male counterparts to have maintained close contact with their children and developed close same-sex friends.

## Relationships Among the Elderly

The three-generation household in which children supported their elderly parents was an exception in North America and Europe in past centuries (Laslett, 1971; Synge, 1980). However, the *modified extended family* is still an important support system for the elderly. By this we mean that elderly parents and children maintain separate households yet retain considerable social contact. However, with the decrease in family size, fewer children are available to assist their elderly parents. With greater geographic mobility, children are more likely to telephone but visit less

*Contact with children and grandchildren is important to the elderly, though the three-generation household was an exception in North America and Europe in past centuries.*
Public Archives Canada/PA-40744.

frequently than in the past. And with higher divorce rates, some grandparents lose contact with grandchildren when a daughter- or son-in-law receives custody.

Elderly parents usually see or speak to their children quite frequently. Yet the frequency of contact does not seem to affect old women's feelings of satisfaction or well-being (Beaudoin et al., 1973; Arling, 1976). On the other hand, contact with friends and neighbours is an important indicator of well-being. As people get old, though, more of their friends and acquaintances die. New friends are harder to make and resources for reciprocating friends' and neighbours' favours may be minimal (Dulude, 1978:72).

Throughout adult life, cross-sex friendships seem difficult to maintain without actual or perceived sexual involvement. Since the elderly are often perceived as "sexless," cross-sex relationships are more acceptable for them. Although these may be encouraged by professionals working with the elderly, sons and daughters do not always encourage their elderly parents to remarry after widowhood.

Mutual help groups and senior citizen clubs provide many elderly with new friendships and activities. Government subsidies provide meeting rooms, transportation and personnel to organize events for seniors. Widows' support groups sometimes help the elderly through bereavement and the adjustment to living alone.

There is a controversy in the literature on aging about how stable the personality remains throughout adult life. Some think that women become more assertive with age and men more nurturant and affiliative (Troll and Parron, 1981). This sex-role change may result from the interaction of biological changes, life events, adult socialization processes and cultural changes in expectations. In old age, women are more likely than men to be living alone and need to be more independent than in earlier years. On the other hand, older men lose their physical strength, stamina and their jobs and may feel the need for stronger relationships than in their younger years.

## Widowhood

In our society, men usually marry women about two years younger than themselves. Since men also have shorter life expectancies than women, wives often outlive their husbands. In North America, the ratio of widows to widowers is about 5:1 for those over age 60. As a result, most of the research on widowhood deals with older women (Lopata, 1973, 1979; Harvey and Bahr, 1980) and focuses on personal adjustment problems and stages in the bereavement process (McPherson, 1983). Although an increasing number of women of preretirement age are in the labour force, most elderly women spent their younger years taking care of their families by doing unpaid domestic work. Consequently, they have no work-related pensions and few savings. It is not surprising that many widowed elderly women live below the poverty line. Policy-oriented research has mainly dealt with how to raise this group above the poverty line.

Although it is statistically common for women to outlive their spouses, there is little preparation for bereavement. Because elderly people have often played complementary roles in their marriage, the death of one spouse often leaves the other helpless. The widower must cook and keep house, and the widow must look after her finances, home and car (if she has one). Children, siblings and neighbours often help out, but many elderly people prefer to be independent. Living in senior-citizens' apartments helps some to cope. Others benefit from more services to enable them to stay in their own homes.

Remarriage after widowhood is becoming increasingly common, but the double standard allows a man to marry a woman his own age or much younger, whereas the older woman generally does not marry a younger man. This makes remarriage more likely for elderly men than for elderly women.

In our culture, death is still not openly discussed. Funeral homes fill their ceremonies with euphemisms to protect clients from the reality of death. Modern medicine has expropriated the free will of the dying and now prolongs life with respirators and other devices. Our lives have been lengthened but not always improved. A person is now likely to die alone in a hospital rather than at home with friends and family. But as a higher proportion of the population reaches old age, perhaps death will become not only an open topic but also a more dignified one.

# SOCIAL THEORIES ON AGING

Many theorists have tried to explain aspects of the social process of aging. Their approaches have been similar to theories in other fields of sociology and can be grouped into structural-functional theories, conflict theories or symbolic interactionist theories. Because so many factors influence the aging process, any type of theory must focus on a particular set of factors, often to the exclusion of others. Thus, different theories explain different aspects of aging and are often based on contradictory assumptions.

In the *structural-functional* tradition, Cumming and Henry (1961) developed the *disengagement theory* to explain the aging process. They suggested that older people gradually withdraw from society by retiring from work and becoming less active in the community. This voluntary withdrawal assists the individual to gradually accept his or her diminishing capacities and allows younger people to fill job and community vacancies. However, critics have suggested that this process is neither universal nor voluntary. The elderly are edged out by colleagues and mandatory retirement policies, poor health or societal neglect. Disengagement in one realm of life does not imply that a person has disengaged generally. Nor is there any indication that this process benefits anyone, least of all the older person. Successful adjustment to aging may involve maintaining high levels of involvement and activity for as long as possible (Havighurst et al., 1968).

In the same tradition, Arnold Rose (1965) described the elderly as a distinct subculture, noting that they often live in age-segregated accommodation, experience common problems and social treatment and consequently often develop a group consciousness. However, socioeconomic, ethnic and life-style differences among the elderly may outweigh the similarities.

*Conflict* theorists have suggested that the elderly, like women, children and certain ethnic groups, have less economic and political power in society than middle-aged white males. With below average incomes after retirement, less formal schooling than younger people and retirement from public positions, the elderly can easily be pushed aside and ignored. Younger people may support early retirement policies to open new positions in the labour force and state-supported residential care to relieve the younger generation from the burden of caring for their elderly relatives. Conflict between generations may be exaggerated under certain economic conditions, such as high unemployment, few promotional possibilities or rapid changes in social values (Tindale and Marshall, 1980). Yet with increased numbers of elderly in North America and many European countries, "grey power" may gain in strength. Senior citizen groups in Canada mustered considerable political strength, for example, in protests against the 1985 pension deindexation.

*Symbolic interaction* theories of aging analyse people's perceptions of the experience of growing old. The self-concept of the elderly may be influenced by how they are treated, by the facilities which are offered to them or by their own psychological reactions to their aging bodies. Lack of friendships due to the death of friends or spouse, social isolation because of the inability to walk or poor health and continual contact with other elderly people in similar situations may explain some of the behaviour and attitudes of the elderly. Simone de Beauvoir (1970) and Neugarten (1968) have used this perspective.

Aging has also been researched from a social policy or social welfare point of view. Considerable work related to mandatory retirement, poverty of the elderly and pensions has been prepared for governments who view the elderly as a vulnerable group in need of special policy attention. Demographers have also investigated the implications of the increasing number of elderly people for social services and social policy.

# THE IMPLICATIONS OF AN AGING POPULATION
## DEPENDENCY RATIOS

In studying the consequences of the demographic shift of the Canadian population, *dependency ratios* are sometimes used as a rough measure of society's needs for social, medical, educational or other facilities. They compare the proportion of the population *assumed* financially dependent (children under 20 and the elderly over 65) with the proportion of the population *presumed* in the labour force (those 20-64 years old). Dependency ratios are used with other demographic data, especially on a provincial or municipal basis, when setting priorities for social programs. While the dependency ratio for children has been declining in Canada, the ratio for the elderly has increased from 8.8 in 1911 to 17 in 1981, and it is expected to be about 33 in 2031 (National Council of Welfare, 1984:21).

TABLE 7-3   Percentage of Population 65 and Older by Country, 1981 (or Nearest Year)

| | |
|---|---|
| Japan | 8.8% |
| Canada | 9.7 |
| United States | 11.4 |
| Netherlands | 11.5 |
| France | 13.5 |
| Italy | 13.5 |
| Denmark | 14.4 |
| Norway | 14.8 |
| United Kingdom | 15.0 |
| West Germany | 15.5 |
| Sweden | 16.3 |

National Council of Welfare, *Sixty-Five and Older*, Ottawa, February 1984, Table 12, p. 19. Reprinted by permission of the National Council of Welfare.

Significant provincial and regional differences are apparent in Canadian dependency ratios, reflecting different levels of economic development, immigration and internal migration. For example, Saskatchewan has experienced high levels of out-migration within the past ten years and consequently has a smaller percentage of working-age people. Since young people searching for work often leave rural areas for larger cities, and since retired people often leave large cities and farms for small towns, smaller communities usually have higher dependency ratios for the elderly

## FOUR MILLION SENIORS BY 2000, REPORT SAYS

By DOROTHY LIPOVENKO

More than one in four Canadians will be older than 65 early in the next century, a federal report released yesterday says.

The report by Statistics Canada says more than four million Canadians will be elderly by the turn of the century and their number will exceed seven million by 2031, when they will "reach an astonishing 27 per cent of the population."

The population projections are based on the current fertility level of 1.4 children a family.

Improvements in life expectancy will alter the numerical imbalance between men and women over 65. By 2006, there will be 76 elderly men for every 100 elderly women—up slightly from the current ratio of 74 to 100.

About equal numbers of dependents—the young and the old—will make up the population early in the twenty-first century, but this pattern will end and not reverse. By 2031, there will be two retired Canadians for every person 18 and younger, the report says.

The bulge in the elderly population is the result of the baby boomers, the generation born in the 15 years after the Second World War ended.

"Canadian society will be substantially different from what it is today" because of changes in the age trends, the report by Anatole Romaniuc concludes.

In 1981, 10 per cent of the population was over 65, while 28 per cent was 17 or younger.

Despite improvements in life expectancy, baby boomers will push the annual death rate to more than 260,000 in the next century from the 1983 level of 180,000.

The aging trend "will be particularly pronounced among elderly women," when the proportion of women over 75 will exceed the number of women between 65 and 74.

Low immigration levels and smaller families will force the population to peak at 28 million at the turn of the century and start to decrease, the report found.

Assuming the current trend of 50,000 immigrants allowed into Canada annually and 1.4 children a family, the population will peak by 2006 and then begin to slide.

"This represents a dramatic shift from the 1950s, when the population was increasing at a high rate of 2 to 3 per cent annually," the report says.

Manitoba, Quebec and the Atlantic provinces will begin to feel the population decline in the late 1990s.

Canada could reverse the trend—and boost its population to 30 million by the turn of the century—if 2.2 children were born to every woman and immigration doubled to 100,000 each year. At those levels, the population would grow to 38 million by 2031.

> At the beginning of the next century, if low fertility and immigration trends continue, there will be more deaths than births. The annual number of births will fall to 258,000 by early next century from 371,000 births in 1983.
>
> The report says 50,000 immigrants a year generate about 1.2 million to Canada's population over a 25-year period.
>
> *The Globe and Mail*, Toronto (June 5, 1985).

than both farm or metropolitan areas (Hodge and Qadeer, 1983:37). The proportion of elderly people in the suburbs of large cities is also growing, especially in neighbourhoods developed in the 1950s.

When reviewing changing dependency ratios, we should remember that, as the ratio for the elderly rises, that for children declines. This leaves the relative size of the working-age population stable. While we usually think that the elderly are more *expensive* to care for than children, this may not be true because much of the cost of rearing children is borne by the family, while the cost of caring for the elderly tends to fall on the state. The high cost of caring for the elderly has been the focus of much public debate, whereas concern about the *higher* cost of rearing children was seldom voiced, either during the high fertility periods of the 1950s and 1960s or at present. Clearly, the controversy is now related to the growing role of the state in the distribution of income and the expansion of the state budget (Myles, 1984).

## SOCIAL POLICY IMPLICATIONS

The social policy implications of these demographic changes are many. For example, the labour force is aging, leaving fewer advancement possibilities for those presently in their 20s or 30s. The increasingly large older population may become a powerful and conservative lobby group. Lodging the elderly in subsidized senior citizens' apartments and nursing homes, which was widely promoted in the 1960s, may prove too costly. Patterns of consumption may change as consumers' needs change with age. Let us look at several of these implications, beginning with the aging of the Canadian labour force.

### The Aging Labour Force
In the 1960s, postsecondary educational facilities were expanded to accommodate the postwar baby-boomers and delay their entry into the labour force. However, few planners anticipated that the proportion of 18- to 24-year-olds enrolled in postsecondary institutions would continue to rise well into the 1980s. Six percent of this age group were enrolled in postsecondary institutions in 1951, but this proportion rose to 22 percent in 1982-83 (Statistics Canada, 1983:65). This will further increase the number of highly educated graduates looking for work at a time of high unemployment and limited job mobility.

TABLE 7-4 Labour Force Participation Rates by Age and Sex, 1961-85, Canada

| | 55 – 64 | | 65 – 69 | | 70 + | |
|---|---|---|---|---|---|---|
| | M | F | M | F | M | F |
| 1961 | 85.9% | 24.6% | 50.4% | 10.8% | 22.0% | 3.8% |
| 1971 | 82.5 | 32.8 | 32.8 | 10.5 | 14.6 | 2.9 |
| 1981 | 75.1 | 33.7 | 21.9 | 8.0 | 8.9 | 2.6 |
| 1985 (Apr.) | 69.8 | 35.0 | 18.7 | 7.4 | 8.1 | 2.5 |

Burbidge, J.B. and A.L. Robb, "Public Pension Plans and the Incentive to Work," Economic Council of Canada, 1980, p. 10. Statistics Canada, *Labour Force Annual Averages 1975-83*, Cat. 71-529, February 1984, p. 15.
Statistics Canada, *The Labour Force*, Cat. 71-001, April 1985, p. 26.

Especially in occupations with life-time career ladders, blocked mobility is becoming a serious problem. Those fortunate enough to find work cannot expect to be promoted with such a large number of middle-aged people occupying the higher ranking positions. Many of these senior employees are not expected to retire for 20 years and are unlikely to change jobs in this economic climate. The lack of promotional possibilities is particularly acute in the civil service and the universities, where job security prevents even the less competent from being fired. With few chances for advancement or job permanence, many professional people are becoming disgruntled and are turning to unions to protect themselves or calling for some system of reviewing the productivity of their older colleagues. For example, five-year reviews of the work of university professors after tenure is granted have been suggested by university administrators and supported by some nontenured faculty members.

Employers have responded to the uncertain economic situation by hiring part-time staff, contract workers or consultants rather than permanent employees with job security and fringe benefits. However, without the security of continuing employment and future pensions, these employees may become dependent on social benefits when they are between jobs and will undoubtedly experience reduced pensions unless they have made private pension arrangements.

## The Changing Sex Ratio
In 1981, 57.2 percent of Canadians 65 years of age and older were female. In the same year, 67.2 percent of those 85 and over were female (National Council of Welfare, 1984:9). This overrepresentation of women among the elderly has been particularly noticeable in recent years, as the life expectancy of women has increased faster than the life expectancy of men. From 1931 to 1981, the average life expectancy at birth for males has increased by about 11 years, but for females it has increased by 17 years (Science Council of Canada, 1976:14; Statistics Canada, 1984). Declining rates of maternal death and increasing rates of male accidental deaths and deaths from stress-related diseases have increased the gap between the life expectancy of the two sexes.

TABLE 7-5 Women as a Proportion of the Aged, By Age, 1901 to 2001

|       | ALL AGED (65 +) | 75 AND OLDER |
|-------|-----------------|--------------|
| 1901  | 48.8%           | 49.3%        |
| 1911  | 49.1            | 50.1         |
| 1921  | 48.8            | 51.3         |
| 1931  | 48.9            | 50.8         |
| 1941  | 49.1            | 51.8         |
| 1951  | 49.2            | 51.8         |
| 1961  | 51.5            | 52.5         |
| 1971  | 55.2            | 58.0         |
| 1981  | 57.2            | 61.6         |
| 1991  | 59.3            | 63.6         |
| 2001  | 60.1            | 65.5         |

National Council of Welfare. *Sixty-Five and Older*, Ottawa, February 1984, Table 4, p. 8. Reprinted by permission of the National Council of Welfare.

Since most women marry men two to four years older than themselves, most wives outlive their husbands, upon whom they have been financially dependent. Only 14 percent of men over 65 were widowed in 1981, compared with 49 percent of women (National Council of Welfare, 1984:14). If most women had been in the labour force all of their adult lives, this would not have such serious economic consequences. Their employer-sponsored pensions would augment their Old Age Security. However, while 70 percent of males aged 55-64 are in the labour force, only 35 percent of females of the same age are working as Table 7-4 indicates.

Since many women of retirement age spent their earlier lives caring for their homes and families, they had little money of their own to set aside for their old age. Even when they worked for pay, they often worked part-time or temporarily in a series of low-paying jobs. Depending on the financial position of their family or husband, their retirement years could be quite comfortable, but more often they were lived in poverty. Elderly women who are still married fare much better in retirement than those who are unmarried or widowed. While only 13.6 percent of couples 70 and over were below the 1981 poverty line, 65 percent of unattached females were officially poor (National Council of Welfare, 1984:26).

This financial dependence on men underlines the importance of state pensions, a state-run system of alimony collection and equitable matrimonial property laws (Dulude, 1978). Because housework has not been remunerated and because women are encouraged to place their family obligations before their paying jobs, many women have not been able to qualify for private pensions or plan their own financial futures.

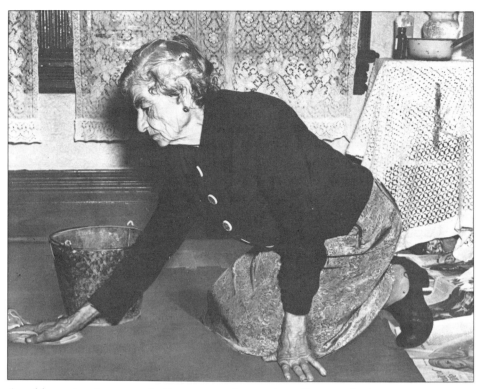

*An old age pensioner scrubs floors to supplement her allowance in 1947.* Public Archives Canada/PA-93924.

Even women who have worked for pay most of their lives likely earned lower wages than men and consequently receive a lower pension. Prior to the mid-1970s, retirement ages for women were often five years earlier than men's. This may have been convenient for the woman who wanted to retire at the same time as her (older) husband, but it also decreased her retirement benefits because of fewer contributing years in the pension plan. Considering the longer life expectancy of most women, they may face 20 years or more on a reduced pension that has not been indexed to the rising cost of living. Women who worked part-time (about 26 percent of female workers, compared to 7 percent of male workers) frequently have no pension at all. Of course, this situation would also pertain to a man in similar circumstances, but most men experience more job stability than women.

The financial dependence of elderly women is compounded by the fact that older women tend to have less formal education than older men. While this often translates into lower wages, it also frequently means less confidence in one's own independent judgement. Older women have been socialized into greater acceptance of dependence and subservience and may have been discouraged from taking the initiative in their work, their relationships and in planning for the future. The negative stereotypes of old women (de Beauvoir, 1970; Dulude, 1978:34, 35) reinforce their dependency and poverty: it requires unusual personal assertiveness to overcome these social expectations.

Thus, we can see that people over 65 are often poor largely because more than half of them are women.

TABLE 7-6  Percentage Distribution of Aged Individuals, By Income Group and Sex (Preliminary Estimates, 1982, Canada)

| INCOME GROUP | AGED WOMEN | | AGED MEN | |
|---|---|---|---|---|
| Under $5 000 | 23.4% | | 7.5% | |
| 5 000 – 6 999 | 35.9 | 80.0% | 23.6 | 53.7% |
| 7 000 – 9 999 | 20.7 | | 22.6 | |
| 10 000 – 14 999 | 9.9 | | 18.8 | |
| 15 000 – 19 999 | 4.2 | | 11.0 | |
| 20 000 – 24 999 | 2.2 | | 5.2 | |
| 25 000 and over | 3.5 | | 11.3 | |
| Total | 100.0 | | 100.0 | |
| Median Income | $6 440 | | $9 349 | |

National Council of Welfare. *Sixty-Five and Older*, Ottawa, 1984, Table 24, p. 39. Reprinted by permission of the National Council of Welfare.

## Retirement Benefits and Pension Funds

With high unemployment, few promotional possibilities, rising life expectancies and a preponderance of poor elderly women, the recent controversies over pensions and retirement policies become more acute. While mandatory retirement frees jobs for younger people and frees employers from having to make judgements about the competency of older workers, it forces the elderly to drastically reduce their standard of living and find new meaningful activity.

Some researchers say that raising the mandatory retirement age from 65 to 70 would increase the size of the labour force by only .01 percent (Morin, 1978). Death and voluntary earlier retirement would keep the size of the elderly working population small. However, if the retirement age were raised, employers might use competency tests to weed out less able workers. Flexibility in the timing of retirement could raise the standard of living of some of the elderly, give them a more useful life and provide employers with loyal and experienced employees.

As more people reach age 65 and fewer workers are contributing to public pension funds, concern is being expressed about the actuarial base of public pensions. Unless contributions are increased or we draw on a larger group of contributors, pensions may not rise with the cost of living. As pension costs rise because of inflation and early retirement, it may be cheaper for an employer to hire younger people. However, the crisis in public pensions could be diverted by raising contributions and by encouraging women to enter and stay in the labour force.

In a report done for the Advisory Council on the Status of Women, Dulude (1981) revealed that women seldom benefit from employer-sponsored pensions,

DE-INDEXATION TO COST POOREST $860 MILLION: EPP

Health Minister Jake Epp says it would cost $860 million over the next five years to reimburse senior citizens receiving the guaranteed income supplement for what they will lose once inflation protection is partially removed from old-age security payments Jan. 1.

Old-age security (OAS) is a monthly federal payment given to most Canadians over 65. The guaranteed income supplement (GIS) is given to those with no other income supplement but old-age security.

Epp defended in a weekend interview the government's controversial budget proposal to drop protection of (OAS) payments for the first 3 percentage-point increase in inflation.

The government estimates de-indexation will save $1.62 billion a year by 1990-91.

The health minister acknowledged that there will be more seniors below the poverty line by the end of the century, partly because seniors as a whole will rise to more than 20 per cent of the population.

Meanwhile, Liberal finance critic Don Johnston said in a weekend interview it would be unwise of Liberal senators to use their majority to block Conservative budget legislation to protest de-indexation.

Johnston suggested the government might decide on its own to rescind the measure.

Patrick Johnston, head of the National Anti-Poverty Association, said the Conservatives will probably admit, "We blew it."

"Some time in the fall, we may see some change—or it may have to wait until the next budget," he said in an interview.

He said the plan won't take effect until the beginning of 1986, so the government has plenty of time to reverse itself while saving face.

*The Gazette*, June 10, 1985. Reproduced by permission of The Canadian Press.

even when they work for pay. For one thing, pension plans usually exclude part-time workers. Not all workers have such plans, and those who do tend to be in the highly paid and organized workforces, where women are underrepresented, or in government employment. Pensions are seldom transferable from job to job and usually require an employee to work at the same place for at least ten years before retaining the employer's contribution. If the employee leaves within this period, his or her own contributions are returned with interest computed at *far below* the prevailing rate. Since women change jobs more often than men, they often have no employer-sponsored pension, or at most a reduced one, by retirement age. This means that they have to rely on Canada/Quebec Pension Plans. Yet in 1976, only 53 percent of women (and 94 percent of men) were contributing to C/QPP (Dulude, 1981: 10). (The 53 percent was comparable to women's labour force participation in that year.) In 1981, 62 percent of women aged 25-54 years were working for pay (and 94 percent of men) (Martin, 1982:149), which suggests that, as women's labour force participation has been rising, so will the pension benefits of future generations of elderly women.

Clearly, better employer-sponsored pensions need to be legislated. But that will not solve the problem of the women who work at home (nearly half of Canadian women). The issue of pensions for housewives has been controversial because of the difficulty of deciding the level of earnings housewives would be presumed to have, who would make the contributions and which women should benefit. Since 1977, the Quebec Pension Plan has allowed parents of either sex to drop out of the labour force to care for their preschool children and to have these low-earning years excluded from their employment record (Dulude, 1981:12). On the assumption that raising the next generation is an important social contribution, the pension benefits for these years would be paid for by the public purse. But a wife without young children who is performing a personal service for her husband should have her contributions paid by her husband rather than by other taxpayers. Until the CPP includes homemakers, the lack of employer-sponsored pensions will be aggravated by the lack of public pensions for a large segment of Canadian women.

In June 1978, it became possible to divide C/QPP pension credits between spouses when a marriage ended in divorce. However, in the two-year period following the change in law, only 1 percent of divorcing couples opted for this division (Dulude, 1981:11). Either the law was not well known or many women could not obtain the necessary information about their ex-husbands to proceed with the division. But likely, most divorcing women preferred an immediate cash settlement rather than a deferred (and larger) payment.

## Facilities for the Elderly

Increasing age is often associated with chronic illness. According to many indicators, women tend to be less healthy than men. Women have more days per year of restricted activity, more days of bed disability, more doctor's visits and higher expenditures for health care than men of the same age. Women are also more likely to experience depression and to be institutionalized. The elderly use more medical services than any other adult age group—the "old elderly" more than the "young elderly" and women more than men (Martin, 1982).

At a time of recession and government cutbacks, attempts are being made to keep new expenditures to a minimum when planning facilities for the elderly. In health care, there are higher levels of institutionalization of the elderly in Canada than in many European countries that have higher proportions of people 65 and over (such as Great Britain). The trend toward home care is evident in both Sweden and Great Britain. Unfortunately, "home care" is often a euphemism for care by women—wives, sisters and daughters (Chappell, 1982:215). In addition to female family members, women in volunteer agencies and churches in Canada have been providing most of the services to the elderly (e.g., Meals on Wheels, home visiting services). The expectation that women will care for sick family members has led many of them to a pensionless, financially insecure old age. The trend toward government-sponsored services and institutionalization takes part of the burden of caring for the elderly away from female family members and volunteer women. Now, this trend may be reversing at a time when women are entering the paid labour force and have neither the time nor the inclination for volunteer work and home care.

Figure 7-1 Percentage Distribution by Age and Sex of Persons Living Alone, Canada, 1981

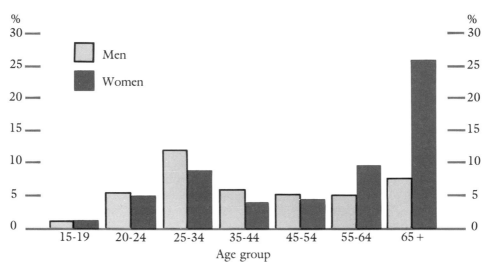

Note:  Excludes population aged less than 15.

Statistics Canada. *Living Alone*. Cat. 99-934. Ottawa: 1984. Reproduced by permission of the Minister of Supply & Services Canada.

In the last 20 years, there has been an increase in the proportion of elderly widows living alone. For one thing, increasing life expectancies for women have meant that more women outlive their husbands. But the construction of more rental apartments and the trend toward greater financial and psychological independence of the elderly has discouraged widows from living with their children. A controversy continues about whether the elderly should be integrated into the larger community or segregated in homes for the aged and retirement communities. Contrary to earlier speculation, recent studies are finding that the elderly usually prefer to maintain contact with their children but to live with elderly people. Living with or even "too near" their children often makes them feel dependent and incapacitated (Canadian Council on Social Development, 1973). Those who live in the same building as other seniors often have more friends, are more independent and participate in more group activities than those who live in the larger community or with their children.

Instead of building either self-contained apartments or hostel accommodation (with laundry, meals and other services) a compromise is often made by providing small, self-contained apartments with the option of using communal facilities for dining, laundry and socializing. But many elderly who move to special housing would not do so if they had inexpensive assistance in housekeeping and home maintenance. Rather than forcing older people to move to senior citizens' apartments to obtain this assistance, it would be cheaper to provide visiting homemakers, grants to remodel a house and better income subsidization.

*This senior citizens apartment housing project is located in Quebec.*
Public Archives Canada/PA-113463

## SUMMARY

As the average of the population rises, our conceptions about aging will inevitably change. Many of the myths and stereotypes about what older people can and want to do will be shattered as the elderly gain political clout. By the time the baby-boomers retire, policies more favourable to their interests may have been passed. Older people will likely be portrayed more frequently and positively in the media. As more women become involved in politics and the labour force, women may be portrayed more accurately, with less focus on youth and physical appearance. Patterns of consumption may change, with markets catering more to middle-aged and older people.

While today's elderly have lower levels of formal education than younger people, the future elderly will be better-educated, more articulate and less trusting of those in authority. Today's elderly women have seldom worked for pay long enough to obtain a pension and have often found that their major life's work has not been rewarded financially in their older years. Because of their better education and employment history, elderly women in the future should be more financially secure and less dependent on government assistance. While today's elderly were brought up during the depression of the 1930s, when there were few social benefits, the elderly of the future will have been raised to expect more from the state (Science Council of Canada, 1976).

Stages in the life cycle are less distinct than they were even 30 years ago. Rather than finish school, work, marry, raise children, see the children leave home and retire, more people will marry and remarry and perhaps start a second family. They may return to school when they are older and change careers or jobs several times. Planning for the future must reflect changing trends in education, family formation, labour force participation and ideology, as well as demography.

Concern about population aging and *demographic stagnation* has been with us since the 1930s. After World War II, the problems and opportunities of rapid population growth began to be recognized. The zero population movement discussed the implications of lower fertility. But the conclusions of these discussions depend very much on the value judgements made about who should benefit or be disadvantaged in the aging population.

Some authors think that the aging of Canada will encourage intergenerational conflict between the young, who are competing for jobs and resources, and the older citizens, who are holding on to their jobs. But the real conflict will more likely break out between groups that have catered to the needs of a youthful population and those whose interests lie with the elderly (Myles, 1982:37). For example, the schools and universities which grew and based their funding requirements on large numbers of students will fight to change the funding formulae when they are no longer to their own advantage. Many of our social organizations have been organized by and for a youthful population, and changing them will create conflict. After all, the young and middle-aged have an interest in improving pensions and benefits for the elderly. If pensions are inadequate, the elderly will stay in the labour fource and block mobility channels for younger people. Improved conditions for the elderly will eventually benefit all individuals but *not* all organizations.

Although the Canadian population is young compared to that of some European countries, our population is aging because of falling birthrates and increased life expectancies. How we treat our children, adolescents and older people has varied through the ages, depending on demographic shifts and economic trends. Stages in the life process are often marked by social rituals, which help us to make the transition in our self-concept and behaviour. With a larger proportion of older people in the population, our social institutions and policies about retirement, pensions, and housing will have to be adapted to this new situation.

## DISCUSSION QUESTIONS

1. Why is the population of Canada becoming older?

2. In what way have we changed our ideas about childhood, adolescence, middle-age and old age over the past hundred years?

3. How are the implications of aging different for men and for women? Why are they different?

4. Why is death surrounded by social rituals and described with euphemisms?

5. Why does the state pay out more money and benefits for the elderly than for children?

# 8

# Control and Deviance

## *Austin T. Turk*

# INTRODUCTION

We are not born knowing right from wrong. This is the basic premise from which the sociology of deviance and its control begins. Against theological or biological determinism, social and behavioural scientists have accumulated an enormous fund of empirical evidence. This chapter will introduce some of the main findings and examine their implications.

As in any developing science, there has been lively controversy among proponents of different theories and research methods. However, most specialists in the study of deviance and social control agree on several issues and are increasingly concerned with complementarity more than conflict among diverse lines of investigation. The following discussion will focus upon 1) the social construction of right and wrong, 2) sources and varieties of deviant behaviour, 3) organizational deviance and 4) changing patterns of social control.

# THE SOCIAL CONSTRUCTION OF RIGHT AND WRONG

There is a very human tendency to take for granted whatever has become familiar, including norms covering the full range of behaviour patterns and nonbehavioural attributes. Furthermore, the familiar tends to become valued so much that we may even begin acting as if the familiar is somehow *right* and better than possible alternatives. Our capacity to accept diversity and change in right-wrong distinctions varies from *absolutism* to *relativism*. Some people find it hard to accept any normative standards other than those which they themselves hold. They consider themselves morally superior because of their beliefs and behaviour, and so may be called *moral absolutists*. Examples include the members of various Christian, Jewish, Islamic and other religious groups. Other people (a far smaller number) think that no one conception of right can legitimately evaluate human ideas or conduct. Such *moral relativists* typically condemn (at least in the abstract) using coercion to prevent, eliminate or punish even harmful conduct. Most people are neither total absolutists nor consistent relativists. Rather, they are absolutist about some things, accept diversity of opinion about other things and are fairly indifferent toward most normative issues.

If most people "live and let live" without concerning themselves too much with questions of morality, how are particular moral boundaries and orders established? To say that moral limits are "natural" or "inevitable" does not explain their existence, but it does remind us that every human relationship generates its own characteristic pattern of normative expectations, failures and controls. No two people can automatically meet each other's expectations. For them to have a relationship (as lovers, parent and child, employer-employee, leader-follower) they must read each other's signals, agree on meanings and priorities and commit themselves to making the relationship work in terms of that agreement. None of this happens automatically; any social relationship is an on-going process. When more people are involved, we speak of "structures" in trying to comprehend their links to one another and the

*Is this sidewalk salesman a social deviant or a respectable member of society? On what do you base your judgement?* Photo courtesy of Catherine Jolly, Toronto.

task of describing and explaining the relationships involved becomes more complex. Insofar as social order is achieved, it tends to become moral order as well.

The boundaries of social relatedness are moral ones to the extent they are used to decide who is subject to the agreed-upon norms of belief and behaviour. Participation in some relationships requires only a limited and perhaps temporary commitment, so that interaction failures produce little sense of outrage or moral indignation. The stronger the commitment, the greater the emotional impact of failures. In both low-commitment and high-commitment relationships, the connection between deviant behaviour and moral boundaries is symbiotic and problematic.

## MORAL BOUNDARIES AND SOCIAL ORDER: THE FUNCTIONS OF STIGMA

When bad, illegal, improper, anomalous and in general disturbing human behaviour began to be studied scientifically in the nineteenth century, investigators assumed that deviation was pathological and conformity was healthy. The aim was to learn how to eliminate deviation, especially in its most disturbing forms, as then perceived: violence, insanity, perversion, dishonesty and idleness. Research since then has led to the startling conclusion that definitions of "deviant" and "normal" are largely subjective and that deviance is "essential to the very organization of society . . . [functioning] to establish and maintain behavioural boundaries and to affirm the value of conformity" (Farrell and Swigert, 1982: 27).

Concepts of deviance vary among individuals and change over time. There is a generalized antipathy toward deviants but considerable variation in the images of them and their attributes. In Simmons's (1969: 25–38) survey research on public stereotyping, respondents were asked to use five words each to characterize "marijuana smokers, adulterers, homosexuals, beatniks, and political radicals." The term "deviant" was not used in presenting the categories. Analysis revealed a fair degree of stereotyping, but the inclination to stereotype was significantly correlated with low education. All categories were seen as "irresponsible," and all except the radical were described as "lonely and frustrated." The more specific images were as follows: marijuana smoker—"an insecure escapist, lacking self-control and looking for kicks"; adulterer—"immoral, promiscuous, and insecure"; homosexual—"perverted and mentally ill"; beatnik—"a sloppy, immature nonconformist"; political radical—"ambitious, aggressive, and dangerous" (Simmons, 1969: 28).

One might suggest that public stereotyping is beside the point. Given that more educated people are less likely to stereotype, maybe the most highly informed, i.e., the social control professionals, accurately identify "real" deviants on scientific, not stereotypical, grounds. Studies of the classification and processing of the mentally ill and criminals do not support this argument. Numerous studies "demonstrate that the behaviour or 'condition' of the person alleged to be mentally ill is not usually an important factor in the decision of officials to retain or release new patients from the mental hospital" (Scheff, 1984: 105). From a flood of research on the criminalization process, "sufficient evidence has accumulated to reject the traditional assumption that distinguishing crime from not-crime merely involves the fitting by competent specialists of legal concepts to observed facts" (Turk, 1984: 319). Deviance, as professionally and officially defined, is the outcome of a complex series of problematic interpretations and discretionary actions.

Historical and comparative studies show that perceptions and assessments of specific forms of deviance are not constant. Demon possession, witchcraft and other once commonly acknowledged phenomena have vanished for more and more people, despite periodic revivals. Conceptions of the nature, causes, types and symptoms of mental illness have become increasingly controversial as the "medical model" has been challenged from within and without the "psy-professions" (Ingleby, 1983; Scheff, 1984). Such crimes as blasphemy, mopery (exposing one's genitals in the presence of a blind man!), abortion and lottery gambling(!) no longer exist, while new crimes such as opium trafficking (since 1908 in Canada, 1914 in the United States) and, most recently, improper disposal of toxic waste are constantly being defined.

## How Deviance Contributes to Social Organization

Though variable and discretionary in its specifics and constantly the target of control efforts, deviance always exists in some form. Moreover, it contributes in several ways to social organization (Cohen, 1966: 6–11).

First, deviance is not necessarily even disapproved of if it is used to circumvent "red tape" (an organization's own rules) to accomplish organizational purposes. Finders, operators and expediters are sometimes legendary for their ingenuity in overcoming military and other bureaucratic constraints to "get the job done." Their wheeling and dealing may be officially condemned and sometimes punished, but it is unofficially tolerated most of the time. Another, rather more serious, example of approved deviance is illegal or ethically questionable behaviour by control agents, such as political security police, which is not merely tolerated but frequently encouraged and even required (Turk, 1981).

Second, deviance may be a *safety valve* for a group or society. The more restrictive and demanding the norms of participation, the more pressure there is upon members to subordinate their personal desires to collective interests. To defuse potentially destructive tensions, social relationships have *norms of patterned evasion* by which usual normative expectations are suspended. Prostitution is a classic example of functional deviance, in that it constitutes an understood though disparaged alternative (for men) to the dissolution of insufficiently gratifying marriages (Davis, 1971). Keeping a mistress or concubine has, in many cultures, been a more accepted, though not fully approved, extramarital solution to the problems generated by traditional (especially arranged) marriage systems. *Moral holidays* (e.g., Mardi Gras and New Year's Eve) and *time outs* also reinforce established relationships by permitting ordinarily disallowed behaviour on the clear understanding that a return to conformity is expected when the party is over.

Third, until moral boundaries are overstepped, they remain abstractions with little or no power to induce conforming behaviour. From vicarious and personal experience, one learns the real meaning of a rule by seeing what happens (and to whom) when it is broken. The meaning of malingering, for example, is clarified when an employee is reprimanded for absenteeism or a soldier sent back to combat. Being physically or psychically fatigued may explain performance failure, but only up to the point where authoritative others, such as employers and military psychiatrists, consider it an acceptable excuse (Daniels, 1970).

Fourth, deviance helps to maintain group solidarity by providing a tangible threat. Much like an external enemy, the deviant is a common enemy against whom others can unite. Child molesting is almost universally despised; a reported incident tends to stimulate "great fear and hysteria in the family, outrage in the neighbourhood, and excitement and vengefulness among the police" (Thio, 1983: 150). Private justice organizations such as neighbourhood patrols and watch committees are a frequent outcome. Demanding more stringent laws, applauding vigilante or police violence against suspected molesters and tolerating the brutal degradation of convicted molesters ("rapos") by other prisoners are other common responses.

Fifth, it is strange but true that deviance can sometimes unite a group *for* rather than *against* the deviant. Though not really approving the deviance, people are often protective of "their" deviant and may go to great lengths to cover for the incompetent, the shirker or the outlaw folk hero (a Robin Hood or John Dillinger, for example). Shielding the deviant has been observed in many settings—families, work units, and military training squads (Dentler and Erikson, 1959: 105).

Sixth, badness and abnormality provide reference points for measuring goodness and normality. The greater the contrast, the more readily people can understand what being good or normal means. This insight may have led to the invention of the traditional Tahitian village *mahu*—a male who, as a child, is selected to spend his life as a woman (Levy, 1971). A village has only one *mahu*, who is expected to have sexual relations with the other men. In a culture marked by the minimal differentiation of gender roles, the *mahu* reminds everyone of their appropriate roles as men and women.

And lastly, deviance indicates that there may be a cultural or organizational problem that needs attention. The *anomie* theory of deviance, as formulated by Merton

*The appearance of this punker draws stares, but its very outrageousness helps to define what is normal in dress and hairstyles.* Photo courtesy of Catherine Jolly, Toronto.

(1957: 131–144), locates the source of deviance in *means–ends discrepancy*—contradictions between culturally encouraged goals and structurally available means for their achievement. A society that teaches people to value themselves and others according to degree of material success but maintains class and racial barriers to legitimate opportunities for success can expect the disadvantaged to seek illegitimate opportunities, such as robbery, theft and fraud. "Double failures," denied illegitimate as well as legitimate oppportunities, may retreat into alcoholism, drug addiction, sexual deviance, mental illness or suicide. Despite its many limitations (Clinard, 1964), there is obvious merit in the proposition that deviance may signal defects in social organization and possibly lead to needed social changes.

Observing that deviance can be functional does not imply that it is always functional. The harmful consequences of some forms (e.g., mass terrorism, sadistic murder) may outweigh their functional payoffs, and less harmful forms of deviance may serve just as well to determine moral boundaries. The amount of deviance required to establish and sustain particular norms is also debatable.

Erikson (1966: 181) has speculated that "societies somehow 'need' their quotas of deviation and function in such a way as to keep them intact." His study of the seventeenth-century New England Puritans examined the three "crime waves" the Massachusetts Bay Colony experienced: the Antinomian (1636) and Quaker (late 1650s) theological challenges to Puritan orthodoxy and later, in 1692, the Salem witchcraft outbreak, which simultaneously violated the normative demands of the theocratic state and provided occasions for brutally but clearly asserting its supreme authority. Erikson's evidence does not directly support his interpretation of it, and his idea of some distinct quota of deviance being needed has been severely criticized. The particular forms and amounts of deviance identified and processed by control institutions are enormously variable, depending heavily upon political-legal policies and economic contexts (Connor, 1972; Turk, 1982; Currie, 1968).

## INTRAGROUP VS. CROSS-GROUP STIGMATIZATION: LABELLING PROCESSES

The drawing of moral boundaries is accomplished by *stigmatizing*, or *labelling*, particular individuals, not merely or necessarily by formulating explicit rules. Variations in the labelling process and in its impact upon the individuals being labelled are associated with the scale and formality of the social order. There are significant differences as well as similarities in labelling within small groups and across group boundaries. In each, the process occurs in a *prior normative context* and has "five analytically distinct but empirically blended phases or dimensions: *identification, justification, negotiation, enclosure*, and *disposition*" (Grimes and Turk, 1978: 41).

Though deviance is a socially constructed reality, it is not constructed on the spot. Through time, a framework is established within which later interpretations and responses occur. Because members of a group share understandings of their own ways, norms are generally tacit. In contrast, where people from different backgrounds and groups are involved, the relevant norms are likely to be explicit agreements or laws.

Criteria for identifying cases of deviance include all sorts of observed or imputed behavioural, anatomical, mental or spiritual attributes. Initial or preliminary definition (*typification*) of deviance is based on little information, which is interpreted largely in accord with stereotypes. Again, the criteria for identification are usually generally understood within groups but must be specified ("reasonable grounds for arrest") in cross-group situations. For the other members of a group, it is enough to sense that something is wrong, but the police officer's hunches must be further substantiated if legal proceedings are to begin.

When a case of deviance is identified, those who must deal with it marshal empirical and theoretical grounds for their actions. Intragroup justification relies upon the commonsense knowledge people have of reality and one another. There are no technical restrictions upon the gathering of evidence. Labelling across groups is a potential source of intergroup conflict, and commonsense understandings cannot be relied upon. Therefore, more limited formal procedures and appeals to legality are ordinarily used to build cases in the absence of intimate knowledge and shared understandings.

Accused persons are pressured to participate in confirming the accuracy of their deviant labels. Negotiation is typically unequal, involving not whether but how the alleged deviant is to be classified. Within groups, the controlling members exert pressure by appealing to group *participation* as a shared value. Across groups, control agents are much more prone to appeal to the suspect's sense of expediency with the inescapable fact of *membership* in the collectivity (usually the state) that binds different groups together.

As the fact and nature of the deviant case are established, controlling others enclose the deviant within physical, social and/or symbolic barriers. Opportunities for normal interaction are closed off and pressure to accept a deviant identity becomes increasingly hard to resist. Enclosure is more often symbolic and social in intragroup labelling (e.g., ostracism, transfer to a lower position, stripping of medals and insignia), more often physical in cross-group labelling (e.g., pretrial detention, confinement to quarters).

The outcome of a case may be rehabilitation, termination, or institutionalization (in a social sense, i.e., demotion to a lower rank). Rehabilitation to normal participation in social interaction is more likely to be a goal within than across groups, and it is far more likely than the other alternatives to be achieved. At the other extreme, termination of social existence by exile or execution is generally decided upon later in intragroup situations and with greater moral indignation, which is heightened by failure to elicit confession and/or achieve rehabilitation. Authentic concern about the individual deviant occurs far less often in cross-group labelling, where "population control" is ultimately more important than personalized control. Consequently, deviants are more often relegated to a permanently inferior status (socially institutionalized) than terminated or rehabilitated. *Career deviants* may even be needed in greater numbers in multigroup collectivities because more bad examples and providers of illicit goods and services may be required to preserve the social order (if not the moral order) of such large organizations.

## COPING AND IDENTITY: THE INDIVIDUAL AS DEVIANT

As we have seen, from an analytical perspective, deviance sometimes helps to construct moral boundaries and maintain social order. Nonetheless, negative labelling (stigmatization) is nearly always intended to eliminate or minimize deviance. And deviance is usually understood as conduct near or beyond a group's *range of tolerance*. Nonbehavioural attributes (such as skin colour, height, weight, mental or spiritual conditions), observed or imputed, are ordinarily of concern only because they are presumed to correlate with or cause unacceptable behaviour. Accordingly, most theorists and researchers have concentrated upon explaining deviant *behaviour*.

The search for explanations of deviant behaviour has led scientists to examine myriad biological, psychological, and social factors as possible causes. Certain behaviours have typically been assumed deviant without much concern about the origins of such assumptions or the problematic nature of labelling processes. *Deviance* has been equated with *variance*, and the specific effort to account for deviant conduct has tended to dissolve into the general effort to explain all human behaviour. One influential attempt to give deviance research a theoretically meaningful focus has been that of Edwin Lemert over the past 35 years.

Lemert's (1972: 62–92) proposal is that we concentrate on the task of explaining secondary rather than primary deviation. He sees *primary deviation* as an essentially unpredictable, polygenetic occurrence

> arising out of a variety of social, cultural, psychological, and physiological factors, either in adventitious or recurring combinations. While it may be socially recognized and even defined as undesirable, primary deviation has only marginal implications for the status and psychic structure of the person concerned (Lemert, 1972: 62).

*Secondary deviation* refers to the patterned responses of individuals to being subjected to labelling processes. The personal problems created by societal reactions to their deviance "become central facts of existence for those experiencing them, altering psychic structure, producing specialized organization of social roles and self-regarding attitudes" (Lemert, 1972: 63). The eventual outcome is the secondary deviant, whose life and identity are organized around the experience of being a deviant in his own and others' eyes.

## ANTICIPATION AND EXPERIENCE: RESPONSES TO LABELLING

Becoming a secondary deviant is neither inevitable nor easy. Learning who one is and coping with that awareness are as hard for the deviant as for the conformist. Many contingencies affect whether an initial deviant act will lead to a deviant identity. We may adapt Lofland's (1969) model of *defensive deviance* to trace the progression from the point where the (primary) deviant feels threatened (by actual or feared control efforts), through *psychosocial encapsulation* (becoming obsessed with "the problem"), to *closure* upon a pattern of action resulting in public and self identification as a (secondary) deviant.

At any time, the individual may stop the progression. The likelihood of going on always depends upon the factors pushing the person on or simply making it easier to go on than to drop out (the *opportunity structure*). These factors include the characteristics of 1) the surrounding others, 2) the places where activities are possible, 3) the "hardware" needed to behave in particular ways and 4) the individual involved.

### The Opportunity Structure: Four Factors Affecting Deviants

1. Other people may inhibit or facilitate secondary deviance. This seems obvious enough until the researcher tries to determine which kinds of behaviour by others will be inhibiting and which facilitating. Does negative labelling deter or produce further deviance? The question has provoked fierce debates (Gove, 1975). The answer, of course, is that labelling may have either effect, so that the real issue is not whether but *when*. Thorsell and Klemke (1972) have suggested that labelling is more likely to deter when certain conditions are met: It occurs early in the deviant career. The deviant is nonprofessional (i.e., not a secondary or socially institutionalized deviant). The labeller's opinion matters to the one who is labelled (as in intragroup labelling). The label is easily removed when deviance stops (i.e., labelling is reversible). Negative labelling results in significant rehabilitative and supportive activities being made available to the deviant. Positive labels are emphasized instead of negative ones. Insofar as such conditions are more often found in intragroup settings, deterrence is more likely to result from intragroup than from cross-group labelling.

Besides *controlling others*, there are also *facilitating others*—people whose behaviour toward the deviant makes secondary deviance more probable. Friends and strangers, accomplices and victims, followers and guides all may facilitate more than inhibit the progression to secondary deviance. Lofland (1969: 212–242) distinguishes between deviant-smiths and normal-smiths. *Normal-smiths* are people who, as supporters (including experienced secondary deviants), deliberately or inadvertently deny that the individual is really or culpably deviant and thereby blur the distinction between normal and abnormal, right and wrong. The individual may then have little reason *not* to be deviant. *Deviant-smiths* are typically controllers who are clearly skeptical about the deviant's being or becoming anything else. They may cut off the deviant from opportunities to escape the progression to secondary deviant. When both normal-smiths and deviant-smiths are present, the deviant is least able to avoid moving on to where deviance is a "master status" overriding all else.

2. Places vary greatly in the extent to which they inhibit or facilitate deviance. It is easier to carry on many forms of deviant behaviour in private than in public, or else in places formally or tacitly set aside for deviant activities. "The strip" is found in cities all over the world. In the 1960s, Toronto's Yorkville ("hippies, weekenders, bikers, and greasers") and Rochdale "free university" were widely known examples of such places (Mann, 1970: 109–128, 207–217). A person living in a small town, known to everyone and expected to be in particular places at specific times, has little chance to experiment or persist in violating local standards. Conversely, people living anonymously in large cities have many opportunities to be deviant and are more likely to encounter both normal-smiths and deviant-smiths. In addition, as the York-ville and Rochdale examples suggest, cities offer many more and varied "deviant places" (bars, clubs, massage and tattoo parlors, hotel rooms, underground garages) where various forms of deviant activity are possible and even expected. Every private, secluded, dark area is a facilitant, especially if people can come and go without anyone's noticing or caring.

Beyond the opportunity structures found in private and public spaces, facilities for enclosing and "correcting" deviants are themselves places where deviants are pressured to accept deviant identities. In one controversial study (Rosenham, 1973), pseudopatients feigned "hearing voices" to gain admission to the psychiatric wards of 12 hospitals on the east and west coasts of the United States. All were admitted for observation, then immediately ceased to feign any abnormality. Eleven were diagnosed as schizophrenic, one as a manic-depressive psychotic (with a more fa-vourable prognosis, given by the only private hospital in the sample). The phony patients were never detected and the initial diagnosis stuck, no matter what they did. Observation periods ranged from 7 to 52 days, averaging 19 days, and were determined by the staff. Despite the absence of any unusual or symptomatic personal history information (all true, excepting names and occupations) and of any observed symptomatic behaviour, all the pseudopatients were discharged with a diagnosis of "in remission" (i.e., still perceived as having been and continuing to be insane).

3. The less a deviant act requires in the way of hardware (weapons, tools, com-puters, vehicles, costumes, substances, sales records), the more likely it is to occur and recur. Many forms of deviance (e.g., casual promiscuity, disorderly public con-duct and incidental assault) require no hardware and so are easy options available to anyone. But to become a professional prostitute, drug dealer, thief, robber, fence or assassin, one must acquire the necessary equipment and learn how to use it. "Road hustlers" (card and dice cheats) advance from the haphazard, crude operations of "rough" hustling to professional standing only after surviving a hard apprenticeship (Prus and Sharper, 1977: 47–59). Much like a professional musician, the road hustler uses hardware (dice, cards, cash, appropriate clothing) and develops extremely com-plex skills until "the ability to manipulate cards or dice is rather commonplace and taken more for granted" (Prus and Sharper, 1977: 47). Only a true virtuoso is considered a "mechanic," and few reach this level.

4. Not all individuals subjected to labelling accept the deviant identity imputed to them. Contrary to some ambiguous formulations and misinterpretations of labelling theory, stigmatization is not always traumatic, deeply and negatively affecting the deviant's self concept. Though exaggerated, Matza's (1969: 144–180) image of the deviant's virtually unquenchable capacity to "mediate the process of becoming" a secondary deviant reminds us that labelling (especially cross-group) may be necessary but is not causally sufficient to produce a secondary deviant. Studies of the impact of official labelling indicate that it is probably *least* traumatic for those people against whom it is most often directed: "maximal for first offenders, the middle-class, and whites, and minimal for prior offenders, the lower class, and blacks" (Liska, 1981: 132).

Some individual deviants may even accept labels without accepting all their negative connotations. Indeed, becoming a "professional" typically involves learning rationalizations (or ego defenses) that discount the "badness" of being a call girl, hustler or hired killer. Call girls, for instance, learn to justify their behaviour on grounds such as counter-exploiting exploitative and cheating men, servicing deserving but deprived men, preventing rapes and murders and keeping marriages and families intact (Bryan, 1965, 1966).

Many prostitutes and ex-prostitutes have organized to seek, not rehabilitation, but improved working conditions, medical services, legal protection, fringe benefits like unemployment compensation and greater public respect for their contribution to society. Acronyms emphasize the message: COYOTE ("Call Off Your Old Tired Ethics") in the United States and BEAVER ("Better End All Vicious Erotic Repression") in Canada.

In some instances, deviants have organized movements to abolish legal and non-legal definitions which label them and their behaviour as deviant. The gay liberation movement is unquestionably the most celebrated example. What was once a largely secretive and fearful subculture has, over the past 20 years, become the increasingly open gay community. The organized gay populace is a growing political force in many cities, such as San Francisco and Toronto, "which may be on its way to becoming the homosexual capital of North America" (Johnson, 1971: 380). Beginning with the decriminalization of private consensual acts between adults, the movement achieved perhaps its most fundamental breakthrough when the American Psychiatric Association voted in 1974 to redefine homosexuality as not, per se, a psychiatric disorder, though the degree of actual change in diagnostic practice remains questionable (Conrad and Schneider, 1980: 204–211).

## DEVIANT WORLDS AND STRAIGHT WAYS: SUBCULTURES, EVASIONS AND HOLIDAYS

Efforts by deviants to find optimum or tolerable combinations of others, places and hardware frequently result in the emergence of *deviant subcultures*. Social scientists, journalists, novelists and other observers have documented the infinite variety of such social constructions. These worlds of deviance are usually pictured as alien, exotic or erotic islands cut off from the rest of society. However, though by no

*Inhabitants of the underside world openly deviate from the prevailing norms of prosperity, appearance, competence and hopefulness.* Photo courtesy of Catherine Jolly, Toronto.

means commonplace to most of us, deviant subcultures are integral (if not necessarily functional) to the straight world of moral evasions and holidays.

Deviant subcultures may centre around a particular form of deviance, but usually incorporate several forms that exist in a symbiotic relationship with one another and the straight world. Such "vices" or "morality offenses" as illicit drug dealing and use, pimping and prostitution and illegal gambling tend to go together, along with theft, mugging and various hustles. The *underworld* is the habitat of institutionalized deviants. These live partly off one another but mostly off the "straights" who visit them seeking fun, relaxation, adventure, information or for other, more sordid reasons. In this uncertain and often dangerous world, few total commitments are possible; interpersonal relationships are usually ephemeral and expedient.

Violence is never far away in the world of institutionalized deviance. For some inhabitants and visitors, violence itself becomes a *focal concern* with its own subcultural meanings. Among biker outlaws, such as the Hell's Angels, violence is routinely used to defend territorial claims ("turf") and discourage business competition, especially in the illegal drug market. It is also used to assert status, demonstrate tough masculinity, maintain internal discipline and enhance sexual gratification (Thompson, 1967).

Overlapping the underworld of pimps, thieves, pushers and other criminal elements is the *underside world* of the assorted "bums, dropouts, freaks, and losers" who openly deviate from the prevailing norms of prosperity, appearance, competence and hopefulness. They are "the disreputable poor . . . who remain unemployed even during periods approaching full employment and prosperity" (Matza, 1975: 198). As the cast-offs of society, they are an affront to "decent people"—who attribute failure to moral shortcomings, blaming the victim instead of society.

Adjacent to the losers' world is the *fringe world* of the semi-respectable, whose occupations or other activities make them suspect and who are in varying degrees excluded from participating in straight society. Carnival workers, circus performers and those who perform the more gruesome and unpleasant services for society deviate from norms of stability, appearance, odour and work (productive, honest, clean, as commonly defined). Denigrated occupations often include gravediggers, executioners, "night soil" (human feces) removers in Asia, as well as surgeons in times past and policemen at all times! An irony of police work is that the implicit threat of police action is disturbing or frightening to many straight people (and, of course, to all deviants), leading them to ostracize and demean police officers for engaging in such "dirty work"—even as it is recognized as necessary. (For representative studies of the police and their problems, see Blumberg and Niederhoffer, 1985.)

Though not ordinarily recognized as such, a large part of the fringe world of deviance is made up of those afflicted with "abominations of the body" (Goggman, 1963: 4). Unusually proportioned, blind, deaf and mentally retarded people typically find themselves relegated to discredited and inferior statuses. An abundance of deviant-smiths and normal-smiths press them to accept deviant identities. Attempts to behave normally may be officially and consciously encouraged but are not ultimately facilitated. In particular, interaction with "normals" tends to be carefully monitored and restricted. Intimate relationships (friends, lovers, spouses, adoptive parents) with normals are generally discouraged and sometimes legally prohibited. The more stringent the standards defining normalcy are, the less able abnormals are to meet them and to count upon continued acceptance in society (Mercer, 1973).

"Respectability" and "normalcy" presumably mean the absence of deviant behaviour in other than exceptional circumstances (moral holidays and time-outs, for example). However, mounting evidence shows that deviance is often hidden within the most sacred bastions of the straight world. Alcoholism and other drug abuse, sexual deviations, mental aberrations and role failures, stealing, fraud, and/or violence characterize the lives of many families. Bryant (1973: 396) has even concluded that "a family may be considered a social collusion system for the maintenance of internal secrets and the concealment of stigma, scandal, and inappropriate behaviour on the part of its members." Other observers have found similar deviant patterns in businesses, factories, schools, government agencies, hospitals, churches—virtually every part of the straight world. This leads many analysts to question whether moral boundaries really differentiate straights and deviants or whether they only signal the relative power of people in a society.

# COMPETITION AND POWER: THE ORGANIZATION AS DEVIANT

Legal and moral boundary construction has long been viewed by many analysts as a "conflict process" or "conflict game" (Lofland, 1969: 13–25). Different categories and groups of people are seen to be openly or implicitly competing for "the means and opportunities to realize their respective visions of the good life" (Turk, 1982: 12). Yet, most studies have examined only individual deviance. The definitional and methodological problems raised by the concepts of structural and organizational deviance have only recently been seriously confronted.

Many researchers (and students) find it hard to think of *collective* behaviour as something other than the sum total of *individual* acts. While it is relatively easy to imagine individuals as deviant, the deviance of organizations and other collectivities—up to and including whole societies—is not as readily visualized. A little thought, however, shows the only real problem is one of scale. Governments, armies, corporations and even social classes and ethnic populations are frequently regarded as acting units and blamed (stigmatized) for "their" actions. In fact, since the Middle Ages, churches, towns and kings ("the crown") and even commercial corporations have been legally considered "juristic persons" rather than 'natural' ones" (Coleman, 1974: 13–31).

Ermann and Lundman (1982: 9–11) observe that corporate entities can produce deviant behaviour in at least three ways. First, leaders may deliberately use their positions to bring about illegal or unethical collective actions. Second, administrative coalitions and compromises may lead to unintended deviant collective behaviour. Third, organizational complexity itself may result in deviant behaviour, even though no individual deviance occurred.

Illegal manipulation of organizational resources by leaders has been described in several studies of corporate and governmental deviance. The Lockheed Corporation, for instance, was recently prosecuted for bribing officials in several countries (Boulton, 1978). Top executives, including the chairman of the board, decided to unload the Starfighter jet, which the American Air Force had rejected as unsafe. The defective plane was sold to various foreign air forces, and a spate of fatal crashes ensued. Probably the best known and documented recent example of governmental deviance in the United States is Watergate, the crimes (breaking and entering, obstructing justice, perjury and others) engineered by then President Nixon and his top aides (Roebuck and Weeber, 1978).

The Ford Pinto story illustrates how administrative procedures can result in organizational deviance (Ermann and Lundman, 1982: 10, 17–18). Lee Iacocca succeeded in pushing for a crash program to develop a small, fuel-efficient car to meet the foreign competition. The Pinto was rushed through design to production in record time. When evidence of a potentially hazardous fault in the fuel tank was found, it was ignored because the design engineers were keenly aware of Iacocca's decree that the car could not exceed 2000 pounds in weight or $2000 in cost. (It was later calculated that the cost of correcting the problem would have added about 11 cents per unit!) Over the next several years, the Pinto fuel tank ruptured in numerous crashes, and several people died in the resulting fires. Ford tried to deny responsibility but lost many suits. In 1978, the company was ordered to repair the nearly 2 000 000 Pintos it produced and became the first corporation ever indicted for homicide. No one at Ford wanted an unsafe vehicle, but organizational policies and hierarchical division of responsibilities produced one.

It is not easy to find concrete examples of entirely inadvertent organizational deviance. Still, many researchers have found that such deviance is often better explained as a product of insensitivity or ignorance rather than intent. Clinard and Yeager's (1980) monumental study of corporate lawbreaking indicates that it varies with the cultural, economic and political-legal environment. Both executives and workers are socialized to be dedicated "organization men" who do not look past the "bottom line" and their particular assignment. Responsibility is diffused through a complex and dehumanizing system, and any lingering personal doubts are discounted as irrelevant to doing business.

Given such findings, it is not surprising that many people see bureaucratic organizations as inherently deviant. Anarchists have developed a political ideology that condemns all varieties of formalism, legalism and hierarchy. Critics of *bureaupathology* and *bureaucratic justice* advocate dismantling organizations and replacing them with informal and egalitarian associations. Social theorists have uncovered dysfunctions and insoluble dilemmas that are characteristic of all formal organizations. And attitude surveys have consistently revealed high levels of hostility toward bureaucracies and a readiness to cheat, attack and otherwise "punish" them (Smigel and Ross, 1970).

Whether complex, necessarily formal organizations of diverse people and groups can ever be fully normal and respectable (*legitimate*) seems doubtful. As long as collective demands and goals take precedence over individual wishes, organizations must deviate from normative expectations developed mainly in interpersonal relationships. Cross-group norms can never be as readily understood and accepted as intragroup norms.

In any case, to explain organizational deviance as simply what organizations are and do is equivalent to imputing original sin to all human beings. We are left with no way to differentiate better from worse, much less to account for the difference. That organizations, like people, *vary* in their deviance indicates a better way: Learn more about the sources of that variation. As was learned in the long search for the causes of individual deviance, the causes of organizational deviance are most likely to be found in the *interactions* between organizations and their social environments.

# SOCIAL CONTROL AND SOCIAL CHANGE

Environments are not constant. It follows that the sources of organizational and individual deviance will change as environmental conditions change. Technological innovations, discovery or depletion of natural resources, economic development or decline, internal and international political realignments—all such factors generate pressures upon whatever social and moral orders have been constructed. Established normative expectations are altered as their social and cultural foundations shift as a result of environmental changes. Whether change is revolutionary or evolutionary, people experiencing it will have to revise or recreate the normative understandings

*Christian morality was a strong force in medieval Europe and continued to be important during the sixteenth and seventeenth centuries. Some say that the morality of the twentieth century is a technological morality, which defines "good" as that which serves the collective interest.* Photo courtesy of Catherine Jolly, Toronto.

by which they relate to one another. The alternative is to lose all sense of meaning in life. In short, structural pressures upon social orders produce pressures upon moral orders.

Jacques Ellul (1969) discerns three great historical transformations in the basic moral order of the Western world. *Christian morality* was a strong force in medieval Europe and continued to be important during the sixteenth and seventeenth centuries. It extolled an other-worldly orientation over this-worldly, material concerns like politics and economics. The inner soul of the individual was the only significant reality, its salvation the only important goal. *Bourgeois morality*, which originated in the Reformation, was an adaptation to the industrial and commercial revolution. It retained the preoccupation with an individual's inner state but developed a new conception of the soul's relationship to the material world. This-worldly success became the outward sign of inner virtue. Attending to one's proper business and rejecting idleness, unproductive pleasures and undue levity became the mark of a good man or woman. Industriousness and propriety were assumed to be the moral preconditions of success, and so they were. Material success in competition with others became the measure of one's worth as a human being. People were responsible for themselves; failure to succeed was a sign of moral weakness.

Today, says Ellul, the once prevailing bourgeois morality is crumbling as individualism is made meaningless by the collectivization of social life. Entrepreneurial skills are irrelevant as individuals become subordinate to massive and complex organizations. What is emerging is a *technological morality*, the morality of the fully collectivized person. Whatever is normally and situationally required to perform one's assigned role is "good." Normalcy and morality are defined not by other-worldly or inner criteria or by any personal standard but by collective interests and demands. "In the last analysis, it appears as a suppression of morality through the total absorption of the individual into the group" (Ellul, 1969: 198).

One does not have to agree entirely with Ellul. The demise of individualism may not be as imminent as he believes. Resistance to governmental and corporate collectivization is widespread, even in totalitarian societies. Individualistic, this-worldly orientations and other-worldly religious movements have acquired new vigour. Everywhere, it appears, people keep trying to construct *moral* as well as social order; everyone hopes to find a "symbolic balance" that will enable them to achieve personally meaningful identities (Klapp, 1969). We are beyond 1984, and no fully effective and eternally unshakeable social structure or control technology is yet on the horizon. Deviance and the need to control persist, as they must, for they are but the two sides of any human relationship.

## SUMMARY

Conceptions of right and wrong are developed in the on-going process of constructing social relationships. Variations beyond what has come to be expected tend to be regarded as not just different but somehow *wrong*. At the extremes, *absolutists* reject anything new or different, while *relativists* are characterized by an indiscriminate tolerance. In time, social orders tend to become moral orders.

Images of deviance are largely subjective, varying among individuals and groups and changing over time. Nonetheless, deviance in some form is always present and may contribute to social order by 1) helping to get around red tape, 2) providing a safety valve, 3) making abstract norms concretely meaningful, 4) uniting groups against a common threat, 5) fostering group solidarity against outsiders, 6) providing reference points for measuring goodness and normality and 7) signaling organizational or cultural problems.

Moral boundaries are drawn by stigmatizing specific individuals. The basic phases of the labelling process, which always occurs in a *prior normative context*, are *identification, justification, negotiation, enclosure,* and *disposition.* Intragroup, compared to cross-group, labelling occurs in a less explicit context and is more subtle, unrestricted, informal and concerned with rehabilitating the individual.

Because *primary deviation* is largely unpredictable and has only marginal social and psychological significance, research on individual deviant behaviour has focused mainly on explaining *secondary deviation*. The process of becoming a secondary deviant is highly problematic, and individuals may halt it at any time. The progression is contingent upon: what kinds of others are involved (controllers vs. facilitating deviant-smiths and normal-smiths); the availability of appropriate or necessary places and hardware; and the capacity of the individual to accept or resist a deviant identity.

Deviant worlds (or subcultures) are integral to the straight world, varying only in the degree to which they are clearly a part of it. The worlds of deviance include the underworld of socially institutionalized deviance, the world of "losers," the fringe world of the semi-respectable and the hidden deviant world within the straight world.

While most studies have focused upon individual deviance, at some point the scale and complexity of social relationships generate *organizational deviance*. Collectivities from groups to corporations and nations may violate legal and other norms. Organizational deviance may be the intended result of elite manipulation, the unintended consequence of policy decisions and administrative procedures or the inadvertent outcome of sheer organizational complexity. Individuals within complex organizations are under pressure to become organization men and women, for whom collective interests and demands override personal moral and other concerns. Awareness of such pressures and their frequent consequences leads many people to see complex organizations as inherently *bureaupathic*. This is equivalent to seeing natural persons as innately sinful. Thus both individual and organizational deviance should be understood as the products of *interactions* between the acting unit and its social environment.

As environments vary, so does the interaction. It follows that patterns of deviance and control shift as people adapt to the changing conditions of their lives. Jacques Ellul suggests that the basic moral order of the Western world has changed from the *Christian morality* of other-worldly, spiritual individualism to the *bourgeois morality* of this-worldly materialistic individualism. Today, he says, the new *technological morality* of the fully collectivized individual is emerging. Yet, people still seek meaning in their lives, despite the pressures of our large, complex society. The human dialectic of control and deviance goes on.

# DISCUSSION QUESTIONS

1. What are some examples of moral absolutism and relativism?

2. How can we know when deviance is functional?

3. In what ways is the social order of a university class also a moral order?

4. Can primary deviation be explained? Why or why not? Give an example of primary deviance.

5. Are all places deviant places?

6. What is insanity? Who is insane?

7. Is it possible to differentiate between organizational and individual deviant behaviour?

8. How can collective deviance be controlled?

# TYPES of SOCIAL ORGANIZATION

All societies consist of social organizations: small and large ones, simple and complex, temporary and permanent, informal and formal.

Some societies are very small and organizationally simple. The earliest human societies, hunter-gatherer groupings, may have numbered mere dozens of people. They were really just extended families, with everyone related to everyone else by birth or marriage. In this sense, early societies could be viewed as a large family, and what was good for the family was good for society. Kinship exchanges bound extended families together through marriage and the exchanges associated with it (dowry, bride-price). Thus, marriage was a more central process of social organization than it is today.

But even today, the family is a fundamental social organization. The modern nuclear family is a small, relatively simple social organization containing three main relationships: parent and child, spouse and spouse and sibling and sibling. A less temporary social organization than some (say, a school class), it is also self-dissolving with the passage of a generation. In time, the parents die, leaving their children to marry and establish new families.

True, some families are very temporary, dissolving because of divorce (or early death) and reconstituting through remarriage. Others may contain many generations, and so be more complex. Grandparent/grandchild alliances tend to undermine and complicate child/parent relationships. Some households may also contain aunts, uncles and other extended kin. Such additional relationships also add complexity to the family and household.

To a larger degree, family complexity is increased by remarriage. More and more households today are nontraditional, containing unmarried or temporarily married spouses and children of different parents. Conflicting rules and role expectations that result complicate matters further.

Much of this is due to the easing of divorce laws, a result of changing ideas about gender and *gender relations*, the relations between men and women. Male and female rights and responsibilities, though far from equalized, have changed enough to modify family roles a great deal. Women are more able, economically and socially, to maintain their own households. Thus, household forms and composition come to vary more. These changes in gender relations, their causes and consequences, will be discussed at length in a later chapter.

## Roles and Interactions

"Role" is a word in common use. However, it has a special meaning for sociologists that is spelled out in the chapter on roles and interactions (Chapter 9) in relation to the so-called *dramaturgical view of society*. This sociological view assumes that "all the world's a stage,/And all the men and women merely players./They have their exits and their entrances,/And one man in his time plays many parts/His acts being seven ages." (Shakespeare, *As You Like It*, Act II, Scene VII, lines 139–143).

Shakespeare's lines suggest the changeability of human identity, the many difficult transformations that come with aging, until finally we are "sans teeth, sans eyes, sans taste, sans everything" (line 166). Sociologists holding the dramaturgical view see human beings in terms of the parts they play on the "stage" of life. People are supposed to move smoothly from one role to another and to retrain themselves as often as necessary to play their assigned parts. This view, though provocative, suggests a disturbing uniformity among us and denies that some of us, at least, may be intent on expressing our "real" selves. Some might also find this view cynical: Individuals ("actors") have real personalities or sincere beliefs that determine how they enact their roles. The dramaturgical view supposes that people are guided more by the immediate prospects of reward and less by scruples, ethics or life purpose. This view also fails to separate the self from the role. What people "really" are when not on stage (how they see themselves, how they view their lives) is ignored.

From a dramaturgical standpoint, interactions between people are determined by the agreed upon "script." The ways a doctor and patient interact, for example, will be largely prescribed in the roles "doctor" and "patient," which are learned by doctors in medical school, by patients in the mass media. Some interactions are complicated by role-conflict, or cross-cutting roles. For example, imagine I am the child of a wealthy family, passing the time with a poor gardener come to rake leaves at our family mansion. By following the rule that age accords the gardener authority, I violate the equally strong norms according me superior authority on the basis of my social standing. How such confusions are resolved is far from clear.

## Top-down, Bottom-up

Yet, even under the simplest, least ambiguous conditions, interactions are not simply determined by social roles. People must frequently respond to new situations by creating new roles and rules. This process particularly interests the sociologists known as symbolic interactionists and phenomen-ologists, who hold that social organization typically proceeds from "the bottom up", not from "the top down." Unlike those who argue that people come into a pre-existing world in which they must learn to play assigned parts, "bottom-up" theorists claim that social order is constantly created or negotiated by interacting people. What is problematic for sociology, in this view, is how people make sense to one another, reach agreements and manage (however provisionally) to make their agreements work.

This approach can be criticised on several grounds where the alternative "top-down" theory seems more appropriate. First, top-down theory is more consistent with a view of society that emphasizes persistent inequalities of power. Such inequalities favour certain roles and interactions over others. The distribution of power, to be discussed at length below, controls the social processes that organize social relationships. But since the distribution of power in a society is rarely renegotiated, neither are the most important social relationships.

Second, top-down theory fits the observed persistence of social order. Though change and conflict are everywhere, they are clearest against a strong backdrop of order. And, to explain the maintenance of order, we need theories that focus on the processes that maintain on-going social organi-zation with little change. Bottom-up theories do not fill the bill. On the other hand, the creativity and spontaneity described by bottom-up theory can be seen in evolving social movements, in the formation and revitalization of ethnic communities and in movements of protest against social inequality, all of which are discussed in this section.

Power is always exercised from above *and* from below. Indeed, the dis-tribution of power between those at the bottom and those at the top helps to account for social movement formation. As well, the resurgence of neigh-bourhoods, networks, informal communities and other new forms of social life in modern cities all show the creativity of human beings facing the supposed "death of community." These social organizations display both "top-down" socialization and "bottom-up" creativity as well as responsive-ness to external pressures for change.

Creativity can be seen clearly in kinship relations. New kinds of families and households create new kinds of relationships, and these relationships demand new social roles: roles that tell us what to expect of step-siblings, of the "spouses" mommy or daddy brings home for a year or a month, of "grandparents by a second marriage." What should a second wife expect of her spouse in relation to what the first wife might have received (in con-sideration, gifts) and what should she expect of her spouse's children by his first marriage? Should she expect to be called (and treated as) "Mommy"? How should we refer to the people living with us conjugally for a month or two? What should other people call them? What is our relationship with their friends, or parents? These questions, asked more frequently all the time, demand creativity from everyone. In time, we all create new social roles, new names for relationships and new forms of interaction in response to a world that has already changed.

## Large Organizations and Small

How are large organizations related to smaller ones? At first glance, many similarities are evident. All organizations arise out of similar social processes. All organizations are composed of roles, interactions and relationships which are similar. Just as all physical objects are composed of similar, though not identical, atoms and are distinguished by how these atoms are aggregated (as solid *versus* liquid, or large object *versus* small), so social organizations are composed of similar, though not identical, social building blocks, gathered together in somewhat different forms.

Secondly, large social organizations are composed of smaller ones. For example, social classes, ethnic groups and urban communities all contain families, genders and roles. In many cases they also include social movements and formal organizations. Thus, smaller organizations are the building blocks of larger ones.

Thirdly, just as large organizations contain smaller ones, so formal organizations include informal ones; permanent organizations, temporary ones; and complex organizations, simpler ones. Thus, a large, complex organization is, in a sense, merely the sum of its small, informal, transitory organizations. For example, the Toronto Jewish community, which has existed for well over a century, comprises many large, formal organizations (schools, synagogues, newspapers, clubs). But it also includes all Jewish individuals, families and temporary groupings who, though organizationally unaffiliated, have some other basis of identification or interaction with the community.

## The Modern Organization Takes Over

Beyond a certain point, a difference of degree becomes a difference of kind. A large, complex, relatively permanent and formal organization is certain to become more than the groups that make it up. Problems of co-ordination, of obtaining required resources (such as personnel, space and supplies), of achieving influence and authority and of enforcing organizational standards become central concerns. For this reason, Max Weber (1864–1920) took modern organization, especially modern bureaucracy and the modern city, as characteristic of modern society. Politics becomes professionalized; organizational roles solidify; often the organization's original purposes are forgotten or replaced by the desire to perpetuate the organization. The organization becomes a thing in its own right, recognized as a "legal person," able to make contracts and protect its chief officers from personal liability for corporate decisions.

In modern societies, more and more social life is lived under the umbrella of ever larger, more enduring and complex social organizations. Of these, the modern welfare state, the international trade union and the multinational corporation are good examples. Their size, complexity and permanence and the protection afforded them as distinct entities under law enable them to amass greater resources than smaller organizations and individuals. In the end, the power these resources command clearly distinguish the large, complex organization from the small, simple one.

As already noted, the resource base of a complex organization is not only material: money, land, buildings and the like. It is also more than special rights written into law and exercised through the intervention of expensive lawyers. These organizations also claim a cultural legitimacy that supports their power and permanence. In short, they dominate the processes of social organization: what is taught in school or shown in the mass media, what laws are enacted and enforced. These processes, in turn, teach and persuade people to accept a view of life that supports, even glorifies, the organization. Modern people are taught to love (or hate) communism, depending on which government controls the schools and mass media; to love (or hate) private enterprise, war, sexual exploitation, depending on who has an interest in and can direct the processes of acculturation, socialization and control.

At this point, understanding power and how it operates is crucial. This will be attempted in the next section, which deals with the central institutions of society. *Central institutions* are the major groupings of social organizations in our society, and that next section simply takes a different approach to the subject matter discussed here: processes, structures and power.

# 9

# Roles and Interactions

*Nancy Mandell*

# INTRODUCTION: SOCIAL ORGANIZATION

## OVERVIEW

Sociologists investigate problems on either the macro or the micro level. *Macro level analyses* examine major institutions and large structures, both as separate parts of the whole society and as interdependent phenomena. Often the connections between these institutions and structures are not readily discernible. Research studies reveal their complex relationships. For example, the close connection between the activities of factories producing essential parts for nuclear power plants, corporate lobbies in Parliament asking for favourable tax breaks and the desire of the military to increase the defense budget is an example of the way the military-industrial complex functions.

While macro studies examine institutional arrangements, *micro-order analyses* expose the unspoken rules of social interaction which make orderly social life possible. How people behave, the groups they form and the rules they live by all shape our society. Micro analyses focus on social interaction, revealing how individuals act out of awareness of others and how they adjust their behaviour according to the perceptions of others.

Both macro and micro studies examine social organization, a term which refers to the variety of interactional patterns found in society. Interactional patterns include structural or institutional relationships (universities, corporations, prisons), group formations (political, leisure and ethnic associations) and interpersonal bonds (friend/friend, neighbour/neighbour, husband/wife). Within each structure, consistent and normative patterns of behaviour guide people's day to day interactions. These arrangements help unify and stabilize the social system, while other stresses and tensions within social organizations promote change.

Canada's health care system is a social organization containing both large- and small-scale behaviour patterns and elements of harmony and discord. Some groups, such as government ministries of health and provincial medical societies, are permanent, formal organizations. Other groups, such as holistic health centres and feminist health collectives, are new, evolving medical alternatives. How these groups interrelate shows the overall character of the health care organization.

Groups within the health system contain distinct interactional configurations. These informal lines of communication are less conspicuous than the formal structure of the organization. But they reveal patterns of power, influence, co-operation and antagonism among the participants. For example, any community health centre produces power struggles between physicians and social workers over clinical areas of responsibility. Within any formal organization, informal relationships mould the character of the system. As these relationships alter, the form and nature of the social unit also changes.

Individuals, then, have an interactive relationship to groups and institutions. Individuals both produce social organizations and are acted upon by them. The family is an example. Couples who establish a joint residence, have children and both contribute financially to the household have created a social unit called a nuclear family. Yet, once in existence, this organization can affect the behaviour of its members. Most people with families insist on fidelity, nurturing of children and financial provision for dependents. Organizations are thus objective entities determining our behaviour. They are also subjective arrangements arising out of the day-to-day interactions of their members. Macro-order analyses reveal how large organizations shape our behaviour. In contrast, micro-order studies examine the interpersonal bonds among organizational participants.

## THE MACRO LEVEL OF ANALYSIS

The macro-order level of analysis includes the systemic or structural organization of a social unit. The term *social system* is interchangeable with *social unit*. Social systems are the actual practices and behaviours of individuals in relationship to each other in particular organizational settings.

Macro level analyses of organizational settings focus on institutions, the conceptual bridge between what people do and what people believe. Institutions include the stable cluster of values, norms, roles and expectations that decide how the needs of a society should be met. Through socialization practices, institutions transfer cultural beliefs, norms, values and roles to each new generation. For example, Canadian studies show how the socialization of doctors (Shapiro, 1978) and chiropractors (Kelner et al., 1980) in formal, institutional settings ensures that students will graduate showing similar behaviour toward their patients, their colleagues and the public.

Within macro analysis, the key concepts are role, status, group and institution. All four are involved in the web of relationships that makes societies possible and predictable. Given the importance of these concepts, they are dealt with in more detail on pages 210–228.

## THE MICRO ORDER OF ANALYSIS

The macro approach is called *structuralist* or *determinist*, meaning that it focuses on how social organizations constrain and determine human activity. In contrast, the micro approach is associated with *interactionists*, who concentrate on the daily exchanges among individuals, which weave the fabric of social life. How determinists and interactionists study social class illustrates their differences. For structural determinists, particularly Marxists, an individual's social class is determined by his relationship to the means of production. Hence, the upper class, or bourgeoise, own the factories, and the working class, or proletariat are employees. Social class is a static concept, defined according to one's relationship to the means of production.

For interactionists, social class is a status designation, but it is also a process. How we eat, talk, maintain friendships, join social clubs, organize our children's after-school activities and monitor their educational progress are but a few examples of the myriad ways we create social class.

Micro-order studies concentrate on this *social construction of reality* (Berger and Luckmann, 1966), or the way individuals and groups create social structure. Situational definitions are called perspectives and are a co-ordinated set of ideas and actions a person or a group uses in dealing with some problematic situation. Perspectives refer to a person's ordinary way of thinking, feeling and acting in such a situation (Becker et al., 1961).

These perspectives constitute patterned behaviours which vary historically. For example, current perspectives about the appropriate behaviour for children differ substantially from medieval ideas on the subject. Situational definitions also vary according to the individual's location in the social structure. Traditionally, upper-class parents have defined children as needing less direct parental stimulation and supervision than have middle-class parents. Upper-class children are likely to have full-time nannies and to be sent to boarding school at an early age.

Within any social situation, there exist rival perspectives. In a study of under-graduate college life, Becker, Geer et al. (1968) concluded that students are most interested in their social life, professors are most concerned with teaching and ad-ministrators are preoccupied with the college making a profit. Within any organi-zation, situational definitions may conflict. College teachers may not, for example, appreciate the perspective of their students. In this situation, as in every other one, the group with the ability to control the actions of others exercises power. Power is a central element in our interpersonal relationships. It affects how we behave and how others manage us. Those who exert power can make their definition of a situation stick. Day-care workers may have the authority to control two-year-olds. But if the children disobey, the teachers must alter their tactics.

Situational definitions are constantly changing. Rules of conduct, agreements and bargains shift, requiring participants to adjust. This behavioural fluctuation is called *negotiation*.

The notion of perspectives as definitions of a situation is rooted in seeing social organizations as negotiated orders. Symbolic interactionists and other negotiation-order theorists outline how interaction patterns are initiated and maintained. Re-search has examined negotiation processes among teachers and students, (Stebbins, 1975), skid row alcoholics (Wiseman, 1979) and professional wrestlers (Turowetz and Rosenberg, 1978). In a classic study, Glaser and Strauss (1965) analysed the emergence of *awareness contexts* among terminally ill patients and the hospital staff. (Awareness contexts describe how patients and the medical staff treat one another. See insert on page 210 about this study.)

Other negotiation-order studies focus on the interactional processes between and among institutions. In a study of the American liquor industry, Denzin (1977) reveals a five-tier economic structure which establishes market policies. In a critical look at health care in the United States, Freidson (1975) illustrates how adminis-trative and political activities affect, but do not determine medical practices. In both studies, the emphasis is on institutional negotiations and their effects on particular social units.

In summary, the macro approach sees the social structure as a self-perpetuating, static arrangement that limits individual behaviour. To a certain extent, social or-ganizations do determine our actions. However, social organizations would not exist without networks of individual and group relationships. Sociologists try to show how individuals co-ordinate their activities and construct group situational defini-tions. The focus of the micro order on interactional activities and the analytic frame of negotiated orders reminds us of the interdependence of institutions and conscious human activity.

AWARENESS OF DYING

The phenomenon of awareness is central to the study of interaction. Barney Glaser and Anselm Strauss (1965) introduced the concept of awareness contexts. Any act of communication contains varying degrees of understanding or awareness between the participants. *Awareness context* refers to the combination of what each person knows about the identity of the other and his own identity in the eyes of the other. Any interaction contains four possible types of awareness. An *open awareness context* occurs when each participant knows his own and the other's true identity. In a hospital, an open awareness context prevails when a patient knows he is dying, identifies himself this way and is defined and treated by the hospital staff as dying. The patient might finalize his will, take care of business and financial matters and settle personal scores. The medical staff, in turn, makes no attempt to disguise the diagnosis.

The complete opposite to this is the *closed awareness context*. In such cases, the patient does not know he is dying and is not aware that the hospital staff has identified him in this way. As Glaser and Strauss state, "The hospital is magnificently organized, both by accident and design, for hiding the medical truth from the patient." Records are not available for scrutiny, the staff conceals information, medical discussion about the patient's condition go on outside his room and the family makes constant reference to future events.

The third context, the *suspicion awareness context,* is a modification of the closed awareness context. One participant suspects the true identity of the other or the other's view of his own identity or both. For example, the patient may suspect he is dying, yet the physician may believe the patient does not know.

Finally, in the *pretense awareness context*, both participants realize that the patient is dying but pretend not to know.

# SOCIAL ROLES AND SOCIAL IDENTITIES

## SOCIAL ROLES

### Roles and Everyday Life

Both macro- and micro-order studies examine the connection between roles and interactions. By participating in collective activities, human beings learn how we behave in particular social situations. *Roles* provide normative expectations and standards for anticipating how strangers will act and for judging how we should adjust our responses.

The smooth transaction of society's daily affairs is greatly facilitated by role playing. In fact, we often do not realize how much we rely on roles to predict others' behaviour until the role prescriptions are violated. Confronting "out of role" behaviour confuses and frustrates us. Harold Garfinkel (1967), an American ethnomethodologist, demonstrated how much humans rely on roles by having his sociology students deliberately break norms in familiar social settings. By breaching customary and unspoken expectations, Garfinkel and his students were scraping below the surface of social behaviour to discover how people understand daily routines. One of Garfinkel's more popular experiments was to have his students act as guests in their parents' home. They asked permission to use household facilities and equipment, addressed their parents formally as Mr. and Mrs. and displayed impeccable manners. This behaviour so violated the norms of usual family interaction that neither the students nor the family members could tolerate it for very long.

## The Structuralist Approach to Roles

All sociologists, it seems, want to know about the origin and transmission of social roles. Macro-order role analyses take a structuralist approach, which stems from the work of Talcott Parsons (1951), Robert Merton (1967) and Ralph Linton (1936). These sociologists viewed society as organized according to a system of roles. The concept of social role became the conceptual link between individual activity and social organization. All individuals have scripts to enact. These scripts are organized into systems of roles. Hence, we have family roles, workplace roles and friendship roles. Social organizations are often analysed by examining their role structure.

The structuralist sees roles as the prescribed pattern of behaviour expected of a person in a given situation by virtue of his position in the transaction. Roles refer to observable behaviour, to what the individual actually does in a given social situation. All roles are socially defined according to the position or status an individual occupies in the social structure. Every social status carries with it a set of norms and expectations that specify how the role it defines ought to be played. The status of doctor suggests a set of behaviour, obligations and privileges that we can all agree upon. Doctors should always act in their patients' best interests. They are obligated to prolong and save lives. In exchange for their dedication and long working hours, they receive the societal privileges of professional autonomy, elevated prestige and high wages.

Roles involve both prescribed behaviours and reciprocal claims and obligations specifying what activities the actor is entitled to expect from others. Patients expect doctors to make every effort to heal them. Reciprocally, doctors expect patients to contribute to the healing process by following their orders. While the patient role specifies ideal role behaviour, our actual role performance often deviates from the norm. For example, studies indicate that over half of all patients ignore their doctor's advice. It is the nature and extent of such deviation that the interactionists study.

We are not always free to choose the parts we play in society. Some scripts, called *ascribed roles*, are assigned to us whether we like it or not. These ascribed roles are given to us at birth on the basis of biological characteristics like race and sex and on the basis of some characteristics of our parents, such as religion, caste or social class. Other parts, called *achieved roles*, require individual choice or talent before they are assumed. Occupational, marital and friendship roles are achieved.

*"Let's play you're a guest, and I'll think of ways of trying to get rid of you."*

Drawing by Whitney Darrow, Jr.; © 1947, 1975. The New Yorker Magazine, Inc.

Both ascribed and achieved roles can be ones we accept but do not enjoy. The role of mental patient may be partially ascribed and achieved and is not likely to be a role we joyfully accept. Other roles are less clearly differentiated according to their voluntary or involuntary assignment. For example, are sex and gender ascribed or achieved? Sex is usually seen as an ascribed status, while gender role behaviour is achieved. *Gender* refers to the cultural, social and psychological characteristics assumed appropriate to one's sex. Thus, gender represents learned behaviour that is acquired over a lifetime. *Sex*, on the other hand, refers to biological features.

Merton (1967) outlined how roles are systematically organized. Each social status involves, not a single associated role, but an array of roles. Physicians play the roles of primary care consultant, scientific researcher, hospital administrator, government consultant and medical school teacher. Upon entering a new status, individuals are confronted with a *role set*, an array of roles to be played in order to meet the expectations of a variety of people.

Role sets differ from multiple roles. *Multiple roles* refer to the fact that each person simultaneously enacts many different roles throughout her life. Hence, the physician is also a mother, a wife, a daughter, a professional weightlifter and a community worker.

Anxiety and stress are pervasive experiences in twentieth-century life. This pressure to succeed, achieve and conform can be analysed as *role strain* or *conflict*. Our actual behaviour does not match our definition of the normative expectations contained in our role prescriptions. We often feel pulled apart by the competing demands within role sets. The role of primary care consultant, for example, may make time claims on a physician that make it difficult for her to fulfill her teaching and research commitments. Peer discussion regularly revolves around strategies for coping with the pressures of role-set demands.

Another source of role strain is the attempt to fulfill multiple roles. Individuals often play two or more roles, each governed by conflicting norms. Consider the working mother. The norm of a wage labourer may periodically conflict with the norm of a domestic labourer. Which norm do women adhere to when their children are sick? Do they stay home and care for the child or go to work? Conformity to one role (staying home) may require deviating from another (going to work). The role overload chart indicates how women respond to role set and multiple role conflicts.

How individuals perform their roles provides another source of potential strain. Role performance can produce conflict when we disagree with others about how we or they ought to behave. Often the norms associated with roles are merely blueprints providing general behavioural guidelines. There are many ways to father, for example. Most of us will find that our definitions of good parenting are sometimes in contradiction to others' definitions. Prolonged discrepancy between actual and situational expectations can cause guilt feelings, frustration and anger. One way to cope with this is to recognize that these feelings result, not from personal inadequacies, but from competing role definitions.

Role performance can also produce strain when the role itself requires inconsistent and diverse conduct. The role of teacher contains a potential conflict in that it requires satisfying both administrators and parents. Educational administrators want teachers to cover all the material outlined by the Ministry of Education for their grade level. Parents may expect a more individualized program tailored to meet the academic and social needs of their child. Teachers sometimes "burn-out" as a result of the frustration they experience in juggling conflicting role demands.

Ambiguous roles create role conflict. The more unclear the role requirements, the more likely it is individuals will disagree over how to play the role. Typically, newly created roles and changing roles are unclear. Alice Rossi (1968) has discussed how women are prepared, through anticipatory socialization and gradual acquisition, to take on occupational and marriage roles. In contrast, transition to the parenting role

## ROLE OVERLOAD AND WOMEN'S ROLE PERFORMANCE

People have a variety of ways of adjusting to overload situations (Miller, 1960). These common overload reactions are defined below. Each is accompanied by an illustration of the way in which an overworked housewife-mother might cope with role overload in her daily life.

*Overload Reaction*

1. Omission: Temporary nonprocessing of demands.

2. Queuing: Delaying response during high overload period.

3. Filtering: Neglecting to process certain types of information while processing others.

4. Cutting categories of discrimination: Responding in a general way to a number of demands.

5. Employing multiple channels: Processing information through two or more parallel channels at the same time.

6. Errors: Processing demands incorrectly.

7. Escape from the task.

*Mother's Response*

1. Forgetting to pick up the cleaning; or not hearing a child's request while talking on the phone.

2. Promising a child that Mother will talk about their problem after dinner; telling someone to call back after the children are asleep.

3. Neglecting household tasks or elaborate food preparation in order to take care of children's needs.

4. Preparing common meals that disregard the food preferences of different family members; having a common bedtime hour for children of different ages; not responding to the unique personality needs of each child.

5. Talking to children or husband while cooking or ironing; changing a diaper while talking on the phone.

6. Confusing the date of a meeting or social engagement; burning the dinner; yelling at a child for something that she/he had gotten permission to do.

7. Going to a movie; falling asleep; leaving home.

Frieze, Irene; J. Parsons; P. Johnson; D. Ruble and G. Zellman. *Women and Sex Roles*, Norton, 1978, p. 161.

occurs abruptly with the birth of a child. Isolated, fatigued and suddenly immersed in 24-hour child care, the caretaking role often feels overwhelming to new mothers.

The structuralist perspective employs the *blueprint* approach when discussing roles and interactions. Individuals are perceived as learning a set of roles in the course of their socialization, which determines their interactional behaviour. Roles are conceptualized as standard, rule-governed actions that individuals automatically and appropriately enact in various settings. Since other organizational members have internalized the same rules, predictable relationships occur. This unified and orderly pattern of interaction becomes codified into characteristic structures.

## The Interactionist Perspective on Roles

While the structural perspective views roles as passive constructions, interactionists emphasize the dynamic aspect of activity formation, performance and conflict. The concept of role was originally employed by George Herbert Mead (1938) to explain co-operative behaviour and communication. Today, symbolic interactionists are reluctant to use the term "role" in analysing micro-order activities because of its structural connotations. Interactionists argue that social interaction cannot adequately be explained by role analysis. Instead, the more inclusive concepts of social acts and situational definitions or group perspectives are used to capture the diverse, situational dimensions of human action.

Interactionists do not analyse events in terms of roles. Rather, they concentrate on the type of experience individuals are having at a particular moment, in a particular place in their social lives. Interactionists ask "What is it that's going on here?" (Goffman 1974:8) and "How are these situational definitions different for various groups in this setting?" Discerning group perspectives means understanding what social acts individuals engage in to create distinct activities, how these activities coalesce into regular patterns and what external or internal forces lead to behavioural changes.

In understanding perspectives, researchers find that *nonverbal behaviour* is as significant as verbal expression. Infants, for example, rely on nonverbal behaviour to communicate.

In conversation, adults use nonverbal cues to tell their partners to continue, repeat, elaborate, hurry up, become more interesting, less salacious, give them a chance to talk. These messages are transmitted by nodding the head, eye contact, raising of eyebrows, slight movements forward and small postural shifts. (Ekman and Frieson 1969:82).

Interactional investigations involve more than ascertaining a set of roles. Individuals and groups are constantly interpreting events. People are always acting on their understandings and responding to the demands and expectations of others. How people mesh together their perspectives constitutes the *analytic focus*.

## ROLE ENACTMENT

Interactionists discuss role enactment as an active, reflective process in which individuals try to figure out what their part in the social exchange is and how others expect them to behave. In his discussion of role enactment, Mead (1938:8–25) identified four phases individuals go through in carrying out any social act.

**Nonverbal Expressions in Spoken English**

The importance of nonverbal behavior and the general understanding of certain nonverbal "communications" has been acknowledged by the incorporation into our spoken language of many nonverbally based expressions. We all know the meaning of the following expressions:

| *Use of the eyes* | *Costume* |
|---|---|
| Catch her eye | Wear the pants |
| Look down at | Dress to the teeth |
| Look down your nose at | |
| Look up to | |
| Admiring gaze | |
| Look ahead | |
| Forward looking | |
| Don't look back | |

| *Mouth* | *Other* |
|---|---|
| Grit your teeth | Sick to his stomach |
| Friendly smile | Land on your feet |
| Smile of satisfaction | Run in circles |
| Stiff upper lip | Keep at arm's length |
| Bare your teeth at | Get your hands on something |
| Grin and bear it | Hold tight |
| | Too close for comfort |

Frieze, Irene; J. Parsons; P. Johnson; D. Ruble and G. Zellman. *Women and Sex Roles*, Norton, 1978, p. 323.

The first involves an *identification with self*. The individual asks who he is or ought to be in that particular situation. Secondly, an individual must then *behave in a manner appropriate* to this identification. We do not simply play roles as puppets; we explore possibilities and choose those most suitable. These decisions are relatively simple when the social norms governing action are clearly defined. Our interactions with shopkeepers and post office workers are based on distinct rules. However, choosing an appropriate stance becomes difficult in ambiguous situations. When we are unsure of someone's sex, considerable confusion results. People greeting new babies always want to know the child's sex because this information determines how they will treat the child.

Thirdly, individuals *use the behaviour of others* as cues to guide their own behaviour. Through their actions, other people convey to us what they expect us to do. By symbolically communicating their expectations, people create a collective definition of the situation. In devising any role performance, we consider the expectations of others. These shared expectations provide countless regulations that we hardly ever think about.

The final element integral to the enactment of roles is an *evaluation* by us and by others of our performance. An individual's part in an exchange provides him with a distinctive position from which to evaluate his own performance and those of others.

The late Erving Goffman (1963, 1967), an American sociologist, analysed the *interaction rituals* people employ in daily life. These rituals include all the taken-for-granted cues we use in dealing with others. *Access* rituals (1967:41), for example, refer to how we greet and take leave of others. The rules governing greetings between intimates differ from those regulating the greetings of boss and employee. Strangers, of course, do not greet one another but rather engage in the ritual of *civil inattention* (1963:84). This ritual can be seen in elevators, where individuals glance at each other only long enough to acknowledge the other's presence. Excessive eye contact is considered inappropriate in such public places. Children, as nonpersons, are permitted to stare.

Interactionists conceptualize roles as negotiable social acts. Social acts are the basic unit of human behaviour, on which all communication is established. By focusing on the social actions among individuals, interactionists can describe the wider dimensions of human exchanges.

## Role Playing and Role Taking

Role enactment is similar to role playing. *Role playing* consists of living up to the obligations of the role one assumes and insisting that others meet your expectations. However, role playing, and indeed all social interaction, would be impossible without role taking. To play a role, you have to understand how others might react to you. You gain this understanding by imaginatively projecting yourself into the point of view of others. A patient, for example, imagines how her complaints will sound to the physician and states her situation vigorously or diffidently, depending on the length and severity of her illness. Mead called this "taking the role of the other toward self" (1938:374). *Role taking* refers to empathizing with others by symbolically assuming their point of view. We observe their behaviour, learn how they think and feel and, simultaneously, see how they are interpreting our behaviour.

We take the roles of others into account so naturally that we never reflect upon this process unless an interactional problem arises. A problem, according to Mead, is some action, word, gesture, thought or physical obstacle that stops the smooth flow of interaction and causes us to think about our situation. When problems arise, we realize that we must put ourselves in the other's shoes and imagine their thoughts and feelings. Greeting friends is done with no reflection, unless one of them snubs you. Most daily exchanges occur on this customary, habitual level. Life would be too exhausting and stressful otherwise. The role of tourist in a foreign country is often tiring because we have to work so hard at comprehending the new cultural system. Similarly, one reason new students at university feel so lost and anxious is the alarming array of new problems they confront. Meeting the demands of professors, finding student hangouts, making new friends and securing dates are all difficult in a strange situation. For the most part, students behave as most people do in new situations. They appear nonchalant, remain silent and closely follow the ways of more experienced students. Often neophytes find people to inform or coach them on how to behave in an unfamiliar setting.

For the interactionists, social change is a gradual, continual and consensual process of mutual realignment of perspectives. Mead (1938:79) outlines exactly how change occurs. In the course of interaction, confusions and misunderstandings between people often arise, effectively ending the exchange. One cannot continue to act until these problems are solved. Resolution occurs when individuals reflect on their situation and come up with alternative ways of behaving. This reflection can occur within minutes or take several years.

Interpersonal negotiation is central to problem-solving. In most situations, degrees and types of bargaining can be identified. Anselm Strauss (1963) has suggested that each situation contains working agreements that broadly outline how individuals should interact. These general agreements do not take on the specificity or the constraining nature of rules. Rather, any agreement can be "stretched, negotiated, argued, ignored and applied at convenient moments" (Strauss 1963:153). Understanding this situational negotiation is essential in analysing social settings.

Wilfred Martin (1976), in a recent Canadian field study of the schooling process, employed the concept of negotiation to explain how teachers view students. Martin (1976:6) defined negotiation as the " . . . total set of processes whereby actors, in pursuit of common interests, try to arrive at a settlement or arrangement with each other or with a third party." The teachers Martin observed classified student role performance according to three categories. The "nonnegotiable" students were those the teachers viewed as problems. Hence, the teachers refused to bargain with them and instead issued explicit directives and stated explicit consequences of disobeying these directives. The second group was labelled "continuously negotiable." These "teachers' pets" joined in open negotiation with the teachers and were often successful in gaining their ends. The third group, the "intermittently negotiable" students, represented the silent majority, whose participation in open or closed negotiation depended on how legitimate their demands were seen to be.

The work of Martin and Strauss demonstrates that role bargaining is a pervasive feature of role enactment. As originally conceived, role taking is falsely based on a model of interaction between equals within neutral settings and leading to mutually satisfying alignments. Interactionists use the concept of negotiation to account for the varying degrees of power which individuals exercise. Negotiation-order theorists acknowledge that most relationships are unequal. Individuals do not have identical power and ability to determine outcomes, and situational definitions are often imposed by those with the most control.

## Roles and Self Identity

Sociologists have linked the concepts of self and role. Through social interaction, we develop a self-identity. Our self-image is closely linked to the roles we enact and reflects how we imagine others characterize us. Just as we perform many diverse roles during our lifetimes, we also have many selves or ways of viewing ourselves.

A classic field-work study by Erving Goffman (1959b) dramatically reveals how roles and situational expectations affect self-behaviour and the behaviour of others. Goffman analysed the effect of being labelled mentally ill and treated as such within the institutional setting of a mental hospital. Mental patients go through a regular sequence of changes in their self- and other definitions. In the first stage, as pre-patients, they typically feel betrayed and skeptical of those who committed them. Once committed, patients are stripped of their rights and liberties. Tension arises between the patients and the staff and family who try to convince the patients that this help is "for their own good."

In the second stage, as inpatients, the patients' self-definitions undergo a transformation. Confronted with unacceptable views of themselves and with isolation, humiliation and stark living conditions, patients present favourable explanations for their past and current behaviours. Patients suggest they were misdiagnosed, overworked or suffer from bad nervous systems. However, the staff and other patients create a social environment that denies these agreeable self-images and forces the patients to constantly review who they are. Over time, patients take on the selves the others present to them. Adopting these self-images is also a more efficient way of coping with their demoralizing situations.

How, then, do we define the self? The self is a social product, an outgrowth of our interaction with others. According to Lindesmith et al. (1977:324), the self is an organization or integration of behaviour imposed upon individuals by themselves and by societal expectations and demands. Selves do not exist except in a symbolic environment from which they cannot be separated. As we move through life, we acquire a succession of selves. William James (1890:294), the noted American social psychologist, first commented on the social and multi-faceted nature of self-identity:

> The individual has as many different social selves as there are distinct groups of persons about whose opinion he cares. Many a youth who is demure enough before his parents and teachers, swears and swaggers like a pirate among his "tough" friends.

Given the situational and changeable nature of self-concepts, is there one true or real self, a unique identity which persists despite the variety of experiences we encounter? Sociologists disagree on this question. But the majority have used role enactment as an explanation for multiple selves. Role enactment allows for a wide variety of acts within a permitted range. Despite individual differences in personality, temperament and life experiences, sociologists emphasize the similarities in role performance. What role variations do exist are seen as resulting from an individual's prior experience or from immediate situational pressures.

Not only do we appear to others as many different people, but often the performance of one role is interrupted by the encroachment of other roles. Given this role diversity, what unifies an individual's behaviour is her controlling conception of what she is doing. This self-direction comes from the ongoing, private dialogues an individual has with herself. By talking with herself, reviewing her behaviour in different situations and evaluating her diverse performances, the individual maintains a consistent sense of self.

Recognition of the *situational self* has led to research on how various environments affect individual and group behaviour. Philip Zimbardo (1971), a social psychologist, demonstrated the effect of the situation on the self in his Stanford County Prison experiment. Zimbardo designed a realistic mock prison in the basement of one of Stanford's buildings. Through a newspaper advertisement, he solicited volunteers who were willing to spend two weeks playing the role of either a prisoner or a guard. The experiment had to be abandoned after six days due to the emotional strain the prisoners were under. Five prisoners had to be released, four because of severe emotional depression or acute anxiety attacks, one because he developed a psychosomatic rash. The prisoners were behaving like "servile, dehumanized robots who thought only of escape, of their individual survival and of their mounting hatred of the guards" (Zimbardo, 1971:3). This happened because, soon after the experiment started, the guards began abusing their power. They made the prisoners obey petty and meaningless rules, forced them to do tedious and useless work, demanded that they laugh and sing on command and ordered them to publicly humiliate each other. In less than a week, ordinary, mature, emotionally stable, middle-class college students became caught up in the traditional prisoner and guard roles.

How do we reconcile an individual's controlling sense of self with his presentation of various and often unpleasant selves? An individual resolves this tension by talking to himself about his seemingly discrepant behaviours, assessing their origin and evaluating their impact on others. This private self-reflection allows an individual to explain current behaviours within the context of his own historical account of past and present acts.

## IMPRESSION MANAGEMENT

In all sorts of exchanges, people employ interactional strategies designed to help them control and impose their definition of the situation on the group. Since group definitions become self-fulfilling prophecies, we recognize the importance of controlling how others interpret events and act on these constructions.

Erving Goffman investigated how people manage their self-impressions. *Self-impressions* include impressions the self makes on others and impressions that others make on the self. (In the course of interaction, selves act, others respond, and selves incorporate these responses into their next act. People are constantly monitoring and evaluating their own behaviour and that of others.) Goffman's approach is thus called *dramaturgical*, based on the idea expressed by Shakespeare as "all the world's a stage and all the men and women merely players."

Building on Mead's notion of role taking, Goffman suggested that actors both empathize with their fellow participants in creating joint social acts and actively strive to manage and control how these others will interpret their behaviour. In all interactional exchanges, we consider our audience expectations and characteristics and attempt to present ourselves favourably. In the *Presentation of Self in Everyday Life* (1959a), Goffman outlined two ways an individual manages impressions. He deliberately gives some impressions. These consist of the information or sign activity an actor wants the audience to receive. An individual also gives off some impressions unwittingly. Both behaviours occur within structurally defined limits. Goffman calls attempting to convey a specific impression *front-stage behaviour*. Deliberately concealing information from our audience is called *back-stage behaviour*. Goffman uses a waiter in a restaurant to illustrate. The front-stage scene for waiters is the formal dining area of the restaurant. Waiters try to convey a sense of sincerity in serving their customers. As in any successful front-stage performance, the actor stages a good performance by acting in role and by manipulating the situational props (the setting and lighting, the food). In some social encounters, such as those that take place in a restaurant, performance teams co-operate in staging a successful and convincing routine for the audience.

Raven and Rubin photo. Permission granted by John Wiley & Sons Ltd.

However, according to Goffman, if we really wanted to know what the waiter was like, we would also have to observe his back-stage, or out of role, behaviour. Kitchens, for example, are back-stage areas for waiters, since that is where the audience does not normally enter. The information a waiter discloses about himself in the kitchen when discussing his customers or arguing with the chef is far more instructive in providing us with a well-rounded picture of this person.

## GENDER DISPLAYS

While we do sometimes willfully manage gender-type impressions, many gender behaviours are not consciously manipulable. Learning appropriate gender displays is a central lesson in childhood socialization, so these behaviours become habitual.

## LANGUAGE AND THE INTERACTION BETWEEN MEN AND WOMEN

Interactionists have studied conversations between men and women. Somehow, in their everyday communications, both sexes reinforce their unequal status. To alter gender inequality, we must understand how, through interaction, men are encouraged to assume positions of dominance and women to fill submissive roles.

One way to tackle this methodological problem is through conversational analysis. People widely believe that women talk much more than men and that they talk about trivial matters. However, there has not been one study to support this notion. In mixed-sex conversations, men talk more than women. In 1972, Jessie Bernard analysed television sitcoms and found that men talked more often than women. In 1977, Nancy Henley noted that it was often impossible for women to talk when men were present, particularly if the males were their husbands. If women wished to talk, they talked to each other. Henley thinks that the stereotype of the talkative woman arises from the role of women in a patriarchal order, where they are required to be submissive and silent. Men wish to dominate and give orders to women. Any amount of talk by a woman is considered excessive.

In a conversational-analysis study, Zimmerman and West (1975) and West and Zimmerman (1977) suggested that the speech behaviour of women interacting with men resembled that of children talking to adults. They found that 98 percent of interruptions in mixed-sex conversations were made by men. Interruptions prevent women from talking and ensure female silence by allowing men to "gain the floor."

Men also denied equal status to women as conversational partners by not pursuing topics of interest to women and by not allowing women an equal number of turns to talk during a conversation. Women maintained longer silences and used a childlike intonation pattern when talking by raising their voices at the end of an exclamation ("I told you so!") instead of dropping their voices, as adult men do.

Pamela Fishman (1978) recorded the daily conversations between three couples who were white, professional and between the ages of 25 and 35. Five of the six were in graduate school. Two of the three women were avowed feminists, while all three men described themselves as sympathetic to the women's movement.

Despite these protestations of gender equality, there was an unequal distribution of work in conversation. The women asked three times as many questions as the men. The women used conversational attention-getters, such as "Do you know what?" or "This is interesting." Women used "yeah," "umm" and "huh" to show they were constantly attending to what was being said. The men also produced over twice as many statements as the women, and they also got responses. The women introduced a number of topics. When they hit one the men wanted to pursue, often the men did so by interrupting and assuming control.

Fishman concluded that women are the "shit workers" of routine interaction. Shit work includes sitting and being a good listener, filling silences and keeping the conversation going, developing others' topics and presenting and developing topics of their own. Women who deviate from this role and successfully control interactions are considered domineering, castrating and aggressive.

Jack Sattel (1982) has analysed "male inexpressiveness" as a strategy men use to maintain their dominant interactional position. Male inexpressiveness refers to behaviour that does not indicate affection, tenderness or emotion. It also includes behaviour that is not supportive of the affective expectations of a wife or female intimate. Sattel suggests that men are inexpressive only when they want to be. From an early age, boys learn that inexpressiveness is a means of assuming and maintaining positions of power. Giving off an affectively neutral impression convinces others of one's rational and calm decision-making ability. By being silent and inexpressive, especially in tense situations, men consolidate their power and "make the effort appear as effortless, to guard against showing the real limits of one's potential and power by making it all appear easy." Sattel further suggests that men are situationally expressive when they see expressiveness as a useful way to exercise control. For example, one way for a man to "come on" to a woman is to show his weaknesses and frailties. Such behaviour is to be read by the woman as a sign of authentic interest in her.

However, in one of his last works (*Gender Advertisements*, 1979), Goffman suggests several ways individuals deliberately use specific strategies to control and manage social encounters involving gender behaviours.

Gender displays are the culturally established gender behaviours that are so stereotypical they can be recognized in almost any social context. Gender displays include the smile, the leer, the seductive posture and the feminine touch. Each display represents typically masculine and feminine behaviour. These displays are part of our everyday life and are easily recognized in television and magazine advertisements.

Using Goffman's analytical frame, Posner (1982) has examined sex-role stereotyping in Canadian magazine advertisements. By examining body postures, facial expressions, eye contact and relationship to physical objects, Posner shows how these advertisements reinforce stereotypical images of women and men. Women are portrayed as childlike, tactile, mentally drifting and passive. Men are aggressive, active, alert and in control. Our uncritical acceptance of these images indicates that we agree that men and women present themselves to others in fundamentally different ways.

# SOCIAL GROUPS AND INTERACTIONS

## THE INDIVIDUAL

### Individuals in Groups

Throughout this chapter, we have stressed the social character of interaction. People have always formed associations and most social interaction occurs within groups. Our behaviour, personality and character are moulded by the groups to which we belong. Moreover, most changes in our lives result from alterations in our group membership. Entering university, working in our first job, getting married, having children and aging are experienced as group events. How we interpret our university life varies tremendously according to our group participation. Women's studies, athletic teams, debating societies, chess clubs and musical societies are examples of different groups in which students can become involved and which can colour their university experience.

### What is a Social Group?

But what is a social group? What, for example, distinguishes a random collection of people at a hockey game from a neighbourhood street gang? Generally, a social group is any collection of two or more people interacting together in an orderly way on the basis of shared understanding about how they and other group members ought to behave. Just because people are together in the same place does not mean that they constitute a social group. Collective behaviour is not group behaviour. For the hockey-game crowd to be regarded as a social group, its members must interact. Instead, crowd members react individually to a central stimulus (the game) and subliminally to each other. In contrast, neighbourhood gangs develop group consciousness and a sympathetic identification with similar groups. Social groups vary in size, organization, durability and flexibility of action.

Sociology contains two distinct approaches to studying group behaviour. The first, a *structuralist* interpretation, focuses on the structural characteristics which distinguish groups from nongroups. Often, only stable aggregates are studied, including ones with a readily identifiable membership, a clearly defined central activity and the binding of one member to another in well-established relationships (Shibutani, 1961:33). This definition of groups includes everything from small peer groups to all members of the Moslem faith.

The second approach, the *interactionist* perspective, defines groups according to their central activity. Interactionists focus on group process, on how the group members work together. A group is thus more than a collection of individuals who happen to be at the same place at the same time. Social groups are units of interacting individuals who have a common sense of identity and a "capacity for common endeavour" (Shibutani 1961:33).

Incorporating both the structuralist and the interactionist views, groups can be said to have the following characteristics:

1. Group members share a sense of identity, co-operation and consciousness of themselves as a group.

2. This identity is established through repeated patterns of interaction, in which group members evolve stable and predictable ways of accomplishing group goals.
3. These interactional patterns are based on shared understandings about definitions of situations, expected situational responses, goals, plans of action and rules of appropriate conduct.
4. Interactional patterns are further differentiated according to the division of labour within the group. The allocation of various group tasks creates a degree of member interdependence and integration within the collective enterprise.
5. Interactional patterns are further differentiated according to the degree of ongoing negotiation, in which group members adjust to situational demands.

Each group has its own norms, roles, status arrangements, rules, shared beliefs, negotiation limits and lines of action. Sociological investigation reveals the internal dynamics of group processes and explores the group's external relationships to other social organizations.

## TYPES OF GROUPS

### Primary Groups

Three main elements significantly affect group interaction. These are group size, the tasks of the group and the nature of the interpersonal relations within it. Based on these three characteristics, groups are classified as either primary or secondary.

Charles Horton Cooley (1909:23), a founder of American sociology, introduced the concept of primary groups to refer to those groups "characterized by intimate face-to-face association and cooperation." Primary groups are based on what Cooley called the primary relation. *Primary relationships* are those small, intimate, co-operative contacts which provide emotional support and teach us our culture. The most common forms of primary bonding are emotionally intense, such as parent-child relationships, love attachments and friendships. In these close primary relationships, we interact by responding to others as unique and whole personalities. These personally satisfying relationships are essential early in life if a person is to learn how to form close relationships with others. Later in life, we participate in primary groups such as families and peer networks.

These primary associations provide affection and security and facilitate personal growth and self-esteem. Given the emotional closeness of these relationships, primary-group members are not interchangeable. The loss of a member through death, divorce or other circumstances requires considerable readjustment. While most primary relations are happy and personally satisfying, others are intensely antagonistic. For example, our experiences within the family are crucial to developing our self-identity, yet, because of child abuse and wife-beating, family relationships are often brutally violent.

Almost any small group can develop primary relations. As Simmel (1955), a German sociologist, pointed out in his brilliant work on *triads* (interactions among three people) and *dyads* (interactions between two people) the size of a group determines its quality and type of interaction. Only small groups can ripen into personal and intimate relationships.

Within any larger organization, such as an army, a college, a factory or a business corporation, small, primary groups may develop. This usually occurs when the members are together for a long time, confronting joint problems and undergoing similar experiences. Friendship networks link the individual to the wider society. The closeness and commitment to other primary group members ultimately sustains small groups and enables their members to accomplish the larger goals of society. William Foote Whyte's classic field work study (*Street Corner Society*, 1961) is perhaps the most thorough treatment of the effect of the primary group on individual behaviour. Whyte graphically details the primary relations among a group of men in the north end of Boston. By living in the area and befriending the group, Whyte discovered how these Italian men, who congregated together on certain street corners, evolved their sense of self-esteem and identity from their gang membership.

## Secondary Groups

While Cooley never discussed the concept of the secondary group, it is a term widely used in sociology today. *A secondary group* is any collection of people who communicate sporadically on an impersonal basis. Often these groups are formed to accomplish a specific purpose. Hence, the group members respond to one another in terms of the limited roles they have taken on to carry out the group's task. Participation in political campaigns, fund-raising organizations, neighbourhood committees or an introductory sociology class are all secondary-group activities. All tend to be unsentimental, instrumental, limited and specific attachments.

Unlike primary groups, secondary-group members are not often emotionally committed to one another. Because of the larger size of secondary groups, it is impossible for all members to know each other personally. Also, the size of the group necessitates specialization of roles and responsibilities. A formal system of decision-making is used to organize the group's tasks. While most social organizations fall somewhere between primary and secondary groups, the distinguishing element between the two types is the relative strength of the sense of identity and attachment to the group which the members feel.

Business organizations are secondary groups that shape workers' behaviour. In a detailed examination of corporate life, Kanter (1977:3) concluded, "Organizations make their workers into who they are." Corporations typically recruit, as managers, people they think will fit into the company. The more individual discretion managerial jobs require, the more likely it is that other managers will hire men they feel they can trust to make responsible decisions. One way of guaranteeing trust is to recruit men from similar educational and social backgrounds. Once in place, "good" managers are defined as those who are good team players, who fit into the organization, who have strong peer acceptance and who make others feel comfortable. In short, good managers evince *general* skills and knowledge which can be adapted to organizational demands.

# GROUP INFLUENCE ON OTHERS

## Reference Groups

Groups modify behaviour, attitudes, character, identity and emotions, and reference groups are particularly influential. *Reference groups* are associations to which individuals refer when formulating and evaluating their own beliefs and actions. The concept stems from interactionist work, which maintains that co-ordinated group action emerges from sharing perspectives.

Reference groups are powerful organizing influences in shaping individuals. They are groups to which people aspire. Thus, individuals do not necessarily belong to their reference group. For people undergoing anticipatory socialization, their reference group is often the group to which they expect eventually to belong. For example, university students enrolled in nursing school may look to nurses who have already graduated for professional standards rather than to other nursing students. Similarly, social climbing and marginality, in which individuals are caught between two social groups with no clear commitment to either, are explained in terms of reference groups.

An early major study of reference groups was undertaken by Theodore Newcomb (1943), who examined the changing attitudes and values of students at the all-female Bennington College in New England. Most of the 250 women came from conservative families. Thus, their family values conflicted with the liberal orientation of the faculty and administration. Following one cohort through their four undergraduate years, Newcomb noticed that the longer the students stayed at the school, the more liberal they became. All but a small minority switched their primary reference group from their conservative families to the liberal faculty. A follow-up study done 25 years later (Newcomb, Koenig, Flacks and Warcick, 1967) indicated that these value changes had persisted. The more liberal students remained committed liberals in their adult life, as measured by their career choices, periodical subscriptions and voting behaviour.

Distinctions are usually drawn between the normative and the comparative functions of reference groups. The *normative function* refers to individuals assuming, either through direct or vicarious participation, the perspectives of the group. The group's norms, values and attitudes are behavioural guides. Teenage friends who dress alike and march in peace demonstrations are examples of the normative influence of groups.

The *comparative function* is exercised when individuals use the beliefs of their reference groups as standards by which to judge the beliefs and actions of others. During the process of assimilation, immigrants gradually acquire the perspectives of the dominant cultural group. Shaffir (1974) studied how religious converts (Jews joining the Montreal Lubavitcher Jewish chassidim movement) adopted the standards and actions of their new reference group.

Why we choose one reference group over another is unclear. From their research on ethnic assimilation, Haas and Shaffir (1978:16) concluded that we are more likely to select groups if we have favourable feelings toward their members and if we are treated in a friendly and sincere manner. Other important factors include the

Following the horrors of World War II concentration camps and the mass extermination of Jews, gypsies, leftists and homosexuals, North American social scientists became fascinated with the phenomenon of people hurting other people. Was the German compliance with Nazi demands a result of some national characteristic? Or was it a result of group influence, which would suggest that such horrors could be carried out by any nation?

To explore these questions, Stanley Milgram (1963) carried out a series of experiments to test to what extent people would obey authority. Milgram assigned the subjects the role of teacher, in what they thought was a study of learning and memory. As the teacher, the volunteer was to administer an ever increasing voltage of electric shocks to a "learner" every time the learner answered a memory question incorrectly. The learner was presumed to be strapped to an electrode, which conducted the electric current. Opposite the learner and separated from him by a wall, the teacher sat in front of an electric shock generator from which he could administer the shocks.

The teacher was told that the experiment would test the effect of punishment on learning. In fact, the real purpose was to ascertain when the teachers would refuse to participate in the experiment despite the researcher's insistence that they continue to administer apparently extremely painful shocks to a learner. Twenty-six of the 40 adult males tested went all the way, administering the most extreme shock of 450 volts to what they thought were real learners.

Milgram explained his results by noting that all of us have spent years being taught to obey those in authority. Most social groups demand conformity to their rules as a condition of membership. Experience in internalizing rules of conduct and obedience in certain group situations increases the likelihood we will "live by the rules" in other group situations.

perceived status and rewards to be gained from membership, individual rates of social mobility (upwardly mobile people choose higher status groups as reference groups) and the individual's own personality and view of himself. We tend to choose groups that seem similar to us in some way (Merton, 1957:288–92).

Reference group theory emphasizes the significance and power of the group in defining and evaluating definitions of social situations. It helps explain behavioural inconsistencies as individuals change groups and make choices between alternatives. (Reference group theory encouraged a wealth of studies that examine the influence of groups on the behaviour of those outside. The issue of social conformity has received special attention and is discussed in the inserts above and opposite.)

# SUMMARY

In this chapter, we have discussed the differences between macro and micro analyses and their approaches to the study of roles and interactions. *Macro-order* studies stress

## JONESTOWN

Reference group theory encouraged a wealth of studies examining the influence of groups on the behaviour of those outside the group. The issue of social conformity has received special attention. Humans conform to and obey others, often in a seemingly blind and unthinking fashion. The following excerpt explains the 1978 Jonestown mass suicide of over 900 people in terms of the types of power exerted in the commune:

### Coercion

It is true that armed guards surrounded the group and some people may have felt that if they didn't drink the poison, they would be killed anyway.

### Informational Power

Jones told them that because of the murders of the congressman and some of those with him, the commune would very soon be attacked either by the Guyanese army or the CIA. There was talk of torture and concentration camps. "When they start parachuting out of the air, they'll shoot some of our innocent babies. Can you let them take your child?" ("Hurry, My Children, Hurry," 1979).

### Referent Power

Jones was a beloved leader for most of his followers. The group, which was composed of many poor blacks, had given up all their possessions, cut off ties with their families, and followed him to the jungles of South America to start a new society. The fact that he felt it was time to "die with dignity" must have motivated many who wanted to emulate him. "To me death is not a fearful thing," Jones said that day. "It's living that's cursed. It's not worth living like this. . . . I like to choose my own kind of death for a change. I'm tired of being tormented to hell. Tired of it." (Applause) (Ibid.). Jones's referent power for one of the members is evident in this statement heard on the tape: "Like Dad (the cultists called Jones "Dad") said, when they come in, they're going to massacre our children. And the ones that they take captive, they're gonna just let them grow up and be dummies. And not grow up to be a person like the one and only Jim Jones." (Applause) ("Hurry, My Children, Hurry," 1979).

### Expert Power

Jones was clearly the expert on what should be done. He controlled everything that happened at Jonestown, and had directed the members' activities for years. Jones's statements to the group emphasize his expertise. "I've tried to keep this thing from happening. But I now see it's the will of the sovereign Being that we lay down our lives in protest against what's been done." As one man said, "I'm ready to go. If you tell us we have to give our lives now, we're ready; all the rest of the sisters and brothers are with me" ("Hurry, My Children, Hurry," 1979).

### Legitimate Power

Jones used many techniques to reinforce the feeling that he was the group's legitimate leader and that they were obligated to obey him. By insisting that they call him "Dad" and call his wife Marcellne, "Mother," he likened his role to that of a parent. Children must obey their parents. At meetings of the commune, he sat on a chair on an elevated platform almost like a king. He laid the groundwork for his legitimacy during the years preceding the tragedy. He had carried out an extensive program of socialization in which group members were called upon to declare, verbally and in writing, how much they loved him and how important he was to them. There were rewards for acceptable behavior and punishment, often in the form of brutal beatings, for unacceptable behavior (Winfrey, 1979).

In addition to this vast store of personal power available to Jones, there was the equally vast force of *peer pressure among the followers themselves*. Seeing their friends and relatives killing their children and then taking their own lives undoubtedly convinced many members that suicide was the only alternative for them.

In summary, by analyzing the influence process of Jonestown, an unbelievable, bewildering event becomes an understandable tragedy.

From SOCIAL PSYCHOLOGY by Daniel Perlan and P. Chris Cozby. Copyright © 1983 by CBS College Publishing. Reprinted by permission.

---

the objective conditions that influence the interpersonal bonds which develop. The social structure or environment within which interaction takes place encourages some types of interaction more than others. The *micro-order* focuses on interactional activities in which individuals learn new behaviours, express their interpretations and adjust to the demands of others.

The *structuralist*, or *blueprint*, approach to roles and interactions sees individuals as passive; they merely learn prescribed patterns through the socialization process. Successfully socialized individuals perform in situationally appropriate ways. Thus, *role sets*, *multiple roles* and *role strain* are defined according to normative standards of role enactment.

In contrast, the *interactionist*, or *process*, perspective emphasizes the dynamic quality of social structure. Individuals are seen as active agents who bring their own meanings to social encounters. Within a general framework of consensus, individuals continually *negotiate* definitions of legitimate behaviour. Roles and interactions are negotiable social acts, patterns which coalesce into group perspectives.

*Social groups* are an intermediate level of social organization linking the macro and the micro orders. *Primary relations* are the most intimate interpersonal bonds. It is from these affiliations that we derive our sense of identity, and in them we experience relationships most intensely. The influence of *reference groups*, one type of primary group, as a source of values and actions attests to the significance of primary relations.

However, most of our behaviour occurs within larger, more impersonal *secondary groups*. We co-operate with larger numbers of people in institutions to accomplish group goals. Analyses of secondary groups reveal the influence of the organizational setting in delineating interactional processes. Focusing on roles and interactions within group settings uncovers the interdependent and reciprocal relationship between individual acts and institutional arrangements.

## DISCUSSION QUESTIONS

1. Devise an experiment to see if the findings of Zimmerman and West and those of Sattel can be replicated *OR* in what conditions might their findings *not* be replicated.

2. Choose a primary and a secondary group to which you belong. Analyse and contrast the roles, norms, status relationships and level of cohesiveness in both groups.

3. Can you recall an awkward social situation you have recently been in? Explain why you felt uncomfortable by analysing the role requirements you were attempting to fulfill.

4. Apply Goffman's ideas of impression management to some social situation you are familiar with.

5. Using the theory of reference groups, discuss some of the changes that have occurred in your life.

# 10

# Gender and Gender Relations

*Maureen Baker*

# INTRODUCTION: MAINTAINING GENDER DIFFERENCES

From the moment a human baby is born, we treat it according to its sex. Wrapping newborns in pink or blue blankets symbolizes this distinction. As soon as people hear a child's name, they usually know whether it is a girl or a boy. Differences in dress, in mannerisms, in personality, in toys and interests are carefully cultivated by parents, who fear they could harm their children by blurring these distinctions. Children themselves are often offended if they are mistaken for a member of the opposite sex.

Segregation of the sexes used to be common in schools, clubs, the workplace and in political life. Until the 1970s, schools usually maintained separate entrances for girls and boys and did not allow the sexes to play together at recess. In some provinces, taverns had one entrance for "ladies and escorts" and one for men only. Private clubs for business and professional men did not admit women. Until just before World War II, a woman was expected to quit her job when announcing her marriage, and until very recently she was expected to leave when she became pregnant. Expectant fathers were not allowed in the delivery room with their wives until a few years ago.

Recently there has been a concerted effort to minimize the differences in the opportunities presented to the sexes in the workplace and to blur the physiological differences. Unisex hairstyling and clothing are fashionable among some segments of the population, yet others exaggerate sexual differences in appearance. Some people tenaciously adhere to the idea that males and females are different in abilities, interests and personality. Others argue that differences between the sexes are "natural," should be respected and accentuated to enhance the quality of life.

## BIOLOGY OR SOCIALIZATION?

How much of the behavioural and attitudinal differences between males and females is caused by physiology? How much is developed through different social treatment? This has been a controversy for many years. Because of the ethical problems involved in doing research on human infants, studies of the innate differences between the sexes are usually performed on animals. These studies, however, have been inconclusive.

Although the origins of gender differences cannot be easily discovered, it is apparent that behavioural differences exist between male and female humans from childhood on. Especially in early adolescence, the aptitudes, personalities, interests and achievement levels of North American girls and boys become more distinct. Males and females develop different verbal abilities by age ten. Girls tend to do better in spelling and boys in mathematics. Girls show less independence in decision-making, less assertiveness and self-confidence and more of an interest in helping people and maintaining relationships. While boys play competitive games with carefully laid-out rules in teams and groups, girls are more likely to play co-operative games in smaller groups.

Many studies of sex differences have had their methods and basic concepts challenged. For example, research on aggressiveness has often considered only physical

*In the summer of 1956, this young boy was learning to use a sewing machine in Ontario.*
Public Archives Canada/PA-137104.

fighting, and not verbal abuse, as evidence of aggressiveness. In studies using children from different cultures, results have varied. In the 1930s, the American anthropologist Margaret Mead found tribes in New Guinea with quite opposite ideas from each other and from North Americans about masculinity and femininity and appropriate activities for the sexes. Even when similar gender distinctions are found in cross-cultural research, the origins of these differences are not easily analysed.

The controversy about innate versus socially induced gender differences reappeared in recent research on the human brain. Some researchers found that the two different sides, or hemispheres, of the brain are developed differently in males and females. One side seems to control language development and the other side spatial relations and analytic abilities. But we do not know whether these developmental differences are innate sex differences or whether they simply result from different training. Since we cannot experiment on human infants or young children, we cannot separate the effects of physiology from the effects of socialization.

The influence of hormones on levels of aggression has also been debated for years, but because experiments have been done on animal primates rather than humans, we do not know if hormone levels influence aggression in humans. We are also unsure if certain hormones are released when we feel anger or whether they cause us to feel anger and to act aggressively.

Without rejecting the thesis of instinctual or innate differences between the sexes, it is clear that North American males and females are socialized very differently. Without realizing it, mothers and fathers talk to and cuddle baby girls more and treat them with more gentleness. Little boys are granted greater independence and personal freedom in decision-making, and they are permitted to stray farther from home than girls. Girls tend to be coddled and protected more and are taught to be neater, cleaner and more obedient. Physical activity is encouraged in boys and curbed in girls by verbal reprimand and by the way they are dressed.

Within the family, girls see their mothers performing most of the child-care and housework while their fathers are away at work. Once small children learn which sex they are, they often imitate the same-sex parent and so develop rigid ideas about sex-appropriate behaviour.

At school, children see that women are the secretaries, nurses and teachers of young children, while men teach older students and become principals. Their guidance counsellors have encouraged them to prepare for sex-appropriate jobs. This occupational segregation is also apparent on the television programs they watch and the glimpses they get of the division of labour in the community. As children spend more time away from home—at school, with their friends, at community functions and later in part-time work—they learn that men and women are expected to behave differently and to perform different jobs.

The physiological differences between the sexes are certainly reinforced by social customs and traditions of gender-related behaviour. Although attitudes toward sexual equality are changing, behaviour has changed less. Inconsistencies between attitudes and behaviour are still apparent: Adolescents *say* they believe in equality yet are often afraid to violate social convention.

Treating boys and girls differently affects their status, income and power as adults. Let us look at male and female participation in education, work and politics as illustrations of the implications of differential socialization and opportunity.

## STATUS AND POWER DIFFERENTIALS IN CANADA BETWEEN MEN AND WOMEN

### THE EDUCATIONAL SYSTEM

The quality and length of education has always varied considerably by sex and social class. In the early 1800s, poorer children received only a rudimentary education. Girls were considered to need formal schooling less and were expected to acquire domestic skills as well as reading and writing. Among the higher classes, young men were often trained in the professions, but young women were excluded from Canadian teachers' colleges until 1849, from universities until the late nineteenth century and from professional schools until well into the twentieth century (MacLellan, 1971:6). In the nineteenth century, many people felt that higher education would make women unfit for their domestic role. Allowing males and females in the same classroom was expected to lead to sexual immorality.

As women's paid labour became more important to the burgeoning factories and businesses of nineteenth-century England and North America, the case for higher education for women became stronger. If women were allowed to work in unskilled jobs, why could they not train for the professions? But the number of women who entered university peaked in the 1920s and tapered off somewhat during the 1930s, when families could not afford to send their daughters to school. Priority was often given to the son's education.

Since 1951, the proportion of females aged 18 to 24 in postsecondary educational institutions has risen from 4.6 percent to 21 percent in 1982–83 (Statistics Canada, 1983). However, the professional schools are still dominated by males, despite the dramatic increase in female students in medicine, law and dentistry in the past decade (Boulet and Lavallée, 1984:30; also see Table 10-1). At the same time that a higher proportion of postsecondary students are female, unemployment rates have soared. The value of education on the labour market has declined, especially for those with undergraduate degrees in general arts, education and law.

Males and females with the same education cannot always find comparable jobs. Because women are more likely to work part-time and to be hired in female job ghettoes, men and women with similar education generally do not make the same wages. The average yearly salary for a woman with a university degree or college diploma is about $2000 less than the average salary for a male graduate (Statistics Canada, 1981).

TABLE 10-1   Proportion of Women Among Full-Time University Students, By Specialization and Level of Study (1972-73 and 1981-82)

| | UNDERGRADUATE LEVEL | | MASTER'S LEVEL | | DOCTORATE | |
|---|---|---|---|---|---|---|
| | 1972-73 | 1981-82 | 1972-73 | 1981-82 | 1972-73 | 1981-82 |
| Medicine | 22.5% | 38.0% | 29.2% | 40.7% | 20.3% | 33.6% |
| Law | 18.0 | 39.9 | 7.7 | 37.0 | 33.3 | 15.9 |
| Education | 49.7 | 57.7 | 43.7 | 57.7 | 29.9 | 48.4 |
| Humanities | 51.9 | 59.5 | 42.5 | 53.6 | 34.2 | 41.4 |
| Engineering | 1.7 | 8.5 | 2.9 | 7.3 | 2.9 | 6.3 |
| Physics | 8.2 | 11.3 | 5.7 | 9.6 | 4.4 | 7.2 |
| Sociology | 57.0 | 67.3 | 36.8 | 51.9 | 32.7 | 46.4 |
| Dentistry | 8.3 | 22.7 | 16.7 | 26.7 | – | – |
| Social Services | 72.4 | 81.4 | 53.7 | 69.2 | 32.7 | 46.4 |

Derived from *The Changing Economic Status of Women* by Jac-André Boulet and Laval Lavallée for the Economic Council of Canada, Ottawa, 1984, p. 30, Table 3-3.

Despite employment inequalities, women have relatively high educational ambitions. In a national study sponsored by the Canadian Advisory Council on the Status of Women in Canada, Baker (1985) found that a similar proportion of adolescent girls and boys (over 75 percent) wanted to go to college or university. Although

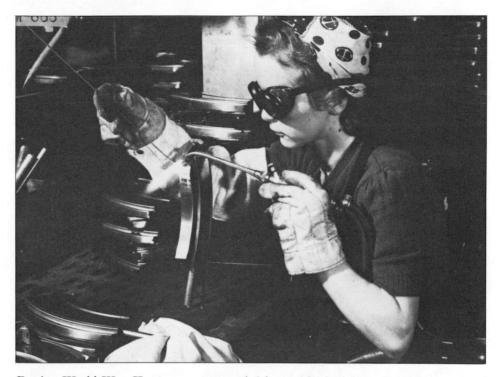

*During World War II, many women took jobs outside the home, often in war-related industries. This girl was a welder at a plant that manufactured Bren guns.*
Public Archives Canada/C-7481.

not all the girls planned to work for pay continuously throughout their adult lives, they realized the importance of higher education.

While an increasing proportion of females are enrolling in higher education in the Western world, illiteracy (especially among women) is still a problem in developing countries (see Table 10-2 on page 240).

## GENDER AND WORK

In the last two decades, the proportion of women in the labour force has risen dramatically. While higher education has kept more young people out of the full-time labour force, more married women have been returning to work or remaining employed throughout their childbearing years. Although only 4 percent of married women were in the labour force in 1941, over 50 percent worked in 1981. This increase has been attributed to an expansion of the service sector of the economy, inflation and the need for two incomes, women's higher education and their increased desire to use this education on the job, lower birth rates and changing attitudes about women's role.

TABLE 10-2    Illiterate Population 15 years and Over by Sex (1980)

| | PERCENTAGE OF ILLITERATES | |
|---|---|---|
| COUNTRY | MALES | FEMALES |
| Afghanistan | 66.8% | 94.4% |
| China (1982) | 20.8 | 48.9 |
| Cuba (1979) | 4.3 | 4.9 |
| Hungary | 0.7 | 1.5 |
| India (1981) | 53.3 | 75.1 |
| Saudi Arabia | 65.5 | 87.8 |
| Yemen | 82.4 | 98.5 |
| United States | −* | − |
| U.S.S.R. | − | − |
| *−less than 0.5% | | |

UNESCO, *Statistical Yearbook 1984*, Paris, 1984.

Although it used to be uncommon for mothers with young children to work outside the home, women are increasingly staying in the labour force and taking short-term maternity leaves. Table 10-3 looks at labour force participation rates since 1901, and Table 10-4 looks at participation rates in 1981 by age.

Recent controversy over equal pay legislation shows that men and women seldom do the same kind of work. While "men's work" covers a broad spectrum, from manual labour, skilled labour and commissioned sales to professional and managerial positions, women are clustered in fewer occupational categories. Most working women are in clerical or service positions, although there are also high proportions in food processing and lower-level professional jobs, such as teaching, nursing and social work (sometimes called the "semiprofessions").

Clerical and service jobs are low paying, have few promotional opportunities and are often temporary or part-time. Regardless of the education achieved by women workers and regardless of their occupational category, women tend to receive lower wages than men. Even women with postgraduate education often start at lower salaries and do not advance as quickly as their male counterparts. Table 10-5 (on page 242) shows the discrepancies between the salaries of males and females two years after graduation.

Men are more likely to graduate from fields which command higher salaries (such as medicine, law, dentistry and engineering). Men are also more likely to work overtime. After age 25, women are much more likely to work part-time. Twenty-two percent of working women aged 25 to 64 work part-time, compared to 1.6 percent of working men (Wallace, 1983:50). Women workers are less often protected by unions. Although the percentage of women union members is increasing, only about 20 percent of women workers and 33 percent of men workers are union members (Boulet and Lavallée, 1984:14). Unions traditionally have been reluctant

TABLE 10-3 Labour Force Participation Rates of Men and Women, Canada (1901-1981)

|  | MEN | WOMEN |
|---|---|---|
| 1981 | 79.4% | 52.9% |
| 1971 | 76.4 | 39.9 |
| 1961 | 81.1 | 29.3 |
| 1951 | 84.4 | 24.3 |
| 1941 | 85.6 | 22.9 |
| 1931* | 78.4 | 19.4 |
| 1921* | 80.3 | 17.7 |
| 1911 | 82.0 | 16.6 |
| 1901 | 78.3 | 14.4 |

* Includes 10-13 year olds

Derived from Statistics Canada, *Historical Statistics of Canada*, 2nd ed., Minister of Supply and Services, Ottawa, 1983, pp. D107-122; 1971 and 1981 figures from J.-A. Boulet and L. Lavallée, *The Changing Economic Status of Women*, Economic Council of Canada, 1984, p. 7.

TABLE 10-4 Participation Rates of Men and Women in the Canadian Labour Force By Age Group (1981)

|  | WOMEN | MEN |
|---|---|---|
| Age group: |  |  |
| 15-19 | 51.2% | 55.0% |
| 20-24 | 78.2 | 92.0 |
| 25-34 | 66.2 | 95.8 |
| 35-44 | 64.6 | 95.6 |
| 45-54 | 55.9 | 92.7 |
| 55-64 | 35.4 | 77.8 |
| 65 and over | 5.3 | 17.1 |
| All age groups | 52.9 | 79.4 |

Derived from *The Changing Economic Status of Women* by Jac-André Boulet and Laval Lavallée for the Economic Council of Canada, Ottawa, 1984, p. 7, Table 2-4.

to include part-time workers and have seen them as unfair competition and cheap labour. More recently, they have realized that, unless part-time workers and women full-time workers are recruited, the gains of the union movement will be eroded.

Generally, women workers are better educated than their male counterparts. Measures of productivity have not revealed consistent differences between the sexes,

TABLE 10-5 Average Annual Salary Two Years After Graduation (June 1978)

|  | MALES | FEMALES |
|---|---|---|
| University Degree | $15 900 | $14 400 |
| Master's or Ph.D. | $21 800 | $17 700 |
| Bachelor's | $15 400 | $14 200 |
| College Diploma | $13 600 | $11 700 |

Derived from Statistics Canada (W. Clark and Z. Zsigmond), *Job Market Reality for Postsecondary Graduates, Employment Outcome by 1978 Two Years After Graduation*. Ottawa: Statistics Canada, Cat. 81-572E, 1981, pp. 141, 142, 144.

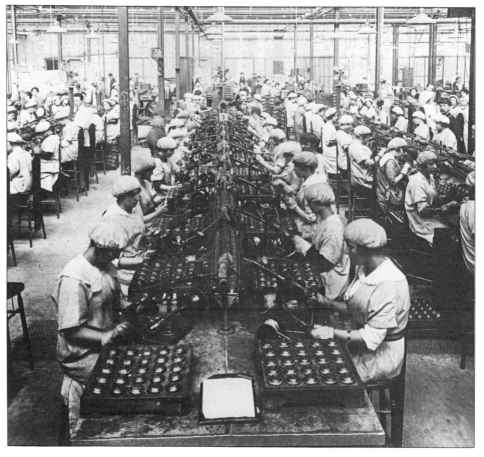

*Workers solder fuses during World War I in the British Munitions Company Ltd. at Verdun, Quebec.* Public Archives Canada/C-18734.

PROMOTE WOMEN, WELCH URGES
By Duncan McMonagle

Deputy Premier Robert Welch has called on private employers to practice "enlightened self-interest" and remove barriers to women's advancement.

Promoting people solely on merit would, in addition to giving women a better chance at advancement, make companies more efficient, he said in a speech yesterday to a conference of the Ontario Human Rights Commission.

Mr. Welch, the minister responsible for women's issues, has been pressing public bodies such as hospitals and boards of education to hire and promote more women, but he has resisted opposition calls to impose affirmative action on private industry.

In a recent annual report on affirmative action in the Ontario public service, Mr. Welch urges private employers to follow the Government's example—promote women and pay them more.

The report noted that the pay for women working for the Ontario Government has crept forward, and they now earn on average 76.8 per cent of what the average man is paid—one percentage point more than a year ago. They continue to do much better than women in private industry, who earn only 63 per cent of what men do, no gain at all from a year ago.

The annual report shows big differences in the way the various Government ministries treat women.

The ministry that paid women best was Correctional Services, at 87.8 per cent of men's salary. But only 27.2 per cent of the ministry's almost 5 000 employees were women.

Women in the Energy Ministry fared worst compared to their male colleagues: They earned only 58.1 per cent of the men's salary. Eighty of the ministry's 164 employees were women, and the ministry is encouraging their promotion to economists' jobs, the report said.

The lowest average salary for women is the $20,250 of the Consumer and Commercial Relations Ministry. By far the highest is the $31,319 paid by the Management Board secretariat.

The men's averages range from $24,569 in Health to $46,301 at the Management Board secretariat.

*The Globe and Mail*, Toronto (February 8, 1985).

except that mothers of preschool children show some decline in productivity because of the extra workload at home.

Studies show that married women working for pay retain most of the routine household tasks (Meissner et al., 1975; Luxton, 1980). Childcare, housecleaning, cooking and shopping have remained women's responsibilities, even when they also work for pay. This double burden of paid and unpaid work interferes with some women's desire for extra hours or responsibility at work. But for other women, who work long hours and wish to be promoted, stereotypes and myths about women workers or women's role may interfere with their opportunities.

The female participation rate in the labour force varies in different countries, depending on the availability of work, child-care facilities, inflation and attitudes about women's role. While less than 30 percent of women over 14 worked for pay in Italy in 1981, over 60 percent of women over 16 were in the labour force in Sweden (Boulet and Lavallée, 1984:49). For many years, Sweden has supported a publicly-funded child-care system and a government policy of equality between the sexes.

In the Soviet Union, nearly all adult women work for pay. Marxist ideology supports the idea that participation in production and financial independence are essential for equality between the sexes. But labour has been in demand in the Soviet Union since the industrialization of the 1930s, and the shortage of men in the population (due to wars and civil unrest) required the acceptance of women as workers.

Women are more widely and evenly distributed in the Soviet economy (Heitlinger, 1979) than in Western industrialized countries. They are extensively employed as manual workers in productive industry, as skilled workers and in the professions (especially medicine).

## POLITICAL RIGHTS AND POSITIONS OF POWER

### Women's Rights in the Nineteenth Century
*Feminism* is an ideology that argues that women should have legal, educational and occupational opportunities that are equal to men's, that women's contribution to public life has historically been downplayed and that the status of women should be raised. If we accept this definition, we could argue that feminism as an ideology has existed for thousands of years. At certain times, women (and some men) have tried to promote feminist goals through government lobbies, demonstrations, public lectures, consciousness-raising groups, publications and individual achievement. The women's movement has never really been a unified social movement but rather a collection of groups with similar goals but different strategies and priorities. Sometimes these groups have worked in tandem and sometimes at cross-purposes.

There has always been a split in the women's movement between *liberal feminists*, who have focused on reforming the existing system, and *socialist feminists*, who want to abolish inequalities based on class along with those based on gender. The socialist feminists have seen gender differences as an example of the inequality of a society organized around profit, where those most vulnerable are exploited. They have argued that equality between men and women is not possible without first eliminating inequalities between rich and poor, the powerful and the powerless. In this chapter, we will refer to both groups of feminists but concentrate on liberal feminism, which has had more impact on government legislation and policy changes in Canada.

### Membership in Feminist Groups
Historically, those who join feminist groups are middle-class women, who have leisure, verbal skills and access to the press. Men affiliated with these women have often been peripherally involved as well, with greater involvement in the nineteenth

THE RIGHTS OF INDIAN WOMEN

After travelling 30,000 kilometres and talking to 300 chiefs and native councils, Indian Affairs Minister David Crombie has struck what he thinks is a fair balance between the rights of Indian women and the rights of bands to self-determination.

Mr. Crombie introduced long-promised legislation in the Commons yesterday under which Indian women would no longer lose their status and associated rights when they marry non-Indians. The estimated 16,000 women who have lost their status and band membership could apply to have it automatically restored.

At the same time, however, the country's 579 Indian bands would retain the right to determine, by majority vote, whether to bestow band membership on the first-generation children of those women who lost their rights.

In the meantime, those 46,000 children would be eligible for registration as status Indians, which would give them access to services now available to Indians living off reserves.

*The Globe and Mail*, March 1, 1985. Full credit to The Canadian Press.

than in the twentieth century. Members of the women's movement have also been active in other social reform or radical movements, such as socialism and the temperance, abolitionist, trade unionism, antiwar and civil rights movements. In fact, the impetus for involvement in feminism sometimes has been a reaction against an experience in another social movement. For example, after helping black American men get the vote in the 1870s, American, British and Canadian women expected blacks to help women win the vote. When it became apparent that black men had no such intentions, the women's suffrage movement gathered strength.

## Issues and Priorities

Since the 1790s, feminist writers such as Mary Wollstonecraft, John Stuart Mill and George Sand have expressed concern about women's lack of public roles, legal rights and education and the double standard of sexual morality. Both the French and the American Revolutions inspired demands for equality for women. But it was the influx of working-class women into the mines and factories of England that led to a widespread public debate about the conditions of work and their potential impact on women's reproduction, the family, morality in the workplace, women's access to higher education and political office and the role of women in general.

Once women began working in factories, the demand for their labour dramatically increased in other areas. The expansion of education in the 1840s and 1850s led to an influx of women teachers, who were usually paid about half the wage of a man because "men supported families" and had teacher's training in "normal school." When women tried to enroll in Canadian teachers' colleges, they met with strong opposition until 1849, when the first woman enrolled in a college in New Brunswick.

In Canada, the fight for coeducation at the postsecondary level lasted over 30 years. While Mount Allison University in New Brunswick admitted women in 1858 (MacLellan, 1971:6), the more prestigious universities, like the University of Toronto, kept women out until 1884, for fear of "lowering their standards." Generally, coeducation was resisted until it was proven financially necessary. The need for more students was often the major motive in allowing women to enter universities. For women, acceptance into professional schools and associations was not accomplished, in some cases, until the twentieth century (MacLellan, 1971:8–12).

Although women were working for pay, they still had no legal rights to keep and administer their own money or to own property. These matters were in the hands of a woman's husband, a fact that put her in a dependent position similar to that of a child. The English *Married Women's Property Act* of 1870 became the impetus for similar laws in Canada. These laws gave married women the right to maintain property they owned prior to their marriage and administer their own finances and property during marriage. Ontario was the first province to legislate this change in 1872.

Leaders of the nineteenth-century women's movement were also concerned with protective legislation, minimum wages and women's and children's working conditions. Dress reform was also an issue, since women's long dresses were cumbersome in some factory jobs and for the new fad of the 1890s—cycling. The right to use birth control was advocated by Margaret Sanger, but little progress was made on this issue until the next century. Generally, women were rebelling against their severely restricted role in society (Kealey, 1979:15).

## Focusing on Voting Rights

Despite interest in improving women's status in several areas, leaders in the movement began to focus on the right to vote, or women's suffrage. They felt that if women could vote and hold public office, women would change the world by abolishing war and human suffering, since women were spiritually and morally superior to men.

The antisuffrage lobby was worried about the alliance between members of the women's movement and temperance groups. They also felt that the husband, as head of the household, voted on behalf of his wife, and she, therefore, had no need for a separate vote. Granting voting rights to women might destroy the harmony of the home and lead to a decline in the birthrate. Since the family was seen as the basic unit of society, anything which threatened it was a serious problem.

In Britain, the lobby for women's suffrage was very controversial from 1905 to 1914. There were demonstrations, and the Pankhurst sisters and other members of the Women's Social and Political Union were imprisoned. But in Canada, the movement was tamer. The first suffrage group, founded in 1876, actually called itself the Toronto Women's Literary Club. By 1883, they had become bolder and renamed themselves the Toronto Women's Suffrage Association. The movement was founded by Emily Howard Stowe, who fought long and hard with the medical association to become Canada's first female doctor. By the turn of the century, there were suffrage groups all across the country, with headquarters in Toronto (Nunes and White, 1973:29–30). Nellie McClung, from Manitoba, was also a prominent leader

# The Women's Canadian Club

## Ottawa

## The boys at the front need socks. Can you knit a pair?

*This sign was part of the war effort campaign in 1917. As a result of the government's eagerness to pass a bill that would allow military conscription, the vote was extended to nurses overseas and the wives and mothers of servicemen in 1917. The next year, it was extended to all women over 21.* Public Archives Canada/PA-125232.

YOU MUSTN'T ASK TO VOTE
You may be our close companion
    Share our troubles, ease our pain,
You may bear the servant's burden
    (But without the servant's gain;)
You may scrub and cook and iron
    Sew the buttons on our coat,
But as men we must protect you—
    You are far too frail to vote.

You may toil behind our counters,
    In our factories you may slave
You are welcome in the sweatshop
    From the cradle to the grave.
    If you err, altho' a woman
    You may dangle by the throat
But our chivalry is outraged
    If you soil your hands to vote.

Courtesy of L. Case Russell and *The Globe and Mail*, Toronto (September 28, 1912).

in the fight for suffrage. She used tactics such as an all-female mock parliament in 1896, lecture tours and publications. The suffragists were supported by western farmers' organizations, organized labour in British Columbia, a substantial number of Protestant clergy, influential sectors of the press and national women's groups such as the Women's Christian Temperance Union, the National Council of Women (established in 1893) and the Women's Institutes (MacLellan, 1971:15). However, the counter lobby was also very strong, strengthened by the brewers and distillers of alcoholic beverages, prominent businessmen and many women.

It was not until 1917 that women could vote in Canadian federal elections (although Australian women could vote in 1902 and New Zealanders as early as 1893). In Canada, the Conservative government of Robert Borden wanted to pass a bill that would allow military conscription for the war raging in Europe. Borden assumed that women who were nurses overseas would support the bill, as would women whose husbands and sons were fighting. So he proposed the extension of the vote to these women in 1917 (and his bill was passed). The next year, in 1918, the vote was extended to all women 21 and over. American women won the right to vote in 1919, and British women in 1921. Women in the Canadian provinces received the vote as early as 1916 (in Manitoba, Saskatchewan and Alberta), but in Quebec, there was no female suffrage until 1940 (Report of the Royal Commission on the Status of Women in Canada, 1970:338).

As early as 1917, Soviet women gained equal rights legislation. Although they are much more likely than women in Canada to be in the labour force and to be represented in politics, only 27.4 percent of Communist party members are women. Although more than 50 percent of the lower echelons of the party structure are held by women, reaching the highest positions in the labour force is easier for men.

In Yugoslavia, which had a woman as president in the late 1970s, women were well represented in both local and national politics. In Albania, one-third of the people's assembly seats were held by women. Generally, in Eastern Europe (as in Western European and North American) countries, women have been elected more often to local rather than national politics (Heitlinger, 1979). Yet, in socialist countries that encourage women to hold office, women's representation is much higher.

## After the Vote

The first woman, Agnes Macphail, was elected to the Canadian House of Commons in 1921 but it was 14 years before the next woman won a federal seat (Cochrane, 1977:10). Several women were elected to the provincial legislatures, but none were appointed to the Senate until a lengthy court case (initiated by five Alberta women) was brought to determine whether or not women were "legal persons." It was decided they were. After the negative decision was appealed by the Judicial Committee of the Privy Council in 1929, women were declared eligible to sit in the Senate. Cairine Wilson was then appointed in 1930 (Royal Commission on the Status of Women, 1970:340).

During the 1920s, some major changes in social legislation occurred that could be attributed to women voters or members of Parliament or may have been just a sign of the times. For example, by 1928, most provinces had passed legislation on mothers' allowances, maintenance for deserted wives, protection of children and

TABLE 10-6   When Women Won the Right to Vote in Federal Elections

| | |
|---|---|
| New Zealand | 1893 |
| Australia | 1902 |
| Finland | 1906 |
| Norway | 1907 |
| Denmark | 1915 |
| U.S.S.R. | 1917 |
| Canada | 1918 |
| U.S.A. | 1919 |
| Britain | 1921 |
| Spain | 1931 |
| Rumania | 1935 |
| Italy | 1945 |
| Greece | 1952 |
| Switzerland | 1971 |
| Liechtenstein* | – |
| Kuwait | – |
| Saudi Arabia | – |

*Women won the right to vote in communal elections in 1976.

equal guardianship of children by both parents. At the federal level, divorce law was equalized for the sexes, and old age pensions were introduced.

From 1920 until the 1970s, the proportion of women MPs did not rise above 1 percent, and the influence of women voters did not produce dramatic changes in political issues. Few women had the educational or occupational background to run for Parliament. Women were also hampered by their domestic responsibilities and by the widespread belief that women belonged in the home. Yet women made inroads into other areas during the 1920s. By the 1930s, more women were enrolled in university undergraduate programs than in the early 1950s. And a greater proportion of postgraduate students were female during the 1920s than throughout the next four decades (Royal Commission on the Status of Women, 1970:168). Because there were fewer men in Canada during and after World War I, new jobs were opened to women, and other jobs were created by an expansion of manufacturing and the service industries. But women's organizations after the 1930s became more concerned with social service than with widening the scope of women in society. The alignment between the women's movement and labour declined as women became more oriented toward issues such as child welfare, juvenile delinquency and mothers' allowance, which were an extension of women's maternal role (*maternal feminism*).

During the 1930s, economic hard times led to legislation that kept married women out of government jobs. Politically, there was little agitation for women's rights, as many people were more concerned about the rising unemployment and increasing number of bread lines. The Great Depression focused on male unemployment, and women were expected to run the households, care for dependent relatives and try to earn some money on the side to assist male breadwinners.

## RECENT ATTEMPTS TO CHANGE WOMEN'S STATUS

During World War II, women again entered the labour force in increasing numbers to work in offices and munitions factories and to fill jobs vacated by men who went to fight overseas. The provision of day nurseries indicated strong government support for women who worked outside the home. Yet, when the war ended in 1945, day-care services were cut back and returning soldiers expected their jobs back. Social pressure forced many women back into the home. The 1950s saw the postwar baby boom, and was a time of high marriage rates and relatively low participation of women in public life. But the proportion of married women in the workforce actually increased from 4.5 percent in 1941 to 11.2 percent in 1951 to 20.8 percent in 1961 (Armstrong and Armstrong, 1978:52). Expansion of the service and industrial sectors of the economy created new jobs, and the demand for labour increased. Despite the popular ideology, which called for mother at home, caring for the children, more working-class wives entered the labour force because of financial pressures caused by inflation.

It was not until the 1960s that the women's movement was revitalized. Simone de Beauvoir published *The Second Sex* in 1949, but her ideas had influenced few North Americans. However, with the expansion of colleges and universities in Canada and the United States, an increasing number of women entered postsecondary institutions and began to aspire to intellectual achievement and paid employment. Rising expectations were also created among American blacks and among native peoples in Canada and the United States. With the expansion of the economy, minority groups and women expected a greater share of the jobs, higher wages and more opportunities for leadership in society. Trade unionism, civil rights, "red power," socialism and protests against American involvement in Vietnam all coincided with the renewal of activism for women. Breakaway groups of women from the "new left" formed the women's liberation movement in the United States and Canada, and these small, leaderless "consciousness-raising" groups spread quickly throughout North America. Reform-oriented lobby groups were formed in many countries. One of the best known was Betty Friedan's National Organization of Women (NOW), formed in 1966 to express dissatisfaction with the results of President Kennedy's Commission on the Status of Women in 1961 (Freeman, 1975:449). Friedan's book, *The Feminine Mystique* (1963), became a best seller because it so clearly identified the problem of so many American women, who were excluded from meaningful social and political participation.

## The Canadian Movement

In Canada, the Committee for Equality for Women was formed in 1966 by Laura Sabia, then president of the Canadian Federation of University Women. This collection of women's groups lobbied for a royal commission on the status of women. With the help of the secretary of state, Judy LaMarsh, the commission was established in February, 1967 (Wilson, 1982:127). Its report was published three years later.

In 1972, a conference to follow up the report gave birth to a new women's group called the National Action Committee. As an umbrella group for 170 women's organizations across the country, it has acted as an important pressure group (Wilson, 1982:127). But smaller and more radical groups also arose out of the Student Union for Peace Action. The Voice of Women, an organization promoting world peace, has also been influential. Other feminists have been involved in organizing women's centres, rape crisis centres, transition houses for battered wives and other specialized counselling services for women. The Women's Press, in Toronto, and women's bookstores across the country have helped transmit feminist ideas and served as a meeting place for like-minded women.

In the 1970s, the Canadian and provincial governments set up advisory councils on the status of women for policy advice, research and publicity on women's issues. The establishment of the Canadian Advisory Council on the Status of Women (CACSW) in 1973 was one of the recommendations of the Royal Commission on the Status of Women. Status of Women Canada and the Women's Bureau of the Department of Labour were set up to initiate and implement government policy related to women. But critics of the advisory councils say they are a diversionary tactic to make it appear that the government is doing something to improve the status of women. While the publications of the CACSW are widely distributed to the public, to schools and to universities, some say they are preaching to the converted. Costly public relations work, political appointees and more conferences than actual changes have been the results of the councils according to critics, who say that the councils carefully avoid anything that is controversial or that approaches socialist feminism.

The Feminist Party of Canada has also been a product of the women's movement. Formed in 1979 by women who had been active in NAC and other women's groups, the party is meant to give a political voice to feminists. Disappointed with women's inroads into the three major political parties, these women assumed that only by creating a new political party could women become more active, gain experience in political office and voice their feminist views without jeopardizing party policy. Although a party with such specialized interests can never hope to win an election, it can provide a strong voice for feminist concerns.

Women's groups all over the world have been heavily involved in antinuclear protests and demonstrations for disarmament. A large portion of protesters in England, Germany and Canada have been women. The effectiveness of these demonstrations against international policy remains to be seen. Women's interest in peace may be an offshoot of maternal feminism. Making military policy and fighting wars have been primarily male activities. Women, as creators of life, do not want to give birth to children who will be killed in war or who will have to live under the threat of nuclear destruction.

Considering that women in Canada could not vote or hold office before 1917, it is not surprising that they do not yet have equal representation in the House of Commons and the Senate. The move toward equality has been extremely slow. From 1920 to 1970, 0.8 percent of elected representatives to the House of Commons were women (Kopinak, 1980:445). In 1984, 9 percent of those elected were women, although 15 percent of the candidates were women. Four of the twenty-two new senators appointed in 1984 were female, which brings the percentage of women senators to 11 percent (Terry, 1984:1).

Why are men overrepresented in politics? One reason relates back to our earlier discussion of education and work. Most members of Parliament have a background in law or business, fields in which women have traditionally been underrepresented. Although only 5 percent of lawyers were female in 1971, this had increased to 15 percent by 1981 (Statistics Canada, 1983a). The recent influx of female law students indicates that this figure may increase dramatically within the next decade. In 1982–83, 42 percent of Canadian law students were female (Statistics Canada, 1983:60). Women have also substantially increased their proportionate enrollment in business and commerce courses over the last few years.

Running for office takes a lot of money, and involves long hours of work, trips away from home, and a single-mindedness that married women with children are seldom able to manage because of their domestic duties. While married men can often count on their spouses to look after the children when they are away in Ottawa, married women seldom can. Consequently, most women who have made their mark in politics have been unmarried, divorced, widowed, married and childless or beyond the years of childrearing.

Other important factors in running for office are confidence, assertiveness and feelings of political effectiveness. We suggested earlier that girls are often socialized to be less assertive and independent than boys and to have less confidence in their abilities.

## CHANGING RELATIONS BETWEEN THE SEXES

A few years ago, a cigarette company that made slim "feminine" cigarettes advertised their product by the slogan "You've come a long way, baby!" How far have women really progressed toward equal opportunity and equal rewards for their efforts? In answering this question, we take on the difficult task of comparing life styles and goals. Whether or not a change is actually a move toward equality or a backward step is often unclear. Even comparing government statistics from one decade to the next can be difficult, since definitions of terms and composition of samples change.

Certainly, dramatic changes have occurred in higher education. In 1951, 5 percent of females aged 18 to 24 were enrolled in postsecondary institutions (Statistics Canada, 1980:81). In 1982–83, this figure had increased to 21 percent (Statistics Canada, 1983:65). However, educational segregation at the university level is still a pattern, in that men tend to specialize in general and applied science, engineering, law, medicine, dentistry and business to a greater extent than women. Most women still study general arts, applied arts, nursing, dental hygiene, physiotherapy and

*These young women attended the Young Women's Christian Association School Girls Camp in 1917.* Public Archives Canada/PA-124245.

home economics (although there has been an increase of women in law, medicine, veterinary science and pharmacy in recent years).

In the workplace, there has been a dramatic increase in the proportion of women working for pay. In 1941, 23 percent of women were in the labour force and 86 percent of men. In 1984, 95 percent of men between 25 and 44 years of age worked for pay, while 70.7 percent of women did (Statistics Canada, 1984). However, despite this influx of women, the gap between the incomes of men and women has changed only slightly. Women have entered the lower echelons of the labour force and have progressed less rapidly than men.

We have already noted that party politics are still dominated by men and that the proportion of women members of Parliament is only 9 percent. However, in the past ten years, there has been more change than in the previous 50 years. Because women are absent from official positions of power, this does not mean that women have no influence in decision-making. The wives and female associates of members of government and business often have some input into political and business decisions. However, those who are in power are not compelled to listen to their comments or advice, and women receive no direct payment or prestige unless they have official positions.

The status of women within the family has also changed in the last two years as a result of reform of laws affecting matrimonial property and divorce settlements. Several provinces now presume that matrimonial property is owned by both spouses, regardless of who paid for it. This gives some financial recognition to the childrearing and housework of the nonearning wife. Marriage is now more likely to be seen as an equal partnership, rather than as a unit headed by a husband, who has a dependent.

The rising labour force participation of married women may have only marginally changed the division of labour in household tasks, but it seems to have given women increased power in their relationships. Some studies suggest that the earning wife has more say in financial decisions and in where the family lives, and she can ultimately leave the relationship if she has her own money. At the same time, she may have given up some control over routine decisions in the home (such as what to eat or how to decorate the house) and some control over the children (who may now be cared for by a sitter).

There is still research evidence that men expect women to defer to them in conversation. For example, men interrupt women more than women interrupt men. People still see men as more authoritative, and women experts are often not trusted by clients or students. Sexual harassment is still a problem in the workplace, and being viewed as "sex objects" still interferes with occupational mobility for many women. Etiquette is still based on the outmoded notions that women are helpless and need protection from men and that women deserve special respect simply because they are women. Perhaps in the past, this respect was intended to make up for women's lower wages and powerlessness in society.

What seems clear from a number of studies is that attitudes toward the equality of the sexes have changed. It is no longer socially acceptable to tell sexist jokes in front of women, to pat bottoms, to admit publicly that a person was not hired *because* she is a woman, to create separate pay scales for men and women or to fire a woman because she is pregnant. Most adolescents believe in equal education for women, in equal pay for equal work and equal promotional opportunities for the sexes. But what people *say* they believe and how they behave are not always consistent.

# WHY ARE WOMEN SUBORDINATED?

## FOUR EXPLANATIONS

The reasons behind the widespread subordination of women have been the subject of many books and articles. Four groups of theories will be briefly discussed here: They are biological, psychological, idealist and economic theories.

### Biological Theories

These explanations of women's subordination focus on the relationship between body size, strength, biochemistry, women's childbearing capacity and social roles and status. Some have argued that male dominance originated in man's larger size and greater strength. This gave him not only a protective role over woman, but also the ultimate power of the threat of physical violence. Theorists such as Lionel Tiger have drawn parallels between primate and human behaviour, referring to men's tendency to group together in hunting, the protection of women by men and the development of a male-oriented culture. Others have focused on dominance hierarchies in animals, which are based on size and strength, and possible parallels with human behaviour. Relationships between male sex hormones, high energy levels and more aggressive behaviour have also been used to explain male dominance.

The biological theorists sometimes claim that pregnancy and lactation have limited women's political and economic contributions to society and led to their more domestic role (Shulamith Firestone). During pregnancy and lactation, women need greater male protection. But, as a radical feminist, Firestone proposes ways to overcome biological inequalities and sexual dependancies.

Menstrual mood changes, postpartem depression and menopausal problems have also been used to explain women's lack of presence and responsibility in public life. However, childrearing itself has served as an alternative (and equally important) contribution by women to society. Women's so-called maternal instincts and ability to breastfeed have made them more appropriate caretakers of children than men.

Critics of these theories say that there is no necessary relationship between smaller body size and lower status, especially in industrialized society. After all, both Hitler and Napoleon were short. Nor does pregnancy necessarily imply an exclusion from paid work or childrearing by women only. Many women now work until their eighth month of pregnancy, and children are frequently raised by sitters or nonrelated caretakers. In hunting and gathering societies, women continue their work until childbirth and are often cared for and protected by other women during and after birthing. Male and female children are often raised by parents or community members of the same sex.

Although sociologists have tended to downplay the role of biology in social life, sociobiologists think that genes, hormones, body size, ability to reproduce and physical strength may strongly influence patterns of social behaviour. However, physical differences between the sexes have been accentuated by differences in diet, exercise and fashion. And the variations within each sex are greater than the differences between them. Some differences, real and imagined, are presumed to exist, and cultural patterns formed around them. For example, women on many Caribbean islands carry very heavy loads on their heads, because of the presumed strength of the female neck. In North America, many precision factory jobs requiring manual dexterity rely on female labour (whereas brain surgeons, requiring similar skills, are almost always men).

## Psychological Theories

According to Sigmund Freud and others influenced by him, the basic nature of men and women is determined by their psycho-sexual development. Because males and females differ sexually, they react differently to their physical maturation, develop different personality characteristics and consequently play different roles in adult life. Some psychoanalysts focus on women's receptive sexuality and supposedly passive personalities, as well as the role of maternal instincts in shaping their abilities and ambitions. Others have argued (Karen Horney, Simone de Beauvoir) that passivity, desire for children and the lack of motivation to compete in the political and economic world are more the result of the way girls are brought up, i.e., passivity and domesticity are rewarded in girl children, while independence and competitiveness are punished. Learning theorists focus on the role models provided for children, the linguistic labels that parents attach to certain behaviours and the ways children imitate and identify with same-sex parents.

What the psychological theories cannot easily explain are the structural barriers to equality of the sexes: the unequal laws, the effect of the economy on equality and why some societies have made more progress toward gender equality than others.

## Idealist Theories

With an emphasis on socialization and cultural tradition, the idealist theories argue that ideas about appropriate behaviour for the sexes are passed down from previous generations. Young children are raised to fit in with these ideas. But where do these ideas come from? When Kate Millett discussed the tradition of patriarchy in *Sexual Politics* (1970), she could not adequately explain the origin of this male dominance. Thus, idealist theories are often ahistorical and usually assume that if people become conscious of the inherent sexism of their attitudes, they will change.

Since women are the main caretakers of children, why do they raise their female children to accept an inferior status? If children were raised to believe that the sexes are equal, would inequalities disappear? Some say that vested interests still encourage men to cling to their advantage by preventing women from gaining more power, jobs or money. After all, if the status of one group is raised, does this not imply that another group is going to have to give up something?

## Economic Theories

Some economic theorists (Friedrich Engels, for example) refer to earlier stages of society and argue that the relative status of the sexes has changed as societies moved from hunting and gathering to agricultural, preindustrial, industrial to postindustrial economies. In hunting and gathering societies, women usually gathered while men hunted. The food gathered formed over half of the diet, and this gave women an important economic and political role. When people became farmers, several social, political and demographic changes occurred. The concept of private property and inheritance became more significant. Consequently, knowledge of paternity became essential, and monogamous marriage was institutionalized. With the increased food supply from farming, the birth rate rose; this kept women in a more domestic role. Gradually, women's role in production shrank until, after the Industrial Revolution, most middle-class women were expected to stay at home to raise their children.

Some theorists argue that capitalist industrial society exploits anyone who is vulnerable. Child and female labour was used at the beginning of the Industrial Revolution to save money, and an ideology was created to provide reasons for

STUDY DISCOVERS ADVERTISERS FAILING TO ELIMINATE
SEXISM
By Dorothy Lipovenko

Self-policing by the Canadian advertising industry is not working because sex-role stereotyping of women persists, a national watchdog group warns in a report to the federal Government.

"Woman continues to be cumulatively portrayed in ways that suggest her place is in the home, her interests do not include issues of the world or public affairs but are limited to interests in other people and her own appearance. Her primary roles are those of caretaker of men and children and sexual object of men," says MediaWatch, a women's group that monitors images of women in the media.

Among the findings of MediaWatch:
• Female characters are more passive and use seductive non-verbal behavior;
• Men outnumbered women more than two to one in voice-overs for commercials;
• Men exclusively pitch products such as cars and financial services while women are more likely to present cosmetics and health care products;
• Women were more likely to be partly or provocatively clothed;
• Men are shown to be more interested in their careers or business, while women are shown to be more interested in clothes and their appearance.

*The Globe and Mail*, Toronto (June 6, 1985).

paying these new workers less. Later, when laws prevented the use of child labour and protected women workers, and there was a surplus of labour, a new ideology was created to justify a more domestic role for women.

The work of housewives was not regarded as real work, since it was not paid. Women's domestic activities were denigrated in a money-oriented society (Eichler, 1973).

The socialist feminist theorists, such as Dorothy Smith and Juliet Mitchell, argue that what women and men do in their work lives affects the way they are valued. If they work at home with children for no direct pay, they are viewed as less important than those who have more public and remunerated positions. If they make an important, visible contribution to the economy, they are seen by others, and see themselves, as more important.

Authors like Blumberg (1978) and O'Kelly (1980) use an economic argument but supplement it with points from psychological, biological and idealist theories. They conclude that women have historically fared better in noncompetitive and nonmilitaristic societies with lower birth rates. Especially in hunting and gathering societies, where women's role in production is significant and birth rates are low, equality between the sexes is more likely. In modern socialist countries with a policy of gender equality, more progress has been made in equalizing laws and participation in public life.

Of the four groups of theories outlined above, the economic explanations seem to be the most persuasive. While the biological and psychological theories focus on the origin of women's subordination, they cannot adequately explain the social structures created to perpetuate male dominance. The idealist theories can account for the continued existence of female subordination but not the origin of patriarchy. Only the economic theories are historical and cross-cultural and deal with both the origin and perpetuation of female subordination.

## DEBATES IN WOMEN'S ISSUES

Now that women's issues have become politically more important, several major issues have surfaced. These include pornography, abortion, sex segregation, pensions for homemakers, divorce laws and affirmative action. Is pornography a form of exploitation of women, or are censorship and sexual freedom more important issues? Should women have the ultimate say over whether or not they will reproduce or do husbands and fetuses have rights that should take precedence? Should women be allowed to work and fight side-by-side with men in all situations, or is some sex segregation still justifiable? Will the problem of poverty among elderly women be partially solved by pensions for homemakers, or will this simply perpetuate a domestic role for women? Who would pay for these pensions? Should women be expected to be self-supporting soon after divorce, or is this an unfair expectation, since many ex-wives lack job experience, and discrimination against women exists in the workplace. Is preferential treatment for qualified female candidates for a job or a promotion a form of reverse discrimination?

Within the women's movement, the divisions between heterosexual and lesbian women, between liberal feminists and socialist feminists and between those who argue that segregation is more productive than integration continue. The questions of whether sex overrides class, of the importance of motherhood and women's traditional roles, of whether children need their mothers at home and whether those who are fighting for equality have just adopted male values continue to be debated. At the same time, many traditional women are arguing that women's status was higher when they concentrated on motherhood and childrearing; they believe that women's maternal contributions should be more highly valued by society. Clearly, the 1960s to the present has been a period of debate and changing relations between the sexes, but with each change there have been voices raised to question the wisdom of disturbing tradition.

Sexism within the educational system continues to be under attack. Many studies have shown that teachers assume males are more serious students and gear classes to them. Textbooks have been found to contain a disproportionate number of examples of male characters and activities. Girls and women have been portrayed as less exciting and powerful characters. Social science courses have been accused of focusing on male activities and ignoring women's less public roles. Women's studies classes have been created to counteract this bias but have often been perceived as ghettoes for female students and faculty.

## BARRIERS TO EQUALITY

The tradition of women having responsibility for childrearing and housework is still a major stumbling block to equality between the sexes. As long as women do most of this unpaid or low-paid work, they will have little motivation and energy to

*What motivation will there be for men to take on a greater share of housework?* Public Archives Canada/C-84798.

increase their responsibilities in public life. Low-paid work stigmatizes the work and the person doing it. Either higher wages could be paid for domestic labour, or both sexes could equally share the unpaid or poorly paid jobs. But what motivation will there be for men to take on a greater share of housework or to work as child-minders or cleaners?

The reasons given for not organizing society to promote equality between the sexes often seem very practical (lack of money for equal pay for work of equal value, lack of washroom facilities to enable the boss to hire women as well as men). But these are often merely excuses. Prejudices and stereotypes still prevent women from being accepted as equals. But guilt feelings, lack of confidence and fear of conflict and controversy keep women from insisting on their right to be treated equally. Without laws to protect their interests or a supportive group to stand up for them, many women accept inequality. Since organizations have a vested interest in maintaining the status quo, women will have to be strong to overcome the barriers that stand between them and equality.

## SUMMARY

Distinctions between males and females are carefully cultivated in North American society and in many other cultures. Although some research suggests that sex differences in aptitude and personality are innate, conclusive evidence is difficult to find because of the ethical problems involved in studying infants and young children and the inability to disregard socialization or upbringing when studying adults.

From birth, parents encourage different traits and interests in their children, depending on their sex, and this socialization continues in school and in the community.

Attitudes about the value of the different roles of and opportunities for the sexes and the division of labour in the family lead to status and power differentials between the sexes in public life. In this chapter, we examined the educational system, paid employment and politics to compare the status of men and women. Although women are approaching equality in education and have dramatically increased their participation in the paid labour force within the last decade, more changes have been apparent in attitudes than in actual behaviour. Structural and psychological barriers still prevent women from attaining equality with men in public life.

## DISCUSSION QUESTIONS

1. Why is it so difficult to determine whether gender differences are cultural or innate?

2. How do television programs and magazines contribute to stereotyped thinking about males and females? How do they blur gender distinctions?

3. What is meant by "women's double day?" Why do married women continue to do most of the housework, even when they work outside the home?

4. Has there been more change in attitudes or behaviour with respect to equality between the sexes?

5. What barriers still exist to gender equality in the workplace and in politics?

# 11

# Families

## Maureen Baker

# INTRODUCTION: THE IMPORTANCE OF THE FAMILY

Despite the publicity about rising divorce rates, over 85 percent of Canadians marry at least once, and most of these couples produce children. Nearly 75 percent of those whose marriages dissolve soon move into new relationships, and second marriages are becoming common. Nonetheless, more Canadians live alone now than ever before. Young people are more likely to live away from their parents and separation and divorce produce more people who are between relationships, choose to live alone or cannot find a new partner. Many women outlive their husbands by ten years or more (considering they marry men older than themselves). Rather than move in with relatives, more widows and widowers choose to live independently. But living alone does not indicate a rejection of family living. Rather, it is for many a temporary stage—before marriage, between marriages and after divorce or the death of a spouse.

Pressure to marry remains high in the 1980s. Especially for lower-income single parents, who find it difficult to pay the bills on their own, pressures for economic and emotional security are strong. High rates of unemployment and job insecurity make shared accommodation essential for many. The desire for regular sex, companionship and love remains strong, as does the urge to reproduce. Although the number of middle-class women choosing to have children out of wedlock has increased slightly, most women find this alternative emotionally and financially stressful. Many more couples now have sex before marriage and live together, but living together often leads to marriage.

The preference for legal marriage is especially strong among religious and older people. Many legal impediments to common law relationships have been removed. Children of such relationships are no longer classified as illegitimate, and both parents must support their children. But social pressures to legalize a relationship in the traditional religious ceremony remain, even for people who are not church-goers.

Employers often see the married man as more emotionally and geographically stable and as a more reliable worker. The unmarried man may pay higher insurance rates because he is thought to be more reckless and carefree. In fact, a prejudice against unmarried people has existed in our culture for hundreds of years. Unmarried people of both sexes are considered less mature, more selfish and less experienced than married people; the unmarried woman over 40 is a "spinster" or an "old maid," both terms which have pejorative connotations.

## FAMILIES AND HOUSEHOLDS

The term "family" refers to the relatives with whom we live or used to live and the larger group to whom we consider ourselves related by blood or marriage. There are different types of families. The husband-wife, or *nuclear family*, has been the most usual arrangement in Canada, yet one in six Canadian families has only one parent (Boulet and Lavallée, 1984:39). A "one-parent family" implies that only one parent raises the children. In actual fact, two parents may participate and even co-operate, although they live apart.

*The term "household" refers to all those sharing a dwelling, whether they are related or not.* Public Archives Canada/PA-128761.

The *extended family* involves several generations, such as grandparents, parents and children, living together. The *census family* used in government documents involves at least one parent living with his or her dependent children. Most definitions of "family," then, involve children, and a distinction is often made between a "childless couple" and a "family." A journalist recently wrote that it has been a long time since we have had a "real family" at 24 Sussex Drive, implying that the former prime minister and his children are not really "a family." Letters to the editor in response to this remark showed that many people today live in one-parent families, and this arrangement is an increasingly acceptable way for a child to be raised (*The Globe and Mail*, December 8, 1984).

The term *household* refers to all those sharing a dwelling, whether they are related or not. Technically, it would be more accurate to call one-parent families one-parent households to avoid the assumption that the absent parent is not involved. The Canadian government gathers statistics on households and families and uses these to plan schools, hospitals and social services. Businesses also use the statistics for future market strategies. Academic researchers often rely on family statistics gathered for other purposes, but they also gather their own information on how families live.

Increasingly, the state is taking over the functions of the family. Educating the young, caring for the sick and assisting the unemployed is now the job of government. Yet family members still provide valuable services for each other. Cleaning houses and caring for preschool children are usually unpaid jobs performed by wives and mothers. Relatives provide accommodation, interest-free loans, child-care, nursing care and other services which are invaluable and would cost millions of dollars if provided by private industry or the state. As long as families provide all these services, they do not have to be organized and financed by the state or employers. Marxists argue that this is one reason the family is such an important social institution.

# CULTURAL VARIATIONS IN FAMILIES

## THE STRUCTURE OF THE FAMILY

In the 1980s, diverse cultures still organize their families differently. However, there is a trend towards a *nuclear* or *conjugal family* with increasing industrialization and urbanization. In the conjugal family, husband and wife live with their children and place more importance on the marital relationship than on ties with their own parents.

The extended family also remains an important unit in some cultures. For example, many Eastern Europeans, Southern Europeans, Latin Americans and Chinese maintain close ties with siblings and parents after they marry. Relatives may provide companionship, child-care or financial assistance; they may be employment partners or simply help out with a problem or crisis. They may visit daily or weekly and, especially in North America, telephone frequently. Close ties with the extended family are also apparent among working class-people and among women of all social classes.

It is unclear whether the extended family used to be more prevalent than the nuclear family. American sociologists such as Talcott Parsons say that the American family of the 1960s was more isolated from kin than in past centuries and that this placed increased pressure on marriages. However, historians have discovered that nuclear families were more prevalent than extended ones even in mid-seventeenth-century Europe (Leslie, 1979: 179). Neither has it been common for married couples to live with their parents at any time in Canadian history. Geographic mobility and short life expectancies encouraged nuclear families, except for short periods during a couple's marriage (Nett, 1981).

In Canada and in most industrialized countries, *monogamy*, or having only one spouse at a time, is the social custom and the law. Yet many Canadians have several spouses throughout their lifetime through divorce and remarriage or consecutive nonmarital relationships. This has led some sociologists to label our current marriage pattern as *consecutive monogamy* or *sequential polygamy*.

Having more than one spouse at a time (*polygamy*) is illegal in all Western developed countries. This is due to the assumed difficulties of providing adequate emotional and financial support to more than one partner and to religious ideas of sexual exclusivity. However, polygamy is practised in some Moslem countries. *Polygyny*, or allowing more than one wife, is the more common arrangement, but it is usually reserved for wealthier men who can afford to pay bride prices and to support more than one woman. For this reason, polygyny is sometimes a status symbol. However, this form of marriage is also prevalent in societies with more females than males, usually where there is a high number of male deaths in hunting accidents and warfare.

*Polyandry*, or marriage with more than one husband, is very uncommon. Confusion about paternity may explain why it is less acceptable. Another reason may be that there are often fewer males than females in any population because it is the men who engage in high-risk activities. But perhaps the most important reason is that males often have a higher status and have organized social life to suit their preferences. Sharing their females may neither suit their sexual nor social needs.

In countries where women's education is low and their labour force participation restricted, such as in Morocco and rural India, dowries are sometimes used as insurance for a woman. She is given money, household goods or land by her parents, and her husband cannot dispose of this property. If they divorce, the ex-wife keeps this dowry to live on or to assist her to find another husband. The larger the dowry and the wealthier the woman's family, the more desirable a marriage partner she is (especially if she is also physically attractive). But providing a dowry is sometimes a financial strain on a woman's family, and this makes it less desirable to have a female child. As women become more educated and enter the paid workforce, they can support themselves and need a dowry less. Yet newspaper reports from India, where the dowry system is declining among the middle-classes, claim that mothers-in-law sometimes want their sons to divorce undowried wives to remarry those with dowries (which would improve the mother-in-law's standard of living). Numerous murders of daughters-in-law were attributed to this motive in New Delhi in 1980.

In countries such as Morocco, it is also very important that the bride (but not the groom) be a virgin on the wedding day. Loss of virginity lowers the reputation of the bride and her family and could cause problems with inheritance if she were pregnant by someone else. Ceremonies surrounding consummation of a marriage (relatives stand outside the bedroom waiting for proof of virginity) are still performed in some Moslem countries. However, in societies with a greater public role for women (higher education, greater participation in politics and the labour force), virginity, dowries and polygyny tend to fade away, at least among middle-class or urban young people.

Population growth has led to policies limiting family size in some developing countries. For example, government policy encouraging one-child families in China has led some rural families to kill female babies in the hope that they will have a male next time. The preference for male children is still strong in many parts of the world: Female children require expensive dowries, and if a daughter becomes pregnant before marriage, she will disgrace the family. In addition only male children perpetuate the family name in many societies. Since women often cannot support themselves or their aging parents, parents prefer male children. Even when females are educated and self-supporting and the need for dowries no longer exists, the preference for male children lingers, since cultural traditions may lag behind their utility.

## MATE SELECTION

Marriages are still arranged in some societies, especially where the extended family is the norm and the new marriage partner affects the functioning of the larger family unit. Parents or aunts and uncles are often involved in negotiating arranged marriages, but marriage brokers may be used if the family has insufficient connections. If status is ascribed by increasing age, older family members may select marriage partners for younger members. The decision is based on family reputation and financial status, the young person's personality and his or her education. But a previous relationship between the new couple would not be necessary. Societies which practise arranged marriages often feel that romantic love is an unsound basis for marriage.

When status is achieved through education and occupation and people live in nuclear families, marriage decisions are usually left to the couple involved. While most of these young people say that they marry because they are "in love," many patterns can be noted in love choices. Several different theories have tried to explain these choices. The *theory of complementary needs* suggests that people fall in love with someone whom they *think* will best fulfill their psychological needs. Their personalities are expected to complement each other. The *theory of social homogamy* proposes that we are attracted to people who are similar to us in life experience, ethnicity, race, religion, age, education or social class. These two theories are sometimes combined to suggest that, from a pool of eligibles who are socially similar to us, we choose someone who seems to satisfy our psychological needs.

Perhaps, though, we become involved with people similar to ourselves simply because those are the people we most often meet. Sociologists have noticed that North Americans often marry someone who lives very close to them (*residential propinquity*). Travelling far from home to visit a potential mate may require too much effort. People sometimes meet by accident and become involved through a process of misunderstanding, conflict, resolution and shared experience. This developmental theory suggests that the process of involvement may be like an escalator that carries us toward marriage. Social pressure to marry is strong at certain times in life, especially after graduation, around the ages of 22 to 24, after a relationship of a few years or when a pregnancy becomes visible.

Sociologists have also found patterns in the relationship of mate selection to marital stability. Marriages that are most likely to be stable take place between the ages of 20 and 30, are not precipitated by premarital pregnancy and are between mature and religious people from similar social backgrounds, whose families approve of the relationship.

## THE BASES OF FAMILY LIFE

During the last century, much of the behaviour of people in families was attributed to human nature. Before cross-cultural studies were done in the early 1900s, we were not aware of the range and variety of human behaviour. People thought that instincts governed behaviour and that "civilized" people behaved in one particular way. The discovery that marriage and family patterns are related to economic and political systems rather than to biology led to relativism in social science. For example, in some societies men have more than one wife not because they like frequent sex, but because wives are status symbols and sound economic investments (because they produce food, services and children).

Of course, there are some biological bases to family life. The human infant needs physical care and a long social-learning period. Living in a family provides some continuity of care. Marriage also provides for regular sex, although this can be and is obtained outside the marriage. Incest taboos prevent genetic abnormalities, but they also maintain the social group. In fact, most of our social customs about whom we can marry and when, and how we should organize our sexual lives have more to do with maintaining social harmony and protecting dependents than with biology. Elaborate wedding ceremonies celebrated with expensive dinners create bonds between families and contribute to the stability of the larger community. Cultures all over the world want to organize personal and sexual life to create a unit in which emotional and material security are maintained and reproduction can take place.

# HISTORICAL CHANGES IN THE FAMILY

The idea that "a man's home is his castle" has become far less true over the centuries. A Roman law called *patria potestas* gave a father the right of life or death over his children and considerable power over his wife. Under English medieval law, men were guardians of their children and their wives. Parents in the eighteenth century had three duties: to maintain, to protect and to educate their children. A man could beat his children or his wife. The wife had no legal rights; instead her husband exercised rights on her behalf (such as the right to administer her own money or property). But gradually, the power of men over family members was reduced as the state intervened more in family life.

## ECONOMIC AND LEGAL CHANGES

In preindustrial society, men, women and children produced goods and services for the family. Early Canadian farms usually operated at a subsistence level, with the husband acting as the representative to the outside world. With the building of factories, many young men left the rural areas to seek wage labour, since it was difficult to make a living from the land. Daughters were usually expected to stay with their parents and do housework until they were married, to enter convents or work as servants in wealthier homes.

With large-scale industrialization in southern and eastern Ontario, wage labour became preferable to personal service or farm work. Many working-class families moved to towns or cities and took factory jobs; children and women worked for a lower wage than men and all family members pooled their financial resources. Gradually, as factory-made goods replaced home-made goods, the family became a unit of consumption rather than one of both production and consumption.

The poor working conditions for women and children in the early days of industrialization led to international controversy about women's role, child labour and the decline of the family. Legislation limiting the labour of children under six years old was introduced in England in 1833, and gradually, with the assistance of trade unionists and women's groups, conditions were improved for women and young workers. These benefits were later extended to men.

Not until 1870 in England and 1872 (or later) in Canada could married women retain their own wages or property without their husbands' permission. Until the

*At one time, a man did his own washing only if he didn't have a wife.* Public Archives Canada/PA-32425.

laws were changed in the provinces (from 1910 to 1922), a husband could also insist on custody of the children if a marriage dissolved. Women were obliged to live where their husbands wanted and they had sole responsibility for child-care and running the home.

The care of children and housecleaning are still the responsibility of women, and these household duties have often been used as a reason to keep women out of paid work and to justify hiring priority for men and lower wages for women. Although both sexes often contribute financially to the family, men are expected to support their wives and children. Thus, unemployment has been considered more of a blow to a man than to a woman.

Family members working for pay outside the home gradually reduced patriarchal authority within the family and public concern about working conditions for women and children led to state intervention in both work and family life. When family members no longer worked together, the husband/father could not supervise them closely, and this eroded his authority. When children were apprenticed, or worked as servants in someone else's house or were in school, parents relinquished some control over them. Protective laws gradually specified the hours and conditions of work for children and women, as well as the laws increasing women's individual rights and requiring compulsory education for children.

Of course, these changes in the structure of the family affected the way family members treated each other. Children became valued more for emotional reasons than for what their labour contributed to the family income. Wives became more confident in asserting their own needs and interests and began to expect more from life than childrearing. Families became protective of their privacy but at the same time grew to expect state assistance with family problems and crises.

The economic changes affecting society have formed the basis of Marxist and political economy theories of the family. For example, Engels thought that monogamy arose when nomadic people became more sedentary and concerned with private property. Knowledge of paternity became important to ensure that this property could be passed on to heirs. Monogamy and private property also led to women's lower status in society, as they became the "property" of men and were restricted to domestic roles.

Anthropologists recently discovered that birth rates often rise when a formerly nomadic people settle on a piece of land and develop large-scale agriculture (O'Kelly, 1980: 80, 156). Rising birth rates tend to keep women in a more domestic role. Recognizing the role of high fertility in lowering the public participation of women has provided motivation for the family-planning movement and direction for feminist strategists.

## DEMOGRAPHIC CHANGES

Since the turn of the century, many demographic, economic and social changes have altered the family structure. In industrializing countries such as Canada, infant mortality and maternal death rates gradually fell as a result of improvements in nutrition, sanitation, housing and health care (see Table 11-1). Life expectancy rose, especially for women. While the average life expectancy at birth was 60 years for males and 62 years for females in 1921 (Urquhart, 1983: B65-74), it increased to 72 years for males and 79 years for females in 1981 (Statistics Canada, 1983: 2).

Birth rates have fallen in most industrialized countries with urbanization, modernization, improved methods of birth control and women's increased participation in the labour force. In the cities, a large family became difficult to accommodate, and children were no longer a financial asset, since they attended school instead of working for pay. With increasing education, women began devoting their time and energy to activities other than childbearing.

Birth rates have generally declined since 1900, but there have been fluctuations (see Table 11-2). During the 1930s, birth rates declined, but they rose again after World War II. The postwar baby boom (from 1945-65) was a time of high marriage rates, high fertility and increasing emphasis on family values. Yet, throughout this period, women's labour force participation gradually rose, as did their level of education.

Birth rates also vary provincially. Quebec, with its large Catholic population and traditional family structures, had a high birth rate until the 1960s. But by 1981 its birth rate was 14.8, compared to the national average of 15.3 (Statistics Canada, Vol. I, 1983: 2). Ontario has the lowest rate (14.2) and the Northwest Territories the highest (28.5), which reflects the higher birth rates among native people.

The age of marriage gradually declined until the early 1970s. With student loans, rising wages, lots of jobs for married women, birth control and more personal freedom, young people had fewer reasons to postpone marriage. Fewer pregnancies and freedom from childrearing enabled women to further their education or enter the labour force. The age of marriage stabilized in the later 1970s and then began

TABLE 11-1   Infant Mortality and Maternal Death Rates from 1921 to 1981 (Canada)

|  | INFANT MORTALITY RATE (PER 1 000 LIVE BIRTHS) | MATERNAL DEATH RATE (DEATHS DURING CHILDBIRTH) (PER 10 000 LIVE BIRTHS) |
|---|---|---|
| 1921 | 102* | 4.7* |
| 1931 | 86 | 5.1 |
| 1941 | 61 | 3.6 |
| 1951 | 39 | 1.1 |
| 1961 | 27 | 0.5 |
| 1971 | 18 | 0.2 |
| 1981 | 10 | 0.2 |

* Excludes the Yukon and Northwest Territories

Urquhart, M.C. (editor). *Historical Statistics of Canada*, 2nd edition, Ottawa: Statistics Canada, 1983, p. B51-58.
Statistics Canada, *Vital Statistics, Births and Deaths*, Ct. 84-204, 1983, p. 2. Reproduced by permission of the Minister of Supply and Services Canada.

TABLE 11-2   Changes in Birth Rates from 1921 to 1981 (Canada)

|  | LIVE BIRTHS (PER 1 000 POPULATION) |
|---|---|
| 1921 | 29.3* |
| 1931 | 23.2 |
| 1936 | 20.3 |
| 1941 | 22.4 |
| 1946 | 27.2 |
| 1951 | 27.2 |
| 1956 | 28.0 |
| 1961 | 26.1 |
| 1966 | 19.4 |
| 1971 | 16.8 |
| 1981 | 15.3 |
| 1982 | 15.1 |

* Excludes the Yukon and Northwest Territories

Urquhart, M.C. (editor). *Historical Statistics of Canada*, 2nd edition, Ottawa: Statistics Canada, Ottawa, 1983, p. B1-14.
Statistics Canada, *Vital Statistics, Births and Deaths 1981*, Vol. I, Cat. 84-204, Ottawa, 1983, p. 2. Reproduced by permission of the Minister of Supply and Services Canada.

*A habitant family poses with its spinning wheel.* Public Archives Canada/PA-112729.

rising again as couples postponed marriage by living together or rejected marriage altogether.

In 1981, the average age of a woman at the birth of her first child was 24.8 years and at the birth of her second child, 27.2 years (Statistics Canada, 1983, Vol. I: 17). Recently, more single women in their thirties have been having babies. This reflects changing norms about unmarried pregnancy and an increasing number of couples living together outside legal marriage. However, it may also be a reflection of the high proportion of couples in their thirties in the population as the baby-boomers approach middle-age. An important long-term change is that childbirth and childrearing take less of a woman's life today than in the past. Since women, on average, live nearly 80 years, they now have over fifty years for other activities after having a family.

## SOCIAL CHANGES

In the early twentieth century, new jobs in manufacturing and office work, with fixed hours and greater personal freedom, made domestic servants scarce and costly. While large houses with servants' quarters were built for the middle-classes until about the 1920s, smaller houses were built for smaller households after that date. After the 1920s, middle-class wives were expected to devote their time to child-care, volunteer activities, needlework or domestic duties. While poorer wives took in sewing, laundry or boarders to help make ends meet, wealthier wives remained out of the labour force. But postwar inflation and the expansion of the service sector of the economy gradually pushed even middle-class women with young children into the work world. As more women entered the labour force, laws and social practices encouraging male dominance declined. Laws equalizing pay, grounds for divorce, division of property after divorce and custody of children have been legislated since the 1920s, and there has been a greater emphasis on marriage as an economic partnership in recent years.

Whether the economic changes led to the women's movement or whether the ideas about liberation arose out of revolutions, such as the French and American Revolutions, the Vietnam War protests or socialist thought has been a controversy for many years. The political economists have argued that ideas are generated from people's material existence—the work they do and the lives they are forced to live. In explaining the division of labour in society and the family, biological determinists and learning theorists have focused on women's reproductive ability and experience and the fact that they are socialized to be passive and domestic. Women's increased interest in education and paid labour and their attempts to become more independent from domestic concerns have certainly influenced the structure of the family and preoccupied family studies for the past two decades.

Marriage has gradually become a less sacred bond and more an institution for personal fulfillment. Increasingly, unsatisfying marriages are dissolved and new liaisons are initiated, combining children from former marriages and creating more complex kin relationships. As divorce and remarriage rates rise, marriage is no longer a permanent bond. More people now go through different marital statuses and living arrangements in their adult lives, moving from single to married to divorced to living together to remarried. These long-term trends in family structure and interaction could be related to Weber's idea that society is moving from traditional to rational-legal authority. We no longer rely simply on tradition and morality but have allowed our family life to be rationalized and demystified.

## RECENT ISSUES IN THE CANADIAN FAMILY

Several family issues have been controversial recently. These include maternal employment and child-care, divorce and remarriage, legal changes in the division of matrimonial property and child custody and increased reports of family violence. Each of these will be discussed in this section.

### CHILD-CARE FOR WORKING PARENTS

Since 47.2 percent of women with children under the age of six were in the labour force in 1981 (Eichler, 1983: 248), many mothers need child-care assistance. Estimates of day-care need are usually based on the number of mothers in the labour force (because researchers assume that women, and not men, care for children). According to the Department of Health and Welfare, most parents make private arrangements for the care of their children. Nearly half of children under the age of six years are cared for by their parents (usually the mother). Only 5.8 percent of children under six attend day-care centres, and 22.3 percent are in a nursery or kindergarten. 18.6 percent are looked after in their own homes by someone other than a parent, and l8.6 percent are cared for in another private home (Eichler, 1983:249). These figures indicate that most preschool children are cared for in shared child-care arrangements. Even though baby-sitters are now frequently used, more parents would take their children to day-care centres if they were available (Johnson, 1977).

TABLE 11-3  Numbers of Children under 6 Requiring Day-care and Licensed Spaces Available, Canada, 1975-1982

| YEAR | ESTIMATED NUMBER OF CHILDREN UNDER 6 WITH MOTHERS IN THE LABOUR FORCE | NUMBER OF CHILDREN UNDER 6 OCCUPYING LICENSED FAMILY AND DAY CARE CENTRE SPACES | PERCENTAGE OF CHILDREN UNDER 6 WITH ACCESS TO LICENSED DAY CARE | NUMBER OF CHILDREN UNDER 6 NOT ACCOMMODATED WITHIN THE FORMAL SYSTEM |
|------|------|------|------|------|
| 1975 | 562,000 | 64,589 | 11.49% | 497,411 |
| 1976 | 620,000 | 75,330 | 12.15% | 544,670 |
| 1977 | 656,000 | 73,865 | 11.26% | 582,135 |
| 1978 | 695,000 | 73,475 | 10.57% | 621,525 |
| 1979 | 721,000 | 86,780 | 12.03% | 634,220 |
| 1980 | 760,000 | 92,423 | 12.16% | 667,577 |
| 1982 | 950,000 | 110,573 | 11.63% | 839,427 |

Health and Welfare Canada, National Day Care Information Centre, Status of Day Care in Canada, 1975-1980; Day Care Spaces in Canada—1982. (Figures for 1981 are not available.) Reprinted from Day Care in Canada: A Background Paper by L. Johnson and N. McCormick, Canadian Advisory Council on the Status of Women, Ottawa, August 1984, Page 20.

The federal government shares day-care costs with the provinces. Despite cuts in other social programs, day-care funding levels have not been altered. However, there is still a shortage of day-care space.

A recent report by the Department of Health and Welfare (1984) claimed that the number of day-care spaces in Canada for children under two is steadily declining despite the influx into the workforce of mothers with children of that age. Of the 123 000 spaces in commercial and nonprofit centres in 1983, less than 7 percent were allocated for children under two years. This is a decrease of about 1200 spaces from 1982 and a decrease of 1600 spaces from 1979. In fact, day-care serves only 10 percent of children under two in families where parents are students or work at least 20 hours a week.

Most working parents rely on baby-sitters. But the high turnover of baby-sitters (many families go through four or five a year) may not be good for children. In fact, weak social support for publicly funded infant day-care may be a result of a previous controversy about the role of the mother in the child's early development. Research from the 1950s and 1960s emphasized the importance of maternal bonding and emotional stability in the child's early years and stressed that all young children are best cared for by their mothers. However, recent comparisons between infants raised within their own families and infants cared for in child-care facilities indicate that many variables affect the development of children (for example, the quality of care and the socioeconomic background of the child).

The number of day-care and family-care spaces (a place allotted to one child in day-care) peaked in 1983 (Lipovenko, 1984). But infant day-care is particularly underfinanced and has not kept pace with the growth in demand. The Health and Welfare study (1984) indicated that when parents must rely on informal child-care arrangements, they are more likely to obtain mediocre and even negligent services.

By April, 1985, 61.4 percent of mothers with children under 16 were in the labour force. Since childbearing benefits *society*, child-care services for employed parents are essential. But recent cutbacks to social programs mean that parents will have to continue to rely on relatives, neighbours or hired sitters to care for their children. Considering that women earn less than two-thirds of men's wages, few female single-parents can afford unsubsidized child-care. The child-care tax deduction (now $2000 per child to a maximum of four children) seldom covers the entire cost of child-care (estimated at $3000 per child per year in 1982). A more realistic tax deduction and increased numbers of day-care spaces are needed.

## DIVORCE AND REMARRIAGE

Although the divorce rate has been rising since World War II, it has soared in Canada since divorce law was liberalized in 1968. Divorce rates are also rising in other industrialized countries, and this has been attributed to increased personal freedom from family and religious tradition, more opportunity for husbands and wives to meet new partners, greater opportunities for women to support themselves if they leave their husbands, less commitment to duty, more emphasis on personal fulfillment in marriage, fewer children (which means that the consequences of a divorce are less complex) and more liberal grounds for divorce. Although Canada's divorce rate has risen dramatically in the past 15 years, the United States and most Eastern European countries have higher divorce rates. Restrictive divorce laws, a traditional role for women, and emphasis on the sacred bond of marriage are often found in Catholic countries. But all societies allow couples to break out of unhappy marriages, even if they are not allowed to remarry. Annulments, separations and desertions took place long before divorce was legalized. However, leaving an un-satisfactory marriage has always been easier for men than for women. Men have been less encumbered with the care of dependent children and more able to support themselves.

Canadian divorce rates fluctuate considerably by province, with higher rates in the West. Frontier areas with a highly mobile labour force and a high proportion of young workers (25-to-40-year-olds) have higher divorce rates, as do large urban centres. Rural areas with a stable population have lower rates. But divorce rates record only a fraction of the number of dissolved or "unsuccessful" marriages. Many people separate with no legal agreement and therefore do not come to the attention of authorities. Others live apart with a separation agreement but without legal divorce. After all, divorces usually involve lawyers and cost money. Other people live in the same household but live separate lives. They stay together to avoid the embarrassment of divorce or because they are afraid to live alone, for financial reasons, for religious reasons or "for the sake of the children." However, research suggests that it may be more harmful for children to live with estranged or hostile parents than to live in a one-parent household (Ambert, 1980: 166-167). Still, some children *are* hurt by divorce, especially if it results in a drop in standard of living or continued parental conflict.

TABLE 11-4  Divorce Rate in Canada By Year
(per 100 000 population)

| YEAR | DIVORCE RATE |
|------|--------------|
| 1921 | 6.4 |
| 1931 | 6.8 |
| 1941 | 21.4 |
| 1951 | 37.6 |
| 1961 | 36.0 |
| 1968 | 54.8 |
| 1969 | 124.2 |
| 1970 | 139.8 |
| 1981 | 278.0 |
| 1982 | 285.9 |
| 1983 | 275.5 |

Statistics Canada, *Vital Statistics, Marriages and Divorces*, Vol. II, 1981, 1982, 1983, Cat. 84-205, Table 1, p. 2; M. Baker (editor), *The Family: Changing Trends in Canada*. Toronto: McGraw-Hill Ryerson, 1984, p. 85.

A decade ago, people without children were more likely to divorce. But increasingly, divorce affects families with children, and 53 percent of divorcing couples in 1983 had one or more children (Statistics Canada, 1985: 26).

The one-parent household is usually headed by the mother. Despite new laws that say custody should go to the parent who is best able to care for the child, 74 percent of children are awarded to the mother, 17 percent to the father and 9 percent to others (Statistics Canada, 1985: 24). Fathers are only slightly more likely to gain custody in 1983 than they were in 1971 (see Table 11-5 on page 278). The non-custodial parent is expected to pay child support but often defaults on these payments after the first year. This means that most separated or divorced women must live on government assistance, their own income or sporadic support payments. Social workers and women's groups recently expressed concern about the high proportion of one-parent families headed by females on welfare. Some provinces, such as Manitoba, automatically garnishee the wages or government benefits of the defaulting parent without action being taken by the custodial parent. But most provinces expect the custodial parent to initiate action.

About three-quarters of divorced men and two-thirds of divorced women remarry. Reasons for this difference in remarriage rates have been debated. Without child

TABLE 11-5    Divorce Rates in Several Industrialized Countries 1981
(per 1 000 population)

| | |
|---|---|
| Japan | 1.3 |
| France | 1.6 |
| Sweden | 2.6 |
| Canada | 2.8 |
| United Kingdom | 2.9 |
| U.S.S.R. | 3.3 |
| United States | 5.1 |

Statistics Canada, *Marriages and Divorces, Vital Statistics*, Vol. II, 1983, Cat. 84-205, Table 21, p. 32, Ottawa, 1985. Reproduced by permission of the Minister of Supply and Services Canada.

TABLE 11-6    Percent of Children Awarded to Mothers, Fathers, or
Others in Custody Cases After Divorce

| | FATHER | MOTHER | OTHER | NO AWARD |
|---|---|---|---|---|
| 1971 | 15.2 | 74.2 | 0.4 | 10.1 |
| 1976 | 15.0 | 78.9 | 0.4 | 5.7 |
| 1980 | 16.0 | 78.2 | 0.2 | 5.5 |
| 1983 | 17.0 | 73.8 | 0.2 | 9.0 |

M. Eichler, *Families in Canada Today*, Gage, 1983, p. 215; Calculated from Statistics Canada, *Marriages and Divorces 1983*, Cat. 84-205, Ottawa, 1985, p. 24. Reproduced by permission of the Minister of Supply and Services Canada.

custody and with higher disposable incomes, most divorced men have greater opportunities to meet new partners; they may also have a greater emotional need to recouple. While women rely on their mothers, sisters and female friends for assistance and companionship after separation, men are less likely to have close emotional bonds with their relatives or with other men (Baker, 1983). They often date widely within the first year after separation and often marry within two years of the legal divorce.

American statistics indicate that remarriages have a higher probability of divorce than first marriages. It may be that people in first marriages simply do not believe that divorce is a possible alternative to an unhappy marriage and would not divorce under *any* circumstances. Those who seek a divorce are less likely to be religious and are more likely to have come from a divorced family. But apart from this, remarriages have different strains and problems than first marriages. Bringing together two sets of children, who may not get along, could certainly cause controversy between the new partners. The husband may be supporting his new family, his former wife and his children from the first marriage, which may result in financial

## JUDGE CONCERNED OVER FATHERS' RIGHTS
By Marina Strauss

Ontario Judge David Steinberg says he is concerned that men who father children as a result of a casual sexual relationship are often not told about the birth and the subsequent adoption.

Legislative amendments are needed to ensure that the biological father is made aware of the birth of his child. The father should have the opportunity to present to a court an alternative plan for his child's upbringing where this is reasonable and practical before the child's placement for adoption, Judge Steinberg of the Unified Family Court in Hamilton said in a recent ruling.

Judge Steinberg nevertheless approved the adoption of a child who was born Jan. 4, 1984, in unusual circumstances after a casual, one-time sexual encounter between the parents.

The mother said in an affadavit that she did not know she was pregnant until the day before the baby's birth.

"No one except my parents knows of my pregnancy or of the baby's birth," the mother's affadavit says.

Her family and the biological father's family have been friends for many years and she knew the father of the baby all her life but they did not have a romantic relationship.

Under the Child Welfare Act, the biological father technically is not a parent because the law defines a parent as a mother of a child or a person who has filed a legal declaration affirming that he is the father, or other provisions—none of which the father qualified for in this case.

The child was placed with the adoptive parents 13 days after his birth and has done well there, the judge found.

"What concerns me is the total withholding of any information concerning the pregnancy and birth of the child from the biological father," Judge Steinberg said.

"The biological father in this case, notwithstanding its unique features, is however in no different position from many other men who have had casual sexual relationships with women who are deliberately excluded from any knowledge of the pregnancy or the birth of their children."

Judge Steinberg acknowledged that most men in that situation would welcome the decision of mothers to place the children for adoption.

Still, he said, "there are some who would cherish the opportunity to care for and raise their offspring."

Under existing laws, the judge said, these biological fathers have no way of getting information about the children or to present a plan prior to their placement in adoptive homes.

*The Globe and Mail*, Toronto (February 8, 1985).

strain and be resented by the second wife. Former marriage partners sometimes continue to plague each other or reappear to dredge up old memories. Relatives may compete with each other to see the children. Arrangements for visiting children or parents may become a problem. All these factors may disrupt the stability of remarriages. Although remarriages have higher rates of dissolution, those who stay together *claim* to be happier and to have matured and learned from their previous marital relationship.

Recent American studies have also suggested that wives with a university education and paid work, whose husbands do not share the housework, are more likely to *consider* divorce than other women (Huber and Spitze, 1980). The fact that women have taken over a part of the traditional male role (earning income) while men are generally not sharing women's traditional role (doing housework) may also be increasing dissatisfaction in marriage.

## FAMILY LAW REFORM

Since 1978, most Canadian provinces have changed their family law. The most publicized changes relate to the division of matrimonial property. After the 1971 Murdoch case, many groups lobbied for change because they felt that women were receiving a smaller share of matrimonial property and that their unpaid contributions to households were not being considered. In the Murdoch case, the wife ran the family farm for several months of each year while her husband worked out of town at another job. The 25-year marriage broke up after he physically assaulted her, but the court gave the farm to the husband because his name was on the deed and most of the money used to purchase it came from him. The wife was given $200 a month alimony and was allowed to continue to live in the farmhouse (Dranoff, 1977: 52). After 25 years, her contributions to the farm and her running of the family household were judged inconsequential.

In Ontario, the property or possessions used within a marriage (i.e., house, car, furniture) are now considered "family assets" and are divided equally if the marriage breaks up. Even if the wife is not working outside the home for pay, she is entitled to one-half of the family assets. But there remains some dispute about whether spouses are entitled to money invested in business ventures. If a woman frees her husband from domestic labour and therefore allows him to work overtime to make extra money, is she entitled to a share of that money? It appears that the answer, so far, is no.

In Quebec, a woman is no longer expected to take her husband's surname at marriage. She may keep her own name or hyphenate her name and her husband's. In other provinces, too, more married women are keeping their own names. Children from the marriage may be given a hyphenated name that includes the surnames of both parents.

The custody of children in a divorce action is no longer automatically given to the mother. The new laws state that each parent has an equal *right* to custody, and each parent is expected to support the children. Yet, in reality, women still usually receive custody, especially of young children.

*Since 1978, most Canadian provinces have changed their family law to recognize the unpaid contributions women make to households.* Public Archives Canada/ PA-115226.

In some provinces, several courts have been consolidated to deal with all family matters (divorce, custody of children, child support and juvenile delinquency). Lawyers defend the child's interests if the parents disagree, are deemed to be negligent or are absent.

A backlog of divorce petitions has led to a new divorce bill that would shorten the separation period to one year (from three or five). Some people think that this would make divorce too easy and not provide adequate support for unemployed wives and dependent children. Initially, this bill cited "marriage breakdown" as the only valid reason for divorce, but amendments added adultery and cruelty as separate reasons that did not require any waiting period. The new divorce bill makes divorce cheaper for the government, eliminating red tape and shortening time spent in the courts. Although spouses are expected to be self-supporting within a few years, allowance will be made for those with no job experience or prospects.

## Family Violence

The recent Badgley Report (1984) on sexual abuse of children was widely publicized because it claimed that one-half of all women and one-third of men had experienced some sexual abuse in their lives. Most incidents occurred when they were children or adolescents, and they often involved male relatives. The growing reports of sexual and physical abuse indicate that it is no longer acceptable to treat children as property and that the state will intervene if a child is deemed to be in danger. However, all studies of child abuse state that reported incidents represent only a small portion of the actual number of cases. Fear of reprisals, lack of knowledge about whom to tell or feelings of guilt discourage many children from reporting incidents. Sexual abuse especially goes unreported.

At least one wife in ten is beaten by her husband at some point. Wife battering is often related to the husband's need to exert his dominance and is often unrelated to the wife's behaviour. In fact, it often occurs when she is sleeping and he returns home drunk. Concern about the inability of the police to deal with domestic violence has led to the creation of temporary shelters and transition houses for battered women, feminist counselling services and a series of government reports investigating the problem. Since 1981, the police in London, Ontario, have been laying charges against abusive husbands wherever possible and the Crown Attorney's office has taken a firm stand against dropping charges. So far, 70 percent of the charges laid have been heard in the courts, with a conviction rate of almost 100 percent (McGraw, 1983). Yet women are often abused many times before they go to the police. A recent Canadian study suggests that abused wives are beaten an average of 35 times before they seek outside help (McGraw, 1983). As with child abuse, fear of reprisals and guilt discourages women from going to the authorities. But in addition, many women lack the financial resources to leave an abusive husband and have nowhere to go. They remain in the situation while deciding what to do, often hoping that things will change

## Cohabitation vs. Legal Marriage

Fifty years ago, a sexually experienced man expected to marry an inexperienced woman. Gradually, this double standard disappeared, and women now have more nonmarital sexual experience. However, women are still more likely than men to have sex with only those they are "in love with" or whom they plan to marry.

Widespread premarital pregnancy and a desire for independence probably led to the earlier marriages of the 1960s and early 1970s. Yet, with improved contraception and changing attitudes, the age of marriage has risen slightly in recent years as more people cohabit without legal marriage. Some believe that this is a new "courting" pattern—living together to see if you are compatible for marriage. Cohabiting is particularly common among divorced people and those worried about the impermanence of marriage.

Studies have found that people who live common-law are less concerned with tradition, organized religion and socially acceptable behaviour and are therefore less likely to oppose the dissolution of the relationship. In other words, although more people cohabit for long periods of time, common-law relationships are even less likely than marriage to be viewed as permanent.

# SUMMARY

Over the last two decades, the age of marriage in Canada has declined and then risen slightly, the birth rate has continued to decline, the divorce rate has risen and levelled off and the labour-force participation of married women (especially young mothers) has increased dramatically. Fewer people live in two-parent families, but more two-parent families have two earners. Mothers are less likely to stay home with their children until they are school-age or adolescents and they are more likely to simply take a maternity leave from work or to stay home for a few years. As women become more educated and jobs become more financially necessary and harder to find, wives and mothers become more committed to paid work. This has led to major changes in family structure and stability.

Although fewer babies are born to each woman now, there has been only a slight rise in childlessness among women. While childlessness by choice is facilitated by effective birth control and the greater availability of abortion, involuntary child-lessness has also been successfully medically remedied so that more people *can* have children. Some unmarried women choose to have children without legal marriage. But having children no longer means an exclusively domestic role for women. Men are slightly more involved in infant and child-care than they were two decades ago, and couples are more likely to hire baby-sitters or to take their children to day-care centres.

Marriage is no longer seen as a life-long commitment, and the remarriage rate after divorce is higher than a few decades ago. The stigma attached to divorce is lessening, and more children live in reconstituted families. The variety of family types, even in a country like Canada, is so great that we can no longer talk about "the family" but of "families." Yet variety always existed within Canadian families. Not only did we experience ethnic variations among immigrant groups and native peoples, but immigration, migrant labour, maternal deaths and high accident rates in the frontier made one-parent families, adoption, boarding and remarriage quite common in the nineteenth century.

In recent years, the sociology of the family as a field of study has been broadened by social historians and feminist scholars. Sociologists such as Jessie Bernard and Margrit Eichler have emphasized that the marital experience is different for males and females. We can no longer assume that couples go through a life cycle together but must acknowledge that individual people experience changes in their lives and marriages which may occur at different times. We no longer become engaged, marry, have children, rear our children and grow old according to the patterns defined for us mainly by American sociologists of the 1950s and 1960s. People sometimes raise other people's children as well as their own. Men sometimes have two sets of children—one from their first marriage and one from their second. Family life has become more complex, with increasing divorce and two-earner families.

Only recently have the laws allowed people to live outside the family with greater ease and protection. It is no longer socially and financially necessary for women to be legally married to reproduce. It is not even necessary to have sexual intercourse to reproduce, as a result of the technology of artificial insemination. Despite the available alternatives in relationships and family life, most people follow social custom rather than create their own alternatives. This is the path of least resistance. Yet enough people have opted out of traditional patterns to force legal and social changes in family life. Now more egalitarian and open to individual preferences and rights, the family continues to be an important institution to both the individual and the state.

Over the past century, the Canadian family has changed as more mothers work for pay and fewer children are born. Children today are cared for by baby-sitters, and divorce and remarriage rates are high. These trends are the consequence of widespread economic and legal changes that began in the late eighteenth century (increasing industrialization, urbanization and demand for labour). In the nineteenth century, families began to produce less for their own consumption, and family members started to work for wages outside the home. As a result, the authority of the father was weakened, and eventually, state regulation of family life increased. Greater participation in public life led to more legal and political rights for women and less emphasis on childbearing. Despite these changes in the family, marriage has remained popular.

## DISCUSSION QUESTIONS

1. Is there a maternal instinct? Discuss the evidence for and against.

2. Why is child abuse and wife battering so underreported?

3. What do we mean when we say there has been social pressure to marry? What evidence is there for this?

4. Why do so few divorced men receive custody of their children?

5. Is there a trend towards the nuclear family with increasing industrialization? Why or why not?

# 12

# Social Movements

*Robert Brym*

# INTRODUCTION

*Social movements* are collective attempts to change some or all aspects of society. Participation in social movements may involve rioting, demonstrating, petitioning, striking, forming new political parties (either reformist or revolutionary) and taking part in other protest activities.

When masses of people conflict with authority they provide fresh material for one of sociology's traditional areas of study. Why do social movements emerge? How are they organized? How does social movement organization change under different social, economic and political conditions? Who participates in social movements? Why are there variations from one movement to the next in the relationship between leaders and followers, between members and nonmembers, between members and authorities? What accounts for the different forms social movements take? What accounts for the wide variety of movement goals, strategies and tactics? What consequences do social movements have for society? These are among the chief questions that have interested students of social movements for two centuries.

In any full account of the field, all these topics would have to be addressed. But a good overview of the subject can be gained by a discussion of a few of these questions. In the following discussion, we will focus on the causes of social movements, their social composition, the relationship between movement partisans and authorities and variations in movement form.[1]

# CAUSES OF SOCIAL MOVEMENTS

Charles Tilly, one of the leading contemporary authorities in this field, has pointed out that two main types of explanations of social movement formation have crystallized over the years (Tilly, Tilly and Tilly, 1975). According to the first type of theory, social movements result from societal and personal *breakdown*. The second type of theory views movements as expressions of new forms of social *solidarity*.

## BREAKDOWN THEORIES

Breakdown theories are rooted in the thinking of nineteenth-century conservatives, who opposed the French Revolution of 1789. Perhaps the most famous codification of this point of view is Gustave Le Bon's *The Crowd*, first published in Paris in 1895 (Le Bon, 1969). The revolutionaries proclaimed *liberté, égalité, fraternité* as their goals; but the conservatives saw the overthrow of the old government and the old ruling class as a great threat to the well-being of the French citizenry. In their writings, they emphasized how existing authority, traditional forms of community and rigid social hierarchy constrained human aspirations and actions, thereby preventing disorganization and anarchy. On the other hand, the migration of peasants to the cities was thought to cause the breakdown of traditional community, the erosion of moral and religious standards, increased crime and the growth of bound-

---

[1] For comprehensive and up-to-date reviews of the entire field, see especially Marx and Wood (1975), Jenkins (1983), and Roy (1984).

less aspirations for material improvement on the part of these new urban poor. The partisans of the revolution—the conservatives labelled them "the dangerous classes," "the criminal classes," "the mob," "the crowd" and the like—were moved largely by impulse rather than reason and could easily be swayed by opportunistic and despotic leaders to commit violent acts against the existing order.

Various aspects of these ideas have found their way into modern sociological thought, albeit stripped of their explicit moral and political messages. Thus, one popular modern variant of the breakdown approach holds that social movements emerge when dissatisfaction with the present fuses with hope for the future. This is frequently called a situation of *relative deprivation* (Davies, 1969; Gurr, 1970). The idea is that people revolt when the gap between what they need and what they expect to receive becomes intolerable. For example, great poverty in itself (or *absolute deprivation*) is not enough to spark rebellion; but poor people whose aspirations are not limited, who want much more than they can get, are likely to act collectively to further their aims.

Such a situation typically arises (according to modern relative deprivation theorists) during periods of rapid industrialization and urbanization. When large numbers of people move from countryside to city, the result has often been

> internal disorder, political unrest, and governmental instability fed by mass misery and frustration in the urban setting. The facts that the differences between the "have" and the "have not" nations, and between the "have" and the "have not" peoples within nations, have become "felt differences", and that we are experiencing a "revolution in expectations", have given huge urban population agglomerations an especially incendiary and explosive character. In the domestic and international settings in which many underdeveloped countries find themselves, huge and rapidly swelling urban populations constitute supersensitive tinderboxes with explosive potential. (Phillip M. Hauser, "The Social, Economic, and Technological Problems of Rapid Urbanization," p. 212 in B. Hoselitz and W. Moore, (eds.) *Industrialization and Society*, The Hague: Mouton, 1963.)

In the allegedly bucolic rural past, nearly everyone was a poor peasant, knew his or her place in society, was well integrated into village and estate and rarely had reasonable hope of improvement. The trouble presumably began only when peasants tore up their roots in the countryside, experienced the hectic and unsettling ways of city life and a painful clash between traditional and modern values and began hoping they could achieve the living standards of the urban "haves." Frustration at failing to advance as rapidly as they hoped led to widespread crime (an attempt to succeed materially by illegal means), suicide (an admission of defeat) and popular rebellion (collective attempts to change conditions perceived as unjust).

## Criticisms of the Theory

This interpretation of the causes of mass social unrest has not gone unchallenged, especially over the past twenty years. One of the main charges lodged against breakdown theories is that they do not fit the available facts. For example, Charles Tilly and his associates (Lodhi and Tilly, 1974; Tilly, Tilly and Tilly, 1975) have collected an enormous cache of relevant data on France and other Western European countries during the period 1830-1930. For each year and for each region, they measured collective unrest (the number of strikes and demonstrations that took place), individual unrest (crime rates) and the level of strain and frustration (urban growth rates). The breakdown interpretation would have been supported if they had discovered that rates of urbanization, collective unrest and crime fluctuated together. But Tilly and his colleagues found no significant covariation. In other words, the best available evidence indicates that personal and social disorganization are unlikely to be the main causes of social movement formation because social movements frequently emerge in the absence of such disorganization.

A second problem with theories that emphasize breakdown and disorganization as causes of social movement formation involves their characterization of the kind of people who typically participate in social movements. Movement partisans are generally viewed as socially rootless types who lack attachments to local communities and secondary associations. For example, the *theory of mass society* was once widely used to explain the rise of many movements, notably Nazism in Germany. According to the theory's chief exponent (Kornhauser, 1959), Germany in the 1930s had relatively few voluntary, civic, religious, occupational and other secondary associations. Large numbers of German citizens were alienated, uprooted and, therefore, unusually susceptible to the influence of extremist groups such as the Nazis. Supposedly, the Nazi appeal would have fallen on deaf ears if more people had been busy attending church, participating in trade unions, running for local office and so forth. This variety of social cross-pressures would have prevented people from having their attention drawn to only one extremist movement.

Subsequent research (well summarized in Oberschall, 1973:102 ff.) has demonstrated this theory is not very accurate. Many studies document the fact that membership in secondary associations may actually *encourage* participation in social movements. Two studies of Canadian social movements illustrate this point strikingly (Lipset, 1968; Pinard, 1971). Consider the Cooperative Commonwealth Federation of Saskatchewan, a radical farmers' and workers' movement and political party that originated in the 1930s and first formed the government of that province in 1944. The early members and chief activists of this movement/party had been leading members of consumers' co-operatives and trade unions before getting involved in the CCF. They were not socially unattached men and women; on the contrary, they were unusually well connected to their communities and to their communities' organizations.

These and other findings raise the question: Under what conditions do secondary associations encourage people to get involved in movements for change, and under what conditions do they suppress such involvement? The answer hinges on how socially diverse the membership of the secondary association is. Members of most *pluralist* secondary associations tend to come from a variety of classes and ethnic groups. In such a situation, secondary associations really do act as the mass-society theorists say: People's class or other group identities and interest are diffused and political behaviour tends to be moderated. However, when secondary associations *segment* the population—when they have *socially homogeneous* memberships—class or group consciousness is sharpened and radicalism is more likely. Thus, research now shows that Germany during the rise of Hitler was not a society full of socially rootless people. Germans had plenty of organizational ties, but these tended to be socially homogeneous organizations that kept major categories of the population separated, or segmented. This militated against political moderation.

## SOCIAL SOLIDARITY THEORIES

To summarize the discussion thus far: The view that social movements arise from the strains and frustrations caused by personal dissatisfaction and social disorganization, and that new movements are internally disorganized collectivities, is an oversimplification. People who press collectively for social change may, as the breakdown theorists say, be angry and/or relatively deprived; but the most recent research on social movement formation demonstrates that only under certain *social structural conditions* can feelings of anger or deprivation be translated into collective protest behaviour (Korpi, 1974). Two such conditions were emphasized above: (a) The more socially segmented potential rebels are from authorities and (b) the more solidarity potential rebels have among themselves, the more likely it is that movements will form.

### Karl Marx's Influence

These are among the core propositions of *solidarity theories* of social movements the second school of thought distinguished by Tilly. If breakdown theorists have conservative intellectual origins, then solidarity theorists may trace their lineage back to the socialism of Karl Marx. Writing in the middle of the nineteenth century, Marx predicted that capitalist industrialization would create a large class of workers. Former peasants, driven from the countryside to work in factories, and former unsuccessful entrepreneurs, unable to compete with wealthier and more adept businesspeople, would compose this proletariat. Furthermore, according to Marx, the concentration of workers in huge factories for reasons of economic efficiency would facilitate the crystallization of working-class consciousness and the establishment of working-class organizations, such as trade unions and political parties. At the same time, wealth would necessarily concentrate in the hands of a small group of capitalists. Consequently, the class structure would become highly polarized, or segmented, as the working-class developed more solidarity. Marx predicted that this situation would result in conflict, both in the workplace and in the political arena, between workers and capitalists. He expected that eventually the working-class would overthrow capitalism—violently, in most cases—and establish a new socialist order (Marx and Engels, 1972).

### Modern Solidarity Theorists

Generally, modern solidarity theorists are not explicitly concerned with the political significance of Marx's work. But they have generalized and extended its sociological implications in interesting and fruitful ways. Some of these sociological developments can best be introduced by considering how social movement formation is influenced by the distribution of *power* in society (Brym, 1979; Korpi, 1974). Imagine a highly simplified situation in which a society consists of just three groups of people: (a) *authorities*, who occupy the strategic command posts of the economy, the military, the political system, the educational system and other major institutions;

(b) *potential partisans* of movements for change, who are disadvantaged, conscious of their disadvantaged position and anxious to improve their lot; and (c) the *uncommitted*, who are sought as recruits and allies by members of groups (a) and (b) (Gamson, 1968). What is the likelihood of potential partisans creating a movement to influence or force authorities to improve the position of the disadvantaged? That depends on how powerful group (a) is relative to group (b). If we think of the distribution of power as the ratio a/b (or authorities' power over potential partisans' power), we can say that the larger this ratio, the less likely it is a movement for change will emerge. But, as the ratio falls, the probability of social conflict and social movement formation increases. In the extreme and infrequent case where the ratio falls to 1 or less, a revolution takes place. This is a violent and rapid upheaval in which potential partisans are sufficiently powerful to take over positions of authority from the previous ruling group and substantially alter the organization of the whole society.

This raises the further question: On what does the relative power of groups depend? One useful definition holds that group power is a function of three factors (Bierstedt, 1974; McCarthy and Zald, 1977; Tilly, 1978). In ascending order of importance, these are: (a) the *size of the group* and its allies, (b) its *level of internal organization* and (c) its *access to scarce resources*. (Such resources may, in turn, be categorized under three headings. *Normative* resources are the newspapers, schools and other means used to teach people beliefs acceptable to the authorities. *Material* resources are means of paying people to behave in desirable ways, i.e., the ability to withhold or bestow jobs or bribes. Finally, *coercive* resources refer to police and military forces, which can be used to compel co-operation.)

## The Power Ratio

These factors help us understand why the power ratio is the central determinant of social movement formation. Consider, for example, the question of resource control. Where the power ratio is very high, authorities are able to influence heavily the content of political norms taught in religious and educational institutions and in the mass media. The point of view of the authorities is so firmly ingrained in the public mind that potential partisans of change are scarcely able to conceive of the possibility of improving their lot. One is reminded here of the totalitarian society depicted in George Orwell's *Nineteen Eighty-Four*, in which a new language was created by the authorities for political ends (see insert). Where the power ratio is very high, authorities also can buy off or co-opt many potentially troublesome people by giving them jobs or threatening to take away their jobs and prevent them from finding employment elsewhere. In the extreme case, authorities who have full control over the means of coercion can call the army or the police into action and suppress dissent violently. However, if the power ratio drops for one or more of these factors, the probability increases that movements for change will develop.

## The Level of Violence

These ideas have also been used to explain the level of violence that may develop once conflict erupts between movement partisans and authorities (Gamson, 1975; Oberschall, 1973:242-345; Tilly, Tilly and Tilly, 1975: 280-290). On the whole,

THE PRINCIPLES OF NEWSPEAK
The purpose of Newspeak was not only to provide a medium for the world-view and mental habits proper to the devotees of Ingsoc [English Socialism], but to make all other modes of thought impossible. It was intended that when Newspeak had been adopted once and for all and Oldspeak forgotten, a heretical thought—that is, a thought diverging from the principles of Ingsoc—should be literally unthinkable, at least so far as thought is dependent on words. Its vocabulary was so constructed as to give exact and often very subtle expression to every meaning that a Party member could properly wish to express, while excluding all other meanings and also the probability of arriving at them by indirect methods. This was done partly by the invention of new words, but chiefly by eliminating undesirable words and by stripping such words as remained of unorthodox meanings, and so far as possible of all secondary meanings whatever. To give a single example. The word *free* still existed in Newspeak, but it could only be used in such statements as 'This dog is free from lice' or 'This field is free from weeds'. It could not be used in its old sense of 'politically free' or 'intellectually free', since political and intellectual freedom no longer existed even as concepts, and were therefore of necessity nameless. Quite apart from the suppression of definitely heretical words, reduction of vocabulary was regarded as an end in itself, and no word that could be dispensed with was allowed to survive. Newspeak was designed not to extend but to *diminish* the range of thought, and this purpose was directly assisted by cutting the choice of words to a minimum.

George Orwell, *Nineteen Eighty-Four*. Harmondsworth, England: Penguin, 1954 (originally, 1949). Courtesy of the estate of the late Sonia Brownell Orwell and Martin Secker & Warburg Ltd.

available evidence indicates that violence is more frequently and massively used by authorities than movement partisans. And, generally speaking, the less powerful authorities are, the more likely they are to respond violently to challenges from movement partisans: Paradoxically, the use of force by authorities is a sign of their weakness. For example, if ruling groups are well organized, they can speak in a binding way, recognize the legitimacy of protesters without feeling threatened, bargain and negotiate with them, and act to institutionalize and tame the conflict. But if ruling groups are disorganized, they may not be able to speak authoritatively, and they may feel threatened by protest activities. This makes bargaining and negotiating with the rebels difficult and undesirable from the viewpoint of the authorities. They may then feel it necessary to use force to maintain order. Similarly, if authorities have not had access to abundant normative resources and have not been able to inculcate their values in the minds of potential movement partisans, and if they have too few available jobs and too little money to co-opt rebels, they will be inclined to put down unrest by force.

Although no society can long rely on force alone to maintain order, if the authorities decide that force must be used, it is more effective if it can be applied in a tough and consistent manner. In contrast, if relatively little force is used to control an aggrieved and unruly population, and if this force is applied in fits and starts, it is likely to increase the violence among movement partisans. Partisans will be angered by the violence directed against them, will sense the inability of the authorities to apply force more severely and will, therefore, take advantage of this perceived weakness.

The violence of movement partisans also varies with the type and level of movement organization. Two broad types of movement organizations may be distinguished: primitive and modern (Tilly, 1979). *Primitive organizations* have communal bases. That is, their members are recruited from particular kinship networks, villages, ethnic groups or tribes. They generate collective violence that is small scale and local in scope and that tends to have inexplicit and apolitical objectives. Bread and tax riots, social banditry, the turn-of-the-century Sicilian Mafia and even millenarian movements, which anticipate the imminent onset of a messianic age, are examples of archaic forms of social protest (Hobsbawm, 1959).

Primitive movements tend to be more violent than *modern movements* because the latter are, in effect, bureaucracies. That is, modern movements are large, specialized associations with well-defined economic and political objectives and routinized procedures and patterns of action. The modern trade union movement provides a good example of how such organizations function. Their leaders tend to enjoy privileged positions which they do not want to see endangered, and their bureaucratic staffs need stability if they are to perform their duties effectively. Violence is likely to disrupt the smooth operation of the movement and threaten the interests of its leaders, so it is avoided.

However, if modern, bureaucratically organized social movements are not monolithic—if, in other words, the movement consists of a number of competing, decentralized organizations—radicalism and even violence is more likely. As Anthony Oberschall points out:

> Competing with each other to gain followers and obtain outside resources and allies, disagreeing with each other on goals, tactics, and ideology, too insignificant to be co-opted and too numerous to be repressed, the leaders and activists in an emerging, decentralized social movement maintain a high level of tension and dynamism that propels the movement forward. Conservative tendencies are not given a chance to build up around vested interests since with each turn of events novel leaders and organizations, ideas and strategies, are thrown up to occupy the center of the stage and to undermine the process of consolidation. New layers of the population hitherto unmobilized become restless and have to be drawn into the movement by formulating new goals and adopting novel tactics. Leaders who wish to rest content with partial gains find that their erstwhile followers are deserting them and are shifting their support to more radical activists. (A. Oberschall, *Social Conflicts and Social Movements*, pp. 260-261, © 1973. By permission.)

To summarize:
(a) The relative power of a social group derives from its comparative size, level of organization and access to politically useful resources.
(b) The frequency of social movement formation varies inversely with the ratio of power between authorities and potential partisans (see Figure 12-1).

(c) When a social movement emerges, authorities are more likely to respond violently if they are relatively disorganized and/or if they have access to few normative and material resources (see Figure 12-1).

(d) Primitive social movements tend to be more violent than modern social movements because the latter are bureaucratically structured. However, radicalism and violence may occur in modern movements that are decentralized.

Figure 12-1   Conflict and the Power Ratio (As the ratio of authorities' to potential partisans' power falls, the rate and intensity of conflict increases.)

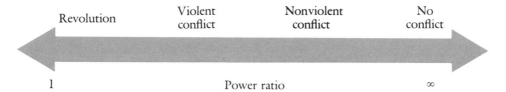

## SOCIAL MOVEMENTS IN CANADA

The discussion to this point has been rather abstract. In order to concretize some of the concepts introduced above, it will prove useful to draw some illustrative material from Canada's experience with social movements.

Is there anything unusual about Canadian social movements that makes them especially worth studying? By international standards, the overall level of collective violence in Canada is not unusually high or low. Several cross-national studies have shown that in the 1950s and 1960s Canada had about the median level of collective violence for all countries and for industrialized countries considered alone. The rate of protest activity was similar to that in England and West Germany (Feierabend, Feierabend, and Nesvold, 1969; Gurr, 1969; Kelly and Mitchell, 1981). Nor has Canada produced an unusually narrow or broad range of types of social movements. Canadians, like the citizens of other Western countries, have formed movements for nuclear disarmament, women's rights, environmental protection, gay rights and so forth.

Canada does stand out in two respects, however. First, since the 1920s, Canadian society has given rise to several social movements that have developed into small *third parties*. These are political parties that have gained up to 20 percent of the vote in national elections but have never constituted a federal government. They have formed provincial governments in British Columbia, Alberta, Saskatchewan, Manitoba and Quebec but have remained unaligned with the "establishment" parties (Liberal and Progressive Conservative) and have generally stood at the left of the political spectrum. This is odd when compared with both the American and the Western European experience. In the United States, third parties have been virtually nonexistent. In most Western European countries, the democratic-socialist third parties that emerged from the labour movement have intermittently won national elections and formed national governments. Canada's exceptional history of weak third parties is intriguing, and it has attracted a great deal of scholarly attention. We shall examine that history shortly.

A second outstanding feature of the Canadian experience with social movements and collective violence concerns the country's record of industrial disputes. The strike movement in Canada is exceptionally robust by international standards. In the 1970s, for example, Canada lost more working days per capita due to strikes than any other country in the world (Ward, 1981). For reasons that are unclear, sociologists have paid much less attention to this remarkable fact than to Canada's history of weak third parties. Nonetheless, the strike movement is worth examining here. As we shall see, its strength is simply the flip side of the weak-third-party syndrome, and we can improve our understanding of social movements in general by understanding the relationship between these two peculiar phenomena. First, however, we turn to the problem of third parties.

## THIRD PARTIES IN CANADA

### Western Parties
The story of Canada's third parties begins on the Prairies in the late nineteenth century (Lipset, 1968; Macpherson, 1962). The Prairies have aptly been called an *internal colony* of Canada. Since Confederation, Montreal and Toronto financiers and industrialists had dreamed about settling Saskatchewan and Alberta with European immigrants. They wished to establish on the Prairies a market for the manufactured goods of central Canada and a source of agricultural exports that would earn revenue for the new dominion. To achieve these aims, they—or, more accurately, the federal government, which they controlled—placed high tariffs on manufactured goods. This protected central Canadian manufacturers and their employees from foreign competition; but from the point of view of the Prairie farmer, it made ploughs and tractors, saws and hammers, shoes and automobiles more expensive. Moreover, the federal government set freight rates so as to ensure that the West would remain an agricultural frontier: The cost of shipping grain out was kept low, as was the cost of shipping manufactured goods into the region. Finally, large central Canadian business interests controlled the marketing of grain and the availability of credit. It was widely felt that this noncompetitive business environment enabled eastern businessmen to set low prices for grain and high prices for loans.

The protective tariff, freight rates policy and price-setting were the issues that galvanized the farmers into collective action. As early as 1906 they formed the Grain Growers' Grain Company. Its purpose: to collect wheat in a collectively owned grain elevator system and sell it directly to the central wheat exchange without going through any middlemen. This was only one of the many important marketing and consumer co-operatives that the farmers created in order to lower their costs of production and increase their incomes.

However, between 1910 and 1920 two developments convinced the Western farmers that collective action on the economic front was inadequate. The price of wheat fell on the world wheat market. Freight rates and the cost of manufactured goods rose. The farmers, caught in a cost-price squeeze, decided that *political* action was necessary: They figured that, by electing members of Parliament to represent their interests, it might be possible to force the government to lower the tariff on manufactured goods, buy grain that could not immediately be sold, establish a floor price for wheat and take other action that would ease the difficulties faced by the agricultural sector. In 1920, the National Progressive Party was formed. In the 1921 federal election, it won 64 seats, over 25 percent of the total. Thirty-nine seats were from the West, twenty-four from rural Ontario and one from rural New Brunswick. However, the party had a short life. This was partly because the elected representatives were unsure whether they should remain a separate party or simply try to influence government policy from within, i.e., by becoming part of an establishment party. And in fact, some of the leaders of the National Progressive Party were given important positions in the Liberal party and were thereby co-opted.

However, the farmers learned from this experience the importance of remaining politically independent. To that end, they created the Co-operative Commonwealth Federation (CCF) in 1933 in alliance with the small Independent Labour Party. The CCF, the forerunner of the New Democratic Party, became the government of Saskatchewan in 1944.

## The CCF

At its origin, the CCF was a democratic-socialist party (see insert). However, in order to appeal to the majority of land-owning farmers, it had to weaken and even abandon some of its more radical socialist principles—notably, the notion that a CCF government would take control of all land for the benefit of the population as a whole. Most farmers considered this equivalent to robbery and therefore rejected it out of hand. Nevertheless, the CCF remained a party that stood for the reform and humanization of the capitalist system, and it championed progressive reforms such as unemployment insurance and Medicare at the provincial and federal levels. It also remained a highly democratic party that stood for the protection of individual and minority rights. In this, it differed from a social movement in neighbouring Alberta that experienced a meteoric rise to political power in 1935. The Social Credit party, like the CCF, railed against eastern business interests and the federal government. In its early years, it, too, aimed to reform the capitalist system. However, for reasons too complex to discuss here (see Brym, 1980; Richards and Pratt, 1979), the Social Credit party eventually lost its reformist zeal. It was never run along particularly democratic lines, and many of its leaders and members had little regard for minority rights, as is evident from the anti-Semitic propaganda the party occasionally distributed.

The emergence of social movements on the Prairies has been explained in terms that correspond closely to the general principles outlined under "Social Solidarity Theories." C. B. Macpherson (1962), for example, stressed two factors that encouraged the success of Social Credit in Alberta: the nature of the province's class structure and the relationship between its economy and eastern Canadian economic forces. Macpherson described Alberta's class structure as relatively homogeneous: In 1941, nearly half of all employed people were farmers. He described the economic system as quasi-colonial, by which he meant that control over its major features was exercised by capitalist interests in the East. The relatively homogeneous class structure meant that a large mass of people in the province faced the same kinds of economic problems, had the same interests, were aware of them and were, therefore,

> **From the *Regina Manifesto*, adopted at the First National Convention of the CCF, Regina, Saskatchewan, July 1933**
>
> The CCF is a federation of organizations whose purpose is the establishment in Canada of a Co-operative Commonwealth in which the principle regulating production, distribution and exchange will be the supplying of human needs and not the making of profits.
>
> We aim to replace the present capitalist system, with its inherent injustice and inhumanity, by a social order from which the domination and exploitation of one class by another will be eliminated, in which economic planning will supersede unregulated private enterprise and competition, and in which genuine democratic self-government, based upon economic equality will be possible. The present order is marked by glaring inequalities of wealth and opportunity, by chaotic waste and instability; and in an age of plenty it condemns the great mass of people to poverty and insecurity. Power has become more and more concentrated into the hands of a small, irresponsible minority of financiers and industrialists and to their predatory interests the majority are habitually sacrificed. When private profit is the main stimulus to economic effort, our society oscillates between periods of feverish prosperity in which the main benefits go to speculators and profiteers, and of catastrophic depression, in which the common man's normal state of insecurity and hardship is accentuated. We believe that these evils can be removed only in a planned and socialized economy in which our natural resources and the prinicipal means of production and distribution are owned, controlled and operated by the people (Young, 1969: 304-305).

in a position to act collectively. The fact that the economy was quasi-colonial meant there was a highly visible group in the East that was perceived as the major source of the population's disadvantaged position. In other words, there was a high degree of social cohesion *within* the major disadvantaged class and a high degree of segmentation *between* that class and external powers. This facilitated the emergence of the Social Credit party.

In his study of the Saskatchewan CCF, Seymour Martin Lipset (1968) also noted the homogeneity of that province's class structure: Nearly 60 percent of the Saskatchewan workforce was employed in agriculture in 1941. Moreover, Lipset showed how the pre-existing dense network of ties among farmers in the co-operative movement and among blue-collar workers in the trade-union movement facilitated their participation in the CCF.[2]

---

[2] The next three paragraphs are reproduced with slight changes by permission of Butterworth & Co. (Canada) Ltd., from "Social Movements and Third Parties," by R. Brym, in S. Berkowitz, (ed.) *Models and Myths in Canadian Sociology*. Toronto: Butterworths, 1984, pp. 36-37.

## One-Party Dominance

Maurice Pinard (1971; 1973), in a study of the rise of Social Credit in Quebec in the early 1960s, generalized Macpherson's and Lipset's arguments. First, Pinard submitted that *class* homogeneity and solidarity among potential partisans of a third party is not the only basis of social cohesion that facilitates protest. Strong social attachments among members of any disadvantaged group—through voluntary or-ganizations, face-to-face contact in small communities, common work contexts and so forth—will have much the same effect. Second, he argued that cleavage between a quasi-colonial economy and a dominant metropolitan economy is not the only form of social segmentation that is conducive to the rise of third parties. Virtually any significant cleavage—for example, between social classes or between ethnic groups—will, in fact, suffice.

In a particularly innovative section of his study, Pinard showed that segmentation is enhanced by unrepresentative political party systems, and he paid special attention to systems of one-party dominance. When Pinard wrote of *one-party dominance*, he referred to a situation where one of the two establishment parties receives less than a third of the vote for some considerable time, or where it suddenly loses popular support as a consequence of, say, the revelation of flagrant corruption among party officials. In either case, only one of the establishment parties has a chance of forming the government. However, when seriously aggrieved segments of the population face a choice between a dominant establishment party and a very weak establishment party, they will be inclined to vote for neither. The dominant party is too closely identified with the sources of the population's grievances, and the other establishment party is not seen as a realistic alternative, since it is so weak. A third, alternative party is then likely to emerge.

Pinard offered compelling evidence to support his thesis. For example, in 88 percent of 33 provincial elections where the main opposition party was strong and received more than a third of the vote, third parties received 20 percent of the vote or less. In 59 percent of 22 provincial elections where the main opposition party was chronically weak and received less than a third of the vote, more than 20 percent of the ballots were cast for the third party. And in 90 percent of 10 provincial elections where the main opposition party was suddenly weakened, third parties received more than 20 percent of the vote.

## Regional Variations

Mention must also be made of the few studies that have tried to explain why different regions or subregions of the country have experienced different rates of social move-ment and third-party formation (Brym, 1979, 1980, 1984, 1986; Brym and Neis, 1978). While the rate of third-party formation has been unusually high on the Prairies, it has been unusually low in Atlantic Canada. This is true even though per capita income and standard of living of Maritimers and Newfoundlanders is the lowest in the country and, according to several public opinion polls, Maritimers and Newfoundlanders feel relatively worse off than other Canadians and are more dis-satisfied with governments.

Absolute and relative deprivation are not enough to cause Atlantic Canadians to rebel because the distribution of power has been so markedly skewed in favour of the ruling circles. Potential partisans of change—traditionally, wage earners and independent commodity producers (farmers, fishermen, etc.)—are relatively weak for several reasons. First, it should be borne in mind that, all else being the same, employed workers are more easily mobilized to participate in social movements than are unemployed workers; and workers employed in large establishments are more easily mobilized than workers in small establishments. This is because employed workers, and especially those employed in settings where they have contact with many people in the same work situation, may easily communicate among themselves, recognize that they are similarly disadvantaged and decide to take collective action to improve their conditions. But there is more unemployment in the Atlantic region than elsewhere in the country, and wage earners who are employed tend to work in relatively small establishments. This is because the region is economically under-developed, and low levels of investment result in high levels of unemployment and relatively small-scale industrial establishments. A second symptom of underdevel-opment is relatively low incomes: Per capita earnings in Atlantic Canada are below earnings elsewhere in the country. This lack of money (a politically useful material resource) also weakens the capacity of potential partisans to mobilize. Third, in-dependent commodity producers tend to be less socially cohesive in Atlantic Canada than elsewhere. Farmers and fishermen in the region tend to produce less for the market and more for their own subsistence than is the case elsewhere in the country. As a result, they have not needed to form many of the economic co-operatives that greatly increased the social cohesion and solidarity of Prairie farmers and served as a vitally important mobilizing force. For all these reasons, Atlantic Canadians have been less likely than Westerners to form social movements and third parties. (There have been a few instances of third-party candidates winning seats in Atlantic Canada. Significantly, this has tended to occur in areas where atypically high levels of capital investment have created relatively solidary and prosperous classes of blue-collar workers, farmers and fishermen at a time when the establishment parties were tem-porarily disunited.)

## HOW ELECTORAL SYSTEMS AFFECT THIRD-PARTY FORMATION

It seems, on the basis of the evidence cited above, that within Canada, there is a positive relationship between the rate of social movement/third-party formation and the degree of social segmentation; and an inverse relationship between the rate of social movement/third-party formation and the value of the power ratio. Do these relationships also hold internationally? There is some evidence, collected mainly by researchers from Israel, Sweden and the United States, (Hibbs, 1978; Korpi and Shalev, 1980; Lipset, 1976; Shalev and Korpi, 1980), that they do.

### Constituency Size
For example, although Seymour Martin Lipset has not stated it in these terms, his evidence shows that the greater the degree to which Western electoral systems segment populations, the more they encourage the growth of democratic-socialist parties (Lipset, 1976; Lipset and Rokkan, 1967). Consider the difference between Canada and the United States in this regard. The American electoral system fosters

parties that contain extremely socially heterogeneous memberships and support bases. This is partly because in the United States, there is a sharp division between the executive and legislative branches of government, i.e., between the presidency and governorships (the executive branch) and state legislatures and the federal Congress (the legislative branch). Separate elections are held for the two branches of government. Elections for the more important executive branch are state- or nation-wide. That these are enormous constituencies containing very heterogeneous populations is usually taken into account by each voter. Generally speaking, a voter does not want to "waste" his or her vote on a presidential or gubernatorial candidate who has little chance of winning, even if the candidate represents policies the voter favours. Thus, a voter will tend to cast a ballot for the candidate who is perceived as (a) having a chance of winning and (b) standing closer to the policies favoured by the voter than any other strong candidate. Because in presidential and gubernatorial contests, Americans must take into account the political complexion of very large and diverse constituencies, voting for a third-party candidate is almost bound to be perceived as a wasted vote. In this manner, the constitutionally enshrined separation of executive and legislative branches ensures that American political parties are socially heterogeneous bodies that bind together people from different classes and ethnic groups and so forth. The Constitution, therefore, makes it difficult for third parties to do well.

This differs from the Canadian situation. In Canada, there is only one elective political arena at the federal and provincial levels—the legislatures. Seats in the legislatures are filled on a constituency-by-constituency basis, and the party that wins a plurality of seats forms the government. These constituencies are relatively small geographical units. This means that, in a Canadian constituency that contains, say, a concentration of democratic-socialists, it "pays" for a left-wing voter to cast a ballot for a democratic-socialist candidate, since the candidate stands a good chance of winning that constitutency, sitting in Parliament and influencing government policy in the legislature. In short, the separation of legislative from executive authority in the United States militates against the success of democratic-socialist and other third parties, while Canada's centralized parliamentary government is more conducive to their growth.

## Party Loyalty

A second way in which electoral systems affect third-party strength has to do with the fact that the British parliamentary principle of party loyalty operates in Canada but not in the United States. In both state legislatures and the Congress, representatives vote according to their individual views, as these are shaped by the interests of the people who support and elect them. This in no way endangers the tenure of the administration. Even if, say, a majority of Republicans votes against a bill favoured by a Republican President, the President does not have to resign and call an election. But in Canada, disputes within a party are resolved outside of Parliament, in caucus, and once the representatives leave caucus and enter the legislature, they are obliged to vote as a bloc. If the representatives of a governing party fail to do so, they may cause the downfall of the government, since failure to pass a government-sponsored bill is likely to be construed as a vote of nonconfidence. In Canada, interests that are not satisfied with the policies of the existing parties thus have little alternative other than forming a third party: The electoral system encourages segmentation. In the United States, diverse interests can be accommodated within existing parties without major difficulties: The electoral system mitigates segmentation. (If space permitted, it could be shown that Western European electoral systems encourage even more social segmentation in political parties than is the case in Canada, which is one reason why, in most of Western Europe, the labour movement has given rise to democratic-socialist third parties that have eventually formed national governments.)

## THE CANADIAN UNION MOVEMENT

### Industrial Disputes in Canada

Also at the international level, the posited relationship between social movement/third-party formation and the power ratio seems to hold.[3] This point is well illustrated by patterns of industrial disputes in Canada and other countries.[4] Let us define the *volume* of strike activity as the number of eight-hour days ("person-days") lost due to strikes in a certain period of time; and the "frequency" of strikes as the number of industrial disputes resulting in work stoppage in a certain period of time. Researchers have shown that, for the post-World War II period, both these measures of strike activity are closely related to fluctuations in the business cycle (Hibbs, 1976; Korpi and Shalev, 1980; Smith, 1981).[5] Why? Largely, it seems, because good business conditions lower the power ratio between employers and employees, while poor business conditions increase the power ratio. During times of low unemployment and steady increases in real wages, workers are in a better position to press their demands. Employers are anxious to maintain high production levels, since profits are up during booms in the business cycle. At the same time, workers have more personal and union financial reserves to sustain them while on strike, and they are likely to have alternative job opportunities to which they can turn if they so desire. However, during economic slowdowns, employers are less anxious to settle disputes. Why should they want to produce at full capacity when there is no market for their products? As far as workers are concerned, strikes are less desirable in bad times because they have less money and fewer alternative job opportunities.

Long-run trends in strike activity can be interpreted in similar terms (Hibbs, 1978; Korpi and Shalev, 1980; Shorter and Tilly, 1971). Figure 12-2 shows the volume of strike activity in Canada from 1901-80. Obviously, the graph reveals a

[3] Electoral systems may themselves be viewed as institutionalized resolutions of past distributions of power among major classes and other groups in society. From this point of view, electoral systems are one means by which ruling groups are able, to varying degrees, to limit the political influence of disadvantaged classes and other groups (Brym, 1985).

[4] If space permitted, the point could also be illustrated by examining cross-national variations in the strength of working-class parties. See the evidence in Lipset (1983) and the evidence and interpretation in Brym (forthcoming, 1986) and in Shalev and Korpi (1980).

[5] The relationship was considerably weaker in the first half of the century, largely because organizational disputes—strikes over the right to form unions and engage in collective bargaining—were common until after World War II. The frequency of organizational disputes is less sensitive to fluctuations in the business cycle than is the frequency of purely economic strikes (Snyder, 1977).

strong upward trend. It also shows that peaks in the volume of strike activity have occurred more frequently with the passage of time. Both tendencies may be interpreted as a result of the increased power of the strike movement's potential partisans. The *size* of the nonagricultural labour force has increased greatly since the beginning of the century, both in absolute terms and as a percentage of the entire labour force. (In 1911, 66 percent of the 2 700 000 people in the labour force were nonagricultural workers; in 1975, 95 percent of the 9 300 000 people in the labour force were nonagricultural workers.) The level of *organization* of the strike movements's potential partisans has also gone up: Workplaces are, on average, much larger, and a steadily increasing proportion of the labour force is unionized. (In 1911, 7 percent of the nonagricultural labour force was unionized. In 1980, the figure was 35 percent. See Figure 12-3.) And the *material resources* of workers have also increased markedly. (Allowing for inflation, there was a 119 percent increase in real average weekly wages and salaries from 1939 to 1980 alone.)

Figure 12-2  The Volume of Strike Activity in Canada, 1901-1980

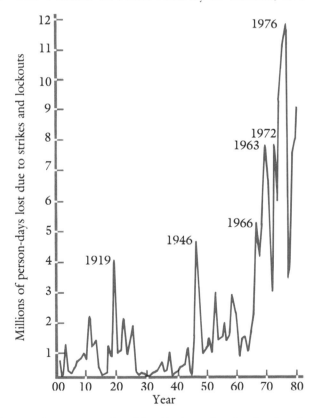

It is also instructive to examine historical tendencies in the *shape* of Canadian strikes. In Figure 12-4, on page 304, strike shapes for four 20-year periods are shown. The boxes are formed by three dimensions: (a) the *weighted frequency* of

Figure 12-3 Trade-Union Growth in Canada, 1921-1980

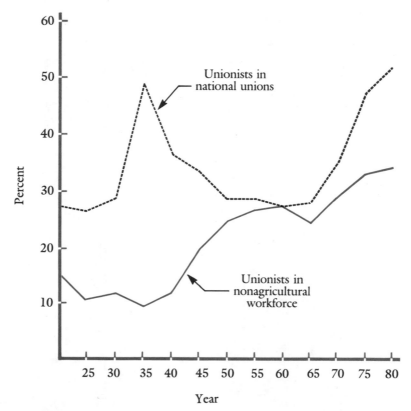

strikes, or strike frequency divided by the number of people in the nonagricultural workforce per year; (b) the *average size* of strikes, or the number of strikers divided by the strike frequency per year; and (c) the *average duration* of strikes, or strike volume divided by the number of strikers per year. Figure 12-4 demonstrates that, over time, there is a tendency for strikes to occur more frequently and a strong tendency towards bigger strikes. Strikes also tend to be of shorter duration.

Although there are wide variations in these dimensions of strike activity from country to country, there is a universal tendency toward more frequent, bigger strikes of shorter duration. Industrialization and urbanization universally have caused working-class power to grow, so that, while strikes used to be tests of endurance, they are now shows of strength.

Despite this general tendency, Canadian strikes tend to last considerably longer than those of any other country in the industrialized world. Indeed, that is the main factor underlying the fact that Canada placed first in the world in the 1970s in person-days lost due to strikes. Here we arrive at an interesting paradox. Above, the pattern of strike activity in Canada was interpreted as a sign of increasing working-class power. However, it may also be suggested that, when Canada is

# Figure 12-4   The Shape of Strikes in Canada, 1901-1980

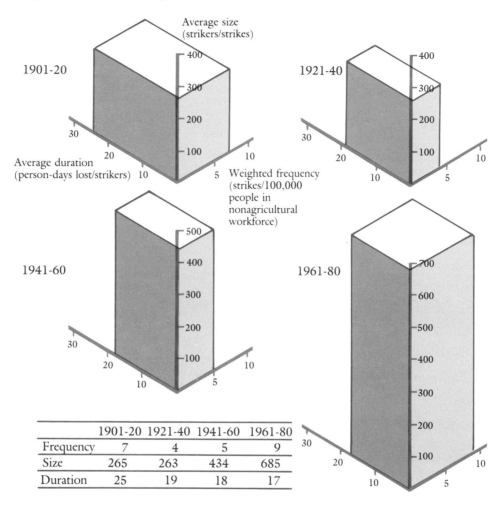

| | 1901-20 | 1921-40 | 1941-60 | 1961-80 |
|---|---|---|---|---|
| Frequency | 7 | 4 | 5 | 9 |
| Size | 265 | 263 | 434 | 685 |
| Duration | 25 | 19 | 18 | 17 |

Data for Figures 2, 3 and 4 taken from the *Census of Canada* (Ottawa: King's and Queen's Printer, decennial, 1901-81); *Report on Strikes and Lockouts in Canada, 1901-1916* (Ottawa: Department of Labour, 1918); *Strikes and Lockouts in Canada* (Ottawa: Department of Labour, annual, 1917-81); *Union Growth in Canada, 1921-1967* (Ottawa: Department of Labour, 1970); *Directory of Labour Organizations in Canada* (Ottawa: Department of Labour, annual 1968-81).

Measures of strike frequency and union density are conservative, since they are based on the number of people in the nonagricultural workforce—a category that includes professionals and businesspeople.

Intercensal labour-force estimates are interpolated.
Labour force estimates between censuses are interpolated.

Figure 12-3 is based on data for five-year intervals, which are adequate, since there are no big year-to year shifts in the data.

compared to most other Western countries, its working-class is unusually weak: A smaller proportion of the working-class is unionized, and trade-union structure is highly decentralized (Ingham, 1974).[6] In most Western countries, strikes by large, powerful and unified trade-union movements can so seriously affect the entire nation's economy that settlements come quickly, and the overall volume of strike activity is low. Not so in Canada (see insert).

---

### "Coyote Condition" Makes our Strikes Long, Spiteful Battles

Industrial experts call it the "coyote condition"—a Canadian on strike would rather gnaw off his leg than go back to work without a satisfactory settlement.

It's the major reason Canada has racked up the industrialized world's worst strike record over the past decade. . . . Canada's unenviable distinction as the industrialized world's strike leader was won on the basis of International Labor Office statistics showing strikes cost this country 1,840 working days for every 1,000 employees over the past decade.

We took the dubious honor by nipping Italy in the stretch.

It was the duration of strikes that catapulted Canada to the top. Other countries had more frequent strikes involving more workers—but shorter in duration.

In Canada, a strike is a matter of endurance, says [John] Crispo [an industrial relations expert from the University of Toronto]. "Once a strike starts, it's a struggle of the will. Each side is determined to outlast the other."

Compared to Canada, strikes in Europe tend to be nasty, brutish and short.

Often, millions of workers in several related unions will walk off the job together.

These common-front strikes hit at the solar plexus of small European countries. Because the entire nation is affected, settlements become a top priority.

On the other hand, strikes in Canada tend to occur union by union within an industry. That's why it seems somebody is always on strike.

It's generally accepted that a Canadian strike—because it is isolated—will seldom inconvenience the public to any great degree . . . .

Ward, 1981. Reprinted with permission Toronto Star Syndicate 1985.

---

## The Union-Democratic-Socialist Alliance

One more international pattern is worth thinking about. Research shows there is a strong inverse relationship between the volume of strike activity and the length of

---

[6] At the same time, the capitalist class in Canada is powerful by international standards, as ownership concentration figures and other indices show. See, for example, Clement (1975).

time democratic-socialist govenments are in power (Hibbs, 1978; but see also Shalev, 1978 and Korpi and Shalev, 1980 for some important qualifications regarding the intervening role played by the institutional framework of industrial relations systems). That is, over the long run, left-wing governments have the effect of lowering strike levels. The countries with the highest levels of strike activity—Canada, the United States and Italy—are also the countries that have had little or no democratic-socialist representation in federal cabinets since World War II. The countries with the lowest levels of strike activity—the Scandinavian nations—have the longest histories of democratic-socialist rule. This is not to suggest that when democratic-socialist governments get elected, fights over the distribution of rewards in society cease. They continue; but their locus shifts. They tend to take place in parliaments or at government-sanctioned negotiating tables, not in the workplace.

It is, of course, uncertain whether Canada will eventually follow the European model, whether its democratic-socialist party will grow beyond minor party status and eventually exert a dampening influence on strike levels. However, there is currently a slow and uneven movement in that direction.

Until the mid-1970s, the great majority of trade unionists in Canada were members of American-dominated unions with American and Canadian members, usually in the ratio 10:1. These "internationals," which began organizing in Ontario before World War 1, were "business unions." They stood for, among other things, the idea that workers should use their votes to punish their political enemies and reward their political friends without, however, forming an independent labour party. Such an approach may have made sense in the American context: Even a labour radical could reasonably argue that the American electoral system makes it more rational for workers to attempt to take over an existing party rather than trying to form a new one. But in the context of Canada's unified parliamentary system, the potential for an independent third party has always been greater than in the United States. Nevertheless, the idea of an independent labour party was slow to take root in Canada. American labour leaders opposed it, and the right to support such a party was expressly denied in some international union charters. Consequently, the trade-union movement in Canada has traditionally had weak ties to the CCF/NDP.

Over the past decade, this picture has altered considerably. In the mid-1970s, some Canadian unionists who were involved in protracted strikes, especially in the aircraft and rubber industries, were angered when their counionists in the United States worked extra shifts to make up for lost production in Canadian plants. The feeling also grew that union funds were being drained from Canadian locals to head offices in the United States. And there was a general rise of nationalist feeling in Canada. These factors all contributed to the so-called "breakaway movement": the resignation of Canadian members from international unions and the formation of independent Canadian unions. By 1977, for the first time in Canadian history, a majority of trade unionists were not members of internationals, and this trend is proceeding apace (see Figure 12-3). Most recently, the autoworkers have broken with their international union. And important gains in Canadianization have been made since the mid-1970s because of the continuing first-time unionization of white-collar workers (public service employees, clerks, nurses).

The Canadianization movement has brought about a strengthening of ties between trade unions and the NDP; there has been increased financial support and election campaigning. This is reminiscent of the strong ties that unite European trade unions and labour parties. Over the next few decades, the weakening influence of American trade-union political practice may result in increased popular support for the democratic left in Canada, which, at the federal level, has risen slowly and unevenly over the past 50 years from just under 9 percent to about 20 percent of the popular vote in the last (1984) election (Jamieson, 1973; Laxer, 1976: Scott, 1978; Smucker, 1976; White, 1975).

All of this should, of course, be tempered by the observation that sociologists' long-range forecasts are rarely as good as those of meteorologists.

## SUMMARY

Solidarity theories of social movements have become increasingly popular over the past two decades and now represent mainstream thinking in the field. This intellectual reorientation has had many important consequences. Twenty years ago, it was still common to view social movements as irrational, spontaneous, short-term, uninstitutionalized phenomena that emerge in conditions of societal and personal strain or breakdown. Given this view, students of the subject tended to focus their attention on crowd behaviour and relatively short-lived "single-issue" movements. Today, the line between social movements and establishment politics has become blurred. It is commonly held that movement partisans behave as rationally as authorities; that the organizational dynamics of movements are no less complex and enduring than those of, say, establishment political parties; that similar conceptual tools ought to be used to analyse all political and prepolitical behaviour, regardless of whether this behaviour originates at the top or the bottom of the stratification system. Marx and Engels clearly oversimplified when they wrote that the "history of all hitherto existing society is the history of class struggles" (Marx and Engels, 1972: 335). But it is just as surely evident that social movements and the conflict they generate always have been and will continue to be a normal and pervasive part of social life.

## DISCUSSION QUESTIONS

1. What are the strengths and weaknesses of breakdown and solidarity theories of social movements?

2. What is the relationship between the distribution of power and the intensity of conflict in society?

3. How has third-party formation in Canada been explained?

4. What accounts for the increasing volume of strike activity and the unusually long duration of strikes in Canada?

5. What is the relationship between economic protest (such as strikes for higher wages) and political protest (such as the formation of parliamentary third parties)?

# 13

# Formal Organizations and Bureaucracy

## R.J. Richardson

# INTRODUCTION

Wherever we turn these days, we are confronted by organizations; they are the most pervasive structures in modern life. We work, study and teach in organizations, and perhaps we play and pray in them too. From the time we wake up with our orange juice and coffee until we leave the pub or watch the late show on television, organizations almost continually invade our daily lives.

Organizations provide many of the good things in life: houses, food, clothing, dishwashers, air conditioning, television sets, health care and so on. But they also cause many of our greatest frustrations. Our lives often seen to be run by organizations in our jobs, our classes, in the constraints we face in the courses we can take or add or drop. Indeed, in virtually everything we do outside the privacy of our own homes we seem to be at their mercy. What can we do, for example, when the airline refuses to honour our ticket because it has overbooked, and we are late for an important date? This chapter is to help us understand these structures that wield such enormous power in every realm of modern life.

# ORGANIZATIONS

What *is* an organization? It can be a giant multinational corporation like General Motors or a small corner variety store, a political party or a government, a church, a school, a sports club or a search party. There is an endless variety of organizational forms and millions of specific examples. What do all these specific examples have in common?

To begin with, we can define an organization as *a group of people participating in a division of labour that is co-ordinated by communication and leadership to achieve a common goal or goals.* But this social group may be spontaneously or deliberately formed, the division of labour may be crude or complex, the communication and leadership may be informal or formal, there may be one goal or several goals. One important distinction to make is between spontaneous and formal organizations. Both types fit our general definition, yet they are different in several significant ways.

## SPONTANEOUS ORGANIZATIONS

Perhaps the most commonly cited examples of spontaneous organizations are a bucket brigade and a search party. Each has but a single goal—keeping a barn from burning down or finding a lost child. They both arise spontaneously, and their leaders emerge through an informal process. They have a relatively crude division of labour: for example, filling buckets, passing them along, emptying them on the fire. Nevertheless, they are infinitely more likely than an unco-ordinated mob to achieve their goals. Imagine the chance of a mob running off in one direction as compared to a group conducting a co-ordinated search pattern, of finding a lost child. Spontaneous organizations will disband as quickly as they form when their goal is achieved or perceived to be beyond reach or when they become absorbed by a formal organization. Our bucket brigade disperses when the fire is quenched, the barn has burned down or the fire department arrives on the scene.

Spontaneous organizations clearly show how the various elements of our definition of organizations develop in an *ad hoc* way, but they are hardly the kind of structure that dominates modern societies. So we will direct our attention for the rest of this chapter to the predominant, formal (or complex) organization.

## FORMAL ORGANIZATIONS

In contrast to spontaneous organizations, formal ones emerge as a result of deliberate planning. Their communication and leadership (which co-ordinates their division of labour) consist of relationships between consciously developed and formalized statuses and roles. They often have multiple goals, and they usually have, or at least intend to have, a long lifespan. The Roman Catholic Church, for example, is a formal organization that has lasted nearly 2000 years. Furthermore, formal organizations normally have access to far greater resources and more complex technologies than spontaneous organizations.

Consequently, we can define a *formal* organization more specifically as *a deliberately formed social group in which people, resources and technologies are consciously co-ordinated through formalized roles, statuses and relationships to achieve a division of labour that is intended to effectively achieve a specific set of objectives*. This is very similar to our broader definition of organizations in general: they both refer to co-ordinated groups; leadership is implied in the more specific definition; and the inclusion of resources and technologies is more a matter of degree than a dichotomy between formal and spontaneous organizations. The differences, however, are important. The broader definition omits any reference to deliberate and conscious intent; it omits the formalized roles, statuses and relationships; and it refers to a *commonality* of goals, a point that is absent from the more specific definition.

This latter point is contentious. Indeed, most definitions of formal organizations refer to common goals. Alan Fox (1966), an English social psychologist, calls this the *unitary view* of organizations and cites a football team as an appropriate example, where all of the organization's members pull together toward the common goal of winning the game. However, he persuasively argues that the greater the degree of formalization in an organization, the less we can assume that there is a single set of common goals and the more appropriate is the *pluralistic view* of the organization. Clearly, a formal organization will have an overarching set of goals that are formulated by its leader(s) and accepted to varying degrees by its members. But we cannot assume that these are the only goals of the membership. Workers may work for pay, job security and because of allegiance to a union, while medical doctors, engineers and accountants may insist on meeting professional standards set by their respective associations. So in all cases, individuals or smaller groups have goals in addition to or different from those of their organizations.

Why are some formal organizations more successful and powerful than others? There is a huge literature addressing this question. Although this literature contains many lively debates, the most common explanations include the degree to which an organization:
(a)  fills a social need (either real or successfully promoted by the organization itself);
(b)  controls or has access to needed resources and technologies;
(c)  tailors its goals to match the goals of its members;

(d) adapts to or causes changes in its environment.

Finally, the predominant form of the large, powerful and long-lived formal organizations of the twentieth century is the *bureaucracy*.

# BUREAUCRACY

## THE EMERGENCE OF THE BUREAUCRATIC FORM OF ORGANIZATION

"Bureaucracy" is a pejorative term to most people; it evokes thoughts of red tape, overemphasis on rules and regulations, inefficiency and ponderous government organizations moving at a tortoise-like pace. To sociologists, though, a bureaucracy is merely a particular type of formal organization that thrives in both the public and the private sector and in capitalist and socialist societies alike. The very fact that bureaucracy is the predominant organizational form that competitive corporations take indicates that it can be very efficient.

The modern form of bureaucracy exists in a money economy, in which the members are paid salaries and wages. Yet, earlier forms of bureaucracy existed. In fact, bureaucratic organizations in various forms have a history almost as long as civilization itself. They existed in ancient Egypt and China, in the Roman Empire and the Inca and Aztec empires in America. However, the modern form owes its prominence to the development of capitalism and the modern state, whose growth, in turn, was facilitated by the rise of modern bureaucracy.

On a broader scale, the rise of bureaucracy, capitalism and the modern state have all been traced by Max Weber to the rationalization of human activity; indeed, rationalization is the central feature of Weber's general conception of history. (Rationalization in this context refers to the movement away from mystical and religious interpretations of the world to the development of human thought and belief based on the systematic accumulation of evidence.) Associated with rationalization is the emergence of legal-rational authority, that is, of impersonal authority based on the universal application of a codified set of rules and laws. (See Chapter 18 for Weber's distinction between this form of authority and other types.)

Just as bureaucracy on the one hand and capitalism and the modern state on the other reinforce each other, so too do rationalization and bureaucracy. Weber proposes that the modern form of bureaucracy could not have emerged in a religious and nonrational world. But, having emerged, it became a rationalizing force in itself, because bureaucracies seek to order their environments systematically and to create predictable patterns (Weber, 1968).

The value system associated with rationalization prizes efficiency and effectiveness in administration and the production of goods and services. These values spurred the growth of bureaucracy, in Weber's analysis, because bureaucracies organize activity in a logical, impersonal manner.

## THE DIVISION OF LABOUR

In earlier eras, production of a society's goods was generally accomplished by individuals, working alone, who handcrafted an article from start to finish. Gradually, though, this type of production process gave way to specialization and the division of labour. The overwhelming productive superiority of specialization was noted by Adam Smith as long ago as 1776. Specialization became the foundation of modern industry and bureaucratization. An automotive assembly line is a typical modern instance of this division of labour: Workers may perform one highly specialized operation every 36 seconds of the working day (Garson, 1972).

Specialization also produces a new basis of social organization and alienation. A central concern of Émile Durkheim was social solidarity. Durkheim (1965) proposed that, in primitive societies, people were bound together by *mechanical solidarity*. In these societies, characterized by a rudimentary division of labour, people performed generally similar tasks, produced goods that met most of their own requirements and were generally self-sufficient. Societies were bound together by kinship, custom and strong systems of common beliefs. As societies become more complex and the division of labour increases, however, people become more dependent on each other. This dependency creates a need for complex social relationships and, therefore, according to Durkheim, produces an entirely different mechanism for binding a society together, one which he calls *organic solidarity*. Some see bureaucracy as the organizational manifestation or organic solidarity.

In contrast to the positive outlooks of Adam Smith and Émile Durkeim, Karl Marx focused on the negative consequences of specialization—exploitation and alienation. Marx (1954) argued that primitive societies, which had only a rudimentary division of labour, were relatively egalitarian because they could barely produce enough to meet their needs for survival. However, as the division of labour approached specialization, societies produced surpluses that were appropriated by an emerging ruling class. How ruling classes expropriated this surplus and exploited the producers became the central dynamic of Marx's materialist conception of history. Similarly, Marx held that this division of labour fundamentally altered the meaning of work. He believed that people fulfill themselves only through productive and creative work. But the combination of capitalism and specialization fundamentally alters the meaning of work. As workers lose control of the labour process and of what they produce, they inevitably become *alienated*, that is, separated from the products of their labour and from any possibility of achieving self-fulfillment.

While Marx associated alienation with capitalism, Weber (1968) associated it with bureaucracy generally. Weber analysed the rise of bureaucracy and proposed that, as bureaucratic institutions began to control increasingly complex technologies, people were forced to work for bureaucracies in order to live. So, in addition to the worker being separated from the means of production and from the products of his labour, the scientist became separated from (did not own) the scientific equipment he needed to work and soldiers were separated from their weapons, in capitalist and noncapitalist societies alike.

In short, alientation was not confined to the workers.

## THE CHARACTERISTICS OF BUREAUCRACY

It is time to identify the particular characteristics of the bureaucratic form of organization, which were first analysed by Weber early in this century. In his study of the major organizations of his day, he identified six essential characteristics of

## ADAM SMITH AND THE DIVISION OF LABOUR

*The greatest improvement in the productive powers of Labour*, and the greater skill, dexterity, and judgment with which it is anywhere directed, or applied, *seem to have been the effects of the division of labour* . . . To take an example . . . a workman could scarce, perhaps, with his utmost industry, make one pin in a day, and certainly could not make twenty. But in the way in which this business is now carried on, not only the whole work is a peculiar trade, but it is divided into a number of branches, of which the greater part are likewise peculiar trades. One man draws out the wire, another straightens it, a third cuts it, a fourth points it, a fifth grinds it at the top for receiving the head: to make the head requires two or three distinct operations; to put it on is a peculiar business; to whiten the pins is another; it is even a trade by itself to put them into the paper; and the important business of making a pin is, in this manner, divided into about eighteen distinct operations, which, in some manufactories, are all performed by distinct hands, though in others the same man will sometimes perform two or three of them. I have seen a small manufactory of this kind where ten men only were employed, and where some of them consequently performed two or three distinct operations . . . Those ten persons, therefore, could make among them upwards of forty-eight thousand pins in a day. Each person, therefore, making a tenth part of forty-eight thousand pins, might be considered as making four thousand eight hundred pins in a day. But if they had all wrought separately and independently . . . they certainly could not each of them have made twenty, perhaps not one pin in a day; that is, certainly, not the two hundred and fortieth, perhaps not the four thousand eight hundredth part of what they are at present capable of performing, *in consequence of a proper division and combination of their different operations.*

Adam Smith, *The Wealth of Nations*, Macmillan and Company, London, Book 1, pp. 57, 1894, (originally published in 1776). Emphasis added.

bureaucratic organizations. These are: a division of labour, a hierarchy of positions, a formal system of rules, a separation of the person from the office, hiring and promotion based on technical merit and the protection of careers (Weber, 1958). Let's examine each of these.

*Division of labour*. As we have seen, a specialized division of labour is the fundamental underpinning of all formal organizations. In bureaucracies, not only does every member perform clearly specified and differentiated duties (like the workers in Adam Smith's pin factory), but also, the bureaucracy itself provides the facilities and resources to carry out these duties. So the worker works with equipment he does not own (is separated from his means of production), and the administrator administers what he does not own. This combination of task specialization based on technical competence and the centralized provision of resources is intended to produce a high degree of efficiency and productivity.

*Hierarchy of positions*. We can visualize the organizational structure as a pyramid, with authority centralized at the top. This authority filters down toward the base through a well-defined hierarchy of command. Thus, the structure explicitly identifies the range and limits of authority for each position. Within this hierarchy, each person is responsible *to* a specific person one level up the pyramid and *for* a specific group of people one level down.

*Rules*. Bureaucracies are run according to written rules. These rules are one manifestation of the rationality and objectivity which permit a bureaucracy to formalize and categorize the myriad circumstances it routinely confronts. For each of these, a rule can be developed which provides for an objective and impersonal response. These rules, aside from providing objectivity, ensure *predictable* responses to specific situations by the bureaucracy's members, and this will promote the achievement of the organization's objectives.

*Separation of the person from the office*. In a bureaucracy, each person is an incumbent of an office in the hierarchy. The duties, functions and authority of this office are all explicitly defined. The relationship between positions in a bureaucracy are impersonal relationships between authorities, *not* personal relationships between people. This separation of person and office means that people are replaceable functionaries in the organization. People come and go, but the organization remains intact. It also means that personal feelings toward other office-holders must be subordinated to the impersonal demands of the office. Furthermore, these relationships are confined to the official duties of office-holders and do not invade their private lives.

To illustrate: Charlie Brown, as sales manager, is empowered to issue specific orders to his sales force. These orders are followed because they come from the sales manager, not because they come from Charlie. And they are followed only to the extent that they relate to the salespersons' official duties. Next week, if Charlie is transferred to a different job, he can no longer issue the same orders to the same people, because he now holds a different office.

*Hiring and promotion based on technical merit*. A bureaucracy's members are hired on the basis of impersonal criteria, such as technical competence, and not because of ascribed characteristics like gender, race or ethnicity. Promotion is also based on technical competence (or sometimes on seniority). People are neither discriminated against nor favoured because of such personal criteria as their personalities or their kinship with someone at the top of the hierarchy.

*Protected careers*. People can look forward to long careers in a bureaucracy, because they are not subject to arbitrary dismissal for personal reasons.

This description of the characteristics of bureaucracy is, in Weber's terminology, the description of an *ideal type*. It is a model, an abstraction from reality. Does any bureaucracy in the real world completely match all of these characteristics? Of course not! People in bureaucracies often bypass the hierarchial chain of command to gain some personal advantage. Rules are bent or broken or simply not applied. Bosses (and indeed whole organizations) often invade the private lives of their subordinates, from whom they may demand *total* commitment and whose life style they may see as reflecting on the credibility of the organization. Women and minority groups are perhaps more often discriminated against than judged by objective criteria for hiring and promotion.

*While impressed by the technical efficiency of bureaucracy, Max Weber and modern sociologists are concerned about bureaucracy's capacity to stifle individuality. Note that these bureaucrats are all of the same gender and are all dressed in a similar fashion.* Permission of Miller Services.

Furthermore, while twentieth-century bureaucracies all exhibit the six elements of Weber's model, they also exhibit important cross-cultural differences (Crozier, 1964). The degree to which they match each individual characteristic reflects the culture in which they exist. For example, the universal application of rules, the separation of the person from the office and the application of impersonal criteria in hiring and promotion are much less pronounced in developing societies, which maintain elements of traditional authority in their cultures (Eisenstadt, 1965). Currently, the success of Japanese industry has been attributed to the adaptation of bureaucracy to an important element of Japanese culture: the primacy of the social group over the individual (Ouchi and Jaeger, 1978).

However, because of its complexity, the real world is hard to analyse. It is much easier to construct a model, as Weber did, and then adjust it to reality. Weber's concept of bureaucracy, then, is a very useful model for the study of these complex organizations. We can, however, identify real problems and benefits of the bureaucratic form of organization.

## Problems and Benefits

Perhaps the most commonly voiced criticism of bureaucracy is the way it can stifle individuality, human freedom and dignity. This results partly from the rigidity of the hierarchy and of the rules and partly from the pressure to conform that seems to be part of bureaucracy. Another problem is the inflexibility and "red tape" that results from the universal application of rules. The bureaucracy's members, customers and clients tend to be slotted into categories and not treated as people with unique needs, desires and personalities. This same inflexibility can also make it difficult for a bureaucracy to react quickly and effectively to changes in its environment. Finally protection from arbitrary dismissal often becomes protection of mediocrity, to the detriment of organizational effectiveness.

On the other side of the coin, the very factors that produce bureaucratic inflexibility and stifle individuality can also result in efficiency, predictability and control. If situations are properly classified (an important proviso), the most efficient response can be developed in advance for recurring situations and applied within the framework of appropriate rules. Thus, the efficiency of all levels of the hierarchy can be enhanced (the wheel need not be constantly reinvented) and the centralized control of the bureaucrats is reinforced.

Weber was ambivalent about bureaucracy. He was extremely impressed by the superiority of bureaucracy over other organizational forms and concluded that it is an extremely powerful tool for whoever controls it. Also, Weber implied that bureaucratic power and effectiveness are related to the degree to which organizations exemplify the characteristics of his model. On the other hand, he expressed great concern over the immense power a bureaucracy can wield in society—for example, the power of the state bureaucracy over German parliamentary institutions (Weber, 1968). He was also concerned about the fate of "grey-faced bureaucrats" and wrote about the "iron cage" of bureaucracy.

## SOME MODERN PERSPECTIVES ON BUREAUCRACY

Modern sociologists have studied this "iron cage" intensively and most have concluded that it is an oppressive structure that has detrimental effects on the people it touches. Here, we will briefly review a few representative studies.

## Merton's "Bureaucractic Personality"

Robert Merton's analysis (1957) of bureaucracy focused on the pressures it places on those within it to act in ways that work against the organization. Bureaucrats, he concluded, are like overtrained athletes. Their intensive training, along with the immense pressures to conform a bureaucracy places on its members, overemphasizes their knowledge of the bureaucracy's rules. This, in turn, makes it comfortable for bureaucrats to habitually act in routine ways, following rules in a "methodical, prudent and disciplined" way. Inevitably, these routines become like blinkers on a horse and prevent the bureaucrat from recognizing new situations in which the old rules are inappropriate. Thus, Merton argued, bureaucrats develop a "trained incapacity."

Furthermore, the routine application of rules requires that all situations must, somehow, be classifiable by objective criteria so they can be made to fit the appropriate pigeonhole. This means that the clients of bureaucrats cannot be seen as individuals with unique wants and needs but only as impersonal categories. The result is, of course, detrimental to the organization since it fails to meet the unique needs of individual clients.

## Blau and Perrow on Rules

Peter Blau's many case studies of bureaucracies included an analysis of an American employment agency (1963). In the branch office of this agency, bureaucrats were to interview job seekers, record their qualifications, search the agency's files to match these with jobs, contact potential employers to arrange job interviews and, ultimately, find employment for clients. Blau concluded that members of the bureaucracy did all this effectively until the agency developed new procedures for appraising their performance. Under the new system, they were judged on the number of interviews they conducted each day. The bureaucrats' rational response was to rush through each interview, make a cursory search of the job files and eliminate the time "wasted" by contacting potential employers—all to maximize their performance under these new rules. Needless to say, the organization's ability to achieve its fundamental goal, which was placing people in jobs, immediately began to decline. From this and many other studies, Blau (1963) discovered a strong tendency for bureaucratic rules—which are intended to facilitate achievement of the organization's ends—to become ends in themselves.

On the other hand, Blau found automatic compliance with *some* rules to be beneficial to bureaucracies, and Perrow provides a spirited defense. In his essay, "Bureaucratic Paradox" (1977), Perrow argues that control by impersonal rules is both more effective and less demeaning than control by obtrusive and personal direct orders. He also demonstrates (1972) that bureaucratic rules provide protection against arbitrary abuse of power.

## Blauner on Technology

Robert Blauner's studies on bureaucracy focused on their capacity to alienate people. He concluded that the degree of workers' alienation was largely determined by the technology the bureaucracy employed (1964). He developed a typology of four basic technologies in the industries he studied—assembly line (automobiles), machine-tending (textiles), continuous process (petrochemicals) and craft (printing)—and studied the impact of each on workers' powerlessness, sense of meaninglessness, self-estrangement and social isolation. Not surprisingly, he found that technology powerfully affected alienation, which was highest among assembly-line workers, diminished through the intermediate technologies in his typology and was lowest among craft workers who enjoyed much more control and self-expression in their work. This raises a real dilemma: Do we want to reduce alienation by automating jobs in Blauner's first two technologies out of existence and by expanding relatively inefficient craft production? Conversely, can we reduce alienation by transcending technological determinism, as the sociotechnical systems approach (see below) proposes?

The profound influence of Max Weber on this small sample of modern sociological perspectives on bureaucracy is clear. They all address the essential characteristics (such as rules, impersonality and hierarchy) that Weber developed, along with his concern about alienation. Nevertheless, Weber's influence has varied substantially as organizational theory has evolved over the years.

# THE EVOLUTION OF ORGANIZATIONAL THEORY

## TAYLORISM: HOMO ECONOMICUS AND THE ONE BEST WAY

Twentieth-century organizational theory has, of course, evolved as we learn more about the nature of human groups and the organizations they form and as social values and social circumstances themselves evolve. One of the earliest approaches to organizational theory was Frederick W. Taylor's *Scientific Management* (1911), which attracted great attention in North America and Western Europe during a period of industrial strife. Taylor's intention was to end labour-management conflict over "shares of the pie" by providing a bigger pie. Taylor saw the worker as *homo economicus*—an economically rational being who works solely for economic rewards, i.e., for money. Therefore, reasoned Taylor, if we show the worker how to produce more and pay him more as profits increase, everyone will be happy—workers, managers and corporate shareholders alike.

To accomplish this, Taylor and his followers trained time-and-motion-study experts to rigorously break down every task into its essential motions, stripping away all the nonessential ones. These experts then trained each worker to perform specific tasks in the precise way their studies showed was the most efficient. Then they timed them with a stopwatch to develop a "standard time," which became the basis of their piecework rates. Workers were then paid (at least partly) on the basis of these rates (i.e., on the quantity produced). The result was often a spectacular, but short-lived, increase in productivity.

Taylorism developed the specialized division of labour to the fullest. Not only was there an extreme vertical division of labour, within which workers repeated their narrowly defined tasks over and over again, but there was a new, horizontal division of labour, as well. No longer could workers use their experience to improve the efficiency of their task performance. Instead, the workplace was now divided into thinkers (managers and experts) and doers (workers). The mindless, repetitive work that *Scientific Management* advocated and the alienation it produced was one reason it gradually faded from prominence. The underlying reason was that human beings are too complex to be defined simply as *homo economicus*. And perhaps the more pressing reason was that "many employers regarded his methods as an unwarranted interference with managerial prerogatives" (Bendix, 1956:280).

## CLASSICAL SCHOOL: THE FUNCTIONS OF MANAGEMENT

The classical school of organizational theory (represented by Chester Barnard, Mary Parker Follett, Lyndal Urwich and Henri Fayol) focused on the functions of management. Fayol and others provided managers with a series of proverbs on managerial

*The modern assembly line, developed under the influence of scientific management principles, has increased productivity enormously, but at tremendous cost to workers' humanity.*
Permission of Miller Services

effectiveness that were far ahead of their time. Barnard developed the important idea that an organizatiaon, if it is to thrive, must maintain a balance between the inducements it offers its members and the contributions it expects from them. On the other hand, one facet of Barnard's work led organizational theory astray for decades.

Barnard, assuming that co-operation is the basic mode of human existence (a controversial assumption that has been debated for centuries), defined organizations as "co-operative systems." Yet, his most influential work (1938) included a treatise on management techniques designed to rid organizations of conflict. Barnard resolved the paradox of conflict in co-operative systems by proposing that only unbalanced people became embroiled in conflict and that these people existed only among the working classes. Barnard saw rational managers dragging humanity forward into modernity against the resistance of the nonrational, emotional and almost subhuman workers. One reason for the profound influence of Barnard was the legitimacy that he provided to the emerging managerial class.

> ### A MISGUIDED COHORT
>
> During the 1960s and early 1970s, the influence of the behavioural school was so strong that virtually every large bureaucracy sent their managers to training courses designed to change leadership styles from "task centred" to "employee centred." Many of these courses were badly conceived, and attempted to change managers' *personalities* to fit the new style. Many managers tried, but failed, to make this change. Others, who had enough confidence in their own self-worth, refused to attempt it.
>
> However, as they returned to their jobs, they came under intense pressure to fit the new behavioural mould. In self-defence, they went through the motions. Managers throughout North America began to keep card files on their subordinates containing personal information such as their spouse's health and occupation, their children's names and ages and the birthdates of every member of the family; a secretary could check the file and send out birthday greetings over the boss's signature.
>
> It became the ritual for managers to look over the file before calling a subordinate into the office. Then the subordinate would be greeted with a "Hi Joe, how's Mary. I hope she's fully recovered from her operation last year. And how is little Cynthia getting along, and Joe Jr.? Say, he must be nearly ready to start school." Then, the ritual over, boss and subordinate would get down to business.
>
> Well, people on the whole are fairly intelligent, and the insincerity of this misguided approach was soon apparent. Those bosses who had a *sincere* concern for the well-being of their subordinates were well-liked, but those who were insincerely going through the motions in self defense soon became disliked and even detested.
>
> It seems that, through the inappropriate application of the tenets of the behavioural school, we systematically trained a whole cohort of North American bosses in the art of insincerity.

## HUMAN RELATIONS AND BEHAVIOURAL SCHOOLS: THE HAPPINESS ERA

In the 1930s, organizational theory shifted away from seeing organization as structure (in the tradition of Weber and Taylor) to seeing it as *people*. This new focus, which can largely be credited to the discipline of psychology, dominated the field through the 1960s.

Growing out of the famous Hawthorne studies (which we will review later in this chapter), the early *human relations school* focused on relationships within informal groups. Assuming that happy group relationships produced job satisfaction, which, in turn, produced high productivity, this school studied the effects of supervision on this equation. Since this school continued to see workers as emotional and nonrational, management's task was to instill both happiness and rationality in these work groups.

Then, in the 1940s and 50s, Abraham Maslow (1954) developed his *hierarchy of needs*, which changed our view of workers forever. No longer were organizations seen to be composed of just two groups—workers and managers. They were associations of complex human beings, who responded to inner drives that Maslow ranked in a hierarchy of needs (physiological, security, social, esteem and self-fulfillment).

Maslow's pathbreaking work was developed and popularized by Douglas McGregor, whose *The Human Side of Enterprise* (1960) is probably the most influential book ever written for managers. McGregor and other members of the *behavioural school* proposed that managers should adopt a democratic/participative/employee-centred leadership style in lieu of the predominant autocractic/task-centred style.

The cumulative result of these two schools was the burgeoning of management-training programs aimed at improving superior-subordinate relationships and workers' happiness. However, subsequent research has shown that happiness and job satisfaction are a function of much more than these relationships, and the correlation between them and productivity is tenuous and indirect at best.

## SYSTEMS THEORY: THE ORGANIZATION AS ORGANISM

Sociological influence on organizational theory re-emerged with *systems theory*, which saw organizations as open systems receiving inputs from the environment (i.e., the relevant organizations and institutions in society with which the focal organizations interact), processing these and producing outputs that must be acceptable to the environment if the organizations are to survive. In fact, *survival* is a basic theme of systems theory, which sees organizations and their goals as shaped by the interests of their participants and their environments. Philip Selznick's justly famous study of the Tennessee Valley Authority (1949) shows how this particular organization "co-opted" important elements of its environment to gain support. However, this support came at a price, as these elements became participants in the TVA's decision-making processes. Systems theory stressed the effects of the environment on organizations, but, as critic Charles Perrow (1972) correctly charges, it tended to ignore the effects of large and powerful organizations on their environments.

Systems theory also saw organizations as analogous to organisms, i.e., as intricately interdependent systems of functional parts. To use an apt analogy: just as blood poisoning from an infected cut on the hand affects the whole human body, so can an ineffective sales department or a hostile workforce endanger the success of an entire organization. This view produced an almost inevitable emphasis on the uniqueness of organizations, accompanied by a case-study methodology that focused on the *ripple effect*, that is, how changes in one part produce (often unforeseen) changes in other parts of an organization. Systems theory also produced the important concept of *equifinality* which simply means there is no "one best way"; indeed, there are many different paths to organizational success.

## THE CONTINGENCY APPROACH: "IT DEPENDS"

Evolving out of both systems theory and the behavioural school, the contingency approach combines sociological and psychological approaches to organizational theory.

It criticizes earlier organizational theories for trying to develop universal principles, whether about the virtues and vices of bureaucracy or the leader-follower relationship. When we try to apply these principles, contingency theorists argue, we run smack up against reality with all its complications. The contingency approach develops the concept of equifinality into its central tenet: *it depends*. It holds that the essential function of organizational theorists is to specify *upon what* it depends and *in which* ways.

Although this approach is still considered deficient in its theoretical development, it has been applied to organizational topics ranging from structural design to leadership and has received a fair amount of research support. Perhaps its greatest contribution has been to analyse the effects of the situational contexts within which leader-follower relations are embedded. For example, contingency theorists conclude—in direct contradiction to the behavioural school—that in a situation as alienating as the assembly line, autocratic and task-centred leadership is the only style that has a hope of success. Fred Fiedler (1965), a prominent contingency theorist, proposes that it is impractical (if not impossible) to get managers to dramatically change their leadership style. Much better, he suggests, to match managers' styles to the jobs they fit.

Some highly influential work straddles the boundary between the contingency and structural approaches. (See below for discussion of the structural approach.) A group of British sociologists have done intensive empirical studies on the differences between *mechanistic* and *organic* organizational structures. Mechanistic structures conform most closely to Weber's concept of bureaucracy, whereas organic structures conform least (Burns and Stalker, 1961). The latter are much more fluid and personal; they contain more lateral than vertical communication, and this communication is more likely to include advice, co-ordination and problem-solving than the giving and receiving of orders. Indeed, these organic structures might be seen as an alternative to conventional bureaucracy. These studies also suggest that organic structures are more effective (i.e., more profitable) in rapidly changing environments, while mechanistic organizations perform best in stable environments. Joan Woodward's (1965) studies of 100 small British corporations suggest that the type of technology an organization employs strongly affects its optimum structure. She found that the most effective firms using mass production technology employ a mechanistic structure, which facilitates the standardization and cost efficiency essential to their success. However, the most successful firms employing unit production (i.e., one-of-a-kind) and process production (e.g., chemical plants) have organic structures because these take advantage of the innovative capacity of their members.

## STRUCTURAL APPROACH: THE ORGANIZATION MAKES THE PERSON

In the evolution of organizational theory, two recently prominent approaches seem to offer the greatest promise. The first is the *structural approach*, which, in the Weberian tradition, focuses on the structural characteristics of organizations and the effect of these on the people within them. One objective of contemporary structural analysis is to devise changes in organizational structures that will make bureaucracies more effective by making them more humane. Charles Perrow (1972), for example, concludes that structural analyses of the famous Hawthorne studies show that bureaucratic effectiveness depends on the degree to which a bureaucracy can implement structural changes that will increase the congruence between the goals of the formal and the informal organizations.

Herbert Simon, the nobel laureate, is an important pioneer of the structural approach. Noted primarily for his work on *decision theory*, Simon also pointed out the importance of structural constraints on organizational decision-making. In doing so, he provided "the muscle and flesh for the Weberian skeleton" (Perrow, 1972: 146) because he showed that Weber's six elements of bureaucracy define the situation for the decision-maker and shape the premises upon which organizational decisions are made. Thus, bureaucratic organizations assist their members to make decisions that are consistent with those made at the top of the hierarchy.

An influential structural analysis of modern bureaucracy is Rosabeth Kanter's *Men and Women of the Corporation* (1977). Kanter uses three key variables to explain the behaviour of people in organizations: the structures of power, opportunities for advancement and proportion of representation. Those who have *power*, her evidence suggests, makes good leaders, not because of the nature of their relationship with subordinates but because they can obtain for their whole group a favourable share of the organization's resources. On the other hand, "accountable but powerless" people react rationally to their unfortunate situation in ways detrimental to both the organization and their leadership. Those who are upwardly *mobile* support the organization and its goals; whereas those whose mobility is blocked salvage their dignity by withdrawing their support from the organization and attempting to gain recognition elsewhere (e.g., from subordinates or from sources outside the organization). Finally, Kanter proposes that those who make up a small *proportion* of a group, such as women and ethnic minorities among managers, are treated as *tokens*. The results (exclusion from leaders' networks, stereotyping and intense scrutiny) produce a self-fulfilling prophecy. Tokens perform moderately well, at best, because of structural constraints, not individual deficiencies, and thus their numbers fail to become large enough to break the bonds of tokenism. Needless to say, Kanter advocates modifying the structures of power, mobility and proportions.

## SOCIOTECHNICAL SYSTEMS: BEYOND TECHNOLOGICAL DETERMINISM

The last of the organizational theories to rise to contemporary prominence is *sociotechnical systems theory*. Founded by a group of British sociologists, it developed out of systems theory. It proposes that we have blindly let technology shape our whole concept of work. Engineers, working in the scientific management tradition, follow the technological imperative and develop the most efficient technology, completely ignoring its dehumanizing effect on the people involved. "To the engineer the perfect machine is the one that an imbecile could operate; he is surprised if the result is a machine only an imbecile is happy operating" (Cherns, 1980: 112). Proponents of this theory argue that this use of technology will ultimately lead to the collapse of the industrial system.

The sociotechnical approach suggests a new context for work, one in which technology sets limits for, but does not create social systems. It sees industrial activity

## ADAPTING TO A CHANGING WORLD

Alienation, a sort of non-work ethic, has been increasing in the postwar period, especially among the younger generation whose expectations and experiences are different from those that arose under the conditions of scarcity that characterized the Depression years. Attitude surveys in several countries indicate that only the older worker continues to be willing to trade off dehumanizing work simply for good wages and employment security . . .

The human individual has work-related needs other than those specified in a contract of employment (such as wages, hours, safety, security of tenure, and so on). These "extrinsic" requirements . . . form the legacy of the old work ethic. In addition, a variety of . . . "intrinsic" factors must also be met if the new work ethic is to develop. These intrinsic factors . . . include:

1. The need for the job to be reasonably demanding in terms other than sheer endurance and to provide a minimum of variety (not necessarily novelty, which is too much for some people though the spice of life for others). This is to recognize enfranchisement in problem-solving as a human right.
2. The need to be able to learn on the job on a continuing basis. Again, this is a question of neither too much nor too little, but of matching solutions to personal requirements. This is to recognize personal growth as a human right.
3. The need for some area of decision-making that the individual can call his own. This recognizes the opportunity to use one's own judgment as a human right.
4. The need for some degree of social support and recognition in the workplace, from both fellow workers and bosses. This recognizes "group belongingness" as a human right.
5. The need to be able to relate what one does and what one produces to one's social life. That is, to have a meaningful occupational identity which gives a man or woman dignity. This recognizes the opportunity to contribute to society as a human right.
6. The need to feel that the job leads to some sort of desirable future (not necessarily promotion). It may involve training or redeployment—a career at shop floor level leading to the development of greater skill. This recognizes hope as a human right . . . .

What have we learned about diffusing a higher quality of working life into the organization as a whole? And what lies ahead?

Permission granted by Eric Trist, *Adapting to a Changing World*, 1977.

as a sociotechnical system comprising social and technological subsystems that can interact positively or negatively. Therefore, in lieu of the old paradigm, which assumes that a technology will be developed first and will determine the nature of work and of the social system, the sociotechnical approach proposes that the social and technological subsystems be developed *simultaneously*. The effect of each upon the other should be continuously considered. This theory has produced the quality-of-work-life movement which tries to implement sociotechnical concepts in practical situations.

The principles of QWL, developed initially by the British Tavistock Institute in 1949, are:

1. The social and technical subsystems should be jointly and coincidentally developed.
2. Representatives of the social system—workers—should be heavily involved in this development.
3. The basic unit of the organization should be the work group (as a social system), not the individual. Thus, tasks should be formally allocated to work groups which will set productivity standards jointly with management.
4. The work group, not the foreperson, should control its own work activities and the way these are allocated to individual members. Aside from providing some worker autonomy, this should make work "variety increasing" and reverse the dehumanizing modern trend toward an excessive division of labour.
5. The role of the foreperson changes dramatically. In lieu of the traditional supervision of individual workers, he or she now oversees the boundaries between work groups and co-ordinates their efforts.

Trist (1981) shows that QWL has had a spotty history. Early successes in the British coal and auto industries were short lived. In each case, management terminated the program and reverted to the traditional bureaucratic system. Another highly successful trial in an American coal mine died an early death when the union became split between the workers involved in the project and those who were not involved.

Eventually, however, the movement took off in Scandinavia, where it was particularly congruent with the developing values of the society. Notable successes have been achieved at Norskhydro (Norway's largest employer) and Volvo (where it was found impossible to recruit Swedes to work on conventional assembly lines). In the past decade or so, hundreds of successful QWL projects have been set up in Western Europe, the United States and Canada, where Eric Trist (one of the originators of the QWL movement) is now associated with York University and the Ontario Ministry of Labour. These projects have clearly improved the quality of work life, as evidenced by such irrefutable empirical evidence as substantial reductions in labour turnover, absenteeism, wildcat strikes and sabotage. They have also provided substantial benefits to the corporations involved by increasing labour productivity.

How can we explain the difficult birth and retarded development of an approach to industrial organization that seems to offer so much to both management and labour? Eric Trist (1981), commenting on the many early projects that were aborted and the snail's pace of QWL development, charges that management is more interested in power than in profits. Because the power of middle management and first-line supervisors is clearly diminished by QWL, management has not been enthusiastic about its success. Nor have unions been universally supportive. Many quasi-QWL projects have attempted to obtain the corporate benefits of the approach without disturbing the traditional organizational structure of the corporations. Many unions argue that if QWL is really as successful as its proponents claim, then surely its very efficiency will ultimately throw their members out of work. Finally, some unions oppose QWL because its fundamental principle of ongoing, direct labour-management consultation and co-operation undermines an important source of union power—the role of intermediary between workers and management.

Nevertheless, despite these important obstacles, the sociotechnical systems approach is an exciting and promising new development in organizational theory, one that combines workplace democracy with industrial efficiency.

# THE INFORMAL ORGANIZATION

Although bureaucracy is intended to be an impersonal form of organization, it is made up of people. And people, it seems, strongly resist becoming faceless cogs in the bureaucratic machine (replaceable cogs, at that). Consequently, they develop complex personal and informal networks that function within the formal organization. Collectively, these networks comprise the *informal organization* or bureaucracy's human face.

These informal networks, which develop among those who interact on the job, serve many purposes. First and foremost, they humanize the organization. They also provide support and protection to those at the lower levels of the hierarchy, serve as active channels of information (the "grapevine") and become mechanisms of personal influence and advantage, through which favours are exchanged.

## THE HAWTHORNE STUDIES

The famous Hawthorne studies were conducted between 1927 and 1932 at the Western Electric plant at Hawthorne, Illinois, under the direction of Elton Mayo, a Harvard management scientist. They provided a massive data base that is still being analysed by social scientists from many different perspectives who are testing a wide variety of hypotheses. They also spawned a huge literature, of which the account by Homans (1951) is probably the most readable. The Hawthorne studies first revealed the importance of the informal organization.

The studies consisted of four phases. *Phase I* began as a simple experiment to test the effect of light intensity on productivity, in the scientific management tradition of the day. However, the research produced some surprising results: For example, when the researchers implied that they were replacing lightbulbs with stronger ones, but in fact replaced them with identical bulbs, productivity increased. The researchers concluded that the psychological and emotional states of the employees were acting as an intervening variable, confounding the simple relationship between lighting and productivity.

To eliminate these intervening variables, the researchers proceeded to *Phase II*, the "relay assembly test room" experiment, in which they isolated six female workers in a workroom, along with a "test-room observer" in lieu of a regular supervisor. This phase lasted for five years, during which time the observers kept daily records of the productivity, health and conversations of each worker, indeed, even how many hours of sleep each reported to have had the previous night. Imagine, if you can, the sheer volume of these records in the days before microfiche and the computer!

Before the test began, the women were conducted to the office of the plant superintendent (next only to God, at Hawthorne) where he explained the importance of the experiment. Later, whenever a change in working conditions was planned, they were recalled to his office to discuss, approve or propose revisions to the planned change. These changes involved implementing rest periods and snacks and reducing the workday and the workweek; there were a total of 12 stages of change. Periodically, and for a substantial period at the end of the experiment, the workers were told to revert to the original, less liberal, working conditions.

The results confounded the researchers! No matter what change they implemented—whether positive or negative from the workers' point of view—productivity continued to rise until it gradually levelled off at a very high rate. The researchers realized that these results could not be the outcome of physical changes in working conditions. Mystified, they fell back on Mayo and Barnard's view of the nonlogical and emotional worker. After all, the experimentees frequently reported that "work was fun." The researchers also realized that an unusual type of supervision was in place (the test-room observer) and decided to investigate the effects of supervision on productivity.

This led to *Phase III*, a massive program of 21 000 worker interviews that concentrated on worker attitudes toward supervision. The researchers noted that, during these unstructured interviews, workers would usually keep returning to whatever topic was uppermost in their minds. They attributed this behaviour to "compulsive neurosis," a pathological condition popularized by Freud. By this time, the workers were viewed not only as nonlogical but as emotionally and even mentally ill. The research team was nearly ready to give up. "The comments elicited from the employees were of only limited use in improving working conditions and methods of supervision. . . . " (Homans, 1951: 229).

Then George Homans and Lloyd Warner (a Harvard sociologist and anthropologist, respectively) were consulted. They suggested that the results of the experiments and interviews needed to be interpreted in the context of social relationships among groups of workers, not as merely the responses of isolated individuals. This insight changed the direction of the studies and ultimately became an important foundation of the human relations school of organizational studies. Hence, *Phase IV* began; it was another study of a workgroup similar to the women in the relay assembly test room.

This fourth phase studied 14 men who were put to work in a separate room, again with a test-room observer in lieu of a formal supervisor. However, there were three important differences between Phase II and Phase IV: Meetings with the plant superintendant were not instituted for the men; comments that "work was fun" were never voiced by the men; and the men's productivity did not climb to unprecedented heights, as the women's did. In fact, the men went to great lengths to keep production constant and in line with the normative conception of "a fair day's work" which the group developed. In fact, they developed various punitive measures to bring "speed kings" and "chiselers" (those who worked too fast or too slowly) back into line.

# THE INFLUENCE OF HAWTHORNE ON ORGANIZATIONAL THEORY

Early conclusions drawn from the Hawthorne studies provided the foundation of the human relations school. One of the first became known as *the Hawthorne effect*, which is that when people know they are subjects of an important experiment and they receive a lot of special attention, they tend to behave the way they think the researchers *expect* them to. Organizational theorists of the day used this effect to explain the anomalous results of the lighting experiments and, to a lesser extent, the women's increased productivity in the relay assembly test room. It has also influenced the design of social psychological experiments ever since, as researchers try to control for this distortion.

The other conclusions drawn from the studies dealt with the social aspect of work, the relationships among the members of the informal group, the norms that informal groups develop and types of supervision. The focus on the social aspect (clearly more important than the physical at Hawthorne) is the basis for the fundamental shift in the emphasis of organizational theory from scientific management to human relations. The relationships among the women in Phase II were happy and supportive, while those among the men in Phase IV were not. This led human relations theorists to conclude that happy group relationships are directly related to productivity. Both the women and the men were paid on the basis of a modified group-piecework incentive scheme. That is, once productivity exceeded a given standard, part of their earnings were determined by the productivity of the group. In this respect, the women appeared to act rationally, but the men did not. Human relations theory then tried to determine the group processes involved in developing nonrational norms. Finally, noting the absence of formal supervision in the relay assembly test room, they concluded that freedom from rigid supervision was as important in increasing the women's productivity as all of the other factors combined. This led to decades of intensive research and theorizing on the efficacy of various leadership styles.

Of course, in retrospect, we can see that supervision was similar in both the men's and women's groups while productivity varied dramatically and that the special attention paid to the women by the plant superintendant could have created the Hawthorne effect on their group. Nevertheless, the Hawthorne studies charted the course of human relations theory and the "happiness era." Assuming that happy group relationships and rational norms produce high productivity, theorists focused on the type of supervision (i.e., the leadership style) that would foster happiness and rationality in group members.

Decades later, reanalyses of these Hawthorne studies (Perrow, 1972) have modified the original conclusions and produced a substantially different conception of informal groups, one that is consonant with the tenets of the structural approach.

Starting from the structuralists' premise that people will respond rationally to the constraints organizations place on them, Perrow and others investigated the objective conditions surrounding the studies. They found that the Hawthorne plant, like most others, had a long history of raising the productivity standard once it had been consistently attained. This meant that, over the long term, workers had to achieve an increasingly fast pace to maintain their incomes. It is also significant that the

*Paul Henderson (with stick raised) scores, with 34 seconds remaining in the final game, to win both the game and the Canada-U.S.S.R. hockey series of 1972. Hockey experts conclude that it was the will to win developed by the players themselves that resulted in this victory.* By permission of the Toronto Star Syndicate.

female workers' productivity climbed duirng the boom of the late twenties and gradually levelled off as the Depression set in, while the study of the male workers in Phase IV began only after the plant began to lay off workers in response to bad times. On both counts then, the male workers' norm of holding to "a fair day's work" seems eminently rational, not irrational, as early human relations theorists implied. It seems entirely logical that they would attempt to maintain a balance between productivity and earnings and to protect their jobs by not producing too much.

We can learn important principles from these reanalyses of the Hawthorne studies that help us to understand the behaviour of informal groups in any organization. First, let us assume (as a working hypothesis) that group members act rationally, in their own collective best interest. Then, by examining the objective situation from the perspective of the group members, we should be able to understand *why* they act the way they do. Finally, organizational success can be directly related to (among other factors, of course) the degree of compatibility between the rational goals of the informal group and of the organization itself.

The informal organization can either help or hinder the attainment of the goals of the formal organization, depending largely on the quality of the relationship between the two. Frequently cited examples of hindrance are the British coal industry and the Canadian Post Office, both of which have a long history of bitter labour-management conflict. Perhaps the most dramatic example of the results of compatible informal and formal goals is Team Canada's victory over the Soviet Union in the eight-game hockey series of 1972. Experts conclude that the Canadian team won, not because of superior management, coaching or even abilities of individual players, but because of an intense will to win generated by the team members themselves.

## SUMMARY

Bureaucracy pervades our daily lives; and large bureaucracies wield enormous power in our society. Large business bureaucracies can ruin their smaller competitors, and governmental bureaucracies often prevail over parliaments. Weber (1968) analysed how the bureaucracy of Bismarck's Germany dominated the weak parliament of the day. Lipset (1950) found that the entrenched bureaucracy aborted many of the newly elected CCF government's reform programs in Saskatchewan in the 1940s. And Campbell and Szablowski (1979) found that Ottawa's "super-bureaucrats" frustrate and circumvent members of our Canadian parliament.

Indeed, Peter Blau (1963), drawing on the work of Michels (1962), points out a paradox in the relationship between two fundamentally different forms of social organization: bureaucracy and democracy. Bureaucracy is an organization formed to achieve predetermined objectives. Its organizing principle is efficiency and its organizing structure is the hierarchical relationship of dominance and subordination. Democracy, on the other hand, is an organization established to *determine* the objectives of a human group. Its organizing principle is the freedom of dissent necessary to permit majority opinions to form and its organizing structure is essentially egalitarian.

While democratic forms of social organization are well suited to making choices between alternative policies, they are *not* well suited to implementing them. This is the role bureaucracy fills so efficiently. So, the two forms of organization complement each other. Democracy depends on bureaucracy to implement its policies and to provide productive units that efficiently produce goods and services for society. But paradoxically, as Blau recognized, by concentrating power in the hands of a very few, bureaucracy is a constant threat to the very survival of democratic institutions.

To a considerable extent, the evolution of organizational theory parallels changes in social values and ideologies. Both the classical theorists (such as Chester Barnard) and the human relations school can be seen as holdovers from the time of the Industrial Revolution, when workers were viewed as children (which, indeed, they often were). As the values of North America and Western Europe changed in the 1960s, the behavioural school, which focused on more enlightened relations between superiors and subordinates in bureaucratic structures, thrived. Then, as we entered the "stagflation" of the 1970s and 1980s, attention turned to structural theories to explain organizational behaviour. Studies began to show that the "happiness era" was over: People would rather work for a powerful boss than a nice one, because a powerful boss can obtain a larger share of the organization's resources for the whole group (Kanter, 1977).

In fact, if we are in the midst of a prolonged period of moderate economic growth and restricted economic rewards for workers, the critical issue of the next decade may concern our ability to change organizations structurally to make them more effective *and* more humane.

## DISCUSSION QUESTIONS

1.  Compare and contrast a successful organization that you know with an unsuccessful one. What major factors account for these differences in effectiveness?

2.  What changes in the structures of power, opportunity and proportions would the structural approach propose? How (if at all) would these make bureaucracies more effective and more humane?

3.  Under what conditions would you expect QWL programs to work well? to work poorly? Why?

4.  Organizations can be seen as *structures* (in the tradition of Weber and Taylor) or as *people* (in the tradition of Maslow and McGregor). What are the relative merits of these opposing viewpoints? Can they be integrated? If so, how? If not, why not?

5.  "Bureaucracy contains the seeds of its own destruction." Comment.

# 14

# Race and Ethnic Relations

*Peter Li*

# INTRODUCTION

With the exception of native people, Canada is made up of immigrants. To the extent that it consists of different races and ethnic groups, Canada is a mosaic. Its society is pluralistic in origin. Roughly speaking, this mosaic is composed of the aboriginal peoples, the two charter groups of English and French Canadians and other immigrants.

The emergence of Canadians as a people was marked by conflict between racial and linguistic groups, although the bases of disputes were frequently not language or culture. Historical examples include: the conquest of Canada's native people in the eighteenth and nineteenth century (Patterson II, 1972); the Riel Rebellion and the execution of Louis Riel in 1885; the colonization of Quebec after the British conquest of 1760 (Milner, 1978); and the antiorientalism of British Columbia around the turn of the century (Ward, 1978). These sad events in our history are a reminder that racial and ethnic problems exist in Canadian society, despite the fact that contemporary Canada did not have a civil rights movement in the 1960s, as the United States did, nor the kind of race riots that hit the United Kingdom in the 1970s. News reports also remind us that racial and ethnic divisions are features of Canadian society. The subject matter of these news items ranges from land claims and demands for self-government by native peoples to discrimination against black taxi drivers in Montreal; from the compensation claims of Japanese-Canadians interned in Canada during World War II to antisemitism in the classroom.

This chapter will provide a sociological basis for understanding race and ethnic relations. Before we discuss how racial and ethnic distinctions operate in Canadian society, we must study some sociological perspectives on this subject.

# THEORETICAL PERSPECTIVES

## WHAT ARE RACE AND ETHNICITY?

There are basically two ways to define race and ethnicity.

Traditionally, sociologists have used *subjective identity* as a basis for defining ethnicity and race. Accordingly, ethnicity is ascribed at birth. Members of an ethnic group share a sense of peoplehood, or identity, based on descent, language, religion, tradition and other common experiences (Weber, 1968:385-398). Ethnic identity allows members of an ethnic group to develop *closures* (Weber, 1968:388), or boundaries, within which ethnic institutions, neighbourhoods, beliefs and cultures are developed and maintained. The members of a racial group also have observable physical traits in common.

More recently, some sociologists have defined race and ethnicity in the context of intergroup relations. For example, according to Wilson, "Racial groups are distinguished by socially selected cultural traits" (1973:6). Physical and cultural traits define social groups only in so far as they are socially recognized as important. In other words, race and ethnicity take on a social meaning only when physical and cultural traits are paired with social attributes, such as intellectual, moral or behavioural characteristics. Whether such associations are alleged or real is often irrelevant. Attaching a social meaning to the physical or cultural characteristics of a group implies that rewards and resources in society are, to some extent, divided along racial and ethnic lines and that the dominant or privileged group can use physical and cultural features of people as a basis of stratification. Some sociologists (van den Berghe, 1984:216-218) use the term *social races* to suggest that they are not genotypical subspecies. Indeed, there is indisputable evidence to indicate that *phenotypes* (superficial physical traits such as skin colour) provide little ground for a scheme of genetical classification (Rex, 1983). The meanings of race and ethnicity, therefore, have to be understood not in terms of phenotypes, but as social constructs based on unequal relations. For example, in South Africa, every person is legally defined in a racial category. However, a person may have fair skin and be classified as black because one of his parents is legally black. This shows that there is no direct correspondence between skin colour, genetical grouping and social classification.

How ethnicity and race are defined affects the questions sociologists ask about ethnic groups and race relations. For example, defining ethnicity as subjective identity raises questions of identity change and persistence in the process of assimilation. In contrast, defining race and ethnicity as products of unequal relations leads to questions about dominant and subordinate groups.

## ASSIMILATION AND PLURALISM

The theme of assimilation dominated race and ethnic studies up until the 1960s. *Assimilation* is the process whereby people of diverse origins conform to a single or amalgamated culture. This concept has been applied to the study of immigrant groups in North America to see how, over time, they become incorporated into the culture of the dominant group.

There are many different versions of assimilation theory. Park (1950) develops the notion of a *race relations cycle*, which takes the form of contacts, competition, accommodation and assimilation. Through migration or conquest, people of different origins meet. After the initial contact, the second stage of the cycle is characterized by conflicts arising from competition over scarce resources. Over time, conflicts are resolved as the competing groups accommodate each other. The final stage is assimilation, out of which a single indistinguishable cosmopolitan population emerges. According to Park, this process is progressive and irreversible. Immigration restrictions and racial barriers may slow down this process, but they can neither stop nor reverse it.

The concept of assimilation has been refined by many sociologists, notably Milton M. Gordon (1964). He distinguishes several versions of the assimilation model as applied to the United States. *Anglo-conformity* refers to the process by which immigrant groups and racial minorities are to conform to the language, behaviours and institutions of the dominant Anglo-Saxon group. A more liberal version of assimilation is the *melting-pot thesis*, which sees all groups as contributing to American culture, as people of every stock are amalgamated into a new nation. Other sociologists (Kennedy, 1952; Herberg, 1955) have proposed a *triple melting pot* to suggest that assimilation in America takes place within the three major religious groups of Catholics, Protestants and Jews.

*Pluralism*, the third assimilation model, refers to both the persistence and assimilation of ethnic groups. In a pluralistic society, ethnic groups may share some aspects of a common culture and participate collectively in economic and political life while retaining unique cultural aspects in their social networks, residential enclaves, churches and languages. Gordon (1964) distinguishes between two types of pluralism: cultural and structural. Cultural pluralism is the retention of ethnic traditions in primary group relations while participating with other ethnic groups in secondary group relations. Structural pluralism, on the other hand, refers to the existence of separate subsocieties along with a massive trend of acculturation to a common culture.

The assimilationist perspective has been criticized on several grounds (Price, 1969; Li and Bolaria, 1979). Park's race relations cycle is simplistic and mechanical. Its prediction of irreversible assimilation is too rigid and is not supported by the experiences of many racial and ethnic groups. A more fundamental objection to assimilation models is that assimilation is loosely defined. Assimilation implies a standard of behaviour and values that immigrant groups have to acquire to become assimilated, yet such a standard is often absent. For example, what does it mean if a person eats spaghetti more often than hamburger? Does it mean that an immigrant is less assimilated if he works and lives like his neighbours but maintains his ethnic friends? Unfortunately, the concept of assimilation is more an ideology calling for Americanization or Anglicization than a realistic description of immigrants' experiences. Thus, the assimilationist perspective has been branded ethnocentric (Rex and Moore, 1967).

The single melting-pot thesis has been challenged by pluralists who argue that racial barriers and ethnic revival have produced persistent ethnic cleavages along religious and racial lines, despite assimilation in some areas (Glazer and Moynihan, 1963). For example, different racial and ethnic groups may have to participate in the same economic and political system, but ethnic distinctiveness is maintained through religious ties and informal social networks. Critiques of pluralism, however, maintain that pluralists downplay the problem of ethnic and racial inequality and that their view of a plural society often assumes a basic equality for all groups (Steinberg, 1981). In a society that is structured on systematic inequalities, pluralism can only be an ideal for some ethnic members, as there is no tenable basis for permanent ethnic preservation (Steinberg, 1981). Even among the upwardly mobile groups, who have the resource base to preserve ethnic pluralism, ethnicity remains expressive or symbolic (Gans, 1979). In other words, there is little support for preserving one's ethnic distinctiveness while participating in the mainstream economic and political life, which is structured unequally, not pluralistically.

The pluralist perspective has also been criticized for unduly emphasizing the transplanted culture from the old country as the principal antecedent and defining characteristic of ethnic groups (Yancey, Ericksen and Juliani, 1976). In doing so, cultural pluralists overlook the importance of the structural conditions of the host society in shaping ethnicity in urban life. Ethnicity is an emergent phenomenon, in that transplanted ethnic cultures may die and new ones evolve, being constantly influenced by the exigencies of survival. Valentine (1968) argues that there is a difference between the material preconditions under which people live and the cultural responses they develop. Culture and ethnicity are variables and not ascribed attributes. The key question is not so much whether immigrants maintain their old-world culture, but under what conditions does ethnicity become particularly salient (Yancey, Ericksen and Juliani, 1976). Hence, the establishment of certain types of businesses among some ethnic groups may have more to do with the conditions and restrictive opportunities in the host society than with a cultural propensity to engage in certain lines of work (Ward and Jenkins, 1984; Bonacich and Modell, 1980; Li, 1979). Differences in historical and structural conditions help to explain why divergent achievements are found even among ethnic groups with similar cultural backgrounds and physical appearances (see insert).

## DOMINANT AND SUBORDINATE GROUPS

A different approach to race and ethnic relations is to examine them as unequal relationships, produced and maintained by power differentials between a dominant group and a subordinate one. In this sense, the terms majority/minority groups in the context of ethnic and race relations are defined by unequal power, and not numeric differences. This approach treats race and ethnicity as relational concepts and not descriptive categories. The focus is on the institutional framework within which groups are defined as racial or ethnic and how social interactions are organized (Bolaria and Li, 1985).

There is a close relationship between labour exploitation and racial categorization (Cox, 1948; Thompson, 1975; Rex, 1983; Miles, 1982), which refers to giving phenotypical traits social meanings. This relationship is best illustrated by colonial and capitalist economies under which labour cost is kept as low as possible in order to maximize profit. The basic structural dilemma in such societies is how to confine a pool of subservient labour to menial tasks when economic accumulation inevitably leads to increased economic activity and opportunities for mobility. Physical and cultural attributes provide the rationale for assigning a group of socially defined undesirables to undesirable jobs. Over time, the cultural and physical characteristics of a subordinate group become inseparable from its work role and its subservient position (Bolaria and Li, 1985).

## Colonial Model

One institutional framework under which race and ethnic relations must function is colonization. The most significant aspect of colonial economies is the massive deployment of nonwhite labour (Rex, 1983). European colonizers transformed previously public resources and brought about economic development in some regions of their colonies at the expense of other sectors. Importing slaves or indentured labourers and inviting in white settlers gradually replaced the indigenous social structure of the colony with a new social order in which race became a dominant feature of stratification (Bolaria and Li, 1985).

The colonization process has seven parts (Frideres, 1983). These are: (1) the incursion of the colonizing group; (2) the social, economic and cultural destruction of the colonized people; (3) the taking of external political control by the colonizers; (4) the establishment of the economic dependence of the colonized people; (5) the provision of low-quality social services for the colonized people; (6) the emergence of racism; and (7) the development of a colour line.

Different aspects of the colonial model have been applied to explain race relations in advanced capitalist societies. For example, Rex (1973, 1983) argues that immigrants from ex-colonies to metropolitan societies such as Great Britain carry the

The historical facts show, for example, that prior to the end of the Second World War, the Chinese were subjected to a discriminatory immigration system which sought to exclude them (see Li, 1979a). One of the consequences of such exclusion was to produce a highly unbalanced sex ratio among the Chinese, even long after the legislative control was removed in 1947. This largely delayed the birth of a second generation which did not begin to emerge in sizable numbers until the sixties (Li, 1979d). In contrast, the immigration system permitted the Japanese to bring their wives as early as 1908 (see Adachi, 1976), and this resulted in a much more balanced sex ratio among the Japanese community as compared to the Chinese (Li, 1979d, Table 3). Furthermore, the experience of relocation and subsequent repatriation of the Japanese in Canada resulted in a large drop in population among the Japanese in Canada (Adachi, 1976). The small volume of Japanese immigration to Canada in the postwar years greatly altered the demographic and social characteristics of the Japanese community (Ujimoto, 1976). These historical factors, and not cultural adaptability, are important in understanding the present demographic structures of the Chinese and the Japanese in Canada.

Historically too, the Japanese and the Chinese entered different occupations in Canada, in part because of different opportunities available to the two groups. The heavy concentration of the Chinese in the service industry as laundrymen and restaurant workers, for example, was largely a result of restricted opportunities in the non-ethnic sector (Li, 1979a). The damage to the Japanese ethnic business during the relocation of the Second World War (see Adachi, 1976) probably resulted in many Japanese having to seek employment in other sectors after the war. These historical experiences must be considered in explaining the differences of the two groups in the occupational structure of today.

What is understood as the adaptive capacity of minority groups then, may be no more than different responses under various constrained situations. Ethnic differences in economic achievements in many cases are probably more related to unequal opportunity structures to which these groups are subjected, than to the adaptive capacity of their old world cultures.

Peter S. Li "Income achievement and adaptive capacity: an empirical comparison of Chinese and Japanese in Canada," in K.V. Ujimoto and G. Hirabayashi (eds.) *Visible Minorities and Multiculturalism: Asians in Canada.*

stigma of colonial workers, which places them in a disadvantaged position. Many immigrants constitute an *underclass*, a bottom stratum below the working-class (Rex and Tomlinson, 1979). Another extension of the colonial model argues that racism facilitates the superexploitation of immigrants and workers in peripheral countries as advanced capitalist countries extend their investments to peripheral markets and transform these countries to neocolonies (Portes and Walton, 1981; Castles and Kosack, 1973). Finally, the concept *internal colonies* has been used to describe the situation of some racial groups in America [the blacks (Blauner, 1972), the Mexicans (Moore, 1970), and the native peoples (Frideres, 1983; Patterson II, 1972)] because of their similarity to colonized people. Internal colonization refers to the political and economic domination of minorities within a country, such that the minorities suffer from exploitation and oppression similar to that endured by indigenous people under classical colonization. For example, Frideres (1983) shows that the native peoples in Canada suffer from colonial status. Such controls as the Indian Act and native reserves produce experiences like those of second-class citizens in colonies and result in lower opportunities and poorer quality of life for native people in Canada.

## Split Labour Market Model

The *split labour market model* is developed by Bonacich (1972, 1979) to explain racial and ethnic conflicts. The source of antagonism is not race and ethnicity, but differences in the price of labour between two groups that are often divided along racial and ethnic lines. Historically, this economically based antagonism surfaced as racial conflict between nonwhite and white labour. The real issue, however, had to do with white workers resisting their replacement by the cheaper labour of nonwhite workers as capitalists tried to lower their labour costs. Depending on the resources of various classes, racial antagonism may be "resolved" by excluding nonwhite workers or by assigning labour by race or ethnic group, as in a caste or near-caste system. The split labour market refers to the price differentials between two groups performing the same task, or in a submerged form in which the higher-paid group monopolizes certain positions, and the lower paid group is restricted to marginal participation.

The emergence of a split labour market is related to two conditions, both of which arose from the development of capitalism in Western Europe (Bonacich, 1979). The first was the rise in the cost of the labour of white workers and the second was the availability of nonwhite labour from the peripheral countries as imperialism accelerated their underdevelopment. The theory of split labour market has been applied to explain racism against blacks in the United States (Bonacich, 1975, 1976) and antiorientalism in Canada (Li, 1979) and Brazil (Makabe, 1981).

The split labour market implies that there is a relationship between class and race. Bonacich's theory also suggests a close tie between labour recruitment and capitalist expansion. Indeed, there are grounds to suggest that Canadian immigration policy, like that of other advanced capitalist countries, is designed to regulate the volume and type of immigrants to suit the country's labour needs. Historically, Canada has favoured immigrants from Britain, the United States and Northern Europe and excluded others from nonwhite countries except in times of severe labour shortage (Li and Bolaria, 1979). A preferential system based on country of origin was maintained until 1967, when a universal point system was introduced (Hawkins, 1972). The change facilitated the recruitment of skilled labour from nontraditional source countries as the economic prosperity of the postwar years increased the demand for technical labour. Despite these changes, postwar Gallup polls show that native Canadians most prefer immigrants from the United Kingdom and northeastern Europe, and least prefer immigrants from Asia (Tienhaara, 1974). According to another study, native Canadians are more willing to accept the services of immigrants in lower-prestige occupations than high-prestige occupations (Jones and Lambert, 1965). During economic hard times, immigrants are often seen as competitors who take away jobs from native Canadians (Li, 1979). These findings give further credence to the split labour market theory. In a later section, we shall examine more closely the relationship between ethnic origin and class in Canada.

So far, we have covered two major approaches to race and ethnic relationships. We can now discuss some empirical studies that use these theoretical positions. The problem of language maintenance and shift represents one aspect of ethnic persistence and assimilation, whereas the question of racial and ethnic inequality is central to the dominant-subordinate group relationship. Before we discuss the empirical findings, we shall examine racial and ethnic patterns in Canada.

## RACIAL AND ETHNIC PATTERNS IN CANADA

Race and ethnicity are important features of Canadian society because: (1) Canadians came from different origins; and (2) racial and ethnic lines cross other cleavages in our society. Canada has seen a decline of the British ethnic group over the past 85 years and an increase in the non-British and non-French population. People of British origin, however, remain the single largest group in Canada. In 1901, for example, 57 percent of the total population were of British origin, and by 1981, they were down to 40.2 percent. The non-British and non-French population increased from 8.5 percent in 1901 to 33.1 percent in 1981. The number of people of French origin declined slightly from 30.7 percent in 1901 to 26.7 percent in 1981.

Canada's ethnic diversity can be seen from Table 14-1. In 1971, the non-English and non-French population (23 percent) came from 31 different backgrounds. The majority of these ethnic minorities were European, with Asians, native peoples and blacks constituting the racial minorities.

Most of the population increase among the ethnic and racial minorities has resulted from changing immigration patterns, especially in the postwar years of industrial expansion. The demand for technical manpower led the Canadian government in 1967 to begin a wider recruitment of skilled labour from nontraditional sources (Hawkins, 1972). Historically, the United Kingdom, northern continental Europe and the United States had been the major sources of immigrants to Canada. The demand for skilled labour from these countries as a result of the postwar economic boom meant that Canada had to compete with other industrial nations for immigrants with professional and technical skills. Third World countries became the main suppliers of skilled labour in what some call the "brain drain" (Parai, 1965). Table 14-2 shows the changing sources of immigrants to Canada. Before 1961, the ten leading sources of immigrants were European countries and the United States, with the British Isles accounting for nearly 30 percent of all immigrants. Between 1971 and 1981, however, the ten leading countries included India, the Philippines, Jamaica, Vietnam, Hong Kong and Guyana. The British Isles, still the largest supplier of immigrants to Canada, accounted for only 13.8 percent of all immigrants entering the country between 1971 and 1981. More recently, the federal government has trimmed the volume of immigrants in response to high unemployment in Canada,

TABLE 14-1   Population by Ethnic Group, 1951, 1961 and 1971

| ETHNIC GROUP | 1951 | | 1961 | | 1971 | |
|---|---|---|---|---|---|---|
| | No. | % | No. | % | No. | % |
| British Isles | 6 709 685 | 47.9 | 7 996 669 | 43.8 | | |
| English | 3 630 344 | 25.9 | 4 195 175 | 23.0 | | |
| Irish | 1 439 635 | 10.3 | 1 753 351 | 9.6 | 9 624 115 | 44.6 |
| Scottish | 1 547 470 | 11.0 | 1 902 302 | 10.4 | | |
| Welsh and other | 92 236 | 0.7 | 145 841 | 0.8 | | |
| French | 4 319 167 | 30.8 | 5 540 346 | 30.4 | 6 180 120 | 28.7 |
| Other European | 2 553 722 | 18.2 | 4 116 849 | 22.6 | 4 959 680 | 23.0 |
| Austrian | 32 231 | 0.2 | 106 535 | 0.6 | 42 120 | 0.2 |
| Belgian | 35 148 | 0.2 | 61 382 | 0.3 | 51 135 | 0.2 |
| Czech and Slovak | 63 959 | 0.5 | 73 061 | 0.4 | 81 870 | 0.4 |
| Danish | 42 671 | 0.3 | 85 473 | 0.5 | 75 725 | 0.4 |
| Finnish | 43 745 | 0.3 | 59 436 | 0.3 | 59 215 | 0.3 |
| German | 619 995 | 4.4 | 1 049 599 | 5.8 | 1 317 200 | 6.1 |
| Greek | 13 966 | 0.1 | 56 475 | 0.3 | 124 475 | 0.6 |
| Hungarian | 60 460 | 0.4 | 126 220 | 0.7 | 131 890 | 0.6 |
| Icelandic | 23 307 | 0.2 | 30 623 | 0.2 | 27 905 | 0.1 |
| Italian | 152 245 | 1.1 | 450 351 | 2.5 | 730 820 | 3 4 |
| Jewish | 181 670 | 1.3 | 173 344 | 1.0 | 296 945 | 1.4 |
| Lithuanian | 16 224 | 0.1 | 27 629 | 0.2 | 24 535 | 0.1 |
| Netherlands | 264 267 | 1.9 | 429 679 | 2.4 | 425 945 | 2.0 |
| Norwegian | 119 266 | 0.8 | 148 681 | 0.8 | 179 290 | 0.8 |
| Polish | 219 845 | 1.6 | 323 517 | 1.8 | 316 425 | 1.5 |
| Portuguese | — | — | — | — | 96 875 | 0.4 |
| Romanian | 23 601 | 0.2 | 43 805 | 0.2 | 27 375 | 0.1 |
| Russian | 91 279 | 0.7 | 119 168 | 0.7 | 64 475 | 0.3 |
| Spanish | — | — | — | — | 27 515 | 0.1 |
| Swedish | 97 780 | 0.7 | 121 757 | 0.6 | 101 870 | 0.5 |
| Ukrainian | 395 043 | 2.8 | 473 337 | 2.6 | 580 660 | 2.7 |
| Yugoslavic | 21 404 | 0.2 | 68 587 | 0.4 | 104 950 | 0.5 |
| Other | 35 616 | 0.2 | 88 190 | 0.5 | 70 460 | 0.3 |
| Asiatic | 72 827 | 0.5 | 121 753 | 0.7 | 285 540 | 1.3 |
| Chinese | 32 528 | 0.2 | 58 197 | 0.3 | 118 815 | 0.6 |
| Japanese | 21 663 | 0.2 | 29 157 | 0.2 | 37 260 | 0.2 |
| Other | 18 636 | 0.1 | 34 399 | 0.2 | 129 460 | 0.6 |
| Other | 354 028 | 2.5 | 462 630 | 2.5 | 518 850 | 2.4 |
| Eskimo | 9 733 | 0.1 | 11 835 | 0.1 | 17 550 | 0.1 |
| Native Indian | 155 874 | 1.1 | 208 286 | 1.1 | 295 215 | 1.4 |
| Negro | 18 020 | 0.1 | 32 127 | 0.2 | 34 445 | 0.2 |
| West Indian | — | — | — | — | 28 025 | 0.1 |
| Other and not stated | 170 401 | 1.2 | 210 382 | 1.2 | 143 620 | 0.7 |
| Total | 14 009 429 | 100.0 | 18 238 247 | 100.0 | 21 568 310 | 100.0 |

Canada Year Book, 1980-81, p. 137. Reproduced by permission of the Minister of Supply and Services Canada.

TABLE 14-2 Ten Leading Countries of Birth of Immigrants for Each Period of Immigration, Canada, 1981

**Before 1961**

| Country of birth | Number | % of total |
|---|---|---|
| Great Britain | 524 900 | 29.8 |
| Italy | 214 700 | 12.2 |
| United States | 136 900 | 7.8 |
| Poland | 118 000 | 6.7 |
| U.S.S.R. | 112 600 | 6.4 |
| Netherlands | 112 400 | 6.4 |
| Federal Republic of Germany | 107 200 | 6.1 |
| Yugoslavia | 39 100 | 2.2 |
| German Democratic Republic | 28 400 | 1.6 |
| Austria | 28 300 | 1.6 |
| Ten leading countries as a percentage of all immigrants who arrived before 1961 | | 80.8 |

**1961-1970**

| Country of birth | Number | % of total |
|---|---|---|
| Great Britain | 195 300 | 21.1 |
| Italy | 141 000 | 15.2 |
| United States | 67 000 | 7.2 |
| Portugal | 57 300 | 6.2 |
| Greece | 40 700 | 4.4 |
| Yugoslavia | 33 200 | 3.6 |
| Federal Republic of Germany | 31 400 | 3.4 |
| India | 28 200 | 3.0 |
| Jamaica | 23 600 | 2.5 |
| France | 19 100 | 2.1 |
| Ten leading countries as a percentage of all immigrants who arrived during the 1961-1970 period | | 68.7 |

**1971-1981**

| Country of birth | Number | % of total |
|---|---|---|
| Great Britain | 158 800 | 13.8 |
| United States | 97 600 | 8.5 |
| India | 75 100 | 6.5 |
| Portugal | 66 400 | 5.8 |
| Philippines | 55 300 | 4.8 |
| Jamaica | 49 900 | 4.3 |
| Socialist Republic of Vietnam | 49 400 | 4.3 |
| Hong Kong | 42 200 | 3.7 |
| Italy | 29 100 | 2.5 |
| Guyana | 27 500 | 2.4 |
| Ten leading countries as a percentage of all immigrants who arrived during the 1971-1981 period | | 56.6 |

1981 Census of Canada, Catalogue 99-936, *Canada's Immigrants*. Reproduced by permission of the Minister of Supply and Services Canada.

but it encourages the immigration of entrepreneurs, who, it is hoped, will create more jobs. In 1982, for example, 449 immigrants entered Canada as entrepreneurs out of 55,472 immigrants destined to enter the labour force.

The immigrant population in Canada is statistically overrepresented in skilled, professional and technical occupations. Figure 14-1 shows the occupational distribution of male immigrants compared to male nonimmigrants. There is a higher percentage of male immigrants in the managerial, professional and technical category and in the processing, machining and assembling group. Figure 14-2 compares female immigrants and nonimmigrants. Female immigrants are clearly overrepresented in the skilled occupations of processing, machining and assembling. These statistics support the earlier claim that the changing immigration pattern is a result of increased demand for technical and skilled labour.

Figure 14-1   Percentage Distribution by Occupation Major Groups of the Immigrant and Non-immigrant Male Labour Force 15 Years and Over Not Attending School Full-time, Canada, 1981

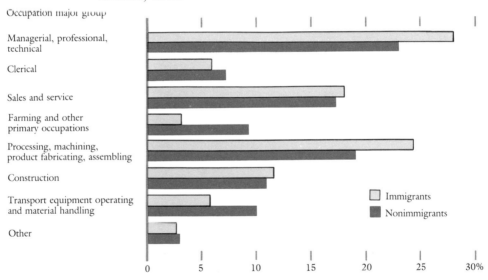

1981 Census of Canada, Catalogue 99-936, *Canada's Immigrants*. Reproduced by permission of the Minister of Supply and Services Canada.

In addition to ethnic diversity, there is linguistic variation in Canada. The 1981 census shows that English is the mother tongue for 60 percent of Canadians. A quarter of all Canadians are of French mother tongue, 85 percent of whom live in Quebec. More than 2 million people speak a language at home that differs from their mother tongue. About 3.7 million Canadians are bilingual, but bilingualism is more common among those whose mother tongue is French. Table 14-3 shows

Figure 14-2    Percentage Distribution by Occupation Major Groups of
the Immigrant and Non-immigrant Female Labour Force
15 Years and Over Not Attending School Full-time,
Canada, 1981

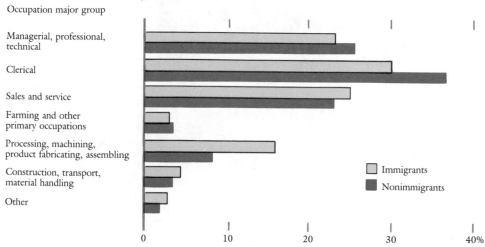

1981 Census of Canada, Catalogue 99-936, *Canada's Immigrants*. Reproduced by permission of the
Minister of Supply and Services Canada.

the linguistic distribution of Canadians by provinces and territories. The figures
show that those whose mother tongue is English are the majority of the population
everywhere in Canada except Quebec and the North West Territories. Compared
to eastern Canada, western Canada has a larger percentage of non-English and non-
French population.

There are marked regional differences in the linguistic patterns in Canada. The
importance of language regions is well summarized in Joy's *bilingual belt* thesis
(1972), according to which the bilingual belt of Soo-Moncton separates the unilingual Francophones of Quebec from the unilingual Anglophones of the rest of Canada. Using 1971 census data, Beaujot (1982) shows that 82.7 percent of the population
in the French zone can speak French only, and 33.5 percent of the population in
the bilingual zone is officially bilingual. This belt has less than one-quarter of Canada's population but over 60 percent of our bilinguals. In the English zone, only
5.8 percents can speak French. The 1981 census indicates that those who are officially
bilingual represent 15.3 percent of the total population. About one-third of those
whose native tongue is French are bilingual, in contrast to 8 percent of the English.
Bilingualism is less common among the English in Quebec than among the French
in the rest of Canada. Figure 14-3 shows the bilingual population as a percentage
of each region. About one-third of the population in Quebec and one-quarter of
the population in New Brunswick are bilingual.

The problem of linguistic and economic inequality is central to understanding
the British/French relationship in Canada. The basis of hostility between the two

TABLE 14-3 Percentage Distribution by Mother Tongue of the Population, Provinces and Territories, 1981

| MOTHER TONGUE | NFLD. | P.E.I. | N.S. | N.B. | QUE. | ONT. | MAN. | SASK. | ALTA. | B.C. | YUKON | N.W.T. |
|---|---|---|---|---|---|---|---|---|---|---|---|---|
| | % | % | % | % | % | % | % | % | % | % | % | % |
| English | 98.8 | 94.0 | 93.6 | 65.1 | 10.9 | 77.3 | 71.7 | 79.7 | 81.1 | 81.9 | 87.4 | 54.1 |
| French | 0.5 | 4.9 | 4.2 | 33.6 | 82.4 | 5.5 | 5.1 | 2.6 | 2.8 | 1.6 | 2.3 | 2.7 |
| Other | 0.7 | 1.1 | 2.2 | 1.2 | 6.7 | 17.2 | 23.1 | 17.7 | 16.2 | 16.5 | 10.3 | 43.2 |

1981 Census of Canada, Catalogue 99-935, *Language in Canada*. Reproduced by permission of the Minister of Supply and Services Canada.

Figure 14-3 Bilingual Population as a Percentage of the Total Population, Canada, Provinces and Territories, 1981

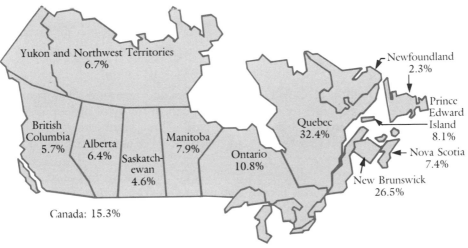

1981 Census of Canada, Catalogue 99-935, *Language in Canada*. Reproduced by permission of the Minister of Supply and Services Canada.

groups is frequently economic, although ethnic antagonism frequently manifests itself in linguistic and cultural terms. To better understand this feature of Canadian society, we shall examine the historical roots of French Canada and its relationship with English Canada.

## HISTORICAL ROOTS OF FRENCH CANADA

Before the British conquest of 1760, New France was a French colony. Although the language of the 90 000 inhabitants was French and their religion was Catholic, the life style in the colony was distinct from that of France (Milner, 1978). Under the *seigneurial system*, land titles were granted by the French crown to *seigneurs*, or land owners, who in turn, parcelled out land to the *Canayens*, or French settlers. The social structure reflected the colonial rule. Fur trade was monopolized by the French regime, and the *habitants* of New France were engaged in subsistence farming. The Catholic Church provided both spiritual and administrative stability to the French settlement.

The conflict in the colony between Great Britain and France was over control of the fur trade; it was not a result of linguistic differences between the French and the British settlers. The French defeat resulted in the Treaty of Paris of 1763, which gave Great Britain control over New France. With the immigration of English-speaking merchants, the English Protestants gradually assumed power in Montreal and Quebec. The French population remained almost exclusively rural. Although the Quebec Act of 1774 recognized the religious and linguistic rights of the French, it also upheld the feudal legacy of the colonial system and the authority of the Church.

The American Revolution of 1776 brought thousands of British Loyalists to Canada. In Montreal, the English Protestant minority became the elites of a unified financial, transportation and staples cartel that dominated subsequent economic development (Milner, 1978). By the time of Confederation, the English oligarchy based in Montreal was well entrenched. Although the British North America Act of 1867 recognized the status of French as an official language in the Parliament of Canada and the legislature of Quebec, commercial enterprises were virtually all in the hands of the English.

The dominance of the Protestant English in Quebec persisted through the first half of the twentieth century. A high birth rate, low education and submission to clerical authority were characteristic of the French population in rural Quebec. The Roman Catholic Church perpetuated a rural mythology that was conservative, fatalistic and passive.

The victory of the Parti Québécois in 1976 indicated the strength of French nationalism in the province, but changes really began during the Quiet Revolution of the 1960s. Industrial expansion after World War II, the increased migration to cities as a result of a high birth rate and the reform of the educational and welfare systems contributed to a new consciousness among the young French intelligentsia (Milner, 1973, 1978). Quebec nationalism was a response to the historical inequality between the British and the French and to the exploitation of labour by English capitalists. Consequently, the independence movement in Quebec was closely tied to labour politics and the political Left (Milner, 1973).

In many ways, the language struggle of the French-Canadians resulted from their economic and political oppression (Jackson, 1977). Generally, when language serves to maintain group boundaries, language conflicts, as Jackson puts it, "also become the focus of class, status and power conflicts" (1977:63).

## LANGUAGE MAINTENANCE AND SHIFT

There is much research available on language use among Canadians. This interest arises partly from the multilingual background of Canadians and partly from the historical rivalry between Francophones and Anglophones. The Official Languages Act of 1969, which made Canada officially bilingual, and the subsequent inclusion in the census of questions on language use also stimulated language research.

The 1981 census found ten major *home languages* of Canadians. A home language is the language spoken by the respondent at home at the time of the census. English is the home language for 68 percent of Canadians and French for 25 percent. The remaining 7 percent speak a home language other than English or French.

*Language maintenance* has to do with whether an ethnic or racial group retains its language over time. *Language shift* refers to a change from the use of one language to another. A study by de Vries and Vallee (1980) distinguishes two types of shifts: ancestral and current. *Ancestral shift* occurs when the mother tongue of a person, or the language he learned in childhood, does not correspond to his ethnic origin, as in the case of a Ukrainian who speaks English as his mother tongue. *Current shift*, refers to the use of a language other than the mother tongue at his present home, for example, a person whose mother tongue is French and who now speaks mainly English at home. *Anglicization* refers to the extent of adopting English as the language used at home by linguistic minorities (Castonguay, 1979). The Language Continuity Index, calculated as the ratio of persons speaking a particular home language to the number of individuals who have the same language as a native tongue, indicates how much a native tongue is gaining or losing in its use as a home language (1981 Census of Canada, Language in Canada).

The data from the 1981 census (Table 14-4) indicate that the English language group has a score of 111.4 percent on the Language Continuity Index, suggesting there are more people speaking English as a home language then there are people whose native tongue is English. Other language groups have varying tendencies to shift to another home language. Although the French have the highest index score among the linguistic minorities, language maintenance is strongest for French in Quebec and New Brunswick and weakest in the Prairies. Vallee (1969) has postulated that the influence of Quebec on French language retention diminishes the further away a region is from Quebec. With respect to other linguistic minorities, the Chinese have the highest score (83.5 percent) on the Language Continuity Index, followed by the Portuguese (79.5 percent). In contrast, language retention is weakest among the Dutch and Ukrainians.

The ability of linguistic minorities to maintain their languages is affected by the demographic-ecological structure of each region, which imposes varying constraints on the linguistic minority (Lieberson, 1970). In regions where the minority is small relative to the majority population, there is greater pressure for minority-group members to learn the language of the majority. For example, the relatively low degree of residential segregation among those of German origin (Richmond and Kalback, 1980:189) may explain their weak language retention.

Language maintenance is sometimes seen as an aspect of ethnic identity (Isajiw, 1976) and language shift as an indication of assimilation (Anderson and Frideres, 1981). Ethnic communities vary according to what Breton (1964) calls their *institutional completeness*, or the extent to which they can offer their members various services through their own separate institutions. In a recent study, Reitz (1980) found a substantial variation in ethnic group cohesion. Similarly, Lieberson (1970)

TABLE 14-4  Language Continuity Index for English, French and Nonofficial Languages Canada and Provinces, 1981

| | ENGLISH | FRENCH | ITALIAN | GERMAN | UKRAINIAN | CHINESE | PORTUGUESE | NETHERLANDIC LANGUAGES | ABORIGINAL LANGUAGES | POLISH | GREEK |
|---|---|---|---|---|---|---|---|---|---|---|---|
| | % | % | % | % | % | % | % | % | % | % | % |
| Canada | 111.4 | 95.9 | 68.6 | 31.7 | 33.1 | 83.5 | 79.5 | 16.8 | 78.0 | 43.7 | 77.0 |
| Newfoundland | 100.5 | 67.5 | 37.5 | 26.9 | 33.3 | 84.8 | 65.8 | — | 58.5 | — | 50.0 |
| Prince Edward Island | 102.7 | 63.0 | 60.0 | 24.1 | 50.0 | 69.0 | 55.6 | 31.6 | — | — | — |
| Nova Scotia | 102.7 | 68.5 | 33.5 | 24.4 | 14.2 | 68.4 | 62.3 | 10.9 | 90.5 | 24.0 | 78.9 |
| New Brunswick | 104.4 | 93.4 | 44.0 | 31.5 | 27.6 | 81.8 | 83.8 | 17.6 | 85.0 | 34.3 | 59.6 |
| Quebec | 116.4 | 100.2 | 75.1 | 36.5 | 54.9 | 84.3 | 82.2 | 23.8 | 88.0 | 50.3 | 85.8 |
| Ontario | 111.2 | 71.2 | 69.1 | 34.2 | 41.6 | 86.1 | 81.1 | 15.8 | 76.0 | 48.2 | 74.0 |
| Manitoba | 119.9 | 59.7 | 59.3 | 42.5 | 34.0 | 85.9 | 78.2 | 20.5 | 78.8 | 34.7 | 67.4 |
| Saskatchewan | 116.4 | 39.8 | 43.8 | 21.9 | 32.4 | 76.1 | 57.0 | 16.5 | 76.6 | 23.2 | 67.2 |
| Alberta | 113.1 | 48.5 | 51.8 | 30.4 | 26.0 | 85.7 | 70.8 | 16.2 | 70.5 | 36.3 | 62.3 |
| British Columbia | 112.0 | 34.6 | 48.4 | 25.0 | 17.9 | 80.1 | 66.4 | 17.9 | 47.0 | 31.6 | 60.4 |
| Yukon | 110.0 | 44.2 | 16.6 | 22.4 | 7.0 | 78.6 | — | — | 27.3 | 12.5 | 100.0 |
| Northwest Territories | 117.4 | 51.2 | 69.6 | 12.2 | 7.1 | 85.7 | 60.0 | 9.5 | 85.6 | 22.2 | 44.4 |

1981 Census of Canada, Catalogue 99-935, *Language in Canada*. Reproduced by permission of the Minister of Supply and Services Canada.

has suggested that highly segregated ethnic minorities have a greater chance of maintaining their languages. The degree of ethnic segregation and cohesion may be measured by in-group interaction, ethnic identification, endogamy (or in-group marriage), ethnic language retention, ethnic neighbourhood residence and ethnic church affiliation (Reitz, 1980).

# RACIAL AND ETHNIC INEQUALITY

Sociologists are interested in why some racial and ethnic groups do better than others socially and economically. Obviously, there are various ways of comparing the performances of racial and ethnic groups, for example, by occupational status, income and membership in the elite. The *explanations* of inequality, however, are more complex. To varying degrees, historical, cultural and institutional factors account for why certain ethnic groups occupy privileged positions in a society, while others are deprived of equal opportunities for advancement.

## THE VERTICAL MOSAIC

John Porter (1965), in *The Vertical Mosaic*, offers several explanations of how ethnicity and class intersect in Canadian society. The title of his book refers to the intimate relationship between ethnicity and class. First, he compares the *charter status* of the British and French with the *entrance status* of later immigrants. The charter group retains many privileges and prerogatives and lays down the conditions and rules under which other groups are admitted. Entrance status implies lower occupational status. Over time, some groups may improve their entrance status, while others may not. The concepts of charter group and entrance status are useful in understanding the privileged positions enjoyed by the English throughout the history of Canada, as compared to the disadvantaged status of the later immigrant groups that were recruited for various economic developments, as in the case of the Irish, who built canals and railways in Upper Canada, the Asians, who opened mines and constructed railroads in the West and the Ukrainians, who homesteaded in the Prairies.

Porter's second point is that, within the charter groups, the British are doing much better occupationally than the French. His analysis of the 1931, 1951 and 1961 censuses shows that the French were underrepresented in professional and financial occupations and overrepresented in the agricultural and primary occupations. By comparison, the English were increasingly overrepresented in the professional and financial occupations. The occupational inequality between the English and French has been shown by many other studies. For example, Hughes (1943), in his ethnographic study of an industrial town in Quebec, found a general pattern of ethnic stratification typical of Quebec, with the English occupying the management positions and the French composing the rank and file. In a study of Francophones and Anglophones in the federal public service in 1965 and 1973, Beattie (1975) reports that Francophones received less pay and had a lower chance of promotion than Anglophones. More recently, Milner (1978) has shown that in

Quebec, the *grande bourgeoisie*, or owners of multinational corporations are still largely Americans and English-Canadians.

Perhaps Porter is best known for his analysis of the economic elite of Canada, in which he shows that the English have overwhelming control. The economic elite are defined as those who hold directorships in dominant corporations in Canada. In 1951, for example, Porter found that, of the 760 individuals in the economic elite, 92.3 percent were British, 6.7 percent were French and 1 percent were from other backgrounds, mainly Jewish. In 1951, the British represented 47.9 percent of Canada's population, the French, 30.8 percent and other ethnic groups, 21.3 percent. The British were clearly overrepresented in the upper echelons of corporations. Porter's findings are supported by Clement's more recent study of the Canadian corporate elite (Clement, 1975). Clement's data show that in 1972, 86.2 percent of the 775 individuals in the economic elite were English, 8.4 percent were French and 5.4 percent were of other origin. The underrepresentation of the French goes back, as we have seen, to the British conquest of 1760, after which the British took over the economic and political insitutions of New France. Subsequent generations of English-Canadians maintained an economic empire in Quebec, largely by relying on the British market and British capital and, more recently, through ties with industrial capitalists in the United States (Clement, 1975).

The fourth point of *The Vertical Mosaic* deals with the relationship between ethnic origin and occupation. Porter suggests that "immigration and ethnic affiliation have been important factors in the formation of social classes in Canada . . . (and) ethnic differences have been important in building up the bottom layer of the stratification system in both agricultural and industrial settings" (1965:73). His analysis of the 1931, 1951 and 1961 censuses showed that people of English and Jewish origin were persistently overrepresented in the professional and financial occupations and underrepresented in agricultural and unskilled jobs. All other racial and ethnic groups were underrepresented in the professional and financial occupations, with the exception of Asians in 1961. Porter's conclusion is that, over this 30 year period, the British maintained their overrepresentation in the white-collar sector, while the French could hardly retain their position relative to other ethnic groups. With the exception of the French, the rough occupational ranking of various groups had remained the same, with the Germans, Scandinavians and Dutch close to the occupational levels of the English, and Italians, Poles and Ukrainians near the lower end of the occupational structure.

More recently, this *blocked mobility thesis* of Porter's has been questioned (Darroch, 1979) because a reanalysis of Porter's data indicates a trend of decreasing occupational dissimilarity among ethnic groups. However, using a more detailed analysis, Lautard and Loree (1984) have shown that, despite declines since 1931, occupational dissimilarity among ethnic groups remains large. Lautard and Loree argue that, although the average, or mean, ethnic inequality declined, the relative ranking of ethnic groups over the three decades remained stable. In other words, the ethnic groups at the top and the bottom of the occupational structure basically retained their positions relative to each other throughout this period. On the basis of their reanalysis, Lautard and Loree conclude that the "relationship between ethnicity and occupation remains a durable feature of Canadian society (1984:342).

# INEQUALITY, RACISM AND VISIBLE MINORITIES

In recent years, it has become fashionable among policy makers and academics to use the term "visible minorities" to refer to nonwhite racial groups (Ujimoto and Hirabayashi, 1980). Evidence suggests that these minorities experience a double jeopardy in the labour market because of their recent immigrant status and racial origin. The 1981 census indicates that, with the exception of people of Japanese origin, a high proportion of other visible minorities in the labour force is foreign born (Abella, 1984). For example, 88.9 percent of black males and 91.5 percent of black females in the labour force were born outside of Canada. Over 90 percent of Indo-Pakistani, Indo-Chinese, Korean, Pacific Islands and Central and South American origin in the labour force are foreign born. Many of them immigrated to Canada after the 1967 change in the Immigration Act. In a recent Royal Commission Report entitled *Equality in Employment*, Abella (1984) found a definite concentration of some racial groups in certain job categories. For example, Indo-Chinese males were largely employed in blue-collar and service occupations, and close to 50 percent of Indo-Pakistani women were in clerical and service jobs. Native people had the highest

TABLE 14-5 Participation Rates and Unemployment Rates of Selected Ethnic Groups by Gender, 1981*

| | MALES | | FEMALES | |
|---|---|---|---|---|
| | PARTICI-PATION RATES | UNEMPLOY-MENT RATES | PARTICI-PATION RATES | UNEMPLOY-MENT RATES |
| British | 77.8% | 5.6% | 51.4% | 7.7% |
| French | 76.2 | 9.7 | 47.9 | 12.4 |
| Other European | 80.9 | 3.9 | 54.0 | 5.9 |
| Indo-Pakistani | 85.7 | 4.5 | 60.3 | 10.0 |
| Indo-Chinese | 77.6 | 8.3 | 58.9 | 12.3 |
| Japanese | 82.4 | 3.1 | 58.6 | 5.0 |
| Korean | 82.2 | 4.9 | 63.7 | 6.6 |
| Chinese | 79.0 | 4.2 | 61.0 | 5.4 |
| Pacific Islands, including Philippines | 84.8 | 3.4 | 75.3 | 4.3 |
| Black | 83.0 | 7.3 | 65.2 | 9.5 |
| Native People | 60.7 | 16.5 | 36.7 | 17.3 |
| Central/South American | 86.2 | 6.9 | 57.9 | 7.1 |
| Total Labour Force | 78.2 | 6.5 | 51.8 | 8.7 |

* Single ethnic origin only.
Royal Commission Report on Equality in Employment, p. 82. The original source is from Statistics Canada, unpublished data from the 1981 Census. Reproduced by permission of the Minister of Supply and Services Canada.

unemployment rate (see Table 14-5). Other groups with high unemployment rates were French females (12.4 percent), Indo-Chinese females (12.3 percent) and Indo-Pakistani females (10 percent).

Table 14-6 shows the income levels of various ethnic and racial groups from the 1981 census. The income level of each group is expressed first as a gross deviation from the grand mean, or national average, and then as a net deviation controlling for sex, nativity, occupation, age, number of weeks worked and education. In other words, the net effect measures the amount of income inequality associated with an

TABLE 14-6    Gross and Net Effect[1] of Racial and Ethnic Origin on Annual Income

| | N | GROSS EFFECT AS DEVIATION FROM GRAND MEAN ($) | NET EFFECT, CONTROLLING FOR SEX, NATIVITY, OCCUPATION, AGE, NUMBER OF WEEKS WORKED AND EDUCATION ($) |
|---|---|---|---|
| Jewish | 159 250 | + 6 261.6 | + 2 936.0 |
| Scandinavian | 176 650 | + 1 859.8 | + 1 034.6 |
| Portuguese | 104 200 | − 2 001.9 | + 626.5 |
| Croatian & Serbian | 71 600 | + 458.6 | + 378.3 |
| German | 708 750 | + 652.4 | + 274.6 |
| Ukrainian | 325 350 | + 794.7 | + 212.7 |
| Italian | 443 100 | − 509.4 | + 148.5 |
| British | 5 365 250 | + 355.8 | + 103.7 |
| Dutch | 251 800 | + 311.3 | + 76.6 |
| Czech & Slovak | 42 500 | + 2 136.9 | + 62.9 |
| Hungarian | 71 750 | + 1 901.6 | + 20.4 |
| Polish | 161 500 | + 720.8 | − 222.7 |
| French | 3 333 800 | − 501.1 | − 240.3 |
| Other[2] | 1 610 400 | − 1 113.3 | − 277.9 |
| Greek | 83 750 | − 1 893.9 | − 796.3 |
| Chinese | 168 100 | − 1 294.6 | − 931.1 |
| Black[3] | 85 900 | − 1 588.0 | − 1 679.5 |
| Canada (all groups) | 13 163 650 | 14 044.9 | 14 044.9 |

[1] Gross and net effects are measured as deviations from the grand mean income, using Multiple Classification Analysis (Andrews et al., 1976).
[2] Includes other single responses and multiple responses of ethnic origin.
[3] Includes African, Caribbean, Haitian, and other Black
Compiled from 1981 Census of Canada Public Use Sample Tape, Individual File. Calculations were based on those 15 years of age and over, who were employed in the Canadian labour force, excluding inmates.

origin when variations in other factors are controlled for. The table indicates that lowest income groups were French, "Other," Greek, Chinese, and black. Their low-income positions did not change, despite controlling for other factors, and this suggests market discrimination on the basis of origin.

The Canadian "vertical mosaic" suggests that structured inequality is associated with ethnic and racial origin. Structured inequality refers to the institutional arrangements by which rewards and privileges are distributed and maintained. The idea of structured inequality contradicts the notion of an open society in which everyone has the same opportunities. One aspect of structured inequality is *institutional racism*, by which racial inequality has become part of social institutions. Wilson (1973:34) says that institutional racism exists "when the ideology of racial exploitation gives rise to normative prescriptions designed to prevent the subordinate racial group from equal participation . . . ." This form of racism differs from individual racism, which may be manifested in various prejudiced dispositions of individuals.

## MULTICULTURALISM IN CANADA

On October 8, 1971, the then prime minister, Pierre Trudeau, announced in the Canadian parliament the policy of multiculturalism within a bilingual framework. The purpose of the policy, according to Trudeau, was "to break down discriminatory attitudes and cultural jealousies . . . (and) form the base of a society which is based on fair play for all" (House of Commons Debates, October 8, 1971:8545). Despite such good intentions, there is little indication that racial prejudice has been less prevalent or ethnic inequality less evident in Canada. The policy has failed to effectively combat racism and discriminatory practices.

Roberts and Clifton (1982) argue that most ethnic groups in Canada do not have the structural resources to promote their cultural heritage, and the policy of multiculturalism simply reinforces the concept of *symbolic ethnicity*, which provides the *appearance* of pluralism. For example, with the exception of French, most minority languages are not recognized in the school system as languages of instruction, and multiculturalism, in practice, mainly means the preservation of ethnic music, crafts and dance. As Li and Bolaria put it, "The irony of multiculturalism is that it furnishes Canadian society with a great hope without having to change the fundamental structures of society. Multiculturalism is the failure of an illusion, not of a policy" (1983:1).

With the Canadian Constitution and the Charter of Rights and Freedoms, there are better prospects for implementing the individual and collective rights of Canadians. However, Evelyn Kallen has suggested that "individual human rights will take precedence over collective (ethnocultural) rights, except in the case of securing the linguistic and religious (cultural) rights of the English and French charter groups" (1982:230).

## SUMMARY

There are two ways to define race and ethnicity: as cultural groups and as conflict groups. The first definition leads to questions of assimilation and pluralism, whereas

## SOUTH AFRICA: THE PLURALIST EXTREME

In many ways, South Africa is clearly at one extreme . . . among most contemporary multiethnic societies. The economic, political, and social inequalities among ethnic groups, specifically, between whites and nonwhites, are unmatched. What is perhaps most peculiar about the South African system in comparison with the others is the officially proclaimed justification of these inequalities and the openly declared intention of dominant whites to sustain them. In none . . . of course, is equality among diverse groups realized; dominant groups in each seek to maximize and protect their disproportionate power. But in contrast to South Africa, there is official acknowledgment in Brazil, Canada, Northern Ireland, and the United States of the desirability of reducing interethnic disparities. Equally anomalous is the shape and degree of institutional separation among South Africa's ethnic groups. In none of the other four societies is the segregation of groups so rigid, and nowhere is it so legitimized. The overwhelming issue of South Africa is thus unambiguous: how will the ethnic disparities in power and privilege be transformed?

Despite the resolve of dominant whites to preserve their supremacy, the forces of change today are drawn unmistakably in South Africa. The end of European colonialism and the assertion of self-determination on the part of indigenous African peoples after World War II marked a power shift in which black political elites replaced white. South Africa has tenaciously resisted this historical drift. Although white South Africans at this point may quite reasonably claim to be indigenous Africans, their objectives and policies seek the perpetuation of white supremacy. Thus, they find themselves portrayed by black Africans as well as Third World peoples everywhere as the sole anachronism of a past colonial era. In a very broad sense, the South African case represents symbolically the confrontation of white and nonwhite peoples globally. The ethnic issues of South Africa today, therefore, have implications not only for South Africa itself or for the larger African continent but also for the entire world.

## CANADA: BUILDING CORPORATE PLURALISM

The Canadian case illustrates most clearly the fact that physical distinctions among groups are not an essential ingredient in the emergence and maintenance of ethnic conflict. Ethnic boundaries can be shaped in a number of ways and, once established, adamantly sustained generation after generation. In Canada, cultural differences, especially language, have served as an effective barrier between its two major ethnic groups. Here is a society, then, that forces us to recognize that ethnic conflict in the modern world is not limited to racially diverse societies.

Another aspect of the Canadian case that distinguishes it from the other four societies is the territorial factor. One of the major ethnic protagonists maintains a territorial base that solidifies its collective consciousness and reinforces its social and economic differences from the larger society. This is unlike the American, Brazilian, or Northern Irish cases, in which ethnic groups are relatively dispersed geographically, or even the South African case, despite attempts by the dominant group there to impose such territorial lines.

The roots to English-French discord in Canada are, as we have seen, historically deep and abiding. But this is a conflict that, by comparison with the black-white conflict in South Africa or even the United States, is subdued. Whatever the nature of its resolution, it is not likely to degenerate into warfare, as is so probable in South Africa, or to erupt periodically in violence, as in the United States. The democratic context of Canada makes ethnic conflict apparently amenable to political solution.

From RACE AND ETHNIC RELATIONS: AMERICAN AND GLOBAL PERSPECTIVES by Martin N. Marger 1985 by Wadsworth, Inc. Reprinted by permission of the publisher.

the second is mainly concerned with domination and subordination. Many views of assimilation and pluralism have been developed by sociologists, including the *melting-pot thesis, Anglo-conformity* and *cultural and structural pluralism*. The assimilationist perspective has been criticized for being mechanical and evolutionary, and in particular, pluralists are unduly accused of emphasizing the transplanted ethnic cultures. From the vantage point of the second definition, race is not a genotype and ethnicity is not primordial. Superficial physical traits, such as skin colour, are only meaningful when social meanings are attached to them. The relationship between a dominant group and a subordinate group is developed in the *colonial model* and the *split labour market model*. Both models relate race and ethnic relations to the process of production.

Race and ethnicity are important features of Canadian society because: (1) Canadians came from different origins and (2) racial and ethnic lines intersect with the class structure. The Canadian population has increased its ethnic and racial diversity as a result of postwar immigration. In addition, linguistic variations in Canada are associated with ethnic origin and geographical region. The linguistic conflicts between the British and the French, however, have historical roots that go back to the conquest of New France and the subsequent economic domination of Quebec by the British.

In *The Vertical Mosaic*, John Porter raised several major points about the relationship between social class and ethnic origin. (1) The charter group retains many privileges and lays down the rules under which other immigrant groups are to be admitted. (2) Within the charter groups, the English are doing much better occupationally than the French. (3) The English have overwhelming control among the Canadian corporate elite. (4) There is a close relationship between ethnic origin and occupation.

Evidence suggests that visible minorities (mostly recent immigrants) encounter a double jeopardy in the labour market because of their immigrant status and racial origin. Despite the multicultural policy and its stated goals to accomplish greater equality, achievements in this area remain limited.

## DISCUSSION QUESTIONS

1. Why is it meaningful to consider the dominant/subordinate group relationship and not just physical traits as defining characteristics of race and ethnicity?

2. What are the similarities and differences of the following models: melting-pot; cultural pluralism; and Anglo-conformity?

3. Why are some ethnic groups more able to maintain their home language than others?

4. How do the concepts of charter and entrance status help us to understand ethnic inequality in Canada?

5. To what extent does institutional racism impede the achievements of visible minorities in Canada? How successful has multiculturalism been in combating racism?

# 15

# Class and Stratification

*Gordon Darroch*

# INTRODUCTION

"Order is Heaven's first law; and, this confessed,
Some are, and must be, greater than the rest."
   —Alexander Pope, *Essay on Man* (1733)

Stephen Jay Gould, in his perceptive *The Mismeasure of Man* (1981), cites Pope to illustrate the argument that "appeals to reason or to the nature of the universe have been used throughout history to enshrine existing hierarchies as proper and inevitable. The hierarchies rarely endure for more than a few generations, but the arguments, refurbished for the next round of social institutions, cycle endlessly" (1981:30).

This chapter has three main objectives. First, it will consider the basic traditions of social thought that continue to inform thinking about contemporary social hierarchies or social inequality. Three basic theoretical perspectives will be reviewed. Secondly, it will show how social hierarchies are sustained or reproduced by specific social processes; they do not merely continue of their own accord nor are they "in the nature of things." On the contrary, social class and stratification are historical phenomena, and an understanding of the historical processes is essential to understanding contemporary forms.

Thirdly, the chapter will review some of the main patterns of inequality in conditions and in opportunities in contemporary Canadian society—distribution of ownership and wealth, of education and income and of the chances to alter one's position or that of one's family. As part of that review, we will consider the relationship between the popular notion that Canada is a middle-class society and the evidence that Canadians have experienced widespread proletarianization in this century. In fact, these are not contradictory notions. A central feature of this chapter is a specific historical interpretation of their relationship. Finally, our focus on class and socio-economic stratification ignores other important forms of inequality, for example, gender inequality and inequality among ethnic groups and regions. These questions are raised in other chapters.

## TWO CONCEPTIONS OF SOCIAL INEQUALITY

There are two distinct ways of thinking about inequality. One considers differences among individuals or social groups by measuring the amount of income, education or status the individuals or groups possess. Social inequality is thought of as a ladder or set of ladders, with groups and individuals standing on different rungs. This view usually implies that people can go up or down the social ladders. This movement is called *social mobility*.

A second conception emphasizes relations between two groups, relations of dominance and subordination or of dependence or exploitation (Ossowski, 1963). This second perspective obviously implies a more explicitly political and, perhaps, moral analysis: After all, the term "exploitation" in everyday speech connotes an unfair exchange—some people getting something for nothing.

This general distinction corresponds broadly to the distinction between the analysis of stratification and the analysis of social class: *stratification* is concerned with forms of social ranking, or relations of order; *class* is concerned with exploitation and relations of dependence. Class analysis and, in particular, Marxist theory, has set the terms of reference historically for discussions of inequality. Stratification theories challenge class analysis—or, as Albert Saloman puts it, "debate with Marx's ghost" (cited by Zeitlin, 1981:127).

# PERSPECTIVES ON INEQUALITY
## THE MARXIST THEORY OF CLASS

Marxist theory of social class is the most elaborate, challenging and radical perspective on social inequality. It is provocative because it carries a political and, ultimately, revolutionary message. It commands attention because it is a complex theoretical system built from detailed historical analyses of the rise and expansion of Western capitalism.

Marx did not formally define class, though there are clarifying remarks at the end of his major work, *Capital*. The term appears in his work in varying contexts, conforming to usage familiar in the nineteenth century. In this, Marx drew from the writing of such English classical political economists as Adam Smith, David Ricardo and Thomas Malthus. Although Marx was German, he fled to London for political reasons in 1849, and he lived there until his death in 1883.

Marx, like David Ricardo, considered the three great classes of English society to be landlords, capitalists and wage-labourers (Zeitlin, 1981:114). These three groups are distinguished by their sources of income, that is, rents for land, profits from production and wages. But Marx looked for a more fundamental difference. What most divides these groups is their relationship to and control of the basic economic resources of the society. Landowners control major blocks of land, capitalists control industrial production and wage-workers' livelihoods depend entirely on selling their skills and their capacity to work. Pressing the analysis further, Marx recognized an even more fundamental division: the division between groups with a proprietary interest in the basic economic resources of society and those who were excluded from ownership and control. In this respect, landowners and manufacturers shared common interests and were sharply divided from the workers. Marx did *not* suggest that the real social world was divided neatly into two competing classes. Rather, there are many class interests and many segments of classes—there are miners and dockworkers, clerks and professionals, small farmers and artisans, financiers, merchants and industrialists and so forth. What he did recognize was that, within this social hierarchy of occupational, income and political groups, there was the more fundamental division between the propertied and nonpropertied.

It is often said that Marxist theory defines class in terms of the ownership of the means of production. The *means of production* include those basic economic resources—land, capital and labour—referred to earlier. This latter definition requires elaboration.

The relations between the private ownership of property and wage labour are only a specific historical form of exploitation in the process of production. "Exploitation" in Marxist theory means a process of extracting *surplus value* from a population. Though these terms are not familiar outside of Marxist theory, the *idea* of exploitation through the extraction of surplus value is quite familiar, for example, when we think of slave-based or feudal societies.

Consider slavery. Slave owners claimed the products of the slaves' labour as a right of their ownership of the slave. The slave-owners still had to deduct from total production the cost of maintaining their slave population. In general, the difference between the value of slave production and the cost of maintaining the slaves was the owners' surplus value. Minimizing maintenance costs, of course, helped to maximize profits.

In the feudal society of medieval Europe, surplus value tended to be extracted from the main producers—the peasants—in the form of surplus products. The peasant gave up a portion of his harvest in return for services from the landowner, for example, protection from marauders and some assurance of help in lean years (Moore, 1969).

Another concept requires clarification. In Marxist analysis, the conventional sociological notions of types of societies are replaced by another concept: the mode of production. *Modes of production* are different historical ways of organizing productive activities by which people develop and maintain a whole way of life. A mode of production is also a specific mode of exploitation. Thus, there are slave, feudal and capitalist modes of production.

Note that a mode of production is an abstract concept and does not actually exist in a pure form. A society (or social formation), in Marxist analysis, is a mixture of modes of production, although a particular mode is usually dominant at any given time. Contemporary Western societies, like Canada are a mixture of a predominantly capitalist mode and a petit-bourgeois, or small property-owning mode. That mixture greatly influences current political debates and social institutions.

What is the core of the Marxist analysis of exploitation in capitalism? The answer lies in an analysis of two capitalist institutions: private ownership of the means of production and the free labour market.

In Marx's words, in capitalism " . . . two very different kinds of commodity-possessors must come face-to-face and into contact; on the one hand, the owners of money, means of production, means of subsistence, who are eager to increase the sum of values they possess, by buying other people's labour-power; on the other hand, free labourers, the sellers of their own labour-power and therefore the sellers of labour" (Marx, *Capital*, vol. I, 714, cited by Zeitlin, 1981:110).

Private property is not simply the ownership of things but a social institution, entailing enforceable claims or rights to use. As C.B. MacPherson says, "What distinguishes property from mere momentary possession is that property is a claim that will be enforced by society or the state, by custom or convention or law" (1978:3). In contemporary society, both social convention and the state enforce property rights. In Marxist analysis, the capitalist class, or bourgeoisie, is composed of those who privately own and effectively control the main means of society's production; the raw materials, energy, land, factories and offices, machinery and equipment. In so doing, they also own, control or influence the main means of making a living of virtually everyone in the society.

Capital is necessarily accompanied by *wage labour*. The class of people dependent on selling their capacity to work—their labour power—is the working class, or *proletariat*. In this theoretical sense, the working class includes all those who are the nonowning class and who are legally "free" to sell their labour power to the owning class. It will be important later to note that this definition includes most of those who consider themselves middle-class, for example, salaried professionals and other white-collar workers. Note, too, that labour power and labour are distinguished. The former is the intrinsic human capacity to work or to create. The latter, in capitalism, is a commodity and is bought and sold on the market. The key to understanding capitalism in Marx's analysis is to recognize that the relationship between classes is exploitative, first, because only in the labour process can value be added to production and, secondly because private ownership means that the owning class can appropriate this additional value in the form of profit. Owners also privately determine the uses of this additional value in investment decisions.

Finally, since the basic relationship between capital and labour is exploitative, it involves a fundamental conflict of interests in the long run. This conflict causes various forms of class struggle and, ultimately, social revolution. There is not space here to outline Marx's political analysis, although it is as important as the theory of exploitation on which it is founded.

In subsequent sections, we will discuss the process of proletarianization in Canada over the last 130 years and what that concept contributes to an understanding of class and stratification in Canada.

We will not attempt a major evaluation of Marx's theory of class and class conflict. However, the major changes in capitalist societies over the last century have important implications for Marxist class theory. A variety of interpretations of Marx's work have emerged. In some cases, there are deep divisions and lively debates among Marxist authors (Althusser, 1969; Poulantzas, 1973; Thompson, 1979). Some critics of Marx have used capitalism's changes to revise or reject Marx's core ideas (Dahrendorf, 1959; Nisbet, 1959; Bell, 1961; Porter, 1965). For example, widespread stock ownership and the growth of a managerial sector, it is said, means that those who own capital don't necessarily control it. The growth of social services and state welfare systems prevents widespread hardship, even during the periodic economic downturns to which capitalism is prone. The general increase in productivity has raised the standard of living of all classes, and, perhaps above all, the growth of middle-class occupations (white-collar jobs)—technicians, bureaucrats, office workers — has increased opportunities for upward mobility for all. Many argue that these changes render obsolete the ideas of progressive proletarianization, a society divided

---

If we stop history at a given point, then there are no classes but simply a multitude of individuals with a multitude of experiences. But if we watch these men over an adequate period of social change, we observe patterns in their relationships, their ideas and their institutions. Class is defined by men as they live their own history, and, in the end, this is its only definition.

Reprinted from THE MAKING OF THE ENGLISH WORKING CLASS, by E.P. Thompson, by permission of Victor Gollancz Limited, England.

---

By class I understand an historical phenomenon, unifying a number of disparate and seemingly unconnected events, both in the raw material of experience and in consciousness. I emphasize that it is an *historical* phenomenon. I do not see class as a "structure," or even as a "category," but as something which in fact happens (and can be shown to have happened) in human relationships.

More than this, the notion of class entails the notion of historical relationship. Like any other relationship, it is a fluency which evades analysis if we attempt to stop it dead at any given moment and anatomize its structure. The finest-meshed sociological net cannot give us a pure specimen of class, any more than it can give us one of deference or of love. The relationship must always be embodied in real people and in a real context. Moreover, we cannot have two distinct classes, each with an independent being, and then bring them *into* relationship with each other. We cannot have love without lovers, nor deference without squires and labourers. And class happens when some men, as a result of common experiences (inherited or shared), feel and articulate the identity of their interests as between themselves, and as against other men whose interests are different from (and usually opposed to) theirs. The class experience is largely determined by the productive relations into which men are born—or enter involuntarily. Class-consciousness is the way in which these experiences are handled in cultural terms: embodied in traditions, value-systems, ideas, and institutional forms. If the experience appears as determined, class-consciousness does not. We can see a *logic* in the responses of similar occupational groups undergoing similar experiences, but we cannot predicate any *law*. Consciousness of class arises in the same way in different times and places, but never in just the same way.

There is today an ever-present temptation to support that class is a thing. This was not Marx's meaning, in his own historical writing, yet the error vitiates much latter-day 'Marxist' writing. "It," the working class, is assumed to have a real existence, which can be defined almost mathematically—so many men who stand in a certain relation to the means of production. Once this is assumed it becomes possible to deduce the class-consciousness which "it" ought to have (but seldom does have) if "it" was properly aware of its own position and real interests. There is a cultural superstructure, through which this recognition dawns in inefficient ways. These cultural 'lags' and distortions are a nuisance, so that it is easy to pass from this to some theory of substitution: the party, sect, or theorist, who discloses class-consciousness, not as it is, but as it ought to be.

But a similar error is committed daily on the other side of the ideological divide. In one form, this is a plain negative. Since the crude notion of class attributed to Marx can be faulted without difficulty, it is assumed that any notion of class is a pejorative theoretical construct, imposed upon the evidence. It is denied that class has happened at all. In another form, and by

> a curious inversion, it is possible to pass from a dynamic to a static view of class. "It"—the working class—exists, and can be defined with some accuracy as a component of the social structure. Class-consciousness, however, is a bad thing, invented by displaced intellectuals, since everything which disturbs the harmonious co-existence of groups performing different "social roles" (and which thereby retards economic growth) is to be deplored as an "unjustified disturbance-symptom." The problem is to determine how best "it" can be conditioned to accept its social role, and how its grievances may best be "handled and channelled."
>
> If we remember that class is a relationship, and not a thing, we cannot think in this way. "It" does not exist, either to have an ideal interest or consciousness, or to lie as a patient on the Adjustor's table. . . .
>
> The question, of course, is how the individual got to be in this "social role," and how the particular social organization (with its property-rights and structure of authority) got to be there. And these are historical questions. If we stop history at a given point, then there are no classes but simply a multitude of individuals with a multitude of experiences. But if we watch these men over an adequate period of social change, we observe patterns in their relationships, their ideas, and their institutions. Class is defined by men as they live their own history, and, in the end, this is its only definition.
>
> Reprinted from THE MAKING OF THE ENGLISH WORKING CLASS, by E.P. Thompson, by permission of Victor Gollancz Limited, England.

between owners and workers and the likelihood, (or certainty) of class conflict and revolutionary change.

Others recognize that the changes are fundamental but argue that they do not render Marx's work irrelevant. Marx was not, after all, trying to set up a simple model of a class society with universal application; what he did want to establish was a method of analysis that revealed the basic contradictions within capitalism and lent itself to the analysis of actual, historical tendencies.

## THE WEBERIAN THEORY OF STRATIFICATION

Max Weber was aware of Marx's conception of class and worked out his more formal theoretical discussion as a critique of, or at least, as a response to it. Weber bridged the nineteenth and twentieth centuries, so he saw the beginning of many of the aspects of contemporary capitalism that challenge Marxist theory. In fact, Weber's understanding of the central institutions of capitalism was much like Marx's: He emphasized the concentration of the means of production in the hands of a few and the growth of a labour market of legally free individuals who hire themselves out to employers (Weber, 1968: vol. I: 300ff.; Gerth and Mills, 1958:180–181).

Despite these common points, two positions clearly distinguish Weber's perspective from Marx's. First, Weber argued that proletarianization was not, as Marx had suggested, creating a homogeneous class of industrial workers with shared conditions of life and political orientations. For Weber, a variety of *class situations*, determined by differing relations to property and by differing positions in the labour market, characterized twentieth-century capitalism. In effect, Weber was reflecting here on the emergence of the propertyless but nonmanual workers, that is, the new middle-classes. As a consequence, Weber doubted that capitalism's development would entail a polarization between bourgeoisie and proletariat. Secondly, Weber analysed forms of power or domination, rather than forms of production and social class. Weber is perhaps best known as the master theorist of the growth of modern bureaucracy (a topic addressed in Chapter 13). It is this concern with bureaucratization that led him to focus on the growth of the "white-collar" sector of propertyless workers. Office and salaried work increased rapidly in the first decades of this century with the growth of both state and private bureaucracies. This growth of bureaucracy led Weber to reject the Marxist focus on the separation of workers from the means of production as a specifically capitalist phenomenon. Rather, this proletarianization was only one example of a general concentration of power in the hands of the few (Weber, 1968:980ff). Finally, although Weber treated ownership of private property and the existence of a labour market as defining characteristics of capitalism, they were not the key to domination in contemporary society. Their elimination, he argued, would only give way to other forms of bureaucratic control: "Also (and especially) every rational socialist economy would retain the expropriation of the workers and would only complete it by expropriating private owners" (Weber, 1956:79, cited by Mommsen, 1977:381). In other words, the state would replace private ownership, deepening and extending the loss of control by individuals over their work and over the means of production.

His concern with forms of power led Weber to clarify the concept of class (Weber, 1968: vol. II: 926ff). He begins with the claim, "Now: 'classes,' 'status groups' and 'parties' are phenomena of the distribution of power within a community" (Gerth and Mills, 1958:181). These are not different dimensions of stratification but different ways in which the interest of individuals and social groups may be pursued in market societies. It is characteristic of Weber not to assert that any one of these ways is necessarily dominant; their relationship varies under different historical conditions.

For Weber a *class* is a group that shares the same economic relationship to markets either in commodities or labour. Class situations, then, result from similar kinds of control over goods or skills that produce income. Weber accepts that possession of property is one, but only one, determinant of class position, i.e., of one's chances on the market and, therefore, of one's life chances (Gerth and Mills, 1958:181–82).

But property ownership is only one among many relations to the market; there are many other forms of marketable skills and resources and, indeed, more than one type of property. For example, ownership may be of natural resources, of money or investment funds, of warehouses, stores, mills, factories, corporations. Each generates a significantly different class situation for the owner.

Thus, in the Weberian tradition, class is a strictly descriptive term; it entails no underlying theory of power, exploitation or value. In fact, Weber sees a class, first of all, as a collection of individuals who happen to be in similar market situations but who by no means share common political orientations. In direct contrast to the Marxist tradition, Weber viewed the transition from a common class situation to a common awareness of interests, organization and class action as a rare occurrence (Giddens, 1973:43).

For Weber, *status groups* are also understood as interest groups, but in contrast to social classes, they are based on shared styles of life, forms of consumption and on prestige or honour accorded by the larger community. They stand in contrast to social class groups, and Weber thought that status groups might sometimes oppose class interests. For example, groups whose power stems from landed or "old" family wealth might oppose the industrially based wealthy or the *nouveau riche*. Another case would be status groups whose claim to privilege is based on ethnic, racial or religious grounds. In each case, the social group marks itself off by its style of life and system of values. These serve as entrance requirements that debar the unworthy.

Weber distinguishes between class and status group to stress that forms of stratification do not rest alone on property or position in economic markets. As Giddens has written: "The theorem informing Weber's position here is his insistence that power is not to be assimilated to economic domination—again, of course, a standpoint taken in deliberate contrast to that of Marx" (1973:44). Weber realized that control of economic resources is one way to maintain status distinctions, as in the case of institutional racism. But he did not think that social interests could be reduced to economic ones (Weber, 1968: II: 935).

Finally, in contrast to the rare conditions under which Weber believed that shared class or market situations generated real social communities of interest, status groups are true communities: They are founded on social criteria of exclusive membership and, as a result, reflect shared ways of life, social interaction and shared values (Gerth and Mills, 1958:186–87). Again, Weber contrasts status groups with class, emphasizing that class consciousness and class politics are historically rare and fragile.

Parties, the third phenomenon noted above, are a form of planned political action. Parties are discussed by Weber as phenomena of the "modern" world, in that they require a staff and modern organizational apparatus. However, Weber's definition of a party includes a range of political organizations, including unions, and formal pressure or lobby groups for professional and manufacturers' associations. For Weber, parties may either represent class interests, status interests or both (Gerth and Mills, 1958: 194–95).

Weber did not formulate a systematic theory of class and stratification. Nor did he attempt to provide an integrated theory of social stratification. His careful discussion of class and status groups tried to separate the two as historical aspects of the way power is distributed in society. There is, however, a theoretical core to the definitions developed elsewhere in his work, and it centres on the process he called *social closure* (Weber, 1968: 342). Social closure has been defined as any social process by which a group restricts access to social resources and opportunities. A group may do this by turning almost any characteristic into a criterion of membership, thereby " . . . restricting access to resources and opportunities to a limited circle of eligibles" (Parkin, 1979: 44). In effect, closure is a social strategy to monopolize social and economic positions.

Forms of social closure may also be developed as a collective means of advancing a group's position in a stratification system. For Weber, property is a form of social closure, since it lets owners monopolize access to the means of production and to their rewards on the market. Status groups are also based on closure strategies, as they are set apart by socially constructed criteria (race, religion, ethnic origin, language).

The central criticism of the Weberian tradition is that the conceptual distinctions are too formal and arid; what they gain in theoretical precision, they may lack in depth of understanding of capitalist society. They have led to a simplistic notion of the multiple dimensions of stratification, without a theory of the relationships among these dimensions. Critics have found Weber's formal distinctions to be of little help in understanding the rise of class consciousness (Giddens, 1973: 79) or in accounting for the realities of class exploitation and power (Stedman Jones, 1976).

## THE FUNCTIONAL THEORY OF STRATIFICATION

A third perspective on class and stratification is supplied by functional theory (see page 23 in Chapter 1). It has two distinguishing features. First, it is founded on the notion that social class divisions and conflict are largely irrelevant in contemporary, industrial societies, although some inequality is both universal and useful (functional).

Secondly, this theory shares basic assumptions with contemporary Western political culture and ideology.[1] The core of that culture is a version of classical liberalism, which emphasized the moral value of rewarding personal merit and individual attainment.

The first, often implicit, assumption of functional theories of stratification is that social class divisions of an earlier era have been dissolved in the more complex society of the mid- and late twentieth century. Usually, functional theorists acknowledge that there was a deep and visible conflict of interests between the working families of the mines, mills and factories of early industrial capitalism and the owners and operators of industrial and commercial property.

But the functionalists assume that these conflicts disappeared as the modern industrial economy spawned four main trends: greatly increased real incomes and purchasing power for working and middle-sector families; a broad increase in the specialization and complexity of jobs; increasing opportunities for upward educational and occupational mobility; and finally, progressive sharing out of capital in the form of a dispersion of stock ownership among many shareholders and a widening gap between owners and managers of firms. Thus, the material and social circumstances of nonowning classes have greatly improved and the power of capital, as a class, has diminished.

It should be obvious how commonplace these functionalist assertions are in contemporary journalism, political rhetoric and in everyday conversation. Familiarity does not make them accurate, of course, but they undoubtedly raise basic questions about the nature of class and stratification in our society.

A second key assumption of functionalist theory is that social inequality is an *essential* feature of any efficient human society. Kingsley Davis put it this way: "Social inequality is, thus, an unconsciously evolved device by which societies insure that the most important positions are conscientiously filled by the most qualified persons" (1949: 367).

[1] By ideology is meant a relatively articulate set of political ideas that serves to justify existing institutions or their change by interpreting the past and prescribing future action. Each of the theoretical perspectives discussed here contains ideological elements.

Davis's central idea contains three separate theoretical tenets. First, certain positions in society are essential to its orderly functioning; it follows that some positions are more important than others, that they require more skill and they impose more onerous responsibilities. This could be called the "demand" side of the division of labour. Secondly, of those able to work, only a limited number have the talent and are willing to pay the costs of being trained to accomplish society's essential tasks. That is, there is a scarcity in the "supply" of talented and trained personnel. Thirdly, there must be inducements, or *differential rewards*, to operate as motivating factors for just enough talented and trained people to fulfill the needs of the economy. In this respect, functional theory is essentially a theory of motivation—it presents social stratification as a system of motivation which fills society's demand for labour from a limited supply of talent (Tumin, 1953; Wesolowski, 1962). The theory relies largely on a market metaphor for its persuasiveness.

Advocates of functional theory insist that the needs of the whole society, not just those of any one interest group, are served by stratification; they say that the theory does not predict any particular level of inequality but just states that some is necessary. Despite such qualifications, the criticisms have been pointed and numerous.

One criticism questions the assumption that positions in the occupational world can be ranked by importance. By what criteria do we compare, say, the importance of farmers and army generals, of lawyers and nurses, of teachers and politicians, of baseball players and bus drivers? Yet these occupations differ widely in the amount of prestige they are accorded, in income and in various "perks" of the job. The point is a telling one, for, despite the wide appeal and the simplicity of functional theory, no adequate response has been offered to this question (Tumin, 1953; Stinchcombe, 1963). In a blunt form, it asks: Why is it that in our society, physically hard, dirty and dangerous work is usually much less well rewarded than safe, clean and physically undemanding work (Wesolowski, 1962); or, why is the work women do (including unpaid domestic labour) less functional for society than mens' work? Certainly, it is less well rewarded.[2]

Regarding Davis's second central assumption, that there is a scarcity of skilled and trained labour, there is a question about whether Western society may not be more wasteful of potential human talent than efficient in recruiting it (Tumin, 1953). Critics point to the relatively few women recruited to managerial positions or to the professions. Others cite the barriers faced by visible minorities in all Western countries as further evidence of a restrictive rather than "functional" system of stratification.

Finally, there is the assumption that stratification helps motivate and recruit the right people for the right jobs. The central criticism here is that there are many ways to motivate individuals in their work beyond material or symbolic rewards (Tumin,

[2] It may be objected that some physically demanding and dangerous work is paid at very high rates, for example, oil rig workers or transport truckers. But a closer look reveals that almost all blue-collar workers have high earnings for a relatively few years of their working lives, when they are young and most healthy. They do not look forward to increasing earnings over a career, nor do they usually enjoy the employer-supported pensions, health, dental and investment plans that are part of the lifetime earnings of many white-collar workers (see the discussion and evidence for England of Westergaard and Resler, 1975: Ch. 5).

1953). To argue otherwise implies, that *our* culture, with an emphasis on tangible, individual rewards, represents a universal form and, that people are not motivated by the intrinsic rewards of work itself or by social, humane or altruistic considerations.

Despite pointed criticism since the 1950s, functionalist theories still hold a central place in contemporary social thought. They do so partly because of the sheer simplicity of the theory and because its main assumptions correspond to core values of Western society, emphasizing the significance of occupational mobility and monetary compensation for individual skill, diligence and self-discipline.

# CLASS FORMATION IN CANADIAN HISTORY

An analysis of class is an analysis of social change. Both the Marxist and Weberian perspectives view class as an historical phenomenon: Class relationships and structures are maintained and changed through specific historical processes.

An analysis of the development of social class relations rests on an analysis of proletarianization, which is a feature of Marxist thought. Recently, however, it has become central to both Marxist and non-Marxist analyses of the rise of capitalism in Western Europe (Tilly 1981; Levine, 1984).

Specifically, what we want to know is how a society dominated by small property-owners—on the land or in their own shops and homes—is transformed into a society divided between big capital and wage labour. As Greer neatly puts it for the Canadian case: "If most producers in early Canada worked 'for themselves,' how and when did the practice of 'working for anyone but themselves' come to be the norm?" (1985:21). We do not yet have an answer, but this section will examine the most widely profferred explanation.

## THE CONVENTIONAL VIEW

Most of the historical and sociological writing on proletarianization in Canada relies on a single interpretation of the changes that took place between 1840 and the decades immediately after Confederation, in 1867.

The Canada of Confederation consisted of three major regions: the Maritimes and Upper and Lower Canada, or Quebec and Ontario, as they are now called. The West was still in an early stage of colonial exploration, settlement and exploitation by the fur-trading companies. It was in central Canada, especially in the major cities (Montreal, Toronto, Hamilton) that industrialization began (Burgess, 1977; Palmer, 1979; Kealey, 1980).

What led to this fundamental turning point in class relations in Canada? Three factors are most often cited (Palmer, 1983: Ch. 2; Pentland, 1959; Teeple, 1972:43–66; Rinehart, 1975).

First, there was the growth of the railways. The railways expanded the market for goods and helped assure regional economic integration. A mere 115 km of track could be counted in all of Canada in 1850; there were over 3200 km in 1865, centred on Montreal and Toronto (Palmer, 1983:61). Secondly, hundreds of small producers—the owners and operators of saw and grist mills, iron forgers, brewers, cabinetmakers, boot- and shoemakers, carriage-makers and tailors—took advantage of the expanded market and began consolidating into larger mechanized factories.

Only a few emerged as major capitalists, of course; the growth of industry was very uneven. Many small shops continued alongside a relatively few large factories. The urban and town industries employed both migrants from rural areas (especially in Quebec, it seems [Robert, 1982]) and recently immigrated skilled workers from Britain (Pentland, 1959). They formed the first Canadian industrial labour force.

Thirdly, and most significantly, the land previously available to immigrants and native Canadian families to farm was, after 1840, more and more restricted. Land policies, it has been argued, reduced access and forced the growth of a class of landless labourers in Ontario (Johnson, 1971): Land speculators held much good land, and the state and the church each had been granted one-seventh of the acreage of the province. In addition, after mid-century, the best land in rural Ontario was already owned and successful farmers were expanding their holdings at the expense of newcomers (Gagan, 1978). In Quebec, after the 1840s, whole families as well as many young, single men and women left rural Quebec to seek city work in Lower Canada and in New England as a result of the over-exploitation of land and the lack of funds for agricultural diversification (McCallum, 1980).

## CRITICISMS OF THE THEORY

In moderately varying versions, this interpretation has influenced virtually every historical account of capitalist class formation in Canada. It is central to both historical (Teeple, 1972; Kealey, 1980; Palmer, 1979; Johnson, 1972) and sociological accounts (Rinehart, 1975; Hunter, 1981: Pt.IV). Important as it is, this perspective causes several problems. Many of the accounts are based heavily on the work of one pioneering scholar, Clare Pentland. His early work was remarkably insightful, but its weaknesses and misconceptions have only recently been given careful attention (Akenson, 1984; Greer, 1985). The questions raised are likely to affect all of the work relying on Pentland's interpretation.

For example, some recent historical evidence for Ontario seriously questions the extent of proletarianization by the time of Confederation. Community studies show that family farming *expanded* in the 1860s and 1870s (Gagan, 1981) and that land speculation, crown and clergy reserves and land policy posed few barriers to acquiring farmland (Akenson, 1983). Table 15–1 presents evidence recently collected for a large area of central Ontario for two census years, 1861 and 1871 (Darroch and Ornstein, 1984). This mobility table shows the percentage of men who stayed in an occupational category or who changed groups between 1861 and 1871.[3] The rows of the table show the proportion who stayed or moved for each group. The main diagonal of the table indicates the occupationally stable groups: For example, 53.4 percent of the merchants, manufacturers and other commercial and industrial property owners stayed in that category over the decade, while 59.3 percent of the professionals and 29.8 percent of the clerks and other white-collar workers were occupationally stable.

[3] These are data for individuals in the labour force. They are available for the 1881 census and earlier censuses only. Individual data for censuses after 1881 are still confidential, though aggregate data, of course, are available in census volumes and disseminated by Statistics Canada.

TABLE 15-1 Occupation in 1871 By Occupation in 1861, For Men, in Central Ontario

| OCCUPATION IN 1861 | PERCENTAGE DISTRIBUTION OF OCCUPATIONS IN 1871 | | | | | | | | NUMBER WITH OCCUPATIONS IN CENSUS OF 1871 | TOTAL NUMBER IN 1861 |
|---|---|---|---|---|---|---|---|---|---|---|
| | MERCHANT ETC. | PROFESSIONAL | OTHER NON-MANUAL | ARTISAN | LABOURER | FARMER | FARMER'S SON | TOTAL | | |
| Not present in 1861 | 5.2 | 3.9 | 3.3 | 20.5 | 20.5 | 30.0 | 16.8 | 100.2 | 6729 | |
| Merchant manufactuers, etc. | 53.4 | 2.5 | 4.9 | 17.8 | 6.1 | 14.7 | 0.0 | 100.0 | 163 | 452 |
| Professional | 12.4 | 59.3 | 2.5 | 8.6 | 2.5 | 14.8 | 0.0 | 100.1 | 81 | 270 |
| Other non-manual (clerks, etc.) | 27.7 | 17.0 | 29.8 | 4.3 | 8.5 | 10.6 | 2.1 | 100.0 | 47 | 165 |
| Artisan-craftsmen | 8.4 | 1.7 | 1.3 | 65.3 | 7.9 | 14.5 | 0.9 | 100.0 | 533 | 1591 |
| Labourer | 4.3 | 1.1 | 1.4 | 13.6 | 36.3 | 39.7 | 3.6 | 100.0 | 705 | 2505 |
| Farmer | 2.3 | 0.4 | 0.1 | 4.3 | 6.1 | 86.4 | 0.6 | 100.0 | 1406 | 2962 |
| Farmer's son (living with fathers) | 3.2 | 1.9 | 0.9 | 7.2 | 6.8 | 39.9 | 40.1 | 100.0 | 531 | 1365 |
| Total, for men with occupations in 1861 | 6.8 | 2.7 | 1.4 | 16.7 | 12.6 | 52.7 | 7.3 | 100.0 | 3466 | 9310 |

From Darroch & Ornstein, 1984: Manuscript Censuses of 1861 and 1871.

There are two main findings of interest here. First, there is a great deal of occupational change. Large numbers of men changed work categories during the ten years. The job changes are major, since jobs are grouped in large and quite different categories. For example, about 18 percent of the merchants and manufacturers and other owners of shops and property became artisans, and fully 15 percent moved into farming. One in three clerks (27.7 percent) or white-collar workers became merchants and manufacturers. And nearly 40 percent of labourers became farmers (most farmed their own land). There is really no evidence of class barriers to the movement between farming, labouring and the work of artisans, merchants or manufacturers. This was a very permeable occupational structure. And there is no obvious class barrier between the distinctly wage-labouring jobs (classified as labouring, which includes semiskilled workers) and nonproletarian work (property owners, including farmers and artisans).

Secondly, most movement was into farming, the one category that people did not leave. Undoubtedly, the predominant ambition and achievement of Canadians in this period was to become a family farmer.

These findings certainly call into question the notion that, by the 1870s, access to Ontario farmland was restricted and a class of landless labourers was established as the core of an emerging capitalist society.

That the vast majority of the population was on the land and the number of farmers was still growing does not imply that this was an egalitarian society. Stratification was startling in Canada and the United States. The best evidence indicates that, in both countries, over 50 percent of adult males owned *no* property whatsoever in 1870 or 1871, including farmland or a home (Soltow, 1975). In the cities, moreover, the inequalities were stark. In Toronto between 1861 and the turn of the century, the richest 10 percent of families owned at least 50 percent of *all* the assessed wealth in each decade; the poorest 20 percent of families never owned more than 2 percent (Darroch, 1983: table III). In addition to being characterized by rapid urban industrialization and marked stratification, nineteenth-century Canadian society was dominated by the values of the petite bourgeoisie, the owners of small businesses, tradespeople and professionals.

It is not yet possible to say how long this social formation persisted. Table 15–2 shows changes in Canada's occupational structure between 1891 and 1961. The data include both men and women in the labour force.

It can be seen that, in 1891, 45.7 percent of the labour force was in farming. Less than a third were industrial workers ("others and operatives").[4] By 1921, one-third of the labour force was still in the farming sector (the majority were small-farm owners). It is not until after 1941 that less than a quarter of the labour force is in farming. It appears that the Depression of the 1930s and the demands for industrial production during World War II contributed to the waning of this sector. The actual number of farms continued to increase from about 370 000 to over 730 000 between 1871 and 1941. But during the 1940s the number of farmers begins to decline. By 1971, it had dropped sharply to fewer than the 370 000 of

[4] The "Other and operatives" is a catch-all category that includes all members of the labour force not classified in the other categories. (See Leacy, 1983, comments on Tables D86–106.)

TABLE 15-2   Work Force by Occupation, Canada, 1891-1961
             (Percentages)

| YEAR | OWNERS & MAN-AGERS | PROFES-SIONS | CLERI-CAL & SALES | FARMERS & FARM WORK-ERS | LABOUR-ERS | OTHERS & OPERA-TIVES | TOTAL | TOTAL WORK-FORCE |
|------|------|------|------|------|------|------|------|------|
| 1891 | 4.9 | 3.4 | 5.3 | 45.7 | 6.8 | 32.9 | 100.0 | 1 607 945 |
| 1901 | 4.7 | 4.7 | 6.2 | 40.1 | 7.1 | 37.2 | 100.0 | 1 782,621 |
| 1911 | 8.0 | 3.1 | 8.3 | 34.1 | 12.2 | 34.3 | 100.0 | 2 275 148 |
| 1921 | 8.3 | 5.5 | 12.3 | 32.8 | 9.7 | 31.4 | 100.0 | 3 173 169 |
| 1931 | 5.7 | 5.9 | 11.9 | 28.7 | 11.6 | 36.2 | 100.0 | 3 927 230 |
| 1941 | 5.4 | 6.7 | 12.4 | 25.8 | 6.3 | 43.4 | 100.0 | 4 195 951 |
| 1951 | 8.1 | 7.3 | 16.3 | 15.9 | 6.7 | 45.7 | 100.0 | 5 218 596 |
| 1961 | 8.6 | 10.0 | 19.7 | 10.3 | 5.0 | 46.4 | 100.0 | 6 305 630 |

From F.H. Leacy (ed.), *Historical Statistics of Canada*, 1983 (Ottawa: Statistics Canada): Table D86-106. Reproduced by permission of the Minister of Supply and Services Canada.

100 years earlier (Leacy, 1983: Table M12–22). Of course, in this century, population, the size of the labour force and production have grown rapidly.

We focus on farming because it has remained the most important segment of the petite bourgeoisie, although it has been shrinking in the last few decades. Farmers may only recently have been replaced as the core of the modern petite bourgeoisie by small businesspeople and self-employed professionals.[5]

## CLASS AND STRATIFICATION IN CONTEMPORARY CANADA

Theoretical debates about inequality in contemporary Western societies are more often debates about root assumptions than about social structure and social experience. Are class divisions and conflict dissolved with the growth of the service industries, white-collar work, rising standards of living and increased individual mobility? Or is contemporary capitalism more deeply divided by the concentration of big capital and the parallel growth of wage and salary work at the expense of

[5] In a national survey in 1981, 13 percent of the employed labour force were self-employed, including farmers and professionals. Nearly twice this number (25 percent) were employed directly by government agencies or by crown corporations, and 6 percent were owners or part-owners of companies with five or more employees (that is, the capitalist class proper). The other 56 percent were distinctly working-class, the salaried and wage employees of private firms (Ornstein, 1983: Table 1). Of course, this class structure is not the same as the subjective identification of class membership: Most Canadians think of themselves as being middle-class.

small businesses? Is our society mainly characterized by individual equality of opportunity or by structural inequality of condition?

## THE CONCENTRATION OF CAPITAL AND WEALTH

That the Canadian industrial system is dominated by a relatively small number of large capitalist enterprises will come as no surprise. For the past 20 years, Canadian political and economic writing has shown that Canadian industry is *controlled* by major corporations and that these are *foreign owned* (Grant, 1965; Levitt, 1970; Naylor, 1972; Clement, 1977). Controversy has largely focused on foreign ownership rather than on the concentration of economic power itself. Evidence shows that foreign interests in major sectors of the economy have increased throughout this century—especially in manufacturing and in the petroleum, natural gas and mining and smelting industries. Fifty-two of the 100 largest industrial firms in Canada were foreign owned in 1979 (*Financial Post*, 1979, cited by Osberg, 1981: 27). In the 1985 report of the largest 500 firms in Canada, 46 (9 percent) were wholly foreign owned and another 87 (17 percent) partly foreign owned, with many of these among the very largest firms (*Financial Post 500*, 1985, May 25).

But despite the prominence of the foreign ownership issue in the press and in academic circles, other analyses do not indicate that foreign-owned industries have disproportionate economic power in Canada. For example, detailed studies of the interlocking directorships of corporate boards in Canada reveal a tight centre of Canadian-owned financial and industrial firms (Carroll, Fox and Ornstein, 1982). Other studies have questioned the prevailing account of the nineteenth-century roots of foreign control, arguing that a Canadian bourgeoisie emerged during the economic expansion between 1896 and the depression of the 1930s and that it still controls the major investments in Canada's economy (Noisi, 1981).

The issue of concentration of economic power receives less attention but the problem is easier to demonstrate. Economic power in Canada is concentrated in the hands of those few families and individuals who control a small number of dominant firms. By economic power, we mean the capacity to affect the livelihoods of large numbers of people through decisions on investment, economic production strategy and expansion or closure of plants. The 100 largest industrial firms in Canada, cited by the *Financial Post* in 1979, had total sales exceeding the combined sales of all other businesses, which made up 97 percent of all firms in Canada (Osberg, 1981: 27–28). Considering the distribution of economic power another way, the 3655 manufacturing firms with 100 or more employees reporting to Statistics Canada in 1978 made up less than 12 percent of all manufacturing firms but produced 76 percent of the *value added in production* (value of production less costs of plant and energy) and employed 68 percent of the labour force in manufacturing (*Manufacturing Industries in Canada: National and Provincial Areas, 1978*, Ottawa; Statistics cited by Ornstein, 1983; Table 4). Those who determine corporate policy clearly affect the lives of a great many people, either directly, as their employers, or indirectly, through the general effect of corporate policy on the economy.

But who controls these major firms? Is stock ownership widely dispersed? Do nonowning managers largely control major firms? These questions have been hotly debated for years. For Canada, however, there is a neat consensus: Raw economic power in Canada may be constrained by a variety of conditions (union organization, the state of the market, legal arrangements), but it is heavily concentrated in the hands of a few families.

In 1970, for example, nearly 90 percent of all Canadian families reported owning no publicly traded stock at all; only about 3 percent owned stocks worth $5000 or more (1970 dollars). However limited the data may be, there can be little doubt that stock ownership is the preserve of a very few families (Osberg, 1981: 36).

John Porter's (1965) pioneering study has been followed by those of Clement (1975), Niosi (1978) and others (Carroll, Fox and Ornstein, 1982; Newman 1975). Porter and Clement established that fewer than 1000 men held the key directorships in dominant corporations and financial institutions in the 1950s and again in 1970s. The avenues into this select circle altered somewhat during the 20 years, but it remained an exclusive and largely self-perpetuating group. Despite some important differences in interpretation, there is no doubt that the economic elites and inter-locking directorates that Porter, Clement and others have traced in Canada are a sufficiently closed and powerful social group to be called the bourgeoisie, a small, dominant economic and social class.

What does the power and cultural closure of a bourgeoisie imply for the Canadian system of stratification, especially for the distribution of wealth? Evidence is not readily available on this question. The holdings of the very wealthy are not recorded in national surveys. However, Table 15–3 shows one estimate of the distribution of wealth measured as family assets (deposits, cash, bonds, stocks, mortgages), total assets, (financial assets, business equity, real estate, automobiles) and net worth (total assets minus debts).

The table shows the proportion of total assets and net worth in 1970 and 1977 that accrues to each 10 percent (deciles) of the family units, starting with the poorest decile and ending with the richest. The poorest 10 percent of families had no measurable assets and a small negative net worth, i.e., debt ($-1.0$ and $-0.6$ in 1970 and 1977). The wealthiest 10 percent of families were exceedingly wealthy: They had about 69.1 and 67 percent of all financial assets, just less than 50 percent of total assets and a little over 50 percent of net worth in the two years. To recognize how much inequality this represents, consider that the less wealthy half of Canadian families (first to fifth deciles) together had just over 5 percent of the net worth of all families in 1977 and only 3.6 percent in 1970. The inequality is even more extreme for people not living in family units.

We can be sure that these patterns of inequality exclude the very wealthiest families, for reasons cited earlier. We can also be fairly certain that the pattern is very stable, though there are no definitive trend studies. If there has been change, it has been at a glacial pace and it is as likely to have increased inequality as to have reduced it since World War II. As we shall see, inequalities in earned incomes, which are distinct from wealth-holding *per se* have also been very stable for several decades.

How can we evaluate these wealth inequalities? They seem extreme: A tiny group owns a huge slice of the whole pie. Marxists and neo-Marxists might ask: Is a just, humane and democratic society compatible with such inequalities? Weberians and neo-Weberians find the inequalities unjustified but acknowledge that they reflect the great differences among the abilities of individuals and social groups to organize and act in their own interests in a market-based and liberal society: Inequality is

TABLE 15-3  The Wealth Distribution of Canada (As Measured by the Survey of Consumer Finance) 1970 and 1977

| | FAMILY UNITS RANKED BY WEALTH | | | | | |
| | FINANCIAL ASSETS | | TOTAL ASSETS | | NET WORTH | |
| Decile (Share of) poorest | 1970 | 1977 | 1970 | 1977 | 1970 | 1977 |
|---|---|---|---|---|---|---|
| 10% | 0.0 | 0.0 | 0.0 | 0.0 | −1.0 | −0.6 |
| 2 | 0.1 | 0.1 | 0.2 | 0.3 | −0.0 | 0.1 |
| 3 | 0.3 | 0.4 | 0.6 | 0.9 | 0.3 | 0.6 |
| 4 | 0.7 | 0.9 | 1.4 | 2.3 | 1.3 | 1.7 |
| 5 | 1.2 | 1.5 | 3.2 | 5.0 | 3.0 | 3.6 |
| 6 | 2.2 | 2.6 | 6.3 | 7.4 | 5.4 | 6.0 |
| 7 | 4.0 | 4.5 | 9.6 | 9.6 | 8.3 | 8.6 |
| 8 | 7.3 | 8.0 | 12.7 | 12.2 | 11.8 | 12.0 |
| 9 | 15.1 | 15.0 | 17.5 | 16.8 | 17.6 | 17.5 |
| (Share of) richest | | | | | | |
| 10% | 69.1 | 67.0 | 48.5 | 45.6 | 53.3 | 50.6 |

Financial assets = deposits, cash, bonds, stocks, mortgages, etc.
Total assets    = financial assets, business equity, real estate, automobiles
Net Worth      = total assets − debts

Adapted from Gail Oja, "Inequality of Wealth Distribution in Canada 1970 and 1977," in *Reflections on Canadian Incomes*, L. Tepperman and J. Richardson et al., Economic Council of Canada, 1980, p.352. Reproduced by permission of the Minister of Supply and Services Canada.

one result of economic and political pluralism. Moreover, they will note, the inequalities in wealth are either unknown to or ignored by most people; they are tolerated, if not accepted as legitimate. Functionalists and other neo-conservatives seldom address the question of inequalities of wealth, focusing instead on occupational and income opportunities. Extreme inequalities present something of a dilemma, since nothing in functional theory suggests that extremely unequal distributions are functional. However, there is a version of the theory invoked increasingly in recent years to suggest that great inequality of wealth is a reasonable consequence of maximizing the efficiency of the economy by rewarding entrepreneurial activity. Michael Wilson, the minister of finance, said in the spring of 1985 that Canada had too few wealthy people for the good of the economy. In fact, recent changes in tax legislation give Canada's wealthy the lightest taxes in the Western world: They are unique in being exempted from both inheritance taxes and capital gains taxes (*Globe and Mail*, 1985, May 30).

The XJ12 Vanden Plas
In every sense~the ultimate Jaguar.

Courtesy Jaguar Canada Inc.

The Globe and Mail, Toronto.
*Canadian society is characterized by marked inequalities in the distribution of wealth.*

How does the unequal distribution of wealth in Canada compare to the distributions in other Western countries? In fact, comparisons are hazardous because of the lack of adequate evidence. So far as the data can be compared, Canada's pattern of wealth concentration is similar to that of other countries, though less unequal than Great Britain's and perhaps slightly less unequal than that of the United States (Atkinson, 1975: Ch. 7 and Table 3).

## THE OCCUPATIONAL DIVISION OF LABOUR

Despite limited evidence, it is clear that a deeply stratified society is generated by the two central institutions of a class society: private ownership of the means of production and the labour market. The ownership of substantial property and of saleable wealth obviously confers opportunities for accumulating assets through investment and choice in life style, residence, and leisure activities, opportunities and choices that the great majority of people simply do not have. But this is not the whole story. Many commentators direct attention to changing occupational patterns, to widespread gains in real family incomes and to increased consumption and leisure. In this context, we should remember that class divisions and experiences are distinct from stratification. It is not unusual in our society to own and control no property (except, perhaps, a little, by mortgage), to be powerless (except for the right to a vote), to work for and be responsible to others and yet to be relatively well educated, moderately well paid and adequately housed. In modern Canadian society, individuals and families experience the (different) processes of class and stratification simultaneously. We saw from Table 15–2 that the change from a largely rural economy of farm families and small craft enterprises to an urban, manufacturing, white-collar economy became clear in the early part of this century and was quite dramatic after 1940. This was a fundamental change in the relationship of class and stratification. Table 15–4 provides another perspective on occupational changes.

The data appear in the conventional categories that distinguish office-oriented, white-collar work from that involved in the direct production of commodities (primary and blue-collar work). Blue-collar work has been stable or has actually *declined* slightly in the labour force. As we saw earlier, the proportion of primary workers, mainly in farming, declined precipitously, especially after 1940. The decline in the primary sector has been mainly offset by the growth of the white-collar sector, notably in professional, technical and clerical jobs.

These data reveal again the extent to which wage and salary work has replaced self-employment and small-property owning as the dominant labour processes and sources of income. In terms of the tripartite division of Marxist analysis, recent estimates (based on census and survey data) classify 5 or 6 percent of the labour force as major productive property-owners, 8 to 13 percent as small-property owners and self-employed and the rest of the employed 81 to 86 percent as working-class (Johnson, 1979 and Ornstein, 1983).

Various wealth, ownership, employment and occupational distributions do not just support different interpretations. It is a key argument of this chapter that they reflect different but simultaneously experienced changes in social conditions, that is, conditions of class and of stratification. Proletarianization has been the dominant

TABLE 15-4   Percentage Distribution of Labour Force 15 Years and Over by Occupation Division, for Canada: 1901, 1921, 1941, 1961, 1971 and 1981

| OCCUPATION DIVISION | PERCENTAGE | | | | | |
|---|---|---|---|---|---|---|
| | 1901[a] | 1921 | 1941 | 1961 | 1971[c] | 1981[d] |
| White Collar | 15.3 | 25.3 | 25.3 | 37.9 | 42.3 | 49.8 |
| Proprietary, managerial | 4.3 | 7.3 | 5.4 | 7.8 | 4.3 | 6.8 |
| Professional | 4.6 | 5.4 | 6.7 | 9.8 | 12.6 | 15.1 |
| Clerical | 3.2 | 6.9 | 7.2 | 12.7 | 15.9 | 18.3 |
| Commercial, financial | 3.1 | 5.7 | 6.0 | 7.6 | 9.5 | 9.6 |
| Blue Collar | 27.8 | 25.8 | 27.1 | 26.6 | 24.3 | 23.9 |
| Manufacturing, mechanical | 15.9 | 11.4 | 16.1 | 16.1 | 17.7 | 17.5 |
| Construction | 4.7 | 4.7 | 4.7 | 5.2 | 6.6 | 6.4 |
| Labourers[b] | 7.2 | 9.7 | 6.3 | 5.3 | – | – |
| Primary | 44.3 | 36.2 | 30.5 | 12.8 | 7.5 | 5.8 |
| Agricultural | 40.3 | 32.6 | 25.7 | 10.0 | 5.9 | 4.2 |
| Fishing, hunting, trapping | 1.5 | 0.9 | 1.2 | 0.6 | 0.3 | 0.3 |
| Logging | 0.9 | 1.2 | 1.9 | 1.2 | 0.7 | 0.7 |
| Mining, quarrying | 1.6 | 1.5 | 1.7 | 1.0 | 0.6 | 0.6 |
| Transportation, communication | 4.4 | 5.5 | 6.4 | 7.7 | 3.9 | 3.8 |
| Service | 8.2 | 7.0 | 10.5 | 12.4 | 11.2 | 11.9 |
| Unknown | – | 0.2 | 0.2 | 2.6 | 10.3 | 4.8 |

[a] 10 years and over in 1901.
[b] Except those in Primary.
[c,d] Divisions not identical to previous years

Derived from Ostry (1967: 50-51); Hunter, 1981: 79; *Census of Canada 1981, Highlight Information on Labour Force*, March 1, 1983, pp. 29 & 30. Reproduced by permission of the Minister of Supply and Services Canada.

structural trend in this century. For many people, this has meant a move into white-collar jobs which entail less physical risk, some promise of shorter hours and greater security, the possibility of greater income and certainly a widely shared sense of increased social status.

## STATUS, EDUCATION AND THE MIDDLE-CLASS

The major occupational shifts in this century have been interpreted as evidence of an "upgrading" of the work process, of job skills and the education and training they require. These assumptions have only recently come under study. There is reason to doubt that industrial work is more skilled than farming and other primary occupations, which often demand mastery of a wide variety of skills (Braverman, 1974: 430ff). Recent studies in the United States indicate that the complexity of many white- and blue-collar jobs may have actually decreased since the turn of the

*In the nineteenth century, Canada had a largely rural economy of farm families and small craft enterprises.* Photos courtesy of Mrs. Dorothy Wilmot, Hamilton, Ontario.

century (Dubnoff, 1978, cited by Hunter, 1981: 83; Horowitz and Herrenstadt, 1966; Spenner, 1979). Clerical and other forms of office work are subject to routinization and supervision. A Canadian survey conducted in 1981 revealed that, although such work was not closely supervised, a great deal was routine. Seventy percent of Canadian workers in all occupations reported that they were completely excluded from planning in their daily work (Ornstein, 1983: Table 6). Contrary to expectations, mobility into white-collar work has not meant increased responsibility or skill on the job, though higher educational credentials are required.

The employment of women warrants a special note. The number of women in the labour force (paid employment) has always been fairly high, but in the 1980s rose for the first time to over 50 percent of women aged 15 and over. Although women work in all sectors of the labour force, they are concentrated in a very few occupations. In 1981, over 50 percent were in clerical, service and related occupations, (Statistics Canada, 1984), and these are jobs with little responsibility, few educational requirements and low pay.

What about education? Since the 1930s, Canadian parents have increasingly invested in the formal education of their children. After World War II, especially, it was widely believed that completing high school and getting some postsecondary education were necessary to compete in the modern work world, and sufficient to ensure a well-placed job and high life-time earnings (Lennards, 1980). The belief

*The shift to an urban, manufacturing, white-collar economy became clear in the early part of this century and was quite dramatic after 1940.* T.M. Wathen/M.D.S.

was as widespread among educational authorities as among the public. The constricted job market of the last few years has had a sobering effect on the public and on authorities alike.

Despite some change in attitude toward education, as a result of the recent recession, enrollment in postsecondary institutions and levels of educational attainment have steadily increased (Lennards, 1980: Table 13–4). Table 15–5 shows the recent trend.

In 1981, 8 percent of the population aged 15 and over had a university degree, an increase of just 3 percent since 1970. Completion of some postsecondary education increased by just over 10 percent in the decade, although a stable 44 to 45 percent completed high school. In 1940, just a little over 30 percent of those over 15 had completed high school (Cuneo, 1980: Table 7–4).

Again, international comparisons are hampered by lack of data, but in the 1970s in the United States, over 40 percent of children obtained a college education (including junior colleges and a wider range of state colleges and universities than there are in Canada). The proportion of children attaining a university education in Great Britain in the 1970s was reported as 9 percent, rather higher than in Canada for the same period (Worsley, 1977: 235–36).

Although access to education has increased in this country and elsewhere, this increase has done little to reduce inequality in educational opportunity, even in the

TABLE 15-5    Educational Stratification, Population Fifteen Years Old
and Over, Canada, 1971-1981

| HIGHEST LEVEL OF SCHOOLING COMPLETED | 1971 | 1976 (PERCENTAGES) | 1981 |
|---|---|---|---|
| Less than Grade 9 | 32.3 | 25.4 | 20.7 |
| Grades 9 to 13 | 45.9 | 44.1 | 43.6 |
| Some Post-Secondary* | 17.1 | 24.1 | 27.6 |
| University Degree | 4.8 | 6.4 | 8.0 |

* Some differences in definition among census years.

Statistics Canada, *1981 Census, Population, Historical Tables for Census Education Data*, June 1984: Table 1. Reproduced by permission of the Minister of Supply and Services Canada.

United States. There were more children from lower-income and working-class backgrounds in institutions of higher education in the 1960s and 1970s, but as a group, they remain as underrepresented as ever. The growth in university attendance by children from middle- or upper-status families has matched or exceeded that of the less privileged in Canada, the United States and Great Britain (Lennards, 1980: 496; Pike, 1980: 124–32; Worsley, 1977: 235–36). As Michael Katz put it, referring to an earlier era, those from lower-status backgrounds have "to run harder than ever just to keep from falling behind" (1975: 284, cited by Pike, 1980: 115).

In addition to questions of access and inequality, is the question of the seeming lack of fit between educational upgrading and the demand for specific occupational skills and training over the last three decades (Berg, 1970; Harvey, 1974; Lennards, 1980). A number of studies have suggested that, rather than teaching knowledge and skills, schools primarily teach the values and attitudes appropriate to an industrial capitalist society (for example, work discipline and respect for authority; see Bowles and Gintis, 1976; Willis, 1977). Others argue that the diplomas awarded for successful school completion serve mainly as devices by which employers can sort out applicants for employment (Collins, 1971). These critical questions arise from both Marxist and Weberian perspectives and have come to undermine the simpler functionalist assumptions regarding rewards for training for skilled work in contemporary society.

## Status, Prestige and Middle Class

The attitude of functionalists toward occupational and educational stratification remains firmly grounded in the view that the occupational division of labour has a distinct and stable status, or prestige order. One of the longest traditions of empirical research in stratification has been that of assessing the prestige rankings of occupations (National Opinion Research Center, 1947; Hodge et al., 1966; Pineo and Porter, 1967; Treiman, 1978). Occupations have been ranked in a similar way in several national studies in the United States, Great Britain, Germany, Japan, the Philippines and some socialist countries of Eastern Europe (Treiman, 1978). But there are important differences, especially for Eastern Europe, where skilled, manual work has come to be rated higher than certain white-collar positions (Parkin, 1971: 156–58). Moreover, the similarity in rankings may result from agreement on the relative prestige of very general categories of work rather than specific positions (Nosanchuk, 1972). Nevertheless, functionalist theory gathers some support from the tendency toward consistent occupational prestige rankings. For Canada, a national study by Porter and Pineo (Pineo, 1981: 617) asked about 800 people to group some 200 occupations into categories that reflected the occupations' general social standing. Table 15–6 shows the results of this survey.

It is readily apparent that the classification of primary, blue- and white-collar jobs given in Table 15–4, closely matches the general social standing accorded occupations by the public. The highest standing was given to the job of provincial premier and the lowest to garbage collectors and newspaper pedlars (Pineo and Porter, 1967, reprinted in Curtis and Scott, 1979: 205–220). Even this selective listing reveals that self-employed professionals command the greatest occupational prestige. A fuller listing would show that owners, managers and officials are accorded less status than the self-employed professional. Although farming is now accorded little prestige— scoring barely above manual work and somewhat below skilled clerical, sales and service work—there is a hint in these data that petit-bourgeois values centered on self-employment still carry a great deal of weight in contemporary Canadian culture.[6]

The general social standing of occupations has been of concern mainly in studies of occupational mobility. We will consider some implications of these studies in a moment. But the prestige rankings also raise questions about a most ambiguous concept—the middle-class.

The concept of the middle-class arose with the growth of white-collar work (Mills, 1956), that is, with the growth of employment in the bureaucracies of corporations and the state. The ambiguity of the concept reflects the ambiguity of the economic, social and political circumstances of this group. They are "middle" only in the obvious, but important, sense that they stand between the upper and lower groups on the scales of wealth, income and life style.

---

[6] These occupational prestige rankings have been generalized to a much larger set of occupations given in censuses by estimating "status" scores for all occupations from their relationships with other factors, such as education and income. These estimates provide socio-economic status scores widely used in research on social mobility (Blishen, 1967 and Blishen and McRoberts, 1976).

The ranking of occupations has seemed stable over time and among countries. This observation lends itself to a functionalist interpretation: The ranking does, indeed, reflect a social consensus on the functional importance of various jobs and on the origins of the stratification of rewards. Marxists have generally ignored this issue. Some Weberians have argued that the ranking of occupations is not the *source* of stratification but the *result* of the differential power of occupational groups, such as professionals, to maintain legal and social exclusivity, thus perpetuating their status and income through social closure (Parkin, 1974). Hence, the ranking simply reflects a public awareness of the realities of stratification. Parkin, for one, also notes that those with relatively low-ranked occupations tend to rank their own occupation more highly then general survey results. This suggests that they recognize the general view but resist its application to their own work (Parkin, 1971: 94).

TABLE 15-6    Occupational Prestige Rankings, Canada 1971

| MAIN STRATA | PRESTIGE OF MAIN STRATA | SUBSTRATA | PRESTIGE OF SUBSTRATA |
|---|---|---|---|
| Professional | 63.8 | Self-Employed Professionals | 78.6 |
| | | Employed Professionals | 68.0 |
| | | Technicians | 67.2 |
| | | Semiprofessionals | 56.7 |
| Managerial and Supervisory | 59.5 | High-level Management | 67.7 |
| | | Middle Management | 64.8 |
| | | Foreman | 51.0 |
| | | Supervisors | 46.3 |
| Clerical, Sales, Service | 37.2 | Skilled | 47.7 |
| | | Semiskilled | 34.2 |
| | | Unskilled | 29.7 |
| Farming | 35.0 | Farmers | 40.9 |
| | | Farm Labourers | 23.3 |
| Manual | 33.4 | Skilled | 40.3 |
| | | Semiskilled | 32.4 |
| | | Unskilled | 24.7 |

Pineo, Peter, John Porter, and Hugh McRoberts. "The 1971 census and the socioeconomic classification of occupations." *Canadian Review of Sociology and Anthropology*, 14(1), 1977, p. 98. Based on the 193 Pineo-Porter-McRoberts titles that matched the 1971 Census Unit Groups.

The concept of the middle-class is poorly developed in both social theory and historical and sociological analysis. In this respect, social and historical research has been badly out of phase with cultural and political reality. Since early in this century, perhaps beginning in the 1920s, Canada, like other Western societies, has been regarded as middle-class as a result of the modestly increased disposable incomes of nuclear families, reduced working hours and an increasingly market- and consumer-oriented society. These developments are accompanied by a pervasive respect for individual effort, competitive educational and occupational opportunities, property and political order.

In fact, we have exceedingly little information about the relationship between the material and historical basis of middle-class consciousness. There are, however, some useful studies of the self-identification of social classes in Canada. Table 15–7 shows the distribution of responses on two related questions from two surveys, a national survey in 1965 and a survey of four major cities in Ontario and Quebec in 1971 (Goyder and Pineo, 1979). The differences between the two survey results suggest that any interpretation of survey questions on this topic requires caution, since results are heavily influenced by the wording of the questions and the nature of the survey (Goyder and Pineo, 1979). In any case, between 60 and 70 percent of the populations surveyed consider themselves "middle-class" or "upper-middle-class," although other studies show that manual workers tend to have a rather more politicized view of Canadian society than nonmanual workers (Rinehart and Okraku,

TABLE 15-7   Distribution of Responses to Class Identification
            Questions, (National Survey 1965; Four Cities, 1971)

OPEN-ENDED QUESTION: "WHAT SOCIAL CLASS DO YOU CONSIDER YOURSELF A
MEMBER OF?"

|      | UPPER | UPPER MIDDLE | MIDDLE | WORKING | LOWER | N/A |
|------|-------|--------------|--------|---------|-------|-----|
|      | %     | %            | %      | %       | %     | %   |
| 1965 | 1.1   | 3.9          | 63.3   | 10.5    | 4.4   | 16.8 |
| 1971 | 0.8   | 5.9          | 53.7   | 16.4    | 1.2   | 22.0 |

CLOSED QUESTION: "IF YOU HAD TO PICK ONE, WHICH OF THE FOLLOWING FIVE
SOCIAL CLASSES WOULD YOU SAY YOU WERE IN—UPPER CLASS, UPPER MIDDLE
CLASS, MIDDLE CLASS, WORKING CLASS, OR LOWER CLASS?"

|      | UPPER | UPPER MIDDLE | MIDDLE | WORKING | LOWER | N/A |
|------|-------|--------------|--------|---------|-------|-----|
|      | %     | %            | %      | %       | %     | %   |
| 1965 | 2.0   | 12.9         | 48.9   | 30.4    | 2.1   | 3.7 |
| 1971 | 1.0   | 13.4         | 46.9   | 27.4    | 0.3   | 11.0 |

Curtis J. and Scott, W. *Social Stratification in Canada*, 2nd edition, p. 434, J. Goyder and P. Pineo,
"Social Class Self-Identification," Table 1. Permission granted by Prentice-Hall Canada, Inc.

1974: 200). One cannot place too much emphasis on these studies, but they indicate
that the popular notion of a broad middle-class also needs to be subjected to class
analysis.

## REAL INCOMES, INCOME INEQUALITY AND OCCUPATIONAL MOBILITY: THE MAKING OF THE MIDDLE-CLASS

The 1920s brought an important historical turning point to Canada. Not until the
late 1920s were the wages of the average manufacturing worker sufficient to raise
a family on one income. And only in the same decade were the wages of women
workers high enough to allow some women to be independent of their own or
other families (Palmer, 1983: 192). In the last century and early in this one, ordinary
families survived by pooling several sources of income and even then they were
often threatened by economic crises.

The Depression of the 1930s cut incomes for many families, but steep declines
in the prices of commodities also meant that wages increased in purchasing power.
In any case, the 1940s and 1950s saw greater gains in real incomes and in consumer
expenditures. These trends continued until the 1970s with important regional variations. This economic expansion brought well-known changes in suburbanization,
transportation, radio and television; it produced a general widening of consumer
culture (Palmer, 1983: Ch. 6). Figure 15–1 shows the general pattern of rising real
incomes.

Figure 15-1   Average Income of Canadian Families and Unattached
              Individuals

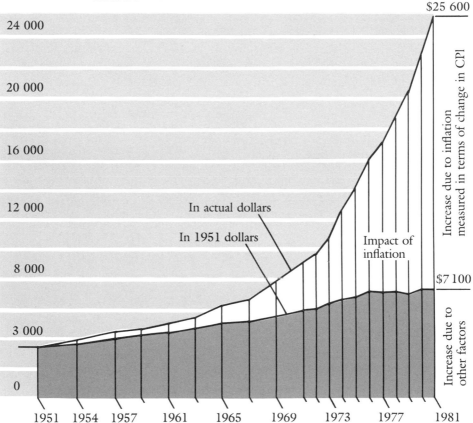

Average income of families and unattached individuals

*Charting Canadian Incomes, 1951–1981*, Ottawa: Statistics Canada, March 1984: p.s. Reproduced by permission of the Minister of Supply and Services.

Figure 15–1 plots the average incomes of families and unattached individuals from 1951 to 1981 and distinguishes *actual* dollar income from *real* income, measured in 1951 dollars. Incomes include earnings from employment and from investments, as well as money from social benefits and pensions.

Actual incomes rose throughout the entire period and grew steeply from about 1965, though inflation accounted for a huge portion of the growth over the last 20 years. But still, real average incomes grew until 1976; they have stagnated since. The recent stability of average real incomes (and hence, declines in income for some segments of the population) is a reversal of historic patterns. Whereas in 1951, 60 percent of all families were one-earner families, that proportion was reduced to 57 percent in 1961, 41 percent in 1971 and just 29 percent in 1981 (Statistics Canada(a), 1984: 11). The return to multiple earners for each family has been a response to economic stagnation and higher unemployment and a means of sustaining purchasing power and middle-class standards of family living. One important economic implication of this trend is the shrunken pool of potential workers, or surplus labour supply, especially of women, as compared to the 1940s, 1950s and 1960s.

The proportion of *married* women in the workforce has grown tremendously, even since 1967, from 35 to 63 percent. Moreover, women have doubled their contributions to family income. Nearly 70 percent of those in the low-income groups in 1981 were unattached people, mainly women under the age of 25 and over 65 who had no earned income. The other 30 percent are mostly single-parent families (Statistics Canada(a), 1984: 15).

Given the origin of the middle-class in rising incomes and purchasing power from the 1920s to the 1970s, it would be more accurate to refer to the growth of the *middle-income society* (Porter, 1965: Part I).

Conceptual niceties apart, the growth of the numbers of people who consider themselves part of a Canadian middle-class almost certainly accompanied higher incomes, suburbanization and increased consumption; these trends have been sustained in recent years by the return to multiple family-income earners. What about inequality in income throughout this period? Has the increased purchasing power of family incomes and spreading commodity markets reduced actual stratification of incomes? In a word, no.

Table 15–8 gives a distribution similar to that for wealth distributions above (see Table 15–3). In this case, five income groups (as defined in the table) are compared; each represents 20 percent of the population (quintiles), ranged from the fifth of the population with highest income to the fifth with the lowest. The distributions over the postwar period are virtually unchanged. The great stability in income distributions comes as some surprise. After all, it flies in the face of all the rhetoric about the expansion of the middle-class and the claims that the Canadian government has been responsible for redistributing income from the upper- to the lower-middle classes and the poor through progressive taxation, social benefit and unemployment insurance programs and the welfare net. This is, as Gillespie aptly called it, one of the great myths perpetuated from the popular podium and in popular literature (Gillespie, 1980).

TABLE 15-8    Income Stratification: Percentage Distribution by Quintiles, Canada, 1951-1981

| FAMILIES AND UNATTACHED INDIVIDUALS | 1951 | 1961 | 1971 | 1981 |
|---|---|---|---|---|
| Poorest Quintile (20%) | 4 | 4 | 4 | 4 |
| Second Quintile | 12 | 12 | 10 | 11 |
| Third Quintile | 18 | 18 | 18 | 18 |
| Fourth Quintile | 23 | 25 | 25 | 25 |
| Richest Quintile | 43 | 41 | 43 | 42 |

Statistics Canada, *Charting Canadian Incomes 1951-1981*, March 1984: 6. Reproduced by permission of the Minister of Supply and Services Canada.

It is valuable to dwell on the fact that the increase in real incomes in the postwar period and stability of income inequality were simultaneous. Individuals and families today experience rising incomes and yet remain in the same *relative* position in the structures of income stratification. In effect, the entire income structure has shifted without losing shape: on average, the rich gained as much as those in the middle or the relatively poor income categories. Recognizing this difference between individual and *structural* conditions is essential to understanding the culture and politics of the middle-class in contemporary capitalist societies like Canada.

## The Role of Cultural Capital in Social Mobility

Perhaps the most important element of a middle-class culture is the value placed on meritocratic principles, i.e., on the rewarding of individual effort and capabilities in a fair and open competition. Historically, these principles were central to the bourgeois and liberal democratic revolutions that assaulted the privileged position of European aristocracies. In our society, these values seem to have taken on a particular importance for middle-class families that are trying to protect and improve the life chances of their children. This adherence to competitive, individualistic principles may be one response to proletarianization, on the one hand, and to the growth of white-collar occupations, on the other. Most Canadians no longer expect to ensure their children's futures through property inheritance or by establishing them in a craft or small business. But they may hope to give their children *cultural capital* in the form of the credentials and social graces of the educated.

Middle-class aspirations and values are founded on a belief in an open and competitive society. Probably no question has attracted as much attention in sociology as that of social mobility in Western countries. The research has relied heavily on the studies of occupational prestige discussed above and on the measurable socio-economic scales of occupations that have been built from them. Increasingly, the research has focused on a specific question in the larger mobility picture. Given that inheritance of property is now so limited and that educational credentials are thought to be so important, the research has asked how parents' statuses are translated into the statuses of sons and daughters. Specifically, it asks how family background and educational attainment are related to a person's occupational status and income (Goyder, 1984).

A major Canadian study conducted in 1973 compared Canadian and United States status attainment processes (Boyd et al., 1981; McRoberts, 1982). In the context of this discussion, the key finding of this study is that education is, indeed, the crucial link between generations in the transmission of occupational status. In contemporary Canada, most parents can do little to directly determine the careers of their children, but both the educational attainments of parents and their occupational status slightly influence their children's education. And, as almost everyone has come to believe, a person's educational attainment is his or her most important (measurable) characteristic when it comes to determining the status of a first job and of subsequent jobs. Whether the weight given to education results from the demand for application of skills on the job or from the use of credentials to screen job applicants cannot be determined from the research (McRoberts, 1982). Another important finding is that the occupational status of women is less closely tied to their family backgrounds and is affected more by educational credentials than is the status of men (Boyd et al., 1981: 662–63). Further, the study showed that status attainment processes are very similar in Canada and the United States (McRoberts and Selbee, 1981).

With respect to the historic growth of the middle-class in Canada and to current patterns of inequality, a particularly useful study is one based on a national survey in 1974. It examines occupational mobility over four generations (Goyder and Curtis, 1977). Table 15–9 shows the correlations between the occupational status scores of the survey respondent, his father, his grandfather and his eldest son (only males were surveyed and "main" occupations recorded; all sons over age 25 were included in these data).

## TABLE 15-9   Occupational Mobility: Four Generations, Canada

INTERCORRELATIONS OF OCCUPATIONAL STATUS SCORES AMONG GRANDFATHERS, FATHERS, RESPONDENTS, AND SONS

| GENERATION | G | F | R | S |
|---|---|---|---|---|
| Grandfather (G) | 1.00 | .49 | .22 | .05 |
| Father (F) | .50 | 1.00 | .38 | .13 |
| Respondent (R) | .27 | .33 | 1.00 | .26 |
| Sons (S) | .03 | .09 | .22 | 1.00 |

* Figures above the diagonal are for the total sample; those below the diagonal are for farmers excluded in each generation.

Goyder and Curtis, 1977: 308.

The correlations measure the degree of association between the socioeconomic scores assigned to occupational titles.

There is a quite rapidly decreasing influence (correlation) of the grandfathers' status on the occupational status (as measured on a socioeconomic scale) of each succeeding generation. As in the national study discussed above, the effect is modest even in the first generation, as the correlation of .49 between grandfathers and fathers indicates. (Statistically, this number can be translated as meaning that 25 percent of the occupational statuses of the fathers is predicted by a knowledge of the grandfathers' statuses.) In other words, the occupational status of a person's grandfather or great-grandfather is almost entirely irrelevant to that person's own job status. This indicates a very open or mobile society. On the other hand, these results are not entirely surprising, since the *structure* of occupations has altered so greatly over these generations.

## Structural Explanations of Social Mobility

Recently there has been much attention paid to the attempt to separate occupational mobility resulting from changes in the distribution of available jobs—called *structural* changes—from changes due to other factors. The task is very difficult, perhaps impossible (Hauser et al. 1975; Sobel, 1983). Studies that undertake the separation indicate that structural changes in the labour force account for a great deal of the individual mobility in Western societies. The study reported in Table 15–9 makes it clear that many of us had grandfathers who were farmers, but few of us have any chance to follow in their footsteps. This is intergenerational mobility due to structural change. There are, of course, many other structural changes. In studies of the United States, England and Wales and Canada, it is suggested that once the structural changes in the economies over time have been accounted for, no other changes in mobility patterns are detected (Hauser and Featherman, 1977: 15; McRoberts and Selbee, 1981). This is a particularly important argument. It means that the *relative* mobility of individuals starting from lower, middle or higher occupational origins has not changed with time, except for the changes resulting from shifts in the occupational structures themselves.[7]

In the present context, these results show again the difference between social structural changes and individual experiences. The transition from farmwork to blue-collar work to white-collar work in three generations tends to be culturally defined as significant upward mobility, given the widely accepted ranking of occupations. However, much of this observed mobility is a direct result of changing labour-force patterns, which are slightly modified by individual aspirations and achievements, job-search strategies, social contacts, employer preferences and other labour-market factors.

Since the early part of this century, and especially after World War II, many Canadians have experienced rising standards of living and the development of a consumer society. At the same time, they have experienced personal and family mobility, moving from rural to urban occupations and, particularly, from farm and manual work to white-collar jobs. These occupational changes have been accompanied by a general upgrading of educational credentials. A sociological understanding of these processes must recognize that individual experiences have been shaped by particular structural changes. The changes in the economy and the division of labour have powerfully moulded the mobility experience. Largely unchanged structures of income and educational inequality have been masked by the widespread sense of intergenerational material gain and personal achievement. It was C.W. Mills (1959) who some years ago insisted that the "sociological imagination" required

---

[7] Although occupational status attainment research finds that the most important individual characteristic influencing occupational status is educational attainment (years of schooling), it is important to recognize that even education has relatively weak effects. That is, there are enormous differences in occupational status and in income among people with the same educational credentials (Jencks et al., 1972). Here, too, one must separate structural effects from individual experience. The whole educational system has expanded over time. Everyone is getting more education. The structure of educational inequality, rather like that of income, remains largely unaltered, though individuals seek and attain additional credentials. Hence, the *relative* position of groups with different starting points is unchanged. Students with lower family income, say, have not much, if at all, improved their representation in higher education relative to those from middle- and higher-income groups (Pike, 1980: Richardson, 1977; Lennards, 1980).

an understanding, not just of personal experiences or of structures and their history, but of the connections between these two realities.

## UNFINISHED BUSINESS: THE TWO FACES OF CLASS EXPERIENCE

Make no mistake, what is described here as the emergence of middle-class patterns of income, consumption, life style and values also describes the growth of the modern working-class. This is not a contradiction. There are two faces to contemporary class experience—proletarianization and the rise of a middle-class life style and culture.

To reiterate, proletarianization is the historic process by which people have experienced increasing dependence on wages and salaries as a sole source of livelihood and loss of control of the means of production and of autonomy in the labour process. A provocative extension of this thesis focuses directly on the labour process (work and the workplace), arguing that, in this century, both manual and white-collar workers increasingly have been subject to supervision and to routinization of their work (Braverman, 1974; Rinehart, 1975). This thesis has not been taken up here, but it has generated an important literature (see Paul Thompson, 1984).

Other recent studies have tried to determine the boundaries between classes and class segments in contemporary Western societies, for example, between working-, middle- and capitalist classes and gradations of those classes. (Poulantzas, 1975; Wright, 1976). This Marxist work has already drawn a biting Weberian response (Parkin, 1979: Ch. 1–3). Again, these issues have not been pursued here, though this chapter argues that, in understanding contemporary Canadian society, it is fruitful to focus on the simultaneous experience of proletarianization and the rise of middle-class culture.

There are, of course, many different labour markets and many visible differences in wealth, education, income and life style among them. But there are also two unifying threads of experience: the dependence on wages and the salience of middle-class aspirations and values. It may be that the common experience of proletarianization is so fundamental that it has the potential to give rise to a modern, mass political movement (Westergaard and Resler, 1975: 401ff). However, it is also possible that the social divisions, relative affluence, individualism and emphasis on family security that are part of middle-class culture will effectively inhibit a working-class movement in the foreseeable future (Runciman, 1966; Parkin, 1974: Ch. 2 and 3; Mann, 1973).

Changes in working conditions and the rise of the modern labour movement in Canada have not been analysed in this chapter, but they are central topics of class analysis. They are addressed elsewhere in this text in reference to economic institutions and to social movements. But it is essential to recognize that the increases in real incomes and the extension of social services, from unemployment insurance to Medicare and pensions, are gains for wage and salary workers and are very much the result of their own political responses and of an active labour movement. They are political gains, that is, they did not come about as natural consequences of economic expansion, the growth of the state or of modernization (Roberts and

Bullen, 1984; Heron, 1984). Thus, central economic features of middle-class life in Canada can themselves be understood as responses to proletarianization.

## SUMMARY

Much research on class and stratification in Canada is recent and scattered, with few works attempting an integrated assessment. From the point of view of class analysis, proletarianization has received little attention, although it is a key to understanding the emergence of advanced, industrial capitalism in Canada. The process appears to have moved forward unevenly from the middle of the last century into the early years of this one and then quickened after 1920 and again after World War II. Whatever the timing of the transition or the crucial turning points, the last three decades or so have seen both an increasing concentration of capital and of wealth, and the growth of wage and salary dependence.

We have argued that the more obvious and immediate experiences of Canadians over the postwar period have been those of increased real incomes and consumption and occupational and educational mobility. These experiences have sustained the strong sense of Canada as a middle-class society and have underwritten the attachment to distinctive middle-class values (social order, the sanctity of property and rewards for individual effort and talent). We have concluded that economic gains and expanded mobility have mediated the processes of property concentration and proletarianization in Canada.

Social class and stratification theory have not been particularly adept at dealing with the concept and the reality of the middle-class. In Marxist theory, the issues have often been treated as distractions from the central concern with conflict between capitalists and the working-classes. Recent research has addressed the topic but has emphasized problems of categorization at the expense of analysis of historical processes (Wright, 1976). Weberian theory contains an implicit analysis of the middle-class in its focus on variations in market positions, life-chances and bureaucratic employment in contemporary societies. But Weber left the analysis unformulated, and it has been developed by very few (Mills, 1956; Parkin, 1979). Functionalists have taken the concept and the reality for granted.

In part this failure is accounted for by the complex and unstable nature of the middle-class as a social, political and cultural amalgam. Even its composition is in need of analysis. Arno Mayer (1975) argues that this social and cultural amalgam (the middle-class) has, in a sense, replaced the older petite bourgeoisie in contemporary Western societies, but we have yet to address adequately its historical implications as a social and political force. For Canada, as for other Western societies, the need for analysis of the middle-class is pressing, since some of the major structural changes lying behind the individual experiences that define the middle-class (economic gain and status attainment) have run their course, especially the historic transition from a rural, petit-bourgeois economy to an urban, industrial one.

# DISCUSSION QUESTIONS

1. The concepts of class and stratification refer to different social phenomena. What is the significance of the distinction?

2. Both Weberian and functionalist theory focus on occupational stratification. Discuss how one is concerned with power and the other with societal needs.

3. Why is the question of the size and character of the small-property-owning class (petite bourgeoisie) so important to understanding the emergence of the Canadian class system?

4. It has been claimed that the two central institutions of capitalism, private property and the labour market, generate deep inequalities in the ownership of productive property and in wealth. Why is this so? How might it be disputed?

5. Canada is often called a middle-class society. What does this mean? How can it be argued that most Canadians are both middle-class and proletarianized?

# 16

# Communities, Cities, and Urbanization

## *William Michelson*

# INTRODUCTION*

What questions do people typically have about communities, cities, and urbanization? It seems four kinds are commonly raised.

1. What are cities and how do they relate to the rest of society? Under what conditions did cities originate, and how did they differ from previous settlements? How have cities evolved over time? Why? To what degree and in what form have Canadian cities developed, and in what ways and for what reasons might this differ from urban development elsewhere? Can national urban development be controlled? The term *urbanization* addresses these and similar questions.

2. Are human experience and behaviour different in cities than in other settlements? If so, how and why? Under what conditions do urban life styles vary from city to city? The study of ways of life associated with cities is known as *urbanism*.

3. Analogous to anatomy, what are the characteristic parts of the city and their interrelationships? Are there regularities underlying growth and change? How segregated are population subgroups within cities? What forms does segregation take, and what are its implications? What do terms like *community* and *neighbourhood* mean? How do the large-scale physical and organizational structures we consciously and unconsciously build influence behaviour in cities? Are some groups more vulnerable than others to the ways we build and run our cities? Studying a city in terms of its subsectors is called taking an *ecological perspective*.

4. What decisions and policies must be made about cities? What do cities do? Does it matter which organizations carry out typical municipal functions? How does the general social structure relate to the structure and functioning of cities? Who controls what gets done within cities? What are urban and community planning, and how do planners relate to the other persons involved in urban decision-making? Where do ordinary citizens fit in? Looking at questions such as these involves a *structural analysis* of cities.

People's interests about cities run the gamut from their place in society to the interiors of dwelling units. They study such different topics as impacts of industrialization, avoidance behaviour among strangers, why suburban youth "hang-out" in shopping centres, and the rationales of metropolitan government. Understanding one concern does not automatically explain others. No single theory is sufficient to describe, explain, or solve all problems. Yet, applying a mixture of sociological perspectives helps us to understand and deal with many unique and challenging situations in urban life.

Let us therefore view communities, cities, and urbanization according to the four perspectives just sketched, keeping the common threads in mind as we proceed.

* I am grateful for comments and suggestions on an earlier draft to Ron Gillis, Jack Richardson, Lorne Tepperman, Alan Wain, and Barry Wellman and to Judy Kjellberg and The Centre for Urban & Community Studies, University of Toronto, for informational and logistical support.

# URBANIZATION

## THE FIRST CITIES

If the most elementary conception of the city is that it contains at least some nonagricultural workers, then its emergence at about 3500 B.C. truly represented "something new under the sun." And its impact on the rest of the society was immediate and direct. The rural sector had to grow a surplus of food to feed the urbanites. Thus, right from the start, urbanization affected whole societies. Creating stable and predictable agricultural surplus required simultaneous developments in technology and social structure, in geographic areas which could support intensive agriculture, e.g., Mesopotamia, The Indus Valley (Adams, 1966).

Important technological innovations included irrigation, bronze metallurgy for plowing and cutting instruments, animal husbandry for use in agriculture, stone mortars, selective cultivation of rich, nonperishable foods like grains and dates, wheeled carts and sailboats for transport and building bricks for permanent settlements.

Social structure evolved and the division of labour beyond age and sex became a legacy to ensuing cities and society. One aspect of the enhanced division of labour was vertical stratification—differential degrees of responsibility and power. Some individuals ensured that the farmers produced surpluses for the nonagricultural workers by providing technological support and controlling delivery. Another aspect was horizontal stratification—specialization at a given stratification level. Full-time soldiers, artists, and consumer goods producers appeared in the urban settlements, while farmers could eventually become even more specialized.

So even from the start, cities had heterogeneous populations with complex, usually coercive relationships with the rest of society. Although farmers did get products and the often dubious benefits of laws and law enforcement from city administrators, they relinquished some of their food under terms not under their control.

Although the relationship between urban and rural people may appear familiar from our own contemporary observations, there have been enormous changes over time in the balance between the two, reflecting developments in the two central elements of technology and social organization. For example, technology was at first barely adequate for the necessary food surplus. It took 50 to 90 farmers to produce enough surplus food for one urbanite. Now one farmer in a technologically developed country produces food for about nine urbanites.

In the first few thousand years of urban life, even the largest cities were very small. Imprecise archeological evidence suggests the largest were between 5000 and 30 000 in population. Their size was limited by how far a labour-intensive transportation technology could bring food, by how far coercion could be extended, and by the state of sanitation and public health.

## GROWTH OF CITIES

With refinements in technology and social structure, some ancient cities grew larger. Athens had about 150 000 residents in 500 B.C. Then Rome grew to between 250 000 and a million inhabitants. Despite such city-states, with dominance over vast tributary areas, the kind of urbanization which we know today took many centuries more to develop.

The static, locally controlled society which predominated through the medieval period was not conducive to the development of large cities. Urbanization became more active in Europe towards the fourteenth century, as areas of peace and civilization started to grow, enhancing international trade. While urban dwellers benefited from agricultural improvements, they became less dependent on rural nobility because of long-distance trade and the development of handicrafts. Trade fairs set up outside city gates, involving merchants and middlemen, turned into quasi-autonomous settlements—literally the first suburbs. These areas and hence the cities grew rapidly because this new economic sector spawned jobs for serfs. It was said that *stadtluft macht frei* (city air makes free); serfs were considered free men if they made it to the city and lived there successfully for a year.

## INDUSTRIALIZATION AND URBANIZATION

Even then, the development of industry, based on inanimate sources of energy, is commonly given credit for shifting the population balance from rural to urban—and for greatly increasing the size of cities. For example, about 200 years ago, only about 3 percent of the world's population lived in settlements of 5000 or more inhabitants, and a city about the size of the current Vancouver metropolitan area would have been the largest in the world.

Power industry reflected societal developments in technology and accentuated the division of labour. The same advances in science and engineering that made possible large-scale factories with machines also led to innovations in agricultural technology which enabled fewer farm workers to grow food more intensively and on larger holdings. In technologically-advanced societies, a surplus of agricultural labour thus became available for newly emerging, specialized city jobs.

Because industrial jobs were so specialized and time-consuming, other specialists had to supply what others needed for living. Specialists built housing, supplied food, provided transportation, and enforced social and political order. Furthermore, factories called for complementary specialties: equipment-makers, wholesalers, transport specialists, and financial services. Thus, the industrial revolution was a wide-ranging urban revolution.

Technically, observers think of urbanization as the percentage of a nation's population living in settlements of a certain minimum size, usually 5000 and over. With industrialization, advanced nations have swung from urbanization levels of only a few percent to beyond 75 percent. The United States had only 6 percent of its population in such urban settlements in 1800, despite the well-known port cities of Boston, New York, Philadelphia and Charleston. By 1850, this reached 15 percent, expanding to 40 percent by 1900, 64 percent by 1950, and 74 percent by 1980 (Palen, 1981, 60).

At Confederation, Canada had an urbanization level just below 20 percent, and Canada's urbanization rate has also expanded surely over the years, to a 1981 level of 75 percent (Kennedy, 1983, 34-35).

Canada and the United States belong to a club of industrial nations with reasonably similar, high rates of urbanization. Recent figures show Belgium at the top with 87.1 percent urbanization and Australia next at 86 percent. Canada lies near the

United Kingdom at 77.9 percent, The Netherlands at 77.7 percent, Japan at 75.9 percent, and France at 73 percent (Statistics Canada, 1984).

Most Eastern European socialist countries lie further back, if only because the industrialization they have undergone has not involved the degree of consumer goods and services typical of capitalist industrialization, with a correspondingly smaller migration to cities. A lower level of agricultural mechanization has occupied nonmigrants in rural areas. Thus, even though the Soviet Union has a number of large cities, its urbanization level is only 58 percent (Statistics Canada, 1984).

Countries with relatively low levels of industrialization show similarly low levels of urbanization, just as Canada did at an earlier time. India and China, despite the presence of some of the world's largest cities, have urbanization levels of 20.1 and 13.2 percent respectively (Statistics Canada, 1984).

Furthermore, the urban population in highly urbanized societies is distributed more liberally around a number of reasonably sized settlements rather than concentrated in just the one obviously large metropolis in a nation or region. In the lesser-developed nations, most of the extremely large cities were centres from which foreign imperial powers exported the nation's or region's raw materials for industrial production back home. Bombay, Calcutta and Shanghai, for example, are gigantic centres on major waterways. They grew to such size as obvious destinations for the rural poor, despite the virtual absence of an industrial economic base there or in the countries at large. Urban populations in such situations are typically underemployed, poor and predominantly male. When more persons reside in a city than would be expected from its economic base, it is called *overurbanization*.

Figure 16-1 shows the majority of people in every Canadian province and territory except Prince Edward Island and the Northwest Territories are urban. High levels of urbanization are hardly confined to Ontario and Quebec and their predominent cities. In both American and Canadian urbanization, economic factors pull people to cities rather than just to push them away from rural areas, and women typically outnumber men.

Before industrialization, Canadian cities were established much like those in today's developing countries—as seaports, trading posts or places to collect resources like furs. Their sites were crucial to their establishment—for access and defence. Later on, once domestic production became a growing reality, a settlement's situation became more central to its vitality. Toronto and Hamilton emerged as financial and industrial centres on this basis with respect to markets, Winnipeg and Thunder Bay as strategically located links in national transportation systems, and Edmonton and Calgary regarding their proximity to petrochemical resources.

Canada thus represents a society whose general technological development has permeated both urban and rural settings (Clark, 1978), promoted a shift of the population to urban settings and influenced the stability of life within cities. Optimists feel that nations which are not yet as technically advanced could, eventually, emulate the nature and pattern of Western urbanization. Unfortunately, it is not clear that countries lacking a historical experience of reaping and reinvesting locally the profits of their resources and products can reach equality in these terms with those already in the highly industrialized category, if all remain in competition with each other. (Frank, 1970).

Figure 16-1  Urban and Rural Living, Canada and the Provinces, 1981

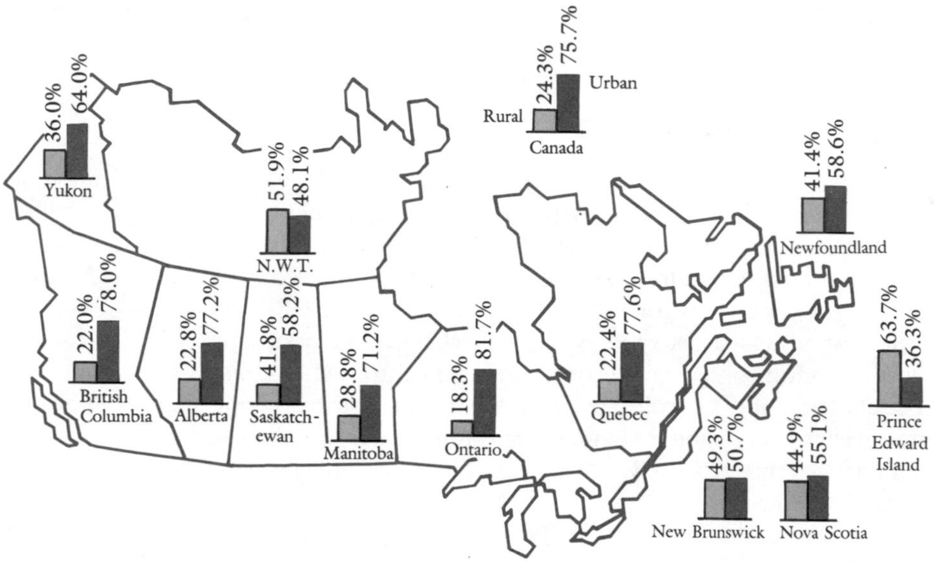

Statistics Canada, *Canada Update*, Vol. 2, No. 4. Reproduced by permission of the Minister of Supply and Services Canada.

## NATIONAL URBAN GROWTH POLICIES

Nations have only recently begun deliberate national urban growth policies. Brazil, Australia and Turkey situated their capitals in Brazilia, Canberra and Ankara to spread urban activity beyond the geographic constraints of existing coastal metropolitan giants. France and Hungary are encouraging industrialization and growth in urban sites apart from the one great star of each country, Paris and Budapest. The Soviet Union has built highly planned new industrial cities in the Caucasus and Siberia, so as to put manufacturing closer to power and raw materials and to avoid undue strains on its already large Western cities. Sweden has created a regionally based network of medium-sized cities, each containing the infrastructure vital to stability and health, going so far as to decentralize the public service away from Stockholm. England has for years had a new town policy that channels population away from the traditionally large cities and into smaller, relatively self-contained, planned cities. The record of success in such conscious efforts to alter urbanization patterns is mixed, since the financial commitments of the participating governments are unequal, as are the national and international economic phenomena which they must confront (Rodwin, 1970; Bourne, 1975).

## URBANISM

Does the way of life associated with urban residence differ systematically from rural living—all else equal?

Although all else is never equal, the question is: Are there crucial aspects of the urban context which explain how behaviour varies from one part of society to another? Max Weber called such tendencies *ideal types*, patterns which set a model for behaviour but which are practically never found unmitigated by other influences on behaviour. Are there *ideal types* of urban life style?

## CLASSICAL APPROACHES

Many analysts have thought so. Weber himself linked the emergence of a middle-class devoted to mercantile activities in the European cities to the development there of bureaucracies. Both cast behaviour into firmly defined roles, with rationality as their most notable feature. In his opinion, exactness and rationally calculated activity became the ideal types for urban behaviour (Weber, 1958).

Sjoberg reviewed historical evidence on changes in city structure which came with industrialization and reached conclusions similar to Weber's. Sjoberg found that job specialization and the complexity of production and marketing that accompanied industrialization required standardization in measures, weights, currencies, pricing and financial interaction. Rational, exact actions became necessary for the system to work (Sjoberg, 1960).

Nonetheless, the best known ideas on urbanism were written by Louis Wirth in "Urbanism as a Way of Life" (1938). Wirth thought that cities had three defining characteristics: large numbers of inhabitants, high densities and heterogeneous populations. Each was felt to account for important aspects of an urban way of life.

Large numbers, for example, lead to the impossibility of knowing all persons, and hence to the relative absence of intimacy in most interpersonal relationships. Human relations become segmented into many largely anonymous, superficial and transitory contacts.

Wirth felt that high density fosters human diversification and specialization to fulfill various human needs within local areas. Due to the inescapable presence of close physical contact with diverse persons, social distance is established to maintain personal space. Nonetheless, accentuated friction inevitably arises, and formal means of social control (e.g., uniformed police) assume prominence in cities. Even with, or perhaps because of, such close proximity, complex patterns of segregation take shape.

Finally, Wirth felt that heterogeneity made it difficult for individuals to be constricted as in rural areas by rigid social structures. Urban individuals more often find themselves in varied social settings and groups. Both upward and downward mobility, with the resultant greater feelings of instability and insecurity, are more likely in cities.

Other early twentieth century observers made parallel assessments. Simmel, for example, found that German urbanites had to continually pay attention to contextual signals: lights, signs, footsteps, whistles and the like. The head rather than the heart dictated behaviours, according to principles of rationality, impersonality, exactness and distrust of others, with a blasé attitude resulting (Simmel, 1950). Plant (1957) discovered psychiatric processes in the inner cities of America, whereby people adapted to unacceptable happenings they could not avoid noticing (fights, muggings, robberies). While people became hardened to such phenomena, they typically also felt insecure, inferior and non-self-sufficient. Illusions die and mental strain sets in.

Although this classic approach to urbanism never achieved a consensus (Dewey, 1960), its legacy was sobering; any societal gains coming from greater division of labour, rationality, large scale and personal freedom seemed counterbalanced by unending suspicion, distrust and isolation.

## MODERN SOCIAL-PSYCHOLOGICAL APPROACHES

Social psychologists have recently taken up these themes with experimental work in American cities. Milgram, for example, developed Simmel's notion of external signals and, using modern systems analysis, put it in the perspective of sensory overload. In his words, "City life, as we experience it, constitutes a continuous set of encounters with overload, and of resultant adaptations" (Milgram, 1970).

One general adaptive strategy is: "Minimize involvement. . . . Maximize social order" (Karp, Stone, and Yoels, 1977: 110). Such guidance applies to overload in several ways.

First, urbanites (at least where observed in the United States) tune out what they find overburdening: drunks, poverty, negative consequences of public or private sector policies or practices which benefit some.

Urbanites avoid aiding strangers who need help so as to avoid trouble themselves. Much research followed public shock when a woman named Kitty Genovese was murdered after appealing for help in front of at least 38 neighbours in a New York City apartment house. This research suggested that the more people are there, the less likely any individual will intervene.

People minimize involvement by removing themselves from easy contact with others. They buy telephone answering devices, fail to list their telephone numbers, filter visitors through secretaries and assistants, travel by private automobile and live in segregated (increasingly guarded) neighbourhoods.

We practise various procedures in public places. We pretend not to see each other (e.g., on beaches) and we tolerate other life styles except where these represent clear and present dangers. We follow unspoken but definite rules about how distant we keep from others for particular purposes, where we sit (e.g., on busses or in libraries) and the way we walk (Hall, 1966; Sommer, 1969).

Similar adaptations facilitate anonymity. Clothing in general and uniforms in particular provide a basis for secure interaction without previous personal acquaintance. Addresses are now thought to provide the same kind of identification. Not only do clothes make the man, but streets and neighbourhoods help complete the introduction.

Some urban settings are heavily patronized because they let people maximize interaction without the usual standards of social order. Thus, bars, sporting events and rock concerts allow activities by their paying customers which many find therapeutic.

## THE DYNAMICS OF URBANISM

Familiar as these situations are, they do not define where urbanism is and is not found. Wirth, for example, put forward the city in ideal-typical form but left other forms of settlement to the imagination. In highly urbanized societies, where is the line drawn?

*Clothing provides a basis for secure interaction without previous personal acquaintance. Addresses also provide identification. Clothes make the man, and streets and neighbourhoods complete the introduction.* Courtesy Costain Limited.

Redfield, an anthropologist, suggested (from work in a less-developed culture) that there is less a line than an urban-rural continuum (1947). In his view, the more remote a settlement is from large-scale centres of production and innovation, the more it shades off into a different way of life. Studies closer to home, however, reveal that the anonymous, segmented and impersonal relations noted by Wirth may reflect people's occupations rather than their precise setting, thus questioning the idea of either an urban-rural dichotomy or continuum. Reiss, for example, found that men living in rural areas but who had nonfarming jobs had much the same daily contact patterns as their urban counterparts (1959).

Questions are therefore raised about the dynamics of behaviour. Is it really determined in some way by cities as the classical observers suggest? If Wirth and his colleagues constitute a *deterministic* school of thought, others employ a *compositional* approach (Fischer, 1976), reflecting the composition of the population. Gans, for example, explained suburban behaviour not in terms of the physical nature of the area but in terms of the social class background and life-cycle characteristics of the population in the suburb he studied (Gans, 1967). The nature and extent of their contact with neighbours, their participation in organizations and their interest in schools reflected middle-class background and families with young children.

Thus, according to the compositional approach, urban life reflects the most salient features of the particular population groups living in cities: by class, ethnic background or race, religion, age or sex.

In his book, *The Urban Experience*, Claude Fischer attempts to reconcile deterministic and compositional perspectives and to go beyond them (1976). Fischer argues that Wirth is right in stressing the significance of large numbers of persons in cities. But rather than the numbers providing various *direct* effects, Fischer sees them as most important in providing the nucleus for various specialized subcultures within cities. It is then the particular composition of the subcultures which influences the so-called urban life styles.

Fischer calls his approach the *subcultural theory of urban life. Which* subcultures become major in any city reflects many macroscopic characteristics of cities—their economic base, sources of migration, climate and more. Within highly urbanized societies, cities of different size and in different locations may be functionally specialized. This does not mean that they are monolithic in their activities or resident populations; but there are distinct tendencies regarding who chooses to live and work there and hence which subcultures take root. It is unusual for even a city specializing in industry to have more than 25 percent of its jobs in manufacturing due to the need for complementary and supportive activities; yet the difference between 25 percent in manufacturing and 10 percent spells a big difference in the critical mass of a blue-collar subculture. Ways of life in Hamilton, with its huge steel mills, are in many ways different than in nearby London, an insurance and financial centre, not to speak of Victoria and its combination of government, weather, retirement and afternoon tea!

The largest national cities, however, are usually diverse economically, with their population size supporting varied subcultures and life styles. It takes a Toronto, not a Truro, to supply the critical masses to support the kind of ethnic centres pictured on page 410—indeed only several blocks apart—as well as major cultural, youth, yuppy, gay, sports, criminal and endless other subcultures side by side.

Does subcultural theory invalidate the kind of generalizations urban social psychologists have been making about problems like overload, anonymity and adaptations made in response? Not really.

A more recent book by Fischer (1982) shows that the personal contact patterns of urbanites are more firmly concentrated in specialized groupings (which in cities means subcultures) than are those of people living in smaller settlements and rural areas. Similarly, big-city dwellers are likely to trust their closest neighbours, but not urbanites in general. While Fischer found that urbanites do not lack contact, however channelled the nature of interpersonal relations, he also confirmed what observers from Wirth on have been suggesting: that individuals and subgroups within large urban areas do not have contact with large numbers and varieties of other persons and groups. Selective interaction and avoidance behaviours are two sides of the same coin—called urbanism.

We have thus seen so far that urban behaviour patterns reflect subcultural cleavages. One would therefore suspect that the physical structure of cities will reflect and reinforce such patterns. Examining the city in ecological terms strongly supports such suspicions.

*Hong Kong? Lisbon? Subcultures flourish in Toronto.*

# ECOLOGICAL STRUCTURE

Looking at communities, cities, and urbanization from an *ecological perspective* turns our attention first to the pattern of urban populations and then to the qualitative nature of the parts within this pattern.

## CITIES, SUBURBS AND METROPOLITAN AREAS

While Canadian urbanization levels show that we live predominantly in cities, this does not tell us in what kind of settlements or where within them we live. Do most Canadians live in large or small cities, in central cities or suburbs?

A common pattern in technologically advanced societies has been the build-up of population beyond the borders of older cities and into newer municipalities immediately adjacent. These are commonly called suburbs, although the word is often applied to areas which simply look newer and less crowded than the centres of the traditional cities; Montreal, for example, has many suburbs, while much of Calgary and Edmonton appears suburban.

Large cities and their suburbs may represent different municipalities, but, in terms of everyday behaviour and economic activity, they form an entity. This entity is called a *metropolitan area*. People commonly live in one part of a metropolitan area and work in another; the interchange between, for example, New Westminster and Vancouver is active.

Statistics Canada defines a Census Metropolitan Area (CMA) as an area with at least 100 000 inhabitants, including one or more large cities at the centre and any other adjacent municipalities having at least 40 percent of their employed residents working in the centre cities or 25 percent of their own labour force commuting from the centre city(ies) (Statistics Canada, 1983: vi). Based on these criteria, some CMAs include a centre city and many municipalities extending a considerable distance from the urban core, while others involve only a single municipality. This reflects not only the size of the urban area but its history and the extent of land suitable for expansion under the control of the centre city. Toronto, for example, extends as a functional entity almost to Hamilton (i.e., through Oakville), while Saskatoon not only includes all the residents in its vicinity but controls undeveloped land for future development.

The term *megalopolis* refers to chains of metropolitan areas which follow major lines of transportation or other stimuli to continuous growth. Megalopolis was first used to describe the succession of metropolitan areas between, roughly, Boston and Washington, along the eastern seaboard of the United States (Gottmann, 1961). It has been projected to other locations, such as the Pittsburgh to Milwaukee industrial belt and Los Angeles to San Diego. While such megalopolises are monumental and interesting in their planning implications, they represent only one part of urban and metropolitan life in the United States. The Canadian equivalent, the so-called Golden Horseshoe from Oshawa to St. Catharines/Niagara in Ontario, is also only one distinct segment on the Canadian urban scene. British scholars use the term *conurbation* to refer to continuous intensive urban land-uses blending together many large cities in England's industrial Midlands.

Whether they live in small or large municipalities, most urban Canadians live in a CMA. Of the 75.5 percent living in cities, 74.3 percent live in a CMA (Statistics Canada, 1983). American figures are similar. While recent census figures in both nations suggest a minor movement from metropolitan to rural areas, most such moves appear to be to areas on the fringe of the major metropolitan areas, in effect extending them further. Canada is thus not only a highly urbanized nation but a highly metropolitan one.

The image many people have of the city is that of an older municipality with high density and buildings which are large and striking or old and grey. The suburbs are somehow something else. This view needs revision. Most residents of Canadian and American metropolitan areas are suburbanites, not even counting the great numbers of persons in the newer cities largely in the western regions of both countries who live in typically suburban conditions. Table 16-1 shows Canada's CMAs by size, indicating the breakdown of the population by residence in either central city or suburban municipality. The over all suburban proportion of 52 percent reflects heavily but not exclusively the largest and oldest of the CMAs. This distribution is essential to understanding the pattern of local areas and life styles in metropolitan areas. Whereas people previously focused on the central city and then spoke in stereotyped terms about the suburbs and suburbanites, now it is essential to recognize that a major share of the population lives outside central cities.

How, then, are people and their subcultures patterned within metropolitan areas?

## INTRAMETROPOLITAN POPULATION AND LAND-USE PATTERNS

An initial land-use and stratification pattern was portrayed by Burgess from studies of Chicago—*concentric rings* (1925). The key dynamic in this scheme was the central business district (CBD), consisting of the major private and public sector offices, department stores and hotels, serviced by public transit to make it the single most accessible place in town. It was assumed that the central business district would be the only major centre in the city and that it would continue to grow indefinitely.

Because of CBD growth, the land around it would be held speculatively, for future profit. Before upgrading, these areas, called *zones in transition*, would be used, without maintenance or improvement, for rooming houses, transient hotels and other impermanent, out-of-the-way uses. The zone in transition would contain the poorest, newest migrants, criminal elements, prostitution and other vices—subcultures requiring short-term, affordable housing and, in many cases, anonymity. The more regularized sectors of the population would be distributed in rings around both the CBD and the zone in transition in proportion to their ability to pay for greater amounts of land increasingly far from these two areas and for the cost and time involved in more lengthy commutes. Working-class communities would be surrounded first by the middle-class and then the upper-class. Hence, major land-uses would claim, through market-mechanism competition, the very centre, and residential areas would be distributed at distances from there according to income.

Within a ring, local communities which were homogeneous by ethnic or religious background would form within major street, railway, park or other boundaries. These communities were called *natural areas* because no people rationally planned

TABLE 16-1 Distribution of Canadian Census Metropolitan Areas by Main City and Suburban Population (1981)

| CENSUS METROPOLITAN AREA | TOTAL POPULATION | % IN MAIN CITY(IES) | % IN SUBURBS |
|---|---|---|---|
| 1. Toronto | 2 998 947 | 20% | 80% |
| 2. Montreal | 2 828 349 | 35 | 65 |
| 3. Vancouver | 1 268 183 | 33 | 67 |
| 4. Ottawa-Hull | 717 978 | 49 | 51 |
| 5. Edmonton | 657 057 | 81 | 19 |
| 6. Calgary | 592 743 | 100 | 0 |
| 7. Quebec (City) | 576 075 | 29 | 71 |
| 8. Winnipeg | 554 842 | 97 | 3 |
| 9. Hamilton | 542 095 | 56 | 44 |
| 10. St. Catharines/Niagara | 304 353 | 64 | 36 |
| 11. Kitchener | 287 801 | 66 | 34 |
| 12. London | 283 668 | 90 | 10 |
| 13. Halifax | 277 727 | 41 | 59 |
| 14. Windsor | 246 110 | 54 | 46 |
| 15. Victoria | 233 481 | 28 | 72 |
| 16. Regina | 164 313 | 99 | 1 |
| 17. St. John's | 154 820 | 54 | 46 |
| 18. Oshawa | 154 217 | 76 | 24 |
| 19. Saskatoon | 154 210 | 100 | 0 |
| 20. Sudbury | 149 923 | 61 | 39 |
| 21. Chicoutimi-Jonquiere | 135 172 | 89 | 11 |
| 22. Thunder Bay | 121 379 | 93 | 7 |
| 23. St. John | 114 048 | 71 | 29 |
| 24. Trois-Rivieres | 111 453 | 45 | 55 |

Adapted from Statistics Canada, *1981 Census of Canada, Census Metropolitan Areas with Components*, Vol. 3 (Profile Series B), 1983. Reproduced by permission of the Minister of Supply and Services Canada.

their location. They were simply a function of land value (thought beyond the control of individuals) and incidental boundaries. Forms of behaviour thought to arise because birds of a feather flocked together were called *community* (Park, 1925).

Unfortunately, the concentric ring pattern was more imageable than universal. It has been demonstrated in few places outside Chicago. Indeed, in many settings outside the United States, the rich occupy the city centres while the poor are left outside the benefits of urban infrastructure. Ironically, it was right in Chicago that a researcher named Hoyt (1939) discovered a rather differnt pattern: *sectors*. These resembled pieces of a pie, extending from the centre outwards without interruption. Hoyt noted that certain amenities and eyesores extend outward, like waterfront parks and freight railroads. People of means try to live within view of the amenities, while those without follow the tracks. Others locate in between. One side of town becomes better than another, if only because it would be upwind from centrally located industries.

A third view is that the location of each land-use or subculture has unique criteria, in terms of location and proximity to other land-uses. Heavy industry wants to be near railroads and highways but doesn't need to be as accessible to consumers as retailing land-uses. Head offices draw fine restaurants, banks and law offices to their vicinity, while universities attract fast-food chains and bookstores. What emerges under this view are cities with many diverse centres whose locations are not in a fixed geometric pattern. This was called the *multiple nuclei theory* (Harris and Ullman, 1945).

A statistical procedure called *social area analysis*, based on many American cities, found that the main dimensions along which local residential areas differ within cities are social rank, size of family and ethnic and racial characteristics (Shevky and Bell, 1955). Another procedure called *factorial ecology* enables the analysis of census statistics based on local areas in a given city to determine the kind of pattern such dimensions are found in there. For example, Murdie's pioneering analysis of Metro Toronto concluded that family size increased with distance from the centre, that social class segregation was in sectors from the centre outwards and that ethnic groups lived in unique clusters, multiple nuclei (Murdie, 1969).

A more systematic analysis of eleven Canadian cities indicated the importance of the same differentiating dimensions as in American cities, as well as the same spatial patterns as in Toronto. Nonetheless, there were variations. In eastern Canada, low social rank and ethnic segregation were more closely associated than in the West (Schwirian and Matre, 1974).

Does this mean everybody lives in a tightly knit neighbourhood with people similar in social class, family size and ethnicity? Not really. But the concepts of neighbourhood and community help clarify the situation.

## NEIGHBOURHOOD AND COMMUNITY

*Neighbourhood* refers to a specific physical area within a city. It may have formal boundaries, though people may have an image of it even without any consensus on its exact territory. *Community* refers to tangible interpersonal contact patterns; it has primarily social connotations.

The traditional idea is that they are synonymous. In the old days, or in small towns, people centred their interpersonal relationships within the physical areas where they lived. The deterministic view of urbanism said this kind of community was lost in the city. Later on, however, researchers found extremely strong ethnic subcultures in cities which appeared to re-establish the identity between community and neighbourhood (Gans, 1962); community was said to be regained (Wellman and Leighton, 1979). More penetrating analyses of people's interpersonal networks went on to show that many people in cities have specific types of contact patterns, often reflecting subcultures but without reference to the boundaries of neighbourhoods (Wellman, 1979; Wellman, Carrington and Hall, 1986). Their close associates may be all over the map yet reached easily by telephone or computer or met at work, bars, parties or conventions. This has been called *community without propinquity*

(Webber, 1963) or community liberated or unbound (Wellman and Leighton, 1979).

Thus, urban neighbourhoods take various forms, starting from the ideal type, where everybody interacts with everyone else (Hallman, 1984; Wireman, 1984). Researchers have shown that the most salient physical area for face-to-face relationships is the so-called *face block*, two sides of the same street. There, territory and contact are reinforced by people seeing each other and by the impact the behaviours of each have on the others (Michelson, 1970: Ch. 8).

The so-called *defended neighbourhood* emerges when people in an area feel besieged by the actions of people in surrounding areas or by, for example, city hall, resulting in newly found local identity (Suttles, 1968).

A *conscious neighbourhood* is something which developers and designers work to achieve in newly built areas. They try to construct unifying symbols, so that residents will treat the area well and interact with each other. Clarence Perry created the *neighbourhood unit plan* in 1927 (1966). It was an area of about 400 homes, surrounded by traffic arteries but with only local roads inside, focusing on an elementary school and communal facilities. Though this plan has been shown ineffective in its most grandiose social engineering objectives (because people often have greater interpersonal loyalties elsewhere), it has been highly influential in suburban development. The picture below shows the use of artifacts and a local area name to create a conscious neighbourhood in Irvine, California—a planned new city.

However, the most common urban neighbourhoods represent what has been called the *community of limited liability* (Janowitz, 1952). People recognize that they

*Uniform housing styles, fencing and subarea names combine to create conscious neighbourhoods in the newly planned city of Irvine, California.*

live in a specific area, which has identifiable institutions. Yet, it is the limit to neither their contact patterns nor their everyday activities.

Regardless of the type of relationship people have with a physical neighbourhood, the terms *neighbour* and *neighbouring* take on relatively independent meanings. Neighbours are still the relatively limited set of persons living on the immediate face block or across a backyard, though some people extend this outward a bit and others, for example in large apartment buildings, contract the range. Neighbouring is a limited set of behaviours, normally centring on borrowing and lending needed ingredients or tools and maintaining friendly relationships at all cost (Keller, 1968).

Community, now liberated from neighbourhood, takes several forms, one of which, of course, is in common territory. A second is with respect to actual inter-action. A third is with respect to personal identification or attachment. Combinations of these may be made.

For example, the intense local subculture may involve territory, attachment and interaction, while a posh commercial area may represent a community involving territory and attachment but not interaction. Both a zone in transition and a faceless suburb may represent a territory but neither attachment nor interaction; however, an alumni or professional association may include attachment and interaction but not territory. Canadians making acquaintance abroad may jump at interaction but have neither real attachment or territory in mind; members of fan clubs share tre-mendous attachment but neither territory nor interaction. Clearly, the communities of most urbanites are neither singular nor unidimensional.

Even if we restrict ourselves to tangible neighbourhoods found in our cities, there are many which are of sociological interest. Let us examine a few to see some of the qualitative differences among parts of the urban pattern.

## SOME SELECTED URBAN NEIGHBOURHOODS

Within the inner cities, planners have noted the crucial differences between actual slums and low-income ethnic subcultural neighbourhoods. The former, typified by the *skid row* (or skid road) is what Burgess had in mind with his zone in transition. People go there to avoid contact, ostensibly, but not always, for short periods of time. Intense personal networks are not common, and there is little or no proprietary interest in buildings or neighbourhood areas apart from their pragmatic function in the short run. Skid rows contrast greatly in their interpersonal communities with other areas that may also have older buildings, poor maintenance and poorer people but where there are well-established kinship and neighbourhood relationships. Gans (1962) and Whyte (1943) have written extremely detailed accounts of the high degree of organization with two Italian-American communities in central Boston. The latter neighbourhoods have been called *urban villages* (by Gans), a term fitting many neighbourhoods with ethnic communities in Canadian cities—e.g., Italian (Sidlofsky, 1969), Jewish (Shaffir, 1974) and Portuguese (Anderson, 1974).

A recent phenomenon is *gentrification*, whereby usually upper-middle class profes-sionals move into and transform formerly working-class areas of the central city (Rosenthal, 1980). Gentrification occurs less frequently in new cities, and its extent is highly variable. Yet it is well developed in Canada, the United States, Britain and other nations. It normally occurs in cities with centralized white-collar and professional jobs, where the suburbs are extending further and further out and where the housing stock in one or more close-in areas is fundamentally sound and with aesthetic potential. At first, on an individual and piecemeal basis, wealthier people purchase, restore and modernize the buildings for personal use or for sale at enormous markups.

As more upper-middle-class persons move in, the neighbourhood changes. Neighbourhood stores, for example, shift to the tastes of well-heeled adults: trendy restaurants, health food stores, art galleries and more. An area in Toronto known for years as Cabbagetown has, with gentrification, assumed the name Don Vale.

City fathers laud gentrification because it improves the condition of neighbourhoods, the tax values of property and the commercial potential of the residents. But they commonly ignore what happens to the former residents, who must commonly make do in more remote areas of their city, where access to most opportunities and necessities is less available. What former owners receive for selling to the gentrifiers does not go far in newer areas of the city, but their situation is still better than that of displaced tenants facing few or no comparable housing opportunities elsewhere.

Residence in suburbs has led to a diversity of area types and influences on behaviour.

The suburban stereotypes came from studies of middle- and upper-middle-class areas. A highly descriptive account of the Forest Hill community in Toronto (Seeley, Sim and Loosley, 1956), for example, was felt to identify traits common to many areas throughout North American metropolitan areas. The authors stressed an emphasis there on providing resources and opportunities for children to advance in business and the professions. Support for schools and recreational facilities is paramount, including the hiring of experts. Housing is less a place for the family to be together than to find privacy, to deposit goods and to show off taste and affluence. New suburbs like these have been called *packaged suburbs* (Clark, 1966).

Yet, other segments of the population seek suburban residence simply for decent, available housing. Many blue-collar families seek affordable housing away from what they regard as disreputable elements in the central city. These so-called *pure suburbs* (Clark, 1966) produce understandably different life styles than do packaged suburbs (Berger, 1960).

Still others move even farther out from the centres than the general range of everyday commuting. The poor seek cheap housing without the physical and social problems of the inner city—*cottage suburbs* (Clark, 1966), jeopardizing their employment and income by living in such remote locations.

Writers and artists have also established settlements in *exurbia* (Spectorsky, 1965). Because exurbanites are by background and training urban people, such remote locations create ongoing dilemmas and extra costs (e.g., for transportation, entertainment and apartments in the city). Indeed, exurban colonies with romantic notions often conflict with the economic interests of long-term residents. This was well described in a study of Elora, Ontario (Sinclair and Westhues, 1974). Moreover, the new residents of a similar area recently passed a by-law preventing farmers from plowing after 9 p.m., so as to safeguard rural tranquility!

Third World nations, whose large cities typically receive in-migrants fleeing rural poverty, add another suburban variation, the *shantytown* (also known as the *favala*, bidonville and more). It is built in extremely short order (usually overnight) with a miscellany of salvaged materials (and little or no infrastructure) on found land in poorly accessible areas outside the actual cities. It is an illegal first foothold, giving residents some access to the city, without the requirements of money, jobs or legitimacy. Planners and other "respectable people" despair of these communities, but development agencies have learned that their most responsible avenue is to try to help install basic aspects of infrastructure such as sewage, water and electricity there. As the economic situation of the population starts to regularize, so, too, does the quality of life in shantytowns: mobility to the city becomes a possibility (Payne, 1977; Lloyd, 1979).

While our view of selected types of subareas within metropolitan areas is extremely partial, it becomes evident that the huge variety of factors accounting for area differentiation goes far beyond the assumption of central business district growth which was advanced to explain natural areas. Many kinds of rational human intervention establish and change local areas, well beyond the invisible hand of land economics. Developers cultivate new neighbourhood images, and real estate agents help reinforce or change the composition of older ones. Banks and insurance companies can influence who enters, leaves and stays in neighbourhoods by their lending and insuring policies. Planning and zoning activities can influence stability and change, while ratepayers' associations, tenants groups and trade organizations can influence planning and zoning bodies.

The parts of our urban pattern are indeed many and complex, as are the forces influencing them. Nonetheless, the social composition of subareas of cities is not the only influence on human behaviour within urban areas. The built environment and the organization of its infrastructure are also important factors.

## BUILT ENVIRONMENTS AND BEHAVIOUR

It is important to note not only which birds flock together, how exclusively and in what pattern, but also the physical parameters of where this occurs. The behaviours flowing from one or more salient characteristics which a person or family may share with neighbours or contacts are extremely diverse, reflecting similarities and priorities involved, for example, life cycle, social rank and ethnicity. In many instances, the way buildings, neighbourhoods and cities are designed and planned facilitates or constrains behaviours (Michelson, 1970).

### Housing
*Housing* is a natural focus for analysis in this regard. Families of different age, composition, size and ethnic background choose or are forced to live in homes of varying size, tenure, density, layout and amenity. Does it matter who lives where, well beyond status and identity connotations?

Enormous amounts of research on families, children, the elderly, women, the handicapped, particular ethnic groups and cultures and modern singles—just for a start—confirm that housing is hardly a matter of indifference. A study of married couples living in high rise apartments and single family homes in both downtown and suburban areas of Metro Toronto indicated that their behaviour differed because of the respective opportunities of their housing (Michelson, 1977).

*Residential mobility* is a highly important factor in people's satisfaction with their housing. It lets them change their residential environments as their wants evolve. Far more people move than can be accounted for by such nonbehavioural factors as cost, landlord actions, size of unit and objectively poor housing conditions.

Intriguing research has suggested that enlightened designs of residential buildings and grounds can mitigate against crimes such as vandalism and muggings that occur where perpetrators believe they can get away with them (Jeffrey, 1971; Newman, 1972). For example, apartment houses that have stairways that are out of public view provide opportunities for muggings; those providing glass walls to their stairways take away the intruder's protection. Long, anonymous hallways make it possible for strangers to lurk unchallenged; not so, small apartment groupings, where residents are more likely to know each other and their respective guests. Well-lit, open lobbies situated in view of many apartments are less of a target than those out of sight.

## Other Institutions

Other institutions besides housing are illuminated by analysing the fit between behaviour and environment. It takes no stretch of the imagination to consider what difference the amount and design of space in schools, hospitals, offices and factories makes to the people there (Porteous, 1977; Rapoport, 1977).

## Neighbourhood Design

On a somewhat greater scale, neighbourhoods have been shown to be of considerable salience to housewives, children and others whose daily routines or resources restrict them to the areas where they live. Consider children. The scope of their world starts with a crib or room and expands slowly; only with teen age does it expand beyond their neighbourhoods (and even then only by the grace of adults in the absence of good public transportation). Thus, proximity to safe, age-appropriate play facilities is important. As children grow older, they seek more specialized, adult-like leisure settings farther from home. Neighbourhoods and urban areas are remiss in recognizing the growing sophistication of teens, just as the developmental differences among younger children—e.g., a physiological inability to react to traffic hazards like adults among children less than about 12 (Sandels, 1964)—are not taken fully to heart. Do teens congregate in shopping plazas because these provide engrossing activities? (Larkin, 1979; Michelson and Roberts, 1979).

Suburban housewives have. been relatively isolated in neighbourhoods zoned residential, where few if any alternative activities can be found for a mother and the young children she is assumed to have. Hence, neighbouring has been accentuated. Women have not been able to travel elsewhere with ease because husbands have traditionally made off for the day with the one family car. Indeed, growing maternal employment has not automatically increased women's flexibility insofar as the husband is still more likely to make off with the family's only car. (Michelson, 1985; Rosenbloom, 1978).

## Urban Design and Organization

It is more difficult to grasp how the urban area at a scale greater than the neighbourhood affects the behaviour of individuals. Fortunately, the Swedish geographer

Hägerstrand provides some insight (1970; Carlstein, 1978). The spatial dimensions of the greater urban area (i.e., the degree of mixture or separation of its land-uses, its densities and the way private and public transportation are laid out and operated) make combining different daily activities like work, shopping and entertainment easier or harder to manage; these are called *coupling constraints*. The time dimensions of community (i.e., working hours, school and day-care hours, medical and bank hours, the opening and closing times of stores, services and bureaucracies, delivery hours, etc.) likewise impinge on what we can do on a given day; these are called *authority constraints*. These two types of constraints combine to limit daily activity and to serve as the basis for habit formation (van Paasen, 1981; Cullen, 1978).

Depending on the part of the population involved, the way our urban areas are laid out and organized can reflect or frustrate the pursuit of daily life. For example, most planners, architects and top-level administrators in North America have been men, and the assumptions behind much land-use planning and timing have reflected traditional sex-role division. With the influx of married women (including those with children) into the paid labour force, many of the arrangements (e.g., low density, segregated land-uses, day-care centres in marginal locations, standard working hours and restricted hours for many public services and stores) are no longer functional (Hayden, 1984; Michelson, 1985). The many other parts of the population which are vulnerable in the greater urban structure include children, the elderly, the handicapped, the poor and many more—indeed everybody at one or another time in their lives.

## URBAN STRUCTURE, POWER, AND PLANNING

Cities must take certain collective actions, both in response to the needs of physical and social subsectors and regarding the formal body politic. Cities face the questions of which actions to take, at what level of aggregation, serving whose interests and at whose initiative.

Cities in North America are formed and get their powers and responsibilities according to the laws and decisions of provincial and state governments. Therefore, what cities "do" and how they are organized to accomplish this are functions of attitudes and actions by higher levels of government. Such delegation of responsibilities assumes decision-making for local concerns is best made "close to home," though additional motivations for delegation involve the shifting of revenue generation and hard choices among policy alternatives into the hands of local politicians.

Schools have traditionally been organized at the municipal level and have always been the single greatest segment of municipal spending. Among other long-standing responsibilities are police and fire protection, public works (roads, parks, water and sewage) and public health (epidemic prevention, sanitary standards and, more recently, pollution control). Among functions developed increasingly this century are planning, transportation, recreation, child-care and welfare. And servicing these specific functions (and more) are central bureaucracies, where the various by-laws, records, permits, licences and the like are written, processed and maintained and where taxes are collected and bills paid.

It is possible to view the functioning of municipal government as a harmonious application of rational laws—if you only read descriptions of how the system is formally structured and you never attend a meeting of city council! There are many reasons, however, why urban structure should be viewed through a conflict perspective, where disagreements emerge naturally within the system.

## CONFLICTS WITHIN THE SYSTEM

First, because money is needed for what cities do and is always limited, different functions are put in conflict with each other. In any given year, a new day-care centre may have to compete with a new stadium for the marginal dollar or with simply maintaining existing facilities and services. It is easy to argue that both could be achieved with increased taxes or new sources of revenue, but others argue that their economic position is more important than either new facility.

Second, while municipalities have a mandate to preserve and enhance health, welfare and safety in terms of the greatest good for the greatest number, specific issues typically carry costs and benefits which impact subsectors of the population differentially. Employed mothers (not to speak of their children and spouses) are affected most by child-care decisions, while building stadiums affects the development and hospitality industries more directly. On many issues, one part of town may receive benefits and another the costs. For example, building a superhighway from a suburb to the centre provides greater access for the suburbanites but gives the highway itself and more cars to the centre.

## POWER

Into this mixture of interests comes the exercise of power—the ability of one person or aggregate to get others to do what they want them to do. The formal structure of government accords power to elected representatives and to those who implement policies and laws. Sociological studies, however, have documented a host of ways in which this formal system is swayed by informal power structures (Hawley and Wirt, 1968; Domhoff, 1980). Some cities have an informally organized power behind the throne which pilots all major policies past the elected officials; in Atlanta, for example, this was once shown to consist of high-ranking regional representatives of national corporations (Hunter, 1953). Some cities have been shown to have their decisions influenced by different interest groups. In New Haven, clearly different groups strongly influenced decision-makers on planning and educational issues (Dahl, 1961). Obviously, no two cities are the same in this regard, reflecting a variety of conditions in each. Long argues persuasively, however, that the city is an "ecology of games" (1958). By this, he means that the outcome of any policy issue is never totally predictable. Each will draw a unique combination of protagonists, whose influence and power are cast in different combinations upon the formal decision-makers. According to this view, urban politics is kaleidoscopic, forming a different pattern with various combinations of elements each time.

Some persons argue that one should focus primarily in this arena on major actors in the economic system and on associated motives for profit and control (Cox, 1978; Pickvance, 1976; Smith, 1979: Ch. 6; Tabb and Sawers, 1984). Does not money talk loudest? Analyses of Toronto, for example, have put the interests of large property developers at the centre (Lorimer, 1978). There is no questioning the presence and impact of economic forces and factors. But they do not always win. Many decisions have been made in recent years in both Vancouver and Toronto, involving so-called reform politicians and citizen groups, which have gone in opposite directions from what an ideologically pure economic determinist perspective would have predicted.

## THE SCOPE OF URBAN FUNCTIONS AND ORGANIZATION

The question of rationality comes into even greater focus, moreover, when recalling the long history of urban growth described earlier. Many municipalities exist side-by-side. Viewed from the other end of the microscope, these metropolitan areas consist of a multitude of local municipalities. To what extent should decisions and operations be kept "close to home" in one municipality after another, or, to the contrary, reorganized at a higher level to represent the metropolitan area?

Many responsibilities of municipal government transcend municipal borders. Polluted smoke or water from one municipality has tangible effects in other jurisdictions; they are not purely local concerns. Similarly, roads, policing, licensing and the like become chaotic without clear co-ordination or reorganization at higher levels.

Furthermore, the tax money individual municipalities can gather has traditionally reflected the intensity and wealth of the buildings and activities within its borders. The needs of a given municipality for money (e.g., for education, welfare, police and fire protection, etc.) are not always in line with its tax base. Indeed, the relationship is often inverse. Municipalities with poor and aging populations may need greater amounts for wider varieties of functions, yet have less basis for raising the money. In contrast, commuters from wealthier suburbs may create the need for central city expenditures for roads and policing, for example, but lack the need to make hefty expenditures in the municipalities to which they bring their paycheques. While the different parts of the metropolitan area may function as an entity in terms of everyday activity, their historical boundaries divide efforts to solve problems facing urban areas as a whole.

While rationality argues in favour of reorganization at higher levels, many people oppose it. More affluent people benefit from channelling tax monies to support their own priorities. When, for example, the Village of Forest Hill was an independent municipality surrounded by the City of Toronto, it was known for its superior schools and snow removal, which its affluent citizens demanded, unburdened by the welfare needs of the surrounding areas. Furthermore, some feel that local control is essential to defending one's own interests.

A purely fiscal solution to the inequitable availablity of tax money is to let higher levels of government (national and provincial or state) collect taxes and then provide grants to municipalities with special needs. Like government in general, however, the idea of such a system can be distorted in its actual operations. School financing has, for example, relied more and more on provincial and state grants in response to local inequities, but many observers doubt that the grants (and the strings attached) have provided net benefits to most of those concerned. Furthermore, when grants are made with few strings, it is uncertain that benefits go where they are most needed.

## Metropolitan Government

One structural response to the underlying problem is metropolitan government. A new level of government is formed from the existing municipalities. The higher level then carries out those functions where metropolitan co-ordination and perhaps financing are instrumental. Which functions are chosen varies from place to place and from time to time. New York City became a metropolitan government in league with its five boroughs in the 1800s and gradually absorbed most functions from the boroughs. Metropolitan Toronto was formed in 1953 to care for water, sewage, arteries, parks, school financing, welfare, co-ordinated planning, policing, business licensing and air-pollution control. Run by a council selected by the various municipal councils and a chairperson it elects, it collects tax money from the cities and boroughs within Metro and distributes it where needed. Periodic reviews since 1953 have increased the powers of the metropolitan government and decreased those of the cities and boroughs. Winnipeg and Montreal have variations on the metropolitan government ideal, with more and less responsibility at the metropolitan level, and the Greater Vancouver Regional District has waxed and waned over past decades.

The sociological lessons of informal systems should not be lost when evaluating formal solutions like metropolitan government. A majority interest can dominate the very minority a structure was set up to assist if the participants (and the interests behind them) so choose. Dade County, Florida (Miami and its suburbs) and Honolulu have had disappointing experiences with metropolitan structures. It is difficult to argue against using the most appropriate levels of response to the kinds of jobs cities must do; but citizens are finding that the formal structures do not do the work without very human interests and influences.

## Other Structural Solutions

It is possible for the original municipalities to be abolished entirely and replaced by the higher level of government, but experiments with this have been relatively few when settlements of any size are involved. People are skittish about becoming part of a larger agglomeration; they fear loss of control in a world that keeps increasing in scale. The opposite strategy, in which existing municipalities remain supreme but join together voluntarily for planning and co-operation, has been shown largely impotent when problems are controversial and costly.

Where people fear alterations in municipal jurisdictions but urgently require area-wide services, special authorities, commissions or districts are commonly set up. These are like crown corporations charged with building and operating specific functions. Depending on their location, they may have taxation rights or public subsidies, as well as the right to charge the public for its services. But, despite elected or selected directors, these bodies are usually shielded from the direct control or scrutiny of city officials. They generally function more efficiently than local municipal services but are often more remote from constituency demands.

There is obviously no perfect form of government. The main factors always involved are what needs to be done, what kind(s) of structures are appropriate to the function(s) and what interests are mobilized in the de facto operation. Just as obviously, when each factor is considered explicitly and faced honestly, local government can be made to serve its purposes.

## URBAN PLANNING IN STRUCTURAL PERSPECTIVE

So far, the discussion has failed to mention urban planning and where it fits into the perspectives of urban structure and power (Simmie, 1974). Planning is a profession practised by persons hired onto municipal staffs or by private consultants hired to contribute services and reports. Planners are not elected. In most municipalities, planning is found in one or more places within city structures. It may be a department of the city, parallel to public works or licensing. It may be advisory to the mayor. It may work under the supervision of an elected or selected commission that reports to city council. Planning activities usually also take place within other organizations like transit agencies, school boards and public housing agencies.

What do planners plan? They help create long-range, comprehensive plans which, if adopted by city governments, should facilitate orderly growth.

Planners also help design transportation networks, the dynamic side of the land-use coin. In addition, they are highly visible when planning interventions within existing city areas.

*Urban renewal* occurs when the nature or use of an area changes. City officials disapprove of areas whose property value and hence, tax base potential are low. When the current buildings or activities are considered outdated or unusable—and unlikely to change through private-sector initiative—cities often intervene. One form of intervention is *redevelopment*; here, the block or larger area is levelled, and a new land-use arranged in co-operation with public- or private-sector bodies. Another type of intervention is *rehabilitation*, where buildings are modernized and either resold or rerented at higher levels.

While American cities have seen much publicly planned and implemented renewal of residential and commercial areas, major Canadian projects have turned increasingly to reuse of older industrial sites and railroad yards whose utility has ceased. The picture on page 425 shows the False Creek area of Vancouver, built on redeveloped railway lands adjacent to downtown yet providing housing with considerable amenities to households varying in income and family structure.

All planning activities do not involve such radical intervention. Preventive medicine is preferred to surgery, and much planning activity is devoted to liaison with specific neighbourhoods in hopes that smaller, site-by-site improvements like off-street parking can maintain or upgrade existing areas.

Yet, whatever they do, planners are caught in a strange structural position. Their recommendations always involve economic benefits to some parties and losses to others. Moreover, they have no political decision-making power. Influences on the essentially redistributive processes with which they deal (Pahl, 1970) can enter the decision-making process above their heads and from any informal source. Furthermore, planners are at the behest of their employers and deviate from the positions of their employers at the risk of their jobs. Yet, the planner in liaison with local neighbourhood residents and groups may honestly support their point of view against that of his or her employers.

*False Creek is an example of new land use for old land in central Vancouver.*

Planners are thus asked to act as lawyers for both prosecution and defense but are paid only by the former and lack judicial powers. Some planners say local groups need their own planners to advance local interests with the same skills as the official city planners. This counter-planning process is called *advocacy planning* (Davidoff, 1965) but has remained relatively minor because corporations and municipalities have a near monopoly on the level of funding needed to hire full-time planners. Many cities assign regular planning staff members to local areas, but these planners still face divided loyalties.

## CITIZEN PARTICIPATION

Others feel that the interests of citizens need to be expressed in an organized and active way to the same forums that now listen to large corporate groups.

The best-known approach is that of the late Saul Alinsky (1971) and his many North American followers. This approach recognizes the difficulty in inducing largely apolitical people to unite in a public stand on technical matters. The answer lies in the uniting effect of *conflict*. People will join together during a crisis. Trained conflict agents are brought in to discover (or invent) problems besetting the local community that could bring them into conflict with others (often the city government). Through such a conflict, latent power can be used to pursue their planning interests. The problem in this approach lies in the difficulty of keeping organizational momentum after resolving the main conflict.

An alternative to the conflict approach is the *coalition* approach. Here, the best effort is made to create a local citizens group such as a ratepayers association or a tenants union. But rather than acting independently, such groups join with other interests and organizations for mutual support. This provides a broader base of support, but it is unclear how broad a coalition can be if interests within it clash on pending issues.

Canadian planners and municipalities have experimented with still another model of citizen participation. Here, the public sector collects and publicizes points of view and recommendations from the various groups with interests involved in a given planning issue. What one person or group says can be the basis for discussion, refutation, counterargument and, perhaps, agreement or compromise. This model uses public funds and initiative to get all arguments onto the table. Halifax, for example, funded a highly successful public encounter on planning issues after more traditional renewal projects had failed (Clairmont and Magill, 1974).

Given that planners have technical expertise and that elected city officials represent the people, it may seem surprising that so many efforts appear necessary to represent the ordinary Canadian's interests in planning issues. Once again, however, one must recognize the diversity of persons and interests in our urban areas, and that informal processes occur within formal urban structures. Insofar as legitimate citizen interests need promotion to the level of strong economic interests, organizational innovation and animation may remain desirable.

## SUMMARY

The diversity in nature and scale of urban considerations and problems taxes the scope of the sociological imagination. This chapter is itself a summary. The interested reader is directed to books dealing exclusively with urban sociology (Berger, 1978; Bollens and Schmandt, 1982; Kennedy, 1983; McGahan, 1982; Palen, 1981; Phillips and LeGates, 1981), which yield to more detailed examinations in yet other books and articles on specific questions and areas of substance. Some of these are indicated by the references in this chapter.

There is no single sociological theory or perspective that addresses all urban problems or phenomena. No two matters are likely to draw on the same combination of factors for their solution or understanding. Yet, it is useful to start thinking through questions about cities and urban living in terms of the logic of four perspectives: 1) *urbanization*—the place of cities in society; 2) *urbanism*—characteristic forms of urban behaviour and their explanation; 3) *ecological structure*—how the physical pattern, environmental design and organization of urban living interact with urban populations, subgroups and individuals; 4) *urban structure, power and planning*—the relationships of diverse interests to formal and informal systems for implementing collective actions by and within cities.

Like other forms of sociological inquiry, analyses and research along these lines helps clarify what goes on around us and helps shape our contexts and structures in useful ways.

# DISCUSSION QUESTIONS

1. What demands do present-day cities make on the nonurban areas of their own societies? Other societies?

2. What role does technology play in contemporary urbanization?

3. How do urbanites avoid most other people even though they are not isolated? Can you give examples of this from your own behaviour?

4. What are the most marked subcultures in your area? How are they reflected in spatial patterns?

5. What are the planning implications of noting (or failing to note) the differences in type and degree of community in inner-city neighbourhoods?

6. Name some subgroups in the population that are poorly served by the current arrangements of built environments. How would you improve matters?

7. Is conflict of interest an inherent part of municipal government? How can citizens balance equity with feelings of local control?

# CENTRAL
# INSTITUTIONS
# of SOCIETY

This section is about institutions, sets of values, activities and resources used to meet important social needs. It builds on what we have covered earlier, illustrating how basic social processes come together to produce order and change. Here, within the central institutions of society, larger structures contain smaller ones; formal structures, informal ones; complex structures, simpler ones; and permanent structures, temporary ones.

The *central* institutions include the economy, the political system, legal system, mass media and educational system. While they differ in important respects, they also share many similarities. For this reason, sociologists typically ask similar questions about them.

That is not to deny that here, as elsewhere in this book, opposing paradigms compete for our attention. These paradigms, especially the Marxist, Weberian and functionalist, define which parts of the central institutions will interest us most.

Yet, within all the main paradigms, the sociological analysis of central institutions means studying *linked, interdependent parts*, the character of these linkages and the ways the parts and the whole system change over time. As well, all are concerned with the place of the institution in society, its relation to society's values, activities and power structure.

## Institutional Outputs

The sociologist's first concern is with what Anthony Giddens calls *structuration* and Paul DiMaggio and Walter Powell call *institutional definition*. Their work suggests that the study of any central institution should, first, specify the institution's parts, or member organizations; then, it should analyse interactions among them, interorganizational control and co-operation, information flow and communication and mutual awareness. The chapters in this section address these issues and others as well.

The focus on structural linkage ignores only the institutional *output*, an identifying feature of any institution and the most important factor in institutional definition. An analysis may begin by asking what the institution is *supposed* to accomplish. What are its *stated* goals and the expectations of its members? Are they met, and if not, why not? Is the institution achieving some other unstated, unintended or hidden purpose? If so, what is it?

How do the *actual* outputs of the institution—programs, laws, decisions, degrees—affect people? How, for example, do television programs influence family life, peer group relations, literacy, mass behaviour? Or how do government policies influence public life, good citizenship, belief in the state, trust among countrymen? How do economic decisions shape material prosperity, class conflict, technological development? Or how does the educational system affect intellectual development, character building and the acquisition of job skills?

The *stated* goals of an institution are usually rooted in a society's dominant values. Every institution claims a strong cultural foundation and, therefore, the right to command large numbers of people and massive resources.

However, an institution's *actual* goals and practices often threaten this right. It must be continuously repaired and regenerated. To do this, central institutions support one another against attack. For example, the media support the political system; the educational system supports the economy; and the legal system supports all of these. How this co-operation comes about and how it is maintained is the subject of much current sociological research.

## Institutional Co-operation

The polity, or political system of a society, is also discussed here. Part of it, the state, plays a major role in protecting and controlling other institutions. The state, as Weber pointed out, enjoys a monopoly of legitimate force or authority. It has the right to give or take away freedoms, to confiscate property, to tax and redistribute wealth and to force compliance with rules by punishing deviance.

For example, the state spells out the conditions under which economic organizations may operate, buy and sell, hire and fire labour. And from the state, educational institutions get the largest part of their operating revenue. At the primary and secondary levels, provincial governments give strong direction to curriculum and other schooling policies. Not surprisingly, all institutions want to control, co-opt or win the favour of the state.

The economy also plays a major part in protecting and controlling other institutions. Indeed, Marxists assert that all social and political institutions rest on an economic base: All are ultimately controlled by the relations of production. People's relations to the means of production determine their opportunities for health, security and self-fulfillment. And an institution's linkages to the economy determine its "life chances" too. One should therefore ask of any institution what its economic foundations or relations with the economic system are. This question has led to an interest in economic elites and the ways they dominate the economy and other institutions. However, elite domination is not limited to the economy. In studying any institution, we want to know who makes up its elite: What group, class, tribe, region or other social unit is in control, and how do they use that control?

This question, in turn, raises a variety of interesting issues: How does the institution further or protect the interests of its controlling group? How does the elite keep control? Who else is contending for control, and how are they kept out? Finally, to what degree does the institution promise change, perhaps even greater equality, yet actually reproduce the existing order of class relations? The success controlling elites enjoy in holding on to and even extending their power as time passes has led to much research on power elites, upper classes and the relations between the two.

## The Institutional System and Its Maintenance

However, too narrow a focus on elites may mislead us. The structure of central institutions is not created by individuals or groups of individuals, all of whom are, in time, replaced. Society is none the better or worse since Conrad Black took E.P. Taylor's place as one of Canada's most powerful and wealthy men; and Black's passing from the scene will probably make as little difference. What sets the pattern is the distribution of power, wealth and legal right that characterizes a modern capitalist, industrial society. Private property, a grossly unequal distribution of wealth and a nominally free market in capital, political decision-making and ideas, all of which benefit the powerful, define such a society. Given these features, strongly interlinked central institutions that reproduce the existing order are bound to result, whoever the elite may be.

Some hold that the key actors are neither elites nor institutions, but dominant organizations within institutions: within the economy, banks; within the polity, political parties; within the media, networks and publishing chains. From this perspective, organizations compete to dominate their own fields as much to ensure their own survival as for the benefit of institutional elites (owners, board members) or dominant social classes.

Power is the enjoyment of and the ability to protect an advantage. We must investigate how a given institution or organization exercises its power. How does a controlling elite or dominant organization control those subordinated to it: its workers, or students, or consumers, or clients, or viewers, or voters? How does the same elite or organization dominate other institutions and *their* elites, workers, clients, and the like? If such control is not exercised—if, instead, institutions co-operate and ally with each other—

how are such arrangements made and enforced? What social structures are protected and helped by a given institution and will, in turn, protect that same institution, thereby serving to maintain the established order?

Again, we must listen to the dialogue between Marx and Weber: Does one institution and one elite, or class, dominate society, as Marx holds; or, as Weber says, do many sources of domination co-exist and compete? If we accept the former, we would expect society to change through conflict between the dominant and subordinate classes; if the latter, through shifting power relationships within the dominant class.

In both paradigms, achieving legitimacy is important. Controlling society is easier if the public co-operates. What, then, structures public awareness of, participation in and perceptions about the institutions in question and their right to control? Is it ignorance? Or what Marx called "false consciousness"? Or even, as Orwell suggested with his Doublethink and Newspeak in *1984*, a distortion of our ability to tell truth from falsehood? Or are people genuinely committed to the goals of the institutions: to educational "excellence," political "good citizenship," media "awareness," and so on? Nothing is harder than trying to sort out such questions from inside a society, yet this is precisely what sociologists try to do. How, then, can we see what an institution is really doing for, or to, a society?

## The Value of Comparative Analysis

Comparative analysis may help us understand. By definition, each central institution is an intimate part of its social environment. To see the unique contribution a particular institution is making, a variety of strategies must be tried.

One strategy is to study how the same kind of institution (for example, a capitalist economy, multiparty political system or adversarial legal system) works in a different cultural, social and economic setting. Another strategy is to study how a given institution has changed historically, relating changes to earlier (therefore, potentially causal) changes in other institutions. A third is to compare institutions within the same society, to see how they adapted differently to the same historical changes in cultural, social and economic contexts.

Still, we cannot minimize the importance of understanding a central institution *within* its own time and place: for example, in Canada, in the late twentieth century.

Many of the generalizations the authors make in this section will hold good for all western, capitalist, industrial societies. But some will need modifying in the light of Canada's peculiar history: its economic dependency, the dominant role of multinational organizations, regional conflict, the twin British and French cultural traditions, high rates of immigration and the resulting multiculturalism, and so on.

History provides a useful backdrop against which to assess contemporary society. Chapters in this section refer to broad historical transformations, such as the shift from preindustrial to industrial society, or early to late (mature) capitalism. Some chapters relate institutional changes to theories of development and modernization, which will be discussed further in the next section. We also find a concern with the changes occurring in the past two decades of economic slowdown. Questions asked include: How are changes in a given institution related to changes in other institutions, and how are they related to social change overall?

The sociologist may want to complete the analysis by considering proposed alternatives to present arrangements, especially after discovering discrepancies between actual and intended outputs. What, the sociologist may ask, are the prospects for future change, and what dynamics are likely to bring such changes about?

Together, these questions and the answers they receive make up the study of central institutions in society.

# 17

# Economic Institutions and Power

*R.J. Richardson*

# INTRODUCTION

What are economic institutions? How are they related to other types of social institutions and to society in general? How do they affect our daily lives? Furthermore, what is economic power and who wields it? This chapter will examine the significance of economic institutions to society and to ourselves as individuals. We will move from general theories of economic institutions and their relationship to society to focus more specifically on North American and then Canadian issues of economic influence and power.

## WHAT ARE ECONOMIC INSTITUTIONS?

Societies consist of people, their relationships with one another, their activities and their values. But the groups people form are not randomly created, nor are their activities or the values they develop arbitrary. In fact, these all are shaped by the central elements of social organization in any society. We call these *institutions*.

More specifically, institutions are collections of organizations or groups that mobilize people and resources in ways consistent with the values of a society. Institutions, in turn, disseminate and reinforce these values. Every society contains familial, political, religious, educational and economic institutions in one form or another. In some societies, these institutions are highly integrated. For example, the Bushmen of the Kalahari subsume virtually all of them under the institution of family and kinship. In others, such as modern Canada, these institutions are highly differentiated. Although they are interrelated in various ways, they each take on a concrete form of their own.

This chapter will focus on economic institutions, which we may define as *the set of organizations, groups and processes by which people in a society produce and distribute goods and services*. Between societies, these economic institutions may vary substantially, depending on:
— the society's basic mode of existence (e.g., hunting and gathering versus manufacturing);
— the technology available (e.g., Stone-Age tools versus nuclear power and the microchip);
— the central values of the society (e.g., co-operation versus competition and the primacy of the individual versus the primacy of the group).

Nevertheless, despite this diversity, economic institutions in any society provide the basic social organization for satisfying the material wants of the society's members. These wants include the necessities of life such as food, clothing and shelter and all of the goods and services that form part of the society's culture.

Economic institutions perform two basic material processes—production and distribution. The production process combines land, labour, capital, technology and organization to produce goods and services. The distributive process recognizes the claims of the members of the society to a share in the benefits of production. In other words, economic institutions produce and distribute a society's wealth.

Economic institutions are the central focus of the discipline of economics, so one might ask: Why should sociology study them too? Is it just empire-building on the part of sociologists? To this, we can answer with a firm "No!" Just as war is too important to leave to the generals, so is the economy too important to leave to the economists. We will see in this chapter that economy and society are intimately related and that economic sociology tends to focus on relationships that cross the boundaries of disciplines. For example, economists tend to study market and sociologists *non*market relationships in economic enterprise.

Marxist sociology looks primarily at the economic base of society and holds that all other institutions are merely superstructure (Marx, 1970). But one need be neither a Marxist nor an economic determinist to recognize that how goods, services and wealth are produced and distributed profoundly affects all the central institutions of any society and, therefore, the quality of human existence. Of course, economic processes are affected by other social institutions as well.

## ECONOMIC POWER

When we think of power, we often think in terms of personal characteristics, as in "He is a powerful man." So, to many of us, power is perhaps merely an abstract form of physical strength. But to sociologists, power is a *relationship*, not an attribute. Weber, for example, defined power as "the probability that one actor in a social relationship will be able to carry out his own will despite resistance . . ." (1968:53). Since power is a relationship, it can also be the inverse of dependence (Emerson, 1962). Thus, your power over me depends on how much I am dependent on you.

Power can be wielded within any of society's institutions, and *economic power* is, of course, wielded in economic institutions and originates in economic relations. It is an aspect of the economy that economists tend to ignore because of their focus on competitive markets and the impersonal laws of supply and demand. But power arises in the economic realm wherever an individual or group controls a significant share of a particular resource. This creates dependence in others who want or need that resource.

Weber (1958) proposed that the distribution of benefits in an economic exchange depends on the relative market power of the parties involved. Market power, in turn, rests on two interrelated factors in Weber's analysis. The first is how much the control of a commodity is concentrated in a few hands. The second is how effectively one party to an exchange can *withhold* a commodity from the market.

We can see these principles at work in the labour market and the wheat market, for example. The labour market contains few capitalists and many workers. Thus, individual workers cannot affect wages by withdrawing their services. A major reason for the rise of unions has been the unionized workers' ability to collectively use the strike to try to reduce this imbalance in economic power. (For a comprehensive analysis of strikes, see Chapter 12.)

Canadian wheat farmers, from the 1880s to World War II, participated in a competitive world market containing millions of independent producers. Throughout this period, wheat prices fluctuated violently because no individual farmer (or group of farmers) could affect the price by withholding wheat from the market. The central Canadian suppliers of their agricultural equipment and machinery, on the other hand, were few in number. Consequently, these suppliers could maintain a substantial degree of price stability by reducing production in times of falling demand. This vast difference in market power between the wheat farmers and their suppliers has been an important element of Prairie society ever since the opening of this Canadian agricultural frontier.

While Weber analysed economic power mainly in terms of the relations of exchange, Marx focused on the relations of production. Marx (1954) proposed that those who control the means of production (the bourgeoisie) dominate and exploit those who do not (the proletariat). Nevertheless, these different analyses of economic power are complementary, not incompatible. For both, the distribution of economic power is determined by economic structures. The complementarity of the analyses by Marx and Weber is not accidental. Much of Weber's work can be seen as a debate with the ghost of Marx (Zeitlin, 1968), or as a positive critique and extension of Marx. (See Chapter 15 for an explanation of some important aspects of this relationship.)

## TYPES OF ECONOMIC INSTITUTIONS

The types of economic institutions that have existed throughout human history are virtually endless, ranging from the primitive communism of many tribal societies, through agricultural societies based on slavery and serfdom to modern industrial capitalism and socialism. Here, we will examine only a few examples to demonstrate the principal variables that differentiate types of economic institutions. These are the technologies employed, the division of labour, the ownership or control of the means of production, the principles under which a society's wealth is distributed and the degree to which economic institutions are separate and distinct.

Tribal societies based on hunting and gathering or primitive agriculture employ restricted technologies suitable to producing what they need. Production is usually based on the kinship unit, which is relatively self-sufficient. The unit contains a rudimentary gender- and age-based division of labour. Yet, there may still be some in the society who specialize in producing specific items, like weapons, and so there is a limited amount of exchange. However, this exchange is based on *who* is involved and what roles they play, unlike the universal and impersonal exchange of commodities. Property, such as the land used for hunting, gathering and tilling, is usually communal and regarded as the property of the group as a whole. Distribution of the products of the society's labour is relatively egalitarian. Any surplus produced tends to be distributed on the basis of noneconomic criteria, such as military prowess and tradition. In these societies, economic activity is densely interwoven with kinship obligations and religious belief, and so economic institutions are indistinct.

Tribal and industrial societies differ in all of these dimensions. Industrial society uses an extremely diverse application of machine technology. This is associated with an intensive division of labour that produces a formalized occupational structure. Whereas in tribal societies, the choice of what to produce is severely restricted by the technology, this choice is virtually unlimited in industrial societies. Yet, since resources are not unlimited, choices must be made and how these are made varies between capitalist and socialist industrial societies.

Under capitalism, there is private ownership of the means of production. Those who own or control these means will make productive choices aimed at maximizing their profits. Profits, in turn, are partly determined by the forces of supply and demand, so production is generally geared toward the goods and services in highest demand. Distribution of wealth generated by economic activity is determined by

*A bushman of the Kalahari brings home a porcupine. Tribal societies based on hunting and gathering meet their needs (often very effectively) by employing restricted technologies.* Irven DeVore/Anthro-Photo.

economic criteria—by the ownership of the means of production, by the commodity value of specific types of labour, expertise and technology and by Weber's "market power." Clearly, in capitalist industrial society, economic activity is secularized, rationalized and distinct from other activities. Economic institutions are much less interwoven with other institutions, such as religion, the family and the political order.

Socialist industrial societies substitute public for private ownership. Productive decisions are based, not on profit maximization, but on centralized planning that aims to meet consumer demand and political objectives, such as development and defence. Economic wealth is distributed (at least in part) according to people's needs rather than according to their position in the economic structure. Although there may be more links between political and economic institutions here than in capitalism, the economic institutions are distinct and well developed.

We have seen that economic institutions can take many forms. But what shapes them? Clearly, they are affected by technology, but we have seen important differences between capitalist and socialist economic institutions that share similar technologies. Furthermore, the Greek, Roman and Chinese civilizations developed many important technologies that were never widely used for economic purposes. Perhaps, then, technology both affects and is affected by the economy. On a broader scale, we might ask: Does the economy shape society, or is it the other way around?

*In industrial societies, the diversity of technology permits an almost unlimited choice of what to produce. Here, oil and gas are extracted from tar sands.* Permission of Miller Services.

# ECONOMY AND SOCIETY

## THE TRANSFORMATION OF ECONOMIC INSTITUTIONS

Marx, Weber and Durkheim all addressed the relationship of economy to society and the transformation from one set of institutions to another. A brief and somewhat oversimplified summary of their analyses follows, working from the simplest to the most complex.

Émile Durkheim (1965) proposes that economy shapes society but that economy, in turn, is shaped by the demographic variable of population density. Primitive societies, he argues, have a sparse population and a rudimentary division of labour. All social institutions, including economic ones, are closely intertwined, and nearly everyone fills similar occupational roles. Because of this common economic base, the members of society behave alike and share a set of beliefs or a *collective conscience*. Hence, there is an idealistic basis for maintaining social order. However, the economic base of self-sufficient production fosters little interdependence among people. Therefore, there is no structural basis for social integration. The collective conscience, then, must be maintained and reinforced by *repressive and punitive laws*, because the society will lose its identity if it tolerates deviance or even individuality. Durkheim calls the economically determined basis for this type of social order *mechanical solidarity*.

If and when the population density increases to the point where a simple division of labour no longer allows the society's members to survive, Durkheim believes that a much more complex division must develop. This high degree of specialization produces a similarly high degree of interdependence among a society's members. Consequently, a new structural basis of social order develops, which Durkheim calls *organic solidarity*. This new, stronger basis of social integration no longer requires repressive law to maintain the collective conscience. In fact, the individualism and uniqueness of personality resulting from specialization are now desirable. So repressive law is replaced by *restitutive law*, which grows out of the new interdependent economic base. Hence, in Durkheim's view, economy shapes society and economic institutions change in response to population pressures.

Marx (1970, 1978) also holds that the economy shapes people and society. "The nature of individuals thus depends on the material conditions determining their production" (1978: 150). In his analysis, not only human nature, but also human ideas, laws, religion and social institutions arise from how people conduct their economic activities. These, in turn, occur within a specific *set* of economic institutions, which he terms a *mode of production*.

This mode of production is the foundation of Marx's conception of history, and changes in it represent distinct historical epochs. It comprises two elements: the *forces of production*, which represent the interaction between human producers, tools, technology and the material environment; and the *relations of production*, which are the class, property and power relationships in a society (Zeitlin, 1968). Marx proposes that to reproduce both themselves and their society, humans enter into social relations of production. These relations are relatively static in any given epoch. The *forces* of production, however, are dynamic. They change with population pressures, the division of labour, technological developments and so on. The friction between these dynamic forces and the static relations of production causes class conflict, which eventually becomes severe enough to produce the objective conditions for social change (that is, change from one mode of production to another). For change to actually happen, these objective conditions must also be accompanied by subjective class consciousness (Zeitlin, 1968). (For a much more comprehensive account of Marx's conception of history, see Cohen, 1978).

Marx's analysis of economic institutions and the relationship of economy to society is much more complex and conditional than Durkheim's. Nevertheless, they agree that economy shapes society. In Weber's analysis, the causal direction is unclear.

Some of Weber's analyses suggest that the change from one set of economic institutions to another is the result of economic processes and that a society is shaped by its economic base. For example, Weber (1976) analysed the decline of the slave-based economy of the Roman Empire and the evolution of that empire into a feudal society. He concluded that the disintegration of the empire was an inevitable political consequence of the decline of commerce. Elsewhere, Weber (1961) proposed that the structure of agricultural societies and their systems of land tenure depend on their economic institutions.

On the other hand, he argued that military and religious motives affect economic developments. For example, he cited the need for large armies in continental Europe as a factor favouring peasant agriculture, which maximized population per acre.

> **KARL MARX ON THE RELATIONSHIP BETWEEN ECONOMY AND SOCIETY**
>
> The general conclusion at which I arrived and which, once reached, became the guiding principle of my studies can be summarised as follows. In the social production of their existence, men inevitably enter into definite relations, which are independent of their will, namely relations of production appropriate to a given stage in the development of their material forces of production. The totality of these relations of production constitutes the economic structure of society, the real foundation, on which arises a legal and political superstructure and to which correspond definite forms of social consciousness. The mode of production of material life conditions the general process of social, political and intellectual life. It is not the consciousness of men that determines their existence, but their social existence that determines their consciousness. At a certain stage of development, the material productive forces of society come into conflict with the existing relations of production or—this merely expresses the same thing in legal terms—with the property relations within the framework of which they have operated hitherto. From forms of development of the productive forces these relations turn into their fetters. Then begins an era of social revolution. The changes in the economic foundation lead sooner or later to the transformation of the whole immense superstructure.
>
> Karl Marx, *A Contribution to the Critique of Political Economy*. Moscow, Progress Publishers, 1970, pp. 20–21.

England, on the other hand, was protected by the Channel, and its navy and had much more modest military needs. This favoured capitalist agriculture, which maximized *production* per acre, rather than population. It also permitted the expropriation of peasants to meet the labour demands of the Industrial Revolution. Elsewhere (1930, 1958) Weber focused on values as the "switchmen" directing social and economic change.

Having examined the classical perspectives on the transformation of economic institutions generally, we will now look at Marx's and Weber's analyses of the emergence of capitalism as the dominant economic institution in the modern western world.

## The Emergence of Capitalism

How and why did capitalism arise when and where it did? These questions were central to the sociology of both Marx (1954) and Weber (1958, 1961). There are many similarities in their conclusions as we should expect, but also some important differences.

Both held that an essential precondition for capitalism was the separation of the labourer from the means of production. This was first seen to occur with the expropriation of the English agricultural producer as feudal tenure was phased out between the sixteenth and eighteenth centuries. It was accompanied by new laws that created a class of labourers free to, indeed *compelled* to, sell their labour power on the market. Labour power, then, became a commodity, like potatoes.

Both Marx and Weber attributed the rise of the prosperous capitalist farmer to European inflation, which was induced by Spain's importation of gold from the New World. Both saw the manufacturing capitalist emerging via two routes. One was a slow process, where independent artisans employed more and more wage labourers; the other, a faster one, where merchants and financiers expanded into manufacturing. Hence, both agriculture and manufacturing increased commodity production for an expanding market.

Marx (1954) concentrated on analysing capitalism as an economic system producing commodities and surplus value (defined in Chapter 15) and continuing to reproduce the relation between the capitalist and the wage labourer.

Weber's analysis was more diverse. For one thing, although Marx certainly did not ignore the emergence of a market, Weber focused much more on it. To Weber, the rise of the mass market was as essential to the emergence of capitalism as the decline of commerce was to the end of the Roman Empire. He also extended Marx's analysis by placing it within a broader sweep of historical dynamics (Zeitlin, 1968). The first of these dynamics was the rise of rationality, which became institutionalized through technology, the marketplace, economic enterprise and the law. The second was the coincident development of bureaucracy, which separated the producer from the means of production, administration, science and war. Thirdly, Weber (1930) examined the influence of religion on the rise of capitalism. He proposed that early Protestantism encouraged the self-discipline, hard work and individualism that fostered competition and investment. This, along with a prohibition against conspicuous consumption, produced the investment in and growth of industry that were the dynamic elements of capitalism.

## From Laissez-Faire to Corporate Capitalism

As capitalism emerged in England, so did the doctrine of *laissez-faire*. This doctrine was taken from the philosophy of Adam Smith (1894) who proposed that the greatest good for the greatest number was served when individuals pursued their own selfish objectives, constrained only by the "unseen hand" of competition. So government, other than acting to bolster capitalism *as a system*, left business alone.

It was from observing laissez-faire capitalism that Marx (1954) formulated his laws of capitalist competition. Marx believed that competition forced capitalist enterprise to continually adopt the latest technology. Firms that did prospered; those that did not failed. Thus, there is a tendency for the economy to be dominated by ever fewer and ever larger firms. Not only is capital concentrated in fewer and fewer hands, but employment is also increasingly to be found only in the few large establishments. Dense concentrations of impoverished wage labourers then provide the conditions for developing the class consciousness and cohesion necessary to overthrow capitalism. Thus, ultimately, "the expropriators are expropriated" (1954: 715).

Although Marx correctly forecast the increasing concentration of capitalist enterprise, the inevitable revolution by the working class that he predicted has not occurred because of several factors he could not have foreseen. Small-scale enterprise survives to this day in labour-intensive sectors of the economy and in new industries where the entry of small, new firms offsets, for a while, the process of concentration. We have also seen that the increased productivity accompanying new technology has reduced living costs, resulting in a higher standard of living for the working class than Marx forecast. Furthermore, concentration has reduced price competition among the few large firms in each industry. This has permitted wages to rise, because the cost of higher wages can be recovered by raising prices. Finally, laissez-faire capitalism has gradually given way to the welfare state.

The modern welfare state evolved out of the massive depression of the 1930s, with the result that—until the advent of President Reagan and Prime Minister Thatcher, at least—there has been ever-increasing government involvement in the economy. The welfare state reduces the economic impact of unemployment, becomes a major employer in its own right and sets minimum wages for the working class. It also provides welfare for businesses through tax breaks and subsidies.

Large modern corporations have immense power. However, their power is not unfettered, as it was in the days of laissez-faire, for they are subject to significant constraints imposed by governments and the judiciary.

## HOW ECONOMY SHAPES MODERN SOCIETY

The massive unemployment of the current decade shows the effect of economic institutions on society. In fact, some claim that robotics and the microchip will make chronic unemployment endemic in future decades as well. Although the unemployed are protected from complete financial ruin by unemployment insurance and other social safety nets, they are robbed of their raison d'être. If work is central to life, as many sociologists conclude, is it any wonder that unemployment breeds psychological disorders, marital breakup, drunkenness, violence, crime and suicide? Truly, private troubles are public issues (Mills, 1959) as the economy affects so many private lives.

The economy affects us all as consumers, as well. The dramatic growth in consumer credit since World War II has induced us to buy more and sooner than we otherwise would. This has produced economic growth and material prosperity. But it has also made us more dependent than ever on economic institutions as we struggle to pay later for what we buy now. As we saw in Chapters 11 and 15, the extension of credit is also a factor in the dramatic growth of the number of families having both parents working outside the home.

Why should so many get caught in the credit trap? Duberman and Hartjen (1979) attribute this largely to the effectiveness of modern advertising. We are bombarded with images of the *affluent society* dozens of times every day. The cumulative result may not induce us to buy a specific product, but it makes affluence seem desirable and achievable. So—we buy our way into it. In a closely related argument, Vance Packard (1960) and Alvin Toffler (1970) state that economic institutions, through advertising, lobbying, influence on the school system and the book publishing industry and so on, have created the *throw-away society*. One element of this tinsel world is planned obsolescence. Industries design products—anything from light bulbs to pantyhose—that have deliberately limited life spans. Or they persuade consumers that their clothes are outmoded and must be replaced, even though still

*In order to "keep up with the Joneses," North Americans contribute to Alvin Toffler's "throw-away society." Yet, what would happen to unemployment if planned obsolescence were eliminated?* Permission of Miller Services.

perfectly functional. Many of us with a closet full of clothes still claim we have nothing to wear.

The North American automobile (up to the late 1970s, at least) is an excellent example of industrial success in promoting Toffler's throw-away society. European cars have an average life span of about 12 years, as the Volvo ads proclaim, and they rarely undergo superficial changes in styling. North American car manufacturers, on the other hand, make major style changes about every two years, with enough trim changes in the intervening years to make last year's car out of date. Because of this successful planned obsolescence, it has become essential for people—if they are going to keep up with their neighbours—to trade in their cars about every two years. This has had two results, just as the automakers planned. First, it has increased the demand for cars. Secondly, cars can be built a lot more cheaply because they are only expected to last a few years.

In the last few years, the throw-away ethos seems to be declining. Perhaps this is a result of changing values. If so, it suggests that society can affect economy, just as we have suggested the reverse. On the other hand, sales of paper plates and drinks in nonreturnable cans continue to grow exponentially, and the ubiquitous, long-wearing blue jeans are threatening to become outmoded. Perhaps the process is circular: Recent hard economic times have affected our values, which has reduced the influence of the throw-away ethos, which has made times even harder by reducing demand and thus employment.

---

### ECONOMIC ORGANIZATIONS AND SOCIETY

Society is adaptive to organizations, to the large, powerful organizations controlled by a few, often overlapping, leaders. To see these organizations as adaptive to a "turbulent", dynamic, ever changing environment is to indulge in fantasy. The environment of most powerful organizations is well controlled by them, quite stable, and made up of other organizations with similar interest, or ones they control. Standard Oil and Shell may compete at the intersection of two highways, but they do not compete in the numerous areas where their interests are critical, such as foreign policy, tax laws, import quotas, government funding of research and development, highway expansion, internal combustion engines, pollution restrictions, and so on. Nor do they have a particularly turbulent relationship to other powerful organizations such as the auto companies, the highway construction firms [and] the Department of Defense. . . .

"Complex Organizations: A Critical Essay," by Charles Perrow. Permission granted by Random House, Inc.

The excerpt illustrates one of the basic arguments Perrow makes in his influential book: Societies adapt to economic organizations more than organizations have to adapt to societies.

---

# ISSUES OF ECONOMIC POWER

## ECONOMIC POWER, CLASS AND THE STATE

Not only does the economy affect society, but many scholars have noted the pervasive economic base of social conflict. Peasants struggling against landowners, workers against employers, the poor against the rich; even racism and wars contain elements of such conflict. World War I can perhaps best be seen as a struggle for access to markets, materials and food—in short, for world economic dominance. From this viewpoint, World War II was merely the second round.

To Marx (1978), the essence of history is the class struggle. This economically based struggle is over the control of property—whether that property is human beings, land or capital. Today, this conflict is most clearly seen in the form of strikes, as discussed in Chapter 12. Class—an economic relationship—is also described as the fundamental element of social stratification in Chapter 15.

The relationship between economic power and the state has been the subject of intensive debate. To Weber (1958) and modern Weberians, it is a complex relationship in which each element affects the other. On the other hand, Marx (1978) held that all struggles within the state are class struggles for political power to represent the economic interests of one class as the general interest. It does happen, of course, that *segments* of a particular class struggle for political power (Marx and Engels, 1950).

Modern, neo-Marxist theory is split between the *instrumentalist* (Miliband, 1969) and the *structuralist* views (Poulantzas, 1978). The former proposes that a cohesive capitalist class (or its dominant element), through formal and informal ties to the polity, is able to manipulate the state into supporting its economic interests. The latter view gives limited autonomy to the state, which can respond to working-class demands while maintaining the long-term economic interests of the capitalist class. For excellent reviews of these positions, see Gold, Lo and Wright (1975) and Cuneo (1979).

However, in a critique of these views, Brym (1985) grants further autonomy to the state. He argues that one source of this autonomy is the simple fact that politicians and bureaucrats want to keep their jobs. To do so, they must not offend any class or group to the point that their re-election or re-appointment is jeopardized. In sum, "States are social structures which reflect the distribution of resources, organization and support—in short, of power—among classes and other groups at given points of time" (Brym, 1985:15). Although economic power greatly influences the state, Brym persuasively argues that it is not the only influence. (For a much broader discussion of the state and political authority, see Chapter 18.)

## MULTINATIONAL ENTERPRISE

An important recent controversy about economic power concerns the emergence of multinational enterprise as the paramount economic fact of the present epoch. Many sociologists argue that these giant conglomerates, which operate in many countries, cannot be effectively controlled by any government. Vernon (1971) points out that a mere 187 American multinational corporations account for one-third of all sales in the United States. The international operations of these giants, he argues, are so vast that they have become a power unto themselves, defying the attempts of their own government to prevent them from exporting jobs while at the same time exporting American economic and political power around the world. As a result of the rapid growth and incredible power of multinational enterprise (MNE), "suddenly, it seems, the sovereign states are feeling naked. Concepts such as national sovereignty and national economic strength appear curiously drained of meaning" (Vernon, 1971:3).

The pervasiveness of MNE has concerned many Canadian sociologists and economists. Since World War II, well over half of Canadian manufacturing and other key industrial sectors have become foreign controlled (see Table 17-1). Although the degree of foreign control has declined slightly in the past decade, it is still the highest among the world's industrialized economies. This has prompted serious concern about the nature of our economy, our society and even our national sovereignty. Scholars such as Clement (1975), Watkins (Canada, 1970) and Brym (1985) have identified the "branch plant" nature of the Canadian economy, which has consequences as diverse as: the serious drain dividend payments place on our

TABLE 17-1  Foreign Control of Canadian Industry Selected Years, 1926-1975

| Sector | % FOREIGN CONTROLLED | | | | | |
| --- | --- | --- | --- | --- | --- | --- |
| | 1926 | 1939 | 1948 | 1958 | 1967 | 1975 |
| Manufacturing | 35 | 38 | 43 | 57 | 57 | 56 |
| Petroleum and natural gas[1] | | | | 73 | 74 | 74 |
| Mines and Minerals | 38 | 42 | 40 | 60 | 65 | 60 |
| Railways | 3 | 3 | 3 | 2 | 2 | 1 |
| Utilities | 20 | 26 | 24 | 5 | 5 | 4 |
| Total of these industries plus commerce | 17 | 21 | 25 | 32 | 35 | 33 |

[1] included in mines and minerals prior to 1958

Statistics Canada, Catalogue 67-202, various years. Adapted from Jorge Niosi, *Les Multinationales Canadiennes,* Montreal, Boreal Express, 1982.

foreign exchange; the retardation of Canadian industrial research; and the barriers to Canadian social mobility created by foreign-controlled branch plants.

A second aspect of the relationship between MNE and Canadian society has, until recently, gone unnoticed. Niosi (1982) points out the startling fact that Canada ranks sixth among the nations which are *home countries* for MNE. In fact, on a per capita basis, it ranks first! So, in two ways—as a host country for foreign MNE and as a home country for our own multinationals abroad—Canada is intimately linked to the world economy. And, to the degree economy shapes society, we are more a world than a national society.

Two further issues involving MNE are important to the relationship between economy and society. These are the questions of extraterritoriality and of values.

Extraterritoriality concerns the application of the home country's laws in the host country. Since the laws of the countries involved often conflict, they can generate a "catch-22" situation for MNE. To obey the law of one country requires breaking the law of another. The Royal Bank of Canada was placed in such a situation when it refused to break Panamanian banking law by releasing banking records of an important client to a Canadian tribunal. The Bank of Nova Scotia found itself in an even more complex and painful situation when it refused to break Bahamian law by releasing client records to a federal grand jury in Florida. It was hit with a $25 000 per day fine. Ford of Canada and M.L.W. Worthington both risked breaking Canadian law and offending Canada when they declined to fulfill orders for trucks to China and locomotives to Cuba respectively. To do so might have resulted in jail terms for the top executives of their American parent firms for breaking the United States' Trading with the Enemy Act. The questions here, of course, are: first, how can nations protect their integrity; and second, how can MNE avoid the Catch-22?

Should a multinational firm be guided by the values of its home society or of the society in which it is operating? Bata finds itself in this dilemma in South Africa, where the position of the legally constituted government and the values of the dominant white society concerning blacks are diametrically opposed to the values and laws of its home country, Canada. So does Northern Telecom, as it restricts the employment of women to the most menial of jobs in Saudi Arabia, in keeping with that country's values and laws concerning gender relations but not our own. Both of these Canadian companies followed the values and laws of their host country, to the chagrin of many Canadians. But an American multinational, ITT, followed the values of its strongly anti-Communist American *home* country by participating in overthrowing the democratically elected Marxist President Allende of Chile (Bosk, 1974). This, too, offended many Canadians.

## WHO CONTROLS ECONOMIC INSTITUTIONS?

We have seen that economic power is wielded, not only within and between economic institutions, but also over other sectors of society. In the early days of capitalism, this power was wielded by the owners of capital and of firms. Many of these were *nouveau riche*, and the rise of this new and powerful class of capitalists was a revolutionary development in rigidly stratified societies. We need only recall the names of Rockefeller, Carnegie and Morgan, for example, to comprehend the extent to which those controlling the rapidly consolidating American corporations wielded economic power. Gradually, this control passed to the descendants of the economically powerful through inheritance, and capitalism became more of a conservative than a revolutionary influence on social stratification. And so, a self-perpetuating capitalist class wielded increasing power from the command posts of the economy.

Then, Berle and Means (1967) argue, this power began to break down because of the very growth in size and power of the major corporations. This growth required massive infusions of new capital, which produced a wide dispersion of stock ownership and loss of control by the original owners. Management now acquired control of (i.e., was able to direct the activities of) the economy's largest corporations and so effected a separation of ownership and control. Berle and Means found that 58 percent of the top 200 American corporations were management controlled in 1929. This proportion rose to 85 percent by 1963. Several other studies supported Berle and Means's proposition that, as a corporation grows, the likelihood of management control also grows, not only among American corporations, but among Canadian and European ones as well.

Many social scientists applauded this development. They believed that management control of the economic power wielded by these dominant corporations would benefit society at large. It would break down the rigid class system and replace it with a new, more flexible, system of stratification. Economic power would now be based on achievement and occupation, not inheritance, and social mobility would be enhanced.

Then, in the 1970s, many sociologists began to refute Berle and Means's findings. They argued that a family can retain control of a corporation with even a small minority ownership, if the remaining shares are widely dispersed. In a reanalysis of

Berle and Means's data, Zeitlin (1974) claimed that roughly two-thirds of the top American corporations were retained under ownership control.

In a 1985 study, the Canadian Bankers Association concluded that nine families control 46 percent of the 300 most important companies on the Toronto Stock Exchange. If valid, this study indicates the strength of family control of the economy in contemporary Canada and an incredible concentration of economic power.

# CANADIAN ECONOMIC INSTITUTIONS

## THE NATURE OF CANADIAN SOCIETY

Are all industrial capitalist societies about the same, or is Canadian society unique? If so, how is it unique?

Canadian sociologists asking these questions see Canadian society as very wealthy, with a per capita production of goods and services among the top half-dozen in the world and not far below that of the United States. Furthermore, they note the flood of American television programs, movies, books and magazines across the border and wonder if a distinct Canadian culture is possible.

On the other hand, several interrelated characteristics of our society distinguish Canadian society from others. These include: the degree of foreign control of our economy; the effect of the regionalism that fragments our society; our unique (and even contradictory) combination of bilingualism and multiculturalism; and our weak sense of national identity. Even Canadian sociology differs from American sociology in its emphasis and approach. An important focus of Canadian sociology is the attempt to explain the nature of our society by determining the effect of our economic institutions on the rest of our social institutions. American sociologists put less emphasis on exploring the uniqueness of their society. When this *is* the topic of their investigations, there is an understandable urge to explain their dominance in terms of the desirable psychological traits of Americans. They contrast these characteristics with the less desirable traits they ascribe to the members of less "advanced" societies, and, *voilà*, the reason for the uniqueness of American society is made clear (Lipset, 1970). Other societies, such as Canada, are naturally less than receptive to explanations based on the shortcomings of their own members. Hence, rather than looking for psychological explanations, we seek institutional ones, such as those developed by economic sociology and political economy.

### Innis and the Staples Perspective

The staples perspective was developed by Harold A. Innis (regarded by many as Canada's greatest scholar) to explain the nature of Canada's economic and social development. He developed his perspective by intensively studying Canada's staples trades (i.e., primary industries), such as the cod fisheries, the fur trade, lumber, wheat and minerals, within the context of the world market.

In essence, Innis (1930, 1956) proposed that the Canadian economy was driven by the demands for raw materials of the metropolitan markets of France, then Britain and then the United States. Canadian exploitation of these raw materials stimulated manufacturing in Europe and the United States, but not in Canada. Indeed, the entire energy of the Canadian economy has been expended in producing raw materials and in providing the infrastructure necessary to process, transport and market them. Furthermore, the demands of other countries for these staples has been highly erratic and beyond our control. This has produced a "boom-bust" economy, as the demand for these staples develops, peaks and then declines. Since different staples are produced in different regions of Canada, regional economic peaks and valleys are even more pronounced than national ones.

Why did Canada not diversify out of its concentration on staples production? Because of the *staples trap*. During good times, there is capital to diversify, but not the will to do so. After all, why meddle with prosperity? In bad times, the will to diversify is present, but not the capital.

Innis and others have used this staples perspective to explain many characteristics of Canadian society. Regionalism is seen to be the result of the different economic interests of Canadian regions and the fact that they are all tied more strongly to foreign economies than to each other. If the lifeblood of British Columbia is the American market for lumber and the Japanese demand for coal, is it not natural that British Columbians are more concerned with political and economic developments abroad than at home?

The boom-bust nature of the Canadian staples economy has historically influenced the Canadian pattern of immigration. As the demand for a particular staple in a specific region boomed, it attracted a flood of immigrants, often from a particular part of Europe. These waves of immigrants could settle together in blocks large enough to develop their own institutions and maintain their own culture. Thus, the Canadian multicultural society can be seen as an outgrowth of our staples economy.

So, too, can our weak sense of national identity. Identity, like culture, is passed on by *tradition carriers*—those who have acquired the identity and the culture of the society. However, the staples perspective suggests that the nature of our economy not only influences Canadians to focus outward, but it also draws a flood of new arrivals during boom periods. Then, as boom turns to bust, there is a surge of emigration. For example, during the last quarter of the nineteenth century, 500 000 more people left Canada than arrived here. This erratic population pattern has produced one of the lowest ratios of tradition carriers to new arrivals of any nation in the world (Bell and Tepperman, 1979). Even had we begun with a strong national identity (and many argue that we did not), this low ratio would tend to weaken it over the course of our history.

The staples perspective, then, attempts to explain the particular nature of the Canadian economy (and of our demographic structure as well). It suggests how Canadian economic institutions have affected other elements of our society. It has had, justifiably, a strong influence on Canadian scholarship, both directly and by influencing the development of subsequent approaches. However, we must be careful to neither oversimplify nor exaggerate its message. There are other persuasive explanations for Canadian regionalism, multiculturalism and weak national identity that draw on a variety of approaches (Bell and Tepperman, 1979; Hiller, 1976; Marsden and Harvey, 1979). Nor are Canadians all hewers of wood and drawers of water in contrast to our highly industrialized American cousins, as the staples perspective suggests. In fact, the contribution of manufacturing to the gross national

TABLE 17-2 Value Added in Manufacturing as a Percentage of Gross National Product, Canada and the United States, Selected Years 1870-1970

| YEAR | MANUFACTURING VALUE ADDED: % OF G.N.P. | | RATIO— US : CANADA |
|---|---|---|---|
| | UNITED STATES | CANADA | |
| 1870 | 23.0 | 20.5 | 1.1:1 |
| 1880 | 23.2 | 21.9 | 1.1:1 |
| 1890 | 27.2 | 25.4 | 1.1:1 |
| 1900 | 26.4 | 23.2 | 1.1:1 |
| 1910 | 24.6 | 24.6 | 1.0:1 |
| 1919 | 28.3 | 27.0 | 1.1:1 |
| 1929 | 29.7 | 27.9 | 1.1:1 |
| 1933 | 25.2 | 26.2 | 1.0:1 |
| 1939 | 27.1 | 27.1 | 1.0:1 |
| 1947 | 32.1 | 26.2 | 1.0:1 |
| 1950 | 31.5 | 33.0 | 1.0:1 |
| 1960 | 32.6 | 28.6 | 1.1:1 |
| 1970 | 30.7 | 25.4 | 1.2:1 |
| 1979 | 30.0 | 24.6 | 1.2:1 |

United States Department of Commerce, 1975: 201, 203, 224, 231, 666, 667; 1984: 431, 746.
Urquhart and Buckley, 1965: 130, 141, 463.
Statistics Canada, various years.

product has been nearly as high in Canada as in the United States ever since Confederation (see Table 17-2). On the other hand, Canadian industry has traditionally emphasized the production of semiprocessed goods for export and the assembly of imported components.

## Political Economy: Beyond the Staples Perspective

As political economy became eclipsed by econometrics within the discipline of economics, it began making a major contribution to sociology. Innis set the initial agenda for this research by analysing the divisive effects of the new staples (e.g., minerals, newsprint, petroleum) on Canadian society. He concluded that, in moving from the orbit of British to American imperialism, "Canada moved from colony to nation to colony" (1956: 405). Canadian sociologists then began trying to explain this return to colonial status.

The staples perspective assumed that Canada was a passive hinterland unable to control its own destiny. The political economy of the 1970s, however, produced a

Canadian ruling class that was an active agent in the takeover of Canadian industry. The most influential analysis was developed by Naylor (1972) and Clement (1975). It proposes that the Canadian staples economy fostered the development of merchant capital to finance the production, transport and export of staples to Britain and the United States. It was not in the interest of the descendants of the early import-export merchants to divert capital from the staples trades into domestic manufacturing. American manufacturers filled this void by expanding into Canada with the blessings of the Canadian merchant capitalists. Perhaps the most forceful proponent of this view is Clement, who declares: "Canadian manufacturers could not survive because the commercial ruling class would not allow them to" (1975:80).

The sociological implications of this analysis are enormous. First, it implies that a small group of merchant capitalists operating in the fields of finance, trade, transportation and utilities shaped Canadian economic development to serve its own selfish ends. This, in turn, suggests that this group wielded enormous economic and political power. In fact, studies have shown that the economically powerful have had close ties to the political system and held many important political posts ever since Confederation (Smith and Tepperman, 1974; Clement, 1975). Secondly, the resulting invasion of American manufacturing enterprises ultimately led to the establishment of American economic power in Canada. Thereafter, the power of Canadian governments was constrained by the economic power of American MNE and the need to maintain good relations with the United States (Levitt, 1970; Marchak, 1979). In all this we can see the influence of the Marxist perspective, which argues that economy shapes society and economic power affects other institutions.

However, this explanation of Canadian economic development (known as the *merchants-against-industry argument*) has not been universally accepted. One study finds, on the contrary, that, historically, there was no cleavage between Canadian merchants and industrialists, for they were often the same people (Richardson, 1982). This same study also contests the supposed dominance of merchants over industrialists.

Another extensive analysis compares industrialization in Canada and several other nations. It finds, in all but Canada, that the landholding and agricultural classes helped shape the political and financial institutions to promote industrialization. To a significant degree then, this study suggests that the Canadian economy was shaped by the defeat of elements of the Canadian farmers in the rebellions of 1837 (Laxer, 1985). On the other hand, Carroll (1985) proposes looking beyond internal class dynamics, and even beyond the relationships between Canadian and American capital to explain the degree of foreign control of Canada's economy and society. Adequate explanation, he contends, will only come within the context of a Marxist theory of imperialism (outlined in Chapter 22).

There have been several objectives in outlining these contending explanations of the development of Canadian economic institutions. First, the foregoing illustrates the dynamic nature of these institutions. Secondly, it presents, within the Canadian context, the contending views of the classical sociologists concerning the interaction of economy and society. We can see that some explanations give primacy to the economy and others, to the polity. And finally, it gives an idea of the complex and fascinating national and international relationships between the economic and political institutions of society.

## ECONOMIC INSTITUTIONS AND REGIONALISM

Innis's staples perspective partly explained the high degree of Canadian regionalism in economic terms. More recently, Canadian sociologists have built upon Innis's theory to significantly extend our understanding of Canadian regionalism.

"The most significant feature of Canadian social organization is not its unity, but its regional diversity" (Matthews, 1980:51). Why should this be? Why should Canadian society be more regionally divided than the societies of Britain, France and the United States? The most persuasive explanations focus on the development of Canadian economic institutions.

There are many objective indicators, such as income and educational attainment, of profound regional differences in Canada. For example, Ontario's per capita personal income has remained almost exactly double the personal incomes in Prince Edward Island and Newfoundland over the past 50 years (Matthews, 1980). These dissimilarities are the result of the different economies of our provinces and regions. The economy of central Canadian society is based on foreign-controlled manufacturing. In fact, nearly three-quarters of all Canadian manufacturing is located within the narrow Montreal-Windsor corridor (Brym, 1985). On the other hand, the Atlantic provinces base their economies on fishing and other primary industries; the Prairies depend on agricultural products and oil for export and British Columbia on forestry and mining.

Regional specialization is partly the result of geography, of course. But it is also partly the result of political action, such as the National Policy of the late nineteenth century and the Crows Nest Pass agreement of 1897. These policies helped open Canada's western agricultural frontier as an internal economic colony of central Canada. Why? Largely because of the need for a new market for central Canadian industry, which was facing bankruptcy at the time.

It should be easy to understand that a wheat farmer, an autoworker, a fisherman and a banker all see the world differently. They earn their daily bread in very different ways, they live in different types of communities and the institutions they are connected with take different forms. Thus, Canadian regionalism is both an economic and a social phenomenon (Matthews, 1980). But, in the tradition of both Marx and Durkheim, it can be seen as ultimately derived from economic activity.

Canadian regionalism can, perhaps, be analysed best in terms of dominance and dependency. Canada itself is dominated by the United States, and this limits our ability to forge stronger interregional ties (Marsden and Harvey, 1979). Within Canada, the economic dominance of the central provinces has been reflected in, and reinforced by, the political dominance of Ontario and Quebec. Those occasions where the location of economic and political power did not coincide, such as the period of rising Quebec nationalism and the Albertan oil boom, have been turbulent times of regionally based social change.

## SUMMARY

This chapter has shown that economic institutions produce and distribute the wealth of a society. Although these functions are common to all societies, they have been fulfilled in very different ways throughout human history. Sociologists are interested in the different forms economic institutions may take, of course. But most of all, sociological curiosity seeks to learn how economic institutions relate to the other institutions of a historically specific society. In other words, sociologists differentiate themselves from economists by setting out to explain the relationship between economy and society. This has been the major objective of this chapter.

Readers may, perhaps, be discouraged by the lack of agreement among Canadian sociologists on a topic as important as the development of the Canadian economy. But actually, this controversy only shows that sociologists are willing to search for answers to extraordinarily complex puzzles. Indeed, it is disagreement that provides excitement in any developing science.

## DISCUSSION QUESTIONS

1. Marx, Weber and Durkheim all studied the conditions under which one form of economic institution will be transformed into another. What are the key elements of the explanations developed by each of these classical sociologists?

2. Using the development and the possible decline of the "throw-away" society as an example, show how economy and society affect each other.

3. Why should Canadians study the impact of multinational enterprise on societies?

4. Does it matter who controls the major economic institutions of a society? If so, why? If not, why not?

5. How does the study of Canadian economic development help us to understand regionalism in Canada?

# 18

# Political Institutions and Authority

*Peter R. Sinclair*

# INTRODUCTION: WHAT IS SOCIAL POWER?

Political institutions are concerned with the exercise of power in society. It is therefore necessary to consider what is involved in the sociological understanding of power and the related concept of authority. Bertrand Russell, the famous philosopher, once defined power as "the production of intended effects," a view that has the advantage of conceptualizing power as performance, not simply the potential to achieve objectives. Social power must involve the control of some actors over others in the pursuit of their objectives or "intended effects."

Sociologists and political scientists have filled countless pages defining power and studying it through empirical research. Perhaps the most provocative and rewarding position is that advocated by Steven Lukes (1974) and by John Gaventa (1980) in his application of Lukes' theory. Lukes challenged the limitations of earlier writing in which the basic (issue was: Under what conditions we should acknowledge that A has power over B?) One group claims that A can be said to exercise power over B when A achieves her objectives over B's opposition, or gets B to do something she would not otherwise do. This definition leads to the study of observable behaviour in concrete decision-making situations, such as Dahl's research on New Haven, Connecticut (1961). The researcher has to find issues on which opposing preferences have been stated, such that A's success involves B's defeat. It is assumed that people's stated preferences represent their actual interest and that silence means consensus.

Dissatisfied with this position, Bachrach and Baratz (1970) pointed to that important source of control in which A manipulates political organizations to keep controversial or threatening topics off the agenda for public debate. They did focus upon decisions, but upon a special kind—those in which "demands for change in the existing allocation of benefits and privileges in the community can be suffocated before they are even voiced . . . " (1970: 44). Thus studies of political power cannot be limited to issues that enter the political arena, but power, in this perspective, is still recognizable only when people consciously challenge the existing order. Consensus is assumed to be genuine, not manipulated.

A more critical position has been adopted by Lukes and Gaventa. The crux of their argument is that even people's perception of their interests (and thus what they take to be an issue) can be controlled with the consequence that they accept the existing state of affairs as legitimate, or at least they see little point in challenging it publicly. To have one's position of control identified as legitimate by those subject to it is the most effective way of exercising power. There is no overt conflict, but the situation nonetheless involves social power. Thus, in studying political power, we should focus not only on open disputes but also on the control of information and on how people acquire values, for in these processes rests the basis for political domination. Such cultural attitudes as fatalism, apathy and self-deprecation should be recognized as psychological adaptations to a system in which people are powerless. And lack of participation leads to a low level of political consciousness, which is summed up in Paolo Freire's evocative concept, "the culture of silence." Unable to express themselves effectively, people may even come to accept the prevailing values, which legitimize their own subordination. A striking example of this occurred when some Jewish inmates of Nazi concentration camps internalized the Nazi definition of themselves as "despicable scum" (Bettelheim, 1961).

The importance of John Gaventa's work is that it demonstrates the validity of this approach in a practical research situation: the investigation of quiescence, the "culture of silence," among Appalachian miners over a prolonged period from the late nineteenth century until 1975, despite a high degree of observable deprivation. Apart from brief periods when the position of landowners and mine operators was weakened by recessions, this local elite wielded effective power by combining each of the mechanisms of power described above. In particular, the compliant behaviour of the poor was explained by (1) lack of resources, because their opponents controlled jobs, houses, land, stores, access to medical facilities and even manipulated local elections; and (2) control by the elite of the opinion-forming institutions of the area, that is, the schools, mass media and churches.

In attempting now to distinguish more clearly the different mechanisms whereby A controls B, the work of one of sociology's distinguished founding figures, Max Weber (1968), provides an excellent starting point. Weber's typology distinguishes in the first instance power based on coercion and power based on authority. Coercion exists in situations where A threatens B with some kind of sanction or deprivation unless B does what A wishes.

Figure 18-1    Max Weber's Typology of Power

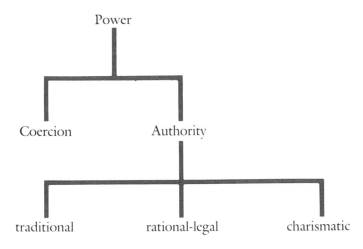

Where power is based on authority, B offers no resistance to A's demand because B accepts that A has the right to command. Thus, authority is power considered legitimate by those subject to it, which makes it far more effective in the long term than power based on coercion. Weber further identifies three abstract or ideal typical forms of authority according to the grounds on which legitimacy is conferred on the powerholder.

Authority may be rooted in *tradition*, in which case people subject to it obey without question because that is the way things have always been done. As long as

A does not try to extend his traditional rights, he is unlikely to meet with opposition. The power of chiefs and elders in tribal societies would be a good example and so too, until recently, would the power of the husband/father in the modern industrial family.

A second source of authority is conveyed in that overused and misunderstood word, *charisma*. An individual enjoys charisma when others believe that he possesses superhuman, supernatural or at least extraordinary powers to resolve problems that are beyond the capacity of ordinary people. Charisma is not something vested in a particular person; rather it is a dimension of a social relationship. As long as B accepts that A has charismatic powers, B will do what A commands. That is what we mean by charismatic authority. Weber sees charisma as a revolutionary force, arising in troubled times, which permits the bonds of tradition to be broken. He does not, however, specify with any clarity the circumstances under which charismatic authority will appear and decline. Some diverse examples of powerful people thought to benefit from charismatic authority are Hitler, Mao Tse-tung and Ghandi.

Weber's third form of authority is characteristic of contemporary industrial societies. *Rational-legal* authority exists when B accepts A's directive because it is just and reasonable, associated with A's office or position, and not personal authority. Generally speaking, the structure of power in modern bureaucracies, both public and private, is supported by rational-legal authority, which permits those in higher ranked positions to command those in subordinate offices within the limits of their officially recognized jurisdiction. Elements of tradition and charisma may enter the relationship, but authority in the modern bureaucracy is primarily rational-legal in form. (Of course, power in such locations may have a coercive dimension as well.) Another example of rational-legal authority is the power of modern professionals over their clients. It is considered just and reasonable by most people that those who are thought to possess specialized knowledge should exercise control within their sphere of competence. The physician, for example, can persuade most patients to engage in unpleasant and undignified behaviour, even when they do not fully understand the reason for it.

Max Weber's classification of social power into coercion and authority is valuable, but needs to be supplemented by two additional mechanisms whereby A can secure B's compliance. Coercion involves the threat of negative sanctions, but A may also get B to do what he wants by the *utilitarian* strategy of offering B a reward in return for B's co-operation. For A to do this, A must possess resources not freely available to B, for example money, goods or information. Finally, *influence* should be mentioned. A may influence B to behave as A wishes by open persuasive argument or by hidden manipulation in which B is not aware of what is taking place. From this brief discussion it should be evident that one of the most fascinating and important tasks of the sociologist is to uncover the distribution of power in society and the mechanisms by which it is exercised.

## POLITICAL INSTITUTIONS

Power is intimately associated with politics. Consider any social relationship and you are sure to observe the making and enforcing of decisions. You are observing a political process. Sometimes, as in a group of friends, the participants appear more or less equal in power; in others, such as employer-emloyee relationships, we observe a marked concentration of power. It is important to recognize that power and politics are aspects of all social relationships, but we are particularly interested here in what are labelled political institutions—the typical patterns of behaviour concerned with the making and implementation of decisions that affect society as a whole. In other words, the political institutions of a society encompass government and administration, law and its enforcement.

Political institutions constitute a network of power relationships and processes open to analysis in terms of their internal structure and also as a system linked to the surrounding society. This conceptualization is abstract, but necessarily so, because the range of concrete forms of political life is enormous across time and space. As sociologists we can, however, begin to understand the character of any society's political institutions by comparing them with others, at least implicitly, and by concentrating on key sociological dimensions. The most important of these are probably the degree of centralization of power, the extent to which the institutional structure is viewed as legitimate (and on what basis), and the pattern of connection between the political and other centres of social action. The sociologist asks questions designed to permit a basic description of any set of political institutions and to provide the possibility of comparison between societies. These questions would certainly include the following.

1. Is the political organization open or closed, democratic or authoritarian?
2. To what degree are political office-holders independent actors in the decision-making process?
3. What groups are best placed to influence political decisions?
4. By what means is political power maintained?
5. How are policies implemented?
6. Under what conditions has the political system developed, and how may it change in the future?

## POLITICAL SYSTEMS AND POLITICAL DEVELOPMENT

Usually sociologists attempt to classify political systems according to a general theory of society and social development, but most contemporary investigators would deny the existence of any single, linear path of political development. At most, it is possible to discern several general trends, such as the increasing scale of government, more political intervention in the conduct of social affairs, the rise of the nation-state and various forms of bureaucratic administration (Bottomore, 1979). Yet these developments proceed at varying paces in different locations and are expressed in a wide variety of concrete forms.

While one does not wish to be accused of advocating a crude historicism, some types of society are historically prior to others and it *is* worth distinguishing between pre-industrial and industrial political systems in that the complex political structures of the contemporary world, both capitalist and socialist, are part of the massive transformation associated with industrialization.

## STATELESS SOCIETIES

Even in the most primitive societies (primitive in the sense of having a rudimentary institutional structure) decisions that affect the society as a whole or that protect society from internal disruption must sometimes be made. In such cases we see government in operation and can learn much about the structure of power in society. Government, the process of effective public decision-making, exists in all societies to some degree, but some societies get by without specialized state structures. With few exceptions, stateless societies have been small, usually hunting and gathering bands of 50 to 200 people. In primitive political systems, government is best understood as an extension of the kinship network. Conflicts and power struggles exist, but there are no special institutions for the exercise of power.

Most of our information about stateless societies comes from the period of early colonization during their incorporation into the European colonial administrations. One such case is the Nuer, who inhabit the valley of the White Nile in the southern Sudan. The Nuer were traditionally a pastoral, migratory people whose central political problem was the maintenance of peace when members of various villages congregated around water holes during the dry season. However, the Nuer had no formal government, law or police force; rather, they relied on the principle that a person who had suffered an offence was entitled to redress by taking cattle in compensation and could expect his kinsmen to aid him. Particularly skilled or experienced men might be respected and their advice followed in difficult situations, but no one could be said to give orders among the Nuer. Thus, power was highly decentralized and followed the fundamental division of lineage (and probably gender as well). Questions regarding access to political institutions do not arise in that the political system of the Nuer consisted simply of "the rules deciding who is to join in, and on which side, in any situation where there has been a resort to force"(Main 1963:38).

## EARLY STATES

States exist if we can identify special institutions that provide the framework for the making, administration and enforcement of decisions that affect society as a whole. Preindustrial states in many variations have flourished in all major regions of the world, but no satisfactory general theory exists to account for their origin. Certainly many states have been the product of conquest in that the conquerers require centralization and control of decisions and the means of force to maintain their dominance. Yet, there are far too many exceptions to permit us to accept conquest as an adequate account of the rise of the state.

An alternative environmental or hydraulic theory claims that the first states all developed in areas where large irrigation projects and flood control were necessary. These works, it is argued, required a degree of collective effort and co-ordination that was only possible through a state structure. This theory may explain the origin of Middle and East Asian states, but clearly breaks down when applied to other independent manifestations of the state.

Perhaps the level of technical development should be considered, for it is evident that only a society capable of generating an economic surplus can support a political/administrative elite that does not itself produce anything directly. The Nilotic herders generated no economic surplus and lived in small groups characterized by primary relationships. They had no need for a state and no means of supporting one. In contrast, the Bantu of central Africa were advanced horticulturalists who measured wealth by the possession of land. To protect their wealth against others, a centralized political system was advantageous. However, there are numerous cases of peoples with similar levels of technical development but different patterns of political life.

Whatever their origin, states involve an obvious centralization of decision-making and require the sociologist to investigate the links between the political institutions and the cleavages in a society in order to evaluate whose interests are best served by the political system. Consider the Bantu states. Many of the Bantu peoples recognized a chief who delegated authority, administered law, collected taxes and organized public activities, especially warfare. With some exceptions, the Bantu states propped up a social structure that was caste-like, that is, the population was divided into several groups each with a particular function and with no movement of individuals between them. Among the Ruanda, these groups constituted a hierarchy of power based on ethnicity. Thus the ruling caste of Tusi warriors and cattle-owners held all powerful state positions and dominated two subordinate castes. The Tusi despised agriculture, which they left to the Hutu, who also looked after Tusi cattle and who could sometimes acquire small herds of their own. Twa pygmies were the pot-makers and were also obliged to entertain the Tusi overlords.

It is wise to remember that the degree of closure is highly variable among the African kingdoms. Lloyd (1965) suggests that a distinction be made between *closed* societies (such as the Ruanda), in which a ruling class is based on lineage and ethnicity, and *open* societies, in which recruitment to the political elite is possible either by election through the royal lineage (the Yoruba) or by royal appointment for which all are eligible (the Buganda).

The administration of the African kingdoms revolved around the "favoured one" or "first minister," whose importance stemmed from his control of access to the king. This official was known as the Katikiro. In the Buganda tribe his duties included the organization of the numerous servants who tended the needs of the royal household, supervision of public works, tax collection, the planning of war and the protection of the king. Administration was channelled through a hierarchy of subordinate chiefs, whose positions were not hereditary. Each chief held his own court and had his own retainers. Only cases that could not be decided at this lower level proceeded to the highest court. Control was possible because of the traditional legitimacy of the king's power and because deviants were severely punished.

A more comprehensive review of preindustrial political institutions and authority would examine the structure of the great bureaucratic empires from China, through the Middle Eastern states, to ancient Rome. Nor should the Inca state be neglected. Described by Eisenstadt (1971:175) as "the first 'archaic' stage of breakthrough from the primitive order," the ancient city-states are an intriguing subject, especially Athens, a democracy built paradoxically on the foundation of slavery. More recent and more directly part of our own social history, the formation and collapse of European feudal institutions are equally worthy of attention.

## MODERN STATES

The appearance of new forms of political organization from the eighteenth century to the present is the subject of an enormous literature. Nation-building and political development are two of the most frequently used terms to capture the theme. Some works, such as Lipset's (1963) account of the United States, focus on individual societies, while others are explicitly comparative (Almond and Powell, 1966; Moore, 1969). Scholars have faced a great challenge in explaining why societies developed the different types of institutions that characterize their political lives. Why should liberal democracy appear so entrenched in Sweden or the United States yet so weak in Germany and Italy that it was overthrown by fascism between the two world wars? What accounts for Chinese or Soviet socialism in contrast with India's capitalist democratic route? Why have so many attempts at nation-building in the Third World ended in military dictatorship and other forms of authoritarian government? And what is to count as political development? What values are embedded in the concept?

### Skocpol's Theory of Social Change

Nobody has been able to answer all of these questions and none of the major works are without substantial limitations; yet such authors as Barrington Moore, Jr. (1969), Reinhard Bendix (1977) and Theda Skocpol (1979) have been stimulating and informative. Consider, for example, the theme of Theda Skocpol's book on the state and revolutionary change. She defines social revolutions as "rapid, basic transformations of a society's state and class structures" (Skocpol, 1979:4). Her theory is developed and tested through an examination of the French, Russian and Chinese revolutions with extensive reference to Germany, Japan and England. Her theory locates the explanation of change in the way that society is structured rather than in the motives or purposes of individuals. In considering structure, states are accorded considerable independent significance in bringing about change, and the importance of the international environment is taken more seriously than in most other works. Thus, Skocpol argues that modern social revolutions occur only in countries situated in disadvantaged positions in the international arena. Like Barrington Moore, Skocpol places great importance on the peasant masses as a factor in the political outcome.

Skocpol demonstrates that France, Russia and China were each characterized by conditions conducive to both political crisis and peasant revolt. For example, prior to 1917, Russia was a bureaucratic, absolutist state with a politically weak nobility and inadequate agricultural development; it was also subject to extreme international pressure that showed up its military and economic weaknesses. Despite the land reforms of the nineteenth and twentieth centuries, peasants remained impoverished by rents and redemption payments, but lived in relatively solidary village communities and were open to mobilization against the existing order. Peasant revolts against private, landed property contributed to the defeat of the old state in 1917 and helped bring the Bolsheviks to power. The tsarist bureaucracy was not defeated

TABLE 18-1 Causes of Social Revolution in France, Russia, and China

A. CONDITIONS FOR POLITICAL CRISES

|  | MONARCHY/ DOMINANT CLASS | AGRARIAN ECONOMY | INTERNATIONAL PRESSURES |
|---|---|---|---|
| France | Landed–commercial dominant class has leverage within semibureaucratic absolute monarchy. | Growing, but no breakthrough to capitalist agriculture. | Moderate. Repeated defeats in wars, especially due to competition from England. |
| Russia | Highly bureaucratic absolutist state; landed nobility has little political power. | Extensive growth; little development in core regions. | Extreme. Defeats in 1850s and 1905. Prolonged participation and defeat in WWI. |
| China | Landed–commercial dominant class has leverage within semibureaucratic absolutist state. | No developmental breakthrough; near limits of growth, given population and available land. | Strong. Defeats in wars and imperialist intrusions. |

*Contrasts*

| Prussia/ Germany | Highly bureaucratic absolutist state; landed nobility has little extralocal political leverage. | Transition to capitalist agriculture. | 1806—Strong 1848—Mild |
| Japan | Highly bureaucratic (though not fully centralized) state. No true landed upper class. | Productivity increasing within traditional structures. | Strong; Imperialist intrusions. |
| England | No bureaucratic state. Landed class dominates politics. | Transition to capitalist agriculture. | Mild |

TABLE 18-1 *(continued)*

B. CONDITIONS FOR PEASANT INSURRECTIONS

| | AGRARIAN CLASS STRUCTURES | LOCAL POLITICS |
|---|---|---|
| France | Peasant smallholders own 30-40% of land; work 80% + in small plots. Individual property established, but peasant community opposes seigneurs, who collect dues. | Villages relatively autonomous under supervision of royal officials. |
| Russia | Peasants own 60% + and rent more; control process of production on small plots; pay rents and redemption payments. Strong community based upon collective ownership. | Villages sovereign under control of tsarist bureaucracy. |
| China | Peasants own 50% + and work virtually all land in small plots. Pay rents to gentry. No peasant community. | Gentry landlords, usurers, and literati dominate local organizational life; cooperate with Imperial officials. |

*Contrasts*

| | | |
|---|---|---|
| Prussia/ Germany | West of Elbe: resembles France. East of Elbe: large estates worked by laborers and peasants with tiny holdings, and no strong communities. | Junker landlords are local agents of bureaucratic state; dominate local administration and policing. |
| Japan | Communities dominated by rich peasants. | Strong bureaucratic controls over local communities. |
| England | Landed class owns 70% +. Peasantry polarizing between yeomen farmers and agricultural laborers. No strong peasant community. | Landlords are local agents of monarchy; dominate administration and policing. |

TABLE 18-1 *(continued)*

## C. SOCIETAL TRANSFORMATIONS

|  | RESULTS OF A PLUS B |
|---|---|
| France | 1787–9: Breakdown of absolutist state; and widespread peasant revolts against seigneurial claims. |
| Russia | 1860s–90s: Bureaucratic reforms from above.<br>1905: Unsuccessful revolutionary outbreak.<br>1917: Dissolution of state; widespread peasant revolts against all private landed property. |
| China | 1911: Breakdown of Imperial state; spreading agrarian disorder, but no autonomous revolts by peasants against landlords. |
| *Contrasts* | |
| Prussia/ Germany | 1807–14: Bureaucratic reforms from above.<br>1848: Failed social revolution; bureaucratic monarchy stays in power. |
| Japan | Political revolution centralizes state; followed by bureaucratic reforms from above. |
| England | Political revolution establishes parliamentary predominance within nonbureaucratic monarchy. |

From STATES AND SOCIAL REVOLUTIONS, by Theda Skocpol, Cambridge University Press, pp. 155–157.

by internal pressure alone, (claims Skocpol) but slipped into its final crisis with military failure during World War I.

Wisely, Skocpol does not conclude her analysis with the rise to power of a new regime; she recognizes that the process of "revolutionary state-building" can last for decades. In her three cases it was encouraged by popular mobilization against counter-revolutionaries and foreign powers. The outcome has consistently meant a state larger, more centralized, more bureaucratic and more concerned to mobilize the masses than was true of the ancien régime.

Despite the majestic sweep of Skocpol's analysis and the range of evidence that she musters in its support, some critical points should be raised. First, the differences in origin and outcome of the three main cases are considerable. One must recognize, for example, that the success of the Chinese Communists depended on their mobilization of the peasantry, whereas the Russian Bolsheviks had no significant rural organization. Indeed, Skocpol pays too little attention to the urban, industrial roots of the Russian revolution. Another point (recognized by Skocpol) is that general theories of nation-building are difficult to square with the historically specific factors that condition each case. Finally, Skocpol leaves almost no role for human agency when she emphasizes so much the general structural conditions of change. It would be better to pay more attention to how those conditions have been judged and acted upon by organizational leaders. These comments are not intended to belittle Skocpol's achievement, but to show that even the best work leaves room for argument and extension.

The Russian revolution spawned a type of industrial society and associated political system that will be labelled here as state socialist. It is socialist in that most productive property is *publicly owned* through the state, but *state* socialist in that control is centralized in the state bureaucracy (effectively, in the Communist Party) rather than decentralized to collectives of workers. At best, working people are consulted before decisions are made at the apex; at worst, they are merely subjected to the decisions of party leaders in a one-party state.

Although the Soviet state and those modelled on it are highly centralized, they are not monolithic entities from which all debate and dispute have been excluded. Interest groups and factions struggle for control within the party. There has, for example, been a long-standing competition between advocates of a more decentralized economic system and those who believe that modern information processing technologies permit centralized planning to a high degree, even in a complex industrial economy. Until recently, the latter position has been dominant.

Nor should the Soviet rulers be considered the equivalent of corporation managers in capitalist societies. The economy is not organized with the prime objective of private profit and state property cannot be inherited by the children of Soviet leaders. Labour does produce wealth that is appropriated by the state, but, allowing for some corruption and parasitic living, it is generally appropriated for subsequent public investment. Officials in the higher circles of the state apparatus may be able to offer educational and political advantages to their kin, but they cannot simply transfer their positions in the state or the wealth accumulated and invested in the name of the state.

Unfortunately, this introduction can provide no more than a glimpse of the fascinating history and structure of such political formations. We must now turn to the institutions associated with capitalist industrialization and to Canadian society in particular.

## POLITICAL INSTITUTIONS OF INDUSTRIAL CAPITALISM

During the early period of capitalist development in Europe, up to the late eighteenth century, the core powers were characterized by absolutist monarchies in which the rulers claimed total power and were advised by aristocratic elites, leaving ordinary people without voice. This system began to crumble, first in seventeenth century England, with the Civil War, later in France and other parts of northern and western Europe as the demands of the rising capitalist class and the ideology of government by consent of the governed proved increasingly irresistible. Despite violent opposition, the remnants of feudalism collapsed before the ideological and economic force of the new order; nor was the most powerful colonial state, Britain, spared from revolutionary upheaval in its North American colonies. Political change went hand-in-hand with the expansion of industrial capitalism in that capitalism could not flourish where the factors of production (land, labour and capital) were restrained by traditional feudal practices. Capitalist development required a radical political break with the past as well as technological and economic transformation.

At a high level of generality, we may note several important features of the modern states that emerged with industrialization. First, the political process became increasingly complex, housed in a distinct institutional structure of legislature, governing executive and administrative apparatus. Second, administration was clearly separated from the household of the rulers in that government was no longer the personal right of any individual. Increasingly action was justified by rational-legal authority, and the era of patrimonial bureaucracy, as Weber might have said, was dead. Third, the new states rather quickly expanded the scope of their involvement in the regulation of social life to an unprecedented level. Fourth, as the means of force became ever more sophisticated and destructive, they were more effectively monopolized within the state apparatus by the formation of standing armies and "professional" police. Fifth, a greater association developed between the boundaries of states and the concept of a national territory to the point where many consider that a nation without its own state is to that degree flawed. Finally, in that minority but powerful group of states classed as liberal democracies, rights of citizenship have been slowly extended to encompass the adult population as a whole (Tilly, 1975; Poggi, 1978; Hechter and Brustein, 1980).

Despite these common features, the political systems that have in fact emerged in the advanced capitalist world exhibit considerable variation. Some states are constitutional monarchies, which means that the formal head of state is a hereditary ruler advised by an elected legislature. Britain, Denmark and Canada (where the governor-general represents the queen) are examples. Others are republics with elected heads of state (for example, the United States, France and West Germany). Some states are unitary, that is, formal power rests with a single central authority (for example, Sweden or Italy), while others are federations in which powers are formally divided between a central authority and the component parts of the state

*Lieutenant Governor John Black Aird, as the representative of the Queen, opens the fourth session of Ontario's thirty-second parliament. Canada's political system is a federal constitutional monarchy and inherits the British parliamentary system.* Reprinted by permission of Ontario Legislative Assembly. Reprinted by permission of the Minister of Government Services and the Ontario Legislature.

(for example, Canada and the United States). Electoral systems are also highly variable, the most important distinction being that between proportional representation and single member, simple majority constituencies. In the former case, political parties are entitled to be represented in the elected assembly in proportion to their support within the electorate. Thus, a party with 15 percent of the votes would expect about 15 percent of the seats, although, to avoid excessive fragmentation in the political system, a party must usually obtain a minimum percentage of votes to qualify for any seats. Societies that utilize such a system include Italy, Sweden, Finland and West Germany. The single member, simple majority system is familiar to Canadians. Here, the electorate is divided into constituencies from which a single member is elected. An absolute majority of votes is not required. Hence, if more than two parties take part, the elected member may have less than 50 percent of the vote. In such a system, a party whose representatives obtained about 15 percent of the vote in all constituencies would never be represented in parliament in contrast with the result under proportional representation.

Sociologists have attempted to explain the politics of the modern bureaucratic state by analysing the connection between the state and civil society, that is, between the state and the social groups of which society as a whole is composed. They do not, however, agree on the nature of that relationship. Some maintain an image of the advanced capitalist societies, particularly the United States, that corresponds closely to the ideology of representative democracy in that they find no clear centre of power. Rather, power is dispersed among a wide range of competing groups, none of which consistently gets its own way. For the obvious reason, this perspective is often called *pluralism* (Bachrach and Baratz, 1970; Lipset, 1960). A much more cynical interpretation was provided by C.W. Mills (1953) and his followers, who identified a ruling elite (composed of the highest levels of the military, political and economic structures) that held sway on all matters of truly national importance. Some Marxists see the state as a conservative force, in effect the instrument of the bourgeoisie, because of its dependence on the major capitalist corporations and the roots of so many officials in middle- and upper-status backgrounds (Miliband, 1969). Other Marxists (Offe, 1972; Poulantzas, 1973; Szymanski, 1978) claim some independence or "relative autonomy" for the state in its relationship with the major capitalist actors because it meets the long-term needs of capitalism as a whole (for example, to maintain the general conditions conducive to the accumulation of wealth), which require action against certain short-term demands of capitalists. Thus, the expansion of public welfare against capitalist opposition is sometimes interpreted as a move to shore up the future of capitalism by smoothing over some of the discontent engendered by unemployment, poor health care and unequal access to education. Yet other authors locate a genuinely independent source of power in the state positions themselves (Skocpol, 1979; Miliband, 1983). No attempt will be made here to evaluate these competing theories, but in developing a sociological perspective on Canadian political institutions, considerable relevant evidence will be referred to.

# CANADIAN POLITICAL INSTITUTIONS

Canada is a federation with a complex state structure in which the powers of legislation are divided between the federal and provincial levels. Although sociologists should analyse the social relationships implied by the formal structures of legislature and government and should certainly be familiar with how decisions are actually made, they have generally left this work to political scientists. A full understanding of the Canadian state would also require tracing its historical development and evaluating the social significance of the division of powers. Nor should the social history of the Canadian political parties, the chief actors in the political system, be ignored. The comments that follow do, however, present some of the most pertinent aspects of a sociology of the contemporary Canadian political system with a focus on the federal state.

## STATE AND SOCIAL STRUCTURE

Political sociology examines the links between political institutions and the structure of society as a whole by assessing the extent to which the system is biased in favour of some groups and against others. In Canadian society, we should consider the groups formed on the basis of class, gender, ethnicity and, with some reservations, region. These are the major social sources of disparate group interests and conflict. The following analysis, drawing on a Marxist-influenced model of the state, paints a rather black picture of social domination, one that is by no means unique to Canada. The Canadian situation differs in detail from other mature capitalist societies, but the general pattern of control has been widely reported in such studies as Dye's (1983) account of the United States and Guttsman's (1974) work on Britain.

In all likelihood, the Canadian state is staffed in the upper echelons by personnel who share the same cultural orientation and ideology as the more privileged social strata. The main basis for this similarity rests in their common social origins and experience of socialization. In the nineteenth century, the wealthy were often directly represented in the state apparatus; in the late twentieth century, this is less common, because they are well served by the middle class. For the period 1961–73, Olsen (1977, 1980) collected biographical data on federal cabinet ministers, provincial premiers, justices of the Supreme Court of Canada and the provincial chief justices. Treated separately were 81 members of the provincial cabinets of Quebec, Ontario, Alberta and British Columbia. Representing only about 1 percent of the general population, the upper class in Olsen's account provided 22.4 percent of the state elite in 1973; the middle class accounted for 69 percent, and the working class only 8.6 percent, a slight decline over the previous decade. These figures are based on the class location of fathers of the 1973 elite.

Considering the previous occupations of cabinet ministers, we find that 86 percent were lawyers, businessmen, doctors or other independent professionals. In 1960, 18 percent of federal cabinet members came from the world of business, while the figure for 1973 was 27 percent. Most would eventually return to corporate boardrooms, there to be joined by other ex-politicians, of whom John Turner and Donald Macdonald are perhaps the best known examples in recent years. Mr. Turner did, of course, re-enter political life in 1984, only to be removed to the opposition benches after a few weeks of power. With this close interaction, it would be quite surprising if the interests of Canadian capitalists were not a prime concern in the upper reaches of the state. Moreover, Wallace Clement (1977) has shown that 33 percent of the senior executives of Canada's dominant corporations in 1975 had been directly involved in state affairs, mostly in appointed positions (for example, as members of advisory councils). This figure rises to 47 percent if positions held by close kin are included. Finally, fully 18 percent had served the state in a full-time capacity. Clement's conclusion is that "this set of people, more than any others, are those taken into account by the state" (1977:233).

So far, only the cabinet and judiciary have been mentioned, but the state is also a bureaucratic structure and the higher civil service is extremely influential, not only because it is responsible for putting government policy into action, but also because the permanent officials are in a strong position to use their knowledge to influence the ministers, who may spend relatively little of their careers in a single department. Olsen researched 318 federal deputy ministers and assistant deputy ministers, provincial deputy ministers, and heads of crown corporations or regulatory boards. The results are similar to those already reported. Thus, in the federal bureaucratic elite, we find 10 percent from the upper class, 75 percent from the middle class and 15 percent from the working class.

There is no doubt that the federal elite is also structured in relation to the ethnic divisions in Canadian society. In 1973, those of British origin were overrepresented in both the political-juridical and bureaucratic segments of the state relative to their share of the total population, although the situation was more equitable than it had been in earlier decades (Olsen, 1977:204-10). Francophones were only slightly underrepresented by 1973. Thus the preponderance of those of British origin was mainly at the expense of Canadians who belonged to ethnic groups other than the French.

Another serious bias in the state's structure is the inadequate representation of women. While there is no reason to expect women to behave differently than men on many issues, it is likely that the interests of women will be more effectively represented by their presence in decision-making positions. Regardless of whether or not women would be better protected by greater political participation, their absence for so long from positions of power is unacceptable, since it seems to have been based purely on the ascriptive criterion of gender. Women did not achieve federal voting rights until 1918 and are still greatly underrepresented in all major branches of the Canadian political institutitional structure. No Canadian prime minister or provincial premier has ever been a woman and, occupying 6 of the 40 positions in Brian Mulroney's first cabinet, women remain drastically underrepresented. They are slowly cracking the bastion of male political dominance, but it is an exceptionally slow process, one that will contribute to, and yet itself depends upon, a general reorientation of attitudes towards gender roles in Canadian society. The socialization process must change before this incipient discrimination will disappear. The position of Canadian women is echoed elsewhere in advanced industrial societies. Thus, only 3.7 percent of the French National Assembly in 1978 and 3.6 percent of the British parliament elected in 1974 were women (Roth and Wilson, 1980:164). Margaret Thatcher has since become prime minister in Britain, but her case remains exceptional.

In his extensive analysis of the special interest groups through which demands are articulated in the Canadian political process, Robert Presthus observed how the unequal distribution of political resources permits those with vested interest in the status quo to enjoy more meaningful and successful political participation. He concluded pessimistically that "the perhaps inevitable inequalities of political resources among interest groups mean that government, to some extent, is pushed into the anomalous position of defending the strong against the weak" (Presthus, 1973:349).

The preceding analysis of the social origins, occupations and connections of the state elite is consistent with the view of the state as a captive of the capitalist class. This oversimplifies the situation in that capitalists and other dominant interests are frequently dissatisfied with the performance of Canadian political institutions. The state elites are not subservient, because they do control key resources, such as legal authority, force and information, which provide scope for independent action, and they are compelled to accommodate deprived groups to some degree to ensure the legitimacy and stability of the political structure in which their own careers are located. Having said that, however, the ideological compatibility of state elites and Canadian capitalists and the complementarity of their interests in maintaining the social structure from which they benfit both inhibit the possibility of radical institutional change.

# POLITICAL PARTIES AND ELECTIONS

Even if the state appears biased in favour of privileged classes, men and anglophones, other classes and marginal groups in Canadian society may still hope to be represented through political parties and special interest groups on the grounds that politicians must be responsive to the electorate as a whole in order to receive their support at periodic elections. Let us examine this pluralist position more closely, since parties and elections are a vital part of the political institutional structure.

First, however, the political party should be distinguished from an interest group. A political party is a voluntary organization that aims to win political power by controlling the institutions of government, a process which, in liberal-democratic systems, requires success in elections. In contrast, interest groups or pressure groups are organized expressions of special interests in society that attempt to achieve their objectives by exerting political pressure on governments, for example, by lobbying cabinet and members of parliament, by influencing senior bureaucrats and by building visible public support for their causes. Interest groups do not attempt to become the government; they are content with influencing policy decisions and the process of implementation.

One obvious problem in the expression of interests is that the electorate is not encouraged by politicians to face the divisive issues. Indeed, the skill of a political leader is often measured according to his or her ability to avoid taking a clear stand or to offer a bland compromise that is open to a wide range of interpretation. Looking specifically at social inequality, we find that only the NDP persistently raises questions in this sphere, although the proposals of the NDP leadership have seldom gone beyond advocating the regulation of capital and the introduction of improved welfare measures. But the NDP has never enjoyed federal political power and has never received more than 20 percent of the popular vote. For the most part, the dominant Liberal and Conservative parties have been able to submerge issues of inequality by tinkering with the rough edges of a system that they claim is basically sound, conducive to material improvements in standards of living and, above all, a protection of basic rights and personal freedoms. The disputes are about the form and amount of the tinkering, or about which person is best suited to engage in it.

## The Problem of Oligarchy

How can the important social issues be submerged in the political parties, given that leaders are now elected and that conventions pass all manner of policy resolutions? Indeed, this has been a classic problem in political sociology since Robert Michels (1915) published his theory of oligarchy in mass political parties. In brief, Michels argued that the division of labour in political organizations combined with the need of mass members for guidance inevitably creates a tendency towards oligarchy, that is, domination by a small inner group. Leaders become more concerned with preserving the organization itself and their position in it than with pursuing the goals for which it was established.[1] Historically, the dominance of the party

---

[1] The inevitability of oligarchy has been challenged by a number of authors. One of the best known is Lipset, Trow and Coleman's (1956) study of competition and democratic practice within an American union.

leaders in policy-making is clear (Whitaker, 1977). How can we explain that dominance? This question leads to more specific ones concerning the internal structure of parties. What kind of people attend conventions and run the political parties? Do they represent the structure of society as a whole or are they drawn from a narrow segment of the social structure?

Regardless of the party, elites and activists come from more privileged social backgrounds. The typical party delegate to a convention will be a male, a businessman or lawyer of above average income and education. The same can be said for candidates for election to the House of Commons and we know it is also true for the higher levels of the state apparatus. NDP activists resemble the Liberals and Conservatives in this regard, whereas Social Crediters tend to have less education and to perceive themselves as working class. Of course, the connection of the NDP with the Canadian labour movement ensures a degree of representation from that source in the inner circles of the party, while business is hardly visible.

Lele, Perlin and Thorburn (1977) provide a valuable three-pronged critique of the limited democracy of conventions in which they refer to the unrepresentative social composition of the delegates, the bias of convention rules and the widespread manipulation by candidates and their agents. Using measures of income, education and occupation, neither the Liberal, Conservative nor NDP conventions were found to be representative of the Canadian population. A person's social background is no guarantee that she will either understand or support the interests that are typical of that group, but it is a disadvantage for less privileged groups to have to rely on the sympathetic perceptions of others. We should also note that Canadian parties try to bring into their elite representatives from regions and cultural groups where the party as a whole is weak. However, since class issues are downplayed, this pattern of recruitment does not extend to social classes.

Convention procedures ensure advantages to party elites through, for example, the practice of permitting a large number of *ex officio* delegates or centrally appointed delegates-at-large. When 30 to 40 percent of delegates fall into these categories it becomes difficult to challenge the party leadership. And what of the remainder, who are selected at the local constituency level? Here, too, the possibility of packing meetings with "instant" members or conducting them with minimal publicity offers opportunities for manipulation, although the extent to which such practices occur is probably impossible to document.

## Canadian Voting Patterns

Yet people can still vote. Are there any relevant social patterns in the voting behaviour of Canadians? It was long believed that Canada constituted an exception to the predominant voting patterns of the western democracies in which the main line of cleavage was based on class position (Bendix, 1977; Alford, 1963). In Canada, ethnicity, region and religion (in the past) have been considered of far greater importance, but none of these factors is decisive when we study the matter in the conventional way by relating people's expressed party preferences to their social positions. However, the relevance of class to voting in Canada has been underestimated because, with the partial exception of the NDP, modern party leaders do not express themselves in class terms and class is a minor factor in predicting party choice. The best national data come from the 1974 election study (Clarke, Jensen, Leduc and Pammett, 1979) which demonstrated that the Liberals and Conservatives both enjoyed support across the major occupational and class divisions.[2] The NDP's low level of total support was also fairly evenly distributed with a tendency to be firmer among semiprofessionals and semiskilled manual workers. However, this apparently weak relationship between socio-economic position and voting was challenged by Ogmundson's (1975) interesting reinterpretation of 1965 election data.

Ogmundson's innovation was to point out that we need to know how people evaluate the class orientation of the political parties before concluding that class is irrelevant. Once parties are classified according to whether people see them as "for the working class" or "for the middle class," then conventional measures of social class are related to voting in Canada in a moderately positive manner similar to that of other western democracies, that is, manual workers who perceived the Liberals as "for the working class" tend to vote Liberal, and so on. If class *appeared* irrelevant to the choice of Canadian voters, this was not due to its actual irrelevance, Ogmundson concluded, but to the tendency of the parties to avoid class issues or to adopt basically similar positions on those issues. Thus it is not surprising that the voters were thoroughly confused, at least in 1965, as to the class orientation of the parties. Forty-one percent of respondents perceived no difference between the major parties, 29 percent considered the Liberals to be more middle class than the Conservatives, while the same percentage judged the Conservatives more middle class. On related questions of political ideology, many Canadians simply could not or would not place the parties on the left or right of the political spectrum.[3] From existing evidence the conclusion is warranted that class, in the sense of socio-economic status, is a genuine though minor factor in accounting for the voting behaviour of Canadians, whereas class in the Marxist sense is a major factor in determining the framework in which other forces operate. The latter point will be developed later.

If socio-economic status is not a good predictor of how Canadians vote, then perhaps ethnic identity can resolve the problem. In Canada, the primary ethnic division is between Francophone and Anglophone. The Liberals have traditionally enjoyed enormous support from Francophone Quebeckers in federal elections and among non-Anglo-Saxon immigrants they have also been stronger than the Conservatives. The Conservatives lost their early hold on Quebec over such issues as the hanging of Louis Riel, the Manitoba school question and the introduction of conscription in World War I. Apart from the brief Diefenbaker interlude after the 1958 election, the Conservatives could not mount a successful assault on the Liberal fortress until, led by a bilingual Quebecker, they swept the Liberals from power in 1984.

Religion is no longer a critical division in the sense that it rarely determines political choice, but, historically, the Liberal Party was more closely associated with Catholic voters, the Conservatives with Protestants. Something more should be said

---

[2] This research is an example of the overlap between quantitative political science and the concerns of political sociologists. Indeed, many of the authors referred to in this chapter are political scientists.

[3] For further development of this line of inquiry see (Lambert and Hunter, 1979).

about region, which is frequently put forward as a decisive factor in Canadian elections. In the 1970s and early 1980s, the Liberal Party was reduced to a handful of seats west of Lake Superior, whereas it dominated Quebec and battled for supremacy with the Conservatives in much of Ontario and Atlantic Canada. The NDP enjoyed strength in Manitoba, Saskatchewan, British Columbia and parts of Ontario, but has been a minor political force east of the Ottawa Valley. The Conservative Party in 1984 surged to the forefront in Quebec and has now become the only truly national party in that it elects MPs from coast to coast. Although regions have been associated with support for particular parties in Canada, one hesitates to identify regionalism as a cause of the structure of representation. It is not region as such, but the economic and social dimensions of past and present life experience, which happen to vary geographically, that are more likely to have some causal impact on politics.

All the preceding sociological factors do not allow us to predict with certainty how individual Canadians will actually vote. In their report of the 1974 survey, Clarke et al. (1979) state that class, ethnicity, religion, region, community size, sex and age all have some effect, but much less than political variables such as prior voting record, concern about immediate issues and the image of the party leader. Should we then conclude that a sociological approach has relatively little to offer on this question? Perhaps not. A crude theory in which voting behaviour somehow inevitably follows from social experience is obviously inadequate. However, it might make for a more interesting sociological account if we start from the assumption that voting is an interpretive action through which people cope with political situations in which they usually possess incomplete information and inadequate understanding of the operation of the political system. As Lukes (1974) might argue, they are not fully aware of their interests and of how those interests can or should be acted upon. Social divisions and conflicts of interest are not unimportant, but they are well camouflaged by political debates that imply a broad social harmony and that contain disputes only over the preferred means and individuals to run the country. Rarely is there any debate about the kind of society that is to be desired. Basically, the structure of society does not encourage adequate political involvement and the low orientation of most of the population to issues compared with personalities makes elite domination easier.[4] Voting does not determine state policy; it provides legitimation for those who do control it.

## POLITICAL PARTICIPATION AND ALIENATION

Political participation has been defined by Verba and Nie (1972:2) as " . . . those activities by private citizens which are more or less directly aimed at influencing the selection of governmental personnel and/or the actions they take." In addition to voting, such participation might include membership in a party, attending a rally

[4] An opposite view is held by authors such as William Kornhauser (1959) or Almond and Verba (1963) who feel that elites need insulation from demands of the masses if they are to be effective and that stability is better ensured if participation is at a moderate level. The dangers of oligarchy and alienation are of lesser significance in such an approach.

or demonstration, active campaigning, directly contacting public officials and seeking election. Generally, political participation is greater among those with advanced education than among those with little education and greater among persons of higher occupational status compared with people of low status.

What is the explanation for those basic sociological observations? Some years ago Robert Lane (1959) provided an extensive review of this subject and his conclusions are still basically sound (but see Milbrath and Goel (1977) for a more recent analysis). The most important factors are:

1. The issues at stake are often clearer to the better informed upper status individual.
2. Lower status people often feel at a disadvantage in contacts with upper status people and tend to withdraw from situations that would accentuate this feeling. It is interesting that such an attitude is unlikely to affect the private act of voting. In fact, casting a vote is the kind of participation that does not deter lower status individuals to anything like the same extent as taking an active part in organizations or writing to a member of parliament.
3. In middle and upper status families (and in the schools that their children attend) more emphasis is placed on the value of participation.
4. Many lower status people are so discouraged by their insecure situation that they simply feel there is no hope and no point in participation.

In Canada, as in most liberal democratic societies, a majority of the population does vote in general elections, but few people are more politically active.[5] Even those who vote often appear to do so out of a sense of obligation rather than the belief that they are exercising any real political control. Indeed, most Canadians feel alienated from the political system. In my own research, I have shown that the experience of lack of control over political affairs is widespread among all major social groups and regions of Canada (Sinclair, 1979). Evidence for this conclusion has been drawn from the 1974 national election survey in which questions were included on political alienation or powerlessness. The results are presented in Table 18-3 where, with one exception, levels of powerlessness are high and also show an increase for three of the four questions that were asked in both 1968 and 1974. This probably reflects the deteriorating situation of the economy during this period. We do know that the most important issues to the electorate were inflation, wage and price controls, general economic issues, pensions and taxes (Pammett et al., 1977:93-126). Thus, economic questions may well have contributed to a growing feeling that government was distant from and could not be influenced by ordinary people. The fifth item ("So many other people vote . . . ") calls for special comment. While most Canadians feel that it matters whether they vote or not, this does not mean that they feel able to exert much influence on the system.

---

[5] See Table 18-2. Based on fieldwork conducted in 1974, this table demonstrates that the level of participation in the Netherlands, Britain, the United States, Germany and Austria was broadly similar and particularly low for those activities that imply greater commitment.

TABLE 18–2  Frequency of Conventional Political Participation*

| | OFTEN | SOMETIMES | RARELY | NEVER | MISSING DATA** |
|---|---|---|---|---|---|
| **The Netherlands** | | | | | |
| Read about politics in papers | 35% | 29% | 20% | 16% | (0)% (= 100%) |
| Discuss politics with friends | 17 | 35 | 27 | 21 | (0) |
| Convince friends to vote as self | 3 | 7 | 12 | 77 | (1) |
| Work to solve community problems | 5 | 13 | 16 | 66 | (1) |
| Attend political meetings | 1 | 5 | 8 | 85 | (1) |
| Contact officials or politicians | 5 | 8 | 13 | 73 | (1) |
| Campaign for candidate | 1 | 2 | 6 | 90 | (1) |
| **Britain** | | | | | |
| Read about politics in papers | 36 | 30 | 19 | 15 | (1) |
| Discuss politics with friends | 16 | 30 | 23 | 30 | (1) |
| Convince friends to vote as self | 3 | 6 | 8 | 82 | (1) |
| Work to solve community problems | 4 | 13 | 13 | 69 | (2) |
| Attend political meetings | 2 | 7 | 12 | 78 | (2) |
| Contact officials or politicians | 2 | 9 | 13 | 74 | (2) |
| Campaign for candidate | 1 | 3 | 3 | 91 | (2) |
| **United States** | | | | | |
| Read about politics in papers | 47 | 27 | 17 | 8 | (1) |
| Discuss politics with friends | 27 | 37 | 24 | 11 | (1) |
| Convince friends to vote as self | 6 | 13 | 21 | 59 | (1) |
| Work to solve community problems | 8 | 28 | 25 | 38 | (1) |
| Attend political meetings | 3 | 15 | 25 | 57 | (1) |
| Contact officials or politicians | 4 | 23 | 24 | 48 | (1) |
| Campaign for candidate | 2 | 12 | 15 | 70 | (0) |

TABLE 18–2 Frequency of Conventional Political Participation*(cont.)

| | OFTEN | SOMETIMES | RARELY | NEVER | MISSING DATA** |
|---|---|---|---|---|---|
| **Germany** | | | | | |
| Read about politics in papers | 46% | 27% | 19% | 8% | (0)% (= 100%) |
| Discuss politics with friends | 13 | 30 | 31 | 26 | (1) |
| Convince friends to vote as self | 7 | 16 | 23 | 54 | (1) |
| Work to solve community problems | 4 | 10 | 21 | 64 | (1) |
| Attend political meetings | 5 | 17 | 24 | 52 | (1) |
| Contact officials or politicians | 3 | 8 | 16 | 72 | (1) |
| Campaign for candidate | 2 | 6 | 13 | 78 | (1) |
| **Austria** | | | | | |
| Read about politics in papers | 30 | 28 | 22 | 19 | (0) |
| Dicuss politics with friends | 13 | 32 | 31 | 25 | (0) |
| Convince friends to vote as self | 5 | 12 | 14 | 69 | (1) |
| Work to solve community problems | 4 | 10 | 12 | 73 | (1) |
| Attend political meetings | 5 | 13 | 20 | 61 | (1) |
| Contact officials or politicians | 2 | 10 | 16 | 72 | (1) |
| Campaign for candidate | 2 | 3 | 7 | 87 | (1) |

*Percentages in this table add row-wise to 100 percent. Rounding errors are possible. The percentages are based on the full samples in each country.
Ns are: The Netherlands: 1201; Britain: 1483; United States: 1719; Germany: 2307; Austria: 1584.
**Missing data includes don't know and not ascertained.

Barnes, Kaase et al., *Political Action*, pages 541–542. Table TA.1.

TABLE 18-3  Level of Political Powerlessness in Canada, 1965–1974.

| Percentage who agree that: | National | | | Atlantic 1974 | Quebec 1974 | Ontario 1974 | Prairies 1974 | B.C. 1974 |
|---|---|---|---|---|---|---|---|---|
| | 1965 | 1968 | 1974 | | | | | |
| Generally, those elected to parliament soon lose touch with the people. | — | 56 | 65 | 64 | 72 | 63 | 62 | 64 |
| I don't think the government cares much what people like me think. | 46 | 42 | 58 | 61 | 67 | 54 | 59 | 42 |
| Sometimes, politics and government seem so complicated that a person like me can't really understand what's going on. | 69 | 69 | 66 | 72 | 66 | 63 | 77 | 56 |
| People like me don't have any say about what the government does. | 49 | 47 | 55 | 54 | 69 | 47 | 58 | 38 |
| So many other people vote in federal elections that it doesn't matter very much whether I vote or not. | — | — | 14 | 20 | 22 | 10 | 14 | 6 |
| N | 2727 | 2767 | 1203 | 252 | 341 | 344 | 198 | 127 |

# OPPOSITION AND CHANGE

At this point the attentive reader may wonder how change is possible at all if the avenues to the decision-making core of the state are structured to favour the dominant classes and if so many people feel powerless to intervene in political affairs. However, it is important to remember that authority and domination can be challenged. People are not doomed to be the passive objects of political manipulation, for the powerful can be weakened by internal division, by the intervention of international forces, by economic failures and by a general loss of legitimacy, while the "powerless" can be mobilized to press for change. At first sight, it appears that stability is assured by the presence of a mass of apathetic, cynical citizens who feel they can have no real political influence. In reality, however, the situation is far less stable, because people can be mobilized when their discontents become articulated by leaders who make them believe that change is possible. This has occurred on

*Peace marchers in St. John's carry banners in English and Russian.*

numerous occasions when disaffected Canadians have formed protest movements on a wide range of issues including labour rights, the status of women, Quebec nationalism, native peoples, agrarian interests, prohibition and poverty (see Chapter 12). Success or failure will subsequently be determined by such considerations as the extent to which the movements themselves can avoid problems of oligarchy, the strategies adopted, and the resources they can command relative to their opponents. The point is simply that the existing structure of political institutions is biased and tends to suppress dissent or to channel it into relatively innocuous activities; the structure, however, does not destroy people's capacity to act in their own interests.

If the argument so far is accepted, the continuation of economic insecurity, the massive changes related to the new microelectronic technologies, the environmental dangers and looming nuclear disaster may threaten the established political institutional structure. The conservatism of so many electorates, including Canada's, may be only temporary. The probable failure of the new right politicians and of policies that are socially divisive (under a rhetoric of national unity and the national interest) may raise the level of discontent and open the door to a period of conflict that the existing institutional structure cannot contain or restrain.

## SUMMARY

This chapter has introduced some of the central concepts in political sociology: power, authority (traditional, charismatic and rational-legal), political institutions, the state, parties, political alienation and participation. Central questions in the analysis of political institutions have been raised. They concern the centralization of power, legitimacy and connections between the political structure and the rest of society. Some attention was then given to several instances of preindustrial political life, followed by a general account of the modern bureaucratic state as the context for an introduction to the sociology of contemporary Canadian politics with special emphasis on the sources of bias built into the institutional structure.

## DISCUSSION QUESTIONS

1. Discuss the ways in which authority can be exercised. Give examples.

2. What is the political significance of the concept of the "culture of silence"?

3. Electoral institutions ensure that political leaders are responsive to the interests of the population as a whole. Discuss.

4. To what extent is class a factor in explaining Canadian voting patterns?

5. Why do so many Canadians experience a sense of political powerlessness?

# 19

# Law and Society

*Austin T. Turk*

INTRODUCTION: WHAT IS LAW?

# INTRODUCTION: WHAT IS LAW?

Legal institutions usually reflect and support the norms underlying organized social life. Political, economic and other institutions operate largely within a framework of justifications, permissions, prohibitions and procedures generally recognized as *the law*.

Sociologists view legal institutions (hereafter, simply *law*) as humanly constructed realities. This means that "legal" behaviour and relationships are empirically studied to learn how they relate to other social phenomena. Whether law is treated as a dependent, independent or intervening variable depends upon the investigator's immediate research question and his general theoretical assumptions about social causation. How law is approached in research also depends in part on whether it is seen as an agency of justice or of injustice.

## THE VIEWS OF MARX, DURKHEIM AND WEBER

When Marx, Durkheim and Weber sought to understand postfeudal social changes, they saw legal changes as somehow important—as products, indicators, correlates or causal factors. Marx's emphasis upon the causal primacy of the economic base relegated law to the epiphenomenal category of *superstructure*, that is, social phenomena generated by the workings of capitalist economics which serve only to obscure the reality of exploitation (Cain and Hunt, 1979). Law, to classical Marxists, is the tool of the capitalist ruling class, an instrument for perpetuating "false consciousness" and criminalizing proletarian resistance. Substantively and procedurally, law obstructs progress toward social justice.

Durkheim's concern with the forms and bases of social order led him to view law as an indicator or correlate of social solidarity. He hypothesized that the *mechanical solidarity* of consensual interpersonal orders is associated with *repressive law*, while the *organic solidarity* of co-ordinated impersonal orders is associated with *restitutive law*. Deviations from basic social norms of *consensual orders* are punished in ritual displays of moral outrage that reinforce the community's values, or *conscience collective*. Violations of *co-ordinated orders*, on the other hand, are dealt with by formal adjudication designed to preserve the links between interest groups, especially those resulting from the division of labour (Durkheim, 1933).

Weber's analysis of the complex historical process of structural rationalization and cultural disenchantment treated law as one factor interacting with many others to generate the stabilities and instabilities of modern society. He noted an affinity between capitalism and formal legal rationality that reflects the need for a predictable context for profitable economic investments and transactions. Comparative and historical studies indicated that both substantively and formally "irrational" legal systems, as well as substantively "rational" ones, are incompatible with capitalist development. Whatever the type of law, its defining attribute is the presence of an *enforcement staff* empowered to use physical or psychological coercion "to bring about conformity or avenge violation" (Rheinstein, 1954: 5).

Despite the work of sociology's early greats, sociological interest in law languished after their era. Marx's followers understandably tended to minimize the significance of law for comprehending and changing the capitalist world. Durkheimians often became preoccupied with the minutiae of positivist research or the abstractions of functionalist theorizing. Weber was almost universally acclaimed; but his intellectual complexity, breadth and pessimism discouraged both the methodologically inhibited and the ideologically committed. Particular concepts and propositions from his writings (especially on religion, bureaucracy, stratification and political domination) became major elements in the theoretical lore of various sociological specialties and major vehicles for ideological polemics on such issues as the evils of bureaucracy. But few tried to understand Weberian sociology as a whole, much less follow in Weber's large footsteps as a distinguished legal historian and social scientist (Kronman, 1983). Regardless of their orientation, sociologists generally left law and "legal sociology" to the jurists (Selznick, 1968).

## MODERN PERSPECTIVES ON THE SOCIOLOGY OF LAW

From the early 1960s, the sociological importance of law began again to be recognized. Since the establishment of the Law and Society Association in 1964, there has been a dramatic increase in theoretical and empirical attention to law. Sociologists and other social scientists, as well as scientifically oriented legal professionals, have become increasingly aware of the issues and options in sociolegal research.

Sociolegal researchers generally agree that law is a human creation instead of an autonomous natural or mystical phenomenon. However, *ius naturalism* (the concept of natural law) persists, in that some analysts view law as having an intrinsic pattern or morality (Fuller, 1964) that is essential for viable social organization. The basic idea is that law reflects and maintains moral order, ensuring social harmony by preventing and resolving conflicts. From such a *moral functionalist perspective*, the aim of sociolegal studies is to help law do its job more effectively. Through law, social life progresses toward realization of an ideal just society.

Of course, there are disagreements over which kind of law is best and what constitutes justice. For instance, Marxist scholars consider *socialist legality* far superior to *bourgeois legalism* as an instrument for achieving social justice, i.e., communism (Mensch, 1982; Fine, 1979). When communism is attained, law (like all instruments of governmental control) is expected to vanish because it will no longer be needed to suppress class enemies and teach social responsibility. While bourgeois law is oppressive and promotes social conflict, socialist law is liberating and resolves conflict.

In contrast, non-Marxist functionalists regard Western legal traditions as guarantors of progress toward an ideal balance of collective and individual interests, i.e., liberal democracy. *The rule of law* is considered the foundation of democracy, or indeed, of civilization itself (Pound, 1942).

Unlike moral functionalism, the *conflict perspective* offers a value-neutral conception of law as power, a set of resources used to favour some interests and values over others, thereby enhancing the lives of some people at the expense of others. Thus, control of the law is itself the object of a struggle, and access to law is greater for some than for others. Accordingly, research aims not to uphold or improve any kind of law but to describe and explain the creation, uses and impact of legal power (Turk, 1976a, 1976b).

The most important question is not whether law is the guarantor of socialist or bourgeois morality or is a neutral source of power. Rather, it is whether one perspective or another leads to useful research and theory. Useful research, quantitative or qualitative, reveals patterns and thereby tests existing ideas and/or suggests new ones. Useful theory explains observations in ways that lead to testable predictions about unobserved situations.

# SOURCES AND DIMENSIONS OF LAW

Descriptions and explanations of law vary in the emphases on culture, social structure and conflict. Although the correspondence between perspectives and research designs is loose, moral functionalists do tend to stress cultural values or structural imperatives, while conflict theorists typically focus upon conflicts of interest.

## CULTURAL FOUNDATIONS AND VALUES ANALYSIS

The key idea is that a society's law is created out of its prelegal or nonlegal culture. Each society's law is considered a unique expression of its basic cultural premises and themes (*jural postulates*). Researchers locate the particular features of law in their cultural contexts, paying special attention to how cultural values are expressed and supported through legal institutions.

Among the most influential cultural studies is E. A. Hoebel's *The Law of Primitive Man* (1954). Hoebel rejects conceptions of law that equate law with custom, or assume that primitive peoples have no law. Instead, he argues that law exists wherever infraction of a social norm "is regularly met, in threat or in fact, by the application of physical force by an individual or group possessing the socially recognized privilege of so acting" (Hoebel, 1954: 28). He sees law as an adaptive response to "trouble cases" arising from conflicts of interest within a framework of shared values. Differing levels of institutionalization are associated with factors such as population size and density, material and technical resources and the proximity of warlike neighbours.

At the most rudimentary level is the law of the widely scattered and highly individualistic Eskimo (as of more than a half-century ago). Even though widely accepted norms prescribed such virtues as productivity, sharing, self-discipline and autonomy, it was up to the aggrieved or injured parties to deal with offenders. The right to demand compliance and punish noncompliance was vested in whoever felt strongly enough about the matter to act. But the risk of blood revenge was great, and even the killing of a universally feared repeat murderer had to be carefully undertaken, for example, by making sure that everyone agreed that he should die, particularly the condemned man's close relatives, who might themselves be enjoined to carry out the execution (Hoebel, 1954: 88–91).

For cultural analysts of the complex legal institutions of modern societies, Japan has been particularly interesting because Japanese law is "underdeveloped" (there are fewer lawyers, laws, courts and cases) relative to other technologically advanced countries (Kidder, 1983: 45–46). The usual cultural explanation is that the Japanese value harmony through compromise and conciliation, shunning formal public adjudication of what are viewed as private matters. However, reluctance to litigate varies with geographic location (isolated rural people are more traditional) and with the social and economic context of a dispute. For example, Japanese victims of mercury poisoning (Minamata disease) did not initially sue the offending Chisso Corporation factory, the major local employer. But when the villagers of Nigata, a fishing village 40 miles away, were victimized by the same factory, they immediatly sued Chisso (with which they had no prior connections) and persuaded several Minamata victims to join the legal attack. Thirteen years after the Minamata victims accepted token compensation and did not sue, the second offense and moral pressure from the Nigatans overcame the cultural (and economic) aversion to legal confrontation (Kidder, 1983: 50–51; Smith and Smith, 1975; and Upham, 1976).

Analysts studying the culture-law relationship have tended to look within a society's culture for the sources of its law. Yet, the assumption in cultural studies that each case must be explained as unique, not by generalizations or comparisons, has always been countered by an inclination to compare cases. To be useful for developing good theories, comparative analysis must consider similarities as well as dissimilarities and the possibility of historical change as well as stability.

The Canadian and American legal cultures have been compared with respect to "how a society's efforts to control criminal behavior may be influenced by national values, historical conditions, and economic constraints" (Hagan and Leon, 1978: 181). Canadian law is closer to the more authoritarian *crime control model*, while the *due process model* better describes the more institutionally fragmented American legal order. The differences are attributed to Canada's counterrevolutionary beginnings and subsequent conservatism and our historically greater need for governmental involvement in resource development. This contrasts with the United States' revolutionary origins, ideology of individualism and more laissez-faire political and economic traditions. "Historically, the Canadian attitude placed a stronger emphasis on social order in relation to individual rights" (Hagan and Leon, 1978: 201).

Whether the Canadian-American differences noted by Hagan and Leon are lessening or persisting is a question for further study. In any case, their analysis demonstrates again the need to consider more than cultural factors in attempting to explain legal phenomena.

## SOCIAL STRUCTURE AND FUNCTIONAL ANALYSIS

Emphasis upon social structure in sociolegal research is usually associated with the de-emphasis of culture. Cultural analysis suggests that culture provides "blueprints" for the creation and operation of law. Structural analysis assumes that law 1) has or develops its own blueprints or 2) is shaped by economic, political, and/or other structural elements in the social environment. The first kind of structural analysis focuses upon *internal* organizational dynamics and imperatives, the second upon law's responsiveness to *external* system requirements or pressures.

Systems analyses of the criminal justice process in Canada and the United States indicate that the processing of cases is significantly influenced by the structural characteristics of the legal system (Connidis, 1982; Saks and Miller, 1979). For instance, the quasi-independence of the police, court and corrections "nodes" means that cases are often passed along on administrative as much as substantive grounds, with inadequate review and feedback and no overall record of the flow of specific cases.

Other structural studies have found that court organization and judicial procedures help ensure that "repeat-players"—usually organizations or wealthy people—will be much more successful litigants than will "one-shotters"—individuals and poor people (Galanter, 1974). In addition, the kinds of disputes and other matters handled by courts and lawyers tend strongly to limit most people's access to law in the first place.

While internal structural analysis typically locates causation in the functioning of law itself, *external* analysis treats such internal causes as effects of structural relationships in the larger social world. Thus, the lack of co-ordination in the criminal justice process may be attributed to the different social origins and positions of police (lower) and judges (higher). Similarly, legal systems may give significant advantages to repeat-players over one-shotters because of institutionalized social inequalities.

The impact of structured inequalities upon the creation and application of law has been the core issue in external, macrostructural research. Three basic kinds of studies are found in the literature: descriptive-empiricist, illustrative-polemical and experimental-analytical.

*Descriptive-empiricist* studies ask whether inequality and legal phenomena are related and—in statistical works—just how strong is the relationship. Mayhew and Reiss (1969) asked whether and how much income and race influence the use of legal professional services. Their survey of the problems and legal experiences of 780 Detroit residents found that 83 percent of respondents with annual family incomes of over $15 000 had contacted a lawyer at some point versus 56 percent of those with incomes of under $7000. Seventy-one percent of the white respondents had seen a lawyer over against 59 percent of the black respondents. After detailed tabular analysis of relationships between the inequality measures and the various types of legal contact, Mayhew and Reiss rejected the common view (the *resources theory*) that differential use of law simply reflects differential access to law because of inequalities in income and other resources. Instead of ability to pay, the crucial determinant was the kind of legal problems facing people. For all socioeconomic categories, contact with lawyers is largely a matter of having legally defined property interests. Because the law and lawyers are heavily oriented to property concerns, those with property-related problems are more likely to seek and receive legal services than are those with other kinds of problems. "The poor have fewer legal problems [but] only in the narrow sense that they have fewer problems that the legal profession habitually serves" (Mayhew and Reiss, 1969: 317).

*Illustrative-polemical* studies assume that social inequality strongly influences law and seek to highlight the injustice of the relationship. McDonald's (1976) landmark treatise includes (along with her descriptive and analytical contributions) numerous examples of such work. After general statements suggesting that Ontario law is biased for employers and against workers in the event of strikes, McDonald dramatizes the point by reporting some details of the 1973 Artistic Woodworking strike in Toronto. During the four-month strike by 120 workers, mostly foreign-born women, 108 strikers and supporters were arrested. "About half" were acquitted, and some cases were still on appeal. Up to 150 police officers were assigned to handle the strike. Twelve charges were laid against the police; there were no convictions. "Yet, while the Labour Relations Board found a prima facie case that the employer had failed to bargain in good faith, an offence under the act, the Attorney-General refused the union's request to prosecute. It would not be 'in the public interest' " (McDonald, 1976:235).

*Experimental-analytical* studies test and develop value-neutral theories integrating many propositions and findings. A recent study by Liska and Chamlin (1984) tested and refined crime control propositions derived from the conflict perspective. Data for 76 American cities were obtained on crime control (arrest rates for property and personal offences), capacity for crime control (number of police employees per capita), racial/economic composition (indices of racial residential segregation and of income inequality) and the control variables of population size, percentage of families below the poverty line and reported crime rates. The major finding was that—as expected—arrest rates were substantially influenced by the racial/economic composition of cities, irrespective of the number of police, reported crime rates and size.

Structural descriptions and explanations of connections between law and society reveal much about *how* the connections work but tell us little about *why* the patterns exist and why they change. The search for causes tends to be side-tracked into the teleologies of functionalism: "Things are as they are because they have to be so in order to . . . " preserve the social order, maintain capitalism or whatever. Something beyond structural inquiries is clearly needed.

## INTEREST GROUPS AND CONFLICT ANALYSIS

Sociolegal research from the conflict perspective generally stresses the causal importance of human interests rather than cultural values of system needs. The law-society connections revealed in cultural and structural studies are seen as the products and instruments of conflicts among diverse groups trying, with different degrees of power and success, to promote their respective interests. Causation is located in the processes of manipulative and exploitative interaction through which social structures—including law—are formed, destroyed and transformed.

Conflict studies vary in the extent to which the causal link is treated as direct or remote, intentional or inertial. *Instrumental* studies emphasize direct and intended causal links: The sources of law are found in the machinations of dominant groups. *Structural* conflict analyses emphasize remote and inertial causation: The conflicts from which law arises are as likely to be historical as current. The causal chains linking them to law are typically lengthy, complex and largely the unforeseen consequences of *conflict moves* that are remote from the legal phenomena under scrutiny.

An example of straightforward instrumental conflict analysis is the Ratner and McMullan (1983) study of the emerging "exceptional state" in Britain, the United States and Canada. They argue that the New Right has successfully mobilized crime, law and order, and punishment in a moralistic ideology that helps justify their political-legal campaign against the liberal democratic welfare state. Legislatively and administratively, the legal obstacles to dismantling or emasculating work, consumer,

*Does an antiabortion rally represent a clash of cultural values or of interest groups?* Photo courtesy of Catherine Jolly, Toronto.

health, safety, environmental, education and other protective social programs are being removed. Facing a developing global economic crisis, the New Right is dramatically expanding the repressive apparatus of the state in order to divert attention from their humanly costly economic policies and to reduce drastically the limits of permissible opposition and dissent. Finding Canada structurally less amenable to rightist authoritarian populism, Ratner and McMullan (1983: 40) conclude that, in this country, "the 'moment' of exceptional state formation must be bureaucratically contrived."

A more complex and empirically better grounded example of instrumental analysis is Thompson's (1975) historical study of the English Black Acts. Beginning in the late seventeenth century, the aristocratic *cum* bourgeois drive to enclose formerly common lands as private estates was extended to abolish the ancient rights of all people to take game on those lands. Poaching and related new crimes were created, including the offence of blacking one's face to make identification more difficult. The standard penalty was death.

In recent years, more "structural" conflict studies have appeared, as theorists and researchers realized the methodological and analytical difficulties of causal analysis. These difficulties are especially acute where cross-cutting issues and interests, shifting coalitions, political compromises, a high degree of legal institutionalization and multiple consequences produce ambiguities and contraditions (Chambliss and Seidman, 1982: 139–169).

Kagan's (1984) study of debt collection illustrates the complexity of structural conflict analysis. His goal was to explain the sharp decline over the past 35 years in contested debt cases in American courts despite 1) large increases in credit transactions and delinquencies, and 2) increases in product liability, malpractice, criminal procedure and public law cases. After tracing the statistical, political and legal history of the decline, Kagan concluded that both debtors and creditors eventually found litigation too costly in relation to alternative tactics. Specifically, he found three factors responsible for shifting creditor-debtor conflicts out of the courts: legal rationalization of contracts, political activity by debtors and their allies and "a trend toward systematic stabilization" (Kagan, 1984: 364–369). Legal rationalization, ostensibly a victory for debtors, actually reduces their opportunities to litigate indebtedness. Pro-debtor political efforts (e.g., by farmer's associations) have shifted the struggle away from the courts and into legislatures and regulatory agencies. And most importantly, systematic stabilization has meant "the development of methods of loss-spreading, diversification, insurance and economic stabilization that prevent financial panics, blunt the edges of individual disputes, and encourage consensual refinancing or absorption of losses rather than protracted litigation" (Kagan, 1984: 365). In short, the creditor-debtor conflict has moved to different legal arenas and generated new legal mechanisms for its handling.

Attempts to identify cultural, structural and conflict sources of law have revealed the limitations of any purist approach to research. In future, sociolegal research is likely to be more fruitful if cultural values, structural relationships and conflict processes are treated, not as optional, but as complementary sources of law.

## USES AND IMPACT OF LAW: SELECTED TOPICS

We have already encountered the question of how much intentions have to do with making law. The problem now is the reverse: How well do the effects of law match the intentions of its creators and users? And how can the consequences of law be measured?

Kidder (1983: 114–116) says many people assume that law is like a medical vaccine. They look for clearly defined injections (of law), into quite specific target populations, with readily observable expected effects. This is an advance over the prescientific assumption that law automatically makes a difference. However, the current technocratic approach runs into several methodological difficulties. First, we "must show that people are choosing actions which, but for the law, are incompatible with their self-interest . . . . [Moreover, we] must show that if people do act in their self-interest in conforming with the law, it is because the law, not other circumstances, has made the action self-serving" (Kidder, 1983: 120). Second, people may obey law out of personal conviction or habit, not from any awareness or concern for the law as such. Third, people may comply because they find useful the information contained in law, as in other advertising and information sources. And fourth, people may react negatively as well as positively to law: They may do things such as drive too fast or use drugs to symbolize their opposition to the law. Overall, the basic problem is "to show either that legal action produces behavior that would not otherwise have happened, or that the behavior commanded by law has not been forthcoming" (Kidder, 1983: 124).

Regardless of the difficulties of showing that law has an impact and of distinguishing intended and direct from unanticipated and remote consequences, nearly all of us believe that law ultimately makes a difference. As noted earlier, moral functionalists tend to view law as an efficacious device for handling disputes, while conflict analysts see it as an instrument of power.

## PREVENTING AND RESOLVING DISPUTES: LAW AS AUTHORITY

The role of law in dispute processing has been examined in a wide range of cultural and political settings. Whether and how the law handles disputes and how well are questions that continue to inspire an enormous amount of research—and considerable controversy. Some analysts (Selznick, 1969) think that law has stimulated administrative and private sector developments that conform in important respects to the legal ideals articulated by moral functionalists such as Fuller (1964). To other analysts (Abel, 1982), the inadequacies and failures of law have led to the emergence of informal and private alternatives for preventing and resolving disputes.

Clearly, a great many people do use the courts and other legal resources for handling their disputes. In a comparative study of litigation rates, Kaupen and Langerwerf (1983) investigated the variations in usage among several countries. Reanalyses of selected empirical studies, supplemented by factor analyses of West German and Belgian data, indicated that litigation is associated with highly competitive economic situations. This relationship was found to be distorted when the "too undifferentiated and/or ideological" concepts of modernization, industrialization or urbanization are used (Kaupen and Langerwerf, 1983:163).

Selznick (1969) has discerned an evolution of *industrial justice* toward structures characterized by fairness, norms of participation and enlightened governance. Though not directly addressing Selznick's thesis, a recent British study (Henry, 1983) investigated the *private justice* systems of several factories and other workplaces. Contrary to Henry's expectations, he found that the private dispute-handling mechanisms of different work organizations were remarkably similar. Hierarchical and cooperative organizations alike combined democratic participatory procedures with executive-elite decision-making procedures for handling disputes. Issues of work discipline in all organizations were dealt with by complementary formal and informal mechanisms. Henry (1983: 220–22) concluded that private justice and state law are the interdependent components of control structures highly resistant to change, especially democratization. Such findings cast doubt on the thesis of progressively evolving industrial justice systems.

Whether state law fosters or impedes the development of private law structures, the ideological appeal of informalism has been compelling for both conservatives and radicals. *Privatization* has appeared to many conservatives as a way to extend and strengthen legal controls while at the same time reducing their cost. Radicals, on the other hand, have perceived in informalism an opportunity to create more effective and politically promising alternatives to bureaucratic justice. Both sides appear to have overestimated the benefits to be derived from private or popular

*Neighbourhood watch has become a popular form of private justice in Canada.* Photo courtesy of Catherine Jolly, Toronto.

justice initiatives. There is little evidence that privatization is any less costly or more effective than formal controls. Similarly, the radical hope that autonomous "liberated zones" can be created has not been realized (Able, 1982; Tomasic and Feeley, 1982).

Instead of a separate private law imitating, augmenting or displacing public law, informal or private justice projects increasingly reveal the tremendous versatility and adaptability of legal institutions. Wherever it has been well established, law permeates society, changing as society changes. Indeed, the idea that truly private law is possible seems from the mounting evidence to be untenable. Black (1976:2) appears to be on the right track in defining law simply as "governmental social control," i.e., an institution whose authority and effectiveness in handling conflict derive from the political organization of society. The authority of law depends upon the power behind it.

## MANIPULATION AND DOMINATION: LAW AS POWER

Not only does law depend upon power, it *is* power. Implicit in every legal definition of rights, duties, liabilities or immunities is the threat that noncompliance will be punished. The threat is most explicit in criminal law but is present in all law. Especially from the conflict perspective, the most important differences among laws and legal structures arise from 1) the varying types and blends of power involved and 2) the varying extent to which legal controls are direct or indirect in their operation and impact.

To say that law is power is not to say that law is merely force. Power is a complex phenomenon for which no universally accepted definition has yet been formulated. One approach is to define it as the control of resources (Turk, 1976a).

## Types of Power

Control of the means of direct physical violence is *war* or *police power*. Having the law on one's side in a dispute implies that one can rightfully use, or call upon authorized others to use, violence to support one's claims against other parties. If a judge's decision does not resolve a dispute, the police are authorized to use force to "uphold the law." Behind the police stand authorities who can call upon the military if police force is insufficient. Under such laws as Canada's War Measures Act, regular laws and procedures can be suspended to remove the usual restrictions on police and military action. As discussed below, law restrains political domination only insofar as legal restraint contributes to political dominance.

To control the production, allocation and/or use of material resources is *economic power*. Property and tax laws, for example, reflect and help implement policy decisions on what kinds of activities, products and people should be rewarded more and what kinds less. In addition, such laws apply decisions on how great the range should be between maximum and minimum rewards. Capitalist and socialist societies differ in how law is used to manipulate economic priorities and rewards: the former encourages free enterprise; the latter promotes collective ownership of the means of production.

*Political power* is control of decision-making processes. State and other organizational decision-making is significantly influenced by and expressed through legal decisions. Law articulates, interprets and implements organizational norms and decisions. It sets forth rules and procedural guidelines, gives legitimacy to agendas and programs and indicates how resources and decision-making responsibilities are to be allocated. Election laws, for instance, prescribe in detail how political leaders and representatives are to be selected, who is to organize elections, how disputes are to be settled and so on. The meaning and validity of elections and other political events and acts are, of course, often at issue. Nonlegal and even obviously illegal factors clearly affect elections and the course of political struggles in general. Still, short of a successful revolution or secession, law is the most definitive model, criterion and arbiter of rightness, which makes it in itself a political resource of major importance.

Controlling definitions of beliefs or values and access to knowledge (as well as definitions of it) is *ideological power*. The law is a potent source of information and ideas about how the world is and ought to be. Over the centuries, it has often successfully challenged or absorbed alternative sources of knowledge, in particular, religion and commonsense. Without at least tacit legal acceptance, particular conceptions of reality, truth and worth tend to wither away. If too contrary to the beliefs and sensitivities of those with legal power, they tend to be suppressed. Beyond promoting, tolerating or censoring particular conceptions, law itself is the cultural bedrock of political order. The very concept of law helps to socialize people to accept the ground rules of conventional politics, which amount to a general agreement not to endanger the political-legal structure.

Finally, having control of people's attention and time is *diversionary power*. As anyone knows who has ever sought legal counsel, been questioned by the police, gone to court or filed a tax return, law takes time. Whatever or whoever has our attention has power over us. This is clear enough when we would rather be doing something else. However, it is equally true when we enjoy the experience as when we are interested in news of or tales about the law. Entrepreneurs of the news, publishing, advertising and entertainment industries have long known that the more reassuring, titillating or lurid aspects of law can (in the name of "information" or "human interest") capture and hold the attention of most of us. There are obviously close links between diversionary and ideological legal power. The more people are preoccupied with the minutiae of law, the less time they have for exploring potentially heretical thoughts, such as the notion that the law is not necessarily legitimate or even real!

## The Imposition of Law

An irony of law is that it lives only as long as it is used and is used only when its validity has been (or may be) challenged. The authority of law exists to the degree that it is taken for granted (respected). When legal demands and claims are ignored or rejected, some form of legal power has to be exercised if legal order is to be maintained. Yet, the idea that law is, or has to be, imposed has had a long and controversial history. Most people (including most legal theorists) have felt that imposed law is a contradiction in terms: Law is "right," imposition is "might." Even when the *idea* has been accepted and thoroughly explored, it has proven hard to specify exactly what is meant by "the imposition of law."

A collection of studies by lawyers, social and behavioural scientists and a philosopher shows how, in various cases, law has operated to the detriment of some people and to the benefit of others (Burman and Harrell-Bond, 1979). In most instances, law has worked against the interests of people who had it imposed upon them. Legal structures and innovations were found to have been created and used by dominant colonial and/or class interest groups with scant regard for the harm done to those subjected to the power of the law. American Indians, Papuans and the Kapauku in New Guinea, various African peoples and the English poor suffered from arbitrary and discriminatory legal treatment. However, several studies also found that mandated legal changes do not necessarily have negative effects, that initially costly innovations may be eventually beneficial, that alien legal devices may be incorporated into indigenous legal structures and that attempts to impose legal constraints may fail. An analysis of the psychology of compliance concluded that internalization of legal norms has little to do with behaviour and that "imposition" is a matter of subjective perception. Whether this is entirely so and whether the imposition of law is necessarily bad are questions for further investigation. Meanwhile, even though imposed law is a tricky concept, it obviously exists in reality.

Whoever controls law or is supported by those who do has power over those who do not exercise control—to the extent that legal power is greater than nonlegal power. Political resistance to legal control raises the question in its sharpest form: Do the authorities have enough power to control those who deny their authority?

An extensive analysis of political crime and its control indicates that established governments are powerful but not all-powerful (Turk, 1982). In using their considerable power to create and alter legal definitions, gather information, manipulate communication channels, punish resistance and intimidate entire populations, dominant interest groups set in motion social processes that work against the control effort (Turk, 1982: 115–66, 171–73). If a government suspends or changes legal rules, this undermines the assumption of legal order, i.e., authority itself. Interfering

*The Ontario Federation of Students protests against cutbacks in the government funding of education. Are they resisting legal control?* Photo courtesy of Catherine Jolly, Toronto.

in people's lives by surveillance and other methods draws attention to the *fact* of legal power as distinct from the *claim* of legal authority. Manipulation of communications (e.g., the news media) destroys public confidence in all sources of information. The use of violence and other sanctions against political resisters frequently drives them to greater efforts and wins them more public sympathy and support. Terrorism and other forms of intimidation may achieve general compliance but at the cost of substituting fear for respect as the basis of legal order.

Law is both power and authority. While every legal relationship has power at the core, it also has some grounding in mutual acceptance of the terms of the relationship. Settling those terms and moving toward their general acceptance is what sociolegal development means.

## DEVELOPMENT, REVOLUTION, AND LAW

Sociolegal development is a difficult process. As the preceding discussion suggests, the transformation of power into authority is a problematic process and can be reversed. When the historical process has been characterized by relatively gradual and continuous movement toward a stable legal order, we speak of *development*. When the movement has been fitful, marked by interruptions and reversals, the term *revolution* is more often used. But note the common tendency to exaggerate the "development" of approved forms of law and society and to condemn the "revolutionary" history of disapproved forms. Most people prefer to believe that the human costs of developing and preserving "good" structures have been relatively low and necessary, while the costs of producing and maintaining "bad" structures are excessively high.

Sociolegal research on development has concentrated mainly on the Third World. Until quite recently, most such work was not value free, in that the assumptions of *liberal legalism* were accepted with little question. The legal systems of the United States and Western Europe were assumed to be good models for developing countries. Liberal legalists believed that these systems promote social equality, democratic participation in public life and economic improvement. Their studies were intended to foster the institutionalization of Western-type law, usually on the foundations of whatever law had been imposed (see page 498) by the former colonial powers. Liberal legalism has now been discredited by its failures, as well as disowned by former proponents under fire from radical critics. (Simon, 1978: 1–44.)

Against liberal legalism, the radical view has been that colonialism and imperialism promoted revolutionary destruction of indigenous law and fostered dependency, not development. A review of the critical literature led radical scholars to conclude that the ideas of imposed dependency and underdevelopment have been far more fruitful for understanding Third World sociolegal (non)development but that further work along these lines should proceed within the Marxist understanding "that legal forms and ideas are secondary and ultimately derivative" (Snyder, 1980: 780).

How to distinguish development from revolution—independently of the moral functionalism of both liberals and Marxists—remains an unsettled question. Most of us hope that sociolegal development leads eventually to *responsive law*, free of repression and formalism (Nonet and Selznick, 1978). And it may be possible to develop indicators of whether particular movements are guiding us toward or away from that idea. For now, however, the lessons of the past may be our best guide: Sociolegal development is a long process in which the basic dynamic is the interaction of *evolution* and *revolution* (Berman, 1983).

## THE FUTURE OF LAW

Depending upon one's perspective, law may or may not have a future; and in either case, the prognosis may or may not be welcomed. Virtually all sociolegal analysts (at least among those working beyond descriptive empiricism) agree that vast changes are occurring in legal institutions and their relationship to society. The decline of legal traditions, the proliferation of interest-group conflicts, the spread of informalism and the increasing awareness of the fact and limits of legal power all lead some analysts to believe that law may disappear.

There are theological, existentialist, anarchist, Marxist, liberal legalist and positivist conceptions of when and why the concept and institutions of law may vanish (Turk, 1979). Some religions anticipate the end of evil and injustice and therefore of conflict, political domination and so of law. Existentialist philosophy implies that the idea of law is meaningless and that legal institutions are doomed to fail and collapse. Anarchists see law as a myth bound to dissipate when the artificial order of politicized society inevitably breaks down. Marxists believe that bourgeois law will be supplanted by socialist law, which itself will wither away as the transition from state socialism to communism occurs. Equating law with Western forms and ideals, liberal legalists see the *rule of law* ending as various trends pave the way for a return to *the logic of tribalism*. And some positivists expect the disintegration of particular forms of political-legal order to result in lawless anarchy.

Opposing such dire predictions are those hardy souls who search for world peace through world law. By and large, they are die-hard liberal legalists and social democrats who seem not to have accepted (or perhaps heard) that sociolegal development is neither guaranteed nor an unmixed blessing. In any case, offering blueprints for world government is hardly a promising tactic. If there is to be a world order, it is unlikely to be what the world peace legalists envision or to be achieved without tremendous conflicts that persist over generations.

The more tough-minded end-of-law conceptions are woefully inadequate because they begin with very literal, idiosyncratic and, thus, ideological definitions of law. Moreover, such definitions are formulated at levels of abstraction that are either too specific or too disembodied to be helpful. Particular forms of law are equated with law, or else law is defined without regard for any body of empirical research. Either way, the prognosticators miss the fundamental point: that the social construction of law is an on-going process by which particular structures of power and authority are created and changed.

## SUMMARY

Social scientists study the relationship between legal and other social phenomena. How they define law varies with their theoretical perspectives, methodological approaches and ideological assumptions. A distinction can be made between *moral functionalist* and *conflict* perspectives. The first seeks justice through law, seen as the guarantor of either bourgeois or socialist morality. Conflict theory, in contrast, offers a value-neutral conception of law as power.

Moral functionalists tend to look for the sources of law in cultural values or structural relationships; conflict analysts view the creation of law as essentially a product of struggles among competing interest groups. The evidence indicates that in future research cultural, structural and conflict factors should be treated as interrelated dimensions of law instead of as alternative sources.

Attempts to learn whether and when law influences behaviour have demonstrated how hard it is to prove that legal factors have effects independently of other factors. Moral functionalists have typically assumed that the authority of law is effective in handling disputes. Where law appears ineffective, the ideology of informalism has suggested that private justice can shore up public, formal legal institutions (the conservative view) or replace them (the radical view). Against both versions of moral functionalism, conflict analysts have emphasized that legal authority depends upon legal power: police, economic, political, ideological and diversionary power. However, efforts to show that law is imposed have revealed the limitations of assuming too readily the fact and meaning of "imposition" and of believing that legal power ensures control. Instead of being one or the other, law turns out to be both authority and power.

Sociolegal development toward stable legal order is problematic. Neither the liberal legalist nor the radical Marxist has adequately defined development, nor distinguished it from revolution independently of moral functionalist assumptions. As for predictions of the demise of law, they are equally lacking in analytical and empirical support. The best starting point is to recognize that past developments have been characterized by the interplay of authority and power and of evolutionary and revolutionary processes. The future of law will be transformation, not extinction.

# DISCUSSION QUESTIONS

1. What is the moral functionalist perspective in sociolegal studies?

2. Why is the Marxist approach in sociolegal studies moral functionalism instead of conflict analysis?

3. How might one integrate cultural, structural and conflict analysis to explain sociolegal development in Canada?

4. Why do repeat-players have an advantage over one-shotters in legal contests?

5. Are there instances of law-making and legal control where everyone's interests are served?

6. How can the impact of law be measured separately from the effects of nonlegal factors?

7. Under what conditions does law prevent and resolve disputes?

8. What is sociolegal development?

# 20

# Mass Media and Influence

*Susannah Wilson*

# INTRODUCTION: MASS MEDIA AND MASS COMMUNICATION

As part of our daily routines, many of us wake up to the radio, read the paper over our morning coffee and read or listen to the radio en route to school or work. During the day we may discuss the news, the game or the soap with our friends or colleagues. Later, in the evening, we may relax by flipping through a magazine or watching a little television. Some of our media consumption will be active and purposeful, as when we make a point of watching *Dallas*, the Leafs or *The National*. At other times, we use the media more as background or company. Yet, whether we use the media as entertainment or as a source of information, we North Americans are avid media consumers.

The mass media are a fundamental part of the social environment. They punctuate our daily routines and fill much of our leisure time. They provide information and interpret world events. In many ways, the media both reflect and shape our definitions of social reality. In this chapter, we will look at some ways sociologists have analysed the mass media and the process of mass communication. Generally, sociologists assume that the media are social institutions which operate within particular cultural and historical contexts. The implications of this assumption will depend on the researcher's particular theoretical orientation. We will begin by looking at two theoretical traditions that have guided research in this field. The first is the empirical tradition, which developed in North America; the second is the European critical tradition. Within the last 10 to 15 years, critical theory has had a considerable influence on North American studies of mass communication.

# PERSPECTIVES ON MASS COMMUNICATION

## THE EMPIRICAL TRADITION

The study of mass communication has been influenced by the introduction of new media and changing images of human nature and the nature of mass society. A major preoccupation has been the media's influence on the attitudes and behaviour of individuals. The effectiveness of wartime propaganda indicated that the mass media were indeed powerful social forces since they apparently played a big part in mobilizing public opinion in support of the war effort. Later, when other tests of the direct effects of the media on behaviour proved inconclusive (see Klapper, 1960), this stimulus-response model was largely abandoned. As researchers began to discover how our families, friends and colleagues (i.e., our social networks) influence media consumption, the social context of mass communication was given greater emphasis. Currently, the influence of the media is seen primarily as shaping definitions of social reality. Effects are now understood to be indirect and cumulative, although no less powerful.

### Lasswell's Model
Lasswell (1948) described the process of mass communication as "who says what, through what channel, to whom, with what effect." This simple statement is no doubt the most frequently quoted definition in the field. It draws attention to three

continuing concerns: 1) the social organization of mass communications; 2) content and 3) effects. Lasswell's model also makes assumptions about the nature of mass communication that are no longer accepted. It assumes a one-way causal relationship and pictures members of the audience as passive recipients. As Carey (1975) describes it, the North American approach to mass communication has been based on a transportation model. In other words, messages are carried from communicator to audience.

## The Functions of the Media

According to Wright (1975), mass communication specialists are engaged in: surveillance of the environment (gathering and distributing information); correlation of the parts of the society (interpreting information and prescribing conduct); transmission of the social heritage (communicating information, values and norms) and, finally, entertainment. Some messages may serve only one of these functions, or the functions may be combined in a single message. Certain messages serve different purposes for different audience members. Because of this, programs such as soap operas or situation comedies, which seem to offer nothing more than fantasy or escape, may also serve the functions of surveillance of the environment and correlation of the parts of society. For example, some evidence suggests that the entertainment media are a source of both normative behaviour and advice in coping with everyday problems. Later in the chapter we will look at a study that suggests that soap opera suicides may trigger imitative behaviour in some members of the audience.

Wright (1975) suggested a framework for the analysis of the media which focuses on these four funtions. This framework provides an inventory for organizing research questions and findings. For Wright, the basic question is:

| | (1) manifest | (3) functions | |
|---|---|---|---|
| What are the | and | and | of mass-communicated |
| | (2) latent | (4) dysfunctions | |

(5) surveillance (news)  for the (9) society
(6) correlation (editorial activity)  (10) individual
(7) cultural transmission  (11) subgroups
(8) entertainment  (12) cultural systems?

McQuail (1983:79) has added a fifth purpose to Wright's list (5 through 8 above): mobilization. "Nearly everywhere, the media are expected to advance national interests and promote certain key values and behavior patterns, but especially so in times of war or other crisis."

The sociology of mass communication in North America until the 1960s was characterized by an accumulation of research findings generated by models like Wright's and Lasswell's. The field was fragmented and lacked a unifying body of theory. Most of the studies were based on large-scale audience surveys or quantitative content analysis and were preoccupied with the question of effects.

# THE CRITICAL CHALLENGE

In Europe, communications studies developed very differently. European studies shared a critical tradition informed by the humanities as much as by the social sciences. This orientation paid more attention to the political, cultural, economic and historical context of communication than was usual in North American research.

Many articles in a special issue of the *Journal of Communication* (Summer, 1983) entitled "Ferment in the Field" dealt with the differences between these two approaches. Some authors saw the rift as a fundamental one. Others identified areas of cross-fertilization. Differences between the empirical and critical approaches are reflected in the selection of problems, the methods used and the ideological orientations of the researchers (Melody and Mansell, 1983; Smythe and Van Dinh, 1983). As Smythe and Van Dinh (1983:117) argue: "All of us have our predispositions, either to criticize and try to change the existing political-economic order or to defend and strengthen it." The first position describes critical research; the second, the empirical (or administrative) tradition.[1] *Administrative research* raises questions that relate to models like Lasswell's and Wright's and uses quantitative methods of analysis. *Critical research* (which includes Marxist analyses) seeks "sharp critical analysis of communications phenomena in their *systemic* context" (Smythe and Van Dinh, 1983:123).

# THE IDEOLOGICAL ROLE OF THE MEDIA

The major difference between administrative research and critical analysis is the "rediscovery of ideology" by critical theorists (Hall, 1982). Critical theorists consider the ideological role of the media in its broadest sense. The media create definitions of reality and thereby shape perceptions of the social world, perceptions that frame and legitimize existing social arrangements.

But the media (except publicly supported media) are also business enterprises and operate under a system of economic constraints. On one level, economic constraints will determine the *range and type* of media available in any community. On another level, economic constraints will determine *budget allocations* within media organizations (Golding and Murdock, 1979). Smythe described the main function of the media as creating audiences for advertisers. "The information, entertainment and educational material transmitted to the audience is an inducement (gift, bribe or 'free lunch') to recruit potential members of the audience and to maintain their loyal attention," (Smythe, 1977:5). Pressure to maximize audience size has a neutralizing effect on content.

The general concern with the ideological role of the media is expressed by researchers in several ways. Some focus on the nature of the content; others, on the protection of class interests by those who own or control the media. The Centre for Contemporary Cultural Studies at Birmingham, England, has developed a unique interdisciplinary approach to media studies. Hall, one of the most influential members of this group is interested in the meanings attributed to content by members

[1] These two terms (critical approach, administrative approach) are used interchangeably by contributors to the symposium, although some (including Smythe and Van Dinh) prefer one or the other term.

of audiences. His method is to concentrate on the *encoding* and *decoding* of media messages. Encoding is the process whereby the media gives meaning to events by putting them in a context that supports dominant interests. Audiences, composed of a number of different groups, decode media messages in terms of their own definitions of reality. In other words, we cannot assume that all members of the audience will interpret media events in the same way.

The Glasgow Media Group (1977, 1980) have approached this issue from a different angle. *Bad News* (1977) studied news coverage of industrial disputes in Britain. The study argues that the way news is handled (i.e., the criteria of newsworthiness and the placement of news items) reflects an antiunion bias. News reports focus on certain key industries, particularly the automotive industry, and disputes that cause the most public inconvenience. Newscasters imply that industrial disputes are not in the public interest. This study also argued that the structure and placement of interviews implicitly supports management's view, although the fact that both views are presented gives the impression of impartiality. For example, interviews with managers were typically conducted in surroundings, such as executive offices, that reinforced management's authoritative role. Interviews with union representatives were conducted out-of-doors or on picket lines, against a background of disorder. Interviewers typically began by asking the union representative to *justify* the union's action. The authors concluded that television news distorts the nature of industrial disputes.

In the following section, we will turn to a second important focus of analyses of the ideological role of the media: the issue of increased concentration of media ownership.

## Media Ownership in Canada

In Canada, the study of media ownership has been addressed in two major studies of the Canadian elite: *The Vertical Mosaic* (Porter, 1965) and *The Canadian Corporate Elite* (Clement, 1975). Two federal commissions have also documented the increased concentration of media ownership in Canada. The Special Senate Committee on the Mass Media—usually called the Davey Report, after its chief commissioner, Senator Keith Davey—was published in 1971. Ten years later, the Kent Commission (The Royal Commission on Newspapers) was published.

Clement has argued that in capitalist societies, control of the media, "whether by the state or big business, places them squarely in the realm of the dominant interest groups already powerful in other fields" (Clement, 1975:280). The ideology articulated in the media supports and maintains existing institutions and social arrangements, and thus acts as an effective agent of social control. "The ideological system must provide the justification for the economic system, the political system, and so forth, and this it does by attempting to show that the existing arrangements conform with the traditional value system (Porter, 1965:460)." The danger of increased concentration is that there are fewer and fewer independent interpretations of the Canadian value system in the mass media.

Privately owned media will only survive if they are financially viable. Newspapers particularly have been hard hit by the introduction of television in Canada (in 1952), by the rising costs of new technologies for typesetting and editing and by the increased costs of raw materials and distribution. These costs make it increasingly difficult for independent owners to survive. Large corporations whose properties are concentrated can more readily take advantage of economies of scale.

When the Davey report was published in 1970, it drew attention to the extent of corporate concentration in the Canadian media. In the 103 communities that supported either a daily newspaper or a primary television station, there were 485 units of mass communication (daily newspapers, radio or television stations). Of these, over half were controlled or partially owned by groups. This included 66 percent of Canada's daily newspapers, 49 percent of our television stations and 47 percent of our radio stations. Furthermore, media control was being concentrated in the hands of fewer and fewer large corporations. The Davey commission rather tentatively concluded that this situation could have the effect of reducing the number of diverse and antagonistic sources from which we derive our view of the social world.

When, on August 27, 1980, a day subsequently referred to in the press as "Black Wednesday," the Winnipeg *Tribune* and the Ottawa *Journal* shut down, concentration became a public concern. Black Wednesday followed a series of takeovers and closings that included the demise of *The Montreal Star*, which ceased publication following a long strike. What made these two closings so contentious was that the closing of the *Tribune* (a Southam paper) and the *Journal* (a Thomson paper) created, in both cases, a monopoly for the other party (for Thomson in Winnipeg and for Southam in Ottawa). Not surprisingly, there were accusations of collusion, and the two companies were charged with conspiracy to reduce competition.

In what many would call a "typical Canadian reaction," the response to increased public concern was the Royal Commission on Newspapers. The commission report, which was tabled in 1981, concluded that concentration of ownership is "entirely unacceptable for a democratic society." Some of its recommendations were that acquisitions be restricted, that ownership of different media in the same city by one person or group be banned and that financial incentives be introduced to encourage independent ownership.

The growth of media conglomerates (see Figure 20-1 on page 510), close connections between the media and corporate and government elites and the extensive use of cost-effective measures, such as wire services, as a source of news make it hard to argue that the view of the world presented in the media will be a diverse one. Although the effects of increased concentration of ownership on media content are difficult to measure, critics generally claim that the media have "tended to become bland, undoctrinaire, unlikely to disturb the status quo" (Kesterton, 1983:13).

## MEDIA CONTENT

In Chapter 6 we talked briefly about the media as agents of socialization: The media reinforce social behaviour and definitions of social reality. In other words, by focusing on some groups and not others or by stereotyping social characteristics, the media provide important lessons about power and influence. For this reason, those concerned about sexual and racial inequality identify the media as major contributors to stereotypes. For example, in a classic study of the portrayal of majority and minority Americans in magazine fiction, Bereleson and Salter (1946) found that

## Figure 20-1   Everywhere in Chains

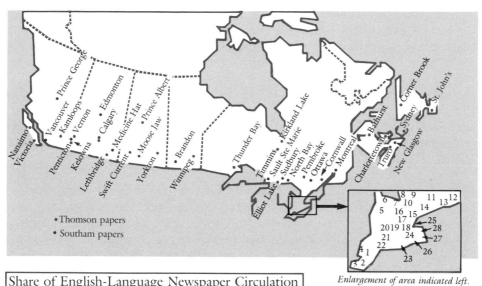

- Thomson papers
- Southam papers

*Enlargement of area indicated left.*

| Share of English-Language Newspaper Circulation by Ownership | | | |
|---|---|---|---|
| | 1970 % Share | 1980 | Share Change |
| Independents | 40.79% | 25.8% | 14.9% |
| Southam | 21.5 | 32.8 | +11.3 |
| Thomson | 10.4 | 25.9 | +15.5 |
| Sun Group | — | 8.3 | + 8.3 |
| Irving | 2.7 | 3.0 | + 0.3 |
| Others | 2.9 | 4.3 | + 1.4 |
| FP Publications | 31.8 | — | −31.8 |
| **Share of French-Language Newspaper Circulation** | | | |
| | 1970 % Share | 1980 | Share Change |
| Independents | 51.0% | 10.1% | −40.9% |
| Quebecor | 11.0 | 40.5 | +29.5 |
| Desmarais | 38.2 | 28.8 | − 9.4 |
| Unimedia | — | 14.7 | +14.7 |

- 1 Chatham
- 2 Leamington
- 3 Windsor
- 4 Sarnia
- 5 Hanover
- 6 Owen Sound
- 7 Collingwood
- 8 Midland
- 9 Orillia
- 10 Barrie
- 11 Peterborough
- 12 Belleville
- 13 Trenton
- 14 Oshawa
- 15 Toronto
- 16 Orangeville
- 17 Brampton
- 18 Georgetown
- 19 Guelph
- 20 Cambridge
- 21 Woodstock
- 22 St. Thomas
- 23 Simcoe
- 24 Brantford
- 25 Hamilton
- 26 Dunnville
- 27 Welland
- 28 Niagara Falls

Permission by *MacLean's* Magazine

native, white Protestant Americans were the most numerous, the richest and most highly approved characters in the stories. In underrepresenting minorities, the media reinforce our views about who counts in our society.

Certainly, we see little evidence of the rich diversity of Canada's cultural heritage in our daily media diet. In part, this is because of our overwhelming dependence on American television and magazines. However, the fact that we can now readily identify black television heroes and heroines, newscasters and models suggest that there has been considerable progress in this area over the last two decades. Yet, in the Canadian media, the underrepresentation of members of Canadian ethnic or racial minorities persists.

Pierre Berton's book, *Hollywood's Canada* (1975), is full of examples of stereotypes of Mounties, French Canadians, native Canadians and of Canada's geography and climate, as the following exerpt shows.

## HAPPY-GO-LUCKY ROGUES IN TUQUES

The impression still persists in some parts of the world and, indeed, in some parts of neighbouring United States, that almost every Canadian speaks French. I have even met, in the course of various travels, some people—again including Americans—who assume that French, and only French, is the mother tongue of Canada. (Others, equally misinformed, believe that Canada is actually a part of the United States. That view is especially prevalent in eastern Europe, where little distinction is made between the two countries.)

That idea could come from one medium only: the movies. In Hollywood's Canada the forest people were almost always French-Canadians, although they weren't confined to Quebec. Actually there appear to have been more French-Canadians outside of Quebec than in the ancient province. As we'll see, Hollywood made several pictures set in Quebec which are remarkable for the absence of French-speaking Canadians. But elsewhere, from southern British Columbia to northern Manitoba, from the Yukon border to the Cypress Hills, they turned up in picture after picture, speaking a kind of pidgin tongue ("Dees Canada, she's lak beeg woom-man!"), sporting their colourful tuques and sashes, smoking their clay pipes, indulging in broad gestures, grimacing and capering, seducing willing women, raping unwilling ones, filching deeds for lost gold mines or simply sitting around in the virgin wilderness scraping away on fiddles.

There were only four classes of forest dwellers who were not French-Canadians: prospectors, mounted policemen, lumbermen, and Hudson's Bay Company factors.

The prospectors were usually Americans, invading Canada in order to strike it rich before retreating to warmer climes. Most were amateurs, such as Clark Gable in The Call of the Wild, while others were really cowboys, like Randolph Scott in The Cariboo Trail or James Stewart in The Far Country.

The mounted policemen tended to be Irish, with names like Moran, Callaghan, O'Rourke, and Shaughnessy. Eleven of the twenty names of policemen which appear in motion-picture titles, for instance, are Irish. O'Malley of the Mounted turns up three times.

The lumbermen were mostly Anglo-Saxons and they came in two models: the Roistering Lumberjack and the Villainous Timber Magnate. The roistering image was indelibly established in 1918 by William S. Hart, the pioneer western star, in the title role of Blue Blazes Rawden, a man with an apparently hollow leg and a legendary reputation ("The boss one time he keel a bear weeth hees hands!").

"Going to hit that Hell hole, Timber Cove, like a blaze of glory!" Rawden shouts at the beginning of the picture as he and his men, firing their pistols into the air, advance upon the little lumber town for an evening of sport. In the saloon Rawden swallows his liquor neat, smashes the empty glasses on the floor, beats up the bartender, one La Barge ("the best rough and tumble fighter in the Cove"), calls for more booze ("Whisky, you frog-eater or I'll swab your own bar with you"), guzzles it straight from the bottle, plucks a half-breed girl, Babette DuFresne, from the arms of the monocled proprietor, Ladyfingers Hilgard, and finally in a *mano a mano* gun-fight shoots Hilgard dead.

It is an exhausting movie—almost as exhausting for the audience as it must have been for Hart, who appears to be engaged in calisthenics to the very end of the picture when, striken by remorse (and also by a bullet), he stumbles off into the storm to Die Alone. No one, certainly not George Brent or even Barton MacLane, who were pitted against each other two decades later in another hard-fisted lumbering yarn, God's Country and the Woman, equalled Hart's portrayal.

From *Hollywood's Canada* by Pierre Berton. Used by permission of The Canadian Publishers, McClelland and Stewart Limited, Toronto.

## THE MEDIA IMAGE OF WOMEN

The media were a particular target of the women's movement in the 1970s. Critiques focused on three interrelated issues: stereotyped portrayals of women in the media; the underrepresentation of women in decision-making positions in media organizations,[2] and the media's trivialization of the movement itself.[3] Literally hundreds

[2] Betty Friedan (1963) pointed out two decades ago that even in the world of women's magazines women have had little impact. The image of the "Happy Housewife Heroine" of 1950s magazine fiction was the creation of *male* writers and editors.

[3] In the 1980s, the number of these kinds of studies dropped. There are several possible explanations for this. Perhaps feminists have turned their attention to violence and pornography in the media, although the change could also be part of the antifeminist backlash.

of studies have documented the numerical underrepresentation and sterotyping of women in the media. These studies have looked at all types of media and all age groups. The results are consistent (although advertisements seem to be the worst offenders and soap operas an exception). Women are underrepresented and trivialized in media content, and they appear in a limited range of roles.

Butler and Paisley (1980:148–169) developed a *consciousness scale* to classify images of women in advertising. They describe the scale as:

| | | |
|---|---|---|
| Level 1 | "Put her down" | (Women portrayed as sex objects, props or decorations) |
| Level 2 | "Keep her in her place" | (Depicts women in the home or in traditional working roles) |
| Level 3 | "Give her two places" | (Shows women as concerned with both career and family) |
| Level 4 | "Acknowledge that she is equal" | (Shows men and women as equally competent in the same roles) |
| Level 5 | "Nonstereotypic" | (Indicates that women and men are able to be superior according to their own talents, motivations and interests, not according to their sex) |

When this scale was tested with magazine advertisements and television commercials, most ads were categorized as at levels 1 or 2.

Gerbner (1978) is very pessimistic about what he sees as the increasingly repressive image of women in the media. This image, he argues, is indicative of the part played by the media in cultivating resistance to change. In Gerbner's view, the media do not reflect changes in women's lives; rather, they are staging a counterattack on the women's movement and its aims. Coining the phrase "women's lib" is one example of such symbolic annihilation (Tuchman, Daniels and Beret, 1978, 1979), for it makes light of the aims of the movement and the fundamental inequalities the women's movement has tried to rectify. In part, the media's response to the women's movement has to do with definitions of what is newsworthy. Legal, political or educational reforms do not make headlines. Bra-burning (if, in fact, this *ever* occurred) does. News is defined in terms of *events*, not *issues*, and reporters make distinctions between "hard" or "soft" news. Hard news receives immediate coverage; soft news can be held over. The founding of the largest and most influential women's group in America, the National Organization of Women, was treated as soft news by *The New York Times*. It was reported on the women's page, several days late, placed between a recipe for turkey stuffing and a fashion bulletin (Tuchman, 1978:201–02).

## CULTIVATION ANALYSIS

The cultural indicators study of Gerbner and his associates was described in Chapter 5 (on page 120). This ambitious research project relies on two sources of data. 1) *Message system analysis* is based on a periodic content analysis of American television drama. 2) *Cultivation analysis* is the investigation (by survey research) of viewer perceptions associated with the recurrent features of television content. The content studies have revealed consistent distortions of a number of aspects of American life. For example, in the world of television, men outnumber women three to one; most of the characters are professionals and law enforcers; and over half of all leading characters are involved in acts of violence. It is Gerbner's contention that "the more time spent 'living' in the world of television, the more likely one is to report perceptions of social reality which can be traced to (or are congruent with) television's most persistent representations of life and society" (1980:14).

While Gerbner's work is not without its critics, some consider it a breakthrough (Van Poecke, 1980). Perhaps the most widely read of Gerbner's studies are the violence profiles (Gerbner et al., 1980). These profiles show a relatively stable pattern of violence and victimization in American television drama from year to year. An average of 70 percent of all prime time programs and 92 percent of all children's programs contained some violence (Gerbner et al., 1980). Surveys found that heavy viewers were more apt to express feelings of mistrust, apprehension and danger.

Gerbner et al. (1980) introduced two additional concepts—mainstreaming and resonance—to clarify the cultivation effect. *Mainstreaming* refers to the common outlook cultivated by television among heavy viewers, which seems to override whatever differences exist among them. In other words, despite differences in race, income or education, heavy television viewers tend to share a relatively homogenous outlook. "*Resonance* may occur when a feature of the television world has special salience for a group, e.g., greater fear among city dwellers, or perceived over-victimization of the elderly" (Gerbner et al., 1980:23).

A Canadian study by Doob and McDonald (1979) found a relationship between heavy television viewing and an expectation of being a victim of violence for residents of Toronto. However, when area of residence was controlled, there was little difference between light and heavy viewers. People who lived in high crime areas were more afraid. *But*, they also tended to be heavy television viewers and to watch more violent television. Doob and McDonald concluded that television was not a direct cause of fear of victimization. Gerbner interprets the findings of the Toronto study in terms of *resonance*. People who live in high crime areas "receive a 'double dose' of messages that the world is violent, and consequently show the strongest association between viewing and fear" (1980:20).

Two American researchers (Beurkel-Rothfuss and Mayes, 1981) tested the cultivation effect of television for soap-opera viewers. People who watch "soaps" are typically young, and a large number are students. They watch them for several reasons, including boredom, escape, companionship, relaxation and advice on problems. Since the soaps usually dramatize many personal and social problems (divorce, infidelity, serious illness, nervous breakdown and criminal involvement), the researchers predicted that heavy viewers would exaggerate the prevalence of these problems in the real world.

Their sample consisted of 290 students, 71 percent of whom watched at least one episode a week. Their findings confirmed their theory. Increased exposure was positively related to exaggerated estimates of the number of people who have been in jail, committed crimes, been divorced and so on. That there was a statistically significant difference between viewers and nonviewers supports the cultivation theory.

# CONTENT ANALYSIS AND SEMIOTICS

Because of its accessibility and consistent form, media content has been widely used for a number of different research purposes. The method typically employed is *content analysis*. In content analysis, the researcher creates a coding scheme, much as the survey researcher creates a questionnaire. Strictly speaking, content analysis cannot be used to make inferences about communicators' intentions or the effects of the message on the audience, although these are often implied.

In the last decade, some sociologists have been influenced by new directions in linguistics and have begun to apply these linguistic models to the study of media content. This approach, known as *semiotics* (the science of signs), is concerned with media messages as structured wholes rather than as fragments of messages that are usually analysed by content analysis. For example, a sign is assumed to have meaning, not because of the number of times it occurs but because of its relational qualities or the context in which it occurs.

McQuail (1983:130–33) has drawn a comparison between this approach and traditional content analysis. Unlike content analysis, semiotics does not comply with the accepted criteria of scientific research. In other words, it is not quantitative, nor are the results generalizable. Semiotics concentrates on the latent meaning of messages, and so is useful for uncovering consistent structures in particular genres of communication, such as detective novels or popular romances. Furthermore, unlike content analysis (which assumes that the meanings of media content are more or less universally perceived), semiotics assumes that communicators and audiences attach different meanings to message systems.

# MANUFACTURING THE NEWS

Several studies have focused on the process of "creating" news. Some (Fishman, 1980; Gans, 1980; and Tuchman, 1978) have approached this research as participant observers. Their interest is in how the news is chosen, covered, produced and disseminated. Others (Glasgow Media Group 1977, 1980) focus on the cultural meaning of news stories and the *methods of signification* used in television news. For example, an impression of impartiality is created by the use of actual footage of events or by on-location interviews, coupled with the "neutral" voice of the newscaster. As described earlier, these signifying conventions disguise underlying biases in the selection and placement of news items.

One interesting conclusion of studies of media content concerns the stability and predictability of news coverage (McQuail, 1983:144–46). This consistency has led some to conclude that news coverage can be described as a particular genre. One of the consistent elements is the regularity of structure. For example, the amount of time devoted to items reported in television news varies little over time or across cultures. "What is striking is the extent to which a presumably unpredictable universe of events seems open to incorporation, day after day, into much the same temporal or spatial frame" (McQuail, 1983:145).

The consistency of news content can be explained in part by the needs of the production process, cost considerations and credibility concerns. Some groups and institutions will have greater access to reporters because they are considered more credible or because they have the resources to package their message in usable form. Consistency is also the result of the way gatekeepers select the news. Gatekeeping includes "all forms of information control that may arise in decisions about message encoding, such as selection, shaping, display, timing, withholding, or repetition of entire message components" (Donohue et al., 1972:43). The consistency of the final product reflects the journalists' professional training, which engenders a particular understanding of the needs of the news organization and the nature of the audience. Journalists see their role as a powerful one. American journalists rank themselves as having less power than business elites but more than other groups, including labour, consumer groups or intellectuals. When asked who *ought* to have power, they rank themselves first (Lichter and Rothman, 1981).

# MEDIA EFFECTS

A key preoccupation in the study of the mass media has been the question of the influence of the media on social behaviour. Early studies of the media assumed that it had a strong influence on social behaviour. Later, this assumption gave way to a more cautious view. Increased skepticism about the media's power was reflected in Bereleson's assessment: "Some kinds of communication, on some kinds of issues, brought to the attention of some kinds of people under some kinds of conditions have some kinds of effects" (1949:500). This shift in thinking resulted from a changing conceptualization of "effects." Early studies looked for *direct* effects of *specific* messages. Now effects are understood to be both *long term* and *indirect*.

As Katz recently proclaimed, "The best thing that has happened to communications research is that it has stopped frantically searching for evidence of the ability of the media to change opinions, attitudes and *actions* in the short run" (1983:52).

On the other hand, many critical theorists object to the separate study of media effects. As Gitlin (1978) argues, trying to measure the impact of a particular media stimulus is like expecting a fish to discover the effects of water. "How can we 'measure' the 'impact' of a social force which is omnipresent within social life and which has a great deal to do with constituting it?" (Gitlin, 1980:9).

In the following sections, we will look at four ways of identifying media effects. Together they suggest the range of concern. The first two, agenda setting and the spiral of silence, describe the role of the media in creating public opinion. The concluding section addresses the issues of the effects of media violence and imitative behaviour.

## AGENDA SETTING

*Agenda setting* refers to the process whereby social issues are brought to the public's attention. "Audiences not only learn about public issues and other matters from the media, they also learn how much importance to attach to an issue or topic from the emphasis the media places upon it" (McCoombs and Shaw, 1976:18). Issues that get more media attention will become increasingly familiar and important to us. Issues that are not identified in the media will decline in importance. Much of the research on agenda setting has concentrated on political campaigns. McCoombs and Shaw (1976) used the media's portrayal of Watergate as an example of agenda setting. The issue of Watergate did not attract public attention until press exposure was accelerated by the televised Senate hearings. Public opinion surveys showed that only 52 percent of Americans knew about Watergate in September, 1972. By June, 1973, 98 percent knew about it.

## THE SPIRAL OF SILENCE

German sociologist Elisabeth Noelle-Neuman (1984) described the media's influence on public opinion as a *spiral of silence*. Her theory rests on the assumption that our opinions depend on what we *perceive* to be the opinions of others. The media help to establish our perceptions of prevailing opinion. Noelle-Neuman argued that most people try to avoid voicing unpopular beliefs. The assessment we make of public opinion will determine our willingness to express our own opinions. It follows that opinions perceived to be unpopular will be less frequently voiced. "The appearance of strength becomes a self-fulfilling prophesy; those who think they are in the majority are more willing to speak out, those who think they are in the minority have an extra incentive to remain silent" (Taylor, 1982:311). This spiralling process establishes *one* opinion as the prevailing one. An example of how this process works is found in the media portrayal of the political climate at election time. During the 1980 presidential campaign, Glynn and McLeod (1984) found that those who believed the political climate *favoured* their candidate said they were more willing to enter into political discussions. Others preferred to remain silent.

## MEDIA VIOLENCE

Questions about media effects reach their most controversial when they deal with the possible negative effects of violence or pornography. This is not a recent concern. Although most attention today centres on television violence (particularly in rock videos), movies, comics and magazines have all been considered potentially dangerous sources of influence, especially for young people. There is a strong feeling among the general public that the negative effects of violent media content are self-evident, that the sheer amount of violence in the media speaks for itself. When this feeling is coupled with anxiety about the increasing number of incidents of violent or antisocial behaviour seemingly triggered by the media, concern is understandably heightened. Gerbner's research (referred to earlier in this chapter) found that people who viewed a lot of television violence had exaggerated feelings about the amount of violence in American society and so were more inclined to favour increased social control.

For the sociologist, this issue presents a particular challenge, for it involves an analysis of content creation, the roles of regulators, cultural autonomy and technological innovation as well as the obvious concern about the effects of media violence. Much of the disagreement among academics has centred on whether or not violent portrayals cause subsequent deviant or antisocial behaviour. This might occur in several ways. Very infrequently, the effect might be direct or imitative, as in the case of *copycat crimes*. A second, more subtle and more pervasive problem is the media's role in creating definitions of social reality. For example, we may tolerate high levels of violence because we have come to think "that's the way life is."

*Ninety-two percent of all children's programs contain some violence.*

Some of the difficulties researchers have faced in sorting out the effects of television violence are methodological. Most effects studies have been done by psychologists in the laboratory. Under laboratory conditions, subjects display more aggressive behaviour than control groups when exposed to television portrayals of violence. It is not clear, however, whether the kinds of imitative behaviour that occur in the laboratory also occur in normal settings. Experiments may confidently conclude that the response (aggressive behaviour) was triggered by the stimulus (violent media portrayals) but not that this will also occur outside of the lab. In natural settings, the difficulty lies in controlling extraneous variables. In other words, how can we be sure that the behaviour we observed was, in fact, triggered by the media and not something else? In methodological terms, experiments have the advantage of control, whereas field studies have the advantage of being able to be generalized. The greater the control, the less the generalizability.

## IMITATIVE BEHAVIOUR

Strong support for the idea that the media plays an important role in triggering imitative behaviour comes from a series of studies done in the United States. These studies looked at the relationship between rates of suicide and violent death and the reporting or fictionalized representation of similar behaviour in the media. Phillips (1979, 1982) and Bollen and Phillips (1982) found that the incidence of suicide rose following newspaper reports of suicides and that the increase was related to the amount of publicity given the suicide story. The effect was greater in the geographic area where the story received greatest coverage. The researchers also investigated accidental deaths, on the assumption that some suicides will be disguised as such. Motor vehicle fatalities and noncommercial airplane crashes also increased following front-page suicide or murder-suicide stories. Increases in accidental deaths were also greatest following highly publicized accounts and were greatest in areas where the stories were most publicized. Similar results occurred whether the stimulus was television news stories or newspaper accounts. "Taken together, all of these findings support the hypothesis that publicized suicides trigger imitative behavior; sometimes this behavior is overt (in the form of an explicit suicide) and sometimes covert (in the form of automobile or airplane accidents)" (Bollen and Phillips, 1982:807).

Phillips looked at this same question using soap-opera suicides. These are relatively easy to track, as they are reported in weekly newspaper plot summaries. Phillips felt that "because they attract large, devoted audiences, soap operas may have the capacity to influence the attitudes and behaviour of many people" (1982:1343). His results showed that his reasoning was correct  The number of suicides, motor vehicle deaths and nonfatal motor vehicle accidents increased in the period following soap-opera suicides. Furthermore, the numbers peaked on the first and sixth days after the soap-opera suicides, which Phillips felt indicated impulsive versus planned reactions.

While it is clear that there are methodological problems in these studies because we cannot determine a causal relationship, it is also clear that the implications are serious. We know that the media influence us in countless insignificant ways, including our consumer behaviour, styles of dress, fads and so on. This research suggests that some people may be predisposed to imitate media behaviour in far more important ways as well.

# SUMMARY

This study of the mass media has been approached from two distinct points of view: The North American empirical tradition has focused on quantitative studies of content and large-scale surveys of audiences; the European critical tradition draws on an interdisciplinary analysis of the ideological role of the media. Both types of analysis are concerned with the social organization of the media and the meaning and influence of media content, although they phrase their questions concerning these issues differently.

The discussion of the image of women and minorities in the media illustrates how media portrayals stereotype certain groups. Gerbner's cultivation theory postulates that media characterizations of behaviour or social groups engenders a view of reality consonant with these portrayals in people who watch a lot of television. Because media portrayals are distortions of reality, heavy viewers develop an unrealistic view of American society. While we understand that television drama is not the real world, we usually have different expectations of news broadcasts. It seems, however, that there is a temporal and cross-cultural consistency in the structure of news reporting, which imposes itself on whatever events are being reported.

Critical theorists define the power of the media as their ability to frame and legitimize a certain view of social reality. In many ways, the role of the media in agenda setting or in creating impressions of public opinion is not incompatible with this view. However, as Gitlin has observed, the omnipresence of the media make it difficult to isolate their effects.

## DISCUSSION QUESTIONS

1. Compare the empirical approaches to the study of mass communication.

2. The Glasgow Media Group study, *Bad News*, described how methods of signification, such as the placement of news items, bias news coverage. Focus on a particular news event and systematically follow its coverage over several days to see if you agree with their finding.

3. Analyse the structure of your favourite news program for several days. Note the length of the broadcast and the length of each report. What proportion of the broadcast is devoted to local, national and international stories? Do you find other consistent elements? If you live in an area where you can watch both American and Canadian news broadcasts, compare their structure.

4. Althouth Ethiopia and other African countries have suffered serious famines for many years, in 1984 famine in Africa became an international issue. Consider the media's coverage of this issue and the overwhelming response it generated as an example of the agenda-setting function of the media.

5. Gerbner found that 70 percent of prime-time television drama and 92 percent of children's programming contain some violence. This proportion has remained relatively stable for the past 15 years, since her study started in 1967. As a member of the audience, how do you explain this preoccupation with violence? How would you imagine it is explained by writers and other communicators?

# 21

# Educational Institutions and Knowledge

*Raymond Murphy*

# INTRODUCTION: THE CRISIS IN CONTEMPORARY EDUCATION

Educational institutions are in a state of crisis, criticized from all quarters. Taxpayers find incomprehensible the increasing cost of elementary and secondary schools at a time of decreasing enrollment. Governments contend that universities are not producing enough "scholar per dollar" of subsidy. University students condemn recent increases in tuition fees. Yet, teachers and administrators of educational institutions claim they are underfunded. Worse still, the financial crisis is merely the tip of the iceberg.

Many employers and parents feel that students are unprepared for their future roles in the labour market because school programs are not in tune with the needs of the market. Others oppose tailoring the school curriculum to job market requirements but nonetheless claim that public educational institutions do not demand enough of themselves and their students and allow too much choice to students not yet ready to choose. A native-student advisor at the University of Manitoba observes that "the emphasis in native education is on quantity not quality . . . Native students are passed from grade to grade almost as a reward for showing up, and when follow-up studies are done, the findings are tragic: high school graduates with grade four reading levels, astounding illiteracy levels among the young, and another generation of native people growing up unprepared for the future" (Krochak, 1985:12). His criticism is that solving the drop-out problem the easy way, by simply passing students regardless of what they have learned, has in fact solved nothing. Researchers have found that the well-intentioned reforms of the 1960s have had many of these counterintuitive effects. These effects have given rise to a back-to-basics movement in education, to the growing popularity of private schools that emphasize discipline and traditional pedagogical methods and even to parents educating their children at home.

In one sense, educational institutions are always in a state of crisis because they are the focal point of conflict over what culture, values and ideas will be transmitted to the next generation and over different conceptions of the good society. The contemporary crisis is, nonetheless, more severe and deeper than usual because it involves a crisis of faith in the very idea that the expansion of the educational system can bring about a more efficient and just society.

Although many criticisms are undoubtedly a product of the wave of conservatism now sweeping late capitalist societies, it would be a mistake to believe that all, or even most, of the critics of educational institutions are right-wing, conservative elitists or that the problems began with the reduced funding of the 1970s. The government promoting most strongly a traditional education based on individual effort, examinations and the transmission of knowledge is the socialist government of Mitterrand in France. Liberal researchers have spent almost two decades debunking the idea that societal reform can be accomplished through educational reform. As early as 1971, conflict theorists drew attention to the fact that the expansion of educational institutions into a mass system has resulted in everyone being placed on an *educational status escalator*: Relative inequalities are perpetuated, but all are forced to remain longer in educational institutions. Marxists have long argued that the so-called democratization of education has been a sham, that the reformed institutions, like their predecessors, are *ideological state apparatuses* which reproduce social classes, instill bourgeois ideology and correspond to the needs of the exploitative capitalist market. Perhaps the severest critic is Ivan Illich, who argued that the mass educational institutions of the late 1960s were not only costly and inefficient in promoting learning (because they mistook teaching for learning), but they were also manipulative (based on bribery and coercion and so unmotivating that they required compulsory attendance), stifling of independence (fostering the idea that a person cannot learn without following a course in a school) and addictive (promoting the belief that the only possible solution to the failures of schooling is more schooling). Thus, he concluded, abolishing educational institutions is a pre-requisite for better learning.

These criticisms of educational institutions are coming from very different quarters. Sociologists, too, have divergent perspectives. To understand their conclusions, it is necessary to understand their overall perspectives.

## THE FUNCTIONALIST-HUMAN-CAPITAL THEORY OF THE EXPANSION OF THE SCHOOL SYSTEM

There has been a great expansion of the school system. Between 1951 and 1977, the proportion of 18- to 21-year-old Canadians enrolled in university jumped from 7 percent to more than 18 percent; in community colleges, enrollment jumped from 3 percent to 13 percent. The most spectacular expansion took place in Quebec; it was also the latest but most rapid, and it constituted the main element of the Quiet Revolution.

The dominant approach in the sociology of education to explaining this expansion during the period when most of it occurred, the 1960s, was the *functionalist approach*. In this perspective, society is seen as a *system* of interdependent parts, much like the human body. Every system has certain needs, so the goal of functionalist analysis is to show how needs are met—how *structures* such as the educational system function to meet the needs of society. Functionalists do not assume that those needs are constant, but they do assume that every system tends toward equilibrium. Hence, the evolution of structures is explained by the changing needs of society. What, it might be asked, determines those needs? Two somewhat different but related versions of functionalism have arisen in answer to that question. The first, *technological functionalism*, focuses on how society's needs have changed in response to its technical development. The second, which could be called *cultural functionalism*, concentrates on how the evolution of society's basic values has modified its needs. Society, in the latter version, is seen as having evolved from, for example *ascriptive values* (based on inherited status or worth) to *achievement values* (which give priority to individual accomplishment). Educational institutions have changed in response to the new needs of society arising from changes in its fundamental values: Modern values have replaced traditional ones.

From the *technological functionalist* viewpoint, the educational system evolves to serve the growing needs of society for skilled labour. Thus, investment in the school system is an investment in *human capital*, which functions to meet the technological needs of the labour market. The massive expansion of the educational system over the past century, and especially since World War II, was caused by technological progress and its need for skilled labour. Modern societies could no longer afford the luxury of an ascriptive school system, which developed the talents of only those already well placed by birth. Societies were pushed by technological change toward an *achievement-oriented school system*, which permitted everyone to develop according to the limit and nature of his or her talents. Modern societies were forced by their growing technical needs for skilled labour to stop basing their school systems on the early selection and *sponsored mobility* of the privileged few and to transform education into a contest that would foster the talents of as many as possible.

The content of education was strongly affected. Vocational and technical education was expanded; subjects judged irrelevant to the needs of the labour market, such as Latin, were dropped. Subjects were made optional on the assumption that students would better develop their talents by following their interests. Academic, technical and commercial education were put under the same roof in large, composite schools to give students the greatest possible chance to find an area in which they had talent and an interest. The pressures and needs of technological development are gradually changing the basis of educational systems in modern societies from *ascription* to *achievement*, from sponsored mobility to contest mobility. *Inequality of results*, stratification and *social class* distinctions remain, but they are based on differential achievement. Technological development pushes modern society toward a *meritocracy*. According to this model, educational institutions in industrial society are liberating individuals from their *ascribed class of origin* and enabling them to enter a new *achieved class of destination*. The expansion of the school system is seen as promoting the maximum development of talents and skills, the maximum contribution by individuals to society and the rational allocation of human capital; hence, it is beneficial (functional) for society as a whole because it produces a more efficient and prosperous society. The functionalist-human-capital perspective was not only a theory for explaining the expansion of the school system; it was also a powerful ideology for promoting such an expansion.

An example of the use of this model to explain and promote the expansion of educational institutions was the widely acclaimed book, *The Vertical Mosaic*, published by John Porter in 1965. He argued that Canada lagged badly behind other industrialized Western societies, particularly the United States and the United Kingdom, in the expansion of educational institutions. The Canadian educational system was small and elitist, and relatively little provision was made for technical and postsecondary education. The classical college system in Quebec was simply an extreme example of what was characteristic of Canadian education generally. Canadians suffered mobility deprivation because a small, elitist education system, inadequate to the needs of industrial society, failed to develop their talents, the human capital of Canadian society. The needs of the labour market were in part met by importing highly trained immigrants, especially from Britain, and this hid the deficiencies of the Canadian educational system. Porter's analysis, as well as one done in Quebec by Guy Rocher from a similar functionalist perspective for the Parent Commission (Commission Royale D'Enquête sur l'Enseignement dans la Province de Québec, 1963), were instrumental in promoting the expansion of the school system in Canada.

Porter's book, which was of central importance in the development of Canadian sociology, is usually thought to be a book about ethnic relations. Its focus is, however, also on the sociology of education. Porter argued that the initial stratification of ethnic groups was determined by conquest (the British, French and native people in Canada) and by immigration (the financial, cultural and social status, on entry, of other ethnic groups). These differences then led to unequal access to an elitist educational system for their offspring, which in turn resulted in differences in educational attainment, therefore in occupation and, hence, the preservation of the vertical nature of the Canadian mosaic from one generation to the next.

The weakness of Porter's study was that it assumed that inequality of educational opportunity was peculiar to Canadian society, and it idealized the educational systems of the United States and the United Kingdom as democratic and egalitarian. Sociologists of education in these societies have documented striking inequalities of educational opportunity, leading them to question the functionalist-human-capital-assumption that an expanded school system results in a meritocratic and prosperous society. But did Canada become prosperous and egalitarian following the expansion of its educational systems? The downturn in the economy of the 1970s and the recession of the 1980s has led to skepticism concerning a direct connection between investment in educational expansion and the prosperity of a society. It would appear that powerful market forces can more than cancel out the economic benefits of educational expansion, if there are such benefits. And what about inequality?

# INEQUALITY

Two different types of equality must be distinguished. The first, *equality of condition*, implies that whatever society values is distributed equally among its members. The second, *equality of opportunity*, suggests that everyone has an equal chance to attain whatever is valued in society (i.e., to attain any particular educational level, enter positions and so on), even though the results of such attempts may be unequal. One of the main arguments to justify the expansion of the public educational system was that it would promote equality of opportunity at least, and hopefully, of condition.

## INEQUALITY OF CONDITION: IN TERMS OF EDUCATIONAL ATTAINMENT

Not only have individuals been classified as, and come to see themselves as, superior or inferior in terms of their school diplomas, but also, groups have had very unequal educational attainment. Ethnic inequalities in university attendance are shown in Figure 21-1. Every ethnic group increased its attendance at university between 1971 and 1976, yet inequality of educational attainment among ethnic groups remained as great after this expansion of university education as before. (Note, though, that some Eastern Europeans, situated low in the "vertical mosaic" have unusually high attendance.)

Women have made substantial gains in undergraduate and professional studies by 1982, with 52 percent of bachelor's and first professional degrees now being awarded to women (Statistics Canada, 1984: 146, Chart 21)—the same as their proportion in the population. Women still received, however, only 41 percent of master's degrees by 1982, but that is, nonetheless, a substantial increase from 24

Figure 21-1    Percentage of 18- to 21-Year-Old Females With at Least Some
University, by Native Tongue

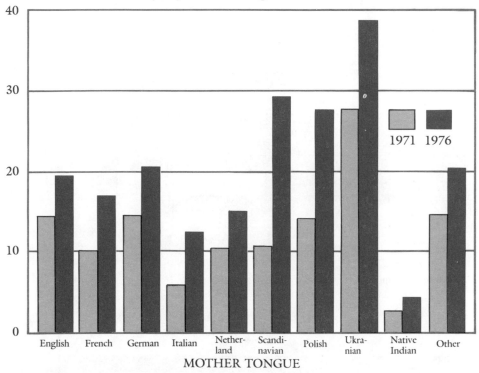

The results for males follow the same pattern. Paul Anisef, Norman Okihiro and Carl James. "The Pursuit of Equality: Evaluating and Monitoring Accessibility to Post-Secondary Education in Ontario," Figure 5.6, 1982. Reproduced by permission of the Ontario Ministry of Education.

percent in 1972. The fact that women were awarded only 24 percent of the doctorates in 1982 demonstrates the striking inequalities between the sexes that still exist at the highest educational levels. Yet this figure is up from only 9 percent in 1972 and demonstrates a considerable improvement from the virtual male monopoly on doctorates which existed previously. Thus, inequality of educational attainment between the sexes has diminished in terms of the quantity of education received but is still very great at the highest levels.

Differences between the sexes in the content of the education received were still enormous in 1982 but not as great as in 1972 (see Figure 21-2). In 1982, women were still very underrepresented in traditionally male areas of study. To name some areas not shown in Figure 21-2, women were awarded only 25 percent of the bachelor's and first professional degrees in architecture, 20 percent in forestry, 33 percent in mathematics and 11 percent in physics. In traditionally female areas, women received 74 percent of the degrees in education, 64 percent in fine and applied arts, 68 percent in sociology, 78 percent in social work, 76 percent in languages, 97 percent in nursing science and 97 percent in household science (Statistics Canada, 1984: 69-72, Table 10). The sexual division of education was far from eliminated by 1982.

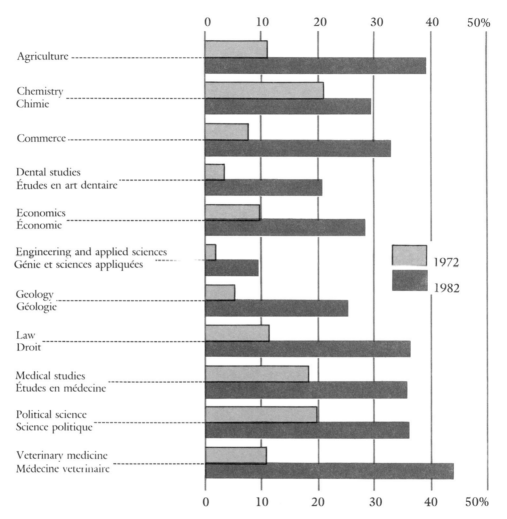

Figure 21-2  Percent of Bachelor's and First Professional Degrees
            Awarded to Women, Selected Specializations, Canada, 1972
            and 1982

Statistics Canada, 1984: Chart 22. Reproduced by permission of the Minister of Supply and Services
Canada.

There is evidence that educational differences between the sexes vary according
to social class. Using enrollment in the general program (leading to university) of
Quebec's colleges (Cegep) as his indicator of inequality, Escande (1973) found no
enrollment inequality between the sexes for the offspring of the upper-class, 11
percent lower enrollment of girls than boys for the offspring of the middle-class and
19 percent lower enrollment of girls than boys for the offspring of the working-
class and of farmers. Seen another way, there was a 22 percent difference between
the enrollment of upper-class and working-class boys in the general program leading

Figure 21-3    Percentage of 18- to 21-Year-Old Females at Home With at Least Some University, by Father's Educational Attainment

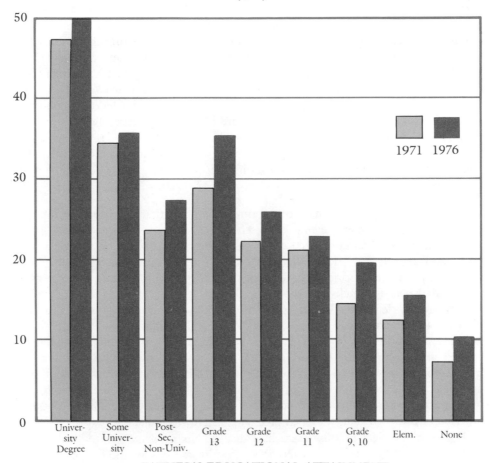

1971   1976

FATHER'S EDUCATIONAL ATTAINMENT

The results for males follow the same pattern. Paul Anisef, Norman Okihiro and Carl James. "The Pursuit of Equality: Evaluating and Monitoring Accessibility to Post-Secondary Education in Ontario," Figure 5.3, 1982. Reproduced by permission of the Ontario Ministry of Education.

to university and a 45 percent difference between the enrollment of upper-class and working-class girls.

The really big inequalities in educational attainment have been and still are among social classes, as shown in Figure 21-3, using father's educational attainment as the indicator of social class. The absolute percentage attending university increased between 1971 and 1976 for all of these categories, yet the relative differences among them were not reduced. There is no evidence that educational inequalities among social classes have been significantly reduced by the expansion of the educational system.

The educational inequalities in Canada are typical of the industrialized world, both capitalist and state socialist. Industrialized countries have attained almost universal literacy: Virtually all of their adult inhabitants have been taught to read and write (admittedly a minimal definition of literacy, since functionally illiterate graduates of the school system are now being discovered). Comparing this literacy rate with that of the Third World reveals the largest educational inequality of all. Thirty percent of the world's population (over 800 million people) are presently illiterate (Oxenham, 1980: 1-5), and illiteracy is concentrated in the Third World. Africa is almost three-quarters illiterate, and so is half of Asia. In Third World countries, nearly four times as many women as men are illiterate, and rural dwellers are four times more likely to be illiterate than urban dwellers.

There are essentially two ways of explaining the above inequalities. Either they are based on differences in merit or on differences in opportunity.

## Merit

Merit is commonly seen to have two components: talent (which usually is taken to mean intelligence when dealing with school success) and effort. Jensen (1969) showed that there are differences in I.Q. test scores among social classes and among races and argued that such differences are, at least in part, the result of genetic dissimilarities. He concluded that school programs seeking to correct deprivation have failed because blacks and the lower-classes are not so much socially deprived as biologically deprived. Williams (1977) presented evidence that purports to show that blacks and Puerto Ricans have less mental ability than Jews and Chinese. He also presented the data in Table 21-1 to show that the mental ability of students in some Canadian provinces is much less than that of students in others. The concrete recommendation of this line of thinking is that the type of instruction should be matched to the I.Q. of the pupils. In practice that would mean, for example, providing many programs to develop the abstract cognitive reasoning abilities of pupils in Alberta but providing few such programs in Newfoundland.

The Achilles' heel of this research is that it fails to demonstrate (and merely assumes) that I.Q. test score differences among these groups indicate biologically determined differences in general mental ability rather than socially based differences in culture and material well-being (Evans and Waites, 1981). For example, I.Q. test questions are selected so that the two sexes are defined as having equal intelligence. Yet there is no scientific basis for screening out differences between the sexes and not screening out such differences among races, ethnic groups, social classes, regional groups and so on. I.Q. test scores tell us more about the preconceptions of the testers than about the genetic capacities of these groups. I.Q. testers also assume that intelligence is fixed at birth and does not change. For example, both the height and the weight of parents and their offspring are correlated. Height is pretty well fixed at birth. Weight, on the other hand, changes, as every weight-watcher knows. The variations in I.Q.s among social classes and other groups suggests that I.Q. can change, like body weight, and is not fixed at birth, like height. Furthermore, I.Q. testing has had a very disreputable history. It has been closely associated with eugenic doctrines and ideas of superior and inferior races which were discredited by Nazi Germany. I.Q. testing became popular in the 1920s in the United States as an

TABLE 21-1  IQ by Province in a National Sample of Canadian High School Students

| PROVINCE | MENTAL ABILITY | | N |
|---|---|---|---|
| | LOW | HIGH | |
| British Columbia | 15.1 | 45.3 | (44 245) |
| Alberta | 17.3 | 44.0 | (35 872) |
| Saskatchewan | 23.1 | 33.5 | (21 790) |
| Manitoba | 18.1 | 40.9 | (22 988) |
| Ontario | 26.3 | 33.0 | (132 235) |
| Quebec | 30.8 | 25.8 | (154 650) |
| New Brunswick | 48.1 | 15.3 | (13 368) |
| Nova Scotia | 28.1 | 25.1 | (13 931) |
| Prince Edward Island | 32.4 | 21.0 | (1 970) |
| Newfoundland | 53.7 | 11.2 | (10 838) |

Williams, 1977: Table 3. Copyright © Gage Educational Publishing Company

ideological weapon in the debate over immigration control: Well-known intelligence testers produced findings claiming to show that immigrants were feeble-minded. (For example, 83 percent of Jewish immigrants, whose offspring have subsequently had remarkable success in the educational system, were classified as having subnormal intelligence, Kamin, 1974.) Recently, I.Q. testing suffered a severe blow when it was demonstrated that the crucial identical-twin and adopted-children studies of Sir Cyril Burt were fraudulent: Sir Cyril invented rather than tracked down his identical twins and adopted children. And he cooked his results to use I.Q. test scores as an ideological weapon to defend the putative need for an elitist educational system based on social origin.

Those who see educational achievement as reflecting merit have not investigated the other component of merit: effort. Effort has not been the object of research; what has been studied instead are aspirations. And it has been found that aspirations vary in a similar way to outcomes: The higher the social-class background, the higher the educational and occupational aspirations (Porter et al., 1982: Figure 5.2). But such findings do not prove that the outcome of the educational contest reflects effort and that the winners and losers merit their fates. A deeper interpretation is that the lack of opportunity to develop high aspirations is itself a form of inequality of opportunity, one in which external constraints become internalized.

## Inequality of Opportunity
There are many reasons why the unequal-opportunity explanation of disparate educational attainment is more plausible than the unequal-merit explanation. Figure 21-3 (on page 529) demonstrated how much attending university depends on having parents who had a high level of formal schooling. As Anisef et al. (1982:102) stated, "A woman whose father had a university degree was about five times as likely to attain some university education as a woman whose father had no schooling." The

offspring of the educated have, by the accident of birth, the opportunity to acquire by osmosis in the family the *linguistic code* (Bernstein 1971, 1975) and culture of the school, whereas the offspring of the less educated are faced in school with the barrier of a linguistic code and culture that are foreign to them. This has been referred to as the *inheritance of the cultural capital* of the school (Bourdieu and Passeron, 1977) by one generation from another. The serious underrepresentation of the offspring of the working-class and lower-middle-class (in universities) is camouflaged by the fact that some university students are from these classes.

The problem is not just one of prohibitive tuition fees at universities. The inequalities appear much earlier. Students of lower-social-class origin who had excellent school records during elementary school only have a one-in-three chance of completing secondary school, a probability lower than that of upper-middle-class pupils with only average elementary school results (Porter et al., 1982: Table 14.2). Follow-up studies have shown that, among pupils who in Grade 8 aspired to and expected to complete secondary school, only 38 percent of lower-social-class pupils, as opposed to 63 percent of upper-middle-class pupils, had the opportunity to translate their aspirations and expectations into reality (Porter et al., 1982: Table 14.6). Fewer (31 percent) high I.Q. lower-social-class pupils attained the last year of secondary school than upper-middle-class pupils of low I.Q. (39 percent) (Porter et al., 1982: Table 14.1). Escande's findings (page 528) on the cumulative effect of sex and social-class origin on enrollment in the university-bound general program are also consistent with an inequality of opportunity explanation. Opportunity for girls in the school system varies enormously according to their social-class origin, even more so than for boys. Sex and social-class origin are cumulative disadvantages in the school system for working-class girls.

Inequality of opportunity is clearly the cause of illiteracy. The poorer the country, the higher the rate of illiteracy: The 25 poorest countries in the world have illiteracy rates above 80 percent (Oxenham, 1980: 1-5). Even within Third World countries, literacy reflects opportunity. In South Korea, for example, the illiteracy rate is 13 times higher among rural females than among urban males, a statistic that reflects opportunity based on both sex and geographic origin. Whether a person learns to read and write depends on where and into which group he or she is born.

Inequality of educational attainment among social groups cannot be explained by variations in mental ability. It can only be accounted for by unequal opportunities. And these differences in opportunity also account for differences in school performance and aspirations.

Equality of opportunity has to be distinguished from *universality*. The former implies that all individuals and groups have an equal chance to enter and succeed in educational institutions. It does not imply the reduction of standards of entrance or promotion, except on a temporary catch-up basis for targeted groups that have been denied equal opportunities. Universality, on the other hand, implies a more or less open door policy, with lower admission and/or promotion standards for all groups. Considerable confusion has existed in the debate over *accessibility* (of universities in particular) because some have used the term accessibility to refer to equality of opportunity, whereas others have taken it to mean universality. Canadian universities between 1960 and 1980 moved toward universality as the university

*In a "separate but equal" school in the southern United States during the Great Depression, two young boys learn to read.* Courtesy of the Library of Congress.

system expanded and marks were inflated at the secondary school level. (For example, the proportion of Ontario grade 13 students receiving an 80 percent average jumped from 1 in 25 in 1959 to 1 in 4 1981, Williams, 1984; *Citizen*, 1984.) The movement toward universality in the 60s and 70s resulted in everyone attending school longer, but it did not change the relative inequalities of educational attainment and opportunity among the offspring of the different social classes.

Although widely used, the term universality is, in fact, a misnomer when applied to institutions such as universities. Even after the expansion of the educational system, more than 80 percent of the 18 to 21 age group do not enroll in university (Statistics Canada, 1984: 125, Table 28). The percentage is still higher for the working-class and certain races and ethnic groups and in particular provinces. The meaning of universality when applied to health care, pensions and so on, that all the population receives the service, is lost when the term is used to refer to university admission.

Inequality of opportunity has another important side-effect. Universities, the pinnacle of the school system, are financed primarily through general taxation. Hence, they are sustained financially primarily by the lower-middle and working-classes because these classes constitute the bulk of the population. But, unlike other social services such as Medicare, which are used by everyone more or less equally, universities are used to a disproportionate degree by the upper-classes. So universities function as Robin Hood in reverse, taking money from the underprivileged and using it to supply a service to the most privileged in society (Meng and Sentance, 1982). This is another reason for promoting equality of opportunity and for making the upper-class pay a larger part of the operating costs of universities.

## Elite Educational Institutions

Elite private schools constitute another important form of inequality of opportunity, a form that exists mainly because of financial barriers. For example, Upper Canada College charges $11 550 per pupil per year in the mid-1980s. "Certificates of character" are often required for entry. In the total environment of this private boarding school, upper-class boys learn the values appropriate to their position during eight of their most formative years. Thus, Clement (1975: 244) argues that "private schools are most appropriately understood as class institutions designed to create upper class associations and maintain class values both by exclusion and socialization; that is, exclusion of the lower classes and socialization of the potential elite."

## Conclusion Concerning Inequality and Educational Expansion

A decade and a half after his first book, Porter (1979) concluded that the educational system has failed to promote either equality of condition or of opportunity, even after the reforms and expansion of the 60s and before the underfunding of the 70s and 80s. "If the question were asked which of the major social innovations of the twentieth century had most failed in its mission a likely answer would be public education. . . . Public education's false promise was that it would be one of the chief instruments to achieve social equality" (Porter, 1979: 242). Therein lies the crisis of the school system. Porter, like many sociologists, began to have serious misgivings concerning the functionalist and human-capital theories of schooling he had espoused earlier.

## EXPLANATIONS OF THE PERSISTENCE OF INEQUALITIES OF EDUCATIONAL OPPORTUNITY AND RESULTS

### Marxist Theory

The persistent nature of inequality after the expansion of the educational system in capitalist societies has caused a different perspective, that of *Marxism*, to become more prevalent in the sociology of education over the last two decades. Marxists argue that the appropriation of unpaid labour from the direct producers of commodities by the owners of capital (the *bourgeoisie*) is the hidden basis of the entire social structure of capitalist societies such as Canada. This exploitation provokes a reaction by the exploited, the working-class. Thus, capitalist social formations are rife with class struggle. Marxists conceive of education as being determined by society's mode of production. They refer to the school in capitalist social formations as an ideological state apparatus that reproduces social classes for *exploitation* in the process of production. The schools reproduce social classes by sorting students into hierarchically structured programs based on the division between mental and manual labour and by inculcating bourgeois ideology in those programs. The way the educational system works is seen to be determined by the needs, not of society as a whole, but of the bourgeoisie and of capital to reproduce the conditions necessary to extract profit and surplus value from the proletariat. Changes in the school system are the result of the changing needs of the capitalist mode of production during its transformation from entrepreneurial capitalism to monopoly capitalism. Business interests "were highly successful in maintaining ultimate control over the administration of educational reform" in order to smother discontent, to legitimize capitalist exploitation and to minimize the erosion of their own power and privilege (Bowles and Gintis, 1976: 240).

The capitalist need to divide and conquer the working-class, to subordinate and motivate workers on jobs and to increase control over its enterprises led it to create a hierarchically structured school system that fosters perseverance, dependability and competitiveness and that mirrors its factories. Even educational innovations, such as progressive education, open classrooms, minimization of grading and free schools are debunked by Marxists as reflecting the temporary needs of monopoly capitalism. Thus, the Marxist perspective postulates a *correspondence principle*, whereby the form, structure and content of education corresponds to the needs of capitalism. Inequality of educational opportunity exists because very unequal social classes exist under capitalism: Educational inequalities reflect inequalities in society, particularly in its economic system. Marxists argue that equality of opportunity requires not educational reform but rather the destruction of capitalism.

## Weberian Conflict Theory

This perspective emphasizes conflicting interests and conceives of the sociological role of schooling as a system of exclusion based on credentials. Weberian conflict theory can be used to analyse not only capitalism but also state socialism—socialism as it exists in societies such as the Soviet Union.

According to this theory, schools socialize individuals into the dominant status culture, with higher education propagating the elite culture and lower levels of education inculcating respect for it. To further their control of their organizations, employers use educational credentials to select members for their managerial positions who have been socialized into their own elite culture and to hire lower-level employees who have internalized an attitude of respect for this elite culture and for those who represent it. For example, studies have found that employers were skeptical of the practical utility of business school training, yet they used business school credentials as a criterion for selection and promotion because they saw them as an important indication of commitment to business attitudes. The association of education with elite status has generated a popular demand for the type of education that facilitates mobility into the elite status culture. Satisfying this demand has resulted in a widely educated population, which in turn has diluted the status value of education. What previously represented an elite level of education (e.g., a high school diploma) has become very common, and the definition of elite education has been pushed to higher levels. Faced with the increasing supply of educated candidates, employers, especially those in the most prestigious organizations, have raised their educational requirements to maintain the relative prestige of their elite group and the relative respectability of their middle ranks. This has in turn resulted in an even greater demand for education. Collins (1971) refers to this spiralling process of educational attainments and requirements as an *educational status escalator*. Every group (races, ethnic groups, social classes) stays longer in school, where the relative differences among them in school attainment do not change and where any particular diploma is progressively devalued in terms of the job openings it brings. The trend toward universality camouflages the persistence of inequality of opportunity. According to Weberian conflict theory, the increasing level of education demanded by employers and the expansion of the school system result, not from the technical needs of jobs, but rather from the increased supply of candidates (Berg, 1970; Collins, 1971).

## Education and the Labour Market
The relationship between education and the labour market is at the centre of functionalist theory, human-capital theory, Marxism and Weberian conflict theory, as described above. There is, in addition, a great deal of empirical research that does not explicitly identify itself with any theoretical perspective. On the empirical level, studies have shown that minority groups do not benefit as much from their schooling as other groups in terms of status of first full-time job, salary and promotions. For a similar diploma, women benefit less than men (Harvey, 1984), French Canadians less than English Canadians (McRoberts et al., 1976), people of lower-class origin less than people of upper-class origin (Clement 1975). Even the moment of entry into the labour market is a major determinant of benefits received. Harvey (1984) has shown that those unfortunate enough to enter the labour market with a university diploma after 1964 (after the expansion of the school system and the baby boom increased the supply of graduates) benefited less than those fortunate enough to enter prior to 1964. Clearly, the belief in ever-increasing *upward mobility* through an expanded school system is a myth. The period from World War II to 1964 may well prove to be the golden age of upward mobility through schooling, in large part because of the job opportunities created by the expansion of the school system itself. The benefit of having diplomas depends not just on individual talents but on the economic context that determines the market value of those diplomas.

# THE POLITICS OF SCHOOL KNOWLEDGE

The new sociology of education often referred to as the *interpretative paradigm*, which was strongly influenced by the sociology of knowledge, focuses on the categories used by educators, on what counts as school knowledge and on the organization of the curriculum. The school is one of the principal institutions for the socialization of the young and for the transmission of culture. Hence, it is one of the foremost instruments for inculcating a group's ideology and for controlling society and the next generation. What is and what is not taught in school not only determine who succeeds in school but also shape the thinking of the successful and the unsuccessful student. School knowledge is a tiny fraction of all knowledge, and it is socially selected in a political context, often becoming the focus of struggle and conflict. Many examples could be used to illustrate this point: the attempt of religions to use the school to instill their doctrines (witness the current conflict in Ontario over the public funding of separate Catholic schools and the very different outcomes of political struggle over that issue from province to province in Canada); the haste of dictators and revolutionaries to make sure that the content of education conforms to their ideology; the teaching of traditional sex roles in the school. The virtual elimination of illiteracy has been one of the principal and most praiseworthy accomplishments of socialist governments in the Third World, yet it would be naive not to recognize that those governments enthusiastically develop the ability to read and write while they strictly control what is published and read. Literacy in such a context is a means to greater social control. Cuba, for example, "was content in 1961 to deem a person literate if at the end of the literacy course he could write a letter of thanks to President Castro" (Oxenham, 1980: 88). Capitalist enterprises have also found literacy a useful tool of control: They discovered that literate workers are more able and willing to follow instructions than illiterate ones. Thus, in the nonsocialist Third World, sectors of the population not employed in factories, such as women and rural dwellers, are left illiterate, whereas their male urban counterparts are taught to read and write.

## THE ORIGIN OF WHAT COUNTS AS SCHOOL KNOWLEDGE

The origin of state control over education in Canada vividly demonstrates the politics of education (Curtis 1983a; 1983b; and 1984). Before 1837, education was provided and controlled by local communities. Books used in the schools were often books read in the home. In the 1830s and 1840s the Reform party, seeking political autonomy, advocated continuing this democratic local control over education and opposed state control of schools, arguing that it would be used for despotic ends by the colonial executive. However, the value of community-controlled schools was called into question by colonial conservatives after the rebellion of 1837, which they blamed on the failure of the school system to shape properly the youthful mind. A more centralized state school system was necessary, they believed, to inoculate the population against the spread of the rebellious, anti-British, antimonarchist, democratic infection that had afflicted the new nation to the south 50 years before. The struggle over education was also a struggle over political rule. The Tory party in particular sought to use education to reconstruct and maintain colonial rule. They brought in a series of school acts that reinforced the state's power to train and license teachers and to specify the curriculum.

The emergence of a state-controlled curriculum around 1846 created a distinction between school and nonschool literature and transformed the schoolbook into an instrument of state policy. The curriculum explicitly aimed to produce sober, reliable and industrious workers who would work under a central authority figure. This school reform sought to maintain political rule through political socialization in the school. Rote learning was rejected because it did not penetrate to the core of consciousness. An inductive pedagogy was proposed, whereby an emotional dependency of the child upon the teacher was created, such that the teacher could govern the child by looks, gestures and tones of voice. Education was to become a pleasurable activity. For example, since vocal music was intrinsically pleasing, teaching children moral songs was stressed. Physical punishment would no longer be necessary. "Students were to become self-disciplining individuals who behaved not out of fear or because of coercion, but because their experience at school had created in them certain moral forms for which they had a positive affection" (Curtis 1983a: 110). Order in both school and society at large would be maintained by manipulating characteristics developed in the student population. Violence and coercion would become unnecessary. Education would produce habits, dispositions and loyalties congenial to the state. Rule would no longer appear to be rule. Power is most effective when it penetrates the consciousness of those ruled in such a way that rule becomes internalized. Educational reform sought to replace governance through the suppression of individual will with governance through the shaping of individual will. It is in this political motivation and process that our present state educational system has its origin.

## THE UNIQUELY CANADIAN INVENTION OF SECOND LANGUAGE IMMERSION

Second language immersion provides another excellent illustration of the politics of and conflict over what is taught in schools. French immersion was begun in 1965 in Montreal by the noted Canadian neurologist Wilder Penfield to enable Anglophone children to participate fully in Quebec's economic life, since French was gaining importance as a language of work. The Quiet Revolution in Quebec and the growing Quebec independence movement, provoked by the English domination of the province's economy, forced the federal government to make Canada officially bilingual to keep it united. This involved recognizing bilingualism as a criterion of merit in the federal public service for positions that involved dealing with the public or supervising French employees. These new job requirements, as well as the ideology of Canadian unity created by the threat of division, produced an enormous demand for adequate French-language training, not only in Quebec but across Canada. The resistance of unilingual English public servants to official bilingualism led to the conclusion that bilingualism could only be achieved through the school system. Pedagogically, French immersion proved to be an enormous success. Rarely has so much research been done to identify problems in a program and yet resulted in such a high degree of unanimity about the project's outstanding success (Genesee, 1983). French immersion has grown rapidly across Canada, and now well over 100 000 students are enrolled in French immersion programs.

Nonetheless, strong evidence shows that the demand is much greater still. In most places, parents had to struggle with their school boards and teachers for the introduction of immersion, and in many localities, their demands have yet to be met. Olson and Burns (1983) argue that French immersion has succeeded because of the interest and efforts of parents and in spite of the resistance of teachers and school boards. Their research shows that school boards have concentrated immersion schools in more affluent areas, so parents of other children must choose between immersion with a long bus trip or a local school without immersion. Many boards have even refused to provide bussing to immersion schools, with the result that children whose families do not have the financial means to provide transportation are excluded from

French immersion. The southern Ontario school board of North York provides a good illustration. Due to a complex regional funding formula, the bussing of immersion pupils would not cost the board anything. In fact, the funds obtained for bussing could support other programs as well. Yet, the board turned the money down because its studies showed that providing transportation would result in a 40 percent growth in immersion enrollment and because of the organized political lobbying against immersion by unilingual teachers. Olson and Burns also "found strong inferential evidence that, at least in some boards, monies obtained through the federal transfer grants for anglophone learning of French were not spent on these programs" (1983:11). The North York school board, like many boards across Canada, provides bilingual learning opportunities for children of affluent and educated parents and refuses to provide those opportunities for children of less affluent, less educated parents "even when the Board's own technical analysis shows that a demand for these programs among less affluent students apparently exists" (Olson and Burns, 1983:4). Thus, the typical finding that immersion students' parents have above average education and income is explained, not by assuming that working-class parents don't want immersion for their children, but rather by the fact that they can't get it and are intimidated by more highly educated teachers and school board members. Political processes such as these determine the school curriculum and the fact that working-class children receive an inferior education, thereby perpetuating inequality of opportunity and reproducing social classes from generation to generation. Such processes have given French immersion programs in the public educational system the exclusiveness characteristic of private schools.

## SOCIALIZATION IN THE CLASSROOM

The culture that is transmitted in school—the culture pupils are being socialized into—is manifested particularly in the curriculum and its selection involves a political process that has been the centre of attention of the interpretative paradigm, as illustrated in the previous section. The *interactionist perspective* is somewhat related, except it focuses on face-to-face interaction in the classroom. It does not see teachers and pupils as dominated by external forces but seeks to bring out their active, creative side as they construct reality and negotiate meanings through their daily activities. Leiter (1974: 73) argues that the everyday routine activities of teachers consist of ad hoc practices that form teachers' "seen but unnoticed . . . methods for locating and producing students of different abilities." Rist (1973) found that, by the eighth day of kindergarten, the teacher had already separated pupils into high-, middle- and low-potential groups, with children with unemployed parents or from welfare and one-parent homes placed disproportionately more often in the low-potential group. Pupils classified as high potential sat at the front of the classroom; those classified as low potential were placed at the rear. The children were socialized to view themselves in terms of these three categories. Three years later, when the study terminated at the end of grade two, teachers still categorized these pupils in the same way: The labels had stuck. Unfortunately, this research glosses over the constraints placed on teachers and pupils by society. Hence, it has been criticized for failing to go beyond blaming the teacher in the classroom.

# ALTERNATIVES TO PRESENT EDUCATIONAL INSTITUTIONS

There have been many suggestions for improving education, ranging from modest reform to radical change. We will examine the more radical proposals to give readers a sense of the range of alternatives to the existing system.

## FREE SCHOOLS

Free schools are founded on the belief of Rousseau that children will mature into happy, co-operative, fully developed human beings if society lets them grow up naturally, without inhibitions. Although many varieties of free schools have been established on this premise, undoubtedly the most famous and durable is Summerhill.

Summerhill was founded in 1921 by A. S. Neill in a village in England about one hundred miles from London. This boarding school usually has about 25 boys and 20 girls enrolled, and they are divided into three age groups: five to seven, eight to ten and eleven to fifteen. No one picks up after the boarders, there is no room inspection, no dress code and they can go to lessons or stay away as they please. (One girl did not attend lessons for three years.) Neill (1960: 4) states: "We set out to make a school to which we should allow children freedom to be themselves. In order to do this, we had to renounce all discipline, all direction, all suggestion, all moral training, all religious instruction." There are no new teaching methods used because Neill believes that teaching does not matter very much, and there are no examinations. Freedom for the children does not imply, however, a total absence of rules. Rules are set by the children themselves at a general meeting held every Saturday night. At that meeting, Neill and the staff have votes, but their votes count no more than a six-year-old child's. Teachers and children are treated as equals at Summerhill. Social control is exercised not by teachers but by the majority, which means the children themselves. Neill says that in such an environment, the children make common-sense rules, particularly concerning their own safety and that of the younger children. They are self-motivated to learn what they are innately interested in. They do end up attending lessons, if only because loafing all the time becomes quite boring.

Freedom at Summerhill has often been mistaken for permissiveness. Neill, however, makes a strong distinction between freedom and licence. He defines licence as interfering with another's freedom. In general meetings and in their daily interaction with pupils, he and his staff speak out against behaviour that amounts to licence: "To let a child have his own way, or do what he wants to at another's expense, is bad for the child. It creates a spoiled child, and the spoiled child is a bad citizen" (Neill, 1960: 167). Neill illustrates how he has been misunderstood with the following story.

> A woman brought her girl of seven to see me. "Mr. Neil," she said, "I have read every line that you have written, and even before Daphne was born, I decided to bring her up exactly along your lines." I glanced at Daphne who was standing on my grand piano with her heavy shoes on. She made a leap for the sofa and nearly went through the springs. "You see how natural she is," said the mother. "The Neillian child!" I fear that I blushed (Neill, 1960: 107).

*Staff and students take part in the Saturday night general meeting at Summerhill.* By permission. From LIVING AT SUMMERHILL (Collier Books) © 1964 by Herb Snitzer.

Thus, Neill is at odds with permissive schools and parents who submit to intimidation by their children: "The whole freedom movement is marred and despised because so many advocates of freedom have not got their feet on the ground" (Neill, 1960: 106). That Neill confronts coercion by children directly is illustrated by the story he tells of a boy who was trying to terrorize others.

> "Cut it out my boy," I said sharply, "we aren't afraid of you." He dropped the hammer and rushed at me. He bit and kicked me. "Every time you hit or bite me," I said quietly, "I'll hit you back." And I did. Very soon he gave up the contest and rushed from the room (Neill, 1960: 167).

Neill cites several cases to show that Summerhill graduates have done well later in life, but he argues that Summerhill should not be judged on these terms but by whether pupils are happy at and after Summerhill. Unfortunately, no systematic studies of either conventional academic success or happiness of Summerhill students exist. There are other reasons to be wary of using Summerhill as a model school to be implemented on a large scale. Bettelheim (1970) suggests that Summerhill has succeeded because of the extraordinary personality of Neill and not because of the principles underlying the school, principles drawn from a naive early version of psychoanalysis. Summerhill's pupils have not been representative of pupils in general: They come largely from upper-middle-class backgrounds, in part because of the tuition fees. And it must be remembered that Neill has expelled some problem children from Summerhill. His school, like all private schools, has an easier task than the public school system.

## SOCIALIST SCHOOLS IN SOCIALIST SOCIETY

A major problem for free schools is that they are constrained by the societies in which they exist, in particular by the entrance requirements of colleges and universities and the job market. Furthermore, such schools are like drops of water in the ocean: They don't lead to large-scale social change. Marxists, as a result, have usually seen free schools and progressive education as mere diversions from more important struggles. They argue that schools cannot be free in an unfree society founded on the exploitation of the working-class, that education can only become free with the destruction of capitalist society and the establishment of socialism.

If we temper the romanticism of the socialist promised land with realism by examining education as it has actually existed after a socialist revolution, there is clearly reason to worry whether the promises of freedom and equality will ever be fulfilled. Many Marxist studies of education in the early 1970s ended by pointing to the cultural revolution of the Red Guards in China as the model to follow. The failure of that model has left Marxists without any example in reality on which to base their hopes. Revolutionary regimes that claim to be socialist have, in fact, taken a particularly authoritarian view of education, using the school system as the means of directly indoctrinating the population in the precepts favoured by the political theorists. Socialist education has tended to be the polar opposite of free schools. Studies show that equality of educational opportunity for the working-class is no greater in industrialized socialist states (the Soviet Union, East Germany, Czechoslovakia) than in the United States and Canada (Dobson 1977). The historical record indicates that the problems of inequality of educational opportunity and an authoritarian school system are not solved by a socialist revolution eliminating private property, profit and the capitalist market. The problems appear to have deeper roots.

## DESCHOOLING SOCIETY

Ivan Illich argues that "schools are fundamentally alike in all countries, be they fascist, democratic or socialist, big or small, rich or poor" (1970: 106-07). All these types of government, Illich argues, are based on *manipulative institutions*. The school, for example, is an institution dispensing compulsory instruction according to a fixed curriculum that defines what counts and what doesn't count as important knowledge. Thus, it creates a sense of inferiority among the unschooled, regardless of how much they have learned. Its hidden curriculum fosters a dependency on institutions. For example, it encourages the belief that one cannot learn unless taught by teachers in school and thereby mistakes teaching for learning. Schools are also addictive: The solution to every school problem is always more schooling (e.g., failure to learn in school is treated by more schooling). Thus, schools are essentially institutions of social control. And these characteristics are true of all educational institutions in both capitalist and socialist societies. Paulo Freire (1971) adds a related criticism of what he calls the *banking conception of education*, in which education is conceived as an act of depositing knowledge in the empty minds of students by the possessor of knowledge, the teacher. This attitude, he argues, is part of a larger context of domination and oppression, particularly in the Third World.

Illich proposes the radical transformation of manipulative institutions to what he calls *convivial institutions*. These would be based not on compulsion and coercion but on freedom, to be used or left unused, much like museums and libraries. Children would be given at birth an edu-credit card entitling them to a certain amount of educational resources, to be used when and how they wished. There would be no schools. *Learning webs* or networks would attempt to match an individual wanting to learn something with the equipment needed to learn it (e.g., laboratories), with people having the skill or knowledge and willing to communicate it and with peers willing to discuss it. Whereas manipulative institutions require people to learn, convivial institutions would facilitate learning for anyone who wants to learn. In a sense, they would be free schools writ large and based on the assumption that people do want to learn. Diplomas as entry requirements for jobs and higher education would be considered discriminatory and ruled illegal. Instead, tests on entry would determine who really has the knowledge required, regardless of how they acquired it. Freire (1971), from a related perspective, advocates a problem-posing pedagogy based on dialogue between students and the teacher, whose goal is to enable the oppressed (in particular, adults in the Third World) to become conscious of the causes of their oppression and committed to its transformation. This he refers to as the *pedagogy of the oppressed* (Freire, 1970: 40).

The problems with deschooling society are similar to the problems with free schools, except on a larger scale. Replacing coercive educational institutions with convivial institutions that presuppose motivation could easily aggravate inequality and have thoroughly conservative consequences because the nature and direction of motivation are shaped by privilege and deprivation. For example, the use of museums and libraries (the prototypes of convivial institutions) varies enormously by social class. Illich's proposal amounts to giving free rein to the market forces of supply and demand in the area of education.

# SUMMARY

Early in the 1960s it was thought that many social problems, not the least being *inequality of opportunity* and of condition, could be solved, or at least alleviated, by reforming and expanding educational institutions. The type of educational reform and expansion that occurred since then have not relieved these problems. Instead of taking steps to equalize opportunity, the school system was simply expanded (this being hailed as universality and accessibility). As a result, it was not so much the bright offspring of the deprived but rather the academically weak offspring of the privileged who marched through the open doors of institutions of higher learning. The expansion of the educational system has proved to be more related to the inflation of marks and diplomas than to the equalization of opportunity. This is not to criticize all forms of educational expansion but rather to criticize an educational system based on inequality of opportunity, whether it has been expanded or not. There is no evidence to show that the inequality of educational attainment among different groups can be explained by inequalities of merit, but there is a great deal of evidence demonstrating that it can be explained by inequalities of opportunity.

Although different theories—*functionalist, Marxist* and *Weberian*—address the relationship between educational institutions and the labour market, all agree that schools are strongly affected by the labour market and by the economic system in general (Murphy 1979). What is learned in educational institutions, how it is learned and by whom it is learned are also strongly affected by the outcome of political struggles. Education is not politically neutral and objective; it is mixed with and is the product of politics.

There is no easy solution to the problem of educational institutions. What is seen as a problem and as a solution is highly influenced by the values of the viewer. Sociologists of education have critically assessed existing systems and expanded the range of new possibilities, but it is up to readers to weigh the options and arrive at their own conclusions. The criticisms of present-day educational institutions have led to calls for radical change. Are the proposed alternatives feasible ways of eliminating current deficiencies?

# DISCUSSION QUESTIONS

1. Recently, there have been political struggles over the funding of education at all levels and in all provinces (especially British Columbia). Discuss the politics of education and the funding question in your province and attempt to uncover the interests and ideologies of the various groups directly or indirectly involved.

2. In the past, teachers did not strike and were not regarded as professionals in the same sense as doctors and lawyers. Over the past 25 years, the

qualifications of teachers have risen; they have become more strongly organized and they go on strike. Should this be seen as the professionalization or as the unionization of teaching? Are teachers professionals or are they educational workers? Are these two terms complementary or contradictory? What are the implications of each?

3. Elite private schools are to be found in virtually every big Canadian city. In English Canada, the acid test of their exclusiveness is whether they belong to the Canadian Headmasters Association. Obtain information about the nearest elite private school. Are such schools better? Why do they exist? What does one need to be admitted? Do they perpetuate inequality of opportunity?

4. Over the last two decades, there has been a great surge in the number of women obtaining advanced degrees. Graduating classes in disciplines such as medicine, which refused women in the past, now contain increasing proportions of women. Sexist stereotypes of male and female jobs and disciplines are being eliminated from schoolbooks. Do female and male students now have equal chances to succeed in the educational system? Do they receive equal treatment? Does what counts as knowledge in educational institutions reflect the culture of women as well as the culture of men?

5. What was the highest school diploma received by your grandparents? Your parents? What diploma do you expect to receive? What was their first job? What is their job now? What will your job prospects be after you finish your studies? Discuss how the relationship between school diplomas and labour market requirements has changed, if it has changed, for the social class and minority group to which your family belongs.

# PROCESSES of CHANGE

Processes of social change deserve a separate section because they are a key to understanding social organization. Many see sociology's central role as the construction of theories about social order; many others see the construction of theories of change as the central task.

Theories of change are usually either evolutionary or revolutionary. Theories of social evolution first appeared in sociology over a century ago. Here the early work of Émile Durkheim (1858-1917) and Herbert Spencer (1820-1903) is most important. They focused on continuity in change, on how things stay the same while changing and how early changes lay the ground work for later ones.

Durkheim examined the social change from primitive, preindustrial to modern, industrial conditions. He noted two main correlates of this process: (1) work and all aspects of life associated with work become specialized, and a division of labour develops; and 2) with a division of labour, the basis of social cohesion changes from *mechanical* to *organic solidarity*.

With mechanical solidarity, people lead similar lives and tend to hold identical views and values. Violation of their values is punished harshly. Conversely, organic solidarity permits many different roles. People lead very different kinds of lives and therefore develop different views and values. Deviance is harder to define, and punishment is less uniform, harsh and automatic. Without moral uniformity, new ways of integrating people must be found. Otherwise, a state of *anomie* (normlessness) exists, which leads to psychological distress and even to higher rates of suicide.

The institutions of a society characterized by mechanical solidarity are typically undifferentiated. Religion, science, law and government may be jumbled up together in a small body of received wisdom, perhaps a holy book, legends or folktales. No mechanisms exist for developing or rejecting this wisdom and such a system has a limited capacity for change.

The emergence of a society based on freedom to contract, rather than on tradition or kinship, is a major development. Yet contractual relations are actually based on *noncontractual elements of contract* rooted in tradition or kinship. These "primitive" elements provide the trust without which rational, voluntary economic activity is impossible. Only later, with the use of strong state protections, do such onetraditional elements become unnecessary. Thus, modern practices rise on the shoulders of older ones.

Theories of dialectical change, or revolution, are theories of discontinuity. They are about radical shifts in social organization. Georg Hegel (1770-1831) and Karl Marx (1818-1883) first used the notion of the dialectic in social analysis. For Marx, the dominant characteristic of a society is its class structure, which arises out of relations of production. Accordingly, the change from one type of society to another involves a change in relations of production and class structure. This fundamental change is accomplished only through the revolutionary overthrow of a ruling class and its replacement by a new ruling class. Such change gives birth to a new order, but not without upheaval and revolution. As Mao said, there is no omelet without broken eggs.

A variety of theorists, of whom Max Weber (1864-1920) is the most eminent, have attempted to combine these two approaches. According to Weber, certain social forms, such as bureaucracy or the city, may radically shift the course of later social development. In that sense, they are revolutionary changes. Yet what typically follows is a return to some kind of routine, or evolution at a new level of complexity. A new social order emerges, then begins to differentiate and integrate again.

Weber gives us the example of a charismatic social movement. A fiery, persuasive leader gathers his followers and proclaims new values, smashing tradition and its guardians. Followers are swept forward by their excitement and the conviction that their leader is right. They risk and share and suffer in ways quite out of the ordinary. Eventually, especially after the prophet dies, this charismatic phase passes. People return to more ordinary lives, although their lives are transformed by their experience. Disciples organize to administer the ideals promoted by the prophet. Both revolutionary (sectarian) religious and political movements follow this pattern, despite their different goals.

*Social differentiation* is an apparently universal process. By "differentiation" we mean that all social organizations, from roles up through central institutions, tend to become more specialized, more different from one another, over time. This process is speeded up immensely by social and technological breakthroughs: by the invention of tools, writing and engines that use artificial sources of energy, among others. The changes associated with modernization show social differentiation in its most dramatic light.

Differentiation proceeds through the specialization of subsystems. Economy, polity, the legal system and other central institutions become more distinct from one another. They develop their own operating rules, agendas, resource bases, patterns of socialization and the like. In turn, they become internally differentiated. The law, for example, is simultaneously a business, a system of courts, a body of knowledge and rules and a self-maintaining culture, with schools, students and a particular "legal" outlook.

Differentiation is only one of the apparently universal processes of social change. Another is *integration*, or co-ordination. Without integration, differentiation leads to confusion and a waste of organizational resources and whatever benefits specialization would otherwise provide.

As social systems differentiate, their goals and interests diverge increasingly. Conflicts between them increase as interests clash. Such conflicts among on-going social units and the kinds of negotiation they lead to produce *dialectical* change. In dialectical change, the force and counterforce (or thesis and antithesis) combine in a synthesis. Thus, for example, conflict over uses of new computerized technology will probably change both the labour movement and management. Each will be thrown off its evolutionary path; new relationships between the two will, eventually, be hammered out. Then, each will return to an evolutionary path of differentiation and integration at a new level of complexity.

## Where Does Change Begin?

In a certain sense, all theories of social change are variations on these few themes. Yet, theories differ in what they see as the cause of change. If all the parts of a society are tied together, it follows that they will tend to keep one another from changing much. This is precisely why many planned attempts at social change fail. An intervention in one subsystem may be offset by counterforces or shifts in an adjacent subsystem. So what kinds of change can break this pattern?

On a descriptive level, the question is easily answered. We know, for example, that capitalism transformed the social life of Western societies from what it was 500 years ago. As well, we can relate the rise of capitalism to changes in religion, warfare and colonization, monetary and economic theory, political organization and other factors. If anything, we have too many explanations but no widely accepted, single theory about the rise of capitalism in the West and its effects on society.

Likewise, we know that technology has significantly affected social life throughout history. People today are feeling the effects of microelectronics and computerization in all parts of their lives. The so-called "information revolution" grows out of the long development of science and technology in the West, associated, like the rise of capitalism, with Protestantism, warfare, the development of nation-states and other factors. In addition, certain new ideas, like efficiency, become new social goals. Where did these new ideas and goals, discussed below by William Vanderburg come from? How do they relate to the other social changes we have mentioned? Again, there are too many explanations of innovation and no widely accepted, single theory of technical innovation and its effect on society.

In historical analyses, theorists tell their story from many different starting points; some begin with the economy, others with religion, still others with the nation-state. A Marxist theory typically sees economic conflicts as basic and value conflicts (e.g., in religion) as superficial or secondary. A Weberian analysis, by contrast, may consider value conflicts as basic as economic or political ones. We can only judge these theories by their thoroughness, economy and agreement with the evidence. Theories of societal change, especially theories aimed at explaining the past, can rarely be verified by prediction and testing. However, not all theories of societal change focus on the past. Increasingly, theories of change aim to predict the future.

Theories about the future are not confined to sociology. They make up a new, interdisciplinary field called *futurology*, to which sociologists contribute both methods and substance. A major work in this area, *The Coming of the Post Industrial Society* (1970), is by sociologist Daniel Bell. It describes a society that, in Bell's view, is already in sight, though far from completion, a society in which knowledge is the most important social resource. To simplify, it predicts that knowledge workers, information technology and educational institutions will have even more importance than they do today.

Other theorists, like Alvin Toffler, whose ideas are similar in many respects to Bell's, predict that technological changes will continue to alter society dramatically. Our lives will supposedly become more prosperous, varied and secure as new microelectronic gadgets revolutionize our homes and workplaces. Of course, our lives have already been improved enormously by modern appliances, electricity, automobiles and the like. More of the same is predicted. Yet, this approach to prediction is missing something important.

## Power and Belief

Amid all the competing sociological theories about past and future, two major concerns emerge time and again: they are power and belief. They come together in the study of ideology and its effect on social change and order.

Changes to a society are largely determined by who controls technology, knowledge and the other agents of change already mentioned. No valid theory of change can limit itself to considering *possible* effects of a change agent while ignoring the way power is actually used. For example, the fact that computers *could* free people from mindless toil tells us little. To predict the future, we must know who controls the computers and what they plan to use them for. Similarly, the fact that knowledge is becoming an evermore important social resource does not ensure that the educated will become more powerful, only that the powerful will make more use of the educated.

Yet, the mere fact of power is not everything. We need to know what people in power are thinking, how they understand the world and what their goals are. Also, how do they exercise their power: To what degree can they project their goals and world view into the minds of people they rule? Power is and will always be exercised as much by persuasion as by force.

Max Weber directed our attention to the continuing contest between power and belief: to the attempts those in power make to control the thinking of the masses; the tendency for disaffection; the rise of prophets with a power to unite and inspire trust, and the ability of disciples to consolidate the achievements of the leader and become new, powerful rivals to the existing order.

Under what conditions will those in power be able to keep control over the thinking of the masses? Will ordinary people become disaffected and rebellious? Will charismatic leaders emerge and succeed in challenging those in power? Some of these questions have already been asked and answered in earlier chapters on social movements and social class. Some will be answered in this section.

Sociology is a science of social relations. But much more preliminary work is needed before we can succeed in that enterprise. This introductory volume is no more than an outline of the sociologist's aims, tools and achievements to date.

# 22
# Historical Patterns of Change and Development
## *Anton L. Allahar*

# INTRODUCTION: DIMENSIONS OF SOCIAL CHANGE

The study of social change is intrinsic to sociology. To understand the nature and functioning of human societies past and present, sociologists have developed many theories on why societies undergo change and why they can resist change. This chapter, then, will be concerned with some of those theories as they relate to change at the *macro* level. It will focus largely on whole societies and attempt to explain why change, or the apparent absence of it, colours so much of the work sociologists do. In this context, small-scale changes, or changes at the *micro* level (for example, changes in styles of dress, musical taste or eating patterns), will not be of central importance.

To talk about social change at the macro or micro levels, however, automatically implies a consideration of its opposite—*social persistence* or *constancy*. Philosophically, the concept of change is *relational* in that it cannot be conceived of without reference to some ideal instance where change is absent. This is not to say that there are actual instances in which it can be demonstrated in an *absolute* way that change is absent. For as we know, change is ubiquitous. It occurs everywhere, always, in some form or fashion.

But, to even speak of change we must ask the question, "Change from what to what?" And in this sense, the phrase "change is relational," as it is used here, can be understood as follows: I cannot come first in a race if I am the only runner. Coming first can only make sense *in relation to* others coming second, third or last. If we all come first, then none of us comes first. So too with change, we may argue. As was said above, change is ubiquitous. Thus, if everything is always changing, nothing is ever changing. The essence of change, then, can only be grasped in relation to that which is constant or that which appears to be constant.

Where, then, does this leave the sociologist who is studying social change? To answer these questions we must introduce three new elements to the discussion: *magnitude, temporality* and *spatiality*. Change is always a matter of degree, it always occurs in time and always relates to space or place. Some things change more than others, faster than others and have a wider impact than others. Thus, we can speak of slow, evolutionary change, quick revolutionary change, micro and macro change, short-term and long-term change.

Certain elements of society or aspects of social structure change more slowly than others and for purposes of description and analysis *may be treated as being more or less constant*. Hence, in looking at the basic structure of the Canadian family over the past century, for example, we may note that it has undergone major changes. But this does not imply that in 1867 the structure of the Canadian family was static. In fact, we can be reasonably certain that in 1867 it already exhibited some of the characteristics that define the modern nuclear family in Canada.

Some changes are more cumulative and can only be fully appreciated in the long-term, while others are more rapid and hence more readily apparent in the short-term. As an example, consider the abrupt changes in family structure among black South Africans caused by their government's policy of apartheid and the creation of homelands that forcibly separate wives, husbands and children from parents. The typical family in the tribal homelands is neither extended nor nuclear. Rather, it is one in which grandparents, aged relatives or aged friends care for the young, who, if fortunate, see their biological parents once or twice each year.

In talking about social change, therefore, we must consider social persistence. The two phenomena are inextricably interwoven. That is why we can say that change is constant and not contradict ourselves. Above all, change is a process that occurs within, between and among social structures that are fluid and dynamic.

## INDUSTRIALIZATION AND DEVELOPMENT

Bearing these general observations in mind, let us look more closely at some major theories of change used by sociologists. All these theories try to describe and explain how human societies have changed from traditional and preindustrial to modern and industrial. The overall shift from simple to more complex forms of social organization is the object of study. And attention is focused on the process of industrial development as the leading indicator of social change. In this context, industrialization is seen as a positive attribute of societies and is closely linked with the idea of progress: More industrialized societies are deemed to have progressed further than less industrialized ones.

Thus, the terms *industrialization* and *development* are often used interchangeably. As Kemp (1978:20) tells us, "It has become common to equate industrialization with economic development, and countries embarking on the path of development have generally assumed that they will have to industrialize."

Conceived of as a process, industrialization implies a matter of degree, and various societies can be located along a continuum from least industrialized to most industrialized. But, in keeping with our introductory comments, we must realize that no society is completely industrialized or completely preindustrial. Even the most industrially backward society has some technology, however rudimentary. And even in a country like Canada, one of the most developed in the world, there remain areas where people lead traditional lives, have low standards of living, sanitation and health care and lack money, education or the material comforts of life. These areas include many reserves, single-industry towns in parts of northern Ontario, the Maritime provinces and various urban slums in Toronto, Montreal and Vancouver.

It is clear, therefore, that when we speak of a society as having developed industrially, we refer to a very uneven process. Surely, there may be a *general tendency* towards industrialization and development, but not all parts of a society will exhibit the same levels of industrial development. In other words, not all parts will have changed to the same degree and at the same pace.

# SOCIAL EVOLUTIONISM

## IDEAL TYPES

### Newton, Darwin and Spencer

During the nineteenth century, when sociology was a fledgling science and when the full force of the Industrial Revolution was beginning to be felt in western Europe, various social theorists on the continent became interested in industrialism. They wanted to understand: a) how societies changed from preindustrial to industrial; and b) what were the essential characteristics of the new order that set it apart from the old. On this score, the works of Sir Isaac Newton, Charles Darwin and Herbert Spencer served as important points of departure.

This is not to say that Newton, as a physicist, Darwin, as a biologist and Spencer, who worked as a railway engineer, were explicitly concerned with explaining *social* change. But these thinkers had ideas that later were adopted by social theorists and incorporated into an explanation of how societies change and develop. By far the most influential of those ideas concerned the question of *evolution*, or *evolutionary change*.

Newton's contribution stemmed from his work on the laws of motion (published in 1687) that showed "how the universe ran of its own accord like a clock" (Collins and Markowsky, 1984: 21). Prior to this time, when people accepted a religious interpretation of natural phenomena, it was generally believed that the universe unfolded according to a plan laid out by God. Unassuming as it may seem, this "discovery" by Newton helped to free the human mind from old ways of thinking and let to the postulation of certain natural (as opposed to religious) laws that regulated the operation of the universe. Having rejected theological explanations, particularly the belief in original sin, thinkers embraced science and rationality, as a means of identifying those natural laws that governed the world, with a view of ordering society in accordance with such laws. In other words, building on the idea that the universe was rationally intelligible and that it unfolded in keeping with natural processes, thinkers began to look outside of religion for an explanation of natural and social phenomena.

Charles Darwin, in his *Origin of the Species* (1859), challenged the Biblical account of creation and theorized that human beings were not descended from Adam and Eve but rather represented a higher form of life that *evolved* out of previously existing lower forms. In his highly controversial *The Descent of Man* (1871), for example, he argued that man shared a common ancestor with animals, most probably the great apes. It is thus said that Darwin, "at a stroke, set the natural world in order, just as Newton had done two centuries earlier in physics" (Collins and Markowsky, 1984: 87).

Building upon the theme of evolutionism, which saw all species of plants, fish and animals and all humans as evolving from common ancestors and not necessarily as the work of God, Herbert Spencer talked about the evolution of societies along a continuum from primitive, to ancient, to modern forms. And the principles of *natural selection* and *survival of the fittest* which were used to describe the evolution and development of living organisms, were also applied to human societies. Such societies were said to be like living organisms. Just as, for example, the human organism has a heart, lungs, liver and so on that function to maintain the whole and ensure its survival, so societies are made up of various parts (institutions) that function interdependently to keep them integrated and healthy. Social theorists who applied the *organismic analogy* to the study of how societies change were called *social Darwinists*.

In describing and accounting for the differences between preindustrial and industrial societies, social evolutionary theorists adopted the *ideal type* approach. This

*Spencer was born in England and, though trained in science, held a number of odd jobs that included inventor, railway engineer, and writer. Between 1860 and 1896 he turned out a massive ten-volume work entitled* **Synthetic Philosophy**, *with volumes six to eight devoted exclusively to the* **Principles of Sociology** *(1872). Spencer subscribed to the organismic analogy and, as an evolutionary thinker, followed Comte's model in arranging primitive, ancient and modern societies along a continuum.*

*Herbert Spencer (1820-1903)*

involves selecting certain features of given societies and classifying them as either preindustrial or industrial, either backward or advanced. Clearly, those in the former category are seen to have evolved and developed *less* than those in the latter category. Consequently, as with the social Darwinists, it may be said that there is an explicit value judgement in this approach, for the more evolved or developed societies are deemed "more fit" or better than the others: "Evolution means *improved capability* to adapt to environmental pressures or changes" (Wilson, 1983: 95, emphasis added).

## Sociology's Contribution

Accepting the basic ideas and assumptions of evolutionism, a great many sociologists have sought ways to marry it to the ideal-type or *bipolar view* of how societies change and develop. Among these, Ferdinand Toennies' (1957) theory of community versus society and Émile Durkheim's (1933) concepts of mechanical and organic solidarity are perhaps the best known. For Toennies, *community* represented a simple way of life in which spontaneity and intimacy characterized the interaction between and among people. Within *society*, on the other hand, social relations were seen to be more complex, impersonal and formal. Durkheim, too, in talking about *mechanical solidarity* or society, posited a fundamental likeness or similarity among people, based upon a common *collective conscience* and morality. Organic solidarity, conversely, describes contemporary society, based on an intricate division of labour and increasing social dissimilarity, differentiation and complexity. In both cases, the move from community to society, from mechanical to organic solidarity, implied evolutionary changes from one ideal type to another.

In a similar vein, as Portes (1976: 62) tells us, a whole host of other social-evolutionary writings on this theme emerged. Charles Horton Cooley (1962), for example, spoke of primary and secondary social attachments in a way that echoed the thoughts of Toennies: *Primary*, face-to-face social encounters were seen to occur in those societies where little social differentiation had taken place; and *secondary*, impersonal, even superficial relations prevailed in advanced societies. From a slightly earlier period, Portes also mentions Henry Maine (1907), who distinguished between societies based on *status* and those based on *contract*; the famous anthropologist Robert Redfield (1965), who opposed *folk* to *urban* cultures; and Howard Becker (1970), who examined the differences between *sacred* and *secular* social orders. In this context, then, even

> the contemporary distinction between "tradition" and "modernity" can be easily conceptualized as a latter-day counterpart of a theme present since the beginnings of sociological thought (Portes, 1976:62).

## PATTERN VARIABLES

### Parson's Four Sets of Pattern Variables

To give more concrete content to the ideal-typical features of traditional and modern societies, several social-evolutionary theorists seized upon the *pattern variable scheme* developed by Talcott Parsons (1954). Although Parsons himself did not initially conceive of the pattern variables in this context, they were adopted by people like Hoselitz (1960) and Chodak (1973) in their descriptions and explanations of social change. But before getting to those descriptions and explanations, we should clarify what the pattern variables are and how it was possible to adapt them to the study of social change. As a central feature of both the social-evolutionary and the *value-orientation* (to be discussed next) theories of change, the pattern variable scheme has coloured much of the work in the sociology of development.

The idea of the pattern variables came to Parsons during a study of the doctor-patient relationship. He observed that in such a highly specialized relationship, the doctor's behaviour toward the patient is guided by the same principles that inform the patient's behaviour toward the doctor: Their interaction is patterned. The patient expects the same degree of concern, dedication and professionalism from the doctor as the doctor affords to all other patients. No favouritism or prejudice should come into play. And the doctor, for his or her part, expects to be judged on the basis of competence and according to the same criteria by which all other doctors are judged. No exceptions or personal considerations should enter the picture.

It thus occurred to Parsons that our patterns of social interaction in modern society increasingly reflect the highly specialized conditions under which we live. Not only the doctor-patient relationship, but teacher-student, employer-employee contacts and many others occur in institutional and bureaucratic settings that more than anything else serve to define contemporary life. And in the public domain we expect, and are expected by others, to act in specific and patterned ways that are established by social convention or accepted practice. And this was the context in which Parsons identified four *variable sets of interaction patterns* among people, known in sociology as *the pattern variables*.

Briefly stated, the four sets of pattern variables, or the four sets of continua along which our social behaviour tends to vary, are: a) particularism-universalism; b) ascription-achievement; c) diffuseness-specificity; and d) affectivity-affective neutrality. In contemporary society, our formal, public behaviour, for example, at work or at school, resembles more closely the universal, achievement-oriented, specific, and affectively neutral types. This means we expect, and are expected by others, to be judged according to impersonal criteria that are equally applicable to all other members of society; we expect, and are expected by others, to move ahead on the basis of merit and knowledge or skills acquired in fair competition; we expect, and are expected by others, to interrelate on the basis of specific roles, such as doctor, student, employee and so on; and finally, we expect, and are expected by others, to interact, not merely on the basis of emotion, but according to reason, following our heads rather than our hearts.

Conversely, our informal, private behaviour, for example, within the family or peer group, will follow more particularistic, ascriptive, diffuse and affective lines. We do not expect our mothers to treat us as our teachers or bosses do. Parents or friends usually take into account the particular attributes of individuals and respond on a more personal level. Further, our status within the family is ascribed; we occupy diffuse roles, such as son, sister, cousin, and we are sensitive to the emotions and moods of other family members. Moreover, homes are supposed to offer love and warmth in a way that offices and schools are not.

## Later Sociological Applications

As was indicated above, the pattern variables were quickly adopted by several sociologists and applied to the study of social change. For Hoselitz (1960), for example, they represented the "sociological aspects of economic growth" (the title of his book). In his study, Portes (1976: 62) says, the underdeveloped, traditional or backward societies were portrayed as those in which "roles were ascribed, functionally diffuse, and oriented toward narrow, particularistic goals." The developed, modern or advanced societies, however, were characterized by "clearly delineated specific roles, acquired through achievement criteria and oriented toward universal norms."

As far as the actual dynamics of change and development are concerned, social-evolutionary theorists focus on two related processes that are internal to societies: social differentiation and social integration. Accepting the Durkheimian view that the developing division of labour simultaneously erodes mechanical solidarity and promotes an integrated organic solidarity, these theorists explain change in traditional societies as a constant interplay between forces or pressures that, on the one hand, make for social differentiation, and on the other, produce structures that enhance greater integration. For example, in a typical agricultural community, there may be a scarcity of food owing to war, drought, famine, flood or overpopulation. This situation causes differentiation, since some people attempt to produce food as farmers, fishermen, hunters, gatherers and so on. If the community is to remain intact, however, the increasing specialization and differentiation has to be integrated at a higher level. And in this respect, one would expect to find the development of networks of interdependence, for example, organizations for distributing or sharing food, that lead to growing societal complexity or *systemness*.

> If this process of differentiation into increasingly specialized units were to continue without other structural modifications, the system would disintegrate. However, the tendencies toward disintegration are counteracted by the evolution of more sophisticated integrative mechanisms (for example) the development of bureaucratic forms of organization (Wilson, 1983: 96).

For Neil Smelser, therefore, change and development are conceived of as a "contrapuntal interplay between differentiation (which is divisive of established society) and integration (which unites differentiated structures on a new basis)" (1968: 138); and for Eisenstadt, social differentiation is a process of "continuous development from the 'ideal' type of primitive society" (1964: 376). According to these social-evolutionary theorists, then, societies change and develop as a result of the gradual passage from less to more differentiated social forms. And in the process, evermore complex structures of specialization and functional interdependence are generated.

## EVOLUTIONISM AND STAGES OF GROWTH

An interesting variant on the theme of evolutionism was presented by W.W. Rostow (1962) in his classic study *The Stages of Economic Growth*. Introduced as a necessary corrective to the prevailing bipolar or two-stage view of change, Rostow's study posited a series of intermediate evolutionary stages in the development from backward to advanced society. From the perspectives of Hoselitz (1960) and Rostow, underdevelopment was seen as the original state of society, the starting point from which all change begins.

Hence, while in basic agreement with the ideal-typical approach, at least as far as the first stage of traditionalism is concerned, Rostow went on to identify four other stages of economic growth: In the first stage, the preconditions for economic "take-off" emerge. This usually occurs as a result of technological diffusion, when a more developed country comes into contact with a less developed one. In Rostow's third stage, actual take-off is experienced in terms of expanded manufacturing, trade and commerce. In the fourth stage, *the drive to maturity*, modern technology is increasingly applied to the bulk of the society's resources, leading ultimately to the fifth stage of *high mass consumption*, as is evidenced in the leading countries of western Europe and North America today.

Although appealing as a descriptive schema, Rostow's stages of economic growth, like other evolutionary views, suffer from two general shortcomings. Firstly, they cannot explain the changes observed. Sure enough, we are presented with descriptions of the various stages, but no attempt is made to specify exactly what causes the transition from one stage to the other. In fact, as Gunder Frank pointed out in a telling critique of this entire school of thought, "No underdeveloped country has ever managed to take off out of its underdevelopment by following Rostow's stages" (1973: 24).

The second general problem inherent in this approach concerns its lack of sensitivity to historical process. To say that all societies begin from a condition of original underdevelopment and proceed along the same path to development ignores the infinite variety of history. The paths to development followed by Britain, the United States and Japan, for example, are very dissimilar: Britain was a colonial power; the United States was a colonial possession; and Japan was never colonized by any foreign power. Yet they are all leading, industrial, capitalist countries. Further, the assertion that underdevelopment is the original stage of all societies directly implies that those societies that have developed have a history, the history of their development, while those that are still underdeveloped have no history, for they are still in the original underdeveloped stage (Gunder Frank, 1973: 19).

These questions will be reconsidered in the section on dependency theory. For the moment, let us turn to the second school of thought on social change and development and examine the ways theorists of that school have used the ideas of evolutionism and pattern variables.

# MODERNIZATION AND VALUE-ORIENTATION SCHOOL

## HOW VALUES INFLUENCE DEVELOPMENT

Evolutionary thinking has also had a marked influence on other theorists of change and development. Emphasizing social-psychological processes, writers such as David McClelland (1963; 1964), Daniel Lerner (1965), Alex Inkeles (1966; 1973) and Seymour Martin Lipset (1967; 1985), among others, have come to be known as value-orientation or *modernization* theorists. For reasons that are somewhat vague, members of this school have identified themselves as the intellectual heirs of Max Weber. Given Weber's insistence on the primacy of ideas and motives in human conduct, modernization theorists view their approach as contributing to the development of a Weberian sociology.

Reacting to Marx's view that much of social life is economically conditioned, Weber attempted to show that, in some instances, ideas, as opposed to material interests, have become effective forces in history. This is the central theme he traced in *The Protestant Ethic and the Spirit of Capitalism* (1958). In essence, Weber linked the emergence of capitalistic behaviour with the religious teachings and ideas of Protestantism, particularly in its Calvinist form. Though *not* arguing that Protestantism *caused* capitalism, he showed that peoples' ideas, motives and values and their outlook on the world, religious or otherwise, have a significant impact on the daily conduct of their lives and their economic dealings.

It is in this context that McClelland seeks to cement the link between Weber and modernization theory by asserting that there is a

> growing conviction among social scientists that it is values, motives or psychological forces that determine ultimately the rate of social and economic development (1963:17).

As was said above, however, the connection is tenuous, for unlike Weber, the modernization theorists are far less sensitive to historical and structural analyses of change. Nevertheless, the latter do draw our attention to some of the noneconomic determinants of human action.

In contrast to the "pure" social-evolutionary thinkers, the writers mentioned above are less concerned with detailed descriptions of traditional or modern social structures. Rather, they stress the actual character of the individuals living in particular societies. Their aim is to assess, in social-psychological terms, how those individuals' actions are informed and how they may bring about or retard change. As Myron Weiner observed, the modernization theorists believe that "attitudinal and value changes are prerequisites to creating a modern society, economy, and political system" (1966: 9).

From the perspective of modernization theory, questions of change, development or industrialization cannot be separated from a consideration of the values underlying those processes. Hence, as Chodak put it:

> Instead of asking "What is development?" or "What happens in its course?", modernization theorists ask *why* it happened, and what specifically *caused* the breakthrough from traditional into modern societies. Thus such theories start with the question "What are the *causes* of industrialization?" (1973: 11, emphasis added).

In answering such queries, modernization theorists look to value orientations. Adopting more of an analytical approach than the earlier evolutionary school, these theorists reason that it is possible to identify certain factors which, when present, lead to development and industrialization and, when absent, cause stagnation. The key factors identified relate to the values and attitudes of members of a given society. Therefore, Western Europe could develop and advance on the basis of its people's value and attitudinal structures, while in the Third World, the people are lacking similarly progressive values and attitudes.

This school is more analytical than descriptive in its approach because it seeks to answer the question "Why?" It does not content itself with merely describing traditional and modern societies but attempts to explain why some societies remain backward and why others advance. As McClelland argued, too much attention has been paid to the external causes of development—favourable trade opportunities, abundant natural resources, conquest of markets and so on. He was more interested in internal factors such as the values and motives that lead people to exploit favourable opportunities and conditions, "in short, to shape their own destiny" (1964: 179-180).

In this respect McClelland examines two other related factors that are supposed to lead to development: a need for achievement (n'Ach) and entrepreneurship. Societies in which people demonstrate a high need for achievement are more likely to develop than those in which traditional values and nonprogressive attitudes prevail. As a psychological factor promoting modernization, the *need for achievement* is defined by McClelland as a desire to do well, not so much for social recognition, but to attain an inner feeling of personal accomplishment or self-satisfaction. This need is thus an internal force that drives individuals

> to work harder at certain tasks; to learn faster; to do their best work when it counts for the record, and not when special incentives like money prizes are introduced; to choose experts over friends as working partners etc. (McClelland, 1964: 180-181).

Arguing that people who have a high n'Ach usually make the most successful entrepreneurs, McClelland goes on to show where those societies that encourage entrepreneurial behaviour and competitiveness tend to be more developed than those in which people "act very traditionally on economic matters" (1964:183). For McClelland, then, entrepreneurs possess the "strategic mental virus" that leads to the establishment of businesses, economic rationality and market innovativeness that are so crucial to the development of society.

Building on these assumptions, another modernization theorist, Daniel Lerner (1965), spoke of "modern man" as having a *mobile personality* that prepares him for dealing with new and challenging situations. For Lerner, "modern man" and "Western man" are one and the same. And among those features that make western man modern are his mental adaptability to change, his rationality, his ability to make independent choices regarding his individual destiny and his disposition to forming and holding political opinions (1965: 47-52).

In a similar vein, Alex Inkeles more or less duplicates Lerner's list of the attributes of modern man (1973: 345). Like McClelland and Lerner, he is concerned with the social-psychological import of values and attitudes and the roles they play in "making men modern" (the title of his study). To this end, he constructed a questionnaire to measure the range of "attitudes, values and behaviours conceived as relevant to understanding the individual's participation in the roles typical for a modern industrial society" (1973: 343). And from that questionnaire, he went on to assert:

> Evidently the modern man is not just a construct in the mind of sociological theorists. He exists and can be identified with fair reliability within any population which can take our test. (1973: 345)

## LIPSET AND THE LATIN AMERICAN VALUE STRUCTURE

With his study "Values, Education and Entrepreneurship in Latin America," Seymour Martin Lipset (1967) combines Parsons' pattern variable scheme with the value orientation approach of McClelland and others. Focusing on culture as the embodiment of societal values, Lipset begins his study by noting that "structural conditions make development possible; cultural factors determine whether the possibility becomes an actuality" (1967: 3).

In Latin America, where particularism and ascriptive criteria are emphasized, Lipset says underdevelopment is the natural result. He thus focuses on the predominant value systems in the region, which foster behaviour antithetical to the systematic accumulation of capital. For the United States, by contrast, the pattern variables of universalism and achievement orientation are the norm. And this specific combination is

> most favourable to the emergence of an industrial society since it encourages respect or deference toward others on the basis of merit and places an emphasis on achievement (1967: 6).

Therefore, in social systems united around kinship and local community, one does not tend to find people who exhibit those characteristics associated with "modern man." Power and authority are decentralized, roles remain diffuse, expressive rather than instrumental behaviour is common, and traditional values are perpetuated. And as we are told, these value orientations are symptomatic of backwardness and underdevelopment.

In trying to explain the origins of these ideas and values among Latin Americans, Lipset is even more explicit. He argues, for example, that we can trace them back to the very institutions and norms the Spaniards and Portuguese took to Latin America during colonial rule. At the time of colonial conquest, we are reminded, both Spain and Portugal were engaged in a long struggle to expel the Moors, who were Moslems, and the Jews, who had for centuries occupied part of the Iberian peninsula. Apart from being non-Christians, the Moors and the Jews were also engaged in economic activities that were seriously frowned upon by the Catholic Church. They monopolized commerce and banking, and the latter particularly was viewed as sinful, for it represented institutionalized usury and a crass preoccupation with material possessions.

Thus, during the colonial period, Lipset observes, the roles of soldier and priest were glorified, while commercial and business pursuits were denigrated (1967:8). As a result, the dominant culture and value system that emerged in Latin America "was not supportive of entrepreneurial activity" (1967: 23), which the modernization theorists view as the cornerstone of economic development. Because the leading political and economic institutions in the society did not encourage pragmatism, materialism and rational business dealings, there was little or no opportunity for the emergence of modern people with modern ideas to direct the development of a modern society.

## CANADIAN-AMERICAN VALUE DIFFERENCES

In a recent update of an earlier study, Lipset (1985) applies the pattern variables to an analysis of cultural differences between Canada and the United States. He begins his comparison with the American Revolution and goes on to discuss differences in the religious, political, legal, socio-economic and ecological spheres of both societies. Unlike the Americans, who embraced the liberal democratic tradition of the French Revolution, Canadians, he says, opted for continued colonial status and dependence on Britain. As a result, Canadian society and its institutions came to exhibit a definite European bias, complete with a conservative political orientation and a healthy respect for the established European churches (Roman Catholic and Anglican). In the United States, conversely, one can see a greater emphasis on the separation of church and state and the growth of nonconformist Protestant sects that opposed state religions.

Politically and philosophically, we are told, Canadians and Americans differ greatly. The former tend to be more elitist and resigned to accepting governmental intervention in their lives, while the latter are more strongly committed to egalitarian thinking and are clearly concerned to limit state interference in the private lives of citizens. Canadian conservatism contrasts sharply with American liberalism and individualism.

In economic matters, these differences are crucial. Reflecting the classic biases of modernization theorists, Lipset argues:

The United States, born modern, without a feudal elitist, corporatist tradition, could create . . . the purest example of a bourgeois society. Canada, as we have seen, was somewhat different, and that difference affected the way her citizens have done business (1985: 42, in manuscript).

Describing Canadian capitalism as *public enterprise* (as opposed to *private enterprise* American capitalism), Lipset implicitly criticizes public or state ownership of parts of the Canadian economy. Because Canada has not experienced "a pure laissez-faire market capitalism," he affirms, Canadian capitalists have grown dependent on government for precisely those things that make American capitalists strong. Canadian capitalists, in comparison to their American counterparts, are less aggressive, less innovative and less willing to take risks. These are exactly the same terms used by McClelland and Lipset himself to describe underdevelopment in Latin America.

Such a situation, we are told, is clearly related to the fact that Canada lags behind the United States in developing a modern society. Stated according to the pattern variables, Canadians are more elitist, ascriptive and particularistic, whereas Americans are more committed to egalitarianism, achievement orientation and universalism: " . . . Canada's economic backwardness relative to the United States is primarily a function of her value system" (1985:15, in manuscript.). See the sections of this chapter on dependency theory for a critique of this perspective.

# POSTINDUSTRIAL SOCIETY

As we have seen, modernization theorists concern themselves mainly with the changes that occur in passing from a preindustrial to an industrial society. Implicit in their approach is the idea that industrialism represents the end point of development, that there is nothing beyond the present stage in which the advanced countries find themselves. New or recent changes within the industrial societies themselves, however, have led to a reconsideration of that position, and the outcome has been a set of analyses and predictions concerning future trends in industrial society; these trends lead to the emergence of "the service society, post-industrial society, technetronic society, post-modern society, post-cultural society and even post-civilized society" (Giddens, 1974:255).

## THE OPTIMISTIC VIEW

The best known exponents of the postindustrial thesis are Alain Touraine (1971) and Daniel Bell (1971; 1973), who identified several key areas in which postindustrial society differs from industrial society. At the base of this new trend is the question of technological advances that have led to a marked shift away from an economy based on the production of *goods* in factories toward one in which the provision of *services* becomes central. Four other features of postindustrial society are identified as accompanying this basic change: an increasing importance of professional and technical workers; emphasis on theoretical knowledge as opposed to manual skills; planning and control of technological growth; and the enhanced use of intellectual technology, such as computers.

In the new society, growing numbers of people are occupied in service sectors such as restaurants and fast-food chains, real estate, banking and insurance, sales, appliance repairs and various clerical jobs. Unlike the industrial society, therefore, where emphasis was placed on blue-collar factory workers who produced the bulk of goods and commodities consumed, postindustrial society has witnessed a pronounced shift to white-collar workers, who are largely engaged in distribution operations (e.g., sales) and the provision of services (e.g., welfare workers).

Changes of this nature are viewed favourably by Bell. He assumes that the most serious problems or contradictions of industrial capitalism for example, high levels of unemployment and militant trade unionism will be overcome once postindustrialism becomes entrenched. Rinehart sums up Bell's position by noting that, as a growing number of the labour force

> is engaged in cleaner, more complex and more desirable white collar jobs, problems growing out of the nature and organization of work subside. Manual jobs, the traditional source of work dissatisfaction and conflict, are scheduled for near extinction (1975: 83-4).

Because the new postindustrial society is one in which the possession of technical knowledge becomes more important than the owning of property, Touraine believes the *technocrats* have become the new dominant class in such societies. As the major forms of decision-making take on an increasingly technical character, industrialists and business leaders look to technical specialists, who occupy key positions of power in the large, formal bureaucracies. And in this context, we are reminded of Weber's very insightful comments on the nature of bureaucracies and the bureaucratic form of domination in advanced societies.

An interesting point, however, is that while Weber focused on the office or the business firm as his main unit of analysis, theorists of postindustrialism single out the university for special attention. For in the "knowledge society," the university is viewed as the main locus of knowledge production.

> Both Bell and Touraine argue that the university, which is the main locale in which theoretical knowledge is formulated and evaluated, becomes the key institution in the newly emerging society (Giddens, 1974: 256).

With the expansion of the service sector and increased demand for technical workers with theoretical knowledge and computer skills, postindustrial society is characterized by a significant growth in the number of white-collar jobs. Simultaneously, if we accept this argument, the decline of the factory as the major centre of economic activity will cause a sharp decrease in blue-collar jobs; for one hallmark of postindustrialism is that "people now deal with other people rather than with machines" (Rinehart, 1975: 84).

## OPPOSING VIEWS

The glowing optimism of postindustrial theorists is thus premised on the belief that the "knowledge society" will eliminate the bulk of the conflicts associated with industrial society. As the number of white-collar jobs increases relative to blue-collar jobs, and as scientific knowledge and information become more widely disseminated, intrinsic job satisfaction will grow and traditional problems related to inequalities in the workplace will disappear. Such optimism, however, has proven to be largely illusory. For, as Blumberg has argued, the new white-collar jobs in the tertiary, or service, sector are neither high paying nor high status. There are more professionals, managers, executives, accountants and so on;

> But a moment's thought is sufficient to realize that the mass of employees in "finance" are bank tellers, not bank presidents; that the majority of employees in retail trade are low paid sales people, not chief executives; that the bulk of employees in insurance are clerical workers, not company executives . . . . (1980: 74).

And even if it is true that labour strife has been minimized (a contentious claim), this is probably due to the fact that, in the tertiary sector (finance, insurance, real estate, trade and services), unions are either very weak or nonexistent.

Another reason for the optimism that greeted the postindustrial thesis has to do with ideology. Coming out of the Cold War era, governments and business leaders in the West were anxious to repudiate the teachings of Marx and to distance themselves from the incisive criticisms that he levelled at industrial capitalism (Blumberg, 1980: 217). And what better way to deal with the situation than to claim that the type of society of which Marx spoke had been transcended? If we have moved from an industrial to a postindustrial order, we have also solved the problems and contradictions that Marx identified in the former.

As we will recall from Chapter 1, Marx felt that worker exploitation and oppression under conditions of industrial capitalism would ultimately lead to a revolt of the workers and the establishment of socialism. For Marx, the exploitation of the worker's labour power was the basis of the capitalist's wealth and power. In fact, Marx's labour theory of value is seen as the key to the rest of his claims regarding the final demise of capitalism (Zeitlin, 1972: 1-17). And it is in this context that Blumberg sees postindustrial theorizing as an attempt to "take the wind out of the Marxist sails" (1980:217).

This charge is given greater credence if one examines Bell's position in "The Social Framework of the Information Society" (1979). Here the author directly challenges Marx's labour theory of value when he contends that knowledge is (intellectual) property. Although knowledge is produced, he argues, it is not to be treated as a commodity in the traditional sense of that term. For unlike a commodity, which can be produced, sold to and consumed by another, knowledge, "even when it is sold, remains with the producer" (1979:174). From Bell's point of view, then, the knowledge society produces knowledge as a *collective good* that is *available to all people*. Commodities, conversely, though socially produced, are privately appropriated—this, we were told by Engels, is the fundamental contradiction of capitalist society. It is at the root of the conflict between capitalists and workers.

Because the production, processing, storage, retrieval and sharing of knowledge is so central a feature of postindustrial society, Bell is convinced that economists can no longer afford to ignore the role of knowledge in market and exchange relations. Knowledge has become part of social overhead capital:

> When knowledge becomes involved in the applied transformation of resources, then one can say that knowledge, not labour, is the source of value. . . . just as capital and labour have been the central variables of industrial society, so

information and knowledge are the crucial variables of postindustrial society (Bell, 1979: 168).

Although Bell's claim to have transcended Marx's labour theory of value remains unconvincing—he does not specify the details of how the *labour* that produces knowledge is organized, and he fails to provide an adequate definition of knowledge (Weizenbaum, 1979: 443-45)—a more challenging set of questions remains to be answered. How, for example, do we know when a society ceases to be industrial and enters its postindustrial phase? Does the logic of capitalism (the pursuit of profit) associated with industrial capitalism disappear in postindustrial society? And, very centrally, in the knowledge society, is it a fact that the knowledge produced is equally accessible and beneficial to everyone?

In sum, the most important attribute of postindustrial theorizing is that it sensitizes us to new and significant societal trends in the advanced countries. It alerts us to the potential problems and social consequences of the information explosion but does not go very far toward proposing solutions.

# DEPENDENCY THEORY AND MARXISM

While the theorists of postindustrialism accepted and extended the assumptions of the evolutionary and value-orientation perspectives, another school of thought was radically opposed to those perspectives and their implications. Known generally as *the dependency school*, these theorists rejected the ideas of Hoselitz, Rostow and McClelland and argued that societal development results from neither natural nor evolutionary processes. Rather, for dependency theorists like Gunder Frank (1967), dos Santos (1970), Cardosdo (1972) and Sunkel (1972), among many others, the overall structure of the world capitalist system makes development possible for some countries but renders it highly unlikely for others. As the very label attached to this school of thought suggests, those countries that are dependent on others, for whatever reasons, are disadvantaged.

## UNDERDEVELOPMENT AS A PRODUCT OF WORLD CAPITALISM

Although there are many variations of theory within the dependency camp, all agree on one key point. Underdevelopment, dependency theorists say, is *not* the original state or stage of all societies. Dependency thinkers make a firm distinction between *underdeveloped* and *undeveloped* societies. Whereas all countries, for example, Trinidad, Britain, Haiti and the United States, were at one point undeveloped, not all of them were underdeveloped. For the dependency theorist, underdevelopment is the *active* socioeconomic and political process of promoting dependence, which, in turn, leads to the establishment of structures and institutions that pre-empt development. Hence, some countries moved from undevelopment to development, while others moved from undevelopment to underdevelopment.

But how does it all come about? Is it because, according to McClelland, Lipset and others, some undeveloped countries fostered entrepreneurial behaviour and progressive values and attitudes in their populations, while others did not? Is it simply because some countries have naturally evolved further than others (Allahar, 1984)? According to Paul Baran, (arguably the precursor of dependency thinking), the answer to these last questions is an unequivocal "No"! Looking at India, he shows that this country was well advanced in its methods of production, industrial and commercial organization and so on *before* conquest by Britain. Apart from having a well-developed handicraft industry, India also exported the finest fabrics and other goods while the ancestors of the British "were leading an extremely primitive life" (1957: 144). Today, however, India is underdeveloped and Britain is not. Why? Was it due to some historical accident or a peculiar inaptitude of the Indian "race"? No, says Baran.

> It was caused by the elaborate, ruthless and systematic despoliation of India by British capital from the very onset of British rule (1957: 145).

In developing his argument that underdeveloped countries also possess a super-abundance of talented and enterprising individuals, Baran is in clear disagreement with McClelland and Lipset. He tells us that in all countries and at all times in history, one can find

> ambitious, ruthless and enterprising men who had an opportunity and were willing to innovate, to move to the fore, to seize power and to exercise authority (1957:235).

It seems, therefore, that, although they possessed many "strategic ingredients" that make for modernization, according to the stipulations of Lerner, Inkeles and McClelland, certain countries have nevertheless failed to realize Rostow's stage of economic "take-off." And this is a point on which most dependency theorists concur. The underdevelopment of the Third World is thus said to result from the economic and political consequences of colonialism and imperialism. The subordination of countries in Asia, Africa, Latin America and the Caribbean by those of Western Europe and North America is seen to have caused dependence. As dos Santos notes:

> By dependence we mean the situation in which the economy of certain countries is conditioned by the development and expansion of another economy to which the former are subjected (1970:231).

Implicit in this definition is the idea that the dominant countries can expand their economies and become virtually self-sustaining, while the dependent countries can only develop in a limited or restricted way within the limits imposed by the dominant-subordinate relationship (dos Santos, 1970).

For the theorists of this school, modern dependency was created by colonial expansion and imperialist penetration into Asia, Africa, Latin America and the Caribbean. Beginning with the voyages that resulted in the so-called "discovery" and the capture of colonial territory, entire countries were brought into the orbit of world capitalist powers and relegated to the status of satellites. In the process, the economies and political structures of the latter were distorted to meet the needs of metropolitan capitalism.

Whether as mining colonies from which gold, silver and other precious metals and minerals are extracted or as plantation colonies that produce commodities such as sugar, coffee, cotton, tobacco, cocoa and bananas for the world capitalist market, the countries of the Third World are not permitted to develop in an *autonomous* fashion. They are viewed solely as producers of raw materials destined for export in foreign-owned ships to the metropolitan centres of manufacturing and industry. Once exported, the raw materials are converted into finished products and sold back to the Third World at greatly inflated prices. In the process, jobs are created for workers in the advanced countries, where most manufacturing and industrial operations are located and where capital is accumulated. Also a consequence, a thriving internal market develops in the centres of advanced capitalism, wages are increased and the spread of commercial activity results in a higher demand for various other goods and services, greater economic differentiation, "modernity" and higher societal complexity.

Within the mining and plantation colonies, however, the picture is quite different. There one finds rather backward techniques of land cultivation, low levels of technological and scientific development, a heavy concentration on raw or unfinished agricultural and mineral exports, very few centres of industrial production and highly labour intensive methods of work (Allahar, 1982: 32-33). Major decisions regarding what to produce, how much to produce and what prices to charge are made outside of the producing countries, thus depriving those countries of any say in determining the structure of their main economic and income-generating sectors. The economies of the Third World countries are thus distorted, or biased, toward activities that favour development in the centres of advanced capitalism. And although the mining and plantation sectors may employ better technology, pay higher wages and afford their workers a generally higher standard of living than the rest of the society in question, the vast bulk of the population in that society continues to live in backwardness, with low levels of skill, education, health care and housing. The economic rape of their country's wealth is thus seen as being directly related to their continued dependence and backwardness.

By tailoring the economies of these countries to meet the needs of the advanced countries, the former become dependent on the latter for supplies of capital, credit, technology, expertise and the very market demand that makes possible continued production. Hence, local needs and local markets tend to be neglected, for the better part of all economic activity is directed toward external markets and consumers.

Such a situation is perpetuated because political leaders in the dependent countries are generally reduced to being mere pawns of international capitalism. Subject to economic and/or political pressure, these leaders come to see their class interests as bound up with those of foreign capital. Hence, as Gunder Frank argues, they "accept dependence consciously and willingly," for as "junior partners of foreign capital," they impose policies that increase dependence on the imperialist metropolis (1972: 3-15).

## Underdevelopment and Social Class

This is the point, therefore, at which the Marxists can be brought into the discussion. For although they agree with the general spirit and thrust of dependency thinking, they find it too descriptive and generally lacking in class analysis. Thus, to take account of the *political* aspects of underdevelopment, Zeitlin, for example, argues that the "full and unhampered" industrial development of the colonies was *not* in the interests of the imperialist forces; hence, it "became the cardinal principle of

every imperialist's policy to prevent and retard" such development (1972: 96).
Realizing that industrialization would eventually lead to the development of national
consciousness, a working-class movement, opposition to both the imperialist presence and domination by local capitalists and, ultimately, to calls for independence,
none of which was in the interests of the imperialists, the latter cultivated allies
among the locally dominant landlord class. And as we are told,

> the imperialist-landlord alliance contributed further to the economic stagnation
> of the colonies because both groups had a powerful interest in preventing
> industrialization and the profound changes that inevitably would follow
> (Zeitlin, 1972:97).

From the Marxist perspective, therefore, the development of capitalism is closely
bound up with the ways in which specific social classes historically have come into
contact with each other, sometimes working together, sometimes working against
each other. It must be pointed out, however, that as an economic system, capitalism
developed unevenly throughout the world. That is to say, a country such as Jamaica
is no less capitalist than the United States, although it may be less economically
developed. Like the United States, Jamaica boasts a free enterprise economic system
and a liberal democratic political system; but nevertheless, these two countries are
at the extremes of the development continuum.

Underdevelopment, then, according to the Marxists, is accounted for in class
terms. The dependent countries are sources of cheap raw materials and viable markets
to which finished goods can be exported. Therefore, specific commercial, manufacturing and industrial classes within the advanced countries are keenly interested in
gaining access to those raw materials and markets. During the early colonial period,
such access was secured by outright conquest and plunder. The politically and
economically powerful classes in the home countries thus benefited at the expense
of the indigenous inhabitants of the colonies. In more contemporary times, however,
the imperialist connection is cemented by the multi-national corporation (MNC).

Acting through their respective MNCs, the above-mentioned classes are seen to
represent imperialist interests that "work out deals" with local governments and
powerful factions of dominant classes in the dependent countries and establish
operations within restricted sectors of those countries. Such operations are usually
focused on mining and agricultural activities and use cheap local labour, which
greatly facilitates the extraction of wealth and the generation of huge profits. Along
with the exploitation of cheap labour, the MNCs also manage to secure attractive
concessions from local governments, e.g., tax incentives, relaxed customs duties on
imported technology and certain monopolistic privileges. Whatever infrastructural
changes they promote are limited generally to transportation and communication
networks that link the mines and plantations with the sea ports, thus producing a
very lop-sided picture of local industrial development.

## The Corporate-Political Imperialist Alliance

An important consideration in this context is the nature of the link between the
economic and political aspects of imperialism. When Marxists speak of the United
States' imperialism, for example, they refer not merely to the economic exploits of
American MNCs abroad but also to the fact that those economic interests are fully

supported by the foreign policy of the United States. Hence, when private American foreign investments are threatened by local uprisings in a dependent country (e.g., Cuba, 1959 to 1962), the American government, *not* the MNCs, dispatches armed forces to that country in an effort to safeguard those private investments.

Such domination, they say, may create the conditions for revolutionary change in the backward countries. Objectively, imperialist exploitation produces increased misery and poverty for the bulk of the population, very few of whom are employed in the foreign-controlled sectors. The constant draining away of national wealth, the monopolization of the best lands by foreign corporations, the recruitment of trained experts from abroad and the underdevelopment of local facilities all accentuate social and economic disparities between the mass of the workers and peasants and the tiny core of privileged classes that benefit from the imperialist connection. Subjectively, this leads to a growing sense of nationalism as local parties, opposition interests and lobby groups see the possibility for change and start mobilizing for more responsible government, better wages and working conditions, greater self-determination and so on. Depending on the extent of such mobilization and the degrees of political education and consciousness that develop, government repression is increased and this deepens the social discontent.

According to the Marxists, then, when *the objective condition of misery* and the *subjective consciousness* simultaneously reach a certain point, a revolutionary situation is created. This is not to say that revolution is a mechanical affair, for other factors can always militate against the effective combination of these two sets of conditions. For example, the Marxists often talk of *false consciousness*, which occurs when workers fail to recognize the true source of their oppression. Such a situation is created by religions that make a virtue of poverty ("The meek shall inherit the earth") and counsel conservatism ("Turn the other cheek"; "You will be rewarded ten-fold in the next world"). Nevertheless, when the objective and subjective conditions are ripe and when the oppressed no longer view their oppressors as legitimate (in the Weberian sense), the Marxists say that the former will rise up against the latter. And tracing the source of their discontent back to the structures of imperialist exploitation, the workers will seek to abolish private property and capitalism and create a workers' state, or socialism.

In sum, therefore, both dependency theorists and Marxists view underdevelopment, poverty and backwardness as products of imperialism. They are diametrically opposed to the evolutionary and value-orientation schools, which see capitalist development as the solution to the problems of premodern or traditional societies. The debate between the various perspectives must thus be judged on the basis of the evidence. And in this context, some relevant questions are: Why does capitalism lead to development in some countries and not in others? Which classes benefit from such development and which classes don't? Can imperialism enhance the possibilities for development in the Third World? Or does it exacerbate problems and create the conditions for revolutionary transformation?

## CANADA: DEPENDENCY THEORY APPLIED

In her book, *Silent Surrender*, Kari Levitt (1970) describes Canada as the world's richest underdeveloped country. Citing numerous examples of American MNCs operating within Canada, Levitt argues that the Canadian economy has become a branch-plant economy, playing host to a wide variety of United States business interests. These branch-plant subsidiaries of parent firms located in the United States drain Canada's wealth and yield a very lopsided picture of industrial development in this country—development that is not locally directed. As Hiller has argued, multinational enterprises are not necessarily concerned with the local problems or priorities of the host country. They are not compelled to reinvest profits locally, and, if pressured by local governments to do so, they often threaten to move their operations elsewhere:

> It is the very nature of corporations to make decisions according to the norms of capitalism and their desire for profit; national sentiments are rarely able to change these norms (Hiller, 1976: 93).

And it was precisely this type of situation that led Levitt to remark:

> Some sixty years ago Sir Wilfrid Laurier declared that the twentieth century belongs to Canada. By the middle of the century it had become clear that Canada belongs to the United States (1970: 58).

In a recent study, Jorge Niosi (1985: 33-60) agrees that the Canadian economy has been subject to external control and dependence on foreign influences; but he does not go so far as Levitt to claim that Canada is underdeveloped. He speaks of Canada's "dependent industrialization" and outlines in very clear detail the processes by which American corporations have "invaded" the Canadian economy and established controlling interests in areas such as telecommunications, utilities, transportation, mining and smelting, oil and gas, lumber and electronics, among many others. Although in recent years various Canadian governments (federal and provincial) have sought to buy back control in several of these areas, the Canadian economy continues to exhibit dependence on foreign technology, foreign markets, foreign capital and foreign expertise:

> Canada, after a century of pursuing a liberal policy towards foreign direct investment and the transfer of technology, now finds itself with half of its technology under outside control—one of the highest percentages of foreign control in the world (Niosi, 1985: 30).

## The Metropolis versus Hinterland View

How do the dependency theorists account for this situation? In recent years, a massive literature has grown around the themes of dependency, regionalism, colonialism and internal colonialism in Canada. Using the basic dependency model of *centre* and *periphery* (Galtung, 1971), *metropolis* and *satellite* (Gunder Frank, 1973) and *metropolis versus hinterland* (Davis, 1971), Canadian scholars have attempted to explain the pattern of dependent development in this country. Focusing on the questions of regionalism and uneven development *within* Canada, writers such as Clement (1980; 1983), Matthews (1982) and Veltmeyer (1978) have looked to the disciplines of economics, geography, history and sociology for answers.

Their basic argument is that historically, Canada's dependence on foreign powers stemmed from its status as a colony of Britain. Being politically, culturally and economically dominated by Britain (Hiller, 1976: 84), Canadians and Canadian society came to exhibit a pronounced European orientation, in contrast to Americans and American society (Lipset, 1985). In economic terms, the Canadian economy was geared to the production and export of raw materials that were processed and manufactured in Britain, thus creating jobs in that country and boosting its industrial development. And, as we saw in the previous section, the host country (Canada) served as a ready market outlet for the manufactured goods produced in the metropole, Britain (Clement, 1983: 55-6). Over the ages, when the United States replaced Britain as Canada's foremost trading partner, Canada's external dependence increased greatly, and the internal disparities between regions were accentuated.

The dependency notion of a chain of metropoles and satellites is useful for explaining the processes involved. As Clement asserts, "Regional economies are tied to national economies and national ones to international ones" (1980: 276). This is the idea of the chain. For Canada is neither developed nor underdeveloped. Some parts or regions are more developed than others. The least developed are linked to the more developed, and the latter, in turn, are tied to even more developed international centres:

> Canada is not unequivocally an industrial country. Part is industrialized—but the rest [is] a resource hinterland. Most of Canada's industrial capacity is located below a line starting at Windsor, encompassing Toronto and moving to Montreal. This is industrial Canada (Clement, 1980:276).

When one speaks of the underdeveloped regions of Canada, one automatically thinks of the Atlantic provinces (Nova Scotia, New Brunswick, Prince Edward Island and Newfoundland). As the so-called hinterland of Ontario and Quebec, the Atlantic provinces are not centres of banking, industry and commerce. As resource-based economies, they are sources of wealth; but that wealth is traditionally accumulated and reinvested elsewhere, bringing jobs to outsiders (Ontarians and Quebeckers, for example) and providing those outsiders with a generally higher standard of living than the Maritimers.

> The traditional wealth of southern Ontario is certainly not attributable to any strong resource base there, as there are few resources within several hundred miles of the area. Conversely the Atlantic provinces have always had abundant iron ore, coal, gold, forests, fish and hydro-electric power, but have remained poor (Matthews, 1982: 105).

The economies of the Atlantic provinces are underdeveloped not because they lack resources but because they are dependent on outsiders for technology, expertise, capital and markets. Because such outsiders usually present themselves as part of MNCs and because they do not necessarily have local interests at heart, it is understandable that peripheral areas and single-industry towns will be seriously disadvantaged. Whatever economic or infrastructural development does occur is highly resource specific and does not lead to integrated development for the region as a whole. Hence, social development (Matthews, 1982) is neglected; schools, hospitals and housing are substandard; and general life chances of the population are not as promising as those of Canadians who live, for example, in the "Golden Triangle" (Toronto-Montreal-Ottawa).

## The Class-Conflict View

To explain further the dynamics of underdevelopment and dependency in Canada, theorists like Matthews, Clement, Niosi, Veltmeyer and Smucker have argued for a class analysis of the situation. Specifically, they direct our attention to the structure of the Canadian capitalist class. That class, which is concentrated largely in the Golden Triangle exerts a growing national dominance in matters of finance, transportation and utilities; and internationally, they are able to compete effectively with the most powerful capitalist enterprises for profits and markets. At the same time, however, the Canadian capitalist class has long played a subordinate role as junior partners of American corporate capital in areas such as mining and manufacturing. As Clement says, by the 1960s, when the bulk of the Canadian economy had fallen into foreign hands,

> [that] development was welcomed by many Canadian capitalists [for] they participated in foreign control in a variety of ways. . . . Canadian capitalists, particularly the powerful ones, have aligned themselves with U.S. corporations and invested heavily in them (1983:58-9).

Within the underdeveloped regions of the country, the economic structures in place do not provide much opportunity for the advancement of the local populations. The jobs that are usually available tend to be of the unskilled or semiskilled variety, and the general content of school curricula reflects the demands of that job market. Housing conditions, health and welfare provisions and overall lifestyles often lag behind those in more developed areas such as Ontario and Quebec. But even within Ontario and Quebec, there are numerous pockets of backwardness, for example, in the single-industry towns and rural areas that are also part of the development-underdevelopment chain. A very clear picture of dependence and uneven development in single-industry towns is painted by Rex Lucas in his classic study, *Minetown, Milltown, Railtown* (1971).

From the above, we can get an idea of how dependency theory can be applied to an understanding of change and development in certain regions of Canada. One must not get the impression, however, that Canada is an underdeveloped society, as Levitt implied. A far more accurate view is supplied by Niosi (1985), who argues that today, Canada is a major imperialist country whose MNCs have extensive control of banking, mining, transportation and communications in many Third World countries. The Canadian capitalist class is allied internationally with other capitalist classes, and together they are responsible for much of the underdevelopment that characterizes large parts of Canada and the Third World.

## SUMMARY

In this chapter, we have examined several approaches to the questions of social change and development. Beginning with the social-evolutionary and value-orientation perspectives, we saw where change was depicted as slow, evolutionary and cumulative. Social-evolutionary theorists, for example, adopt an ideal-typical view of traditional and modern societies, in which the former follow more or less the same path to development as the latter. The more developed societies today are those that have evolved more than the rest. In this respect, the sociological aspects of economic growth are seen to be captured by Parsons' pattern variable scheme of particularism-universalism, ascription-achievement, role diffuseness-specificity, and affectivity-affective neutrality.

The value-orientation theorists emphasize psychological factors as the key to explaining change and development. They thus examine the values and attitudes held by individuals in specific societies, with a view to determining whether those values and attitudes are likely to produce behaviour that will lead to development. In this context, they identify *achievement motivation* as a crucial variable that gives rise to entrepreneurial behaviour, which, in turn, results in greater overall development. The solution to the problems of backwardness and underdevelopment, therefore, lies in a society's ability to modernize its value and attitudinal structures.

Finally, dependency theorists and Marxists are not convinced that underdevelopment is an original or natural state in which all societies once found themselves. Nor are they convinced that underdevelopment results merely from a given population's lack of progressive values and attitudes. Rather, for these theorists, underdevelopment is the social, political and economic outcome of colonialism and imperialism. When capitalism spread across national boundaries to tap the resources of the Third World, they say, the Third World countries were drained of their resources and wealth through alliances between foreign capitalists and locally dominant classes. This situation will ultimately lead to the revolutionary overthrow of the local bourgeoisie and the severance of the imperialist connection.

## DISCUSSION QUESTIONS

1. In what sense can the social-evolutionary and value-orientation schools be seen to promote a conservative approach to the questions of change and development?

2. Why do dependency theorists think it important to make a distinction between undeveloped and underdeveloped societies?

3. What are the benefits of trying to understand change and development as historical processes? Which of the theories discussed take account of history, and which do not?

4. How can the pattern variable scheme be applied to an understanding of Canadian society in historical and contemporary times?

5. How does a consideration of the social processes of colonialism and imperialism affect Rostow's stages-of-growth thesis?

# 23

# Technology and Social Change

*Willem H. Vanderburg*

# INTRODUCTION

Before reading this chapter, make a list of all the technologies and their products that you directly or indirectly depend on during a typical day. Do many of your interactions with individuals, groups and institutions involve a technology or its products? What is the overall effect of technology on us as individuals and on our society? Who controls this technology and to what ends is it used? How many of the major problems now facing humanity relate to the growing power our technology give us over our social and natural environments? Do our responses to these problems make sense? (Think, for example, of our attempts to avoid war by developing evermore powerful weapons; or the efforts to remedy our economic problems by improving productivity through automation.) It is important to reflect on your own experiences in light of our attempt here to understand the influence technology is having on individual and collective human life.

From a historical perspective, the role played by modern technology in our present world is highly unique. Technology today is increasingly widely used. Together with science, it is helping to create a knowledge base that is no longer exclusively linked to any society, that is utilized by a growing number of nations as a basis for similar ways of life aimed at economic development. For the first time in history, all the nations of the world can be classified in terms of their degree of success in achieving similar goals. They are now all underdeveloped, developing or developed nations. The growing importance of computers and the associated techniques for accessing, processing, applying and transmitting information will undoubtedly reinforce these trends.

Many aspects of the transformation of the relationship between technology and society have been studied. It has been noted, for example, that before a traditional society can utilize modern technology, it must fundamentally change its culture and organization (Goulet, 1977; Pelto, 1973; and Richardson, 1975). This is evident from the literature on the transfer of technology to Third World societies and indigenous peoples. Some authors argue that intermediate or appropriate technologies must be designed which require fewer and less substantial changes in the recipient societies (Jéquier, 1976; Rybczynski, 1980). Societies already far advanced along the road of economic development appear to acquire very similar social, economic and political structures, although the degree of similarity has been disputed (Aron, 1967; Bell, 1973; Ellul, 1977; Richta, 1969; Touraine, 1971; Winner, 1977). There is also a considerable literature on the implications of individual technologies for specific human activities. Less work has been done on using these studies to establish a comprehensive theory on how modern technology as a whole contributes to social and cultural change (Badham and Davies, 1984). It has also been recognized that technology undergoes profound changes when it begins to play a new role in society (Galbraith, 1978; Noble, 1979; Touraine, 1965). All these aspects of technology in our modern world must be accounted for in a perspective on technology and social change.

# THE INDUSTRIAL REVOLUTION

Most theories of the Industrial Revolution focus on the mechanization of human work and the accompanying proliferation of machines throughout society. This overemphasis on machines obscures the fact that the technical approach and orientation to material production was also part of a general technical orientation in the cultures of many Western European societies.

In the political domain, for example, the state emerged as a product of the French Revolution. In France, the state developed its military technique by taking a rational approach to strategy, organization, logistics and recruitment. It also developed rational methods of administration to harness the resources and energies of the nation for the transformation of society. The state's attempts under Napoleon to systematize and rationalize the legal system, which led to the Napoleonic Code, are well known. It sought to suppress or alter laws based on custom. These legal transformations were quickly adopted by other Western European nations, except for England. Weights and measures were standardized. A systematic approach was adopted for the planning of roads. Science also was rationalized in the eighteenth century. This chapter will argue that the Industrial Revolution was but one facet of a larger technical revolution that manifested itself in a technical mentality concerned with rationality, efficiency, power and profits.

Many people at the time of the Industrial Revolution clearly understood that machines were only one aspect of a new society in which everything would become rational and efficient. Ths conception is manifested, for example, in the Encyclopaedia of Diderot. It clearly showed that people wished to master the world with reason by making things clear and precise, by quantifying the qualitative and by bringing rational order to chaos (Ellul, 1964). The technical orientation was most strongly embodied in the social classes and institutions that spearheaded the Industrial Revolution. They greatly enhanced their social position and power by applying it.

It should be remembered that the technology of a society contains much more than just machines. It is constituted of many elements that may be arranged along a spectrum ranging from the *hardware* on one end to *software* on the other. In other words, on one end we find instruments, machines, tools, bridges and so on, while on the other we find concepts, processes, theories, organizations, institutions, attitudes, ways of conceptualizing, values and so on. Complex machines had been invented and applied earlier in history, but never were they used in the context of a widespread technical orientation in the culture, which included a mechanistic world view, a rational conception of human life and society and a sense of the possibility of human progress. The development of each element of a technology is often a response to the conditions prevalent in a society. The technology is then made workable through innovation and finds its way into the mainstream of society by application. It diffuses into and becomes a part of the way of life of a society and, finally, is displaced from that society. All these processes are an integral part of the fabric of a society.

The failure to see the Industrial Revolution as only one aspect of the larger technical revolution can perhaps be explained by the fact that the transformations of various areas of society by the technical approach did not come together in a relatively coherent pattern until the mechanization of human work and the proliferation of machines began. This could not have happened, however, without the rationalization of the entire fabric of society. To explain this, we will first look at the *structural* characteristics of industrialization. We will examine a case study of the chain reaction of events set off in England by the mechanization of textile production—a process that completely transformed English society. Remember that each technology, from its invention until its displacement, is embedded in the fabric of a society. It both affects and is affected by the structure of the society.

## THE TECHNICAL REVOLUTION

The highly interrelated character of a society is partly reflected in the network of its flow of goods. The nodes of the network represent a process in the production, transportation, consumption or disposal of some commodity. Each node is connected to others by its inputs and outputs. Societies generally organize themselves so that the output of one process is practically identical to the input of the next process a commodity undergoes. For example, in the putting-out system, where the technical revolution probably began in England, the preparation of raw materials— spinning this material into yarn, weaving yarn into cloth and finishing the cloth— was done by rural families under contract to an entrepreneur. The system was like a decentralized factory, with a technological division of labour in which families worked at home using a simple, inexpensive device such as a spinning wheel or handloom to complete a single stage of production. The system had become an integral part of rural life, where it complemented subsistence farming, particularly during times when the land required relatively little attention. The four stages of production formed a chain, with inputs of cloth on the other end, which may, in turn, have constituted the inputs for the manufacturing of clothes or other goods. Processes of transportation interposed themselves everywhere. Each process in the chain also required other goods that were often produced elsewhere, such as spinning wheels, handlooms, bleaches and dyes. In other words, the network of the flow of goods in the putting-out systems was only a small part of a much larger one. The putting-out system did not respond well to a sudden increase in the demand for textiles, which occurred, for example, when a war ended and overseas markets opened up once again. As entrepreneurs looked for ways of better controlling the work process to increase profits, the technical orientation, including the mechanistic world view of the time, brought to the fore the idea of mechanizing human work.

> The flying shuttle of 1733 made a greater production of yarn necessary. But production was impossible without a suitable machine. The response to this dilemma was the invention of the spinning jenny by James Hargreaves. But then yarn was produced in much greater quanitities than could possibly be used by the weavers. To solve this new problem, Cartwright manufactured his celebrated loom. In this series of events we see in its simplest form the inter-action that accelerated the development of machines. Each new machine disturbs the equilibrium of production; the restoration of equilibrium entails the creation of one or more additional machines in other areas of operation.
>
> Production becomes more and more complex. The combination of machines within the same enterprise is a notable characteristic of the nineteenth century. It is impossible, in effect, to have an isolated machine. There must be adjunct machines, if not preparatory ones. . . . The need for organization of machines is found even in the textile industry. A large number of looms must be grouped together in order to utilize the prime mover most effectively, since no individual loom consumes very much energy. To obtain maximum yield, machines cannot

be disposed in a haphazard way. Nor can production take place irregularly. A plan must be followed in all technical domains (Ellul, 1964: 111-112).

Landes also recognizes the patterns that draw together many events of the time when he writes:

> In all of this diversity of technological improvement, the unity of the movement is apparent: change begat change. For one thing, many technical improvements were feasible only after advances in associated fields. The steam engine is a classic example of this technological interrelatedness: it was impossible to produce an effective condensing engine until better methods of metal working could turn out accurate cylinders. For another, the gains in productivity and output of a given innovation inevitably exerted pressure on related industrial operations. The demand for coal pushed mines deeper until water seepage became a serious hazard; the answer was the creation of a more efficient pump, the atmospheric steam engine. A cheap supply of coal proved a godsend to the iron industry, which was stifling for lack of fuel. In the meantime, the invention and diffusion of machinery in the textile manufacture and other industries created a new demand for energy, hence for coal and steam engines; and these engines, and the machines themselves, had a voracious appetite for iron, which called for further coal and power. Steam also made possible the factory city, which used unheard-of quanitites of iron (hence coal) in its many-storied mills and its water and sewage systems. At the same time, the processing of the flow of manufactured commodities required great amounts of chemical substances: alkalis, acids, and dyes, many of them consuming mountains of fuel in the making. And all of these products—iron, textiles, chemicals—depended on large-scale movements of goods on land and on sea, from the sources of raw materials into the factories and out again to near and distant markets. The opportunity thus created and the possibilities of the new technology combined to produce the railroad and steamship, which of course added to the demand for iron and fuel while expanding the market for factory products. And so on, in ever-widening circles (Landes, 1969:2,3).

Clearly, all these events could not happen without larger amounts of capital. To accomplish this required that existing financial institutions develop a variety of new techniques. In fact, capital became the scarcest and therefore most crucial input into the new system of production. The accumulation of capital produced by machines and also necessitated by them led to a national and later international financial organization. It also required a new legal invention, namely the corporation, with limited liabilities. Marketing of the growing quantities of goods also needed to be rationalized, and this led to a range of commercial techniques. The development of improved transportation systems, such as railroad systems, required better organizational techniques for scheduling trains. The failure of any of these techniques to rationalize a variety of other activities could have produced a major bottleneck in the technical revolution.

Because of the size and expense of the new textile machines and their need for more power than human beings could supply, work could no longer be done at home along with subsistence farming. As the mechanization of work spread, the concentration of machines in factories in the industrial centres grew, requiring the uprooting of a growing portion of the rural population. The change from a rural to an urban society intensified as industrialization advanced, with obvious social consequences. As people began leaving their families to find work in the industrial centres, their lives were totally transformed. The conditions under which they worked were different, as exemplified by factory discipline. They became wage-earners who bought the basic necessities for life as opposed to producing most of them themselves. They had escaped the social control of their families and villages and had to rely on their own individual resources. No longer was their traditional morality, which was essentially the normalized behaviour of their own group, of much use. Under these circumstances, an individualistic morality slowly emerged over many generations. The new social fabric that began to constitute itself in the industrial centres was based on greatly weakened family units, which were no longer the context for most human activity. We see here the beginning of a reconstitution of the social fabric of traditional societies, which would eventually produce a mass society. The growing importance of capital as the most crucial input into the process of industrialization made the owners of capital increasingly influential and powerful. They soon began to constitute the dominant class, controlling the capital on which everything else depended. They built the new society for their own profit. In other words, the fundamental reconstitution of the social fabric of these societies was accompanied by, and depended on, major economic, political and moral transformations.

The massive relocation of the population from the countryside to the new industrial centres created large cities.

> At the beginning, the big city engendered no particular technique; people were merely unhappy in it. But it soon appeared that megalopolis represented a new and special kind of environment, calling for special treatment. The technique of city planning made its appearance. At first, urban planning was only a clumsy kind of adaptation which was little concerned, for example, with slums (despite the efforts of the utopian planners of the middle of the century). Somewhat later, as big city life became for the most part intolerable, techniques of amusement were developed. It became indispensable to make urban suffering acceptable by furnishing amusements, a necessity which was to assure the rise, for example, of a monstrous motion-picture industry (Ellul, 1964:113,114).

The transformation of technology and society during the technical revolution created a period of immense human and social dislocation. There was massive exploitation of the workers who laboured for long hours under inhumane conditions. Each new problem created by applying new techniques required the development of further techniques. The proliferation of techniques itself raised still other problems. Human beings do not adapt easily to the rational order of machines, factories and industrial towns. The state had to constrain the individual in several ways. External constraints were not sufficient. The individual had to be adjusted to the new society, and thus the techniques of education, propaganda and psychological manipulation began to develop. As the techniques of production became more developed, human techniques became necessary. Each new technique required still others, whose development in turn permitted the further extension of the technique. It is the ensemble of techniques present in almost every sphere of human life that eventually began to characterize the new societies. We will define technique as the totality of methods rationally arrived at and having maximum possible efficiency for a given stage of development, in every field of human activity (Ellul, 1964:xxv).

The structure of the patterns of events we have described occurs in every society regardless of where mechanization is initiated. Mechanization will produce a local disturbance in the fabric of a society that can only be resolved by a further mechanization and rationalization. This in turn produces new disturbances in adjacent areas of the sociocultural fabric, and so on. These changes gradually transform the daily lives of the members of a society. As the new patterns of life are internalized by each new generation, they affect human consciousness as well as the culture of the society. We will turn now to these cultural aspects of the technical revolution.

## CULTURAL TRANSFORMATIONS

The description of some of the changes in the fabric of society as a result of the technical revolution would be incomplete without considering the retroaction on the individual and on the culture of the society. By growing up in a particular society, we acquire language, and along with it, the images and stereotypes by which we think and apprehend reality. Socialization also furnishes us with a mode of behaviour and a life style. It also provides the structures for our emotional life and our memory. These are individually unique and yet culturally typical. In other words, the members of a society interpret their experiences and shape the relationships between themselves and the world by means of what we shall call a culture, following the tradition of American sociology.

Babies and children acquire the culture of their society by internalizing experiences. They thus develop their minds, which function as a kind of mental map, permitting them to live in reality in a way that is individually unique and yet typical of their culture and time. The culture integrates the lives of the members of a society into a social order based on a hierarchy of values absolutized by means of a sacred set of myths. In this way, the culture of a society permits the members to live together on the basis of a unique way of life.

The massive changes in people's daily lives implied in the above description of the technical revolution thus gradually altered not only individual consciousness but also the very foundations of the traditional cultures. Thus, a new set of values and a new morality emerged, while the myths of progress and happiness helped constitute a new ultimate value or sacred belief. This may explain, for example, the appearance of liberal Christianity, as well as changes in the art, music and literature of society. The transformations in the culture that underlie these and other phenomena are extremely slow, lasting many generations. They helped in laying the foundation for a new epoch in the history of Western civilization and, increasingly, in many other societies.

Once completed, the cultural transformation further reinforced and accelerated the technical revolution. It reunified society in a fundamental way, although it did not end exploitation. During its early phases, industrial society was built up by a social class, the bourgeoisie, who shaped it to further their own interests and power. They did so by exploiting other social classes. The bourgeoisie incarnated the spirit of the new age, while the other classes still largely lived according to the values and

Courtesy of IBM Canada Ltd.

Because of the high value industrially advanced societies place on technology, there is a tendency to play down or ignore the losses that accompany the gains. This promotional photograph shows one side of the so-called information revolution. However, the human costs are substantial. The new electronic assembly lines, where the keystrokes and other operations of each worker can be monitored, are considered by some observers to be more oppressive than the early factories. The new information technology is integrating institutions and society in new ways, based on information flows rather than on human interaction, and this fundamentally affects the social fabric. While creating many new jobs, the new technologies appear to eliminate an even greater number. They are also speeding up military activities, leaving less time for human decisions and interventions, which, in a nuclear age, is a very serious matter. The new "postindustrial industries" may lack smokestacks, but they do produce significant quantities of dangerous chemical wastes. The industrially advanced nations will not be very successful in solving their problems if they do not treat technology more realistically. The strategy of divide and conquer applied to separating the positive from the negative implications of technology is a dangerous one.

ways of preindustrial culture. Through the processes described earlier, the other classes eventually also embraced the myths of progress and happiness through technology. Thus, the social classes were transformed into social strata of the emerging industrial societies. All these strata increasingly agreed on the desirability of the promises offered by technology, but conflict over the distribution of the benefits of technology continued, along with much exploitation.

## The Third World

The massive transformation of society that we have described requires many resources. These were largely present in Western European societies due to the historically unique conditions that prevailed on the eve of the technical revolution. Since these conditions do not exist in most Third World societies, the chain reaction of transformation tends to get stuck for lack of resources of one kind of another. As a result of colonialism, the transfer of technology, the operation of the multinationals, the education in the West of their elite and so on, this process of transformation has been started in many sectors in these societies. Once the process of transformation stops, these societies can neither move forward nor return to their traditional way of life. They become societies literally divided against themselves, comprising modern and traditional elements that are incompatible with one another. This is at the heart of the problem of so-called "underdevelopment."

## Some Additional Facets of the Technical Revolution

Our critique of the concepts of the Industrial Revolution and of industrial society is, of course, made with the benefit of hindsight. It permits us to place the transformation of Western Europe in the eighteenth and nineteenth centuries in a broader historical context, which reveals new patterns and thus sheds new light on the events of that time. For the people who lived during this great change, it was a challenging intellectual task to make sense of what exactly was happening. It is instructive to briefly look at these efforts, because some of them continue to profoundly influence sociology.

Henri de Saint-Simon (1760–1825) published a journal, *L'Industrie*, in 1816, in which he developed a vision for an industrial society when Europe was still mostly agricultural. He largely shared this vision of what lay ahead with Auguste Comte (1798–1857): Human and social progress could be achieved through developing and applying scientific and technical reason. As a result, society was on the threshold of the most fundamental transformation in human history, namely, the passage from a military and theological past to a scientific and industrial future. To ensure this future, Comte saw the need for a new science of society that he called sociology. Social evolution was seen to be inevitable, but by discovering its laws, social and political activity could speed up the process by preparing the prerequisites for tomorrow and by making the changes as orderly as possible. All thought and action were to be directed toward establishing an industrial society. These visions contained many ambiguities about the dynamics of industrialization and its regulation, in part because the central roles of both scientific ideas and social classes were emphasized (Comte, 1974).

When we turn to thinkers who experienced much of the actual transformation and who were therefore *analysing* what was going on, we find that what they were describing was much more than what can be covered by concepts such as industrialization, Industrial Revolution and industrial society. Their interpretations have had a great influence on the development of sociology, including the perspective presented in this chapter.

Karl Marx (1818–1883) created the concept of capital as the key to understanding what was happening at that time. Everything was directly or indirectly structured to preserve and accumulate capital. This was true in two essential ways. The social class that was building the new system required ever larger amounts of capital to build the machines, factories and the vast infrastructure of roads, canals, railroads, mines, houses and so on. Secondly, the lives of those who worked in the factories became equally determined by capital. They had to sell their capacity to work for a wage and it was with this "capital" that they had to procure all the necessities of life in the market. The workers became appendages to machines. They could no longer depend on themselves. They became totally dependent on the capitalist system. Their only resource was their ability to work—an ability that had value only if someone was willing to buy it because it was profitable, and this in turn was determined by world markets. Thus, workers totally depended on a system that they were unable to control. Because of long working hours, the lives of the workers were dominated by work, which reduced them to a mere commodity to be bought and sold.

The workers were alienated, which for Marx had a two-fold meaning: to be possessed by someone or something (like a master possesses the body and soul of a slave) and to be self-alienated by being transformed into another and not being oneself. To characterize the condition of the workers as alienated is therefore to suggest much more than simply that they were exploited. The workers had become less than human, possessed by a system over which they had no say and which did not allow them to be themselves. The descriptions of some European travellers of life in the industrial centres leave little doubt as to the accuracy of Marx's characterization of the condition of early industrial workers.

There was an additional component of economic alienation resulting from the central role capital played in society. It applied to both rich and poor. Marx showed that the amount of money possessed became the only essential quality of people in the capitalist system. Money became the common measure of all things, and virtually everything could be obtained with money. Relations between people and between people and nature were determined by money, which became an active power. One was what one had, and this is a negation of what it is to be human.

Alienation in capitalism also included an ideological and religious dimension. The new human venture based on the exploitation of human beings and nature could not be seen for what it was. People therefore had to perceive everything by means of a false consciousness and create an ideology that concealed the true situation. It is here that people were most deeply divested of themselves. The accuracy of Marx's description of the human condition (Marx, 1972, 1977) during the time of the Industrial Revolution is in no way negated by the fact that today the causes of alienation have changed. This is a matter to which we shall return.

Émile Durkheim (1858–1917) did not think that industry was the primary determinant of social change or that it could constitute a goal for future development. The characteristics of the new societies had their root in the growing division of labour in all spheres of human life under the pressure of population growth. For Durkheim, earlier societies were characterized by a measure of *mechanical solidarity*. Individuals largely shared the same experiences, emotions and values; they were therefore similar enough to give society a great deal of coherence.

The increasing social differentiation that came with a complex division of labour greatly accelerated the trend toward the opposite of mechanical solidarity, which Durkheim called *organic solidarity*. It is based on a relationship of complementarity between very different individuals analogous to that between organs of the human body, which are all different yet all indispensable. In a society where mechanical solidarity is very strong, the individual consciousness is largely coextensive with the collective consciousness. In a highly differentiated society, this is not the case. Individuals have more choice and are much more conscious of their uniqueness but this also makes them less well integrated into society, so that the collective consciousness may be weaker. The absence or disintegration of norms, often accompanied by a weakening of the moral order and religion creates *anomie*. The individual senses a lack of meaning and purpose resulting from his or her insufficient integration into the collectivity. Durkheim thought that most of the important problems of his time could be understood in terms of fundamental social processes that made a greater division of labour necessary. For him, industrialization could not provide a meaningful sense of individual and social purpose. As members of a mass society, we are no strangers to these problems, and Durkheim's work continues to be of interest (Durkheim, 1964).

Max Weber (1864–1920) did not think that industry was the key phenomenon in terms of which all the new social realities could be understood. For him, industrialization was a part of the more general phenomenon of the rationalization of social life. The rationalization of one or more areas of human life had occurred in earlier societies and took a variety of directions, depending on the culture. Rationality, for Weber, must be understood in relation to the individual actor as a social being and not in relation to the observer. However, most action in the past was largely based on internalized custom and tradition.

What was historically new at this time and significant for Weber was the widespread application of logical, systematic thought and calculation in the pursuit of conscious goals. He observed this in a growing number of areas: the economy, politics, public administration, law and culture. He examined the spread of machine technology, the rise of bureaucracies, rational capitalism, the rationalization of intellectual life and the rise of science. This rationalization led to a whole range of new problems that could not be resolved by further industrialization. As Weber put it: "Together with the machine, the bureaucratic organization is employed in building the houses of bondage of the future, in which perhaps men will one day be like peasants in the ancient Egyptian State, acquiescent and powerless, while a purely technical goal, that is, rational, official administration and provision becomes the sole, final value, which sovereignty decides the direction of their affairs" (Weber, 1974: 181). He feared that rationalization had become an end in itself by undermining all other goals that might have given it meaning. The means was becoming an end, thus profoundly alienating the people subjected to it. This was the new, harsh reality of human life as Weber masterfully portrayed it in his work (Weber, 1968).

Marx, Durkheim and Weber each gave a systematic and internally coherent interpretation of what was happening in the nineteenth century. All three saw the extraordinary coherence in the patterns of events of that time. Although they interpreted very differently the origin, nature and future of these developments, they all recognized that no simple or piecemeal solutions existed to the enormous problems posed by the technical revolution. The problems and dislocations experienced intensely by Germany, probably the most technically advanced society around the turn of the century, would be a significant factor in shaping the conditions that led to two world wars and, indirectly to the Russian Revolution. There were several new developments in the making, however, of which Marx, Durkheim and Weber experienced only the beginning. It is to these that we will now turn.

# THE TRANSFORMATION OF THE TECHNICAL KNOWLEDGE BASE

We have thus far described how introducing industrial technology into Western European societies fundamentally disturbed the social, economic, political, legal, moral and religious dimensions of society; massive restructuring was required, which forced the various efforts at rationalization (until then largely piecemeal) into a chain-reaction transformation. Out of this emerged a diversity of societies that shared many important features and which resembled each other much more than they resembled earlier societies. They are often called *industrial* societies, but this is an oversimplification that will become particularly evident when we examine the so-called advanced industrial, or *postindustrial* societies. The transformation that produced the latter is rooted in a fundamental change in the technical knowledge base. This change, beginning ever so slowly toward the end of the nineteenth century (after the death of Marx) became sociologically significant only after World War II. It radically changed society once again by means of a new chain reaction. The new patterns of social change were less driven by industrialization and machine technology than those of the nineteenth and early twentieth centuries.

Until the late nineteenth century, the development and application of the various techniques was largely empirical. They were passed on from one generation to the next by apprenticeship arrangements, in which one learned a technique by working with someone who had a great deal of experience. Formal education played an almost insignificant role until the end of the nineteenth century. Take technology as an example. The increasing precision and complexity of machines, as well as the growing pressure from competition to eliminate any inefficiency, required a technological knowledge base that was as much as possible scientifically founded. The Germans were far ahead of the English in this respect, and as a result, Germany began to overtake England in its technological and industrial capacity toward the end of the nineteenth century.

This was the beginning of a complete transformation of the way technological knowledge is transmitted, developed and applied. There is clearly a discontinuity between knowledge acquired from experience and knowledge acquired by formal education. No amount of experience and on-the-job training can lead to a knowledge of the applied sciences. These can only be learned in the classroom. As a result, the knowers and the doers are more and more frequently different people.

By way of example, consider a welder with many years of experience erecting high-rise buildings. One day, as the crane is bringing up another beam for the twenty-sixth floor structure, the welder may alert the crane operator and the foreman by saying, "I've never seen such a light beam being used on this large a span. Are you sure we aren't making a mistake?" The foreman may then decide to call the engineer in the field office to check the calculations. On the basis of many years of experience, the welder has obtained a certain knowledge of the strength of beams. Yet he will never learn to calculate the strength of a beam by means of stress analysis, because this is not learned from experience but from books or classroom instruction. Without it, all the welder can say is that a beam does not look strong enough to him. It should be remembered, however, that virtually all the technical accomplishments of the past were based on a body of knowledge built up from the experience of many generations.

The changes in the knowledge base of technology were accompanied by similar changes in other areas. A greater precision of one technique necessitates similar developments in other techniques. By the end of World War II, changes in the technical knowledge base had necessitated the restructuring of a variety of institutions in society. Galbraith (1978) has examined the restructuring of large corporations after World War II. Since Galbraith did not sufficiently appreciate the interdependence of industrial technology with a whole range of other techniques, we will briefly reinterpret his findings.

At the core of the large, modern corporation, we find what Galbraith has called its *technostructure*, essentially the brain of the enterprise, in which most activities are based on knowledge acquired by the formal education of its members. Together they have an expertise in the techniques necessary for the efficient running of all parts of the corporation, such as marketing, production, engineering, management, personnel and public relations. Thus, the latest technical knowledge is applied to all aspects of the corporation. Since the expertise of each member of the technostructure is highly specialized, each task must be so subdivided that every part is coterminous with a particular body of specialized technical knowledge. A knowledge of metallurgy, for example, cannot be applied to the design of a whole automobile. It can be applied only to the selection and design of appropriate materials for its parts. Thus, technical knowledge is applied to each and every part of the task, then to each subpart in combination with another, and then in combination with still others to ensure a coherent synthesis of the whole task. All aspects of the problem must be considered at the same time. For example, an automobile manufacturer does not spend millions of dollars on designing a new car only to discover that it cannot be produced economically or that, during the years spent designing the car and building the production facilities, substantial market changes have taken place. It is by means of a technostructure, therefore, that a large corporation takes advantage of the latest formal, technical knowledge.

The technostructure is surrounded by the body of the corporation, in which most tasks can be performed without any advanced formal education. Most tasks can be learned on the job (such as those of assembly-line workers), while others require some technical training (such as those of the operators of word processors). In all these tasks, knowledge acquired from experience plays an essential role.

The gradual restructuring of large corporations during the first half of the twentieth century was, therefore, in part a response to the emergence of the new technical knowledge base. Without this restructuring, large corporations would not be able to take advantage of the latest developments in the natural, applied and social sciences. All corporate operations became extremely effective. The development of any new product, for example, now required the collaboration of a great many people with complementary types of expertise relevant to the task. Since these people must be paid, provided with support staff, have offices and so on, the capital investment needed to bring any new product to market skyrocketed. A competitively priced product could be produced only if this investment could be written off over a large number of units manufactured. In other words, restructuring the technical knowledge base necessitated a further acceleration in the trend toward mass production. This trend in turn, required highly specialized production facilities. It was no longer possible to economically mass produce a product using general purpose machines, which were typically used for only one or two operations, although they were capable of doing many more. Production costs could be lowered by designing specialized production facilities, but this greatly added to the investment necessary to bring a new product to market.

All these factors greatly increased the risk involved in developing a new product. During the considerable length of time it took to design and develop a new product and prepare the production facilities, market conditions could change. If sales fell far below the projected figures, however, the investment in design and development of the new product and the highly specialized production facilities could not be transferred to another product. In order to protect themselves from such risks, companies diversified, so that the losses in one division could be offset by profits in another and not endanger the survival of the firm.

The corporations that exploited the new technical knowledge base, therefore, required a much greater concentration of capital than did the entrepreneurial firms of the nineteenth century. This made it virtually impossible for a family or a small group of shareholders to own these new firms. A modern corporation is usually owned by a large number of shareholders, who each own only a small part of the corporation. At shareholders' meetings, they tend to approve the plans put forward and prepared by the technostructure, which essentially controls the operation of the firm as long as it earns sufficient profits to pay reasonable dividends to the shareholders and to generate enough capital to finance its own internal operations. The greatly weakened link between ownership and control also affects the economic behaviour of the large corporation, whose goals are now much more complex than a simple profit maximization. Its relationship with the market also undergoes a profound transformation. No longer can it rely on the market to supply the specialized materials and machines that may be unique to one of its products. On the output side, the corporation attempts to manage consumer demand through a variety of techniques, including advertising. It relies on the state to create the educational institutions necessary to graduate specialists for its technostructure.

The growth and development of the new technical knowledge base required an expansion in the role of the modern state. It alone could create the educational system necessary to ensure that the nation would produce specialists in the various areas of technical expertise. Before the development of the new technical knowledge base, access to higher education was typically restricted to the upper-classes of society. In order to advance the development of the new technical knowledge base, access to the educational system had to be based not on social status, but on the intellectual capability of the individual. Hence, a person's position in the social hierarchy was increasingly determined not by his or her social status at birth, but by the amount of education he or she had received. Particularly when there was a scarcity of technical experts, equality of educational opportunities became a necessity. The result was that children from the same family could rise to very different social positions. This greater social mobility contributed to the birth of a mass society.

To provide the large corporation with a stable economic environment in which it could plan new products that would not come onto the market until years later, the state had to regulate the economy. It did so by creating a large public sector that it expanded or contracted to offset the fluctuations in the private sector. In the most advanced industrial nations, this public sector is in part occupied by projects not directly affecting the mainstream of society, such as defence, space programs and the development of nuclear energy. To ensure the development of the new technical knowledge base, the state also became involved in scientific and technical research. In order to efficiently carry out its new tasks, as well as to improve its effectiveness in more traditional domains, the state began to depend on the technical knowledge of experts. They brought their expertise to bear on these tasks, using patterns of collaboration very similar to the ones found in the technostructures of large corporations.

Developing the new technical knowledge base and the techniques derived from it did not only affect large corporations and the state, however. A growing number of activities in society were increasingly structured and restructured in accordance with the latest technical knowledge. In fact, all the characteristics of "postindustrialism" or "advanced industrialism" derive directly from the proliferation of techniques throughout society. We have already suggested that modern technology could not have emerged without a whole range of developments in other industrial techniques. Similarly, industrial techniques could not have been refined without the restructuring of many other areas of society. The transformations of technology and society are interdependent and reciprocally determine one another. The concepts of the Industrial Revolution and industrial society have obscured the many-faceted technical developments and necessitated the concepts of postindustrialism and advanced industrialism.

Courtesy of Ontario Hydro

Beginning with the Industrial Revolution, the proliferation of machines and the associated societal restructuring helped create an evergrowing demand for energy. Nuclear energy was initially thought to solve this problem once and for all. However, more and more people are becoming convinced that we have too often trusted technology to solve its own problems. In return for the electricity produced by a nuclear power plant during its lifetime (a maximum of 25 to 30 years), society is left with a vast quantity of highly dangerous radioactive waste, tailings from mining uranium and the radioactive housing of the reactor. How can we ever be totally sure that the methods proposed for storing these wastes will not be found inadequate 50, 100 or 200 years later? This raises fundamental moral questions about our responsibility to future generations. Some analysts have estimated that the total energy involved in all the activities associated with the production of electricity from nuclear energy exceeds the quantity of energy produced. The construction of some 70 nuclear power plants in North America has been stopped at varying stages. The photo shows Canada's first full-scale nuclear power station at Douglas Point, on Lake Huron. It came on line in 1967 and is now permanently out of service.

# THE PHENOMENON OF TECHNIQUE[1]

It would appear that, in the debate over the nature of modern society (whether it is industrially advanced, postindustrial, technological or something else) an important point has been overlooked. Surely, one thing that sets modern societies apart from all others is that a wide range of activities is no longer based on custom or tradition grounded in a culture. They systematically research virtually every sphere of human activity in order to render it more effective, rational and efficient or to eliminate problems. They do this on the assumption (and this is a cultural hypothesis that underlies modern societies) that the quality of life can be improved by making all facets of our existence more efficient. Research takes the form of what we will call the *technical operation*, which is constituted of four stages.

The first stage involves studying some area of human life for a particular purpose. The study's results are used in the next stage to build a model that can range from a precise mathematical theory to a theory that is largely qualitative. In the third stage, the model is examined to determine what happens when its parameters are altered, in order to discover when it functions optimally. The technical operation concludes with the reorganization of the area of human life studied originally, to achieve the highest efficiency and rationality demonstrated to be possible by the model. It is by means of this pattern of events that modern societies seek to improve the productivity of a plant, the running of a large office or hospital, the effectiveness of classroom instruction, the performance of a professional athlete or hockey team, the functioning of a group and even the satisfaction derived from a sexual relationship. As a result, the technical operation deeply permeates the fabric of technologies or techniques. The French sociologist Jacques Ellul first drew our attention to this fact.

Increasingly in modern societies, almost every sphere of human activity is organized not on the basis of custom or tradition, but on the basis of a variety of techniques that ensure that everything is done as effectively as possible. Technology is only one part of the larger phenomenon of technique.

The reason the "industrially advanced" nations began to generate a mass of information at a certain point is now evident. When techniques increasingly began to replace tradition as the basis of human activities, much information was generated as a result of the technical operation. As these developments gained momentum, new technologies or techniques became necessary to deal with the mass of information. The computer and associated techniques were developed to meet this challenge and immediately found a wide range of applications. This in turn greatly accelerated the patterns of development described above.

The information economy, the proliferation of theoretical services, the rise of new intellectual techniques, the emergence of a new class of technical experts, the growth of the service sector and other phenomena taken to be signs of the "post-industrial age" (Bell, 1973) are simply the result of the proliferation of techniques in society.

---

[1] The following is largely based on W.H. Vanderburg, "Some Implications of Modern Technology for Culture and Knowledge", presented at the 1983 AAAS annual meeting in Detroit, later published under the same title in *Man-Environment Systems*, Vol. 13, no. 5, Sept. 1983.

Speculation on what the computer could perhaps make possible is often voiced in total disregard of the sociocultural context in which the computer was invented and applied. This leads to a serious misunderstanding of the forces behind its diffusion throughout society. The new utopias predicted for tomorrow do not take into account the continuity in the patterns of development of modern societies made possible by the computer.

## THE CONSEQUENCES OF THE
## TECHNICIZATION OF LIFE

When we reflect on the above description of the technical operation, we see that techniques are not neutral; they do not merely make an activity more effective. An area of human life is studied not holistically but for a specific purpose. As a result, certain aspects of the situation will be externalized (i.e., excluded from consideration) in the technical operation. Although a greater efficiency will be achieved in some area, this will be at the expense of significant *externalities*. Furthermore, the techncial operation separates knowing from doing, knowledge from experience and the knower from the doer. Consider a simple example.

Around the turn of the century, as machines in factories became increasingly efficient, the operations carried out by human beings caused a bottleneck. It made no sense to further improve the efficiency of the machines when the workers could not keep pace. In this context, studies were done on how to rationalize human work to make it more efficient. Some of the most famous studies were done by Gilbreth (Giedion, 1969: 102-105). By fastening a small electric light bulb to the wrist of a worker performing some task, it was possible to record the trajectory traced out by the bulb with three cameras mounted along three perpendicular axes. From the photographic records, wire models were constructed that showed exactly how the worker moved his or her hand. By analysing these models, it was possible to optimize the movements, and once this was accomplished, the worker was taught to perform the task more efficiently.

Gilbreth's technique perfectly illustrates the technical operation. As expected, rationalizing traditional work by this or other techniques creates an important externality. It can readily be identified when we compare traditional with technicized work. If we observe a traditional craftsperson at work, the gestures reflect a variety of things, such as the person's state of mind, personality, previous experience (including apprenticeship training) and culture. Once the "one best way" was determined by means of the technical operation, all this had to be suppressed as much as possible by the worker. This led to the well-known consequence of physical fatigue largely being replaced by nervous fatigue in technicized work. Normally, even in the most routine movements, something of our personality comes through, as is evident in the characteristics of our handwriting. This can be explained if we recall what we said earlier about the role of culture (Vanderburg, 1985). Since the relationship between human beings and reality is not predetermined genetically, the limited organization of the brain present at birth is expanded by experience. The mind that thus emerges in relation to the brain is the symbolic basis for mediating all relationships with reality. Since the mind is first shaped during socialization into a culture, it functions as a kind of mental map that the members of a culture use to interpret their experience and relate to one another and reality. While the mental map of each member of a culture is unique, it is sufficiently similar to those of other members to make communication possible. In traditional work, this mental map is the symbolic basis on which the craftsperson performs his or her operations.

Once work is technicized on the basis of the technical operation, the situation changes fundamentally. When workers are taught the one best way of moving their hands, they are being asked to suppress as much as possible their personality, state of mind, past experience and culture. Of course, this is not entirely possible, since their cultural mental map continues to play a role, although it is a reduced one. In a nontechnicized relationship, the mind makes it possible for each moment to be lived holistically, that is, in the context of and in relation to a person's whole being. This is not to say that alienation is impossible. In technicized relationships, on the contrary, a person must constantly suppress the way he or she would spontaneously act on the basis of his or her mental map. In technicized work, a person's mind must make a special effort to suppress his or her subjectivity. The result is nervous fatigue, which generally characterizes technicized work, as physical fatigue did traditional work. We must not absolutize these findings but remember that we are building an ideal type following Max Weber. As far as knowledge is concerned, it follows that traditional workers knew their work differently than people engaged in technicized work.

## Technique as Milieu

The illustration of the technicization of work can now be generalized to determine some implications the phenomenon of technique has for individual and collective life. There is a long tradition of thinking about technology as a means to accomplish human ends. This is true, of course, but it is only a part of the picture. Technology and techniques also mediate relationships between human beings or between human beings and anything in their environment. Consider the telephone. It mediates between many people who may never meet face-to-face. This is obvious, but we often forget that this mediation is not neutral. It fundamentally transforms the relationship, since many sociocultural dimensions of a typical face-to-face relationship are stripped away, requiring a change in the relationship. The culture's facial expressions, gestures and body language (Hall, 1977) are not transmitted by the telephone. Yet these dimensions play an important part in face-to-face conversation, to the point that many people are uneasy talking to a blind person face-to-face because he or she typically does not respond to or transmit all the nonverbal dimensions of conversation. Young children using the telephone for the first time will also behave as though it were a face-to-face encounter. They quickly learn, however, that the telephone does not mediate in a neutral fashion.

What is true for the telephone is equally true for television. It mediates between producer and consumer, between the politician and the voter, between events around the globe and the viewer, and so on. These mediated relations are also transformed in a nonneutral way. A politician may come across well in person but may have to rely on a media consultant to ensure that she projects the right image. Advertising is not a neutral diffusion of information about products. By linking a product to certain symbols alive in the minds of people, it affects them subconsciously on the level where these symbols have become a part of their being, thus partly displacing the culturally mediated and conscious process of choice. All this is well known and need not be elaborated upon. What we have said thus far is equally true for computer-mediated relationships.

Techniques do not necessarily mediate relationships on the basis of some device. Many relationships are technically mediated with devices playing little or no essential part. Take a large office, for example. Here organization theory is applied to large numbers of people collectively performing a variety of tasks as effectively as possible. Here again, organizational techniques have been developed to find the best way of identifying, executing and interconnecting the functions of the organization. By making use of job descriptions and organizational charts, an optimal model is created that specifies how the relationships between the people in that office are to be technically mediated. People no longer primarily behave spontaneously, on the basis of their cultural mental maps. The relationships have been transformed, as the studies of bureaucracy by Max Weber and others have shown. We are not suggesting that mediation on the basis of culture is totally eliminated in a modern office, but technically mediated relationships predominate. If the cultural mediation entirely disappeared, we would find the human and social transformation described by Aldous Huxley in *Brave New World* (Huxley, 1932) or what Lewis Mumford calls the *megamachine society* (Mumford, 1970). Human beings would be completely adapted to society as mere pieces in a social mechanism. Such a transformation is far more radical than the one we are describing, and there is little sociological evidence of the possibility of that situation coming about. In fact, many problems of contemporary societies are the result of tensions between their technicized and nontechnicized elements.

A society changes fundamentally once most of the relationships in which its members are engaged become technically mediated. At this point, technique becomes the primary milieu for its members. It is in relation to this milieu that life evolves. This means much more than that the members of these societies live in an urban technical environment. Human existence has known only three primary milieus: nature in prehistory, society during much of our history and technique for the "industrially advanced" nations during the past two decades. In other words, it is in relation to the primary milieu that human life evolves. The milieu completely permeates all experience and presents human beings with almost everything they need to maintain their way of life, but it also threatens their existence. It fundamentally affects how people symbolically mediate their relationships with reality. This is evident when we recall that the mind develops by expanding the genetically established organization of the brain on the basis of internalized experiences. Hence, the characteristics of the resulting mental map (and thus, human consciousness), is decisively influenced by the primary milieu.

In prehistory, human beings lived in small groups totally dominated by nature. The natural milieu provided them with everything necessary for life, but it also posed the most serious threats in the form of droughts, wild beasts or storms, for example. Nature permeated almost every experience, producing a unique type of consciousness characterized by a certain kind of mental map.

When human beings began to live in societies at the dawn of history, the im-

Courtesy of R. Vanderburg

Courtesy of R. Vanderburg

Industrialization has also transformed war. Mass production made large armies possible. This totally transformed the nature of war, which in the past was fought with armies that were small by modern standards and which often left much of the population of warring societies relatively unaffected. War based on high technology will almost certainly destroy life on our planet. Rather than dealing with the root causes of war, however, nations are pushing expenditures on arms to unprecedented levels. If even a fraction of these resources were spent on peaceful pursuits, the world would be a safer place. The arms race is a good example of technology out of control. Here are some chilling statistics from the *UNESCO Courier* (March, 1982):

Number of persons directly or indirectly involved in military activities worldwide: 50 million

Global military industrial production costs: $100 billion

Global military consumption of aluminum, copper, nickel and platinum exceeds total demand for these materials in Africa, Asia and Latin America

Global land use for military purposes: 500 000 square kilometres

Percentage of world's scientists and engineers involved in military work exceeded 20 percent in the 1970s

Percentage of global research and development expenditures in 1980 used for military purposes: 25 percent

Per capita military expenditures for every man, woman and child on earth in 1980: $110 (US)

portance of the natural milieu became overshadowed by the social milieu. The latter interposed itself between the individual and nature. This made it possible for a society to better defend itself against natural dangers, but the new primary milieu also introduced a new series of dangers, such as war and economic or political instability, that could lead to the collapse of a society or civilization. Once the social milieu became the primary and nature the secondary milieu, a new type of consciousness emerged with correspondingly different mental maps.

When the phenomenon of technique began to transform a growing number of relationships, structures and institutions within a society, the first steps toward another transition commenced. It may well be as sweeping as the one from prehistory to history. Technically mediated relationships eventually dominated culturally mediated ones, and technique displaced society as the primary milieu. Society now constituted the secondary milieu and nature moved to third place. Life in a modern society, and particularly in its large urban centres, is impossible without a variety of technical support systems, while at the same time technique presents all societies with new ultimate threats: nuclear holocaust, the destabilization and poisoning of the ecosystem and the growing inability to provide meaningful work for all people. Again, a new consciousness emerges as techniques permeate almost every experience.

# SUMMARY

The following selected references examine the effects technique and/or technology are having on various areas of contemporary society. See the bibliography at the back of this text for complete references. For an introduction, see *Perspectives on Our Age: Jacques Ellul Speaks on His Life and Work,* edited by W.H. Vanderburg. In art, see *Art and the Industrial Revolution,* by F.D. Klingender; *The Voices of Silence,* by A. Malraux; *Art and Technics,* by L. Mumford. In music, see *The Tuning of the World,* by R.M. Schafer, and *Music-Society-Education-Literature,* by C. Small. In literature, see *Literature Against Itself,* by G. Graff; *Language and Silence: Essays on Language, Literature and the Inhuman,* by G. Steiner; and *Literature and Technology,* by W. Sypher. On language, see an article by T.B. Farrell and G.T. Goodnight, "Accidental Rhetoric: The Root Metaphors of Three Mile Island," in *Communication Monographs; The State of the Language,* by L. Michaels and C. Ricks; and *The Technological Conscience,* by M. Stanley. On *weltanschauung,* see *Ways of Seeing,* by J. Berger et al.; *Mechanization Takes Command,* by S. Giedion; and *Technology and the Canadian Mind: Innis/McLuhan/Grant.* For thoughts on the effects of technique and/or technology on religion, see *The Orwellian World of the Jehovah's Witnesses,* by H. Botting and G. Botting; *The New Demons,* by J. Ellul; and by J.S. Glen, *Justification by Success.* On morality and values, see *The Collective Definition of Deviance,* edited by F. James Davis and Richard Stivers. Also, *Culture Against Man,* by J. Henry and "Values in Engineering," by M.W. Thring, in *Science and Public Policy.* In education, see *Education and the Cult of Efficiency,* by R.E. Callahan; *Deschooling Society,* by I. Illich; and *Education and the Rise of the Corporate State,* by J. Spring. On technique and/or technology and leisure, see *Of Time, Work and Leisure,* by S. de Grazia; *Leisure and Work,* by S. Parker; and *Sport and Work,* by B. Rigauer. On sexuality, see *Sex and Dehumanization,* by D. Holbrook; and an article by R. Stivers entitled "A Festival of Sex, Violence and Drugs: The Sacred and Profane in our World," which appeared in *Katallagete.* On agriculture, see *The Unsettling of America,* by W. Berry; *Food for Nought,* by R.H. Hall; and *Dry Cereals,* hearings held by the U.S. Senate Committee on Commerce, Consumer Subcommittee. And finally, on war, see *War and Industrial Society,* by R. Aron; *The Baroque Arsenal,* by M. Kaldor; and *War and Human Progress,* by J.U. Nef.

The proliferation of technicized relationships in modern societies has a profound influence on human life. The separation of knowing from doing and knowledge from experience causes us to depend on experts in almost every domain of life. Since we have devalued daily life knowledge that is embedded in experience, we need to turn to experts who supposedly know much more about the various aspects of our lives than we can know ourselves. If we are responsible and know what is good for us, we live in accordance with the objective body of technical experience. Experts make their living by giving us access to that knowledge, which is believed to be vital for our existence. They do this personally or via the multitude of how-to-do-it books that tell us how to treat our babies, how to talk to our teenage children, how to save a marriage, improve our sex life, sleep better, eat a balanced diet, organize a good vacation, cope with stress and so on. Apparently, we cannot be trusted to do these things ourselves anymore.

We are not saying, of course, that in the past, people did not rely on experts, we are saying that the phenomenon was on a completely different scale. We have created a society in which all of us, including the experts, must rely on others in important matters to the point that we have become spectators of much of our own lives. This phenomenon is taking on new proportions as a result of the proliferation of information services accessed through personal computers. It is fundamentally alienating, whether we are exploited or not. The fact that the control over one's own life has become largely external is a threat to human freedom, and it is also very stressful. The difficulty of participating in technicized relationships and the loss of control over one's life leads to the reification of the human subject—a fact powerfully portrayed in modern abstract art, which developed as the phenomenon of technique began to manifest itself. The human subject disappeared from art.

The technicization of life produces a new kind of alienation that is superimposed on economic alienation.

> Consider the average man as he comes home from his job. Very likely he has spent the day in a completely hygienic environment, and everything has been done to balance his environment and lessen his fatigue. However, he has had to work without stopping and under constant pressure; nervous fatigue has replaced muscular fatigue. When he leaves his job, his joy in finishing his stint is mixed with dissatisfaction with a work as fruitless as it is incomprehensible and as far from really productive work. At home he "finds himself" again. But what does he find? He finds a phantom. If he ever thinks, his reflections terrify him. Personal destiny is fulfilled only by death; but reflection tells him that for him there has not been anything between his adolescent adventures and his death, no point at which he himself ever made a decision or initiated a change. Changes are the exclusive prerogative of organized technical society, which one day may have decked him out in khaki to defend it, and on another in stripes because he had sabotaged or betrayed it. There was no difference from one day to the next. Yet life was never serene, for newspapers and news reports beset him at the end of the day and forced on him the image of an insecure world. If it was not hot or cold war, there were all sorts of accidents to drive home to him the precariousness of his life. Torn between this precariousness and the absolute, unalterable determinateness of work, he has no place, belongs nowhere. Whether something happens to him, or nothing happens, he is in neither case the author of his destiny. . . . But amusement techniques have jumped into the breach and taught him at least how to flee the presence of death. He no longer needs faith or some difficult asceticism to deaden himself to his condition. The movies and television lead him straight into an artificial paradise. Rather than face his own phantom, he seeks film phantoms into which he can project himself and which permit him to live as he might have willed. For an hour or two he can cease to be himself, as his personality dissolves and fades into the anonymous mass of spectators. The film makes him laugh, cry, wonder, and love. He goes to bed with the leading lady, kills the villain, and masters life's absurdities. In short, he becomes a hero. Life suddenly has meaning (Ellul, 1964:376-377). This and all other excerpts from THE TECHNOLOGICAL SOCIETY, by Jacques Ellul, translated by John Wilkinson. Copyright © 1964 by Alfred A. Knopf, Inc. Reprinted by permission of the publisher.

During its initial phases, the web of techniques was built up in the self-interest of a specific social class. As more and more techniques linked together during the technical revolution, they became increasingly difficult to control, due to the technical alienation produced. Such alienation was experienced even by the powerful and wealthy.

The patterns of development of the "industrially advanced" world are those of the growth of technique. Many of the problems faced by present-day societies derive from these very patterns of development, yet we continue to seek new techniques in an attempt to solve the problems created by earlier ones. It is impossible, however, to solve problems by simply doing more of the kinds of things that created these problems in the first place. This approach merely replaces one problem with another, inevitably leading to a top-heavy and unstable technical order. Yet, because of the way technique as milieu influences human consciousness, societal values and myths, we continue to turn to technique to solve the problems created by it. There can, however, be no security in evermore powerful weapons, and there can be no real solution to our economic problems without addressing the challenge technique poses to human life and society. We need to create a civilization that includes technique but is based on a culture not permeated by it. This will determine the kind of world we will leave for future generations.

## DISCUSSION QUESTIONS

1. When a society faces certain problems, it attempts to solve them by extending its institutions, way of life and means of existence. During the beginning of a new epoch in the history of a society, this makes a lot of sense since its problems become an opportunity for expanding and strengthening the basis on which its members live together. There soon comes a point in its development, however, when this approach becomes counterproductive because it often amounts to solving problems by doing more of the kinds of things that helped to produce them in the first place. This "inertia" in a society is not just a matter of powerful vested interests; it is, more importantly, the consequence of the myths and values that orient the members of a culture in a certain direction by valuing certain options and thereby devaluing others. Our modern society greatly values science and technology, and we consequently look for technical solutions to the challenges we face. We have difficulty seeing that technique is useful for certain things but useless for others. Critically assess the approaches that modern societies are taking to the following challenges:

   (a) *Our approach to defense.* Beyond a certain point, the application of modern science and technique to defense and weapons development creates a threat to human survival. Is the new Star Wars research an example of attempting to solve a problem by doing more of the kind of thing that helped to produce that problem in the first place? What alternative options are available to us? Do the Canadian, American or Russian people freely decide who their enemies really are, or is this all decided for us?

(b) *Our approach to underdevelopment.* Is this a problem with a technical solution, i.e., can it be solved by the transfer of techniques of all kinds?

(c) *Our approach to unemployment.* Is a strategy of ongoing economic growth based on scientific and technical development able to solve the problems of unemployment and the need to find meaningful ways for the members of a society to participate in its way of life? What about the problems of depleting resources and environmental pollution?

(d) Can the ongoing development of technique deal with the reification of modern life?

2. At international conferences it is common to hear delegations of so-called underdeveloped nations say that they wish to acquire the science and technology of the industrially advanced world but not the materialistic, consumer-oriented culture of the democratic nations or the bureaucratic and authoritarian state of the socialist countries. Do you think that this is possible, and, if so, what has the analysis presented in this chapter overlooked?

3. We have argued that in a culture permeated by technique, the minds of the members of each new generation acquire values which essentially define "the good" as everything that directly or indirectly advances technique and the power of the institutions that are the primary agents for applying, developing and transmitting techniques. Can this be explained in Marxist terms as being a part of the ideology created by the ruling class to justify and defend its power and position? If the mind is formed by internalized experiences, to what extent do you think such arguments are plausible? Can these values be explained from a functionalist-structuralist perspective, and, if so, how do we account for such problems as: environmental pollution and its threat to human health; the increased power of our weapons and the threat it poses to human survival; and the alienation and reification of human life?

4. Who or what controls modern technique and for what purpose? Who gains and who loses? Illustrate your argument with some examples.

# 24

# Ideology, Social Order and Social Change

*Anton L. Allahar*

# INTRODUCTION

Social scientists use several terms which, though widely employed, generate a great deal of controversy as to their precise meanings. Ideology is such a term. One often hears of ideological debates, ideological presuppositions, ideological biases and so on, but there is little agreement as to what ideology is or what it does. The concept is at best a contentious one. It is applied generally to those whom we wish to discredit, for, whatever other meaning the term may convey, it is usually employed in a negative or pejorative sense. In everyday parlance, for instance, when someone is accused of "being ideological" in a discussion, it implies that he or she is deliberately distorting the "facts," concealing the "whole truth" or being overly narrow in outlook.

In one respect, ideology is like charisma. While it is difficult to define charisma, most people can recognize it. We say, for example, that former prime minister Pierre Trudeau has it—he has that "something special" that former prime minister Joe Clark lacks. But exactly what that something special is, is difficult to pinpoint; so too with ideology. As Marchak (1975: 1) observes, ideologies "are seldom taught explicitly and systematically."

This chapter has two goals. The first is to move toward a definition of ideology that can be agreed upon by social analysts. This will entail considering numerous statements about the nature and essence of ideology and the process by which it is acquired. Our second goal is to assess the social and political functions of ideology. In other words, once we understand what it is, we will examine what it does. Nevertheless, it must be borne in mind that, although the questions of definition and function may be separated for analytical purposes, they will not be that clearly distinguishable in actuality.

# CLASSICAL VIEWS ON IDEOLOGY

## KUHN'S VIEW

The basic theme of this chapter concerns the relationship between ideology, order and change. To develop this theme we will use the concept of *revolution*, which implies both order and change, as a point of departure. For the moment, however, revolution will not be understood in the political sense. Rather, we will talk more philosophically, in the manner that Thomas Kuhn (1970) spoke of *scientific revolutions*.

When discussing revolutionary changes in the realm of scientific knowledge, Kuhn contended that the process involved the "rejection of one time-honored scientific theory in favour of another" (1970: 6). But such a process is not without considerable struggle and resistance, for the scientist who practises "normal science" has a commitment to the established methods of his or her trade. "Normal science" is thus seen as inherently conservative:

> Normal science, for example, often suppresses fundamental novelties because they are necessarily subversive of its basic commitments (Kuhn, 1970: 5).

Revolutionary breaks with past practice and the acceptance of new methods and knowledge are thus conceived of by Kuhn as "tradition-shattering complements to the tradition-bound activity of normal science" (1970: 6). This commitment of a scientific community to a well defined and coherent set of established practices and beliefs is referred to as a *paradigm* (1970: 176-81). And science is replete with examples of outmoded, current and emerging paradigms. In fact, the basic "stuff" of scientific revolutions and progress entails conflicts between paradigms, between communities of scholars, their ideas, and their findings.

Kuhn's observation that changes in the dominant paradigm "cause scientists to see the world of their research-engagement differently" and that "after a revolution scientists are responding to a different world" (1970: 111) is crucial to the student of ideology and social change. For, as Hagopian has pointed out:

> Scientists are, after all, opinion makers and their views ultimately affect the general state of beliefs in society. . . . And it is quite likely that the new world harbours many aspects that are not in keeping with the view of the world associated with the traditional society (1974: 140).

Building on the insights of Kuhn, we can discuss some of the classical views on ideology. If normal science is conservative and scientific revolutions are radical, we can expect each to have its own ideological justifications of and defenses for its right to exist. The conservatives, those associated with the traditional society, will argue for the wisdom and correctness of tradition; the radicals, who have no stake in the existing order, will insist on the need for change.

## MARX'S AND WEBER'S VIEWS

For Marx, ideology is viewed negatively as a set of beliefs that serves to justify and legitimize the rule of the few over the many. He sees the economic structure of capitalism, the system under which commodities produced by workers are appropriated by capitalists, as the basis for the development of class conflict and ideology. By ideology he means the moral codes, philosophies, art, law, religion and even literature that comprise a society's *superstructure*, the glue that binds together the economic base or *substructure* of that society. For example, the religious injunction, "Thou shalt not steal," clearly serves the interests of those who own property. When the propertyless worker who is compelled to sell his labour power to the capitalist internalizes and abides by this religious exhortation, potential conflict is minimized, and both worker and capitalist can go about their daily affairs.

Because Marx gave primacy to economic dealings and how they colour the greater part of all social interactions, and because he linked ideology with domination and the class structure of society, he underestimated the autonomous role that ideas and ideology can play in everyday life. His use of the term "ideology" is very general, and it was left to other scholars, most notably Max Weber and Karl Mannheim, to attempt a more complete treatment of it. We must point out, however, that neither Weber nor Mannheim managed completely to divorce ideology from class (Gerth and Mills, 1958: 61-63; Abercrombie et al., 1980: 30-36).

From Weber's point of view, it is not that Marx was wrong to emphasize the economic basis of domination, for on that score he applauds many of the insights of Marx. As Zeitlin says,

He was not concerned with refuting Marx . . . nor did he see himself as having bested Marx. On the contrary, he looked upon Marx's analytical concepts and methodological principles as extraordinarily fruitful (1981: 28).

Weber's main quarrel with Marx, however, was that he did not go far enough to take account of the noneconomic bases of human action. For Weber, human behaviour is informed largely by meanings, subjective perceptions and personal assessments of goals. Psychological states, he felt, are as important as material interests in guiding that behaviour. This is a central theme in his *Protestant Ethic and the Spirit of Capitalism* (1958). In that study, he shows how the Calvinist doctrine of predestination rendered believers psychologically anxious: There was no way of knowing whether one was saved or damned. Hence, literally to preserve their sanity, members of the faith sought to do things to convince themselves that they were worthy of salvation. They worked hard, saved their money, led ascetic lives and so on, all of which complemented the ethos of early capitalism. Weber's point, then, is that the religious ideas and teachings of Calvinism had a definite impact on how Calvinists conducted their economic lives. It was not that capitalism as an economic form came into existence and later gave rise to the ideology of ascetic Protestantism.

Weber, therefore, was concerned with "rounding out" the Marxian thesis, with demonstrating the nonmaterial bases of action and showing how, under certain circumstances, "ideas become effective forces in history" (Weber, 1958: 90). Thus, "with Marx he shares the sociological approach to ideas: they are powerless in history unless they are fused with material interests" (Gerth and Mills, 1958: 62). But where Marx emphasizes an almost one-to-one correspondence between ideas and interests, Weber is also eager to recognize possible tensions between them. In other words, though ideas and class interests are often linked, Weber leaves the door open to the possibility of a conflict between ideas and material interests.

Applying the concept of *elective affinity* to ideology, Weber would argue that human beings are not total prisoners of social or class structures. They have some freedom to choose and discard ideas as they suit their purposes:

> Ideas do gain an affinity with the interests of certain members of special strata; if they do not gain such affinity, they are abandoned (Weber, 1958: 63).

In linking the views of Weber and Mannheim on ideology, Abercrombie et al. are quick to point out their connection to Marxism. Marx's contention that the dominant ideas of every age are the ideas of the dominant class, the *dominant ideology thesis*, represents his attempt to reduce ideas to concrete economic and political interests. But for Weber and Mannheim also, class is a crucial variable:

> The sociology of knowledge tradition of Weber and Mannheim attempts to show how beliefs can be reduced to social groups . . . . the sociology of knowledge which tries to develop a non-Marxist theory of ideology in fact arrives at similar class-theoretical conclusions to the dominant ideology tradition with Marxism (Abercrombie et al., 1980: 30).

And as far as Mannheim himself is concerned, writers like Wolff (1969: 508) and Remmling (1975: 44) show that his sociology of knowledge is firmly rooted in the

Marxian tradition. This much Mannheim would not deny, for he often acknowledged his intellectual debts to Marx (Mannheim, 1936:75-77).

## MANNHEIM'S CONTRIBUTION

But Mannheim, like Weber, rejected Marx's overly economic definition of class. As Coser tells us,

> Mannheim did not limit himself to a programme of study inherited from Marxian class analysis. He included a variety of other social factors such as status groups and occupational categories as existential determinants of ideas (1977: 433).

The important point, however, is that Mannheim, though sensitive to the non-material bases of thoughts and actions, nevertheless constantly referred back to the class (or what he called *group*) origins of ideas and actions. Nowhere is this made more clear than in his discussion of *ideology* and *utopia*.

For Mannheim, the everyday conditions of existence and the conflicts that they generate between various groups and classes lead to two opposing kinds of ideas. Such ideas he termed *situationally transcendent*, or unreal, for they do not fit into the prevailing order (Mannheim, 1936: 194). Situationally transcendent ideas are of two types: they are either ideological or utopian, depending on the *social location*, or *perspective*, from which they are viewed. The rulers, oppressors or members of the upper strata, who have a vested interest in maintaining the status quo, dismiss the claims of the ruled or oppressed strata as unrealistic, or *utopian*. The oppressed, conversely, see the oppressors' defense of the status quo as *ideological*: The appeal to divine law, the sanctity of tradition or the natural order of things are all deemed ideological, for they are inherently conservative and defend the existing order (Hagopian, 1974: 256).

In elaborating on his ideas, Mannheim separates the *particular* conception of ideology from the *total* conception. The first deals with the micro situation and operates at the psychological and individual level: "Since the particular conception never actually departs from the psychological level, the point of reference in such analyses is always the individual" (Hagopian, 1974: 58). The particular conception also refers to the scepticism we feel about the ideas of an opponent whom we suspect of telling lies in order to prevent us from seeing a given situation in its true light. Supposedly, it is in the interest of our opponent that we do not see the situation as it really is. Hence, at the level of individuals, the *particular* conception of ideology concerns the conscious distortion of the truth.

The *total* conception of ideology concerns the thoughts of whole classes, epochs, civilizations and ages. The ideologies of democracy and liberalism are instances of the total conception. For example, when Prime Minister Mulroney talks of his commitment to democratic principles, he speaks a language that all of Canada, North America and the Western world can understand. But in rounding out his discussion, Mannheim makes one further qualification.

The total conception, we are told, can further be divided into two types: special and general formulations. Quite simply, the *special* formulation of the total conception of ideology involves our ability to identify our opponent's ideas as ideologically and situationally determined. The *general* formulation, conversely, concerns our "courage to subject not just the adversary's point of view but all points of view, including [our] own, to ideological analysis" (Hagopian, 1974: 77).

We will now look at some contemporary views on and uses of ideology, beginning with an attempt to provide a comprehensive definition of that term.

# DEFINING IDEOLOGY

## THE PRIMACY OF FAITH IN IDEOLOGY

Ideology is a body of systematic beliefs and ideas. By systematic, however, we do not mean that the beliefs and ideas are necessarily *logically* interconnected in a scientific and empirical manner. The central doctrines in Christianity, for example, include belief in the Holy Trinity, belief that there is one God and that Christ is both God and the son of God, belief in the virgin birth, and belief in the resurrection. Of course, to converts who unquestioningly accept that "miracles do happen" and who accept on faith the existence of an all-powerful and all-knowing God, these beliefs are not problematic. But sociology is a social science concerned with empirical proof, and such beliefs are nonscientific and cannot be proved empirically.

We know that the virgin birth, for instance, is a logical and biological impossibility. But even if we accept that it happened, there is a further problem. In biological reproduction, the female carries the XX chromosome while the male contributes the XY chromosome which determines the sex of the offspring. Now, even if the Virgin Mary became pregnant without sexual intercourse, if the male XY chromosomal contribution were absent, her child (Jesus) logically would have had to be female. Similar logical and biological arguments could be made about the resurrection and the Holy Trinity.

The point is, nonetheless, that as an ideology, Christianity consists of a series of beliefs that are connected, though not necessarily *logically*. And what is more, Christian doctrine is accepted by hundreds of millions of people around the world as an integral part of their lives. The strength with which the ideology is embraced and its persistence in light of scientific evidence to the contrary, however, leads us to consider another feature of ideology.

The earlier observation that ideology is a body of systematic beliefs and ideas should be modified to stress that it is *primarily* a body of beliefs and *secondarily* a body of ideas. The distinction is more than semantic. For ideas are open to scientific testing and verification; beliefs are not (Rejai, 1971: 3). Hence, ideologies, as systems of beliefs, are difficult and maybe even impossible to refute or challenge on empirical grounds. Scientifically speaking, one can neither prove nor disprove the existence of God. It is purely a matter of faith: Either one believes or does not believe.

This raises a third consideration in defining ideology: the relationship between ideology and science or ideology and truth. Ideologies are like dogmas. They claim to be true but do not propose a method to substantiate their claim. Science, on the other hand, pursues knowledge and truth in a demonstrable fashion. Scientific truth can be questioned, tested, refuted, upheld or disproven. As Bergmann suggests, an ideological statement is "a value judgement disguised as, or mistaken for, a statement of fact" (1951: 210). McCain and Segal equate ideology with dogma:

You are being too ideological so let's now examine this whole matter OBJECTIVELY from MY point of view.

One way of contrasting science and dogma is to say that a scientist accepts facts as given and belief systems as tentative, whereas a dogmatist accepts the belief systems as given; facts are irrelevant (1969: 31-32).

This does not mean, however, that certain scientific truths have not been made dogma by those who accept them as absolute. Nor does social science only deal with "facts as given." For facts are never free of theory. They are always interpreted and screened subjectively as human beings seek to impart *meaning* to them.

## THE FIVE DIMENSIONS OF IDEOLOGY

Based on our discussion so far, we can clarify our understanding of ideology a bit more. An ideology usually consists of five dimensions: the cognitive, affective, evaluative, programmatic, and social (Rejai, 1971: 3-10). The *cognitive* dimension refers to the fact that ideologies embody a significant element of myth, which simplifies a complex social reality (Lasswell and Kaplan, 1950: 116-33). Such simplification is usually accomplished by using symbols (for example, the crucifix) that "package" meanings of and responses to reality:

Whether linguistic (words or speech) or nonlinguistic (flags, insignia, monuments, holidays, ceremonies, anthems), symbols capture in an economical fashion large expanses of meanings and communicate these meanings in an instantaneous fashion (Rejai, 1971: 6).

As might be imagined, the cognitive and *affective* dimensions are closely related. To the extent that ideologies elicit emotive responses, they are embraced blindly and sometimes passionately. This is clearly seen in political, religious and nationalist ideologies: "One might say, in fact, the most important, latent function of ideology is to tap emotion" (Bell, 1960: 371).

The *evaluative* dimension of ideology concerns the question of "the good society." In this context, an ideology will either criticize the existing status quo or defend it by appealing to high-sounding moral principles. Particularly in political ideology, one hears explicit references to regimes that suppress or support human rights, liberty, equality and dignity. Ideologies often involve value judgements aimed at discrediting those who do not support a particular ideology. This is accomplished by masking the truth in some cases and by exaggerating it in others.

Thus, United States' President Ronald Reagan, for example, describes the Soviet Union as an "evil empire" bent on destroying the "free world." In fact, so evil are the Soviets that their government oppresses its own citizens. Here one is given to understand that in the United States, there is no inequality, no racial oppression, no social barriers to limit individual mobility and success. Internationally, too, we are led to believe that American foreign policy is designed with the interests of oppressed peoples at heart, whereas Soviet foreign policy is motivated by self-interest.

Many ideologies also have a *programmatic* dimension, in that they call for action that translates specific values, norms and ideas into practice. Such actions, as was hinted above, will be aimed either at maintaining a given status quo or transforming it. The ideologies of conservatism, black power and feminism are cases in point. And, as we might expect, the call to action will also have a *social* component. Hence, ideologies are associated with social groups and classes whose members represent specific interests, ambitions, hopes, dreams, ideals and preferences. As the two fundamental units of subjective action in any society, individuals and social groups or classes are creators and carriers of ideology. This is why Daniel Bell referred to ideologies as "mobilized belief systems" that seek to

> simplify ideas, establish a claim to truth, and, in the union of the two, demand a commitment to action. Thus not only does ideology transform ideas, it transforms people as well (Bell, 1960: 372).

Later in this chapter, we will take a closer look at the relationship between ideology, social class and change. But for the moment, we may take the following as a working definition of ideology that will be refined during our discussion. An ideology is a system of mobilized beliefs that claims to represent the truth and reality but does not make any provision for assessing the veracity of those claims. To make itself accessible to the majority of the population, ideology simplifies its depiction of truth and reality by using symbols, appeals to emotions, socially accepted values and high-sounding moral principles. Finally, the values and principles embraced in an ideology usually imply some course of social action if they are to be adhered to and if they are to successfully represent the interests and ambitions of their promoters.

# FUNCTIONS OF IDEOLOGY

On a practical level, ideology serves two general functions. Ideologies help to either maintain social *order* or to promote social *change*. As we saw in Chapter 1, an understanding of order and change is intrinsic to the sociological enterprise. In any society, an uneasy tension exists between forces that make for stability and forces that threaten to disrupt stability and bring about change.

Without social order, social living would be impossible. As human societies grow larger and more complex, the tasks of planning and regulation at the international, national, regional and subregional levels assume increasingly bureaucratic forms. And in the liberal democratic states particularly, those tasks are plagued by a constant dilemma: How do we strike the delicate balance between individual liberty and social harmony? In one way or another, this has been the central issue in the writings of the great political philosophers such as Thomas Hobbes, John Locke, Jean Jacques Rousseau, John Stuart Mill, Jeremy Bentham, Alexis de Tocqueville and many others. At what point does the pursuit of individual self-interest conflict with the collective well-being of society? How much and what kinds of freedom can individuals be allowed without jeopardizing the whole society? Are individual liberty and social control incompatible? Can there be social order without social control?

We will see in the next section how ideology is used for social control. Of course, control may also be effected by using overt force or coercion. But using force *alone* is both costly and cumbersome and cannot guarantee long-term stability. No social system can afford to rely exclusively on force to control its members—not even in a prison or a concentration camp.

Shifting our attention to social change, we may also note the key role played by ideology. In the same way that one may speak of "ideologies of order" (for example, conservatism), one may also identify "ideologies of change" (for example, radicalism). To the extent that social change is often (though not always) associated with social movements, it is clear that ideology will have an important part to play. For it is in the ideology of such a movement that its goals are explicitly stated. And, as was said before, since ideologies usually encompass a call to action, no social movement lacks an ideological component. The ideologies of social movements give those movements a sense of coherence, identity and purpose. These issues will be reviewed when we consider the student movement and the FLQ movement in Quebec during the 1960s and early 1970s.

## IDEOLOGY, LEGITIMACY AND SOCIAL CONTROL

In this study, it is assumed that social control can either deny group and individual liberty or support it. But far from being a zero-sum phenomenon, control and freedom are multidimensional and are matters of degree. Further, they are not mutually exclusive and contradictory, for some degree of control is indispensable to freedom, both individual and collective. The central questions, therefore, are control by whom and freedom for whom? These, in turn, are questions of power and social class, for the dominant class, or a fraction of that class, in any society is advantageously placed to exact obedience or compliance from the subordinate classes.

The observation by Marx and Engels that "the ideas of the ruling class are in every epoch the ruling ideas" (1969: 39) is usually taken as those authors' summary statement on ideology. Among other things, it implies a relationship between both class and ideology and between power and ideology—the organized and structured power of a given class:

> The class which is the ruling material force of society is at the same time its ruling intellectual force. The class which has the means of material production at its disposal, has control at the same time over the means of mental production. . . . The ruling ideas are nothing more than the ideal expression of the dominant material relationships grasped as ideas; hence of the relationships which make the one class the ruling one, therefore the ideas of its dominance (Marx and Engels, 1969:39).

In this context, ruling class ideologies set limits to the consciousness of the ruled classes or, stated differently, they create *false consciousness*. Since ruling class ideologies are linked to practical political and economic interests, they will portray those interests as universal. To maintain social order and stability, it is important that those who benefit from such order and stability, those with a direct stake in maintaining the status quo, convince the less privileged that the system works to the mutual benefit of everyone in it.

The related ideologies of liberalism, individualism and free enterprise are cases in point. As essential underpinnings of the capitalist system, it is crucial for the working-class and the unemployed in that system to accept that their lots in life are arrived at fairly. The so-called "system" must not be perceived as being "rigged against them" but rather must be seen as being free and open, rewarding individual merit and ensuring the survival of the fittest. Such people, therefore, must be convinced that their apparent "failure" is due to their own shortcomings. They have only themselves to blame, since the system's integrity, its commitment to fair play and equal opportunity are beyond reproach.

Thus, as was said earlier, ideologies are the intellectual and emotional justifications used by individuals, groups and classes to organize their cultural symbols, to interpret their world and to give focus and meaning to their common actions (Gramsci, 1971: 377; Simon, 1982:58-66). But at this point, a new element in the definition of ideology must be added, for ideologies do not seek to depict social reality pure and simple. They emphasize certain aspects of reality while masking other aspects. Ideologies, therefore, in serving or legitimizing the interests of the dominant class, cannot be neutral. They actively mask or distort those aspects of social reality that do not correspond to the claims advanced by those in power.

Ideology has thus been viewed as a tool for social control which the ruling or dominant class has at its disposal. Hence, the definition of the situation embodied in the dominant ideology will reflect the concerns of that ruling class. In the previously cited example of capitalism, for instance, the ideology of equal opportunity is widely propagated and embraced by the population at large. Although individual members of the society may actually be less privileged and less mobile than others, the population as a whole believes that all people compete fairly and equally for scarce resources or rewards.

In Canada, for example, we are told that "education is a means to mobility." Further, we are told that education is free, at least up until the end of high school. Thus, those who are not mobile, those who are not "successful," have only themselves to blame. The ideology of equal opportunity, premised as it is upon the ideologies of liberalism and individualism, thus becomes accepted as true, even by those lacking the various trappings of success. Accepting the blame for their lack of mobility or success, various individuals and groups rationalize their situation by saying such things as, "I did not work hard enough"; "It's my fault for not applying myself"; "Nature dealt me a rotten hand"; "The fates are against me"; "That's the luck of the draw," and so on.

Such responses do not question whether or not there *is* equal opportunity. People channel the blame either onto themselves or remove it entirely from the realm of human control and talk about such things as fate and luck. Thus, those in control, those who promote the myth of equal opportunity, those who mask the fact that class, race, religion and sex are important determinants of mobility and success, escape unscathed. The ideology persists and social order is maintained. (This point will be reconsidered in the last section on ideology and democracy.)

Any discussion of ideology, then, will also involve considerations of social control. As a mechanism of control, it is far more efficient and less costly than physical coercion. Not only does it obviate the need for close supervision, but it also makes for more social and political stability. If a given population or specific social class can be made to act in ways that run counter to its own interests (whether immediate or long-term) without perceiving those actions to be harmful to itself, then there is no need to embark upon an elaborate program to control that population or class. It is rendered so blind to its particular interests that it fails to grasp them as class interests, while simultaneously embracing the interests of its oppressor as its own. And herein lies the question of legitimacy: The rule of the oppressor goes uncriticized.

## Ideology of Nationalism as Social Control

To elucidate the above points further, we may consider the ideology of nationalism in a class-divided society, particularly during times of war or large-scale social and political upheaval. Witness, for example, the reactions of the masses of Argentine and British citizens to the conflict between those two countries in 1982 over the Malvinas, or the Falkland Islands. Putting aside the grave domestic economic and political problems in their respective countries, both populations rallied solidly behind their governments and went to war for an idea—an idea that evoked a sense of patriotism and pride in their homelands.

For a brief moment, in Argentina particularly, the government did not have to worry about local uprisings and protests against the brutal and dictatorial treatment that it had been meting out to its citizens; nor did it have to worry about the immediate consequences of an unemployment rate in excess of 40 percent and inflation that topped the 200 percent mark. All energies were channelled to uphold national pride and dignity. Opposition parties, political prisoners, the unemployed and various youth groups were all prepared to put aside local differences and were mobilized against the British. And even within Britain, also a class-divided society, where Prime Minister Margaret Thatcher was losing a large measure of her popular support, similar trends were noted. Her decisive action in sending the navy and other armed forces to the Falklands boosted her political fortunes at home so much that she called national elections soon after the war and won a resounding victory.

In such situations, public sentiments can be manipulated simply by invoking the threat of a common external enemy. Another clear example of this, though in a slightly different context, occurred during the American invasion of the tiny Caribbean nation of Grenada in October, 1983. In that case, Grenada was said to have been undermined by an enemy identified as "international communism." The citizens of Grenada were given to understand that the enemy had taken control of their leaders and their country and that the only hope of salvation lay in the American Marines. Hence, during the invasion, the Grenadian people openly embraced the Marines and thanked God for having delivered them from the hell of communist perversion.

As we were told by United States President Ronald Reagan, the "popular response" of the Grenadian people showed their firm "commitment to liberal democratic traditions and institutions." However, prior to the "communist" government's coming to power, Grenada had been ruled by Eric Gairy, a dictator who had been in office for over 30 years and whose personal reign of terror was never once questioned by the American government. Thus, the firm commitment to democracy of which President Reagan spoke must be seen as an attempt to mask the absence of democratic traditions in that country. For even before Gairy, Grenada was a colonial possession of Britain, and during colonial rule local input into political and economic decisions was restricted to the point of being virtually nonexistent.

Ideologically speaking, it was important for the American government to retain Grenada as a faithful ally. The geopolitical significance of the country was enhanced even further because the Soviet Union already had ideological and military allies in Cuba and Nicaragua. Hence, the Americans could not afford another Soviet "base" in so sensitive an area, so close to its own shores. Invading Grenada was, therefore, politically necessary in order that a government more favourably disposed (ideologically) to Washington could be reinstalled. And this has, in fact, been accomplished.

But even if we grant the political and ideological interests of Washington, how can we explain the so-called "popular response" of the Grenadians to the Marines on ideological grounds? And what does this have to do with the ideology of nationalism? The answers can be found in what was said earlier about invoking the threat of an external enemy: Communism and communists are "evil." Hence the "free world" (note the ideological content of the term) must be forever vigilant lest the enemy infiltrate and take control of our countries, ourselves and our minds. And the Grenadians were made fully aware of the dangers of communism.

As far as the American Marines in particular are concerned, Grenadians had been socialized to accept them as liberators, as "good guys" whose patriotic and unselfish duty it was to save the world from communist and other "forces of evil." Grenadians, like so many others in their circumstances, wholly identified with and revered such Hollywood heroes as Audie Murphy, John Wayne and Alec Guinness and their heroic deeds in such films as *Back to Bataan*, *The Battle of the Bulge*, *The Longest Day* and *Bridge on the River Kwai*. Generations of colonialism and cultural domination had programmed the bulk of the Grenadian population to accept Washington's definition of what was in Grenada's best interests.

As an ideology, nationalism transcends class boundaries and unites an otherwise divided population in the defense of a common idea or ideal. Nowhere is this point made more clearly than in George Orwell's classic best seller, *Nineteen Eighty-Four*. In Orwell's discussion of public rallies and reactions in the fictitious society of Oceania, we can see how the citizens were constantly mobilized by the threat of foreign invasion by Eastasia and Eurasia alternately. Living with such threats, their attention and energies were cleverly directed away from their more immediate domestic problems, and the authorities did not have to worry about local dissent, uprisings or revolts against their rule:

> All that was required of them [the proles] was a primitive patriotism which could be appealed to whenever it was necessary to make them accept longer working hours or shorter rations. And even when they became discontented, their discontent led nowhere, because being without general ideas, they could only focus it on petty specific grievances. The larger evils invariably escaped their notice (Orwell, 1984: 66, courtesy of the estate of the late Sonia Brownell Orwell and Secker & Warburg Limited).

Evidently, Oceania was a special case. It was a situation in which the ruling authorities relied heavily in the short-term on coercion to secure social order. Such coercion, however, was viewed merely as a stop-gap measure to be used *only* until the government's full program could be realized. And that program aimed at total thought (ideological) control. It was designed, as we will see presently, to eliminate all conflict, opposition or threats to the social order as defined by those in power.

## Social Control and Complementarity

A final point in our theoretical treatment of social control and legitimacy concerns the issue of complementarity, which is systematically elaborated in the work of Bernd Baldus (1975, 1977). This author argues that social control can be effected in two ways: either via the deliberate intervention of some body or agency or via the manipulation of *complementary conditions*. Under the rubric of interventive control, Baldus includes both *physical coercion* and *ideological persuasion*. Our use of the term *interventive control* is slightly different. We reserve it solely for physical coercion, since it seems to imply more direct and immediate attempts at controlling behaviour than does ideological persuasion. As indicated in the above discussion of Orwell's Oceania, physical and ideological control differ in both form and content. Ideological control is slower, more subtle, less easily resisted and hence, more difficult to escape once it is established. And those subject to ideological control tend to be less aware of the fact than those subject to physical control. The former is less likely to produce protest on the part of the controlled, while those in control do not suffer the loss of legitimacy. It does not occur to the controlled to question the controllers' motives and intentions.

The manipulation of *complementary conditions* represents the specific insight of Baldus. As a strategy of control "it involves the use of already existing conditions" (Baldus, 1977: 250) within the population and society at large. In essence, it seeks to discover patterns of behaviour in the target population to see whether such behaviour *complements* the interests of the authorities or the ruling class. Where it is complementary, it will be used or exploited; and where such patterns of behaviour do not exist beforehand, the ruling class may attempt to create them.

An example of the deliberate use of complementarity is reported to us by Baldus, based on his reading of Philip Agee's (1975) *Inside the Company*. As an ex-CIA agent turned critic, Agee could give incisive insights into the daily operations of the American Central Intelligence Agency. And Baldus claims that in his devastating exposé of the CIA, Agee

> shows the planned and systematic search by the Agency for complementary conditions which can be employed to weaken leftist political movements and to prevent significant social change. The financial support of existing conservative parties, the use of local mass media to disseminate false information and to conceal its origins, or the bombing of churches in such a way that it is likely to be attributed to "radical subversives" take advantage of existing conditions which are favourable to the Agency's goals. These conditions have *not* been created by the CIA, but they represent important complements essential to the success of the Agency's operations. In the ideal case, they require only minimal efforts of guidance or exposure to have their desired effects (From the *Canadian Journal of Sociology*, Vol. 2 (3), 1977, pp. 250-51. Reprinted by permission).

In a similar vein, we may refer again to *Nineteen Eighty-Four* for another example of the use of complementarity. Among the "proles" of Oceania, who made up 85 percent of the population of 300 million (Orwell, 1984: 64, 67), Orwell tells us there existed a fairly high level of apathetic behaviour. Even the mass rallies were carefully orchestrated and had an air of superficiality about them. The proles were fatalistic and resigned to their lot in life. They were mostly apolitical and interested only in the minute irrelevant details of daily life. In fact, as Winston, the main character, remarked after an aborted conversation with one of them: "The old man's memory was nothing but a rubbish-heap of details. One could question him all day without getting any real information" (1984: 82).

Using the pervasive mood of apathy and disinterestedness, the government of Big Brother realized its program of mass control by staging certain public happenings, such as the Lottery, which further distracted the proles from the reality of their condition.

> The Lottery, with its weekly pay-out of enormous prizes was one public event to which the proles paid serious attention. It was probable that there were some millions of proles for whom the Lottery was the principal if not the only reason for remaining alive. It was their delight, their folly, their anodyne, their intellectual stimulant. Where the Lottery was concerned, even people who could barely read or write seemed capable of intricate calculations and staggering feats of memory. There was a whole tribe of men who made a living simply by selling systems, forecasts and lucky amulets (Orwell, 1984: 82, courtesy of the estate of the late Sonia Brownell Orwell and Secker & Warburg Limited).

With a largely uninformed, distracted and ignorant population, the job of social control is that much easier. If those conditions are already in existence, they will be viewed as complementary to the interests of those in control or those who wish to exercise control. If, on the other hand, such conditions do not already exist, they may be created by manipulating public education systems and the mass media. Again, the techniques of subtle ideological persuasion will be used.  ·

Using complementarity as a strategy of social control, then, will yield two benefits to the ruling authorities. The first, according to Baldus, concerns expense, for complementarity secures the desired behaviour at costs much lower than those that would be incurred if the same behaviour were secured by interventive (coercive) control.

The second benefit is that the interests of the dominant class are protected while simultaneously permitting a wide variety of behaviours among the population at large to continue. For, as Baldus observes, "Complementary behaviour is judged primarily by its instrumentality or utility for dominant class interests" (Baldus, 1977:251). Hence, it is of no immediate importance if the proles in Orwell's Oceania, for example, attributed meanings to their behaviour that were totally different from those assigned by the dominant interests:

> So long as they continued to work and breed, their other activities were without importance. Left to themselves . . . they reverted to a style of life that appeared to be natural to them. . . . They were born, they grew up in the gutters, they went to work at twelve, they passed through a brief blossoming period of beauty and sexual desire, they married at twenty, they were middle-aged at thirty, they died, for the most part, at sixty. Heavy physical work, the care of home and children, petty quarrels with neighbours, films, football, beer, and above all, gambling, filled up the horizon of their minds. *To keep them in control was not difficult* (Orwell, 1984: 65, emphasis added).

It is thus clear that the behaviour of the proles was complementary to the interests of the Party—and they were forever distracted:

> Even the civil police interfered with them very little. There was a vast amount of criminality in London, a whole world-within-a-world of thieves, bandits, prostitutes, drug-peddlers, and racketeers of every description; *but since it all happened among the proles themselves, it was of no importance* (1984: 66, emphasis added. Courtesy of the estate of the late Sonia Brownell Orwell and Secker & Warburg Limited).

Quite apart from the subjective and personal meanings assigned to their behaviour, therefore, what really mattered was the final outcome of that behaviour—its contribution to the goals of the dominant class:

> Consequently, periphery units *often are not aware of the complementarity of their own behaviour*. Moreover, the use of complementary periphery behaviour does not require an interaction between dominant class and periphery. It is often the very absence of actions in the periphery, for instance as a result of ignorance or because internal strife weakens or preoccupies the periphery, which facilitates the realization of dominant class interests. The use of complementary behaviour therefore allows the dominant class to obtain needed means from a periphery which *appears to pursue goals of its own choice, and free of outside interference* (Baldus, emphasis added. From the *Canadian Journal of Sociology*, Vol. 2(3), 1977, p. 251. Reprinted by permission).

Again, this appearance of freedom is important from the point of view of legitimacy, control and order. The less conscious one is of being controlled or manipulated and the more one feels in charge of one's destiny, the more effective is that control and the more secure the social order.

## IDEOLOGY, ROUTINIZATION AND CHANGE

Before discussing the direct relationship between ideology and change, it is important that we examine the question of *routinization*, or the process by which the extraordinary becomes ordinary. In Weber's political sociology, he paid a great deal of attention to the issues of domination and authority in society. He spoke of three basic ideal types: charismatic, traditional and legal. Here we will be concerned mainly with charismatic leadership and domination. As Bendix tells us, Weber used the term *charisma* to designate

> an extraordinary quality possessed by persons . . . that is thought to give these persons a unique magical power. . . . the man who possesses genuine charisma exercises domination, but this power of command differs from legal and traditional domination in that it is extraordinary (Bendix, 1962: 299).

The rise of charismatic leaders is closely associated with times of crisis, social unrest or revolution. When the routine of everyday life is upset and traditional or legal forms of domination can no longer restore order, the situation is ripe for the appearance of someone with that "gift of grace" called charisma. Charismatic leaders are truly revolutionary in that they challenge established practice and manipulate public sentiments in a manner that often transcends traditional class, status and ethnic divisions in society. Examples of charismatic leaders from history are Jesus, Mohammed, Napoleon and Hitler.

After the passage of the initial crisis that brings the charismatic leader to the fore, there begins a process of institutionalization of the new order that Weber refers to as *routinization*. The cooling off of extraordinary states of devotion and fervour paves the way for the development of institutions, which Weber says can lead to either traditionalism or bureaucratization (Gerth and Mills, 1958: 54). The petty and mundane issues of everyday life thus lead to the routinization of charisma, as offices, rules and regulations are put in place to handle the particular concerns and needs of ordinary citizens.

Such institutionalization and bureaucratization for Weber is a necessary evil. It is necessary in order to meet the numerous and diverse demands of individuals, especially in large and differentiated societies; and it is evil in that it leads to cold, impersonal and antidemocratic institutions. Bureaucratic organizations, as we know, concentrate decision-making in the hands of the few. And this is the context in which Weber spoke of the "iron cage" of bureaucracy. It makes for greater overall efficiency but at the expense of direct mass input.

Expressing similar sentiments, Robert Michels talks of the "iron law of oligarchy" in his analysis of *Political Parties* (1962). Along with Gaetano Mosca and Vilfredo Pareto, Michels is known as an *elite theorist*. These authors believe that democracy in the strict sense of rule by the majority is impossible. There always has to be a small, cohesive minority that will make the rules to govern the masses. This is what is meant by oligarchy: "The principal cause of oligarchy is to be found in the technical indispensability of leadership. . . . The mass will never rule except *in abstracto*" (Michels, 1962: 365, 366). Like the other elite theorists, therefore, Michels is convinced that the masses are inferior to their leaders and follow them out of blind devotion:

> Taken in the mass, the poor are powerless and disarmed vis-à-vis their leaders. Their intellectual and cultural inferiority make it impossible for them to see whither the leader is going, or to estimate in advance the significance of his actions (1962: 369).

On the basis of these observations, Michels argues for "the historic necessity of oligarchy." Oligarchy is the natural outcome of political organization (or *bureaucratization*, in Weber's terms), for "the social wealth cannot be satisfactorily administered in any other manner than by the creation of an extensive bureaucracy" (Michels, 1962: 347). Thus, in analysing political parties, even socialist ones, Michels contends that oligarchy is inescapable: "It is organization which gives birth to the domination of the elected over the electors. . . . who says organization, says oligarchy" (1962: 365).

In addressing the socialist parties particularly, Michels raises the question of the relationship between socialism and democracy. Because of the social distance between the leadership and the masses, he feels that the socialist party leaders will succumb to *bureaucratic conservatism* and place the needs of organizational survival over ideology or adherence to doctrine. "Knowing what is best for the masses," the leaders of socialist parties will thus undertake a revolution that inevitably results in a "dictatorship in the hands of those leaders who have been sufficiently astute and sufficiently powerful to grasp the sceptre of dominion in the name of socialism" (1962: 19). And once in power, institutions and bureaucracies will develop and their rule will become routinized.

Picking up this theme, Crane Brinton discusses *The Anatomy of Revolution* (1965). He identifies three phases of a revolution: the rule of moderates, the reign of terror and virtue, and the Thermidor. We are concerned here with the last of the three, *the Thermidor*, which refers to the new French calendar at the time of the French Revolution and the fall of Robespierre on July 27th, 1794. Briefly summarized, the rule of moderates, or the *moderate interregnum*, covers the first phase of the revolution when the moderate rulers are sandwiched between the ousted ruling class and the more extremist tendencies within the revolutionary movement. In the second phase, the extremists take power from the moderates and institute a *reign of terror* to stamp out all opposition and inculcate new revolutionary sensibilities (virtues) in the masses.

The Thermidorian reaction, according to Brinton, begins with the leaders of the radical movement, who, after the terror and

> once the crisis period is over, will, save for the few born martyrs, cease to be crusaders, fanatics, ascetics. Their revolutionary beliefs will be softly cushioned in a comfortable ritual, will be a consolation and a habit rather than a constant prick of the ideal (Brinton, 1965: 191).

Describing the Thermidor as "a convalescence from the fever of revolution" (1965: 205), Brinton argues that during this third phase, as the revolutionaries grow old and feeble or simply die and as the revolution becomes more institutionalized, bureaucratized and routinized, a period of conservatism sets in: Revolutionary passion wanes; strict laws are relaxed; concessions to opposition interests are made; and many of the more radical economic measures are toned down. At this point, Edwards says,

> The revolutionary government itself, as it gets older, ceases to be revolutionary and presently ceases to think of itself as revolutionary. The revolution is complete (Edwards, 1970: 200).

## Marxism and Change

The ideology of change most often referred to is Marxism. The ideology of Marxism is seen to be opposed to the social and economic system of capitalism: Based on Marx's critique of the dehumanizing consequences of capitalism, the ideology of Marxism has come to represent, in general terms, the interests of those who are unhappy with economic exploitation, class inequality and political impotence, as these derive from the structure of capitalist society. Like all ideologies, Marxism has a general appeal. But as a specific ideology, it is most attractive to those who are less privileged or who have most reason to be critical about the capitalist system.

This does not imply, however, that the less privileged are automatically the most critical. People in this category are often unaware of the causes of their misery. Hence, one will find poor, uneducated and unemployed people in the United States, for example, extolling the virtues of capitalism and liberal democracy. This is a condition referred to by Marx as *false consciousness*. It occurs because the pervasive influences of early socialization, schooling, religious teaching and the mass media are able to portray social inequality in such a way that the less privileged members of society come to see their problems in personal rather than in systemic terms. They internalize the definition of themselves that is embodied in the dominant ideology. And it is precisely this false consciousness that Marxism seeks to dispel.

Because ideologies are presented in ways that have a mass appeal, many people embrace them at a very superficial level of understanding. Such is the case with Marxism. Many disadvantaged individuals and groups can identify with the general sentiments Marxism expresses and see it as championing their cause. Hence, although they may not be familiar with the precise details of the Marxian critique of capitalism, they nevertheless embrace its general thrust. Thus, we must be careful not to confuse the ideology of Marxism as it has been summarized here with Marxism as a social scientific critique of capitalism.

Let us, therefore, consider the student movement to assess how it incorporated elements of Marxist ideology and used those elements, albeit superficially, to inform its purpose.

## The Student/Youth Movement

During the 1960s, Western Europe and North America witnessed a period of social upheaval that altered many of their deep-seated ways of thinking and behaving. The mood of the day was aptly captured in Bob Dylan's song "The Times They are a' Changing," which served as an impetus for the rebirth of protest music, particularly in the United States. Amidst such cries as "Power to the people," "Give peace a chance," and "Hell no, we won't go" (to Vietnam), a variety of social movements took root as people began to demand changes in governmental and other social institutions. Many adopted the slogan "Question authority" as their official motto.

In this context, one might think of the student movement, the youth or hippie movement, the civil rights or black power movement, the antiwar movement and the women's liberation movement. All shared a concern with where contemporary society was heading. All argued that elected political leaders and the men who controlled the big corporations had lost sight of their social responsibilities. In relentlessly pursuing political domination and economic profits, government and business leaders were trampling the "little man," and a genuine concern for the quality of human life took a back seat to the dictates of corporate profitability. The rich were getting richer and the poor were getting poorer.

The student and youth movements, in particular, attracted young, idealistic people, the products of the postwar baby boom, who were largely of comfortable middle-class origin and who were growing up in a time of prosperity. Hearing horror stories of the war from their parents, seeing the films and learning about the Nazi holocaust, among other things, these young people were determined to avoid the excesses of their parents' generation. They organized peace marches, love-ins, and antinuclear demonstrations, all with a view to overcoming the sense of alienation that characterized the "generation gap" between themselves and the older members of society. In the process, they embraced an anti-imperialist stance, formed organizations in solidarity with Cuban revolutionaries, the Vietnamese people, the blacks of South Africa and the victims of capitalist oppression and exploitation everywhere. To this extent, the ideology of Marxism, with its *humanistic* content, was appealing to the youth of the time and to those who wrote sympathetically about them.

Among the most influential writings of the period are John and Margaret Rowntree's, *The Political Economy of Youth* (1968) and Herbert Marcuse's, *One-Dimensional Man* (1964), *An Essay on Liberation* (1969) and *Counter-Revolution and Revolt* (1972). A common theme reflected in these and other works was the implicit, and often explicit, Marxian critique of industrial capitalism. As Marcuse observed, the popular movements of the day were inspired by Marxist ideology and sought principally to unite young people and workers in opposition to economic exploitation and political repression:

> The real interest, the attainment of conditions in which man could shape his own life, was that of no longer subordinating his life to the requirements of profitable production, to an apparatus controlled by forces beyond his control. And the attainment of such conditions meant *the abolition of capitalism* (Marcuse, 1969: 15, emphasis added).

An identification with the more humanistic content of Marxism was also revealed in the youth-as-class notion of Rowntree and Rowntree (1968). Using the general sentiments associated with Marxian "class analysis" (though ignoring the theoretical rigour of the term), these authors described students and young people in general as a separate class. Armed with statistics, they argued that in the United States, at least half of the males between the ages of 18 and 24 could be found within the ranks of students, soldiers and the unemployed. Their point was that the schools and the military functioned to keep the unemployment rate at an acceptably low level, thus diffusing the potential for mass dissatisfaction and frustration among young people: "The young are exploited as soldiers, as students, and as unemployed workers" (Rowntree and Rowntree, 1968: 13). In summarizing this point, Levitt (1984: 5) notes that students came to view themselves as a new "youth proletariat," exploited by capital and manipulated by the state:

> As unemployed they are robbed of their productive potential; as young soldiers they are underpaid and trained to kill; as students they are forced to produce and reproduce themselves as skilled labour to suit the wants of corporate capital (Levitt, 1984: 122).

As with most opposition ideologies, the student movement incorporated both a moral critique of existing society and a call to action, concerning itself with such issues as nuclear testing and disarmament, environmentalism, militarism and civil rights. In claiming to transcend narrow political and ideological positions, the students saw themselves as moral crusaders armed with Truth: "Speak truth to power and the truth shall set you free." They challenged the traditional institutions and practices of the older generation, established communes, engaged freely in premarital sex, experimented with all kinds of drugs and rejected the outer trappings of material success in their society. They grew long hair, wore beards, went barefoot and generally sought to embarrass or shock the guardians of the old order. As opposed to military and economic power, they favoured flower power.

At the ideological level, the student youth identified their social and moral rejection of established society with Marxism. For them, Marxism represented everything the older generation eschewed; hence, Marxism had to be good. This is not to say that they were totally blind or ignorant of what Marxism was, but their understanding of it was very superficial and even distorted. As Levitt tells us, among the students, very few converts to the Marxism of the New Left were won as a result of a "careful presentation and sifting of evidence, through reasoned debate, or by weighty intellectual argument" (1984: 139). Rather, the appeal was more emotional given its moralistic content and its call to action and involvement. Hence, in spite of their Castro beards, their guerrilla army fatigues, their revolutionary slogans and posters of Ché Guevara, all the student radicals needed to know was that the general sentiments attributed to Marxism coincided with theirs.

But, having said all of this, what actual changes did the movement manage to effect? Although it is not easy to answer such a question in precise terms, suffice it to say that by the time the movement died in the early 1970s, an entire generation of thinking had been changed. There was much greater social awareness about nuclear war, imperialist control of Third World countries, poverty, racism, sexism, women's rights and native rights within the leading liberal democratic countries. On many high-school and university campuses, students were able to elect their own representatives; they won a voice in determining some of the content of their curricula, in recruiting teachers and in the provision of recreational, food and housing services. Sex education clinics, campus day-care facilities and offices of ombudsmen are also among the gains. And last but not least is the political awakening of students and other youth, whose votes are now actively sought by professional politicians.

## The FLQ Movement

In Canada, the *Front de Libération du Québec* (FLQ) may serve as an example of an attempt at revolutionary change that embraced the ideology of Marxism. The French-speaking people of Quebec, particularly the workers, have long complained that they are second-class citizens in their own country. They charge that the owners, managers and top executives of the large corporations and businesses are English Canadians, that the huge corporate profits are not reinvested in Quebec, that they are discriminated against in matters of language and religion and that the federal government has always worked in complicity with the Anglo-Saxon capitalist interests to the detriment of *les Québecois*. In fact, their grievances were well summed up in the title of a book written by one of their leaders, Pierre Vallieres, and called *The White Niggers of America* (1971).

Arguing that Quebec was a nation separate from Canada and that Quebec was a colony of Canada, the "white niggers of America" sought to do what the "black niggers" had been doing for many years. They began a struggle aimed at the decolonization and total independence of their country—Quebec. In the process, the FLQ emerged as the militant wing of the independence movement. They employed tactics similar to those used by other groups in various parts of the world that were struggling toward the same goal: clandestine meetings, kidnappings, terrorist bombings, urban guerrilla attacks on targets that symbolized colonial tutelage, underground press releases that denounced federalism and Anglo-Saxon capitalism and so on. They even issued a manifesto outlining the philosophy of the movement, its major goals and demands.

The use of Marxist ideology and rhetoric in the *FLQ Manifesto* is clear. Its style and content bear a striking resemblance to the *Communist Manifesto* written by Marx and Engels in 1848. But it is interesting to note that while the FLQ called for an end to Anglo-Saxon capitalism, it did not call for the abolition of capitalism per se, nor did it mention anything about socialism. This reinforces the earlier point made in connection with the student movement and the notion of a "youth proletariat": Both movements embraced Marxism as an ideology, *not* as a social scientific critique of capitalism. They both had a superficial appreciation of the humanistic content of Marxism, and that was sufficient to sustain them ideologically. An excerpt from the *FLQ Manifesto* (opposite) clearly shows the extent to which the movement adopted that ideology in its demands for social change in Quebec.

## IDEOLOGY AND DEMOCRACY

In closing, it will be instructive to reflect briefly on the relationship between ideology and democracy as practised in our Western liberal societies. It is instructive because for many people, the term "democracy" has a very rigid meaning, and it is reserved almost exclusively for reference to the countries of Western Europe and North America. This point was brought home to me recently upon my return from a trip to Cuba, when someone asked me, "Is Cuba socialist or democratic?" Implicit in the question is the idea that socialism and democracy are antithetical to each other— a country cannot be both socialist and democratic at the same time. The same idea, albeit in an altered form, was reflected in President Reagan's comments following the American invasion of Grenada, which were referred to earlier. Mr. Reagan said, "We (the Marines) arrived in Grenada just in time to save democracy." Apparently,

### THE FLQ MANIFESTO

The people in the *Front de Libération du Québec* are neither Messiahs nor modern-day Robin Hoods. They are a group of Quebec workers who have decided to do everything they can to assure that the people of Quebec take their destiny into their own hands, once and for all.

The *Front de Libération du Québec* wants total independence for Quebeckers; it wants to see them united in a free society, a society purged for good of its gang of rapacious sharks, the big bosses who dish out patronage and their henchmen, who have turned Quebec into a private preserve of cheap labour and unscrupulous exploitation.

. . . what is called democracy in Quebec has always been, and still is, nothing but the "democracy" of the rich. . . . Consequently we wash our hands of the British parliamentary system; the *Front de Libération du Québec* will never let itself be distracted by the electoral crumbs that the Anglo-Saxon capitalists toss into the Quebec barnyard every four years. Many Quebeckers have realized the truth and are ready to take action. . . .

We are fed up with the taxes we pay that Ottawa's agent in Quebec would give to the English-speaking bosses as an "incentive" for them to speak French, to negotiate in French. Repeat after me: "Cheap labour is *main d'oeuvre à bon marché* in French."

Workers in industry, in mines and in the forests! Workers in the service industries, teachers, students and unemployed! Take what belongs to you, your jobs, your determination and your freedom. And you, the workers at General Electric, you make the factories run; you are the only ones able to produce; without you, General Electric is nothing!

Workers of Quebec, begin from this day forward to take back what is yours; take yourselves what belongs to you. Only you know your factories, your machines, your hotels, your universities, your unions. . . .

Make your revolution yourselves in your neighbourhoods, in your places of work. . . . Only you are capable of building a free society.

We are Quebec workers and we are prepared to go all the way. . . . we want to replace this society of slaves by a free society, operating by itself and for itself, a society open on the world.

Our struggle can only be victorious. A people that has been awakened cannot long be kept in misery and contempt.

Long live Free Quebec!
Long live our comrades the political prisoners!
Long live the Quebec Revolution!
Long live the *Front de Libération du Québec!*

the government of Grenada, which had developed close relations with the Soviets and Cubans, had placed Grenadian democracy in jeopardy.

Democracy is understood to be a unique social and political attribute of countries in "the free world," itself an ideological term. But what does democracy really mean? Could one argue that the word "democracy," in spite of its apparent neutrality, has ideological functions, that it masks certain aspects of social reality, that the theory and practice of democracy do not necessarily coincide?

The answers to such questions can be found by analysing liberalism and the rise of the capitalist market economy. As far as Western countries are concerned, their form of democracy is best described as *liberal democracy*. The term "liberal" is meant to indicate that before they became democratic, before the vote was extended to all adult citizens, these countries had evolved what we know today as the liberal market economy. In Britain, France and the United States, for example, this type of economy existed long before slaves were freed or women and nonpropertied people had the right to vote.

The maturation of the market society and economy and its eventual democratization, Macpherson says, coincided with the creation of a) the society and politics of choice; b) the society and politics of competition; and c) the society and politics of the market (1965: 6). Indeed, a striking feature of these countries is that they are all capitalist. Liberal democracy and capitalism appear to go well together, for, with few exceptions, the capitalist countries of today can generally boast a liberal democratic political system.

Ideologically, freedom of choice and the freedom to compete are cornerstones of capitalism. In addition, the emphasis on these freedoms is closely linked to the idea of individualism, as was discussed earlier. We speak, for example, of *individual* free choice as a major tenet of liberalism. Freedom is defined as the *individual's* ability to choose; and the society that permits the greatest personal freedom and range of choice is seen as the best society. We are told that competition is healthy. A society that does not encourage competition does not encourage excellence. Thus, the "free" and "fair" competition among individuals for desired goods and services contributes to the overall well-being of the system. And finally, there is the market, the arena of fair play in which individual freedom of choice and competition among equals can be realized.

From the point of view of ideological control, the beauty of the free enterprise, liberal, market society is that not only is success attributed to *individual* initiative and effort, but failure also is easily explained as the result of too little *individual* initiative and effort. The key point, masked by the liberal ideology, is that the system is not necessarily free and fair and competition does not necessarily take place among equals.

We are dealing here with capitalist market society, and one thing is certain: As an economic system, capitalism is premised upon a fundamental inequality between those who own and those who do not own the major means of production. All other inequalities are derived from this one. The point, therefore, is that, by definition, capitalism is a system of entrenched inequality; and while all may be free to choose and compete, *some will always be freer than others*. And this is the crucial aspect of social reality that is masked by the ideology of liberal democracy.

# SUMMARY

In this chapter, we have defined ideology as a system of beliefs and ideas that orients the patterns of thought and the actions of human beings in the world. Ideologies are rooted in society, and no person anywhere can be without them. It is generally the case that ideologies are promoted by specific groups and classes with a view to protecting their own interests. In the process, ideologies mask and distort certain aspects of social reality which, if they were not masked, would threaten the security of the dominant group's interests. Finally, to be effective, ideologies must have a mass appeal. They must also claim a higher morality, a truth, with which most people can subjectively identify. And in this respect, ideologies seek not only to distort social reality but also to simplify it by using symbols whose meanings are readily understood by the population at large.

After defining ideology, we analysed its specific social and political functions. The first function was social control. We observed that some control is essential for the preservation of social order, for as populations increase and societies become more complex, social co-ordination and planning also grow in complexity. Contrary to the utilitarian view, which holds that the surest guarantee of social order is the pursuit of individual self-interest, we argue that social order must be created deliberately. It does not come about as the automatic result of each individual doing what is best for him or her. For it is not certain that what is in one person's best interest will necessarily be advantageous to another. Hence, if we all tried to maximize our own interests, there is no guarantee that the greatest good for the greatest number would automatically follow.

Ideology can also promote social change. In this context, we examined the radical, revolutionary ideologies that inform certain social movements that are aimed at restructuring the existing society or parts of it. Ideologies of change, it was said, embrace a call to action on the part of individuals and groups who perceive the status quo as somehow working against their own interests. Ideologies of change, however, can become quite conservative once the movements that they inspire and sustain gain power. This is the case with the once revolutionary ideology of Marxism-Leninism in the Soviet Union, where the status quo appears to be very intolerant of change. In terms of the analysis presented here, therefore, the government of the Soviet Union, at least in domestic matters, acts very conservatively.

# DISCUSSION QUESTIONS

1.  From the point of view of ideology, why are the questions of social control and social order seen to be of paramount importance?

2.  In talking about ideology, Marx once remarked that "religion is the opiate of the masses." What do you think he meant? Your answer should make reference to the social functions of religion.

3.  Apart from the three examples in this chapter, give a fourth example of how the ideology of nationalism has been used by a government to further its own political or economic interests.

4. Under what conditions do ideologies of change become conservative? Provide and discuss an example.

5. In what ways does the ideology of liberal democracy complement the economic system we call capitalism?

# BIBLIOGRAPHY

Abel, Richard L., ed. *The Politics of Informal Justice*. New York: Academic, 1982.

Abercrombie, Nicholas; Stephen Hill; and Bryan S. Turner. *The Dominant Ideology Thesis*. London: George Allen & Unwin, 1980.

Adams, Robert M. *The Evolution of Urban Society*. Chicago: Aldine, 1966.

Akenson, Donald. *The Irish in Ontario: A Study in Rural History*. Kingston and Montreal: McGill-Queen's University Press, 1984.

Alford, Robert R. *Party and Society*. Chicago: Rand McNally, 1963.

Alinsky, Saul. *Rules for Radicals*. New York: Vintage Books, 1971.

Allahar, Anton. "Colonialism and Underdevelopment." *Two-thirds,* Vol. 3, No. 2, 1982.

———. "The Cuban Sugar Planters (1790-1820)." *The Americas,* Vol. XLI, No. 1, July 1984.

Almond, Gabriel, and G. Bingham Powell. *Comparative Politics: A Developmental Approach*. Boston: Little Brown, 1966.

——— and Sidney Verba. *The Civic Culture: Political Attitudes and Democracy in Five Nations*. Princeton: Princeton University Press, 1963.

Althusser, L. *For Marx*. Harmondsworth: Penguin Books, 1969.

Alwin, Duane F. "Trends in Parental Socialization, Detroit, 1958–1983." *American Journal of Sociology,* Vol. 90, No. 2, pp. 359-382, 1984.

Ambert, Anne-Marie. *Divorce in Canada*. Toronto: Academic, 1980.

Anderson, Alan B., and James S. Frideres. *Ethnicity in Canada: Theoretical Perspectives*. Toronto: Butterworth, 1981.

Anderson, Grace. *Networks of Contact: The Portuguese and Toronto*. Waterloo: Wilfred Laurier University, 1974.

Andrews, F.M.; J.N. Morgan; and J.A. Sonquist. *Multiple Classification Analysis*. Ann Arbor, Mich.; Survey Research Centre, University of Michigan, 1976.

Anisef, Paul; Norman Okihiro; and Carl James. *Losers and Winners*. Toronto: Butterworth, 1982.

Ariès, Philippe. *Centuries of Childhood: A Social History of Family Life*. New York: Vintage Books, 1962.

Arling, Greg. "The Elderly Widow and Her Family, Neighbours and Friends." *Journal of Marriage and the Family,* pp. 757-768, November 1976.

Armstrong, Pat, and Hugh Armstrong. *The Double Ghetto*. Toronto: McClelland and Stewart, 1978.

Aron, R. *Eighteen Lectures on Industrial Society*. London: Weidenfeld & Nicolson, 1967.

Atkinson, A.B. *The Economics of Inequality*. London: Oxford University Press, 1975.

Bachrach, Peter, and Morton S. Baratz. *Power and Poverty*. New York: Oxford University Press, 1970.

Badham, R., and C. Davies. "The Sociology of Industrial and Post-Industrial Societies." *Current Sociology,* Vol. 32, No. 1, pp.1-145, Spring 1984.

Baer, Douglas. "Cultural Indicators Research: Canadian Prospects." In *Communication Studies in Canada*, edited by Liona Salter, pp. 212-231. Toronto: Butterworth, 1981.

Baker, Maureen. "Concerns and Controversies Within Family Sociology." In *The Family: Changing Trends in Canada*, pp. 1-20. Toronto: McGraw-Hill Ryerson, 1984.

———. "Divorce: Its Consequences and Meanings." In *The Canadian Family*, edited by K. Ishwaran, pp. 289-300. Toronto: Gage, 1983.

———. *What Will Tomorrow Bring? A Study of the Aspirations of Adolescent Women*. Ottawa: Canadian Advisory Council on the Status of Women, 1985.

Balakrishnan, T.R.; G. Edward Ebanks; and Carl Grindstaff. *Patterns of Fertility in Canada, 1971*. Ottawa: Statistics Canada, 1979.

Baldus, Bernd. "Social control in capitalist societies: an examination of 'the problem of order' in liberal democracies." *Canadian Journal of Sociology,* Vol. 2, No. 3, 1977.

———. "The study of power: suggestions for an alternative." *Canadian Journal of Sociology,* Vol. 1, No. 2, 1975.

——— and Verna Tribe. "The development of perceptions and evaluation of social inequality among public school children." *Canadian Review of Sociology and Anthropology,* Vol. 15, No. 1, pp. 50-60, 1978.

Baran, Paul. *The Political Economy of Growth.* New York and London: Monthly Review Press, 1957.

Barnard, Chester. *The Functions of the Executive.* Cambridge, Mass.: Harvard University Press, 1938.

Barnes, Samuel H. et al. *Political Action: Mass Participation in Five Western Democracies.* Beverly Hills: Sage Publications, 1979.

Beattie, Christopher. *Minority Men in a Majority Setting.* Toronto: McClelland and Stewart, 1975.

Beaudoin, A. et al. "Non-institutional Housing Conditions for the Aged." *Urban Renewal and Low-Income Housing,* Vol. 9, No. 2, pp. 14-22, 1973.

Beaujot, Roderic. "The decline of official language minorities in Quebec and English Canada." *Canadian Journal of Sociology,* Vol. 9, No. 4, pp. 367-389, 1982.

——— and Kevin McQuillan. *Growth and Dualism: The Demographic Development of Canadian Society.* Toronto: Gage, 1982.

Becker, Howard S. "Problems of inference and proof in participant observation." *American Sociological Review,* 23, pp. 652-660, 1958.

———. *Sociological Work.* New Brunswick, N.J.: Transaction Books, 1970.

———; Blanche Geer; and Everett C. Hughes. *Making the Grade: The Academic Side of College Life.* New York: Wiley, 1968.

———; Blanche Geer; Everett C. Hughes; and Anselm L. Strauss. *Boys in White: Student Culture in Medical School.* New Brunswick, N.J.:Transaction Books, 1961.

Bell, Daniel. *The Coming of Post-Industrial Society.* New York: Basic Books, 1973.

———. *The End of Ideology.* London: Collier Books, 1961.

———. "The Social Framework of the Information Society." In *The Computer Age: A Twenty-Year View,* edited by Michael L. Dertouzos and Joel Moses. Cambridge, Mass.: The MIT Press, 1979.

———. "Technology and Politics." *Survey,* No. 16, 1971.

Bell, David, and Lorne Tepperman. *The Roots of Disunity.* Toronto: McClelland and Stewart, 1979.

Bem, Sandra. "The Measurement of Psychological Androgyny." *Journal of Consulting and Clinical Psychology,* Vol. 42, pp. 155-162, 1974.

Bendix, Reinhard. *Max Weber: An Intellectual Portrait.* New York: Anchor Books, 1962.

———. *Nation-Building and Citizenship.* Berkeley and Los Angeles: University of California Press, 1977.

———. *Work and Authority in Industry.* New York: Harper and Row, 1956.

Bereleson, Bernard, and Patricia Salter. "Majority and Minority Americans." *Public Opinion Quarterly,* Vol. 10, pp. 168-190, 1946.

Berg, Ivar. *Education and Jobs: The Great Training Robbery.* New York: Beacon Press, 1970.

Berger, Alan S. *The City.* Dubuque: Wm. C. Brown Company, 1978.

Berger, Bennett. *Working Class Suburb.* Berkeley & Los Angeles: University of California Press, 1960.

Berger, Peter, and Brigette Berger. *Sociology: A Biographical Approach.* 2d ed. New York: Basic Books, 1975.

——— and Thomas Luckmann. *The Social Construction of Reality.* Garden City, N.Y.: Doubleday, 1966.

Bergmann, Gustav. "Ideology." *Ethics,* LX1, April 1951.

Berle, Adolphe A., and Gardiner C. Means. *The Modern Corporation and Private Property,* rev. ed. New York: Harcourt, Brace and World, 1967.

Berman, Harold J. *Law and Revolution: The Formation of the Western Legal Tradition.* Cambridge, Mass.: Harvard University Press, 1983.

Bernard, Jessie. *The Sex Game.* New York: Atheneum, 1972.

Bernstein, Basil. *Class, Codes and Control: Theoretical Studies Towards a Sociology of Language,* Vol. 1. London: Routledge and Kegan Paul, 1971.

———. *Class, Codes and Control: Towards A Theory of Educational Transmissions,* Vol. 3. London: Routledge and Kegan Paul, 1975.

Berton, Pierre. *Hollywood's Canada.* Toronto: McClelland and Stewart, 1975.

Bettelheim, Bruno. *The Informed Heart.* London, 1961.

———. In *Summerhill: For and Against,* pp. 98-118. New York: Hart, 1970.

Beurkel-Rothfuss, Nancy and Sandra Mayes. "Soap Opera Viewing: The Cultivation Effect." *Journal of Communication,* Vol. 31, No. 3, pp. 108-115, 1981.

Bierstedt, Robert. "An analysis of social power." In *Power and Progress: Essays in Sociological Theory,* by R. Bierstedt, pp. 220-241. New York: McGraw-Hill, 1974.

Black, Donald. *The Behavior of Law.* New York: Academic, 1976.

Blalock, Hubert M., Jr. *Causal Inferences in Nonexperimental Research.* New York: Norton & Co., 1972.

Blau, Peter M. *The Dynamics of Bureaucracy.* Chicago: University of Chicago Press, 1963.

Blauner, Robert. *Alienation and Freedom.* Chicago: University of Chicago Press, 1964.

———. *Racial Oppression in America.* New York: Harper & Row, 1972.

Blishen, Bernard. "Perceptions of National Identity." *Canadian Review of Sociology and Anthropology,* Vol. 15, No. 2, pp. 128-132, 1978.

———. "A Socio-economic Index for Occupations in Canada." *Canadian Review of Sociology and Anthropology,* Vol. 4, No. 1, pp. 41-53, 1967.

——— and Hugh McRoberts. "A Revised Socio-economic index for Occupations in Canada." *Canadian Review of Sociology and Anthropology,* Vol. 13, No. 1, pp. 71-79, 1976.

Blumberg, Abraham S., and Elaine Niederhoffer, eds. *The Ambivalent Force: Perspectives on the Police.* 3d ed. New York: Holt, Rinehart & Winston, 1985.

Blumberg, Paul. *Inequality in an Age of Decline.* New York: Oxford University Press, 1980.

Blumberg, Rae L. *Stratification: Socioeconomic and Sexual Inequality.* Wm. Brown, 1978.

Blumer, Herbert. *Symbolic Interactionism.* Englewood Cliffs, N.J.: Prentice-Hall, 1969.

Bolaria, B. Singh, and Peter S. Li. *Racial Oppression in Canada.* Toronto: Garamond Press, 1985.

Bollen, K.A., and D. P. Phillips. "Imitative Suicides: A National Study of the Effects of Television News Stories." *American Sociological Review,* Vol. 47, pp. 802-809, 1982.

Bollens, John C., and Henry J. Schmandt. *The Metropolis: Its People, Politics, and Economic Life.* 4th ed. New York: Harper & Row, 1982.

Bonacich, Edna. "Abolition, the extension of slavery, and the position of free blacks: a study of split labor markets in the United States, 1830-1863." *American Journal of Sociology,* Vol. 81, pp. 601-628, 1975.

———. "Advanced capitalism and black/white race relations in the United States: a split labor market interpretation." *American Sociological Review,* Vol. 41, pp. 34-51, 1976.

———. "The past, present, and future of split labor market theory." In *Research in Race and Ethnic Relations,* Vol. 1, edited by C.B. Marrett and C. Leggon. Greenwich, Conn.: JAI Press, 1979.

———. "A theory of ethnic antagonism: the split labor market." *American Sociological Review,* Vol. 37, pp. 547-559, 1972.

——— and John Modell. *The Economic Basis of Ethnic Solidarity.* Berkeley: University of California Press, 1980.

Boon, James A. "Further operations of culture in Anthropology: a synthesis of and for debate." *The Idea of Culture in the Social Sciences,* edited by L. Schneider and C.M. Bonjean, pp. 1-32. Cambridge: Cambridge University Press, 1973.

Bosk, P.G. "The Transnational Corporation and Private Foreign Policy." *Society,* J/F, pp. 44-49, 1974.

Bottomore, Tom. *Political Sociology.* London: Hutchinson University Press, 1979.

Boughey, Howard. *The Insights of Sociology.* Boston: Allyn and Bacon, 1978.

Boulding, Kenneth E. *Ecodynamics: A New Theory of Societal Evolution.* Beverly Hills: Sage Publications, 1981.

Boulet, Jac-André, and Laval Lavallée. *The Changing Economic Status of Women.* Ottawa: Economic Council of Canada, 1984.

Boulton, David. *The Grease Machine: The Inside Story of Lockheed's Dollar Diplomacy.* New York: Harper & Row, 1978.

Bouma, Gary D., and Wilma J. Bouma. *Fertility Control: Canada's Lively Social Problem.* Toronto: Longman's Canada, 1975.

Bourdieu, Pierre, and Jean-Claude Passeron. *Reproduction in Education, Society and Culture.* Beverly Hills: Sage Publications, 1977.

Bourne, L.S. *Urban Systems: Strategies for Regulation.* New York: Oxford University Press, 1975.

Bowles, Samuel, and Herbert Gintis. *Schooling in Capitalist America: Educational Reform and The Contradictions of Economic Life.* New York: Basic Books, 1976.

Boyd, Monica et al. "Status Attainment in Canada." *Canadian Review of Sociology and Anthropology,* Vol. 18, No. 5, pp. 657-673, 1981.

Brace Research Institute and Canadian Hunger Foundation. *A Handbook on Appropriate Technology.* Ottawa: Canadian Hunger Foundation, 1976, 1977.

Brake, Mike. *The Sociology of Youth Culture and Youth Subculture.* London: Routledge & Kegan Paul, 1980.

Braverman, Harry. *Labor and Monopoly Capital: The Degradation of Work in The Twentieth Century.* New York: Monthly Review Press, 1974.

Breton, Raymond. "Institutional completeness of ethnic communities and personal relations to immigrants." *American Journal of Sociology,* Vol. 70, pp. 193-205, 1964.

———. "The production and allocation of symbolic resources: an analysis of the linguistic and ethnocultural fields in Canada." *Canadian Review of Sociology and Anthropology,* Vol. 21, No. 2, pp. 123-124, 1984.

Brinton, Crane. *The Anatomy of Revolution.* New York: Vintage Books, 1965.

Bryan, James H. "Apprenticeships in Prostitution." *Social Problems,* Vol. 12, No. 3, pp. 287-297, 1965.

———. "Occupational Ideologies and Individual Attitudes of Call Girls." *Social Problems,* Vol. 13, No. 4, pp. 441-450, 1966.

Bryant, Clifton D. "The Concealment of Stigma and Deviancy as a Family Function." In *Deviancy and the Family,* edited by Clifton D. Bryant and J. Gipson Wells, pp. 391-397. Philadelphia: F.A. Davis Co., 1973.

Brym, Robert J. "An introduction to the regional question in Canada." In *Regionalism in Canada,* edited by R. Brym. Toronto: Irwin, 1986.

———. "Incorporation vs. Power Models of Working-Class Radicalism: with Special Reference to North America." *Canadian Journal of Sociology,* 11(4), 1986. Forthcoming.

———. "The Canadian Capitalist Class, 1965-1985." In *The Structure of the Canadian Capitalist Class,* edited by R. Brym. Toronto: Garamond Press, 1985.

———. "Political conservatism in Atlantic Canada." In *Underdevelopment and Social Movements in Atlantic Canada,* edited by R. Brym and R. Sacouman, pp. 59-79. Toronto: New Hogtown Press, 1979.

———. "Regional social structure and agrarian radicalism in Canada: Alberta, Saskatchewan, and New Brunswick." In *People, Power and Process: A Reader,* edited by A. Himelfarb and C. Richardson, pp. 344-353. Toronto: McGraw-Hill Ryerson, 1980.

———. "Social movements and third parties." In *Models and Myths in Canadian Sociology,* edited by S. Berkowitz, pp. 29-49. Toronto: Butterworth, 1984.

——— and Barbara Neis. "Regional factors in the formation of the Fishermen's Protective Union of Newfoundland." *Canadian Journal of Sociology,* Vol. 3, pp. 391-407, 1978.

Buckley, Kenneth. "The Role of Staple Industries in Canada's Economic Development." *Journal of Economic History,* Vol.18, pp. 439-450, December 1958.

Burgess, Ernest. "The Growth of the City: An Introduction to a Research Project." In *The City,* edited by Robert E. Park and Ernest Burgess, pp. 47-62. Chicago: University of Chicago Press, 1925.

Burgess, Joanne. "L'Industrie de la chaussure à Montréal, 1840-1870. Le Passage de l'artisan a la fabrique," *Revue d'Histoire de l'Amerique Francaise,* 31 (Sept.) 1977: 187-210.

Burman, Sandra B., and Barbara E. Harrell-Bond, eds. *The Imposition of Law.* New York: Academic, 1979.

Burns, Tom, and G.M. Stalker. *The Management of Innovation.* London: Tavistock, 1961.

Burstyn, Varda. "The Age of Women's Liberation." *Canadian Dimension,* Vol. 18, pp. 21-26, October/November 1984.

Butler, Matilda, and William Paisley. *Women and the Mass Media.* New York: Human Sciences Press, 1980.

Cain, Maureen, and Alan Hunt, eds. *Marx and Engels on Law.* New York: Academic, 1979.

Campbell, C., and G. Szablowski. *The Superbureaucrats.* Toronto: Macmillan, 1979.

Campbell, Donald T., and Julian C. Stanley. *Experimental and Quasi-experimental Designs for Research.* Chicago: Rand McNally, 1966.

Campbell, Ernest Q. *Socialization, Culture and Personality.* Englewood Cliffs, N.J.: Prentice-Hall, 1975.

Canada, Government of. *Royal Commission on Bilingualism and Biculturalism.* Ottawa: Queen's Printer, 1969.

———. *The Status of Day Care in Canada.* Submission to the Federal Task Force on Day Care. Ottawa: Department of Health and Welfare, November 1984.

———. *Report of the Royal Commission on Equality in Employment.* Ottawa: Minister of Supply and Services, 1984.

———. *Royal Commission on Health Services.* Ottawa: Queen's Printer, 1964.

———. *Directory of Labour Organizations in Canada.* Ottawa: Department of Labour, 1968-81. Annual.

———. *Language Use in Canada.* Ottawa: Minister of Supply and Services, 1980.

———. *Report of the Special Senate Committee on the Mass Media.* Ottawa: Queen's Printer, 1970.

———. *Royal Commission on Newspapers.* Ottawa: Ministry of Supply and Services, 1981.

———. *Cultural Tradition and Political History of Women in Canada.* Studies of the Royal Commission on the Status of Women in Canada, Ottawa: Information Canada, 1971.

———. *Sexual Offences Against Children.* Report of the Committee on Sexual Offences Against Children and Youth. Ottawa, 1984.

———. *Strikes and Lockouts in Canada.* Ottawa: Department of Labour, 1917-81.

———. *Union Growth in Canada, 1921-1967.* Ottawa: Department of Labour, 1970.

Canada, Privy Council Office. *Foreign Ownership and the Structure of Canadian Industry.* Ottawa: Information Canada, 1970.

Canadian Council on Social Development. *Beyond Shelter — A Study of NHA-Financed Housing for the Elderly.* Ottawa, July 1973.

Cardoso, Fernando Henrique. "Industrialization, Dependency and Power in Latin America." *Berkeley Journal of Sociology,* Vol. 18, 1972.

Carey, James W. "Communication and Culture." *Communication Research,* Vol. 2, pp. 176-191, 1975.

———. "Harold Adams Innis and Marshall McLuhan." *Antioch Review,* Vol. 27, pp. 5-39, 1967.

Carlstein, Tommy. "A Time-geographic Approach to Time Allocation and Socio-ecological Systems." In *Public Policy in Temporal Perspective,* edited by William Michelson, pp. 69-82. The Hague: Mouton, 1978.

Carroll, William K. "Dependency, Imperialism and the Capitalist Class in Canada." In *The Structure of the Canadian Capitalist Class,* edited by Robert J. Brym. Toronto: Garamond Press, 1985.

————; John Fox; and Michael Ornstein. "The Network of Directorate Interlocks among the Largest Canadian Firms." *Canadian Review of Sociology and Anthropology,* Vol. 19, No. 1, pp. 44-69, 1982.

Cashmore, E. Ellis, and Bob Mullan. *Approaching Social Theory.* London: Heinemann Educational Books, 1983.

Castles, Stephen, and Godula Kosack. *Immigrant Workers and Class Structure in Western Europe.* London: Oxford University Press, 1973.

Castonguay, Charles. "Exogamie et anglicisation chez les minorités canadiennes-françaises." *Canadian Review of Sociology and Anthropology,* Vol. 16, pp. 21-31, 1979.

*Census of Canada.* Ottawa: King's and Queen's Printer, decennial, 1901-81.

Chambliss, William and Robert Seidman. *Law, Order, and Power.* 2d ed. Toronto: Addison-Wesley, 1982.

Chappell, Neena L. "The Future Impact of the Changing Status of Women." In *Canada's Changing Age Structure, Implications for the Future,* edited by Gloria M. Gutman. Vancouver: Simon Fraser University Publications, 1982.

———— and Nina L. Colwill. "Medical Schools as Agents of Professional Socialization." *Canadian Review of Sociology and Anthropology,* Vol. 18, No. 1, pp. 67-79, 1981.

Charbonneau, Hubert. *Vie et mort de nos ancêtres.* Montreal: Les Presses de l'Université de Montréal, Collection Demographie Canadienne 3, 1975.

Cherns, A.B., "Speculations on the Social Effects of New Microelectronics Technology." *International Labour Review,* Vol. 119 No. 6, pp. 705-22, 1980.

Chodak, Szymon. *Societal Development.* New York: Oxford University Press, 1973.

Cicourel, Allen V., and John I. Kitsuse. *The Educational Decision-Makers.* Indianapolis: Bobbs-Merrill, 1963.

*Citizen.* "Ontario suspects scholarships out of hand." Ottawa, Jan. 27, 1984: 2.

Clairmont, Donald H., and Dennis W. Magill. *Africville: The Life and Death of a Canadian Black Community.* Toronto: McClelland and Stewart, 1974.

Clark, S.D. *The New Urban Poor.* Toronto: McGraw-Hill Ryerson Ltd., 1978.

————. *The Suburban Society.* Toronto: University of Toronto Press, 1966.

Clarke, H.D. et al. *Political Choice in Canada.* Toronto: McGraw-Hill Ryerson, 1979.

Clement, Wallace. *The Canadian Corporate Elite.* Toronto: McClelland and Stewart, 1975.

————. *Class, Power and Property.* Toronto: Methuen Publications, 1983.

————. *Continental Corporate Power.* Toronto: McClelland and Stewart, 1977.

————. "The Corporate Elite, the Capitalist Class, and the Canadian State." In *The Canadian State,* edited by L. Panitch. Toronto: University of Toronto Press, 1977.

————. "A Political Economy of Regionalism in Canada." In *Structured Inequality in Canada,* edited by John Harp and John R. Hofley. Toronto: Prentice-Hall, 1980.

Clinard, Marshall B., ed. *Anomie and Deviant Behavior.* New York: The Free Press, 1964.

———— and Peter C. Yeager. *Corporate Crime.* New York: The Free Press, 1980.

Coale, Ansley J. "The decline of fertility in Europe from the French Revolution to World War II." In *Fertility and Family Planning,* edited by S.J. Behrman, L. Corsa, and R. Freedman, pp. 3-24. Ann Arbor: University of Michigan Press, 1969.

————. "Population and economic development." In *The Population Dilemma,* edited by Philip Hauser, pp. 46-69. Englewood Cliffs, N.J.: Prentice-Hall, 1963.

———— and Edgar M. Hoover. *Population Growth and Economic Development in Low Income Countries*. Princeton: Princeton University Press, 1958.

Cochrane, Jean. *Women in Canadian Life — Politics*. Toronto: Fitzhenry and Whiteside, 1977.

Cohen, Albert K. *Deviance and Control*. Englewood Cliffs, NJ: Prentice-Hall, 1966.

Cohen, G.A. *Karl Marx's Theory of History*. Oxford: Clarendon Press, 1978.

Coleman, James C. *Power and the Structure of Society*. New York: W.W. Norton, 1974.

Coleman, James S. *The Adolescent Society*. New York: The Free Press, 1961.

———— et al. *Equality of Educational Opportunity*. Washington, D.C.: U.S. Department of Health, Education and Welfare, 1966.

Collins, Randall. "Functional and Conflict Theories of Educational Stratification." *American Sociological Review,* Vol. 36, No. 6, pp. 1002-19, 1971.

———— and Michael Markowsky. *The Discovery of Society*. 3rd ed. New York: Random House, 1984.

Commission royale d'enquête sur l'enseignement dans la province de Québec. *Rapport de la Commission royale d'enquête sur l'enseignement dans la province de Québec*. Québec: Imprimeur de la Reine, 1963.

Comte, A. *The Positive Philosophy*. New York: AMS Press, 1974.

Connidis, Ingrid. *Rethinking Criminal Justice Research: A Systems Perspective*. Toronto: Holt, Rinehart, and Winston, 1982.

Connor, Walter D. "The Manufacture of Deviance: The Case of the Soviet Purge, 1936-1938." *American Sociological Review,* Vol. 37, pp. 403-413, August 1972.

Conrad, Peter, and Joseph W. Schneider. *Deviance and Medicalization: From Badness to Sickness*. Toronto: C. V. Mosby Co., 1980.

Cooley, Charles H. *Human Nature and Social Order*. New York: Scribner, 1902.

————. *Social Organization*. Glencoe, Ill.: The Free Press, 1962.

Coser, Lewis, A. *Masters of Sociological Thought*. 2nd ed. New York: Harcourt, Brace and Jovanovich Inc., 1977.

Coulson, Margaret, and Carol Riddell. *Approaching Sociology*. 2nd ed. London: Routledge and Kegan Paul, 1980.

Cox, Kevin R., ed. *Urbanization and Conflict in Market Societies*. Chicago: Maaroufa Press, Inc., 1978.

Cox, Oliver C. *Caste, Class, & Power: A Study in Social Dynamics*. New York: Doubleday, 1948.

Crozier, Michael. *The Bureaucratic Phenomenon*. Chicago: University of Chicago Press, 1964.

Cullen, Ian. "The Treatment of Time in the Explanation of Spatial Behavior." In *Human Activity and Time Geography,* edited by T. Carlstein et al., pp. 27-38. New York: Halstead Press, 1978.

Cumming, Elaine, and William Henry. *Growing Old: The Process of Disengagement*. New York: Basic Books, 1961.

Cuneo, Carl. "Class, Stratification and Mobility." In *Sociology,* edited by R. Hagedorn, pp. 237-77. Toronto: Holt, Rinehart and Winston, 1980.

————. "State, Class and Reserve Labour: The Case of the 1941 Canadian Unemployment Insurance Act." *Canadian Review of Sociology and Anthropology,* Vol. 16, No. 2, pp. 147-170, 1979.

Currie, Elliott P. "Crimes Without Criminals: Witchcraft and Its Control in Renaissance Europe." *Law and Society Review,* Vol. 3, No. 1, pp. 7-32, 1968.

Curtis, Bruce. "Capitalist Development and Educational Reform." *Theory and Society,* Vol. 13, pp. 41-68, 1984.

————. "Preconditions of the Canadian State: Educational Reform and the Construction of a Public in Upper Canada, 1837-1846." *Studies in Political Economy,* Vol. 10, pp. 99-121, 1983.

————. "Schoolbooks and the Myth of Curricular Republicanism: The State and the Curriculum in Canada West, 1820-1850." *Histoire sociale — Social History,* Vol. 16, pp. 305-329, 1983.

Curtis, James and William Scott, eds. *Social Stratification: Canada*. Toronto: Prentice-Hall, 1979.

Dahl, Robert. *Who Governs? Democracy and Power in an American City*. New Haven: Yale University Press, 1961.

Dahrendorf, Ralf. *Class and Class Conflict in Industrial Society*. Palo Alto, Calif.: Stanford University Press, 1959.

Daniels, Arlene K. "Normal Mental Illness and Understandable Excuses: The Philosophy of Combat Psychiatry." *American Behavioral Scientist*, Vol. 14, No. 2, pp. 169-178, 1970.

Darroch, Gordon A. "Another look at ethnicity, stratification and social mobility in Canada." *Canadian Journal of Sociology*, Vol. 4, pp. 1-25, 1979.

———. "Early Industrialization and Inequality in Toronto, 1861-1899." *Labour/Le Travailleur*, Vol. 11, pp. 31-61, Spring 1983.

——— and Michael Ornstein. "Ethnicity and Class, Transitions Over a Decade: Ontario, 1861-1871." *Canadian Historical Association, Papers 1984*, pp. 111-137.

Davidoff, Paul. "Advocacy and Pluralism in Planning." *Journal of the American Institute of Planners*, Vol. 31, pp. 331-338, 1965.

Davies, James C. "Toward a theory of revolution." In *Studies in Social Movements: A Social Psychological Perspective*, edited by B. McLaughlin, pp. 85-108. New York: Free Press, 1969.

Davis, Arthur K. "Canadian Society and History as Hinterland versus Metropolis." In *Canadian Society: Pluralism, Change and Conflict*, edited by R.J. Ossenberg. Toronto: Prentice-Hall, 1971.

Davis, James A. *Elementary Survey Analysis*. Englewood Cliffs, N.J.: Prentice-Hall, 1971.

Davis, Kingsley. *Human Society*. New York: Macmillan, 1949.

———. "Sexual Behavior." In *Contemporary Social Problems*, edited by Robert K. Merton and Robert Nisbet, pp. 313-360. 3rd ed. New York: Harcourt, Brace, Jovanovich, 1971.

———. "The world demographic transition." *Annals of the American Academy of Political and Social Science*, Vol. 237, January 1945.

——— and Wilbert E. Moore. "Some Principles of Stratification." *American Sociological Review*, Vol. 10, No. 2, pp. 242-249, 1945.

Dawe, Alan. "Two Sociologies." *British Journal of Sociology*, Vol. 21, pp. 207-218, 1970.

de Beauvoir, Simone. *Old Age*. Harmondsworth: Penguin Books, 1970.

———. *The Second Sex*. New York: Bantam, 1952.

Dentler, Robert A., and Kai T. Erikson. "The Functions of Deviance in Groups." *Social Problems*, Vol. 7, No. 2, pp. 98-102.

Denzin, Norman. *Childhood Socialization*. San Francisco: Jossey-Bass, 1977.

de Vries, John, and Frank G. Vallee. *Language Use in Canada*. 1971 Census of Canada, Catalogue 99-762E. Ottawa: Statistics Canada, 1980.

Dewey, Richard. "The Rural-Urban Continuum: Real but Relatively Unimportant." *American Journal of Sociology*, Vol. 66, pp. 60-66, 1960.

Dobson, Richard B. "Social Status and Inequality of Access to Higher Education in the USSR." In *Power and Ideology in Education*, edited by Jerome Karabel and A.H. Halsey, pp. 254-275. New York: Oxford, 1977.

Domhoff, G. William, ed. *Power Structure Research*. Beverly Hills: Sage Focus Editions, No. 17, 1980.

Donohue, George et al. "Gatekeeping: Mass Media Systems and Information Control." In *Current Perspectives in Mass Communication Research*, edited by G.F. Kline, pp. 49-69. Beverly Hills: Sage, 1972.

Doob, A., and G.E. McDonald. "Television Viewing and the Fear of Victimization: Is the Relationship Causal?" *Journal of Social Psychology and Personality*, Vol. 37, pp. 170-179, 1979.

dos Santos, Theotonio. "The Structure of Dependence." *American Economic Review*, May 1970.

Douglas, Jack et al. *Introduction to the Sociologies of Everyday Life*. Boston: Allyn and Bacon, 1980.

Dranoff, Linda Silver. *Women in Canadian Life — Law*. Toronto: Fitzhenry and Whiteside, 1977.

Driedger, Leo, and Rodney A. Clifton. "Ethnic Stereotypes: Images of Ethnocentrism, Reciprocity or Dissimilarity." *Canadian Review of Sociology and Anthropology*, Vol. 21, No. 3, pp. 287-301, 1984.

Drucker, Peter. *The Age of Discontinuity*. New York: Harper and Row, 1968.

Drummond, Ian. *The Canadian Economy: Structure and Development*. Georgetown, Ont.: Irwin-Dorsey, 1972.

Duberman, Lucile, and Clayton A. Hartjen. *Sociology*. Glenview, Ill: Scott, Foresman, 1979.

Duff, R.S., and A.B. Hollingshead. *Sickness and Society*. New York: Harper and Row, 1968.

Dulude, Louise. *Pension Reform with Women in Mind*. Ottawa: Canadian Advisory Council on the Status of Women, 1981.

————. *Women and Aging*. Ottawa: Canadian Advisory Council on the Status of Women, April 1978.

Durkheim, Émile. *The Division of Labour in Society*. New York: Free Press, 1965.

————. *The Rules of Sociological Method*. New York: Free Press, 1964.

Dye, Thomas R. *Who's Running America? The Reagan Years*. Englewood Cliffs, N.J.: Prentice-Hall, 1983.

Easterlin, Richard A. *Birth and Fortune: The Impact of Numbers on Personal Welfare*. New York: Basic Books, 1980.

Edwards, Lyford P. *The Natural History of Revolution*. Chicago: The University of Chicago Press, 1970.

Eichler, Margrit. *Families in Canada Today*. Toronto: Gage, 1983.

————. "Women as Personal Dependents." In *Women in Canada,* edited by Marylee Stephenson, pp. 38-55. Toronto: New Press, 1973.

Eisenstadt, S.N. *Essays on Comparative Institutions*. New York: John Wiley & Sons, 1965.

————. *Political Sociology*. New York: Basic Books, 1971.

————. "Social Change, Differentiation and Evolution." *American Sociological Review,* No. 29, June 1964.

Ekman, Paul, and Wallace V. Friesen. "The repertoire of nonverbal behaviour: Categories, origins, usage and coding." *Semiotica,* Vol. 1, p. 82, 1969.

Elkin, Frederick. "Communications Media and Identity Formation in Canada." In *Communications in Canadian Society,* edited by B. Singer, pp. 147-157. Toronto: Addison-Wesley, 1983.

————and Gerald Handel. *The Child and Society*. New York: Random House, 1978.

Ellis, Godfrey; Gary Lee; and Larry Petersen. "Supervision and Conformity: A Cross-Cultural Analysis of Parental Socialization Values." *American Journal of Sociology,* Vol. 84, No. 2, pp. 386-402, 1979.

Ellul, J. *The Technological Society*. Translated by J. Wilkinson. New York: Alfred A. Knopf, 1964.

————. *The Technological System*. Translated by J. Neugroschel. New York: Continuum, 1980.

————. *To Will and To Do*. Philadelphia: United Church Press, 1969.

Emerson, Richard M. "Power-Dependency Relations." *American Sociological Review,* Vol. 27, pp. 31-41, 1962.

Erikson, Kai T. *Wayward Puritans*. New York: John Wiley & Sons, 1966.

Ermann, M. David, and Richard J. Lundman. *Corporate Deviance*. New York: Holt, Rinehart & Winston, 1982.

Escande, Claude. *Les Classes Sociales au Cegep*. Montreal: Parti Pris, 1973.

Evans, Brian, and Bernard Waites. *IQ and Mental Testing*. London: Macmillan, 1981.

Farrell, Ronald A., and Victoria L. Swigert. *Deviance and Social Control*. Glenview, Ill.: Scott, Foresman, 1982.

Feierabend, Ivo K.; Rosalind L. Feierabend; and Betty A. Nesvold. "Social change and political violence: cross-national patterns." In *Violence in America: Historical and Comparative Perspectives,* edited by H. Graham and T. Gurr, pp. 632-687. New York: Bantam Books, 1969.

Fiedler, Fred E. "Engineer the Job to Fit the Manager." *Harvard Business Review,* Vol. 43, No. 5, 1965.

Fine, Bob. "Law and class." In *Capitalism and the Rule of Law,* edited by Bob Fine et al., pp. 29-45. London: Hutchinson, 1979.

Firestone, Shulamith. *The Dialectic of Sex.* New York, Bantam, 1970.

Fischer, Claude S. *The Urban Experience.* New York: Harcourt Brace Jovanovich, 1976.

———. *To Dwell Among Friends.* Chicago: University of Chicago Press, 1982.

Fischer, Linda, and J.A. Cheyne. *Sex Roles.* Ontario: Ministry of Education, 1977.

Fishman, Mark. *Manufacturing the News.* Austin: University of Texas Press, 1980.

Fishman, Pamela. "Interaction: The work women do." *Social Problems,* Vol. 25, pp. 397-406, 1978.

Foot, David K. *Canada's Population Outlook: Demographic Futures and Economic Challenges.* Toronto: James Lorimer and Company, in association with the Canadian Institute for Economic Policy, 1982.

Fox, Alan, "Management's Frame of Reference." In A. Fox, *Industrial Sociology and Industrial Relations.* London: H.M.S.O., 1966.

Frank, Andre Gunder. "The Development of Underdevelopment." In *Dependence and Underdevelopment,* edited by James D. Cockcroft et al., pp. 3-17. Garden City, N.Y.: Doubleday Anchor Press, 1970.

Freeman, Jo, ed. *Women: A Feminist Perspective.* Palo Alto, Calif.: Mayfield Publishing Company, 1975.

Freidson, Eliot. *Doctoring Together: A Study of Professional Social Control.* New York: Elsevier, 1975.

Freire, Paulo. *Pedagogy of the Oppressed.* New York: Herder and Herder, 1971.

Frideres, James S. *Native People in Canada: Contemporary Conflicts.* 2d ed. Toronto, Ontario: Prentice-Hall, 1983.

Friedan, Betty. *The Feminine Mystique.* New York: Dell, 1963.

Fuller, Lon L. *The Morality of Law.* New Haven, Conn.: Yale University, 1964.

Gacas, Victor. "The Influence of Social Class on Socialization." In *Contemporary Theories About the Family.* Vol. 1, edited by W. Burr et al. New York: The Free Press, 1982.

———. "The Self Concept." *Annual Review of Sociology,* Vol. 8, pp. 1-33. Palo Alto: Annual Reviews Inc., 1982.

Gagan, David. "The 'Critical Years' in Rural Canada West." *Canadian Historical Review,* Vol. 59, No. 3, pp. 293-318, 1978.

———. *Hopeful Travellers: Families, Land and Social Change in Mid-Victorian Peel County, Canada West.* Toronto: University of Toronto Press, 1981.

Galanter, Marc. "Why the 'Haves' Come Out Ahead: Speculations on the Limits of Legal Change." *Law and Society Review,* Vol. 9 (Fall), pp. 95-160, 1974.

Galbraith, J.K. *The New Industrial State.* 3d revised ed. New York: Mentor, 1978.

Galtung, Johan. "Structural Theory of Imperialism." *Journal of Peace Research,* Vol. 2, 1971.

Gamson, William. *Power and Discontent.* Homewood, Ill.: Dorsey Press, 1968.

———. *The Strategy of Social Protest.* Homewood, Ill.: Dorsey Press, 1975.

Gans, Herbert, J. *Deciding What's News.* New York: Vintage Books, 1980.

———. *The Levittowners.* New York: Pantheon Books, 1967.

———. "Symbolic enthnicity: the future of ethnic groups and cultures in America." *Ethnic and Racial Studies,* Vol. 2, pp. 1-20, 1979.

———. *The Urban Villagers.* New York: The Free Press, 1962.

Garfinkel, Harold. *Studies in Ethnomethodology.* Englewood Cliffs, N.J.: Prentice-Hall, 1967.

Garson, Barbara. *All the Livelong Day.* New York: Doubleday, 1972.

Gaventa, John. *Power and Powerlessness: Quiescence and Rebellion in an Appalachian Valley.* Urbana, Ill.: University of Illinois Press, 1980.

Gee, Ellen. "Population." In *Sociology,* 2d ed., edited by Robert Hagedorn. Toronto: Holt, Rinehart and Winston, 1983.

Genesee, Fred. "Bilingual education of majority language children: The immersion experiments in review." *Applied Psycholinguistics,* Vol. 4, pp. 1-46, 1983.

Genovese, Eugene. *Roll Jordon Roll: The World the Slaves Made.* New York: Pantheon Books, 1974.

Gerber, Linda M. "The Development of Canadian Indian Communities: a two-dimensional typology reflecting strategies of adaptation to the modern world." *Canadian Review of Sociology and Anthropology,* Vol. 16, No. 4, pp. 404-421, 1979.

Gerbner, George. "The Dynamics of Cultural Resistance." In *Hearth and Home: Images of Women in Mass Media,* edited by G. Tuchman, A.K. Daniels, and J. Benet, pp. 46-50. New York: Oxford University Press, 1978.

———— and L. Gross. "Living with Television: the violence profile." *Journal of Communication,* Vol. 26, No. 2, pp. 173-199, 1976.

———— et al. "The Mainstreaming of America: Violence Profile No. 11." *Journal of Communication,* Vol. 30, No. 3, pp. 10-29, 1980.

Gerth, H.H., and C. Wright Mills. *From Max Weber: Essays in Sociology.* New York: Oxford University Press, 1958.

Giddens, Anthony. *Capitalism and Modern Social Theory.* London: Cambridge University Press, 1971.

————. *The Class Structure of the Advanced Societies.* London: Hutchinson University Library, 1974.

————. *Sociology: A brief but critical introduction.* New York: Harcourt, Brace and Jovanovich Inc., 1982.

Giedion, S. *Mechanization Takes Command.* New York: Norton, 1969.

Gillespie, Irwin. "On the Redistribution of Income in Canada." In *Structured Inequality in Canada,* edited by John Harp and John R. Hofley, pp. 22-53. Toronto: Prentice-Hall, 1980.

Gillis, John R. *Youth and History.* New York: Academic, 1974.

Gitlin, Todd. "Media Sociology: The Dominant Paradigm." *Theory and Society,* Vol. 6, pp. 205-253, 1978.

————. *The Whole World is Watching.* Berkely: University of California Press, 1981.

Glascow Media Group. *Bad News.* London: Routledge and Kegan Paul, 1977.

————. *More Bad News.* London: Routledge and Kegan Paul, 1980.

Glaser, Barney A., and Anselm L. Strauss. *Awareness of Dying.* Chicago: The University of Chicago Press, 1965.

Glazer, Nathan, and Daniel P. Moynihan. *Beyond the Melting Pot.* Cambridge, Mass.: M.I.T. Press, 1970.

Glynn, Carroll, and Jack McLeod. "Public Opinion du Jour: an Examination of the Spiral of Silence." *Public Opinion Quarterly,* Vol. 48, pp. 731-740, 1984.

Goffman, Erving. *Behavior in Public Places: Notes on the Social Organization of Gatherings.* New York: The Free Press of Glencoe, 1963.

————. *Frame Analysis.* New York: Harper and Row, 1974.

————. *Gender Advertisements.* New York: Harper and Row, 1979.

————. *Interaction Ritual: Essays on Face-to-Face Behavior.* Garden City, N.Y.: Doubleday Anchor Books, 1967.

————. "The Moral Career of the Mental Patient." *Psychiatry,* Vol. 22, pp. 123-142, 1959.

————. *Presentation of Self in Everyday Life.* Garden City, N.Y.: Doubleday, 1959.

————. *Stigma: Notes on the Management of Spoiled Identity.* Englewood Cliffs, N.J.: Prentice-Hall, 1963.

Gold, David; Clarence Lo; and E.O. Wright. "Recent Developments in Marxist Theories of the Capitalist State." *Monthly Review,* Vol. 27, No. 5, pp. 29-43, 1975.

Golding, Peter, and Graham Murdock. "Ideology and the Mass Media: the Question of Influence." In *Ideology and Cultural Production,* edited by M. Barrett et al., pp. 198-224. New York: St. Martin's Press, 1979.

Gordon, Milton M. *Assimilation in American Life.* New York: Oxford University Press, 1964.

Gottman, Jean. *Megalopolis: The Urbanized Northeastern Seaboard of the United States.* New York: Twentieth Century Fund, 1961.

Gould, Stephen Jay. *The Mismeasure of Man.* New York: Norton, 1981.

Goulet, D. *The Uncertain Promise.* IDOC/North America, 1977.

Gove, Walter R., ed. *The Labelling of Deviance: Evaluating a Perspective.* New York: John Wiley & Sons, 1975.

Goyder, John C. "Social Mobility or status attainment, or social mobility and status attainment?". *Canadian Review of Sociology and Anthropology,* Vol. 21, No. 3, pp. 331-343, 1984.

———— and James E. Curtis. "Occupational Mobility Over Four Generations." *Canadian Review of Sociology and Anthropology,* Vol. 14, No. 3, pp. 303-19, 1977.

———— and Peter Pineo. "Social Class Self-Identification." In *Social Stratification: Canada,* edited by James E. Curtis and William G. Scott, pp. 431-447. Toronto: Prentice-Hall, 1979.

Grabb, Edward G. *Social Inequality: Classical and Contemporary Theorists.* Toronto: Holt, Rinehart and Winston, 1984.

Gramsci, Antonio. *Selections from the Prison Notebooks.* New York: International Publishers, 1971.

Grant, George. *Lament for a Nation.* Toronto: McClelland and Stewart, 1965.

Greenglass, Esther R. *A World of Difference: Gender Roles in Perspective.* John Wiley and Sons, 1982.

Greer, Allan. "Wage Labour and the Transition to Capitalism." *Labour/Le Travail,* Vol. 15, Spring, pp. 7-22, 1985.

Greer, Scott. *The Logic of Social Inquiry.* Chicago: Aldine Publishing, 1969.

Griffin, John H. *Black Like Me.* Boston: Houghton Mifflin Co. 1977.

Grimes, Ruth-Ellen M., and Austin T. Turk. "Labeling in Context: Conflict, Power and Self-Definition." In *Crime, Law, and Sanctions: Theoretical Perspectives,* edited by Marvin D. Krohn and Ronald L. Akers, pp. 39-58. Beverly Hills: Sage, 1978.

Gunder Frank, Andre. *Capitalism and Underdevelopment in Latin America: Historical Studies of Chile and Brazil.* New York: Monthly Review Press, 1967.

————. "The development of underdevelopment." *Monthly Review,* Vol. 18, No. 4, pp. 17-31, September 1966.

————. *Lumpenbourgeoisie: Lumpendevelopment: Dependence, Class and Politics in Latin America.* New York: Monthly Review Press, 1972.

————. *Sociology of Development and Underdevelopment of Sociology.* London: Pluto Press, 1973.

Gurevitch, M. et al., eds. *Culture, Society and the Media.* London: Methuen, 1982.

Gurr, Ted Robert. "A comparative study of civil strife." In *Violence in America: Historical and Comparative Perspectives,* edited by H. Graham and T. Gurr, pp. 572-632. New York: Bantam Books, 1969.

————. *Why Men Rebel.* Princeton, NJ: Princeton University Press, 1970.

Gutman, Gloria M. *Canada's Changing Age Structure, Implications for the Future.* Vancouver: Simon Fraser University Publications, 1982.

Guttsman, W.L. "The British Political Elite and the Class Structure." In *Elites and Power in British Society,* edited by P. Stanworth and A. Giddens. London: Cambridge University Press, 1974.

Haas, Jack, and William Shaffir. *Shaping Identity in Canadian Society.* Toronto: Prentice-Hall, 1978.

Habakkuk, H.J. "English population in the Eighteenth Century." In *Population in History,* edited by D.V. Glass and D.E.C. Eversley, pp. 269-284. London: Edward Arnold, 1965.

Hagan, John and Jeffrey Leon. "Philosophy and Sociology of Crime Control: Canadian-American Comparison." In *Social System and Legal Process,* edited by Harry M. Johnson, pp. 181-208. San Francisco: Jossey-Bass, 1978.

Hagedorn, Robert. *Sociology.* 2d ed. Toronto: Holt, Rinehart and Winston of Canada, Ltd, 1983.

Hägerstrand, Torsten. "What About People in Regional Science." *Papers of the Regional Science Association,* Vol. 24, pp. 7-21, 1970.

Hagopian, Mark N. *The Phenomenon of Revolution.* New York: Harper and Row, 1974.

Hajnal, J. "European marriage patterns in perspective." In *Population in History,* edited by D.V. Glass and D.E.C. Eversley, pp. 101-143. London: Edward Arnold, 1965.

Hall, Edward T. *Beyond Culture.* New York: Anchor Books, 1977.

————. *The Hidden Dimension.* Garden City, N.Y.: Doubleday, 1966.

Hall, Stuart. "The Rediscovery of Ideology: Return of the Repressed in Media Studies." In *Culture, Society and the Media,* M. Gurevitch et al., pp. 56-90. London: Methuen, 1982.

Hallman, Howard W. *Neighborhoods: Their Place in Urban Life.* Beverly Hills: Sage Library of Social Research, 1984.

Haralambos, Michael, and Robin M. Heald. *Sociology: Themes and Perspectives.* Slough, G.B.: University Tutorial Press, 1980.

Harris, Chauncy, and Edward L. Ullman. "The Nature of Cities." *Annals of the American Academy of Political and Social Science,* Vol. 242, pp. 7-17, 1945.

Harvey, C., and H. Bahr. *The Sunshine Widows.* Lexington, Mass.: Lexington Books, 1980.

Harvey, Edward B. *Barriers to Employer Sponsored Training in Ontario.* Toronto: Ministry of Education, 1980.

————. "The Changing Relationship Between University Education and Intergenerational Social Mobility." *The Canadian Review of Sociology and Anthropology,* Vol. 21, pp. 275-286, 1984.

————. *Educational Systems and The Labour Market.* Toronto: Longman, 1974.

————; L.R. Marsden; and A. Woodsworth. *Project Progress: A Study of Canadian Public Libraries.* Ottawa: Canadian Library Association, 1981.

Haskell, M. *From Reverence to Rape: The Treatment of Women in Movies.* New York: Holt, Rinehart and Winston, 1974.

Hauser, Philip M. "The population of the world: recent trends and prospects." In *Population: The Vital Revolution,* edited by Ronald Freedman. Garden City, N.Y.: Anchor Books, 1964.

————. "The social, economic, and technological problems of rapid urbanization." In *Industrialization and Society,* edited by B. Hoselitz and W. Moore, pp. 199-215. The Hague: Mouton, 1963.

Hauser, Robert M. et al. "Temporal Change in Occupational Mobility: Evidence for Men in the United States." *American Sociological Review,* Vol. 40, No. 3, pp. 279-97.

———— and David L. Featherman. *The Process Stratification.* New York: Academic, 1977.

Havighurst, Robert J. et al. "Disengagement and Patterns of Aging." In *Middle Age and Aging,* edited by B. Neugarten. Chicago: University of Chicago Press, 1968.

Hawkins, Freda. *Canada and Immigration: Public Policy and Public Concern.* Montreal: McGill-Queen's University Press, 1972.

Hawley, Willis, and Frederick M. Wirt. *The Search for Community Power.* Toronto: Prentice-Hall, 1968.

Hayden, Dolores. *Redesigning the American Dream.* New York: Norton, 1984.

Hechter, M. and W. Brustein, "Regional Modes of Production and Patterns of State Formation in Western Europe." *American Journal of Sociology,* Vol. 85, pp. 1061-1094, 1980.

Heitlinger, Alena. *Women and State Socialism, Sex Inequality in the Soviet Union and Czechoslovakia.* Montreal: McGill-Queen's University Press, 1979.

Henley, Nancy. *Body Politics.* Englewood Cliffs, N.J.: Prentice-Hall, 1977.

Henripin, Jacques. *Immigration and Language Imbalance. Canadian Immigration and Population Studies*. Ottawa: Information Canada, 1974.

———— and Evelyne Lapierre-Adamcyk. *La Fin de la revanche des berceaux: qu'en pensent les Québecoises?* Montréal: Les Presses de l'Université de Montréal, Collection Demographie canadienne 2, 1974.

Henry, Stuart. *Private Justice*. London: Routledge & Kegan Paul, 1983.

Herberg, Will. *Protestant, Catholic, Jew*. New York: Doubleday, 1960.

Heron, Craig. "Labourism and the Canadian Working Class." *Labour/Le Travail*, Vol. 13, pp. 45-76, Spring 1984.

Hibbs, Douglas A. "Industrial conflict in advanced industrial societies." *American Political Science Review*, Vol. 70, pp. 1033-1058, 1976.

————. "On the political economy of long-run trends in strike activity." *British Journal of Political Science*, Vol. 8, pp. 153-175, 1978.

Higgins, Ronald. *The Seventh Enemy: The Human Factor in the Global Crisis*. London: Pan Books, 1980.

Hiller, Harry H. *Canadian Society: A Sociological Analysis*. Toronto: Prentice-Hall, 1976.

Hobsbawm, E.J. *Primitive Rebels: Studies in Archaic Forms of Social Movement in the 19th and 20th Centuries*. New York: Norton, 1959.

Hodge, G.D., and M.A. Qadeer, *Towns and Villages in Canada: The Importance of Being Unimportant*. Toronto: Butterworth, 1983.

Hodge, Robert W.; P. Siegel; and Peter H. Rossi. "A Comparative Study of Occupational Prestige." In *Class, Status and Power*. 2d ed. Edited by R. Bendix and S.M. Lipset, pp. 322-334. New York: Free Press, 1966.

Hoebel, E. Adamson. *The Law of Primitive Man*. Cambridge, Mass.: Harvard University Press, 1954.

Homans, George. "The Western Electric Researchers." In *Human Factors in Management,* edited by S.D. Hoslett, pp. 210-241. New York: Harper, 1951.

Horney, Karen. "The Flight from Womanhood." In *Feminine Psychology*, K. Horney, pp. 54-70. New York: Norton, 1973.

Horowitz, M., and I. Herrenstedt. "Changes in Skill Requirements of Occupations in Selected Industries." *The Employment Impact of Technological Change*, Vol. 2, Appendix. Washington: U.S. Government Printing Office, 1966.

Hoselitz, Berthold F. *Sociological Aspects of Economic Growth*. Glencoe, Ill.: Free Press, 1960.

Hoyt, Homer. *The Structure and Growth of Residential Neighborhoods in American Cities*. Washington, D.C.: Federal Housing Administration, 1939.

Huber, Joan, and Glenna Spitze. "Considering Divorce: An Expansion of Becker's Theory of Marital Instability." *American Journal of Sociology*, Vol. 86, No. 1, pp. 75-89, 1980.

Hughes, E.C. *French Canada in Transition*. Chicago: University of Chicago Press, 1943.

Hunter, Alfred A. *Class Tells: On Social Inequality in Canada*. Toronto: Butterworth, 1981.

Hunter, Floyd. *Community Power Structure*. Garden City, N.Y.: Doubleday, 1953.

Illich, Ivan. *Deschooling Society*. New York: Harrow, 1970.

Ingham, Geoffrey K. *Strikes and Industrial Conflict: Britain and Scandinavia*. London: Macmillan, 1974.

Ingleby, David. "Mental Health and Social Order." In *Social Control and the State*, edited by Stanley Cohen and Andrew Scull, pp. 141-188. Oxford: Martin Robertson & Co., 1983.

Inkeles, Alex. "The Modernization of Man." *Modernization: The Dynamics of Growth*, edited by Myron Weiner. New York: Basic Books, 1966.

————. "Making Men Modern." *Social Change: Sources, Patterns, and Consequences,* edited by Amitai Etzioni. New York: Basic Books, 1973.

Innis, Harold A. *The Bias of Communication*. Toronto: University of Toronto Press, 1951.

————. *Essays in Canadian Economic History*. Toronto: University of Toronto Press, 1956.

————. *The Fur Trade in Canada*. New Haven, Conn.: Yale University Press, 1930.

Isajiw, S.. "Multiculturalism and the Integration of the Canadian Community." *Canadian Ethnic Studies,* Vol. 15, No. 2, pp. 107-117, 1983.

Isajiw, W.W. *Identities: The Impact of Ethnicity in Canadian Society.* Toronto: Peter Martin Press, 1976.

Jackson, John D. "The functions of language in Canada: on the political economy of language." In *The Individual, Language and Society in Canada,* edited by W.H. Coons, D.M. Taylkor, and M. Tremblay, pp. 59-76. Ottawa: The Canada Council, 1977.

James, William. *The Principles of Psychology in Two Volumes.* New York: Holt, 1890.

Jamieson, Stuart. *Industrial Relations in Canada,* 2d ed. Toronto: Macmillan, 1973.

Janowitz, Morris. *The Community Press in an Urban Setting.* Chicago: University of Chicago Press, 1980.

Jeffrey, C. Ray. *Crime Prevention Through Environmental Design.* Beverly Hills: Sage Publications, 1971.

Jencks, Christopher et al. *Inequality: A Reassessment of the Effect of Family and Schooling in America.* New York: Harper Colophon Books, 1972.

Jenkins, Craig J. "Resource mobilization theory and the study of social movements." *Annual Review of Sociology,* Vol. 9, pp. 527-553, 1983.

Jenkins, David. *QWL — Current Trends and Directions.* Toronto: Ontario Ministry of Labour, 1981.

Jensen, Arthur. "How much can we boost I.Q. and Scholastic Achievement? *Harvard Educational Review,* Vol. 39, pp. 1-123, 1969.

Jéquier, N. *Appropriate Technology: Promises and Problems.* Paris: Development Centre of the Organization for Economic Co-operation and Development, 1976.

Johnson, Laura. *Who Cares? A Report on the Project Child Care, Survey of Parents and Their Child Care Arrangements.* Toronto: Social Planning Council, 1977.

Johnson, Leo A. "The Development of Class in Canada in the Twentieth Century." In *Capitalism and the National Question,* edited by Gary Teeple, pp. 141-183. Toronto: University of Toronto Press, 1972.

———. "Land Policy, Population Growth and Social Structure in the Home District 1793-1851." *Ontario History,* Vol. 67, pp. 41-60, March 1971.

———. *Poverty in Wealth.* Toronto: New Hogtown Press, 1977.

Johnson, William. "The Gay World." In *Social Deviance in Canada,* edited by W.E. Mann, pp. 380-389. Toronto: Copp Clark, 1971.

Jones, Frank E., and Wallace E. Lambert. "Occupational rank and attitudes towards immigrants." *Public Opinion Quarterly,* Vol. 29, pp. 137-144, 1965.

Jones, Landon Y. *Great Expectations: America and the Baby Boom Generation.* New York: Ballantine Books, 1980.

Jones, Robert A. "Myth and Symbol Among the Nacirema Tsigoliocos." *The American Sociologist,* Vol. 15, pp. 207-212, November, 1980.

Joy, Richard J. *Languages in Conflict: The Canadian Experience.* Toronto: McClelland and Stewart, 1972.

Kagan, Robert A. "The Routinization of Debt Collection: An Essay on Social Change and Conflict in the Courts." *Law and Society Review,* Vol. 18, No. 3, pp. 323-371, 1984.

Kalbach, W.E. *The Impact of Immigration on Canada's Population.* Ottawa: Queen's Printer, 1970.

——— and W. McVey. *The Demographic Bases of Canadian Society.* 2d ed. Toronto: McGraw-Hill Ryerson, 1979.

Kallen, Evelyn. *Ethicity and Human Rights in Canada.* Toronto: Gage, 1982.

Kallen, Horace M. "Functionalism." In *Encyclopaedia of the Social Sciences,* Vol. 3, edited by Edwin R.A. Seligman. New York: Macmillan, 1937.

Kanter, Rosabeth Moss. *Men and Women of the Corporation.* New York: Basic Books, 1977.

Karp, David; Greogry P. Stone; and William C. Yoels. *Being Urban.* Toronto: D.C. Heath, 1977.

Katz, Elihu. "The Return of the Humanities and Sociology." *Journal of Communication,* Vol. 33, No. 3, pp. 51-52, 1983.

Kaupen, Wolfgang, and Étienne Langerwerf. "The Comparative Analysis of Litigation Rates." In *Disputes and the Law,* edited by Maureen Cain and Kálmán Kulcsár, pp. 147-164. Budapest: Akadémiai Kiadó, 1983.

Kealey, Gregory S. *Toronto Workers Respond to Industrial Capitalism 1867-1892.* Toronto: University of Toronto Press, 1980.

Kealey, Linda, ed. *A Not Unreasonable Claim, Women and Reform in Canada, 1880s-1920s.* Toronto: Women's Press 1979.

Kehoe, Jack. "Ethnocentrism, Self-Esteem and Appreciation of Cultural Diversity." *Canadian Ethnic Studies,* Vol. 14, No. 3, pp. 69-78, 1982.

Keller, Suzanne. *The Urban Neighbourhood.* New York: Random House, 1968.

Kelly, Michael J., and Thomas H. Mitchell. "The study of internal conflict in Canada: problems and prospects." *Conflict Quarterly,* Vol. 2, pp. 10-17, 1981.

Kelner, Merrijoy; Oswald Hall; and Dan Coulter. *Chiropractors: do they help? a study of their education and practice.* Toronto: Fitzhenry and Whiteside, 1980.

Kemp, Tom. *Historical Patterns of Industrialization.* New York: Longman, 1978.

Kennedy, Leslie W. *The Urban Kaleidoscope: Canadian Perspectives.* Toronto: McGraw-Hill Ryerson Ltd., 1983.

Kennedy, Ruby Jo Reeves. "Single or triple melting-pot? Intermarriage in New Haven, 1870-1950." *American Journal of Sociology,* Vol. 58, pp. 56-59, 1952.

Kesterton, Wilfred. "The Growth of the Newspaper in Canada." In *Communications in Canadian Society,* edited by B. Singer, pp. 3-16. Toronto: Addison-Wesley, 1983.

Keyfitz, Nathan, and Wilhelm Flieger. *Population: Facts and Methods of Demography.* San Francisco: W.H. Freeman, 1971.

Kidder, Louise. *Selltiz, Wrightsman and Cook's Research Methods in Social Relations.* 4th ed. New York: Holt, Rinehart and Winston, 1981.

Kidder, Robert L. *Connecting Law and Society.* Englewood Cliffs, N.J.: Prentice-Hall, 1983.

Kimball, M. "Socialization of Women: A Study in Conflict." In *Marriage, Family and Society,* edited by S.P. Wakil, pp. 189-201. Toronto: Butterworth, 1975.

Kirk, Dudley. "A new demographic transition?". In *Rapid Population Growth: Consequences and Policy Implications,* National Academy of Sciences, pp. 123-147. Baltimore: Johns Hopkins Press, 1971.

Klapp, Orrin E. *Collective Search for Identity.* New York: Holt, Rinehart & Winston, 1969.

Klapper, Joseph. *The Effects of Mass Communication.* New York: The Free Press, 1960.

Kohlberg, Lawrence. "A Cognitive-Developmental Analysis of Children's Sex-role Concepts and Attitudes." In *The Development of Sex Differences,* edited by E. Maccoby, pp. 82-172. Stanford, Calif.: Stanford University Press, 1966.

Kopinak, Kathryn. "Polity." In *Sociology,* edited by Robert Hagedorn, pp. 429-473. Toronto: Holt, Rinehart and Winston, 1980.

Kornhauser, William. *The Politics of Mass Society.* Glencoe, Ill.: The Free Press, 1959.

Korpi, Walter. "Conflict, power and relative deprivation." *American Political Science Review,* Vol. 68, pp. 971-984, 1974.

———— and Michael Shalev. "Strikes, power, and politics in the Western nations, 1900-1976." *Political Power and Social Theory,* Vol. 1, pp. 301-334, 1980.

Kotler, Philip. *Marketing for Nonprofit Organizations.* Englewood Cliffs, N.J.: Prentice-Hall, 1975.

Krochak, Kevin. "Native Education." *The Fulcrum,* Ottawa, Feb. 14, 1985, pp. 12-13, (reprinted from The *Manitoban*).

Kroeber, A. L., and T. Parsons. "The Concepts of Culture and of Social System." *American Sociological Review,* Vol. 23, pp. 582-583, 1958.

Kronman, Anthony T. *Max Weber.* Stanford, Calif.: Stanford University Press, 1983.

Kuhn, Thomas S. *The Structure of Scientific Revolutions.* 2d ed. Chicago: The University of Chicago Press, 1970.

Lachapelle, Rejean. "Evolution of ethnic and linguistic composition." In *Cultural Boundaries and the Cohesion of Canada,* edited by R. Breton, J. Reitz and V. Valentine, pp. 15-43. Montreal: Institute for Research on Public Policy, 1980.

Lambert, R.D., and A.A. Hunter. "Social Stratification, Voting Behaviour, and the Images of Canadian Federal Political Parties." *Canadian Review of Sociology and Anthropology,* Vol. 16, pp. 287-304, 1979.

Landes, D.S. *The Unbound Prometheus.* London: Cambridge University Press, 1969.

Lane, Robert E. *Political Life.* The Free Press, Glencoe, Ill.: 1959.

Langness, L.L. *The Study of Culture.* San Francisco: Chandler & Sharp Publishers, Inc., 1974.

Larkin, Ralph. *Suburban Youth in Cultural Crisis.* New York: Oxford University Press, 1979.

Larson, Lyle E. *The Impact of Resource Development on Individual and Family Well Being.* Edmonton: Alberta Oil Sands Environmental Research Program, 1977.

Laslett, Peter, ed. *Household and Family in Past Time.* London: Cambridge University Press, 1972.

———. *The World We Have Lost.* 2d ed. London: Methuen, 1971.

Lasswell, Harold. "The Structure and Function of Communication in Society." In *The Communication of Ideas,* edited by L. Bryson. New York: Harper, 1948.

——— and Abraham Kaplan. *Power and Society.* New Haven, Conn.: Yale University Press, 1950.

Lauer, Robert. "Socialization into Inequality: Children's Perception of Occupational Status." *Sociology and Social Research,* Vol. 58, No. 2, pp. 176-183, 1974.

Lautard, Hugh E., and Donald J. Loree. "Ethnic stratification in Canada, 1931-1971." *Canadian Journal of Sociology,* Vol. 9, pp. 333-343.

Lavoie, Yolande. *L'émigration des Canadiens aux Etats-Unis avant 1930.* Montréal: Les Presses de l'Université de Montréal, Collection Demographie canadienne 1, 1972.

Laxer, Gordon. "Class, Nationality, and the Roots of Foreign Ownership." In *The Structure of the Canadian Capitalist Class,* edited by Robert J. Brym. Toronto: Garamond Press, 1985.

Laxer, Robert. *Canada's Unions.* Toronto: James Lorimer, 1976.

Leacy, F.H., ed. *Historical Statistics of Canada:* Ottawa: Statistics Canada, 1983.

Le Bon, Gustave. *The Crowd: A Study of the Popular Mind.* New York: Ballantine, 1969.

Leiter, D.C.W. "Ad hocing in the Schools: A Study of the Placement Practices in the Kindergartens of Two Schools." In *Language Use and School Performance,* edited by A. Cicourel et al., pp. 17-75. New York: Academic, 1974.

Lele, J., G.C. Perlin; and H.G. Thorburn. "The National Party Convention." In *Political Parties in Canada,* 4th ed., edited by H.G. Thorburn. Toronto: Prentice-Hall, 1979.

Lemert, Edwin M. *Human Deviance, Social Problems, and Social Control.* 2d ed. Englewood Cliffs, N.J.: Prentice-Hall, 1972.

Lennards, J. L. "Education." In *Sociology,* edited by Robert Hagedorn, pp. 475-514. Toronto: Holt, Rinehart and Winston, 1980.

Leonard, J.S. "What Promises are Worth: The Impact of Affirmative Action Goals." *The Journal of Human Resources,* Vol. 20, No. 1, pp. 3-20.

Lerner, Daniel. *The Passing of Traditional Society.* New York: The Free Press, 1965.

Leslie, G.R. *The Family in Social Context.* 4th ed. New York: Oxford, 1979.

Levine, David. "Production, Reproduction, and the Proletarian Family in England, 1500-1851." *Proletarianization and Family History,* edited by David Levine, pp. 87-128. New York: Academic, 1984.

Levine, Robert, and Ellen Wolff. "Social Time: The Heartbeat of Culture." *Psychology Today,* pp. 28-35, March 1985.

Levinson, D. *The Seasons of a Man's Life.* New York: Alfred Knopf, 1978.

Levitt, Cyril. *Children of Privilege: Student Revolt in the Sixties.* Toronto: University of Toronto Press, 1984.

Levitt, Kari. *Silent Surrender: The Multinational Corporation in Canada*. Toronto: Macmillan of Canada, 1970.

Levy, Robert I. "The Community Function of Tahitian Male Transvestism: A Hypothesis." *Anthropological Quarterly* Vol. 44, pp. 12-21, January 1971.

Lewis, Oscar. "The Culture of Poverty." *Scientific American,* Vol. 215, No. 4, pp. 19-25, 1966.

Li, Peter S. "A historical approach to ethnic stratification: the case of the Chinese in Canada, 1858-1930." *Canadian Review of Sociology and Anthropology* Vol. 16, pp. 320-332, 1979.

———. "Canadian immigration policy and assimilation theories." In *Economy, Class and Social Reality,* edited by J.A. Fry, pp. 411-422. Toronto: Butterworth, 1979.

———. *Social Research Methods.* Toronto: Butterworth, 1981.

——— and B. Singh Bolaria. *Racial Minorities in Multicultural Canada.* Toronto: Garamond Press, 1983.

Lichter, S. Robert, and Stanley Rothman. "Media and Business Elites." *Public Opinion Quarterly,* Vol. 45, pp. 42-60, 1981.

Lieberson, Stanley. *Language and Ethnic Relations in Canada.* New York: John Wiley & Sons, 1970.

Liebow, Elliot. *Tally's Corner.* Boston: Little, Brown & Co., 1967.

Lindell, Susan. "Role Expectations of Adolescent Women." *Canadian Women's Studies,* Vol. 4, No. 1, pp. 67-70, 1982.

Lindesmith, Alfred R.; Anselm L. Strauss; and Norman K. Denzin. *Social Psychology.* New York: Holt, Rinehart and Winston, 1977.

Linton, Ralph. *The Study of Man: An Introduction.* Englewood Cliffs, N.J.: Prentice-Hall, 1936.

Lipovenko, Dorothy. "Day Care Spaces for Infants Steadily Declining, Study Says." *Globe and Mail,* November 1984.

Lipset, Seymour Martin. *Agrarian Socialism: The Cooperative Commonwealth Federation in Saskatchewan.* rev. ed. Berkeley, Calif.: University of California Press, 1968.

———. "Canada and the United States: The Cultural Dimension." In *Canada and the United States,* edited by Charles F. Doran and John H. Sigler. Toronto: Prentice-Hall, 1985.

———. *The First New Nation.* Garden City, N.Y.: Doubleday, 1963.

———. *Political Man.* London: Heinemann, 1960.

———. "Radicalism in North America: a comparative view of the party systems in Canada and the United States." *Transactions of the Royal Society of Canada,* Series IV, Vol 14, pp. 19-55, 1976.

———. "Radicalism or reformism: the sources of working-class politics." *American Political Science Review,* Vol. 77, pp. 1-18, 1983.

———. *Revolution and Counterrevolution.* New York: Anchor Books, 1970.

———. "The Value Patterns of Democracy: A Case Study in Comparative Analysis." *American Sociological Review,* Vol. 28, 1963.

———. "Values, Education and Entrepreneurship." In *Elites in Latin America,* edited by S.M. Lipset and Aldo Solari. New York: Oxford University Press, 1967.

——— and Stein Rokkan. "Cleavage structures, party systems and voter alignments: an introduction." In *Party Systems and Voter Alignments: Cross-National Perspectives,* edited by S. Lipset and S. Rokkan, pp. 1-64. New York: Free Press, 1967.

———; M.A. Trow; and J.S. Coleman. *Union Democracy.* Glencoe, Ill.: The Free Press, 1956.

Liska, Allen E. *Perspectives on Deviance.* Englewood Cliffs, N.J.: Prentice-Hall, 1981.

——— and Mitchell B. Chamlin. "Social Structure and Crime Control among Macrosocial Units." *American Journal of Sociology,* Vol. 90, No. 2, pp. 333-395, 1984.

Lloyd, Peter C. "The Political Structure of African Kingdoms." In *Political Systems and the Distribution of Power,* edited by M. Banton. London: Tavistock, 1965.

———. *Slums of Hope? Shanty Towns of the Third World.* New York: St. Martin's Press, 1979.

Lodhi, Abdul Qaiyum, and Charles Tilly. "Urbanization, crime, and collective violence in 19th-century France." *American Journal of Sociology*, Vol. 79, pp. 296-318, 1973.

Lofland, John. *Deviance and Identity*. Englewood Cliffs, N.J.: Prentice-Hall, 1969.

Long, Norton. "The Local Community as an Ecology of Games." *American Journal of Sociology,* Vol. 64, pp. 251-261, 1958.

Lopata, H. *Widowhood in an American City.* Cambridge, Mass.: Schenkman Publishing Co., 1973.

———. *Women as Widows: Support Systems.* New York: Elsevier, 1979.

Lorimer, James. *The Developers*. Toronto: James Lorimer & Co., 1978.

Lowery, S., and Melvin L. DeFleur. *Milestones in Mass Communications Research*. New York: Longmans, 1983.

Lucas, Rex. *Minetown, Milltown, Railtown.* Toronto: University of Toronto Press, 1972.

Lukes, Steven. *Power: A Radical View*. London: Macmillan, 1974.

Luxton, Meg. *More Than a Labour of Love: Three Generations of Women's Work in the Home*. Toronto: Women's Press, 1980.

Lyell, Ruth G. "Adolescent and Adult Self-Esteem as related to Cultural Values." *Adolescence,* Vol. 8, pp. 85-92, Spring 1973.


Maccoby, Eleanor, and Carol Jacklin. *The Psychology of Sex Differences*. Stanford, Calif.: Stanford University Press, 1974.

Mackie, Marlene. *Exploring Gender Relations*. Toronto: Butterworth, 1982.

———. "Socialization: Changing Views of Child Rearing and Adolescence." In *The Family, Changing Trends in Canada,* edited by Maureen Baker, pp. 35-62. Toronto: McGraw-Hill Ryerson, 1984.

——— and Merlin B. Brinkerhoff. "Measuring Ethnic Salience." *Canadian Ethnic Studies,* Vol. 16, No. 1, pp. 114-131, 1984.

Macpherson, C.B. *Democracy in Alberta: Social Credit and the Party System*. 2d ed. Toronto: University of Toronto Press, 1962.

———. *The Real World of Democracy*. Toronto: Canadian Broadcasting Corporation, 1965.

———, ed. *Property: Mainstream & Critical Positions*. Toronto: University of Toronto Press, 1978.

Madigan, Francis C. "Are sex mortality differentials biologically caused?". *Millbank Memorial Fund Quarterly,* Vol. 35, pp. 202-223, 1957.

Maine, Henry. *Ancient Law*. London: 1907.

Mair, Lucy. *Primitive Government*. Harmondsworth: Penguin, 1963.

Makabe, Tomoko. "The theory of the split labor market: a comparison of the Japanese experience in Brazil and Canada." *Social Forces,* Vol. 59, pp. 786-809, 1981.

Malinowski, Bronislaw. "Review of Six Essays on Culture by Albert Blumenthal." *American Sociological Review,* Vol. 4, pp. 588-592, 1939.

Malthus, Thomas R. *Population: The First Essay*. Ann Arbor: University of Michigan Press, 1959.

———. "A summary view of the principle of population." In *Malthus: An Essay on the Principle of Population,* edited by Anthony Flew. New York: Penguin Books, 1970.

Mann, Michael. *Consciousness and Action among the Western Working Class*. London: Macmillan, 1973.

Mann, N.E., ed. *The Underside of Toronto*. Toronto: McClelland and Stewart, 1970.

Mannheim, Karl. *Ideology and Utopia*. New York: Harcourt, Brace and Company, 1936.

Marchak, Patricia. *Ideological Perspectives on Canada*. 2d ed. Toronto: McGraw-Hill Ryerson, 1981.

———. *In Whose Interests*. Toronto, McClelland and Stewart, 1979.

Marcuse, Herbert. *Counter-Revolution and Revolt*. Boston: Beacon Press, 1972.

———. *An Essay on Liberation*. Boston: Beacon Press, 1969.

———. *One-Dimensional Man*. Boston: Beacon Press, 1964.

Marger, Martin N. *Race and Ethnic Relations.* Belmont, Calif.: Wadsworth, 1985.

Marsden, Lorna, and Edward Harvey. *Fragile Federation.* Toronto: McGraw-Hill Ryerson, 1979.

Marshall, Victor W. *Aging in Canada. Social Perspectives.* Toronto: Fitzhenry and Whiteside, 1980.

——— and Joseph Tindale. "A Generational Conflict Perspective for Gerontology." In *Aging in Canada,* Victor W. Marshall, pp. 43-50. Toronto: Fitzhenry and Whiteside, 1980.

Martin, James K. "Social Policy Concerns Related to Retirement: Implications for Research." In *Canada's Changing Age Structure,* G. Gutman. Vancouver: Simon Fraser University Publications, 1982.

Martin, W.B.W. *The Negotiated Order of the School.* Toronto: Macmillan, 1976.

——— and Allan J. Macdonell. *Canadian Education.* 2d ed. Toronto: Prentice-Hall, 1982.

Marx, Gary T., and James L. Wood. "Strands of theory and research in collective behavior." *Annual Review of Sociology,* Vol. 1, pp. 363-428, 1975.

Marx, Karl. *Capital,* Vol. 1. Moscow: Foreign Languages Publishing House, 1954.

———. *A Contribution to the Critique of Political Economy.* Moscow: Progress Publishers, 1970.

———. "The German Ideology." In *The Marx-Engels Reader,* edited by R.C. Tucker, pp. 146-200. New York: Norton, 1978.

———. *Pre-Capitalist Economic Formations.* New York: International Publishers, 1965.

———. *Early Texts.* Edited by D. McLellan. Oxford: Basil Blackwell, 1972. *Selected Writings.* Edited by D. McLellan. Oxford University Press, 1977.

——— and Frederick Engels. "The Class Struggles in France." In *Selected Works,* 2 vols., K. Marx and F. Engels. Moscow: Foreign Languages Publishing House, 1950.

———. *The Communist Manifesto.* Edited by Samuel H. Beer. New York: Appleton Century-Crofts, 1955.

———. *The German Ideology.* New York: International Publishers, 1969.

Maslow, Abraham. *Motivation and Personality.* New York: Harper & Row, 1954.

Matthews, Ralph. "Regional Differences in Canada." In *Social Issues: Sociological Views of Canada,* edited by Dennis Forcese and Stephen Richer. Toronto: Prentice-Hall, 1982.

———. "The Significance and Explanation of Regional Divisions in Canada: Toward a Canadian Sociology." *Journal of Canadian Studies,* Vol. 15, No. 2, pp. 43-61, 1980.

Matthews, Robin. "Regional Differences in Canada: Social versus Economic Interpretations." In *Social Issues: Sociological Views of Canada,* edited by D. Forcese and S. Richer, pp. 82-123. Toronto: Prentice-Hall, 1982.

Matza, David. *Becoming Deviant.* Englewood Cliffs, N.J.: Prentice-Hall, 1969.

———. "The Disreputable Poor." In *The Collective Definition of Deviance,* edited by F. James Davis and Richard Stivers, pp. 197-221. New York: The Free Press, 1975.

Mayer, Arno. "The Lower Middle Class as Historical Problem." *Journal of Modern History,* Vol. 47, pp. 409-36, September 1975.

Mayhew, Leon, and Albert J. Reiss, Jr. "The Social Organization of Legal Contacts." *American Sociological Review,* Vol. 34, No. 3, pp. 309-318, 1969.

McCain, Garvin, and Erwin M. Segal. *The Game of Science.* Belmont, Calif.: Brooks/Cole Publishing Company, 1969.

McCallum, John. *Unequal Beginnings: Agriculture and Economic Development in Quebec and Ontario until 1870.* Toronto: University of Toronto Press, 1980.

McCarthy, J., and M. Zald. "Resource mobilization and social movements," *American Journal of Sociology,* Vol. 82, pp. 1212-1241, 1977.

McClelland, David. "The Achievement Motive in economic growth." In *Development and Society: The Dynamics of Economic Change,* edited by David Novack and Robert Lekachman. New York: St. Martin's Press, 1964.

———. "Motivational Patterns in Southeast Asia." *Journal of Social Issues,* Vol. 29, No. 17, January 1963.

McCoombs, Maxwell E., and Donald L. Shaw. "Structuring the Unseen Environment." *Public Opinion Quarterly,* Vol. 40, No. 1, pp. 18-22, 1976.

McDonald, Lynn. *The Sociology of Law and Order.* London: Faber and Faber, 1976.

McGahan, Peter. *Urban Sociology in Canada.* Toronto: Butterworth, 1982.

McGraw, Garet. "Wife Assault." *Canadian Forum,* Vol. 63, pp. 16-17, December 1983.

McGregor, Douglas. *The Human Side of Enterprise.* New York: McGraw-Hill, 1960.

McKeown, Thomas, and R.G. Brown. "Medical evidence related to English population changes in the Eighteenth Century." In *Population in History,* edited by D.V. Glass and D.E.C. Eversley, pp. 285-307. London: Edward Arnold, 1965.

McLuhan, Marshall. *Understanding Media: The Extensions of Man.* New York: McGraw-Hill, 1965.

McPherson, Barry D. *Aging as a Social Process.* Toronto: Butterworth, 1983.

McQuail, Denis. *Mass Communication Theory.* London: Sage, 1983.

———— and Sven Windell. *Communication Models.* London: Longmans, 1981.

McRoberts, Hugh A. "Family of Origin and Social Mobility in Canada." pp. in Stephen Richer and Dennis Forcese (eds.)

———— et al. "Differences dans la mobilite professionnelle des francophones et des anglophones." *Sociologie et Societes,* Vol. 8, pp. 61-79, 1976.

———— and Kevin Selbee. "Trends in Occupational Mobility in Canada and the United States: A Comparison." *American Sociological Review,* Vol. 46, No. 4, pp. 406-21.

Mead, George H. *Mind, Self and Society.* Chicago: University of Chicago Press, 1934.

————. *The Philosophy of the Act.* Edited by Charles Morris. Chicago: The University of Chicago Press, 1938.

Mead, Margaret. *Sex and Temperament in Three Primitive Societies.* New York: Dell, 1935.

Meadows, D.H. et al. *The Limits to Growth.* New York: Universe Books, 1972.

Meek, Ronald L., ed. *Marx and Engels on Malthus.* New York: International Publishers, 1954.

Meissner, Martin et al. "No Exit for Wives: Sexual Division of Labour and the Cumulation of Household Demands." *Canadian Review of Sociology and Anthropology,* Vol. 12, Part 1, pp. 424-439.

Melody, W., and Robin Mansell. "The Debate over Critical vs. Administrative Research: Circularity or Challenge." *Journal of Communication,* Vol. 33, No. 3, pp. 103-116, 1983.

Meltzer, B.N.; J.W. Petras; and L.T. Reynolds. *Symbolic Interactionism.* London: Routledge and Kegan Paul, 1975.

Meng, Ronald, and Jim Sentance. "Canadian Universities: Who Benefits and Who Pays?". *The Canadian Journal of Higher Education,* Vol. 12, pp. 47-58, 1982.

Mensch, Elizabeth. "The History of Mainstream Legal Thought." In *The Politics of Law: A Progressive Critique,* edited by David Kairys, pp. 18-39. New York: Pantheon, 1982.

Mercer, Jane R. *Labeling the Retarded.* Berkeley, Calif.: University of California Press, 1973.

Merton, Robert K. *Social Theory and Social Structure.* New York: The Free Press, 1957.

————. *On Theoretical Sociology.* New York: The Free Press, 1967.

Michels, Robert. *Political Parties.* New York: The Free Press, 1962.

Michelson, William. *Environmental Choice, Human Behavior, and Residential Satisfaction.* New York: Oxford University Press, 1977.

————. *From Sun to Sun: Daily Obligations and Community Structure in the Lives of Employed Women and their Families.* Totowa, N.J.: Rowman & Allanheld, 1985.

————. *Man and his Urban Environment: A Sociological Approach.* Toronto: Addison-Wesley, 1970.

———— and Ellis Roberts. "Children and the Urban Physical Environment." In *The Child* in the City: Changes and Challenges, W. Michelson, S. Levine and A. Spina. Toronto: University of Toronto Press, 1979.

Mifflen, Frank J. and Sydney C. Mifflen. *The Sociology of Education: Canada and Beyond.* Calgary: Detselig, 1982.

Milbrath, L.W. and M.L. Goel. *Political Participation.* 2d ed. Chicago: Rand McNally, 1977.

Miles, Robert. *Racism and Migrant Labour.* London: Routledge & Kegan Paul, 1982.

Milgram, Stanley. "The Experience of Living in Cities." *Science,* Vol. 167, pp. 1461-1468, 1970.

Miliband, Ralph. *The State in Capitalist Society.* London: Weidenfeld and Nicolson, 1969.

———. "State Power and Class Interests." *New Left Review,* No. 138, pp. 57-68, 1983.

Millett, Kate. *Sexual Politics.* New York: Avon Books, 1970.

Mills, C. Wright. *The Power Elite.* New York: Oxford University Press, 1953.

———. *The Sociological Imagination.* London: Oxford University Press, 1959.

———. *White Collar: The American Middle Classes.* New York: Oxford, 1956.

Milner, Henry. *Politics in the New Quebec.* Toronto: McClelland and Stewart.

Miner, Horace. "Body Ritual among the Nacirema." *The American Anthropologist,* Vol. 58, pp. 503-507, 1956.

Miyamoto, Frank S., and Sanford M. Dornbusch. "A Test of Interactionist Hypotheses of Self-Conception." *American Journal of Sociology,* Vol. 61, 1956.

Mommsen, Wolfgang J. "Max Weber as a critic of Marx." *Canadian Journal of Sociology,* Vol. 2, No. 4, pp. 373-398, 1977.

Moore, Barrington Jr. *Social Origins of Dictatorship and Democracy.* London: Peregrine, 1969.

Moore, Joan W. "Colonialism: the case of Mexican Americans." *Social Problems,* Vol. 17, pp. 463-472, 1970.

Morgan, N.S. *No-where to go?* Montreal: Institute for Research on Public Policy, 1981.

Morin, A. "The Impact of Change to the Mandatory Retirement Age." Ottawa: Library of Parliament, August 23, 1978.

Mortimer, Jeylan T., and Roberta G. Simmons. "Adult Socialization." In *Annual Review of Sociology,* Vol. 4, pp. 421-454. Palo Alto: Annual Review Inc., 1978.

Mumford, L. *The Pentagon of Power,* New York: Harcourt, Brace, Jovanovich, 1970.

Mungham, Geoff, and Geoff Pearson. *Working Class Youth Culture.* London: Routledge and Kegan Paul, 1976.

Murdie, Robert A. *Factorial Ecology of Metropolitan Toronto.* Chicago: University of Chicago, Department of Geography Research Paper No. 116, 1969.

Murdock, G., and G. Phelps. *Mass Media and the Secondary School.* London: Macmillan, 1973.

Murphy, Raymond. *Sociological Theories of Education.* Toronto: McGraw-Hill Ryerson, 1979.

Myles, John. *Old Age in the Welfare State.* Toronto: Little Brown, 1984.

———. "Social Implications of Canada's Changing Age Structure." In *Canada's Changing Age Structure,* G. Gutman. Vancouver: Simon Fraser University Publications, 1982.

National Council of Welfare: *Sixty-Five and Older: Report on the Income of the Aged,* Ottawa: February 1984.

National Opinion Research Centre. "Jobs and Occupations: A Popular Evaluation." *Opinion News,* Vol. 11, pp. 3-13, 1947.

Naylor, R.T. "The Rise and Fall of the Third Commercial Empire of the St. Lawrence." In *Capitalism and the National Question,* edited by Gary Teeple, pp. 1-41. Toronto: University of Toronto Press, 1972.

Neill, A.S. *Summerhill: A Radical Approach to Child Rearing.* New York: Hart, 1960.

Neill, Robin. *A New Theory of Value: The Canadian Economics of H.A. Innis.* Toronto: University of Toronto Press, 1972.

Nett, Emily. "Canadian Families in Social-Historical Perspective." *Canadian Journal of Sociology,* Vol. 6, No. 3, pp. 239-260, 1981.

———. "The Family and Aging." In *The Family, Changing Trends in Canada,* edited by Maureen Baker, pp. 129-161. Toronto: McGraw-Hill Ryerson, 1984.

Neugarten, B. *Middle Age and Aging: a Reader in Social Psychology.* Chicago: University of Chicago Press, 1968.

Neuman, W. Russell. "Television and American Culture: the Mass Medium and the Pluralist Audience." *Public Opinion Quarterly,* Vol. 46, pp. 471-487, 1982.

Newcomb, T.M. *Personality and Social Change.* New York: Dryden, 1943.

Newcomb, T.M. et al. *Persistence and Change: Bennington College and its students after 25 years.* New York: Wiley, 1967.

Newman, Oscar. *Defensible Space.* New York: Macmillan, 1972.

Newman, Peter C. *The Canadian Establishment,* Vol. 1. Toronto: McClelland and Stewart, 1979.

Nichols, Peter C. and Associates. *Service Delivery in the Athabasca Oil Sands Region since 1961,* Edmonton: Alberta Oil Sands Environmental Research Program.

Niosi, Jorge. *Canadian Multinationals.* Ontario: Garamond Press, 1985.

———. *The Economy of Canada: A Study of Ownership and Control.* Montreal: Black Rose Books, 1978.

Nisbet, Robert A. "The Decline and Fall of Social Class." *Pacific Sociological Review,* Vol. 2, pp. 11-17, 1959.

———. *The Sociological Tradition.* New York: Basic Books, 1966.

——— and Robert G. Perrin. *The Social Bond.* 2d ed. New York: Alfred A. Knopf, 1977.

Noble, D. *America by Design.* New York: Knopf, 1979.

Noelle-Neuman, Elisabeth. *The Spiral of Silence.* Chicago: University of Chicago Press, 1984.

Nonet, Philippe, and Philip Selznick. *Law and Society in Transition: Toward Responsive Law.* New York: Harper Torchbooks, 1978.

Nosanchuk, Terrance A. "A Note on the Use of the Correlation Coefficient for Assessing the Similarity of Occupational Rankings." *The Canadian Review of Sociology and Anthropology,* Vol. 9, No. 4, pp. 357-67, 1972.

Nunes, Maxine, and Deanna White. *The Lace Ghetto.* Toronto: New Press, 1973.

Oakley, Ann. *Subject Women.* New York: Pantheon Books, 1981.

Oberschall, Anthony. *Social Conflict and Social Movements.* Englewood Cliffs, N.J.: Prentice-Hall, 1973.

O'Connell, Agnes. "The Social Origins of Gender." In *Female and Male: Psychological Perspectives,* R. Unger, pp. 146-166. New York: Harper and Row, 1979.

Offe, Claus. "Political Authority and Class Structure: an Analysis of Late Capitalist Societies." *International Journal of Sociology,* Vol. 2, pp. 73-108, 1972.

Ogmundson, Rick. "Party Class Images and the Class Vote in Canada." *American Sociological Review,* Vol. 40, pp. 506-512, 1975.

———. "Toward study of the endangered species known as the anglophone Canadian." *Canadian Journal of Sociology,* Vol. 5, No. 1, pp. 1-12, 1980.

O'Kelly, Charlotte G. *Men and Women in Society.* New York: Van Nostrand, 1980.

Olsen, Denis. *The State Elite.* Toronto: McClelland and Stewart, 1980.

Olson, Paul, and George Burns. "Politics, Class, and Happenstance: French Immersion in a Canadian Context." *Interchange,* Vol. 14, pp. 1-16, 1983.

Ontario, Government of. *Changing Organizations: The Quality of Working Life Process.* Toronto: Ontario Ministry of Labour, 1983.

Orbach, Susie. *Fat is a Feminist Issue II: A Program to Conquer Compulsive Eating.* New York: Berkley Books, 1982.

Ornstein, Michael D. "The Development of Class in Canada." In *Sociology: An Alternative Approach,* edited by Paul Grayson, pp. 216-259. Toronto: Gage, 1983.

Orwell, George. *Nineteen Eighty-Four.* New York: Penguin Books, 1984.

Osberg, Lars. *Economic Inequality in Canada.* Toronto: Butterworth, 1981.

Osherow, Neal. *"Making Sense of the Non-sensical. An Analysis of Jonestown."* In *Readings About the Social Animal*, edited by Elliot Aronson, pp. 69-88. San Francisco: W.H. Freeman, 1981.

Ossowski, S. *Class Structure in the Social Consciousness*. Translated by S. Patterson. New York: The Free Press, 1963.

Ouchi, William G., and Alfred M. Jaeger. "Type Z Organization: Stability in the Midst of Mobility." *Academy of Management Review*, Vol. 3, pp. 35-14, April 1978.

Overbeek, Johannes. *History of Population Theories*. Rotterdam: Rotterdam University Press, 1974.

Oxenham, John. *Literacy: Writing, Reading and Social Organisation*. London: Routledge & Kegan Paul, 1980.


Packard, Vance. *The Waste Makers* New York.: David McKay, 1960.

Pahl, R.E. *Whose City? and Other Essays on Sociology and Planning*. New York: Longman, 1970.

Palen, John. *The Urban World*. Toronto: McGraw-Hill, 1981.

Palmer, Bryan D. *A Culture in Conflict: Skilled Workers and Industrial Capitalism in Hamilton, Ontario, 1860-1914*. Montreal: McGill-Queen's University Press, 1979.

———. *Working Class Experience: The Rise and Reconstitution of Canadian Labour, 1800-1980*. Butterworth (Canada) Ltd., 1983.

———. "Social Formation and Class Formation in North America, 1800-1900." In *Proletarianization and Family History*, edited by David Levine, pp. 229-309. New York: Academic Press, 1984.

J.H. Pammett et al. "The Perception and Impact of Issues in the 1974 Federal Election." *Canadian Journal of Political Science*, Vol. 10, pp. 93-126, 1977.

Pappert, Ann. "Today's Women, Yesterday's Dreams." *Homemaker's Digest,* pp. 166-180, October 1980.

Parai, L. *Immigration and Emigration of Professional and Skilled Manpower During the Post-War Period*. Ottawa: Queen's Printer, 1965.

Park, Robert E. "The City: Suggestions for the Investigation of Human Behavior in the Urban Environment." In *The City*, edited by R.Park, E. Burgess, and R. McKenzie, pp.1-46. Chicago: University of Chicago Press, 1925.

———. *Race and Culture*. Glencoe, Ill.: Free Press, 1950.

Parkin, Frank. *Class Inequality and Political Order*. London: Macgibbon and Kee, 1971.

———. *Marxism and Class Theory: A Bourgeois Theory*. New York: Columbia University Press, 1979.

———, ed. *The Social Analysis of Class Structure*. London: Tavistock, 1974.

Parsons, Talcott. "Age and Sex Structure of the United States." *American Sociological Review*, Vol. 7, pp. 604-616, 1942.

———. "Culture and Social System Revisited." In *The Idea of Culture in the Social Sciences*, edited by L. Schneider and C. Bonjean, pp. 33-46. Cambridge University Press, 1973.

———. *Essays in Sociological Theory*. Glencoe, Ill.: The Free Press, 1954.

———. "A Revised Analytic Approach to the Theory of Social Stratification." In *Class, Status and Power*, edited by R. Bendix and S.M. Lipset, pp. 92-128. Glencoe, Ill.: The Free Press, 1953.

———. *The Social System*. New York: The Free Press, 1951.

Patterson, E. Palmer II. *The Canadian Indian: A History since 1500*. Toronto: Collier-Macmillan Canada, 1972.

Payne, Geoffrey K. *Urban Housing in the Third World*. Boston: Routledge & Kegan Paul, 1977.

Pearson, Judy L. *Gender and Communication*. Wm. Brown, 1985.

Pelto, P.J. *The Snowmobile Revolution: Technology and Social Change in the Arctic*. Menlo Park: Cummings, 1973.

———. "The Development of The Capitalist Labour Market in Canada." *The Canadian*

*Journal of Economic and Political Science,* 25 (November), 1959.

Pentland, Clare H. *Labour and Capital in Canada 1650-1860.* Toronto: University of Toronto Press, 1981.

Perrow, Charles. "The Bureaucratic Paradox." *Organizational Dynamics,* Spring 1977.

⸺. *Complex Organizations: A Critical Essay.* Chicago: Scott, Foresman, 1972.

Perry, Clarence. "The Neighborhood Unit Formula." In *Urban Housing,* edited by William Wheaton et al., pp. 94-109. New York: The Free Press of Glencoe, 1966.

Peters, John F. "Reciprocal Socialization." forthcoming, *Adolescence,* 1985.

Petersen, William. *Population.* 3d ed. New York: Macmillan, 1975.

Peterson, Richard A. "Revitalizing the Culture Concept." *Annual Review of Sociology,* pp. 137-166. Palo Alto: Annual Reviews Inc., 1979.

Phillips, D.P. "The Behavioral Impact of Violence in the Mass Media: A Review of Evidence from Laboratory and Nonlaboratory Investigations." *Sociology and Social Research,* Vol. 66, pp. 560-568, 1982.

⸺. "Suicide, Motor Vehicle Fatalities, and the Mass Media: Evidence Toward a Theory of Suggestion." *American Journal of Sociology,* Vol. 84, pp. 1150-1174, 1979.

Phillips, E. Barbara, and Richard T. LeGates. *City Lights.* New York: Oxford University Press, 1981.

Phillips, Paul. *Regional Disparities.* 2d ed. Toronto: James Lorimer and Co., 1982.

Pickersgill, J.W., and D.F. Forster. *The Mackenzie King Record, Volume 4, 1947-1948.* Toronto: University of Toronto Press, 1970.

Pickvance, C., ed. *Urban Sociology.* London: Tavistock, 1976.

Pike, Robert M. "Education, Class and Power in Canada." In *Power and Change in Canada,* edited by Richard Ossenberg, pp. 106-145. Toronto: McClelland and Stewart, 1980.

Pinard, Maurice. *The Rise of a Third Party: A Study in Crisis Politics.* Englewood Cliffs, N.J.: Prentice-Hall, 1971.

⸺. "Third parties in Canada revisited: a rejoinder and elaboration of the theory of one-party dominance." *Canadian Journal of Political Science,* Vol. 6, pp. 439-460, 1973.

Pineo, Peter. "Prestige and Mobility." *Canadian Review of Sociology and Anthropology,* Vol. 18, No. 5, pp. 615-626, 1981.

⸺ and John Porter. "Occupational Prestige in Canada." *Canadian Review of Sociology and Anthropology,* Vol. 4, No. 1, pp. 24-40, 1967.

Plant, James S. "The Personality and an Urban Area." In *Cities and Society,* edited by P.K. Hatt and A.J. Reiss, pp. 647-665. New York: The Free Press, 1957.

Poggi, G. *The Development of the Modern State.* Stanford: Stanford University Press, 1978.

Porteous, J. Douglas. *Environment and Behavior.* Toronto: Addison-Wesley, 1977.

Porter, John. "Ethnic Pluralism in Canadian Perspective." In *The Measure of Canadian Society,* John Porter, pp. 103-138. Toronto: Gage, 1979.

⸺. *The Vertical Mosaic.* Toronto: University of Toronto Press, 1965.

⸺; Marion Porter; and Bernard Blishen. *Stations and Callings: Making it Through the School System.* Toronto: Methuen, 1982.

Portes, Alejandro. "On the Sociology of National Development: Theories and Issues." *American Journal of Sociology,* Vol. 82, No. 1, July 1976.

⸺ and John Walton. *Labor, Class, and the International System.* New York: Academic Press, 1981.

Posner, Judy. "From Sex role Stereotyping to SadoMasochism." *Fireweed,* Vol. 14, 1982.

Poulantzas, Nicos. *Classes In Contemporary Capitalism.* London: New Left Books, 1975.

⸺. *Political Power and Social Classes.* London: Verso, 1978.

Pound, Roscoe. *Social Control Through Law.* New Haven, Conn.: Yale University Press, 1942.

Presthus, Robert V. *Elite Accommodation in Canadian Politics.* Toronto: Macmillan, 1973.

Price, Charles. "The study of assimilation." In *Migration,* edited by J.A. Jackson, pp. 181-237. Cambridge: Cambridge University Press, 1969.

Prus, Robert C., and C.R.D. Sharper. *Road Hustler.* Toronto: Gage, 1977.

Quarentelli, E.L., and J. Cooper. "Self Conceptions and Others: A Further test of Median Hypotheses." *Sociological Quarterly,* Vol. 7, Summer 1966.

Rapoport, Amos. *Human Aspects of Urban Form.* Toronto: Pergamon Press, 1977.

Ratner, R.S., and John L. McMullan. "Social Control and the Rise of the 'Exceptional State' in Britain, and the United States, and Canada." *Crime and Social Justice,* No. 19, pp. 31-43, 1983.

Raven, Bertram H., and Jeffrey Z. Rubin. *Social Psychology: People in Groups.* New York: Wiley, 1976.

Real, Michael R. *Mass Mediated Culture.* Englewood Cliffs, N.J.: Prentice-Hall, 1977.

Redfield, Robert. "The Folk Society." *American Journal of Sociology,* Vol. 52, pp. 233-308, 1947.

————. *Peasant Society and Culture.* Chicago: University of Chicago Press, 1965.

Reiss, Albert J., Jr. "Rural-Urban and Status Differences in Interpersonal Contacts." *American Journal of Sociology,* Vol. 65, pp. 182-195, 1959.

Reitz, Jeffrey G. *The Survival of Ethnic Groups.* Toronto: McGraw-Hill Ryerson, 1980.

Rejai, M. "Political Ideology: Theoretical and Comparative Perspectives." In *Decline of Ideology,* edited by M. Rejai. Chicago: Aldine and Atherton Inc., 1971.

Remmling, G.W. *The Sociology of Karl Mannheim.* London: Routledge and Kegan Paul, 1975.

Rex, John. *Race, Colonialism and the City.* London: Routledge & Kegan Paul, 1973.

————. *Race Relations in Sociological Theory.* 2d ed. London: Routledge & Kegan Paul, 1983.

———— and Robert Moore. *Race, Community, and Conflict: A Study of Sparkbrook.* London: Oxford University Press, 1967.

———— and S. Tomlinson. *Colonial Immigrants in a British City.* London: Routledge & Kegan Paul, 1979.

Reynolds, Barbara P. "Mandatory Retirement at Age 65: Summary of Arguments." Ottawa: Unpublished paper for the Research Branch, Library of Parliament, October 16, 1978.

Rheinstein, Max, ed. *Max Weber on Law in Economy and Society.* Cambridge, Mass.: Harvard University, 1954.

Richards, John, and Larry Pratt. *Prairie Capitalism: Power and Influence in the New West.* Toronto: McClelland and Stewart, 1979.

Richardson, B. *Strangers Devour the Land.* New York: Macmillan, 1975.

Richardson, C. James. "Education and Social Mobility: changing conceptions of the role of the educational systems." *Canadian Journal of Sociology,* Vol. 2, No. 4, pp. 417-33, 1977.

Richardson, R. Jack. " 'Merchants Against Industry': An Empirical Study of the Canadian Debate." *Canadian Journal of Sociology,* Vol. 7, No. 3, pp. 279-295, 1982.

Richmond, Anthony H., and Warren E. Kalback. *Factors in the Adjustment of Immigrants and their Descendants.* Ottawa: Statistic Canada, Catalogue 99-761E, 1980.

Richta, R. *Civilization at the Crossroads.* New York: International Arts and Science, 1969.

Rinehart, James W. *The Tyranny of Work.* Toronto: Longman, 1975.

———— and Ishmael O. Okraku. "A Study of Class Consciousness." *Canadian Review of Sociology and Anthropology,* Vol. 11, pp. 197-213, 1974.

Rioux, Marcel. *Quebec in Question.* Toronto: James Lorimer and Company, 1978.

Rist, Ray C. *The Urban School: Factory for Failure.* Cambridge, Mass.: The M.I.T. Press, 1973.

Ritzer, George. *Sociology: A Multiple Paradigm Science.* Boston: Allyn and Bacon, 1975.

Roadburg, Alan. *Aging, Retirement, Leisure and Work in Canada.* Toronto: Methuen, 1985.

Robert, Jean-Claude. "Urbanisation et population. Le Cas de Montreal en 1861." Revue d'Histoire de l'Amerique Francaise, 35(Mar.) 1982.

Roberts, Lance W., and Rodney A. Clifton. "Exploring the ideology of Canadian multiculturalism." *Canadian Public Policy* Vol. 8: pp. 88-94, 1982.

Roberts, Wayne, and John Bullen. "A Heritage of Hope and Struggle: Workers, Unions and Politics in Canada, 1930-1982." In *Modern Canada: 1930-1980's*, edited by Michael S. Cross and Gregory S. Kealey, pp. 105-143. Toronto: McClelland and Stewart, 1984.

Rodwin, Lloyd. *Nations and Cities.* Boston: Houghton Mifflin, 1970.

Roebuck, Julian, and Stanley C. Weeber. *Political Crime in the United States.* New York: Praeger, 1978.

Rogoff, Natalie. *Recent Trends in Occupational Mobility.* Glencoe, Ill.: Free Press, 1953.

Rose, Arnold. "The Subculture of Aging: a Framework for Research in Social Gerontology." In *Older People and their Social World*, edited by A. Rose and W. Peterson. Philadelphia: F.A. Davis Co., pp. 3-16, 1965.

Rosenbloom, Sandra, ed. *Women's Travel Issues: Research Needs and Priorities.* Washington, D.C.: U.S. Department of Transportation, 1978.

Rosengren, Karl. "Mass Media and Social Change: Some Current Approaches." In *Mass Media and Social Change*, edited by E. Katz and T. Szecsko, pp. 247-263. London: Sage, 1981.

Rosenham, D.L. "On Being Sane in Insane Places." *Science,* Vol. 179, pp. 250-258, January 19, 1973.

Rosenthal, Donald B., ed. *Urban Revitalization.* Vol. 18. Beverly Hills: Sage Urban Affairs Annual Reviews, 1980.

Rossi, Alice. "Gender and Parenthood." *American Sociological Review,* Vol. 49, No. 1, pp. 1-19, 1984.

———. "Transition to Parenthood." *Journal of Marriage and the Family,* Vol. 30, pp. 26-39, 1968.

Rossi, Peter H., and Sonia R. Wright. "Evaluation Research: An Assessment of Theory, Practice, and Politics." *Evaluation Quarterly,* Vol. 1, No. 1, pp. 5-52, February 1977.

Rostow, W.W. *The Stages of Economic Growth: A Non-Communist Manifesto.* Cambridge: Cambridge University Press, 1962.

Roth, D.F., and F.L. Wilson. *The Comparative Study of Politics.* Englewood Cliffs, N.J.: Prentice-Hall, 1980.

Rowntree, John, and Margaret Rowntree. "The Political Economy of Youth." *Our Generation,* Vol. 6. Nos. 1-2, 1968.

Roy, William G. "Class conflict and social change in historical perspective." *Annual Review of Sociology,* Vol. 10, pp. 483-506, 1984.

*Royal Commission on Newspapers,* Ottawa: Supply and Services Canada, 1981.

Rubin, J.; F. Provenzano; and Z. Luria. "The Eye of the Beholder: Parents' Views on Sex of Newborns." *American Journal of Orthopsychiatry,* Vol. 44, No. 4, pp. 512-519, 1974.

Runciman, W.G. *Relative Deprivation and Social Justice.* London: Routledge and Kegan Paul, 1966.

Russell, Louise B. *The Baby Boom Generation and the Economy.* Washington, D.C.: The Brookings Institution, 1982.

Rybczynski, W. *Paper Heroes: A Review of Appropriate Technology.* Garden City, N.Y.: Anchor Press/Doubleday, 1980.

Saks, Michael J. and Meridith Miller. "A Systems Approach to Discretion in the Legal Process." In *Social Psychology and Discretionary Law*, edited by Lawrence E. Abt and Irving R. Stuart, pp. 71-91. New York: Van Nostrand Reinhold, 1979.

Salter, Liona. *Communication Studies in Canada.* Toronto: Butterworth, 1981.

Sandels, Stina. *The Skandia Report II: Why Are Children Injured in Traffic: Can We Prevent Child Accidents in Traffic?* Stockholm: Skandia Insurance Co. Ltd., 1964.

Sattel, Jack. "The Inexpressive Male: Tragedy or Sexual Politics?". In *Women and Work:*

*Problems and Perspectives,* edited by Rachel Kahn-Hut, Arlene Kaplan Daniels, and Richard Colvard, p. 160, New York: Oxford University Press, 1982.

Scheff, Thomas J. *Being Mentally Ill: A Sociological Theory.* 2d ed. New York: Aldine, 1984.

Schneider, Joseph W., and Sally L. Hacker. "Sex Role Imagery and the use of generic man in Introductory texts: A case in the sociology of sociology." *American Sociologist,* Vol. 8, pp. 12-18, January 1973.

Schneider, L., and Charles M. Bonjean, eds. *The Idea of Culture in the Social Sciences.* Cambridge: Cambridge University Press, 1973.

Schwartz, Mildred. *Politics and Territory: The Sociology of Regional Persistence in Canada.* Montreal: McGill-Queen's University Press, 1974.

Schwirian, Kent P., and Marc Matre. "The Ecological Structure of Canadian Cities." In *Comparative Urban Structure,* edited by Kent P. Schwirian, pp. 309-323. Toronto: D.C. Heath, 1974.

Science Council of Canada. *Implications of the Changing Age Structure of the Canadian Population.* Ottawa, July 1976.

Scott, Jack. *Canadian Workers, American Unions.* Vancouver: New Star Books, 1978.

Seeley, John R.; R.; R. Alexander Sim; and E.W. Loosley. *Crestwood Heights.* New York: Basic Books, 1956.

Seiber, Timothy R., and Andrew J. Gordon. *Children and Their Organizations.* Boston: G.K. Hall and Co., 1981.

Seidman, Steven. *Liberalism and the Origins of European Social Theory.* Berkeley, Calif.: University of California Press, 1983.

Selznick, Philip. *Law, Society, and Industrial Justice.* New York: Russell Sage Foundation, 1969.

————. "The Sociology of Law." In *International Encyclopedia of the Social Sciences.* Vol. 9. Edited by David Sills, pp. 50-59. New York: Macmillan, 1968.

————. *TVA and the Grass Roots.* Berkeley, Calif.: University of California Press, 1949.

Shaffir, William. *Life in a Religious Community: The Lubavitcher Chassidim in Montreal.* Toronto: Holt, Rinehart and Winston, 1974.

Shalev, Michael. "Strikers and the State: A Comment." *British Journal of Political Science,* Vol. 8, pp. 479-492, 1978.

———— and Walter Korpi. "Working class mobilization and American exceptionalism." *Economic and Industrial Democracy,* Vol. 1, pp. 31-61, 1980.

Shapiro, Martin. *Getting Doctored: Critical Reflections on Becoming a Physician.* Kitchener, Ont.: Between the Lines Press, 1978.

Sheehy, Gail. *Passages: Predictable Crises in Adult Life.* New York: Dutton, 1974.

Shevky, Eshrev, and Wendell Bell. *Social Area Analysis.* Berkeley: University of California Press, 1955.

Shibutani, Tamotsu. *Society and Personality: An Interactionist Approach to Social Psychology.* Englewood Cliffs, N.J.: Prentice-Hall, 1961.

Shorter, Edward, and Charles Tilly. "The shape of strikes in France, 1830-1960." *Comparative Studies in Society and History,* Vol. 13, pp. 60-86, 1971.

Shryock, H.S., and J. Siegel. *The Methods and Materials of Demography.* Washington: U.S. Bureau of the Census, Government Printing Office, 1973.

Sidlofsky, Samuel. "Post-War Immigrants in the Changing Metropolis, with Special Reference to Toronto's Italian Population." Toronto: University of Toronto, Ph.D. Dissertation in Sociology, 1969.

Siegal, Arthur. *Politics and the Media in Canada.* Toronto: McGraw-Hill Ryerson, 1983.

Simmel, Georg. "The Metropolis and Mental Life." In *The Sociology of Georg Simmel,* edited by Kurt Wolff, pp. 400-427. New York: The Free Press, 1950.

————. *The Web of Group Affiliation (1908).* Translated by K.H. Wolff. New York: The Free Press, 1955.

Simmie, J.M. *Citizens in Conflict: The Sociology of Town Planning.* London: Hutchinson, 1974.

Simmons, J.L. *Deviants*. Berkeley, Calif.: Glendessary Press, 1969.

Simon, Rita J., ed. *Research in Law and Sociology: An Annual Compilation of Research*. Vol. 1, Greenwich, Conn.: JAI, 1978.

Simon, Roger. *Gramsci's Political Thought*. London: Lawrence and Wishart Limited, 1982.

Sinclair, P.R. "Political Powerlessness and Sociodemographic Status in Canada." *Canadian Review of Sociology and Anthropology*, Vol. 16, pp. 125-135, 1979.

—— and Kenneth Westhues. *Village in Crisis*. Toronto: Holt, Rinehart & Winston of Canada, 1974.

Sjoberg, Gideon. *The Preindustrial City*. New York: The Free Press, 1960.

Skocpol, Theda. *States and Social Revolutions*. Cambridge, Mass.: Harvard University Press, 1979.

Smelser, Neil. *Essays in Sociological Explanation*. Englewood Cliffs, N.J.: Prentice-Hall, 1968.

Smigel, Erwin O., and H. Laurence Ross, eds. *Crimes Against Bureaucracy*. New York: Van Nostrand Reinhold, 1970.

Smith, Adam. *The Wealth of Nations*. London: Macmillan, 1894.

Smith, David, and Lorne Tepperman. "Changes in the Canadian Business and Legal Elites, 1870-1970." *Canadian Review of Sociology and Anthropology*, Vol. 11, No. 2, pp. 97-109, 1974.

Smith, Michael P. *The City and Social Theory*. New York: St. Martin's Press, 1979.

——."Industrial conflict in post-war Ontario or one cheer for the Woods Report." *Canadian Review of Sociology and Anthropology*, Vol. 18, pp. 370-392, 1981.

Smith, Eugene W., and Aileen Smith. *Minamata*. New York: Holt, Rinehart & Winston, 1975.

Smucker, Joseph. *Industrialization in Canada*. Ontario: Prentice-Hall, 1980.

——. "Reformist themes in the Canadian Labour Congress." *Sociological Focus*, Vol. 9, pp. 159-197, 1976.

Smythe, Dallas. "Communications: Blindspot of Western Marxism." *Canadian Journal of Political and Social Theory*, Vol. 1, pp. 120-127, 1977.

—— and Tran Van Dinh. "On Critical and Administrative Research: A New Critical Analysis." *Journal of Communication*, Vol. 33, No. 3, pp. 117-127, 1983.

Snyder, David. "Early North American strikes: a reinterpretation." *Industrial and Labor Relations Review*, Vol. 30, pp. 325-341, 1977.

Snyder, Francis G. "Law and Development in the Light of Dependency Theory." *Law and Society Review*, 14 (3), pp. 723-804, 1980.

Sobel, Michael E. "The Analysis of Occupational Mobility." *American Sociological Review*, Vol. 48, No. 5, pp. 721-27, 1983.

Soltow, Lee. *Men and Wealth in the United States: 1850-1870*. New Haven: Yale University Press, 1975.

Sommer, Robert. *Personal Space*. Toronto: Prentice-Hall, 1969.

Sorokin, Pitrim A. *Society, Culture and Personality: Their Structure and Dynamics*. New York: Cooper Square Publications Inc., 1969.

Spectorsky, A.C. *The Exurbanites*. Philadelphia: J.B. Lippincott Co., 1955.

Spenner, Kenneth I. "Temporal Changes in Work Content." *American Sociological Review*, Vol. 44, pp. 968-975, 1979.

Statistics Canada. *Births and Deaths*. Cat. 84-204. Ottawa, May 1985.

——. *Canada Update*. Vol 2, No. 4 Ottawa, March 1984.

——. *Canada's Immigrants*. Cat. 99-936. Ottawa: Minister of Supply and Services, 1984.

——. *Canadian Yearbook*. Ottawa: Information Canada, various years.

——. *Charting Canadian Incomes. 1951-1981*. Ottawa: Supply and Services Canada, 1984.

——. *Current Demographic Analysis: Report on the Demographic Situation in Canada 1983*. Cat. 91-209E. Prepared by Jean Dumas, Demography Division. Ottawa: Minister of Supply and Services, 1984.

———. *Education in Canada: A Statistical Review for 1982-83*. Cat. 81-229. Ottawa: Minister of Supply and Services, 1984.

———. *Historical Statistics of Canada*. 2d ed. Edited by M.C. Urquhart. Ottawa.

———. *Job Market Reality for Postsecondary Graduates, Employment Outcome by 1978 Two Years After Graduation*. Cat. 81-572E. By W. Clark and Z. Zsigmond, Ottawa, 1981.

———. *The Labour Force*. Cat. 71-001. Ottawa, April 1985.

———. *Life Tables 1980-82*. Cat. 84-522, Ottawa, 1984.

———. *Living Alone*. Cat. 99-934. Ottawa, 1984.

———. *Perspectives Canada III*. Ottawa: Minister of Supply and Services, 1980.

———. *Population. Labour Force-Occupation Trends*. 1981 Census of Canada. Cat. 92-920, Vol. 1, pp. 1-3 and 1-37. Ottawa, 1983.

———. *Vital Statistics*. Vol. 1. *Births and Deaths, 1981*. Cat. 84-204. Ottawa, 1983.

———. *Vital Statistics*. Vol. 2. *Marriages and Divorces, 1982*. Cat. 84-205. Ottawa, 1983.

———. *Women in the Work World*. Chart 10(a). Ottawa: Supply and Services Canada, 1984.

Stebbins, R.A. *Teachers and Meanings: Definitions of Classroom Situations*. Leiden: E.J. Brill, 1975.

Stedman Jones, Gareth. "From Historical Sociology to Theoretical History." *British Journal of Sociology,* Vol. 27, No. 3, pp. 295-305, 1976.

Steinberg, Stephen, *The Ethnic Myth: Race, Ethnicity, and Class in America*. Boston: Beacon Press, 1981.

Stevens, Stanley S. "Mathematics, measurement and psychophysics." In *Handbook of Experimental Psychology,* edited by S.S. Stevens, pp. 1-49. New York: Wiley, 1951.

Stinchecombe, Arthur L. *Constructing Social Theories*. New York: Harcourt Brace Jovanovich, 1968.

———. "Some Empirical Consequences of the Davis-Moore Theory of Stratification."

*American Sociological Review,* Vol. 28, pp. 805-808, 1963.

Stirling, Robert, and Denise Kouri. "Unemployment indexes—the Canadian context." In *Economy, Class and Social Reality,* edited by J.A. Fry, pp. 169-205. Toronto: Butterworth, 1979.

Stolnitz, George J. "The Demographic transition." In *Population: The Vital Revolution,* edited by Ronald Freedman. Garden City, N.Y.: Anchor Books, 1964.

Stone, Leroy O., and Claude Marceau. *Canadian Population Trends and Public Policy Through the 1980s*. Institute for Research on Public Policy. Montreal: McGill-Queen's University Press, 1977.

Strauss, Anselm et al. "The Hospital and its Negotiated Order." In *The Hospital in Modern Society,* edited by Eliot Freidson, pp. 147-169. New York: The Free Press, 1963.

Sudnow, David. *Passing On: The Social Organization of Dying*. Englewood Cliffs, N.J.: Prentice-Hall, 1967.

Sunkel, Osvaldo. "Big Business and 'Dependencia.'," *Foreign Affairs,* Vol. 50, No. 3, April 1972.

Suttles, Gerald D. *The Social Order of the Slum*. Chicago: University of Chicago Press, 1968.

Synge, Jane. "Work and Family Support Patterns of the Aged in the Early Twentieth Century." In *Aging in Canada,* edited by Victor W. Marshall, pp. 135-144. Toronto: Fitzhenry and Whiteside, 1980.

Synnott, Anthony. "Little Angels, Little Devils: A Sociology of Children." *The Canadian Review of Sociology and Anthropology,* Vol. 20, No. 1, pp. 79-95, 1983.

Szymanski, Albert. *The Capitalist State and the Politics of Class*. Cambridge, Mass: Winthrop, 1978.

Tabb, William K., and Larry Sawyers. *Marxism and the Metropolis*. 2d ed. New York: Oxford University Press, 1984.

Tanner, Julian. "Youth Culture and the Canadian High School: an Empirical Analysis." *Canadian Journal of Sociology,* Vol. 3, No. 1, pp. 89-102, 1978.

Taylor, D. Garth. "Pluralistic Ignorance and the Spiral of Silence." *Public Opinion Quarterly,* Vol. 46, pp. 311-335, 1982.

Taylor, Frederick W. *Principles of Scientific Management.* New York: Harper, 1911.

Teeple, Gary. "Land, Labour and Capital in Pre-Confederation Canada." In *Capitalism and the National Question in Canada,* edited by G. Teeple, pp. 43-66. Toronto: University of Toronto Press, 1972.

Terry, John. "The Gender Gap: Women's Political Power." Ottawa: Research Branch, Library of Parliament, October 1984.

Thio, Alex. *Deviant Behavior.* 2d ed. Boston: Houghton Mifflin, 1983.

Thomas, William Isaac, and Florian Znaniecki. *The Polish Peasant in Europe and America.* New York: Dover, 1958.

Thompson, E.P. *The Poverty of Theory and Other Essays.* New York: Monthly Review Press, 1979.

Thompson, E.P. *Whigs and Hunters: The Origin of the Black Act.* New York: Pantheon, 1975.

Thompson, Edgar T. *Plantation Societies, Race Relations, and the South: The Regimentation of Populations.* Durham, N.C.: Duke University Press, 1975.

Thompson, Hunter S. *Hell's Angels.* New York: Ballantine, 1967.

Thompson, Paul. *The Nature of Work: An Introduction to Debates on the Labor Process.* Atlantic Highlands, N.J.: Humanities Press, Inc., 1984.

Thorsell, Bernard A., and Lloyd W. Klemke. "The Labeling Process: Reinforcement and Deterrent?". *Law and Society Review,* Vol. 6, No. 3, pp. 393-403., 1972.

Tienhaara, Nancy. *Canadian Views on Immigration and Population: An Analysis of Post-War Gallup Polls.* Ottawa: Manpower and Immigration, 1974.

Tiger, Lionel. *Men in Groups.* New York: Random House, 1969.

Tilly, Charles. *As Sociology Meets History.* New York: Academic, 1981.

———. "The Chaos of the living city." In *An Urban World,* edited by C. Tilly, pp. 86-133. Boston: Little, Brown, 1974.

———. "Collective violence in European perspective." In *Violence in America: Historical and Comparative Perspectives,* 2d ed., edited by H. Graham and T. Gurr, pp. 83-118. Beverley Hills: Sage Publications, 1979.

———. *From Mobilization to Revolution.* Reading, Mass: Addison-Wesley, 1978.

———; Louise Tilly; and Richard Tilly. *The Rebellious Century, 1830-1930.* Cambridge, Mass: Harvard University Press,, 1975.

———, ed. *The Formation of National States in Western Europe.* Princeton: Princeton University Press, 1975.

Tindale, J.A., and V. Marshall. "A Generational Conflict Perspective for Gerontology." In *Aging in Canada,* edited by V. Marshall, pp. 43-50. Toronto: Fitzhenry and Whiteside, 1980.

Toennies, Ferdinand. *Community and Society.* East Lansing: Michigan State University Press, 1957.

Toffler, Alvin. *Future Shock.* New York: Bantam, 1971.

Tomasic, Roman and Malcolm M. Feeley. *Neighborhood Justice: Assessment of an Emerging Idea.* New York: Longman, 1982.

Touraine, Alain. *The Post-Industrial Society.* New York: Random House, 1971.

———. *Workers' Attitudes to Technical Change.* Paris: Organization for Economic Co-operation and Development, 1965.

Treiman, Donald J. *Occupational Prestige in Comparative Perspective.* New York: Academic, 1977.

Trist, Eric. "Adapting to a Changing World." Montreal: paper presented at the 6th International Personnel Conference, November 1977.

———. *The Evolution of Socio-Technical Systems.* Toronto: Ontario Ministry of Labour, 1981.

Troll, L., and E. Parron. "Age Changes in Sex Roles Amid Changing Sex Roles: the Double Shift." In *Annual Review of Gerontology and Geriatrics,* Vol. 2, edited by C.

Eisdorfer, pp. 118-143. New York: Springer Publishing Co., 1981.

Tuchman, Gaye. *Making News.* New York: The Free Press, 1978.

———; and A.K. Daniels; and J. Benet, eds. *Hearth and Home: Images of Women in Mass Media.* New York: Oxford University Press, 1978.

Tumin, Melvin M. "Some Principles of Stratification: A Critical Analysis." *American Sociological Review,* Vol. 18, pp. 387-393, 1953.

———, ed. *Readings on Social Stratification.* Englewood Cliffs, N.J.: Prentice-Hall, 1970.

———. "Conceptions of the Demise of Law." In *Structure, Law, and Power: Essays in the Sociology of Law,* edited by Paul J. Brantingham and Jack M. Kress, pp. 12-26. Beverly Hills, Calif.: Sage, 1979.

Turk, Austin T. "Criminology and Socio-Legal Studies." In *Perspectives in Criminal Law,* edited by Anthony N. Doob and Edward L. Greenspan, pp. 309-334. Aurora, Ont.: Canada Law Book, Inc., 1984.

"Law as a Weapon in Social Conflict." *Social Problems,* 23 (3) pp. 276-291, 1976.

———. "Law, Conflict, and Order: From Theorizing Toward Theories." *Canadian Review of Sociology and Anthropology,* 13 (3) pp. 282-294, 1976.

———. "Organizational Deviance and Political Policing." In *Organizational Police Deviance,* edited by Clifford D. Shearing, pp. 111-125. Toronto: Butterworth, 1981.

———. *Political Criminality: The Defiance and Defense of Authority.* Beverly Hills, Calif.: Sage, 1982.

Turowetz, Allan, and Michael Rosenberg. "Exaggerating Everyday Life: The Case of Professional Wrestling." In *Shaping Identity in Canadian Society,* edited by Jack Haas and William Shaffir, pp. 87-100. Toronto: Prentice-Hall, 1978.

Tylor, Edward. *Anthropology: An Introduction to the Study of Man and Civilization.* London: Macmillan, 1924.

UNESCO. *Statistical Yearbook 1984.* Paris, 1984.

Unger, Rhoda. *Female and Male: Psychological Perspectives.* New York: Harper and Row, 1979.

United Nations. *Determinants and Consequences of Population Trends.* Vol. 1. New York: United Nations Department of Economic and Social Affairs, 1973.

———. *Manual IV, Methods of Estimating Basic Demographic Measures from Incomplete Data.* ST/SOA/Series A/42, Population Studies, No. 42. New York, 1967.

United States Department of Commerce. *Historical Statistics of the United States, Colonial Times to 1970.* Washington: United States Government Printing Office, 1975.

Upham, Frank K. "Litigation and Moral Consciousness in Japan: An Interpretive Analysis of Four Japanese Pollution Suits." *Law and Society Review,* 10 (4) 1976, pp. 579-619.

Urquhart, M.C., ed. *Historical Statistics of Canada.* 2d ed. Ottawa: Statistics Canada, 1983.

——— and K. Buckley. *Historical Statistics of Canada.* Toronto: Macmillan, 1965.

Vallee, Frank G. "Regionalism and ethnicity: the French-Canadian case." In *Perspectives on Regions & Regionalism,* edited by B.Y. Card, pp. 19-25. Western Association of Sociology and Anthropology Proceedings, 1969.

Vallieres, Pierre. *White Niggers of America.* Toronto: McClelland and Stewart, 1971.

van den Berghe, Pierre. *Race and Racism: A Comparative Perspective.* New York: John Wiley & Sons, 1967.

Van de Berghe, Pierre L. "Race, perspective two." In *Dictionary of Race and Ethnic Relations,* E. Ellis Cashmore, pp. 216-218. London: Routledge and Kegan Paul.

Vanderburg, W.H. *Culture and Technique: I — The Growth of Minds and Cultures.* Toronto: University of Toronto Press, 1985.

van de Walle, Etienne, and John Knodel. "Europe's Fertility transition: New evidence and lessons for today's developing world." *Population Bulletin,* Vol. 34, No. 6, Feb. 1980.

van Paasen, C. "The Philosophy of Geography: From Vidal to Hägerstrand." In *Space and Time Geography: Essays Dedicated to Torsten Hägerstrand,* edited by A. Pred, pp. 17-29. Lund: C.W.K. Gleerup, 1981.

Van Poecke, Luc. "Gerbner's Cultural Indicators." In *Mass Communication Review Yearbook,* Vol. 1, edited by Wilhoit and de Bock, pp. 423-431, 1980.

Veevers, Jean E. *Childless by Choice.* Toronto: Butterworth, 1980.

Veltmeyer, Henry. "The Underdevelopment of Atlantic Canada." In *The Review of Radical Political Economics,* Vol. 10, No. 2, 1978.

Verba, S., and N.H. Nie. *Participation in America.* New York: Harper and Row, 1972.

Vermeersch, Etienne. "An Analysis of the Concept of Culture." In *The Concept and Dynamics of Culture,* edited by B. Bernardo, pp. 9-73. The Hague: Mouton Publishers, 1977.

Vernon, Raymond. *Sovereignty at Bay.* New York: Basic Books, 1971.

Wallace, Joan, Commissioner. *Part-time Work in Canada.* Report of the Commission of Inquiry into Part-time Work. Ottawa: Labour Canada, 1983.

Ward, Bruce. "Coyote condition makes our strikes long, spiteful battles." Toronto: *Toronto Star,* p. A20, August 5, 1981.

Ward, W. Peter. *White Canada Forever.* Montreal: McGill-Queen's University Press, 1978.

Ward, Robin, and Richard Jenkins, eds. *Ethnic Communities in Business.* Cambridge: Cambridge University Press, 1984.

Watkins, M.H. "A staple theory of economic growth." *Canadian Journal of Economics and Political Science,* Vol. 29, No. 2, pp. 141-158, May 1963.

Webber, Melvin M. "Order in Diversity: Community Without Propinquity." In *Cities and Space,* edited by L. Wingo, pp. 23-54. Baltimore; The Johns Hopkins Press, 1963.

Weber, Max. *The Agrarian Sociology of Ancient Civilizations.* London, New Left Books, 1976.

———. *The City.* Translated by D. Martindale and G. Neuwirth. New York: Free Press, 1958.

———. *Economy and Society.* New York: Bedminster Press, 1968.

———. *From Max Weber: Essays in Sociology.* Translated by H.H. Gerth and C. Wright Mills. New York: Oxford University Press, 1958.

———. *General Economic History.* New York: Collier Books, 1961.

———. *The Protestant Ethic and the Spirit of Capitalism.* London: George Allen and Unwin, 1974.

Weiner, Myron, ed. "Introduction". *Modernization: The Dynamics of Growth.* New York: Basic Books, 1966.

Weiss, Carol H. *Evaulation Research.* Englewoods Cliffs, N.J.: Prentice-Hall, 1972.

Weitzman, Lenore J. "Sex Role Socialization: A Focus on Women." In *Women: A Feminist Perspective,* edited by J. Freeman, pp. 157-237. Palo Alto: Mayfield Publishing Co., 1984.

Weizenbaum, Joseph. "Once More: The Computer Revolution." In *The Computer Age: A Twenty-Year View,* edited by Michael L. Dertouzos and Joel Moses. Cambridge, Mass.: The MIT Press, 1979.

Wellman, Barry. "The Community Question: The Intimate Networks of East Yorkers." *American Journal of Sociology,* Vol. 84, pp. 1201-1231, 1979.

———; Peter Carrington; and Alan Hall. "Networks and Personal Communities." In *Structural Sociology,* S.D. Berkowitz and Barry Wellman. New York: Cambridge University Press, expected publication 1986.

——— and Barry Leighton. "Networks, Neighborhoods, and Communities: Approaches to the Study of the Community Question." *Urban Affairs Quarterly,* Vol. 14, pp. 363-390, 1979.

Wesolowski, W. "Some Notes on the Functional Theory of Stratification." *Polish Sociological Bulletin,* Vol. 3-4, pp. 28-38, 1962.

West, Candace, and Don. H. Zimmerman. "Women's place in everyday talk: Reflections on parent-child interaction." *Social Problems,* Vol. 24, pp. 521-529, 1977.

Westergaard, John, and Henrietta Resler. *Class in A Capitalist Society: A Study of Contemporary Britain.* London: Heinemann Educational Books Ltd., 1975.

Whitaker, Reginald. *The Government Party.* Toronto: University of Toronto Press, 1977.

White, Robert A. "Mass Communication and Culture: Transition to a New Paradigm." *Journal of Communication,* Vol. 33, No. 3, pp. 279-301, 1983.

White, Terence H. "Canadian labour and international unions in the seventies." In *Prophecy and Protest: Social Movements in Twentieth Century Canada,* edited by S. Clark, P. Grayson, and L. Grayson, pp. 288-305. Toronto: Gage, 1975.

Whitehead, Alfred North. *Science and the Modern World.* New York: Cambridge University Press, 1948.

Whyte, William Foote. *Street Corner Society.* Chicago: The University of Chicago Press, 1961.

Wilber, Charles K., ed. *The Political Economy of Development and Underdevelopment.* New York: Random House, 1973.

Williams, Kenneth S. "Uniform Province-Wide Test Best for University Admission." *Citizen,* Ottawa, Jan. 12, 1984, p. 9.

Williams, Raymond. *Culture.* Glascow: William Collins Sons and Company, 1981.

Williams, Thomas R. *Socialization.* Englewood Cliffs: N.J.: Prentice-Hall, 1983.

Williams, Trevor. "Education and Biosocial Processes." In *Education, Change, and Society: A Sociology of Canadian Education,* edited by Richard Carlton, Louise Colley, and Neil MacKinnon, pp. 248-280. Toronto: Gage, 1977.

Willis, Paul. *Learning to Labour.* Farnborough: Saxon House, 1977.

Wilson, John. *Social Theory.* Englewood Cliffs, N.J.: Prentice-Hall, 1983.

Wilson, S.J. *Women, The Family, and the Economy.* Toronto: McGraw-Hill Ryerson, 1982.

Wilson, Seymour V. "The Role of Royal Commissions and Task Forces." In *The Structures of Policy Making in Canada,* B.G. Doern and P. Aucoin, pp. 113-129. Toronto: Macmillan, 1971.

Wilson, William J. *Power, Racism, and Privilege: Race Relations in Theoretical and Sociohistorical Perspectives.* New York: Free Press, 1973.

Winner, L. *Autonomous Technology.* Cambridge, Mass.: MIT Press, 1977.

Wireman, Peggy. *Urban Neighborhoods, Networks, and Families.* Toronto: Lexington Books, 1984.

Wirth, Louis. "Urbanism as a Way of Life." *American Journal of Sociology,* Vol. 44 pp. 1-24, 1938.

Wiseman, Jacqueline. *Stations of the Lost: The Treatment of Skid Row Alcoholics.* Chicago: The University of Chicago Press, 1979.

Wolff, K.H. "The Sociology of Knowledge and Sociological Theory." In *Symposium on Sociological Theory,* edited by L. Gross. New York: Row, Peterson, 1969.

Woodward, Joan. *Industrial Organization.* London: Oxford University Press, 1965.

Worsley, Peter et al. *Introducing Sociology.* 2d ed. Harmondsworth: Penguin, 1977.

Wright, Charles R. *Mass Communication: A Sociological Perspective.* 2d ed. New York: Random House, 1975.

Wright, Erik Olin. "Class Boundaries in Advanced Capitalist Societies." *New Left Review,* Vol. 98, pp. 3-41, 1976.

Wrigley, E.A. *Population and History.* New York: McGraw-Hill, 1969.

————, ed. *An Introduction to English Historical Demography.* London: Weidenfeld and Nicolson, 1966.

Wrong, D.H. "The Oversocialized Concept of Man in Modern Sociology." *American Sociological Review,* Vol. 26, pp. 183-193, 1961.

Wuthrow, Robert et al. *Cultural Analysis.* Boston: Routledge and Kegan Paul, 1984.

Yancey, William L.; E.P. Ericksen; and R.N. Juliani. "Emergent ethnicity: a review and reformulation." *American Sociological Review,* Vol. 41, pp. 391-403, 1976.

Yankelovich, D. "New Rules in American Life: Searching for self-fulfillment in a World Turned Upside Down." *Psychology Today,* Vol. 15, No. 4, pp. 35-91, 1981.

Young, M.F.D., ed. *Knowledge and Control: New Directions for the Sociology of Education.* London: Collier-MacMillan, 1971.

Young, Walter D. *The Anatomy of a Party: The National CCF, 1932-61.* Toronto: University of Toronto Press, 1969.

Zeitlin, Irving M. *Capitalism and Imperialism.* Chicago: Markham, 1972.

————. *Ideology and the Development of Sociological Theory.* ed. Englewood Cliffs, N.J.: Prentice-Hall, 1981.

————. *The Social Condition of Humanity.* New York: Oxford University Press, 1981.

Zeitlin, Maurice. "Corporate Ownership and Control: The Large Corporation and the Capitalist Class." *American Journal of Sociology,* Vol. 79, pp. 1073-1119, March 1974.

Zimbardo, P. "The psychological power and pathology of imprisonment." Unpublished paper. Stanford University, 1971.

Zimmerman, Don, and Candace West. "Sex roles, interruptions and silences in conversation." *Language and Sex: Difference and Dominance,* edited by B. Thorne and N.M. Henley, pp. 105-129. Rowley, Mass.: Newbury House, 1975.

# INDEX

Skocpol, Theda, 465–69
Smelser, Neil, 561
Smith, Adam, 314, 315, 444
Smythe, Dallas, 507
Snowball sampling, 54
Social area analysis, 414
Social bond, 1
Social closure (Weber), 370–71
Social construction of reality, 208
Social control, *see* Control.
Social Credit Party, 296–97
Social critic, applied sociology as, 77
Social Darwinists, 557–58
Social differentiation, 548–49, 560
Social evolutionism, 547–48, 556–62.
    *See also* Evolution, social, theories of.
Social homogamy, 267
Social identity, 129
Social impact assessment, 63–65
Social institutions, 24, 25, 207, 208
    economic institutions, *see* Economic
    institutions; institutional co-operation,
    430–31; institutional negotiations, 209;
    institutional outputs, 429–30; mainte-
    nance of the institutional system, 431–
    32; political institutions, *see* Political
    institutions; total institutions, 150;
    *See also* Education; Law; Media.
Social interaction, 207, 209
Socialism, 440
    in Marxist thought, 28, 117; state
    socialism, 469; strike activity and
    democratic-socialist governments,
    305–307
Socialist schools in socialist society, 542–43
Socialization, 83–84, 116, 137–51
    adolescent, 146–48; adult, 148–51; class
    and, 141–42; media and, 146; in
    schools, 536, 539; sex role, 142–46,
    162–63, 237; theories of, 138–41
Socializing organizations, 150
Social learning theory, 144
Social mobility, 363
    cultural capital and, 392–93; structural
    explanations of, 393–95
Social movements, 287–307, 483, 548
    breakdown theories on, 287–90; of the
    1960s, 625–27; social solidarity theo-
    ries on, 290–94, 307; third parties in
    Canada, 294–301; union movement in
    Canada, 301–307
Social organization:
    defined, 207; macro level analyses of,
    207, 208, 209; micro order analyses of,
    207, 208–209; overview, 207–208
Social programs, 61, 248–49, 445
Social relations, 1

Social solidarity theories, 290–94.
    *See also* Mechanical solidarity; Organic
    solidarity.
Social structure:
    Coulson and Riddell on, 16–17; defined,
    89; population processes and, 89–90;
    roles in, 211; in sociolegal research,
    490–92
Social system, 5–6, 208
    Parsons' concept, 24–25, 116
Societies, defined, 1
Sociological imagination (Mills), 15–16
Sociology:
    Canadian sociology, 31–33; contending
    perspectives within, 22–31, 37; con-
    trasted with other disciplines, 3–4, 9;
    as a science, 19–22; subject matter of,
    4–5, 20
Sociotechnical systems theory, 325–28
Sorokin, Pitrim A., 21
South Africa, 357
Spencer, Herbert, 547, 557
"Spiral of silence," 517
Split labour market model, 342–43
Spontaneous organizations, 311–12
Stable population theory, 106
Staples perspective (Innis), 451–53
Stateless societies, 463
State and social structure, 472–74
    growth in role of state in technical
    society, 594
Static-group comparison, 42
Statistical regression, as source of internal
    invalidity, 43
Statistics, official, 51–52
Statuses, 16–17, 25, 211
Status groups (Weber), 370
Stereotypes, 129, 143, 146, 170, 180–81
    sex-role stereotyping, 222, 223, 257,
    512–13
Stigmatization, *see* Labelling processes.
Stirling, Robert, 51–52
Stowe, Emily Howard, 246
Stratification:
    in Canada, 376, 379–80, 382; distin-
    guished from class, 363–64; functional
    theory of, 371–73; by income (Canada),
    389–92; vertical and horizontal, 402;
    Weberian theory of, 368–71
Stratified sampling, 53–54
Strauss, Anselm, 209, 210, 218
Strikes, 295, 301–306
Structural approach to organizational theory,
    324–25
Structural functionalism, 23–26
    approach to roles, 211–13, 215;
    approach to study of organizations,